CORPORATE FINANCE AND PORTFOLIO MANAGEMENT

CFA® PROGRAM CURRICULUM
2014 • Level I • Volume 4

WILEY

Photography courtesy of Hector Emanuel and Justin Runquist.

ISBN 978-1-937537-63-0 (paper)
ISBN 978-1-937537-84-5 (ebk)

10 9 8 7 6 5 4 3 2 1

Please visit our website at
www.WileyGlobalFinance.com.

CONTENTS

Corporate Finance

◙ indicates an optional segment

indicates an optional segment

Portfolio Management

◙ indicates an optional segment

◙ indicates an optional segment

How to Use the CFA Program Curriculum

Congratulations on your decision to enter the Chartered Financial Analyst (CFA®) Program. This exciting and rewarding program of study reflects your desire to become a serious investment professional. You are embarking on a program noted for its high ethical standards and the breadth of knowledge, skills, and abilities it develops. Your commitment to the CFA Program should be educationally and professionally rewarding.

The credential you seek is respected around the world as a mark of accomplishment and dedication. Each level of the program represents a distinct achievement in professional development. Successful completion of the program is rewarded with membership in a prestigious global community of investment professionals. CFA charterholders are dedicated to life-long learning and maintaining currency with the ever-changing dynamics of a challenging profession. The CFA Program represents the first step towards a career-long commitment to professional education.

The CFA examination measures your mastery of the core skills required to succeed as an investment professional. These core skills are the basis for the Candidate Body of Knowledge (CBOK™). The CBOK consists of four components:

- A broad topic outline that lists the major top-level topic areas (CBOK Topic Outline)
- Topic area weights that indicate the relative exam weightings of the top-level topic areas
- Learning outcome statements (LOS) that advise candidates about the specific knowledge, skills, and abilities they should acquire from readings covering a topic area (LOS are provided in candidate study sessions and at the beginning of each reading)
- The CFA Program curriculum, readings, and end-of-reading questions, which candidates receive upon exam registration

Therefore, the key to your success on the CFA exam is studying and understanding the CBOK™. The following sections provide background on the CBOK, the organization of the curriculum, and tips for developing an effective study program.

CURRICULUM DEVELOPMENT PROCESS

The CFA Program is grounded in the practice of the investment profession. Using the Global Body of Investment Knowledge (GBIK) collaborative website, CFA Institute performs a continuous practice analysis with investment professionals around the world to determine the knowledge, skills, and abilities (competencies) that are relevant to the profession. Regional expert panels and targeted surveys are conducted annually to verify and reinforce the continuous feedback from the GBIK collaborative website. The practice analysis process ultimately defines the CBOK. The CBOK contains the competencies that are generally accepted and applied by investment professionals. These competencies are used in practice in a generalist context and are expected to be demonstrated by a recently qualified CFA charterholder.

A committee consisting of practicing charterholders, in conjunction with CFA Institute staff, designs the CFA Program curriculum in order to deliver the CBOK to candidates. The examinations, also written by practicing charterholders, are designed to allow you to demonstrate your mastery of the CBOK as set forth in the CFA Program curriculum. As you structure your personal study program, you should emphasize mastery of the CBOK and the practical application of that knowledge. For more information on the practice analysis, CBOK, and development of the CFA Program curriculum, please visit www.cfainstitute.org.

ORGANIZATION OF THE CURRICULUM

The Level I CFA Program curriculum is organized into 10 topic areas. Each topic area begins with a brief statement of the material and the depth of knowledge expected.

Each topic area is then divided into one or more study sessions. These study sessions—18 sessions in the Level I curriculum—should form the basic structure of your reading and preparation.

Each study session includes a statement of its structure and objective, and is further divided into specific reading assignments. An outline illustrating the organization of these 18 study sessions can be found at the front of each volume.

The reading assignments are the basis for all examination questions, and are selected or developed specifically to teach the knowledge, skills, and abilities reflected in the CBOK. These readings are drawn from CFA Institute-commissioned content, textbook chapters, professional journal articles, research analyst reports, and cases. All readings include problems and solutions to help you understand and master the topic areas.

Reading-specific Learning Outcome Statements (LOS) are listed at the beginning of each reading. These LOS indicate what you should be able to accomplish after studying the reading. The LOS, the reading, and the end-of-reading questions are dependent on each other, with the reading and questions providing context for understanding the scope of the LOS.

You should use the LOS to guide and focus your study, as each examination question is based on an assigned reading and one or more LOS. The readings provide context for the LOS and enable you to apply a principle or concept in a variety of scenarios. The candidate is responsible for the entirety of all of the required material in a study session, the assigned readings as well as the end-of-reading questions and problems.

We encourage you to review the material on LOS (www.cfainstitute.org/programs/cfaprogram/courseofstudy/Pages/study_sessions.aspx), including the descriptions of LOS "command words" (www.cfainstitute.org/programs/Documents/cfa_and_cipm_los_command_words.pdf).

FEATURES OF THE CURRICULUM

OPTIONAL SEGMENT

Required vs. Optional Segments   You should read all of an assigned reading. In some cases, however, we have reprinted an entire chapter or article and marked certain parts of the reading as "optional." The CFA examination is based only on the required segments, and the optional segments are included only when they might help you to better understand the required segments (by seeing the required material in its full context). When an optional segment begins, you will see text and a dashed vertical bar in the outside margin that will continue until the optional segment ends, accompanied by another icon. *Unless the material is specifically marked as optional, you should assume it is required.* You should rely on the required segments and the reading-specific LOS in preparing for the examination.

Problems/Solutions *All questions and problems in the readings as well as their solutions (which are provided directly following the problems) are part of the curriculum and are required material for the exam.* When appropriate, we have included problems within and after the readings to demonstrate practical application and reinforce your understanding of the concepts presented. The questions and problems are designed to help you learn these concepts and may serve as a basis for exam questions. Many of these questions are adapted from past CFA examinations.

Margins The wide margins in each volume provide space for your note-taking.

Six-Volume Structure For portability of the curriculum, the material is spread over six volumes.

Glossary and Index For your convenience, we have printed a comprehensive glossary in each volume. Throughout the curriculum, a **bolded** word in a reading denotes a term defined in the glossary. Each volume also contains an index specific to that volume; a combined index can be found on the CFA Institute website with the Level I study sessions.

Source Material The authorship, publisher, and copyright owners are given for each reading for your reference. We recommend that you use this CFA Institute curriculum rather than the original source materials because the curriculum may include only selected pages from outside readings, updated sections within the readings, and contains problems and solutions tailored to the CFA Program.

LOS Self-Check We have inserted checkboxes next to each LOS that you can use to track your progress in mastering the concepts in each reading.

DESIGNING YOUR PERSONAL STUDY PROGRAM

Create a Schedule An orderly, systematic approach to examination preparation is critical. You should dedicate a consistent block of time every week to reading and studying. Complete all reading assignments and the associated problems and solutions in each study session. Review the LOS both before and after you study each reading to ensure that you have mastered the applicable content and can demonstrate the knowledge, skill, or ability described by the LOS and the assigned reading. Use the LOS self-check to track your progress and highlight areas of weakness for later review.

As you prepare for your exam, we will e-mail you important exam updates, testing policies, and study tips. Be sure to read these carefully. Curriculum errata are periodically updated and posted on the study session page at www.cfainstitute.org. You may also sign up for an RSS feed to alert you to the latest errata update.

Successful candidates report an average of over 300 hours preparing for each exam. Your preparation time will vary based on your prior education and experience. For each level of the curriculum, there are 18 study sessions, so a good plan is to devote 15–20 hours per week, for 18 weeks, to studying the material. Use the final four to six weeks before the exam to review what you've learned and practice with sample and mock exams. This recommendation, however, may underestimate the hours needed for appropriate examination preparation depending on your individual circumstances, relevant experience, and academic background. You will undoubtedly adjust your study time to conform to your own strengths and weaknesses, and your educational and professional background.

You will probably spend more time on some study sessions than on others, but on average you should plan on devoting 15-20 hours per study session. You should allow ample time for both in-depth study of all topic areas and additional concentration on those topic areas for which you feel least prepared.

CFA Institute Question Bank   The CFA Institute topic-based question bank is intended to assess your mastery of individual topic areas as you progress through your studies. After each test, you will receive immediate feedback noting the correct responses and indicating the relevant assigned reading so you can identify areas of weakness for further study. The topic tests reflect the question formats and level of difficulty of the actual CFA examinations. For more information on the topic tests, please visit www.cfainstitute.org.

CFA Institute Mock Examinations   In response to candidate requests, CFA Institute has developed mock examinations that mimic the actual CFA examinations not only in question format and level of difficulty, but also in length and topic weight. The three-hour mock exams simulate the morning and afternoon sessions of the actual CFA exam, and are intended to be taken after you complete your study of the full curriculum so you can test your understanding of the curriculum and your readiness for the exam. You will receive feedback at the end of the mock exam, noting the correct responses and indicating the relevant assigned readings so you can assess areas of weakness for further study during your review period. We recommend that you take mock exams during the final stages of your preparation for the actual CFA examination. For more information on the mock examinations, please visit www.cfainstitute.org.

Preparatory Providers   After you enroll in the CFA Program, you may receive numerous solicitations for preparatory courses and review materials. When considering a prep course, make sure the provider is in compliance with the CFA Institute Prep Provider Guidelines Program (www.cfainstitute.org/partners/examprep/Pages/cfa_prep_provider_guidelines.aspx). Just remember, there are no shortcuts to success on the CFA examinations; reading and studying the CFA curriculum is the key to success on the examination. The CFA examinations reference only the CFA Institute assigned curriculum—no preparatory course or review course materials are consulted or referenced.

SUMMARY

Every question on the CFA examination is based on the content contained in the required readings and on one or more LOS. Frequently, an examination question is based on a specific example highlighted within a reading or on a specific end-of-reading question and/or problem and its solution. To make effective use of the CFA Program curriculum, please remember these key points:

1   All pages printed in the curriculum are required reading for the examination except for occasional sections marked as optional. You may read optional pages as background, but you will not be tested on them.

2   All questions, problems, and their solutions—printed at the end of readings—are part of the curriculum and are required study material for the examination.

3   You should make appropriate use of the online sample/mock examinations and other resources available at www.cfainstitute.org.

4 You should schedule and commit sufficient study time to cover the 18 study sessions, review the materials, and take sample/mock examinations.

5 **Note:** Some of the concepts in the study sessions may be superseded by updated rulings and/or pronouncements issued after a reading was published. Candidates are expected to be familiar with the overall analytical framework contained in the assigned readings. Candidates are not responsible for changes that occur after the material was written.

FEEDBACK

At CFA Institute, we are committed to delivering a comprehensive and rigorous curriculum for the development of competent, ethically grounded investment professionals. We rely on candidate and member feedback as we work to incorporate content, design, and packaging improvements. You can be assured that we will continue to listen to your suggestions. Please send any comments or feedback to info@cfainstitute.org. Ongoing improvements in the curriculum will help you prepare for success on the upcoming examinations, and for a lifetime of learning as a serious investment professional.

Corporate Finance

TOPIC LEVEL LEARNING OUTCOME

The candidate should be able to analyze a capital budgeting problem; to estimate a company's cost of capital; to evaluate a company's operating and financial leverage, working capital management, and corporate governance policies; and to describe the mechanics of dividends and share repurchases.

11

Corporate Finance

This study session covers the principles that corporations use to make their investing and financing decisions. The first reading covers capital budgeting. Capital budgeting is the process of making decisions about which long-term projects the corporation should accept for investment and which it should reject. Both the expected and required rate of return for a project should be taken into account. The second reading explains how the required rate of return for a project is developed economically sound methods. The third reading discusses measures of leverage and how they affect a company's earnings and financial ratios. In managing or evaluating the riskiness of earnings, analysts and corporate managers need to evaluate operating leverage (the use of fixed costs in operations) and financial leverage (the use of debt in financing operations). The fourth reading deals with important features of alternative means of distributing earnings. Earnings may be distributed to shareholders by means of dividends and share repurchases. The fifth reading discusses short-term liquidity and working capital management.

The final reading in this study session is on corporate governance practices. Inadequate corporate governance can expose a company to negative effect, including damage to reputation and loss of business and market value.

READING ASSIGNMENTS

Reading 36   Capital Budgeting
              by John D. Stowe, CFA, and
              Jacques R. Gagné, CFA, CIPM

(continued)

Capital Budgeting

by John D. Stowe, CFA, and Jacques R. Gagné, CFA, CIPM

LEARNING OUTCOMES

Mastery	The candidate should be able to:
☐	**a.** describe the capital budgeting process, including the typical steps of the process, and distinguish among the various categories of capital projects;
☐	**b.** describe the basic principles of capital budgeting, including cash flow estimation;
☐	**c.** explain how the evaluation and selection of capital projects is affected by mutually exclusive projects, project sequencing, and capital rationing;
☐	**d.** calculate and interpret the results using each of the following methods to evaluate a single capital project: net present value (NPV), internal rate of return (IRR), payback period, discounted payback period, and profitability index (PI);
☐	**e.** explain the NPV profile, compare the NPV and IRR methods when evaluating independent and mutually exclusive projects, and describe the problems associated with each of the evaluation methods;
☐	**f.** describe expected relations among an investment's NPV, company value, and share price.

INTRODUCTION

1

Capital budgeting is the process that companies use for decision making on capital projects—those projects with a life of a year or more. This is a fundamental area of knowledge for financial analysts for many reasons.

■ First, capital budgeting is very important for corporations. Capital projects, which make up the long-term asset portion of the balance sheet, can be so large that sound capital budgeting decisions ultimately decide the future of many corporations. Capital decisions cannot be reversed at a low cost, so mistakes are very costly. Indeed, the real capital investments of a company describe a company better than its working capital or capital structures, which are intangible and tend to be similar for many corporations.

■ Second, the principles of capital budgeting have been adapted for many other corporate decisions, such as investments in working capital, leasing, mergers and acquisitions, and bond refunding.

■ Third, the valuation principles used in capital budgeting are similar to the valuation principles used in security analysis and portfolio management. Many of the methods used by security analysts and portfolio managers are based on capital budgeting methods. Conversely, there have been innovations in security analysis and portfolio management that have also been adapted to capital budgeting.

■ Finally, although analysts have a vantage point outside the company, their interest in valuation coincides with the capital budgeting focus of maximizing shareholder value. Because capital budgeting information is not ordinarily available outside the company, the analyst may attempt to estimate the process, within reason, at least for companies that are not too complex. Further, analysts may be able to appraise the quality of the company's capital budgeting process—for example, on the basis of whether the company has an accounting focus or an economic focus.

This reading is organized as follows: Section 2 presents the steps in a typical capital budgeting process. After introducing the basic principles of capital budgeting in Section 3, in Section 4 we discuss the criteria by which a decision to invest in a project may be made.

2   THE CAPITAL BUDGETING PROCESS

The specific capital budgeting procedures that a manager uses depend on the manager's level in the organization, the size and complexity of the project being evaluated, and the size of the organization. The typical steps in the capital budgeting process are as follows:

■ Step One: Generating Ideas—Investment ideas can come from anywhere, from the top or the bottom of the organization, from any department or functional area, or from outside the company. Generating good investment ideas to consider is the most important step in the process.

■ Step Two: Analyzing Individual Proposals—This step involves gathering the information to forecast cash flows for each project and then evaluating the project's profitability.

■ Step Three: Planning the Capital Budget—The company must organize the profitable proposals into a coordinated whole that fits within the company's overall strategies, and it also must consider the projects' timing. Some projects that look good when considered in isolation may be undesirable strategically. Because of financial and real resource issues, the scheduling and prioritizing of projects is important.

■ Step Four: Monitoring and Post-auditing—In a post-audit, actual results are compared to planned or predicted results, and any differences must be explained. For example, how do the revenues, expenses, and cash flows realized from an investment compare to the predictions? Post-auditing capital projects is important for several reasons. First, it helps monitor the forecasts and analysis that underlie the capital budgeting process. Systematic errors, such as overly optimistic forecasts, become apparent. Second, it helps improve business operations. If sales or costs are out of line, it will focus attention on bringing performance closer to expectations if at all possible. Finally, monitoring and post-auditing recent capital investments will produce concrete ideas for future investments. Managers can decide to invest more heavily in profitable areas and scale down or cancel investments in areas that are disappointing.

Planning for capital investments can be very complex, often involving many persons inside and outside of the company. Information about marketing, science, engineering, regulation, taxation, finance, production, and behavioral issues must be systematically gathered and evaluated. The authority to make capital decisions depends on the size and complexity of the project. Lower-level managers may have discretion to make decisions that involve less than a given amount of money, or that do not exceed a given capital budget. Larger and more complex decisions are reserved for top management, and some are so significant that the company's board of directors ultimately has the decision-making authority.

Like everything else, capital budgeting is a cost–benefit exercise. At the margin, the benefits from the improved decision making should exceed the costs of the capital budgeting efforts.

Companies often put capital budgeting projects into some rough categories for analysis. One such classification would be as follows:

1 Replacement projects. These are among the easier capital budgeting decisions. If a piece of equipment breaks down or wears out, whether to replace it may not require careful analysis. If the expenditure is modest and if not investing has significant implications for production, operations, or sales, it would be a waste of resources to overanalyze the decision. Just make the replacement. Other replacement decisions involve replacing existing equipment with newer, more efficient equipment, or perhaps choosing one type of equipment over another. These replacement decisions are often amenable to very detailed analysis, and you might have a lot of confidence in the final decision.

2 Expansion projects. Instead of merely maintaining a company's existing business activities, expansion projects increase the size of the business. These expansion decisions may involve more uncertainties than replacement decisions, and these decisions will be more carefully considered.

3 New products and services. These investments expose the company to even more uncertainties than expansion projects. These decisions are more complex and will involve more people in the decision-making process.

4 Regulatory, safety, and environmental projects. These projects are frequently required by a governmental agency, an insurance company, or some other external party. They may generate no revenue and might not be undertaken by a company maximizing its own private interests. Often, the company will accept the required investment and continue to operate. Occasionally, however, the cost of the regulatory/safety/environmental project is sufficiently high that the company would do better to cease operating altogether or to shut down any part of the business that is related to the project.

5 Other. The projects above are all susceptible to capital budgeting analysis, and they can be accepted or rejected using the net present value (NPV) or some other criterion. Some projects escape such analysis. These are either pet projects of someone in the company (such as the CEO buying a new aircraft) or so risky that they are difficult to analyze by the usual methods (such as some research and development decisions).

3   BASIC PRINCIPLES OF CAPITAL BUDGETING

Capital budgeting has a rich history and sometimes employs some pretty sophisticated procedures. Fortunately, capital budgeting relies on just a few basic principles. Capital budgeting usually uses the following assumptions:

1   Decisions are based on cash flows. The decisions are not based on accounting concepts, such as net income. Furthermore, intangible costs and benefits are often ignored because, if they are real, they should result in cash flows at some other time.

2   Timing of cash flows is crucial. Analysts make an extraordinary effort to detail precisely when cash flows occur.

3   Cash flows are based on opportunity costs. What are the incremental cash flows that occur with an investment compared to what they would have been without the investment?

4   Cash flows are analyzed on an after-tax basis. Taxes must be fully reflected in all capital budgeting decisions.

5   Financing costs are ignored. This may seem unrealistic, but it is not. Most of the time, analysts want to know the after-tax operating cash flows that result from a capital investment. Then, these after-tax cash flows and the investment outlays are discounted at the "required rate of return" to find the net present value (NPV). Financing costs are reflected in the required rate of return. If we included financing costs in the cash flows and in the discount rate, we would be double-counting the financing costs. So even though a project may be financed with some combination of debt and equity, we ignore these costs, focusing on the operating cash flows and capturing the costs of debt (and other capital) in the discount rate.

6   Capital budgeting cash flows are not accounting net income. Accounting net income is reduced by noncash charges such as accounting depreciation. Furthermore, to reflect the cost of debt financing, interest expenses are also subtracted from accounting net income. (No subtraction is made for the cost of equity financing in arriving at accounting net income.) Accounting net income also differs from economic income, which is the cash inflow plus the change in the market value of the company. Economic income does not subtract the **cost of debt** financing, and it is based on the changes in the market value of the company, not changes in its book value (accounting depreciation).

In assumption 5 above, we referred to the rate used in discounting the cash flows as the "required rate of return." The required rate of return is the discount rate that investors should require given the riskiness of the project. This discount rate is frequently called the "opportunity cost of funds" or the "cost of capital." If the company can invest elsewhere and earn a return of r, or if the company can repay its sources of capital and save a cost of r, then r is the company's opportunity cost of funds. If the company cannot earn more than its opportunity cost of funds on an investment, it should not undertake that investment. Unless an investment earns more than the cost of funds from its suppliers of capital, the investment should not be undertaken. The cost-of-capital concept is discussed more extensively elsewhere. Regardless of what it is called, an economically sound discount rate is essential for making capital budgeting decisions.

Although the principles of capital budgeting are simple, they are easily confused in practice, leading to unfortunate decisions. Some important capital budgeting concepts that managers find very useful are given below.

- A **sunk cost** is one that has already been incurred. You cannot change a sunk cost. Today's decisions, on the other hand, should be based on current and future cash flows and should not be affected by prior, or sunk, costs.

- An **opportunity cost** is what a resource is worth in its next-best use. For example, if a company uses some idle property, what should it record as the investment outlay: the purchase price several years ago, the current market value, or nothing? If you replace an old machine with a new one, what is the opportunity cost? If you invest $10 million, what is the opportunity cost? The answers to these three questions are, respectively: the current market value, the cash flows the old machine would generate, and $10 million (which you could invest elsewhere).

- An **incremental cash flow** is the cash flow that is realized because of a decision: the cash flow *with* a decision minus the cash flow *without* that decision. If opportunity costs are correctly assessed, the incremental cash flows provide a sound basis for capital budgeting.

- An **externality** is the effect of an investment on other things besides the investment itself. Frequently, an investment affects the cash flows of other parts of the company, and these externalities can be positive or negative. If possible, these should be part of the investment decision. Sometimes externalities occur outside of the company. An investment might benefit (or harm) other companies or society at large, and yet the company is not compensated for these benefits (or charged for the costs). **Cannibalization** is one externality. Cannibalization occurs when an investment takes customers and sales away from another part of the company.

- **Conventional cash flows** versus **nonconventional cash flows**—A conventional cash flow pattern is one with an initial outflow followed by a series of inflows. In a nonconventional cash flow pattern, the initial outflow is not followed by inflows only, but the cash flows can flip from positive to negative again (or even change signs several times). An investment that involved outlays (negative cash flows) for the first couple of years that were then followed by positive cash flows would be considered to have a conventional pattern. If cash flows change signs once, the pattern is conventional. If cash flows change signs two or more times, the pattern is nonconventional.

Several types of project interactions make the incremental cash flow analysis challenging. The following are some of these interactions:

- **Independent projects** versus **mutually exclusive projects**—Independent projects are projects whose cash flows are independent of each other. Mutually exclusive projects compete directly with each other. For example, if Projects A and B are mutually exclusive, you can choose A or B, but you cannot choose both. Sometimes there are several mutually exclusive projects, and you can choose only one from the group.

- **Project sequencing**—Many projects are sequenced through time, so that investing in a project creates the option to invest in future projects. For example, you might invest in a project today and then in one year invest in a second project if the financial results of the first project or new economic conditions are favorable. If the results of the first project or new economic conditions are not favorable, you do not invest in the second project.

▪ **Unlimited funds** versus **capital rationing**—An unlimited funds environment assumes that the company can raise the funds it wants for all profitable projects simply by paying the required rate of return. Capital rationing exists when the company has a fixed amount of funds to invest. If the company has more profitable projects than it has funds for, it must allocate the funds to achieve the maximum shareholder value subject to the funding constraints.

4   INVESTMENT DECISION CRITERIA

Analysts use several important criteria to evaluate capital investments. The two most comprehensive measures of whether a project is profitable or unprofitable are the net present value (NPV) and internal rate of return (IRR). In addition to these, we present four other criteria that are frequently used: the payback period, discounted payback period, average accounting rate of return (AAR), and profitability index (PI). An analyst must fully understand the economic logic behind each of these investment decision criteria as well as its strengths and limitations in practice.

4.1 Net Present Value

For a project with one investment outlay, made initially, the net present value (NPV) is the present value of the future after-tax cash flows minus the investment outlay, or

$$\text{NPV} = \sum_{t=1}^{n} \frac{\text{CF}_t}{(1 + r)^t} - \text{Outlay} \tag{1}$$

where

$$\text{CF}_t = \text{after-tax cash flow at time } t$$
$$r = \text{required rate of return for the investment}$$
$$\text{Outlay} = \text{investment cash flow at time zero}$$

To illustrate the net present value criterion, we will take a look at a simple example. Assume that Gerhardt Corporation is considering an investment of €50 million in a capital project that will return after-tax cash flows of €16 million per year for the next four years plus another €20 million in Year 5. The required rate of return is 10 percent. For the Gerhardt example, the NPV would be[1]

$$\text{NPV} = \frac{16}{1.10^1} + \frac{16}{1.10^2} + \frac{16}{1.10^3} + \frac{16}{1.10^4} + \frac{20}{1.10^5} - 50$$
$$\text{NPV} = 14.545 + 13.223 + 12.021 + 10.928 + 12.418 - 50$$
$$\text{NPV} = 63.136 - 50 = €13.136 \text{ million.}$$

---

[1] Occasionally, you will notice some rounding errors in our examples. In this case, the present values of the cash flows, as rounded, add up to €63.135. Without rounding, they add up to €63.13627, or €63.136. We will usually report the more accurate result, the one that you would get from your calculator or computer without rounding intermediate results.

The investment has a total value, or present value of future cash flows, of €63.136 million. Since this investment can be acquired at a cost of €50 million, the investing company is giving up €50 million of its wealth in exchange for an investment worth €63.136 million. The investor's wealth increases by a net of €13.136 million.

Because the NPV is the amount by which the investor's wealth increases as a result of the investment, the decision rule for the NPV is as follows:

Invest if $\quad\quad\quad\quad\quad$ NPV > 0

Do not invest if $\quad\quad\quad$ NPV < 0

Positive NPV investments are wealth-increasing, whereas negative NPV investments are wealth-decreasing.

Many investments have cash flow patterns in which outflows may occur not only at time zero, but also at future dates. It is useful to consider the NPV to be the present value of all cash flows:

$$NPV = CF_0 + \frac{CF_1}{(1+r)^1} + \frac{CF_2}{(1+r)^2} + \cdots + \frac{CF_n}{(1+r)^n}, \text{ or}$$

$$NPV = \sum_{t=0}^{n} \frac{CF_t}{(1+r)^t}$$

(2)

In Equation 2, the investment outlay, CF_0, is simply a negative cash flow. Future cash flows can also be negative.

4.2 Internal Rate of Return

The internal rate of return (IRR) is one of the most frequently used concepts in capital budgeting and in security analysis. The IRR definition is one that all analysts know by heart. For a project with one investment outlay, made initially, the IRR is the discount rate that makes the present value of the future after-tax cash flows equal that investment outlay. Written out in equation form, the IRR solves this equation:

$$\sum_{t=1}^{n} \frac{CF_t}{(1+IRR)^t} = \text{Outlay}$$

where IRR is the internal rate of return. The left-hand side of this equation is the present value of the project's future cash flows, which, discounted at the IRR, equals the investment outlay. This equation will also be seen rearranged as

$$\sum_{t=1}^{n} \frac{CF_t}{(1+IRR)^t} - \text{Outlay} = 0$$

(3)

In this form, Equation 3 looks like the NPV equation, Equation 1, except that the discount rate is the IRR instead of r (the required rate of return). Discounted at the IRR, the NPV is equal to zero.

In the Gerhardt Corporation example, we want to find a discount rate that makes the total present value of all cash flows, the NPV, equal zero. In equation form, the IRR is the discount rate that solves this equation:

$$-50 + \frac{16}{(1+IRR)^1} + \frac{16}{(1+IRR)^2} + \frac{16}{(1+IRR)^3} + \frac{16}{(1+IRR)^4} + \frac{20}{(1+IRR)^5} = 0$$

Algebraically, this equation would be very difficult to solve. We normally resort to trial and error, systematically choosing various discount rates until we find one, the IRR, that satisfies the equation. We previously discounted these cash flows at 10 percent and found the NPV to be €13.136 million. Since the NPV is positive, the IRR is probably greater than 10 percent. If we use 20 percent as the discount rate, the NPV is −€0.543 million, so 20 percent is a little high. One might try several other discount rates until the NPV is equal to zero; this approach is illustrated in Table 1.

Table 1	Trial and Error Process for Finding IRR
Discount Rate (%)	**NPV**
10	13.136
20	−0.543
19	0.598
19.5	0.022
19.51	0.011
19.52	0.000

The IRR is 19.52 percent. Financial calculators and spreadsheet software have routines that calculate the IRR for us, so we do not have to go through this trial and error procedure ourselves. The IRR, computed more precisely, is 19.5197 percent.

The decision rule for the IRR is to invest if the IRR exceeds the required rate of return for a project:

Invest if   IRR > r

Do not invest if   IRR < r

In the Gerhardt example, since the IRR of 19.52 percent exceeds the project's required rate of return of 10 percent, Gerhardt should invest.

Many investments have cash flow patterns in which the outlays occur at time zero and at future dates. Thus, it is common to define the IRR as the discount rate that makes the present values of all cash flows sum to zero:

$$\sum_{t=0}^{n} \frac{CF_t}{(1 + IRR)^t} = 0 \tag{4}$$

Equation 4 is a more general version of Equation 3.

4.3 Payback Period

The payback period is the number of years required to recover the original investment in a project. The payback is based on cash flows. For example, if you invest $10 million in a project, how long will it be until you recover the full original investment? Table 2 below illustrates the calculation of the payback period by following an investment's cash flows and cumulative cash flows.

Table 2		Payback Period Example					
Year	0	1	2	3	4	5	
Cash flow	−10,000	2,500	2,500	3,000	3,000	3,000	
Cumulative cash flow	−10,000	−7,500	−5,000	−2,000	1,000	4,000	

In the first year, the company recovers 2,500 of the original investment, with 7,500 still unrecovered. You can see that the company recoups its original investment between Year 3 and Year 4. After three years, 2,000 is still unrecovered. Since the Year 4 cash flow is 3,000, it would take two-thirds of the Year 4 cash flow to bring the cumulative cash flow to zero. So, the payback period is three years plus two-thirds of the Year 4 cash flow, or 3.67 years.

The drawbacks of the payback period are transparent. Since the cash flows are not discounted at the project's required rate of return, the payback period ignores the time value of money and the risk of the project. Additionally, the payback period ignores cash flows after the payback period is reached. In the table above, for example, the Year 5 cash flow is completely ignored in the payback computation!

Example 1 is designed to illustrate some of the implications of these drawbacks of the payback period.

EXAMPLE 1

Drawbacks of the Payback Period

The cash flows, payback periods, and NPVs for Projects A through F are given in Table 3. For all of the projects, the required rate of return is 10 percent.

Table 3		Examples of Drawbacks of the Payback Period					
	Cash Flows						
Year	**Project A**	**Project B**	**Project C**	**Project D**	**Project E**	**Project F**	
0	−1,000	−1,000	−1,000	−1,000	−1,000	−1,000	
1	1,000	100	400	500	400	500	
2		200	300	500	400	500	
3		300	200	500	400	10,000	
4		400	100		400		
5		500	500		400		
Payback period	1.0	4.0	4.0	2.0	2.5	2.0	
NPV	−90.91	65.26	140.60	243.43	516.31	7,380.92	

Comment on why the payback period provides misleading information about the following:

1   Project A.

2   Project B versus Project C.

3   Project D versus Project E.

4   Project D versus Project F.

Solution to 1:

Project A does indeed pay itself back in one year. However, this result is misleading because the investment is unprofitable, with a negative NPV.

Solution to 2:

Although Projects B and C have the same payback period and the same cash flow after the payback period, the payback period does not detect the fact that Project C's cash flows within the payback period occur earlier and result in a higher NPV.

Solution to 3:

Projects D and E illustrate a common situation. The project with the shorter payback period is the less profitable project. Project E has a longer payback and higher NPV.

Solution to 4:

Projects D and F illustrate an important flaw of the payback period—that the payback period ignores cash flows after the payback period is reached. In this case, Project F has a much larger cash flow in Year 3, but the payback period does not recognize its value.

The payback period has many drawbacks—it is a measure of payback and not a measure of profitability. By itself, the payback period would be a dangerous criterion for evaluating capital projects. Its simplicity, however, is an advantage. The payback period is very easy to calculate and to explain. The payback period may also be used as an indicator of project liquidity. A project with a two-year payback may be more liquid than another project with a longer payback.

Because it is not economically sound, the payback period has no decision rule like that of the NPV or IRR. If the payback period is being used (perhaps as a measure of liquidity), analysts should also use an NPV or IRR to ensure that their decisions also reflect the profitability of the projects being considered.

4.4 Discounted Payback Period

The discounted payback period is the number of years it takes for the cumulative discounted cash flows from a project to equal the original investment. The discounted payback period partially addresses the weaknesses of the payback period. Table 4 gives an example of calculating the payback period and discounted payback period. The example assumes a discount rate of 10 percent.

Year	0	1	2	3	4	5
Table 4 — **Payback Period and Discounted Payback Period**						
Cash flow (CF)	−5,000	1,500.00	1,500.00	1,500.00	1,500.00	1,500.00
Cumulative CF	−5,000	−3,500.00	−2,000.00	−500.00	1,000.00	2,500.00
Discounted CF	−5,000	1,363.64	1,239.67	1,126.97	1,024.52	931.38
Cumulative discounted CF	−5,000	−3,636.36	−2,396.69	−1,269.72	−245.20	686.18

The payback period is three years plus 500/1,500 = 1/3 of the fourth year's cash flow, or 3.33 years. The discounted payback period is between four and five years. The discounted payback period is four years plus 245.20/931.38 = 0.26 of the fifth year's discounted cash flow, or 4.26 years.

The discounted payback period relies on discounted cash flows, much as the NPV criterion does. If a project has a negative NPV, it will usually not have a discounted payback period since it never recovers the initial investment.

The discounted payback does account for the time value of money and risk within the discounted payback period, but it ignores cash flows after the discounted payback period is reached. This drawback has two consequences. First, the discounted payback period is not a good measure of profitability because it ignores these cash flows. Second, another idiosyncrasy of the discounted payback period comes from the possibility of negative cash flows after the discounted payback period is reached. It is possible for a project to have a negative NPV but to have a positive cumulative discounted cash flow in the middle of its life and, thus, a reasonable discounted payback period. The NPV and IRR, which consider all of a project's cash flows, do not suffer from this problem.

4.5 Average Accounting Rate of Return

The average accounting rate of return (AAR) can be defined as

$$AAR = \frac{\text{Average net income}}{\text{Average book value}}$$

To understand this measure of return, we will use a numerical example.

Assume a company invests $200,000 in a project that is depreciated straight-line over a five-year life to a zero salvage value. Sales revenues and cash operating expenses for each year are as shown in Table 5. The table also shows the annual income taxes (at a 40 percent tax rate) and the net income.

	Year 1	Year 2	Year 3	Year 4	Year 5
Table 5 — **Net Income for Calculating an Average Accounting Rate of Return**					
Sales	$100,000	$150,000	$240,000	$130,000	$80,000
Cash expenses	50,000	70,000	120,000	60,000	50,000
Depreciation	40,000	40,000	40,000	40,000	40,000
Earnings before taxes	10,000	40,000	80,000	30,000	−10,000

(continued)

Table 5	(Continued)				
	Year 1	**Year 2**	**Year 3**	**Year 4**	**Year 5**
Taxes (at 40 percent)	4,000	16,000	32,000	12,000	−4,000[a]
Net income	6,000	24,000	48,000	18,000	−6,000

[a]Negative taxes occur in Year 5 because the earnings before taxes of −$10,000 can be deducted against earnings on other projects, thus reducing the tax bill by $4,000.

For the five-year period, the average net income is $18,000. The initial book value is $200,000, declining by $40,000 per year until the final book value is $0. The average book value for this asset is ($200,000 − $0) / 2 = $100,000. The average accounting rate of return is

$$\text{AAR} = \frac{\text{Average net income}}{\text{Average book value}} = \frac{18,000}{100,000} = 18\%$$

The advantages of the AAR are that it is easy to understand and easy to calculate. The AAR has some important disadvantages, however. Unlike the other capital budgeting criteria discussed here, the AAR is based on accounting numbers and not based on cash flows. This is an important conceptual and practical limitation. The AAR also does not account for the time value of money, and there is no conceptually sound cutoff for the AAR that distinguishes between profitable and unprofitable investments. The AAR is frequently calculated in different ways, so the analyst should verify the formula behind any AAR numbers that are supplied by someone else. Analysts should know the AAR and its potential limitations in practice, but they should rely on more economically sound methods like the NPV and IRR.

4.6 Profitability Index

The profitability index (PI) is the present value of a project's future cash flows divided by the initial investment. It can be expressed as

$$\text{PI} = \frac{\text{PV of future cash flows}}{\text{Initial investment}} = 1 + \frac{\text{NPV}}{\text{Initial investment}} \tag{5}$$

You can see that the PI is closely related to the NPV. The PI is the *ratio* of the PV of future cash flows to the initial investment, whereas an NPV is the *difference* between the PV of future cash flows and the initial investment. Whenever the NPV is positive, the PI will be greater than 1.0; conversely, whenever the NPV is negative, the PI will be less than 1.0. The investment decision rule for the PI is as follows:

Invest if	PI > 1.0
Do not invest if	PI < 1.0

Because the PV of future cash flows equals the initial investment plus the NPV, the PI can also be expressed as 1.0 plus the ratio of the NPV to the initial investment, as shown in Equation 5 above. Example 2 illustrates the PI calculation.

EXAMPLE 2

Example of a PI Calculation

The Gerhardt Corporation investment (discussed earlier) had an outlay of €50 million, a present value of future cash flows of €63.136 million, and an NPV of €13.136 million. The profitability index is

$$PI = \frac{PV \text{ of future cash flows}}{\text{Initial investment}} = \frac{63.136}{50.000} = 1.26$$

The PI can also be calculated as

$$PI = 1 + \frac{NPV}{\text{Initial investment}} = 1 + \frac{13.136}{50.000} = 1.26$$

Because the PI > 1.0, this is a profitable investment.

The PI indicates the value you are receiving in exchange for one unit of currency invested. Although the PI is used less frequently than the NPV and IRR, it is sometimes used as a guide in capital rationing. The PI is usually called the profitability index in corporations, but it is commonly referred to as a "benefit–cost ratio" in governmental and not-for-profit organizations.

4.7 NPV Profile

The NPV profile shows a project's NPV graphed as a function of various discount rates. Typically, the NPV is graphed vertically (on the y-axis), and the discount rates are graphed horizontally (on the x-axis). The NPV profile for the Gerhardt capital budgeting project is shown in Example 3.

EXAMPLE 3

NPV Profile

For the Gerhardt example, we have already calculated several NPVs for different discount rates. At 10 percent the NPV is €13.136 million; at 20 percent the NPV is –€0.543 million; and at 19.52 percent (the IRR), the NPV is zero. What is the NPV if the discount rate is 0 percent? The NPV discounted at 0 percent is €34 million, which is simply the sum of all of the undiscounted cash flows. Table 6 and Figure 1 show the NPV profile for the Gerhardt example for discount rates between 0 percent and 30 percent.

Table 6	Gerhardt NPV Profile
Discount Rate (%)	**NPV (€ Millions)**
0	34.000
5.00	22.406
10.00	13.136
15.00	5.623
19.52	0.000
20.00	−0.543

(continued)

Table 6	(Continued)
Discount Rate (%)	**NPV (€ Millions)**
25.00	−5.661
30.00	−9.954

Figure 1   **Gerhardt NPV Profile**

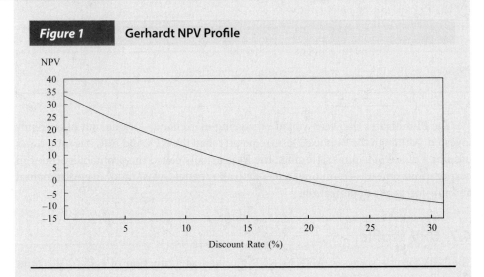

Three interesting points on this NPV profile are where the profile goes through the vertical axis (the NPV when the discount rate is zero), where the profile goes through the horizontal axis (where the discount rate is the IRR), and the NPV for the required rate of return (NPV is €13.136 million when the discount rate is the 10 percent required rate of return).

The NPV profile in Figure 1 is very well-behaved. The NPV declines at a decreasing rate as the discount rate increases. The profile is convex from the origin (convex from below). You will shortly see some examples in which the NPV profile is more complicated.

4.8 Ranking Conflicts between NPV and IRR

For a single conventional project, the NPV and IRR will agree on whether to invest or to not invest. For independent, conventional projects, no conflict exists between the decision rules for the NPV and IRR. However, in the case of two mutually exclusive projects, the two criteria will sometimes disagree. For example, Project A might have a larger NPV than Project B, but Project B has a higher IRR than Project A. In this case, should you invest in Project A or in Project B?

Differing cash flow patterns can cause two projects to rank differently with the NPV and IRR. For example, suppose Project A has shorter-term payoffs than Project B. This situation is presented in Example 4.

EXAMPLE 4

Ranking Conflict Due to Differing Cash Flow Patterns

Projects A and B have similar outlays but different patterns of future cash flows. Project A realizes most of its cash payoffs earlier than Project B. The cash flows, as well as the NPV and IRR for the two projects, are shown in Table 7. For both projects, the required rate of return is 10 percent.

| Table 7 | Cash Flows, NPV, and IRR for Two Projects with Different Cash Flow Patterns |

| | | Cash Flows | | | | | |
Year	0	1	2	3	4	NPV	IRR (%)
Project A	−200	80	80	80	80	53.59	21.86
Project B	−200	0	0	0	400	73.21	18.92

If the two projects were not mutually exclusive, you would invest in both because they are both profitable. However, you can choose either A (which has the higher IRR) or B (which has the higher NPV).

Table 8 and Figure 2 show the NPVs for Project A and Project B for various discount rates between 0 percent and 30 percent.

| Table 8 | NPV Profiles for Two Projects with Different Cash Flow Patterns |

Discount Rate (%)	NPV for Project A	NPV for Project B
0	120.00	200.00
5.00	83.68	129.08
10.00	53.59	73.21
15.00	28.40	28.70
15.09	27.98	27.98
18.92	11.41	0.00
20.00	7.10	−7.10
21.86	0.00	−18.62
25.00	−11.07	−36.16
30.00	−26.70	−59.95

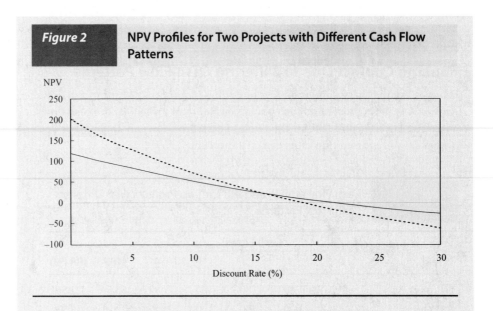

Figure 2   NPV Profiles for Two Projects with Different Cash Flow Patterns

Project B (broken line) has the higher NPV for discount rates between 0 percent and 15.09 percent. Project A (solid line) has the higher NPV for discount rates exceeding 15.09 percent. The crossover point of 15.09 percent in Figure 2 corresponds to the discount rate at which both projects have the same NPV (of 27.98). Project B has the higher NPV below the crossover point, and Project A has the higher NPV above it.

Whenever the NPV and IRR rank two mutually exclusive projects differently, as they do in the example above, you should choose the project based on the NPV. Project B, with the higher NPV, is the better project because of the reinvestment assumption. Mathematically, whenever you discount a cash flow at a particular discount rate, you are implicitly assuming that you can reinvest a cash flow at that same discount rate.[2] In the NPV calculation, you use a discount rate of 10 percent for both projects. In the IRR calculation, you use a discount rate equal to the IRR of 21.86 percent for Project A and 18.92 percent for Project B.

Can you reinvest the cash inflows from the projects at 10 percent, or 21.86 percent, or 18.92 percent? When you assume the required rate of return is 10 percent, you are assuming an opportunity cost of 10 percent—that you can either find other projects that pay a 10 percent return or pay back your sources of capital that cost you 10 percent. The fact that you earned 21.86 percent in Project A or 18.92 percent in Project B does not mean that you can reinvest future cash flows at those rates. (In fact, if you can reinvest future cash flows at 21.86 percent or 18.92 percent, these should have been used as your required rate of return instead of 10 percent.) Because the NPV criterion uses the most realistic discount rate—the opportunity cost of funds—the NPV criterion should be used for evaluating mutually exclusive projects.

---

2 For example, assume that you are receiving $100 in one year discounted at 10 percent. The present value is $100/$1.10 = $90.91. Instead of receiving the $100 in one year, invest it for one additional year at 10 percent, and it grows to $110. What is the present value of $110 received in two years discounted at 10 percent? It is the same $90.91. Because both future cash flows are worth the same, you are implicitly assuming that reinvesting the earlier cash flow at the discount rate of 10 percent has no effect on its value.

Another circumstance that frequently causes mutually exclusive projects to be ranked differently by NPV and IRR criteria is project scale—the sizes of the projects. Would you rather have a small project with a higher rate of return or a large project with a lower rate of return? Sometimes, the larger, low rate of return project has the better NPV. This case is developed in Example 5.

EXAMPLE 5

Ranking Conflicts due to Differing Project Scale

Project A has a much smaller outlay than Project B, although they have similar future cash flow patterns. The cash flows, as well as the NPVs and IRRs for the two projects, are shown in Table 9. For both projects, the required rate of return is 10 percent.

Table 9	Cash Flows, NPV, and IRR for Two Projects of Differing Scale						
	Cash Flows						
Year	**0**	**1**	**2**	**3**	**4**	**NPV**	**IRR (%)**
Project A	−100	50	50	50	50	58.49	34.90
Project B	−400	170	170	170	170	138.88	25.21

If they were not mutually exclusive, you would invest in both projects because they are both profitable. However, you can choose either Project A (which has the higher IRR) or Project B (which has the higher NPV).

Table 10 and Figure 3 show the NPVs for Project A and Project B for various discount rates between 0 percent and 30 percent.

Table 10	NPV Profiles for Two Projects of Differing Scale	
Discount Rate (%)	**NPV for Project A**	**NPV for Project B**
0	100.00	280.00
5.00	77.30	202.81
10.00	58.49	138.88
15.00	42.75	85.35
20.00	29.44	40.08
21.86	25.00	25.00
25.00	18.08	1.47
25.21	17.65	0.00
30.00	8.31	−31.74
34.90	0.00	−60.00
35.00	−0.15	−60.52

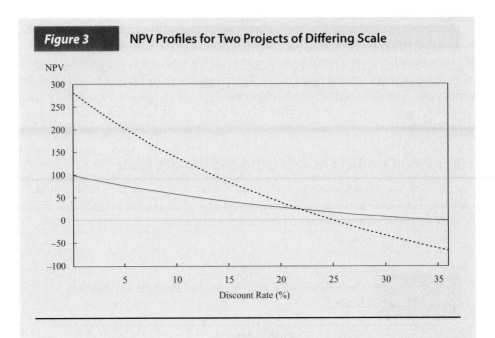

Figure 3   NPV Profiles for Two Projects of Differing Scale

Project B (broken line) has the higher NPV for discount rates between 0 percent and 21.86 percent. Project A has the higher NPV for discount rates exceeding 21.86 percent. The crossover point of 21.86 percent in Figure 3 corresponds to the discount rate at which both projects have the same NPV (of 25.00). Below the crossover point, Project B has the higher NPV, and above it, Project A has the higher NPV. When cash flows are discounted at the 10 percent required rate of return, the choice is clear—Project B, the larger project, which has the superior NPV.

The good news is that the NPV and IRR criteria will usually indicate the same investment decision for a given project. They will usually both recommend acceptance or rejection of the project. When the choice is between two mutually exclusive projects and the NPV and IRR rank the two projects differently, the NPV criterion is strongly preferred. There are good reasons for this preference. The NPV shows the amount of gain, or wealth increase, as a currency amount. The reinvestment assumption of the NPV is the more economically realistic. The IRR does give you a rate of return, but the IRR could be for a small investment or for only a short period of time. As a practical matter, once a corporation has the data to calculate the NPV, it is fairly trivial to go ahead and calculate the IRR and other capital budgeting criteria. However, the most appropriate and theoretically sound criterion is the NPV.

4.9 The Multiple IRR Problem and the No IRR Problem

A problem that can arise with the IRR criterion is the "multiple IRR problem." We can illustrate this problem with the following nonconventional cash flow pattern:[3]

Time	0	1	2
Cash flow	−1,000	5,000	−6,000

The IRR for these cash flows satisfies this equation:

---

3 This example is adapted from Hirschleifer (1958).

$$-1,000 + \frac{5,000}{(1 + \text{IRR})^1} + \frac{-6,000}{(1 + \text{IRR})^2} = 0$$

It turns out that there are two values of IRR that satisfy the equation: IRR = 1 = 100% and IRR = 2 = 200%. To further understand this problem, consider the NPV profile for this investment, which is shown in Table 11 and Figure 4.

As you can see in the NPV profile, the NPV is equal to zero at IRR = 100% and IRR = 200%. The NPV is negative for discount rates below 100 percent, positive between 100 percent and 200 percent, and then negative above 200 percent. The NPV reaches its highest value when the discount rate is 140 percent.

It is also possible to have an investment project with no IRR. The "no-IRR problem" occurs with this cash flow pattern:[4]

Time	0	1	2
Cash flow	100	−300	250

The IRR for these cash flows satisfies this equation:

$$100 + \frac{-300}{(1 + \text{IRR})^1} + \frac{250}{(1 + \text{IRR})^2} = 0$$

For these cash flows, no discount rate exists that results in a zero NPV. Does that mean this project is a bad investment? In this case, the project is actually a good investment. As Table 12 and Figure 5 show, the NPV is positive for all discount rates. The lowest NPV, of 10, occurs for a discount rate of 66.67 percent, and the NPV is always greater than zero. Consequently, no IRR exists.

Table 11	NPV Profile for a Multiple IRR Example

Discount Rate (%)	NPV
0	−2,000.00
25	−840.00
50	−333.33
75	−102.04
100	0.00
125	37.04
140	41.67
150	40.00
175	24.79
200	0.00
225	−29.59
250	−61.22
300	−125.00
350	−185.19
400	−240.00
500	−333.33

(continued)

---

4 This example is also adapted from Hirschleifer.

Table 11	(Continued)

Discount Rate (%)	NPV
1,000	−595.04
2,000	−775.51
3,000	−844.95
4,000	−881.62
10,000	−951.08
1,000,000	−999.50

Figure 4	NPV Profile for a Multiple IRR Example

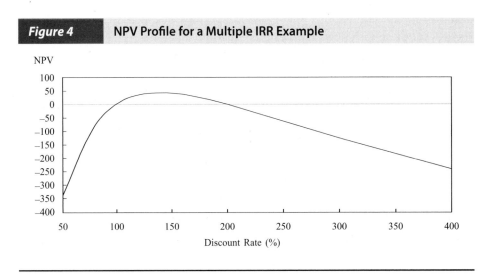

Table 12	NPV Profile for a Project with No IRR

Discount Rate (%)	NPV
0	50.00
25	20.00
50	11.11
66.67	10.00
75	10.20
100	12.50
125	16.05
150	20.00
175	23.97
200	27.78
225	31.36
250	34.69
275	37.78
300	40.63

Table 12	(Continued)
Discount Rate (%)	**NPV**
325	43.25
350	45.68
375	47.92
400	50.00

Figure 5 **NPV Profile for a Project with No IRR**

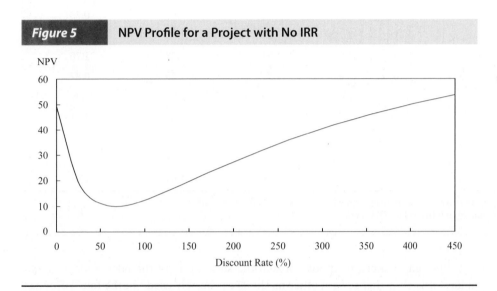

For conventional projects that have outlays followed by inflows—negative cash flows followed by positive cash flows—the multiple IRR problem cannot occur. However, for nonconventional projects, as in the example above, the multiple IRR problem can occur. The IRR equation is essentially an nth degree polynomial. An nth degree polynomial can have up to n solutions, although it will have no more real solutions than the number of cash flow sign changes. For example, a project with two sign changes could have zero, one, or two IRRs. Having two sign changes does not mean that you *will* have multiple IRRs; it just means that you *might*. Fortunately, most capital budgeting projects have only one IRR. Analysts should always be aware of the unusual cash flow patterns that can generate the multiple IRR problem.

4.10 Popularity and Usage of the Capital Budgeting Methods

Analysts need to know the basic logic of the various capital budgeting criteria as well as the practicalities involved in using them in real corporations. Before delving into the many issues involved in applying these models, we would like to present some feedback on their popularity.

The usefulness of any analytical tool always depends on the specific application. Corporations generally find these capital budgeting criteria useful. Two recent surveys by Graham and Harvey (2001) and Brounen, De Jong, and Koedijk (2004) report on the frequency of their use by U.S. and European corporations. Table 13 gives the mean responses of executives in five countries to the question "How frequently does your company use the following techniques when deciding which projects or acquisitions to pursue?"

| Table 13 | Mean Responses about Frequency of Use of Capital Budgeting Techniques |

	U.S.	U.K.	Netherlands	Germany	France
Internal rate of return[a]	3.09	2.31	2.36	2.15	2.27
Net present value[a]	3.08	2.32	2.76	2.26	1.86
Payback period[a]	2.53	2.77	2.53	2.29	2.46
Hurdle rate	2.13	1.35	1.98	1.61	0.73
Sensitivity analysis	2.31	2.21	1.84	1.65	0.79
Earnings multiple approach	1.89	1.81	1.61	1.25	1.70
Discounted payback period[a]	1.56	1.49	1.25	1.59	0.87
Real options approach	1.47	1.65	1.49	2.24	2.20
Accounting rate of return[a]	1.34	1.79	1.40	1.63	1.11
Value at risk	0.95	0.85	0.51	1.45	1.68
Adjusted present value	0.85	0.78	0.78	0.71	1.11
Profitability index[a]	0.85	1.00	0.78	1.04	1.64

[a]These techniques were described in this section of the reading. You will encounter the others elsewhere.
Note: Respondents used a scale ranging from 0 (never) to 4 (always).

Although financial textbooks preach the superiority of the NPV and IRR techniques, it is clear that several other methods are heavily used.[5] In the four European countries, the payback period is used as often as, or even slightly more often than, the NPV and IRR. In these two studies, larger companies tended to prefer the NPV and IRR over the payback period. The fact that the U.S. companies were larger, on average, partially explains the greater U.S. preference for the NPV and IRR. Other factors influence the choice of capital budgeting techniques. Private corporations used the payback period more frequently than did public corporations. Companies managed by an MBA had a stronger preference for the discounted cash flow techniques. Of course, any survey research also has some limitations. In this case, the persons in these large corporations responding to the surveys may not have been aware of all of the applications of these techniques.

These capital budgeting techniques are essential tools for corporate managers. Capital budgeting is also relevant to external analysts. Because a corporation's investing decisions ultimately determine the value of its financial obligations, the corporation's investing processes are vital. The NPV criterion is the criterion most directly related to stock prices. If a corporation invests in positive NPV projects, these should add to the wealth of its shareholders. Example 6 illustrates this scenario.

---

5 Analysts often refer to the NPV and IRR as "discounted cash flow techniques" because they accurately account for the timing of all cash flows when they are discounted.

> **EXAMPLE 6**
>
> ### NPVs and Stock Prices
>
> Freitag Corporation is investing €600 million in distribution facilities. The present value of the future after-tax cash flows is estimated to be €850 million. Freitag has 200 million outstanding shares with a current market price of €32.00 per share. This investment is new information, and it is independent of other expectations about the company. What should be the effect of the project on the value of the company and the stock price?
>
> ### Solution:
>
> The NPV of the project is €850 million − €600 million = €250 million. The total market value of the company prior to the investment is €32.00 × 200 million shares = €6,400 million. The value of the company should increase by €250 million to €6,650 million. The price per share should increase by the NPV per share, or €250 million / 200 million shares = €1.25 per share. The share price should increase from €32.00 to €33.25.

The effect of a capital budgeting project's positive or negative NPV on share price is more complicated than Example 6 above, in which the value of the stock increased by the project's NPV. The value of a company is the value of its existing investments plus the net present values of all of its future investments. If an analyst learns of an investment, the impact of that investment on the stock price will depend on whether the investment's profitability is more or less than expected. For example, an analyst could learn of a positive NPV project, but if the project's profitability is less than expectations, this stock might drop in price on the news. Alternatively, news of a particular capital project might be considered as a signal about other capital projects underway or in the future. A project that by itself might add, say, €0.25 to the value of the stock might signal the existence of other profitable projects. News of this project might increase the stock price by far more than €0.25.

The integrity of a corporation's capital budgeting processes is important to analysts. Management's capital budgeting processes can demonstrate two things about the quality of management: the degree to which management embraces the goal of shareholder wealth maximization, and its effectiveness in pursuing that goal. Both of these factors are important to shareholders.

SUMMARY

Capital budgeting is the process that companies use for decision making on capital projects—those projects with a life of a year or more. This reading developed the principles behind the basic capital budgeting model, the cash flows that go into the model, and several extensions of the basic model.

- Capital budgeting undergirds the most critical investments for many corporations—their investments in long-term assets. The principles of capital budgeting have been applied to other corporate investing and financing decisions and to security analysis and portfolio management.

- The typical steps in the capital budgeting process are: 1) generating ideas, 2) analyzing individual proposals, 3) planning the capital budget, and 4) monitoring and post-auditing.

- Projects susceptible to capital budgeting process can be categorized as: 1) replacement, 2) expansion, 3) new products and services, and 4) regulatory, safety and environmental.

- Capital budgeting decisions are based on incremental after-tax cash flows discounted at the opportunity cost of funds. Financing costs are ignored because both the cost of debt and the cost of other capital are captured in the discount rate.

- The net present value (NPV) is the present value of all after-tax cash flows, or

$$NPV = \sum_{t=0}^{n} \frac{CF_t}{(1+r)^t}$$

  where the investment outlays are negative cash flows included in the CF_ts and where r is the required rate of return for the investment.

- The IRR is the discount rate that makes the present value of all future cash flows sum to zero. This equation can be solved for the IRR:

$$\sum_{t=0}^{n} \frac{CF_t}{(1+IRR)^t} = 0$$

- The payback period is the number of years required to recover the original investment in a project. The payback is based on cash flows.

- The discounted payback period is the number of years it takes for the cumulative discounted cash flows from a project to equal the original investment.

- The average accounting rate of return (AAR) can be defined as follows:

$$AAR = \frac{\text{Average net income}}{\text{Average book value}}$$

- The profitability index (PI) is the present value of a project's future cash flows divided by the initial investment:

$$PI = \frac{\text{PV of future cash flows}}{\text{Initial investment}} = 1 + \frac{NPV}{\text{Initial investment}}$$

- The capital budgeting decision rules are to invest if the NPV > 0, if the IRR > r, or if the PI > 1.0 There are no decision rules for the payback period, discounted payback period, and AAR because they are not always sound measures.

- The NPV profile is a graph that shows a project's NPV graphed as a function of various discount rates.

- For mutually exclusive projects that are ranked differently by the NPV and IRR, it is economically sound to choose the project with the higher NPV.

- The "multiple IRR problem" and the "no IRR problem" can arise for a project with nonconventional cash flows—cash flows that change signs more than once during the project's life.

- The fact that projects with positive NPVs theoretically increase the value of the company and the value of its stock could explain the popularity of NPV as an evaluation method.

PRACTICE PROBLEMS

1 Given the following cash flows for a capital project, calculate the NPV and IRR. The required rate of return is 8 percent.

Year	0	1	2	3	4	5
Cash flow	−50,000	15,000	15,000	20,000	10,000	5,000

	NPV	IRR
A	$1,905	10.9%
B	$1,905	26.0%
C	$3,379	10.9%

2 Given the following cash flows for a capital project, calculate its payback period and discounted payback period. The required rate of return is 8 percent.

Year	0	1	2	3	4	5
Cash flow	−50,000	15,000	15,000	20,000	10,000	5,000

The discounted payback period is:

A   0.16 years longer than the payback period.

B   0.51 years longer than the payback period.

C   1.01 years longer than the payback period.

3 An investment of $100 generates after-tax cash flows of $40 in Year 1, $80 in Year 2, and $120 in Year 3. The required rate of return is 20 percent. The net present value is *closest* to:

A $42.22.

B $58.33.

C $68.52.

4 An investment of $150,000 is expected to generate an after-tax cash flow of $100,000 in one year and another $120,000 in two years. The cost of capital is 10 percent. What is the internal rate of return?

A   28.39 percent.

B   28.59 percent.

C   28.79 percent.

5 Kim Corporation is considering an investment of 750 million won with expected after-tax cash inflows of 175 million won per year for seven years. The required rate of return is 10 percent. What is the project's:

	NPV?	IRR?
A	102 million won	14.0%
B	157 million won	23.3%
C	193 million won	10.0%

6 Kim Corporation is considering an investment of 750 million won with expected after-tax cash inflows of 175 million won per year for seven years. The required rate of return is 10 percent. Expressed in years, the project's payback period and discounted payback period, respectively, are *closest* to:

A 4.3 years and 5.4 years.

B 4.3 years and 5.9 years.

C 4.8 years and 6.3 years.

7 An investment of $20,000 will create a perpetual after-tax cash flow of $2,000. The required rate of return is 8 percent. What is the investment's profitability index?

A 1.08.

B 1.16.

C 1.25.

8 Hermann Corporation is considering an investment of €375 million with expected after-tax cash inflows of €115 million per year for seven years and an additional after-tax salvage value of €50 million in Year 7. The required rate of return is 10 percent. What is the investment's PI?

A 1.19.

B 1.33.

C 1.56.

9 Erin Chou is reviewing a profitable investment project that has a conventional cash flow pattern. If the cash flows for the project, initial outlay, and future after-tax cash flows all double, Chou would predict that the IRR would:

A increase and the NPV would increase.

B stay the same and the NPV would increase.

C stay the same and the NPV would stay the same.

10 Shirley Shea has evaluated an investment proposal and found that its payback period is one year, it has a negative NPV, and it has a positive IRR. Is this combination of results possible?

A Yes.

B No, because a project with a positive IRR has a positive NPV.

C No, because a project with such a rapid payback period has a positive NPV.

11 An investment has an outlay of 100 and after-tax cash flows of 40 annually for four years. A project enhancement increases the outlay by 15 and the annual after-tax cash flows by 5. As a result, the vertical intercept of the NPV profile of the enhanced project shifts:

A up and the horizontal intercept shifts left.

B up and the horizontal intercept shifts right.

C down and the horizontal intercept shifts left.

12 Projects 1 and 2 have similar outlays, although the patterns of future cash flows are different. The cash flows as well as the NPV and IRR for the two projects are shown below. For both projects, the required rate of return is 10 percent.

	Cash Flows						
Year	**0**	**1**	**2**	**3**	**4**	**NPV**	**IRR (%)**
Project 1	−50	20	20	20	20	13.40	21.86
Project 2	−50	0	0	0	100	18.30	18.92

The two projects are mutually exclusive. What is the appropriate investment decision?

A   Invest in both projects.

B   Invest in Project 1 because it has the higher IRR.

C   Invest in Project 2 because it has the higher NPV.

13 Consider the two projects below. The cash flows as well as the NPV and IRR for the two projects are given. For both projects, the required rate of return is 10 percent.

	Cash Flows						
Year	**0**	**1**	**2**	**3**	**4**	**NPV**	**IRR (%)**
Project 1	−100	36	36	36	36	14.12	16.37
Project 2	−100	0	0	0	175	19.53	15.02

What discount rate would result in the same NPV for both projects?

A   A rate between 0.00 percent and 10.00 percent.

B   A rate between 10.00 percent and 15.02 percent.

C   A rate between 15.02 percent and 16.37 percent.

14 Wilson Flannery is concerned that this project has multiple IRRs.

Year	**0**	**1**	**2**	**3**
Cash flows	−50	100	0	−50

How many discount rates produce a zero NPV for this project?

A   One, a discount rate of 0 percent.

B   Two, discount rates of 0 percent and 32 percent.

C   Two, discount rates of 0 percent and 62 percent.

15 With regard to the net present value (NPV) profiles of two projects, the crossover rate is *best* described as the discount rate at which:

A   two projects have the same NPV.

B   two projects have the same internal rate of return.

C   a project's NPV changes from positive to negative.

16 With regard to net present value (NPV) profiles, the point at which a profile crosses the vertical axis is *best* described as:

A   the point at which two projects have the same NPV.

B   the sum of the undiscounted cash flows from a project.

    C   a project's internal rate of return when the project's NPV is equal to zero.

17 With regard to net present value (NPV) profiles, the point at which a profile crosses the horizontal axis is *best* described as:

    A   the point at which two projects have the same NPV.

    B   the sum of the undiscounted cash flows from a project.

    C   a project's internal rate of return when the project's NPV is equal to zero.

18 With regard to capital budgeting, an appropriate estimate of the incremental cash flows from a project is *least likely* to include:

    A   externalities.

    B   interest costs.

    C   opportunity costs.

SOLUTIONS

1 C is correct.

$$\text{NPV} = -50{,}000 + \frac{15{,}000}{1.08} + \frac{15{,}000}{1.08^2} + \frac{20{,}000}{1.08^3} + \frac{10{,}000}{1.08^4} + \frac{5{,}000}{1.08^5}$$

$$\text{NPV} = -50{,}000 + 13{,}888.89 + 12{,}860.08 + 15{,}876.64 + 7{,}350.30$$
$$+3{,}402.92$$

$$\text{NPV} = -50{,}000 + 53{,}378.83 = 3{,}378.83$$

The IRR, found with a financial calculator, is 10.88 percent.

2 C is correct.

Year	0	1	2	3	4	5
Cash flow	−50,000	15,000	15,000	20,000	10,000	5,000
Cumulative cash flow	−50,000	−35,000	−20,000	0	10,000	15,000
Discounted cash flow	−50,000	13,888.89	12,860.08	15,876.64	7,350.30	3,402.92
Cumulative DCF	−50,000	−36,111.11	−23,251.03	−7,374.38	−24.09	3,378.83

As the table shows, the cumulative cash flow offsets the initial investment in exactly three years. The payback period is 3.00 years. The discounted payback period is between four and five years. The discounted payback period is 4 years plus $24.09/3{,}402.92 = 0.007$ of the fifth year cash flow, or $4.007 = 4.01$ years. The discounted payback period is $4.01 - 3.00 = 1.01$ years longer than the payback period.

3 B is correct.

$$\text{NPV} = \sum_{t=0}^{3} \frac{CF_t}{(1+r)^t} = -100 + \frac{40}{1.20} + \frac{80}{1.20^2} + \frac{120}{1.20^3} = \$58.33$$

4 C is correct. The IRR can be found using a financial calculator or with trial and error. Using trial and error, the total PV is equal to zero if the discount rate is 28.79 percent.

		Present Value			
Year	Cash Flow	28.19%	28.39%	28.59%	28.79%
0	−150,000	−150,000	−150,000	−150,000	−150,000
1	100,000	78,009	77,888	77,767	77,646
2	120,000	73,025	72,798	72,572	72,346
Total		1,034	686	338	−8

A more precise IRR of 28.7854 percent has a total PV closer to zero.

5 A is correct.

$$\text{The NPV} = -750 + \sum_{t=1}^{7} \frac{175}{1.10^t} = -750 + 851.97 = 101.97 \text{ million won.}$$

The IRR, found with a financial calculator, is 14.02 percent. (The PV is –750, N = 7, and PMT = 175.)

6 B is correct.

Year	0	1	2	3	4	5	6	7
Cash flow	–750	175	175	175	175	175	175	175
Cumulative cash flow	–750	–575	–400	–225	–50	125	300	475

The payback period is between four and five years. The payback period is four years plus 50/175 = 0.29 of the fifth year cash flow, or 4.29 years.

Year	0	1	2	3	4	5	6	7
Cash flow	–750	175	175	175	175	175	175	175
Discounted cash flow	–750	159.09	144.63	131.48	119.53	108.66	98.78	89.80
Cumulative DCF	–750	–590.91	–446.28	–314.80	–195.27	–86.61	12.17	101.97

The discounted payback period is between five and six years. The discounted payback period is five years plus 86.61/98.78 = 0.88 of the sixth year cash flow, or 5.88 years.

7 C is correct.

$$\text{The present value of future cash flows is PV} = \frac{2{,}000}{0.08} = 25{,}000$$

$$\text{The profitability index is PI} = \frac{\text{PV}}{\text{Investment}} = \frac{25{,}000}{20{,}000} = 1.25$$

8 C is correct.

$$\text{PV} = \sum_{t=1}^{7} \frac{115}{1.10^t} + \frac{50}{1.10^7} = 585.53 \text{ million euros}$$

$$\text{PI} = \frac{585.53}{375} = 1.56$$

9 B is correct. The IRR would stay the same because both the initial outlay and the after-tax cash flows double, so that the return on each dollar invested remains the same. All of the cash flows and their present values double. The difference between total present value of the future cash flows and the initial outlay (the NPV) also doubles.

10 A is correct. If the cumulative cash flow in one year equals the outlay and additional cash flows are not very large, this scenario is possible. For example, assume the outlay is 100, the cash flow in Year 1 is 100 and the cash flow in Year 2 is 5. The required return is 10 percent. This project would have a payback of 1.0 years, an NPV of –4.96, and an IRR of 4.77 percent.

11 A is correct. The vertical intercept changes from 60 to 65 (NPV when cost of capital is 0%), and the horizontal intercept (IRR, when NPV equals zero) changes from 21.86 percent to 20.68 percent.

12 C is correct. When valuing mutually exclusive projects, the decision should be made with the NPV method because this method uses the most realistic discount rate, namely the opportunity cost of funds. In this example, the reinvestment rate for the NPV method (here 10 percent) is more realistic than the reinvestment rate for the IRR method (here 21.86 percent or 18.92 percent).

13 B is correct. For these projects, a discount rate of 13.16 percent would yield the same NPV for both (an NPV of 6.73).

14 C is correct. Discount rates of 0 percent and approximately 61.8 percent both give a zero NPV.

Rate	0%	20%	40%	60%	61.8%	80%	100%
NPV	0.00	4.40	3.21	0.29	0.00	−3.02	−6.25

15 A is correct. The crossover rate is the discount rate at which the NPV profiles for two projects cross; it is the only point where the NPVs of the projects are the same.

16 B is correct. The vertical axis represents a discount rate of zero. The point where the profile crosses the vertical axis is simply the sum of the cash flows.

17 C is correct. The horizontal axis represents an NPV of zero. By definition, the project's IRR equals an NPV of zero.

18 B is correct. Costs to finance the project are taken into account when the cash flows are discounted at the appropriate cost of capital; including interest costs in the cash flows would result in double-counting the cost of debt.

Cost of Capital

by Yves Courtois, CFA, Gene C. Lai, and Pamela Peterson Drake, CFA

LEARNING OUTCOMES

Mastery	The candidate should be able to:
☐	**a.** calculate and interpret the weighted average cost of capital (WACC) of a company;
☐	**b.** describe how taxes affect the cost of capital from different capital sources;
☐	**c.** explain alternative methods of calculating the weights used in the WACC, including the use of the company's target capital structure;
☐	**d.** explain how the marginal cost of capital and the investment opportunity schedule are used to determine the optimal capital budget;
☐	**e.** explain the marginal cost of capital's role in determining the net present value of a project;
☐	**f.** calculate and interpret the cost of debt capital using the yield-to-maturity approach and the debt-rating approach;
☐	**g.** calculate and interpret the cost of noncallable, nonconvertible preferred stock;
☐	**h.** calculate and interpret the cost of equity capital using the capital asset pricing model approach, the dividend discount model approach, and the bond-yield-plus risk-premium approach;
☐	**i.** calculate and interpret the beta and cost of capital for a project;
☐	**j.** describe uses of country risk premiums in estimating the cost of equity;
☐	**k.** describe the marginal cost of capital schedule, explain why it may be upward-sloping with respect to additional capital, and calculate and interpret its break-points;
☐	**l.** explain and demonstrate the correct treatment of flotation costs.

1   INTRODUCTION

A company grows by making investments that are expected to increase revenues and profits. The company acquires the capital or funds necessary to make such investments by borrowing or using funds from owners. By applying this capital to investments with long-term benefits, the company is producing value today. But, how much value? The answer depends not only on the investments' expected future cash flows but also on the cost of the funds. Borrowing is not costless. Neither is using owners' funds.

The cost of this capital is an important ingredient in both investment decision making by the company's management and the valuation of the company by investors. If a company invests in projects that produce a return in excess of the cost of capital, the company has created value; in contrast, if the company invests in projects whose returns are less than the cost of capital, the company has actually destroyed value. Therefore, the estimation of the cost of capital is a central issue in corporate financial management. For the analyst seeking to evaluate a company's investment program and its competitive position, an accurate estimate of a company's cost of capital is important as well.

Cost of capital estimation is a challenging task. As we have already implied, the cost of capital is not observable but, rather, must be estimated. Arriving at a cost of capital estimate requires a host of assumptions and estimates. Another challenge is that the cost of capital that is appropriately applied to a specific investment depends on the characteristics of that investment: The riskier the investment's cash flows, the greater its cost of capital. In reality, a company must estimate project-specific costs of capital. What is often done, however, is to estimate the cost of capital for the company as a whole and then adjust this overall corporate cost of capital upward or downward to reflect the risk of the contemplated project relative to the company's average project.

This reading is organized as follows: In the next section, we introduce the cost of capital and its basic computation. Section 3 presents a selection of methods for estimating the costs of the various sources of capital. Section 4 discusses issues an analyst faces in using the cost of capital. A summary concludes the reading.

2   COST OF CAPITAL

The **cost of capital** is the rate of return that the suppliers of capital—bondholders and owners—require as compensation for their contribution of capital. Another way of looking at the cost of capital is that it is the opportunity cost of funds for the suppliers of capital: A potential supplier of capital will not voluntarily invest in a company unless its return meets or exceeds what the supplier could earn elsewhere in an investment of comparable risk.

A company typically has several alternatives for raising capital, including issuing equity, debt, and instruments that share characteristics of debt and equity. Each source selected becomes a component of the company's funding and has a cost (required rate of return) that may be called a **component cost of capital**. Because we are using the cost of capital in the evaluation of investment opportunities, we are dealing with a *marginal* cost—what it would cost to raise additional funds for the potential investment project. Therefore, the cost of capital that the investment analyst is concerned with is a marginal cost.

Let us focus on the cost of capital for the entire company (later we will address how to adjust that for specific projects). The cost of capital of a company is the required rate of return that investors demand for the average-risk investment of a company. The most common way to estimate this required rate of return is to calculate the marginal cost of each of the various sources of capital and then calculate a weighted average of these costs. This weighted average is referred to as the **weighted average cost of capital** (WACC). The WACC is also referred to as the marginal cost of capital (MCC) because it is the cost that a company incurs for additional capital. The weights in this weighted average are the proportions of the various sources of capital that the company uses to support its investment program. Therefore, the WACC, in its most general terms, is

$$\text{WACC} = w_d r_d (1 - t) + w_p r_p + w_e r_e \qquad \textbf{(1)}$$

where

w_d = the proportion of debt that the company uses when it raises new funds

r_d = the before-tax marginal cost of debt

t = the company's marginal tax rate

w_p = the proportion of preferred stock the company uses when it raises new funds

r_p = the marginal cost of preferred stock

w_e = the proportion of equity that the company uses when it raises new funds

r_e = the marginal cost of equity

EXAMPLE 1

Computing the Weighted Average Cost of Capital

Assume that ABC Corporation has the following capital structure: 30 percent debt, 10 percent preferred stock, and 60 percent equity. ABC Corporation wishes to maintain these proportions as it raises new funds. Its before-tax cost of debt is 8 percent, its cost of preferred stock is 10 percent, and its cost of equity is 15 percent. If the company's marginal tax rate is 40 percent, what is ABC's weighted average cost of capital?

Solution:

The weighted average cost of capital is

$$\text{WACC} = (0.3)(0.08)(1 - 0.40) + (0.1)(0.1) + (0.6)(0.15)$$
$$= 11.44 \text{ percent}$$

There are important points concerning the calculation of the WACC as shown in Equation 1 that the analyst must be familiar with. The next two sections address two key issues: taxes and the selection of weights.

2.1 Taxes and the Cost of Capital

Notice that in Equation 1 we adjust the expected before-tax cost on new debt financing, r_d, by a factor of $(1 - t)$. In the United States and many other tax jurisdictions, the interest on debt financing is a deduction to arrive at taxable income. Taking the tax-deductibility of interest as the base case, we adjust the pre-tax cost of debt for this tax shield. Multiplying r_d by $(1 - t)$ results in an estimate of the after-tax cost of debt.

For example, suppose a company pays €1 million in interest on its €10 million of debt. The cost of this debt is not €1 million because this interest expense reduces taxable income by €1 million, resulting in a lower tax. If the company is subject to a tax rate of 40 percent, this €1 million of interest costs the company (€1 million) (1 – 0.4)

= €0.6 million because the interest reduces the company's tax bill by €0.4 million. In this case, the before-tax cost of debt is 10 percent, whereas the after-tax cost of debt is (€0.6 million)/(€10 million) = 6 percent.

Estimating the cost of common equity capital is more challenging than estimating the cost of debt capital. Debt capital involves a stated legal obligation on the part of the company to pay interest and repay the principal on the borrowing. Equity entails no such obligation. Estimating the cost of conventional preferred equity is rather straightforward because the dividend is generally stated and fixed, but estimating the cost of common equity is challenging. There are several methods available for estimating the cost of common equity, and we discuss two in this reading. The first method uses the capital asset pricing model, and the second method uses the dividend discount model, which is based on discounted cash flows. No matter the method, there is no need to make any adjustment in the cost of equity for taxes because the payments to owners, whether in the form of dividends or the return on capital, are not tax-deductible for the company.

EXAMPLE 2

Incorporating the Effect of Taxes on the Costs of Capital

Jorge Ricard, a financial analyst, is estimating the costs of capital for the Zeale Corporation. In the process of this estimation, Ricard has estimated the before-tax costs of capital for Zeale's debt and equity as 4 percent and 6 percent, respectively. What are the after-tax costs of debt and equity if Zeale's marginal tax rate is:

1   30 percent?

2   48 percent?

	Marginal Tax Rate	After-Tax Cost of Debt	After-Tax Cost of Equity
Solution to 1:	30 percent	0.04(1 − 0.30) = 2.80 percent	6 percent
Solution to 2:	48 percent	0.04(1 − 0.48) = 2.08 percent	6 percent

Note: There is no adjustment for taxes in the case of equity; the before-tax cost of equity is equal to the after-tax cost of equity.

2.2 Weights of the Weighted Average

How do we determine what weights to use? Ideally, we want to use the proportion of each source of capital that the company would use in the project or company. If we assume that a company has a target capital structure and raises capital consistent with this target, we should use this target capital structure. The **target capital structure** is the capital structure that a company is striving to obtain. If we know the company's target capital structure, then, of course, we should use this in our analysis. Someone outside the company, however, such as an analyst, typically does not know the target capital structure and must estimate it using one of several approaches:

1   Assume the company's current capital structure, at market value weights for the components, represents the company's target capital structure.

2   Examine trends in the company's capital structure or statements by management regarding capital structure policy to infer the target capital structure.

3   Use averages of comparable companies' capital structures as the target capital structure.

In the absence of knowledge of a company's target capital structure, we may take Method 1 as the baseline. Note that in applying Method 3, we use an unweighted, arithmetic average, as is often done for simplicity. An alternative is to calculate a weighted average, which would give more weight to larger companies.

Suppose we are using the company's current capital structure as a proxy for the target capital structure. In this case, we use the market value of the different capital sources in the calculation of these proportions. For example, if a company has the following market values for its capital

Bonds outstanding	$5 million
Preferred stock	1 million
Common stock	14 million
Total capital	$20 million

the weights that we apply would be

$$w_d = 0.25$$
$$w_p = 0.05$$
$$w_e = 0.70$$

Example 3 illustrates the estimation of weights. Note that a simple way of transforming a debt-to-equity ratio D/E into a weight—that is, D/(D + E)—is to divide D/E by 1 + D/E.

EXAMPLE 3

Estimating the Proportions of Capital

Fin Anziell is a financial analyst with Analytiker Firma. Anziell is in the process of estimating the cost of capital of Gewicht GmbH. The following information is provided:

Gewicht GmbH

Market value of debt	€50 million
Market value of equity	€60 million

Primary competitors and their capital structures (in millions):

Competitor	Market Value of Debt	Market Value of Equity
A	€25	€50
B	€101	€190
C	£40	£60

What are Gewicht's proportions of debt and equity that Anziell would use if estimating these proportions using the company's:

1 current capital structure?

2 competitors' capital structure?

3 Suppose Gewicht announces that a debt-to-equity ratio of 0.7 reflects its target capital structure. What weights should Anziell use in the cost of capital calculations?

Solution to 1:

Current capital structure

$$w_d = \frac{€50 \text{ million}}{€50 \text{ million} + €60 \text{ million}} = 0.4545$$

$$w_e = \frac{€60 \text{ million}}{€50 \text{ million} + €60 \text{ million}} = 0.5454$$

Solution to 2:

Competitors' capital structure:[1]

$$w_d = \frac{\left(\dfrac{€25}{€25 + €50}\right) + \left(\dfrac{€101}{€101 + €190}\right) + \left(\dfrac{£40}{£40 + £60}\right)}{3} = 0.3601$$

$$w_e = \frac{\left(\dfrac{€50}{€25 + €50}\right) + \left(\dfrac{€190}{€101 + €190}\right) + \left(\dfrac{£60}{£40 + £60}\right)}{3} = 0.6399$$

Solution to 3:

A debt-to-equity ratio of 0.7 represents a weight on debt of 0.7/1.7 = 0.4118 so that $w_d = 0.4118$ and $w_e = 1 - 0.4118 = 0.5882$. These would be the preferred weights to use in a cost of capital calculation.

2.3 Applying the Cost of Capital to Capital Budgeting and Security Valuation

With some insight now into the calculation of the cost of capital, let us continue to improve our understanding of the roles it plays in financial analysis. A chief use of the marginal cost of capital estimate is in capital-budgeting decision making. What role does the marginal cost of capital play in a company's investment program, and how do we adapt it when we need to evaluate a specific investment project?

A company's marginal cost of capital (MCC) may increase as additional capital is raised, whereas returns to a company's investment opportunities are generally believed to decrease as the company makes additional investments, as represented by the **investment opportunity schedule** (IOS).[2] We show this relation in Figure 1, graphing the upward-sloping marginal cost of capital schedule against the downward-sloping investment opportunity schedule. In the context of a company's investment decision, the optimal capital budget is that amount of capital raised and invested at which the marginal cost of capital is equal to the marginal return from investing. In other words, the optimal capital budget occurs when the marginal cost of capital intersects with the investment opportunity schedule as seen in Figure 1.

The relation between the MCC and the IOS provides a broad picture of the basic decision-making problem of a company. However, we are often interested in valuing an individual project or even a portion of a company, such as a division or product line. In these applications, we are interested in the cost of capital for the project, product, or division as opposed to the cost of capital for the company overall. The cost of capital in these applications should reflect the riskiness of the future cash flows of the project, product, or division. For an average-risk project, the opportunity cost

---

1 These weights represent the arithmetic average of the three companies' debt proportion and equity proportion, respectively.

2 The investment opportunity schedule originates with Fisher's production opportunities [Irving Fisher, *The Theory of Interest* (New York: MacMillan Co.), 1930] and was adapted to capital budgeting by John Hirshleifer ["On the Theory of Optimal Investment Decision," *Journal of Political Economy*, Vol. 66, No. 4 (August 1958), pp. 329–352.]

of capital is the company's WACC. If the systematic risk of the project is above or below average relative to the company's current portfolio of projects, an upward or downward adjustment, respectively, is made to the company's WACC. Companies may take an *ad hoc* or a systematic approach to making such adjustments. The discussion of a systematic approach is a somewhat advanced topic that we defer to Section 4.1.

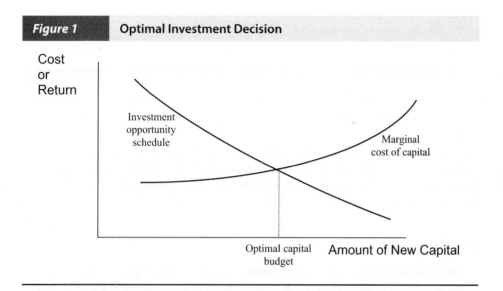

Figure 1	**Optimal Investment Decision**

The WACC or MCC corresponding to the average risk of the company, adjusted appropriately for the risk of a given project, plays a role in capital-budgeting decision making based on the **net present value** (NPV) of that project. Recall from the reading on capital budgeting that the NPV is the present value of all the project cash flows. It is useful to think of it as the difference between the present value of the cash inflows, discounted at the opportunity cost of capital applicable to the specific project, and the present value of the cash outflows, discounted using that same opportunity cost of capital:

NPV = Present value of inflows − Present value of outflows

If an investment's NPV is positive, the company should undertake the project. If we choose to use the company's WACC in the calculation of the NPV of a project, we are assuming that the project:

- has the same risk as the average-risk project of the company, and
- will have a constant target capital structure throughout its useful life.[3]

These may not be realistic or appropriate assumptions and are potential drawbacks to using the company's WACC in valuing projects. However, alternative approaches are subject to drawbacks as well, and the approach outlined has wide acceptance.[4]

---

3 WACC is estimated using fixed proportions of equity and debt. The NPV method assumes a constant required rate of return, whereas a fluctuating capital structure would cause WACC to fluctuate. The importance of this issue is demonstrated by James A. Miles and John R. Ezzell, "The Weighted Average Cost of Capital, Perfect Capital Markets, and Project Life: A Clarification," *Journal of Financial and Quantitative Analysis*, Vol. 15, No. 3 (September 1980), pp. 719–730.

4 See the reading on capital budgeting for a discussion.

For the analyst, the second key use of the marginal cost of capital is in security valuation using any one of several discounted cash flow valuation models available.[5] For a particular valuation model, if these cash flows are cash flows to the company's suppliers of capital (that is, free cash flow to the firm), the analyst uses the weighted average cost of capital of the company in the valuation.[6] If these cash flows are strictly those belonging to the company's owners, such as the free cash flow to equity, or dividends, the analyst uses the cost of equity capital to find the present value of these flows.[7]

In the next section, we discuss how an analyst may approach the calculation of the component costs of capital, focusing on debt, preferred stock, and common equity.

3   COSTS OF THE DIFFERENT SOURCES OF CAPITAL

Each source of capital has a different cost because of the differences among the sources, such as seniority, contractual commitments, and potential value as a tax shield. We focus on the costs of three primary sources of capital: debt, preferred equity, and common equity.

3.1 Cost of Debt

The **cost of debt** is the cost of debt financing to a company when it issues a bond or takes out a bank loan. We discuss two methods to estimate the before-tax cost of debt, r_d: the yield-to-maturity approach and debt-rating approach.

3.1.1 Yield-to-Maturity Approach

The **yield to maturity** (YTM) is the annual return that an investor earns on a bond if the investor purchases the bond today and holds it until maturity. In other words, it is the yield, r_d, that equates the present value of the bond's promised payments to its market price:

$$P_0 = \frac{PMT_1}{\left(1 + \frac{r_d}{2}\right)} + \dots + \frac{PMT_n}{\left(1 + \frac{r_d}{2}\right)^n} + \frac{FV}{\left(1 + \frac{r_d}{2}\right)^n} = \left(\sum_{t=1}^{n} \frac{PMT_t}{\left(1 + \frac{r_d}{2}\right)^t}\right) + \frac{FV}{\left(1 + \frac{r_d}{2}\right)^n} \qquad (2)$$

where

P_0 = the current market price of the bond
PMT_t = the interest payment in period t
r_d = the yield to maturity[8]

---

5 See John Stowe, Thomas Robinson, Jerald Pinto, and Dennis McLeavey, *Analysis of Equity Investments: Valuation* (AIMR 2002) for a presentation of such models.

6 Free cash flow to the firm (FCFF) is the cash flow available to the company's suppliers of capital after all operating expenses (including taxes) have been paid and necessary investments in working capital (e.g., inventory) and fixed capital (e.g., plant and equipment) have been made.

7 Free cash flow to equity (FCFE) is the cash flow available to holders of the company's common equity after all operating expenses, interest, and principal payments have been paid and necessary investments in working capital and fixed capital have been made. See John Stowe, Thomas Robinson, Jerald Pinto, and Dennis McLeavey, *Analysis of Equity Investments: Valuation* (AIMR 2002) for more details on FCFF and FCFE and valuation models based on those concepts.

8 r_d is expressed as an annual rate and is divided by the number of payment periods per year. Because most corporate bonds pay semi-annual interest, we divided r_d by 2 in this calculation. The interest payment for each period thus corresponds with the bond's semi-annual coupon payment.

n = the number of periods remaining to maturity

FV = the maturity value of the bond

This valuation equation assumes the bond pays semi-annual interest and that any intermediate cash flows (in this case the interest prior to maturity) are reinvested at the rate $r_d/2$.

Example 4 illustrates the calculation of the after-tax cost of debt.

EXAMPLE 4

Calculating the After-Tax Cost of Debt

Valence Industries issues a bond to finance a new project. It offers a 10-year, 5 percent semi-annual coupon bond. Upon issue, the bond sells at $1,025. What is Valence's before-tax cost of debt? If Valence's marginal tax rate is 35 percent, what is Valence's after-tax cost of debt?

Solution:

Given:

$$PV = \$1,025$$
$$FV = \$1,000$$
$$PMT = 5 \text{ percent of } 1,000 \div 2 = \$25$$
$$n = 10 \times 2 = 20$$

$$\$1,025 = \left(\sum_{t=1}^{20} \frac{\$25}{(1+i)^t} \right) + \frac{\$1,000}{(1+i)^{20}}$$

Use a financial calculator to solve for i, the six-month yield. Because i = 2.342 percent, the before-tax cost of debt is r_d = 2.342 percent × 2 = 4.684 percent, and Valence's after-tax cost of debt is $r_d (1 - t)$ = 0.04684 (1 − 0.35) = 0.03045 or 3.045 percent.

3.1.2 Debt-Rating Approach

When a reliable current market price for a company's debt is not available, the **debt-rating approach** can be used to estimate the before-tax cost of debt. Based on a company's debt rating, we estimate the before-tax cost of debt by using the yield on comparably rated bonds for maturities that closely match that of the company's existing debt.

Suppose a company's capital structure includes debt with an average maturity (or duration) of 10 years and the company's marginal tax rate is 35 percent. If the company's rating is AAA and the yield on debt with the same debt rating and similar maturity (or duration) is 4 percent, the company's after-tax cost of debt is[9]

$$r_d(1 - t) = 4 \text{ percent}(1 - 0.35) = 2.6 \text{ percent}$$

A consideration when using this approach is that debt ratings are ratings of the debt issue itself, with the issuer being only one of the considerations. Other factors, such as debt seniority and security, also affect ratings and yields, so care must be taken to consider the likely type of debt to be issued by the company in determining the

---

9 Duration is a more precise measure of a bond's interest rate sensitivity than maturity.

comparable debt rating and yield. The debt-rating approach is a simple example of pricing on the basis of valuation-relevant characteristics, which in bond markets has been known as evaluated pricing or **matrix pricing**.

3.1.3 *Issues in Estimating the Cost of Debt*

3.1.3.1 Fixed-Rate Debt versus Floating-Rate Debt
Up to now, we have assumed that the interest on debt is a fixed amount each period. We can observe market yields of the company's existing debt or market yields of debt of similar risk in estimating the before-tax cost of debt. However, the company may also issue floating-rate debt in which the interest rate adjusts periodically according to a prescribed index, such as the prime rate or LIBOR, over the life of the instrument.

Estimating the cost of a floating-rate security is difficult because the cost of this form of capital over the long term depends not only on the current yields but also on the future yields. The analyst may use the current term structure of interest rates and term structure theory to assign an average cost to such instruments.

3.1.3.2 Debt with Optionlike Features
How should an analyst determine the cost of debt when the company used debt with optionlike features, such as call, conversion, or put provisions? Clearly, options affect the value of debt. For example, a callable bond would have a yield greater than a similar noncallable bond of the same issuer because bondholders want to be compensated for the call risk associated with the bond. In a similar manner, the put feature of a bond, which provides the investor with an option to sell the bond back to the issuer at a predetermined price, has the effect of lowering the yield on a bond below that of a similar nonputable bond.

If the company already has debt outstanding incorporating optionlike features that the analyst believes are representative of the future debt issuance of the company, the analyst may simply use the yield to maturity on such debt in estimating the cost of debt.

If the analyst believes that the company will add or remove option features in future debt issuance, the analyst can make market value adjustments to the current YTM to reflect the value of such additions and/or deletions. The technology for such adjustments is an advanced topic that is outside the scope of this reading.[10]

3.1.3.3 Nonrated Debt
If a company does not have any debt outstanding or if the yields on the company's existing debt are not available, the analyst may not always be able to use the yield on similarly rated debt securities. It may be the case that the company does not have rated bonds. Though researchers offer approaches for estimating a company's "synthetic" debt rating based on financial ratios, these methods are imprecise because debt ratings incorporate not only financial ratios but also information about the particular bond issue and the issuer that are not captured in financial ratios.

3.1.3.4 Leases
A lease is a contractual obligation that can substitute for other forms of borrowing. This is true whether the lease is an operating lease or a capital lease, though only the capital lease is represented as a liability on the company's balance

---

10 See, for example, *Fixed Income Analysis for the Chartered Financial Analyst® Program*, by Frank Fabozzi, for an introduction. Fabozzi discusses the estimation of an option-adjusted spread (OAS) to price the call option feature of a callable bond.

sheet.[11] If the company uses leasing as a source of capital, the cost of these leases should be included in the cost of capital. The cost of this form of borrowing is similar to that of the company's other long-term borrowing.

3.2 Cost of Preferred Stock

The **cost of preferred stock** is the cost that a company has committed to pay preferred stockholders as a preferred dividend when it issues preferred stock. In the case of nonconvertible, noncallable preferred stock that has a fixed dividend rate and no maturity date (**fixed rate perpetual preferred stock**), we can use the formula for the value of a preferred stock:

$$P_p = \frac{D_p}{r_p}$$

where

P_p = the current preferred stock price per share
D_p = the preferred stock dividend per share
r_p = the cost of preferred stock

We can rearrange this equation to solve for the cost of preferred stock:

$$r_p = \frac{D_p}{P_p} \tag{3}$$

Therefore, the cost of preferred stock is the preferred stock's dividend per share divided by the current preferred stock's price per share. Unlike interest on debt, the dividend on preferred stock is not tax-deductible by the company; therefore, there is no adjustment to the cost for taxes.[12]

A preferred stock may have a number of features that affect the yield and hence the cost of preferred stock. These features include a call option, cumulative dividends, participating dividends, adjustable-rate dividends, or convertibility into common stock. When estimating a yield based on current yields of the company's preferred stock, we must make appropriate adjustments for the effects of these features on the yield of an issue. For example, if the company has callable, convertible preferred stock outstanding, yet it is expected that the company will issue only noncallable, nonconvertible preferred stock in the future, we would have to either use the current yields on comparable companies' noncallable, nonconvertible preferred stock or estimate the yield on preferred equity using methods outside the scope of this reading.[13]

---

11 In the United States, an operating lease is distinguished from a capital lease in Statement of Financial Accounting Standards No. 13, *Accounting for Leases* (FASB, November 1976). (IAS No. 17 similarly distinguishes between operating and finance leases, another term for capital-type leases.) These two forms of leases are distinguished on the basis of ownership transference, the existence of a bargain purchase option, the term of the lease relative to the economic life of the asset, and the present value of the lease payments relative to the value of the asset. In either case, however, the lease obligation is a form of borrowing, even though it is only in the case of a capital lease that the obligation appears as a liability on the company's balance sheet. The discount rate applied in the valuation of a capital lease is the rate of borrowing at the time of the lease commencement; therefore, it is reasonable to apply the company's long-term borrowing rate when estimating the cost of capital for leasing.

12 This is not to be confused, however, with the dividends-received deduction, which reduces the effective tax on intercorporate preferred dividends received.

13 A method for estimating this yield involves first estimating the option-adjusted spread (OAS). For further information on the OAS, see, for example, Frank Fabozzi's *Fixed Income Analysis for the Chartered Financial Analyst® Program.*

EXAMPLE 5

Calculating the Cost of Preferred Equity

Alcoa has one class of preferred stock outstanding, a $3.75 cumulative preferred stock, for which there are 546,024 shares outstanding.[14] If the price of this stock is $72, what is the estimate of Alcoa's cost of preferred equity?

Solution:

Cost of Alcoa's preferred stock = $3.75/$72.00 = 5.21 percent.

EXAMPLE 6

Choosing the Best Estimate of the Cost of Preferred Equity

Wim Vanistendael is finance director of De Gouden Tulip N.V., a leading Dutch flower producer and distributor. He has been asked by the CEO to calculate the cost of preferred equity and has recently obtained the following information:

- The issue price of preferred stock was €3.5 million and the preferred dividend is 5 percent.
- If the company issued new preferred stock today, the preferred coupon rate would be 6.5 percent.
- The company's marginal tax rate is 30.5 percent.

What is the cost of preferred equity for De Gouden Tulip N.V.?

Solution:

If De Gouden Tulip were to issue new preferred stock today, the coupon rate would be close to 6.5 percent. The current terms thus prevail over the past terms when evaluating the actual cost of preferred stock. The cost of preferred stock for De Gouden Tulip is, therefore, 6.5 percent. Because preferred dividends offer no tax shield, there is no adjustment made based upon the marginal tax rate.

3.3 Cost of Common Equity

The cost of common equity, (r_e), usually referred to simply as the cost of equity, is the rate of return required by a company's common shareholders. A company may increase common equity through the reinvestment of earnings—that is, retained earnings—or through the issuance of new shares of stock.

As we discussed earlier, the estimation of the cost of equity is challenging because of the uncertain nature of the future cash flows in terms of the amount and timing. Commonly used approaches for estimating the cost of equity include the capital asset pricing model, the dividend discount model, and the bond yield plus risk premium method.

---

14 Alcoa Annual Report 2004, Footnote R, p. 56.

3.3.1 *Capital Asset Pricing Model Approach*

In the capital asset pricing model (CAPM) approach, we use the basic relationship from the capital asset pricing model theory that the expected return on a stock, $E(R_i)$, is the sum of the risk-free rate of interest, R_F, and a premium for bearing the stock's market risk, $\beta_i(R_M - R_F)$:

$$E(R_i) = R_F + \beta_i \left[E(R_M) - R_F \right] \tag{4}$$

where

β_i = the return sensitivity of stock i to changes in the market return

$E(R_M)$ = the expected return on the market

$E(R_M) - R_F$ = the expected market risk premium

A risk-free asset is defined here as an asset that has no default risk. A common proxy for the risk-free rate is the yield on a default-free government debt instrument. In general, the selection of the appropriate risk-free rate should be guided by the duration of projected cash flows. If we are evaluating a project with an estimated useful life of 10 years, we may want to use the rate on the 10-year Treasury bond.

EXAMPLE 7

Using the CAPM to Estimate the Cost of Equity

Valence Industries wants to know its cost of equity. Its CFO believes the risk-free rate is 5 percent, equity risk premium is 7 percent, and Valence's equity beta is 1.5. What is Valence's cost of equity using the CAPM approach?

Solution:

Cost of common stock = 5 percent + 1.5(7 percent) = 15.5 percent.

The expected market risk premium, or $E(R_M - R_F)$, is the premium that investors demand for investing in a market portfolio relative to the risk-free rate. When using the CAPM to estimate the cost of equity, in practice we typically estimate beta relative to an equity market index. In that case, the market premium estimate we are using is actually an estimate of the **equity risk premium** (ERP).

An alternative to the CAPM to accommodate risks that may not be captured by the market portfolio alone is a multifactor model that incorporates factors that may be other sources of **priced risk** (risk for which investors demand compensation for bearing), including macroeconomic factors and company-specific factors. In general

$$E(R_i) = R_F + \beta_{i1} \left(\text{Factor risk premium} \right)_1$$
$$+ \beta_{i2} \left(\text{Factor risk premium} \right)_2 + \ldots \tag{5}$$
$$+ \beta_{ij} \left(\text{Factor risk premium} \right)_j$$

where

β_{ij} is stock i's sensitivity to changes in the jth factor

(Factor risk premium)$_j$ is expected risk premium for the jth factor

The basic idea behind these multifactor models is that the CAPM beta may not capture all the risks, especially in a global context, which include inflation, business-cycle, interest rate, exchange rate, and default risks.[15,16]

There are several ways to estimate the equity risk premium, though there is no general agreement as to the best approach. The three we discuss are the historical equity risk premium approach, the dividend discount model approach, and the survey approach.

The **historical equity risk premium approach** is a well-established approach based on the assumption that the realized equity risk premium observed over a long period of time is a good indicator of the expected equity risk premium. This approach requires compiling historical data to find the average rate of return of a country's market portfolio and the average rate of return for the risk-free rate in that country. For example, an analyst might use the historical returns to the TOPIX Index to estimate the risk premium for Japanese equities. The exceptional bull market observed during the second half of the 1990s, and the bursting of the technology bubble that followed during the years 2000–2002, reminds us that the time period for such estimates should cover complete market cycles.

Elroy Dimson, Paul Marsh, and Mike Staunton conducted an analysis of the equity risk premiums observed in markets located in 16 countries, including the United States, over the period 1900–2002.[17] These researchers found that the annualized U.S. equity risk premium relative to U.S. Treasury bills was 5.3 percent (geometric mean) and 7.2 percent (arithmetic mean). They also found that the annualized U.S. equity risk premium relative to bonds was 4.4 percent (geometric mean) and 6.4 percent (arithmetic mean).[18] Note that the arithmetic mean is greater than the geometric mean as a result of the significant volatility of the observed market rate of return and of the observed risk-free rate. Under the assumption of an unchanging distribution of returns through time, the arithmetic mean is the unbiased estimate of the expected single-period equity risk premium, but the geometric mean better reflects growth rate over multiple periods.[19] In Table 1 we provide historical estimates of the equity risk premium for 16 developed markets from Dimson, Marsh, and Staunton's study.

---

15 An example of the multi-factor model is the three-factor Fama and French model [Eugene Fama and Kenneth French, "The Cross-Section of Expected Stock Returns," *Journal of Finance*, Vol. 47, No. 2 (1992), pp. 427–465], which includes factors for the market, equity capitalization, and the ratio of book value of equity to the market value of equity.

16 These models are discussed in more detail by Robert F. Bruner, Robert M. Conroy, Wei Li, Elizabeth O'Halloran, and Miquel Palacios Lleras [*Investing in Emerging Markets*, AIMR Research Foundation monograph (August 2003)] and by Eugene F. Fama and Kenneth R. French, "The Capital Asset Pricing Model: Theory and Evidence," *Journal of Economic Perspectives*, Vol. 18, No. 3 (Summer 2004), pp. 3–24.

17 Elroy Dimson, Paul Marsh, and Mike Staunton, "Global Evidence on the Equity Risk Premium," *Journal of Applied Corporate Finance* (Fall 2003), pp. 27–38.

18 Jeremy Siegel presents a longer time series of market returns, covering the period from 1802 through 2004, and observes an equity return of 6.82 percent and an equity risk premium in the range of 3.31 to 5.36 percent. See Jeremy J. Siegel, "Perspectives on the Equity Risk Premium," *Financial Analysts Journal*, Vol. 61, No. 6 (November/December 2005), pp. 61–73. The range depends on the method of calculation (compounded or arithmetic) and the benchmark (bonds or bills).

19 Aside from the method of averaging (geometric versus arithmetic), estimates of the historical equity risk premium differ depending on the assumed investment horizon (short versus intermediate versus long), whether conditional on some variable or unconditional, whether U.S. or global markets are examined, the source of the data, the period observed, and whether nominal or real returns are estimated.

Table 1	Equity Risk Premiums Relative to Bonds (1900 to 2002)	
	Mean	
Country	**Geometric**	**Arithmetic**
Australia	6.3%	7.9%
Belgium	2.8	4.7
Canada	4.2	5.7
Denmark	1.8	3.1
France	4.6	6.7
Germany	6.3	9.6
Ireland	3.1	4.5
Italy	4.6	8.0
Japan	5.9	10.0
The Netherlands	4.4	6.4
South Africa	5.4	7.1
Spain	2.2	4.1
Sweden	4.9	7.1
Switzerland	2.4	3.9
United Kingdom	4.2	5.5
United States	4.8	6.7
World	4.3	5.4

Note: Germany excludes 1922–23. Switzerland commences in 1911.
Source: Dimson, Marsh, and Staunton (2003).

To illustrate the historical method as applied in the CAPM, suppose that we use the historical geometric mean for U.S. equity of 4.8 percent to value Citibank Inc. (NYSE: C) as of early January 2006. According to Standard & Poor's, Citibank had a beta of 1.32 at that time. Using the 10-year U.S. Treasury bond yield of 4.38 percent to represent the risk-free rate, the estimate of the cost of equity for Citibank is 4.38 percent + 1.32(4.8 percent) = 10.72 percent.

The historical premium approach has several limitations. One limitation is that the level of risk of the stock index may change over time. Another is that the risk aversion of investors may change over time. And still another limitation is that the estimates are sensitive to the method of estimation and the historical period covered.

EXAMPLE 8

Estimating the Equity Risk Premium Using Historical Rates of Return

Suppose that the arithmetic average T-bond rate observed over the last 100 years is an unbiased estimator for the risk-free rate and amounts to 5.4 percent. Likewise, suppose the arithmetic average of return on the market observed over the last 100 years is an unbiased estimator for the expected return for the market. The average rate of return of the market was 9.3 percent. Calculate the equity risk premium.

> **Solution:**
>
> $$ERP = \overline{R}_M - \overline{R}_F = 9.3 \text{ percent} - 5.4 \text{ percent} = 3.9 \text{ percent}.$$

A second approach for estimating the equity risk premium is the **dividend discount model based approach** or implied risk premium approach, which is implemented using the Gordon growth model (also known as the constant-growth dividend discount model). For developed markets, corporate earnings often meet, at least approximately, the model's assumption of a long-run trend growth rate. We extract the premium by analyzing how the market prices an index. That is, we use the relationship between the value of an index and expected dividends, assuming a constant growth in dividends:

$$P_0 = \frac{D_1}{r_e - g}$$

where P_0 is the current market value of the equity market index, D_1 are the dividends expected next period on the index, r_e is the required rate of return on the market, and g is the expected growth rate of dividends. We solve for the required rate of return on the market as

$$r_e = \frac{D_1}{P_0} + g \tag{6}$$

Therefore, the expected return on the market is the sum of the dividend yield and the growth rate in dividends.[20] The equity risk premium thus is the difference between the expected return on the equity market and the risk-free rate.

Suppose the expected dividend yield on an equity index is 5 percent and the expected growth rate of dividends on the index is 2 percent. The expected return on the market according to the Gordon growth model is

$$E(R_m) = 5 \text{ percent} + 2 \text{ percent} = 7 \text{ percent}$$

A risk-free rate of interest of 3.8 percent implies an equity risk premium of 7 percent – 3.8 percent = 3.2 percent.

Another approach to estimate the equity risk premium is quite direct: Ask a panel of finance experts for their estimates and take the mean response. This is the **survey approach**. For example, one set of U.S. surveys found that the expected U.S. equity risk premium over the next 30 years was 5.5 percent to 7 percent forecasting from 2001 as the baseline year and 7.1 percent using 1998 as the baseline year.

Once we have an estimate of the equity risk premium, we fine-tune this estimate for the particular company or project by adjusting it for the specific systematic risk of the project. We adjust for the specific systematic risk by multiplying the market risk premium by beta to arrive at the company's or project's risk premium, which we then add to the risk-free rate to determine the cost of equity within the framework of the CAPM.[21]

---

20 We explain Equation 6 in more detail in Section 3.3.2.
21 Some researchers argue that the equity risk premium should reflect a country risk premium. For example, a multinational company or project may have a higher cost of capital than a comparable domestic company because of political risk, foreign exchange risk, or higher agency costs. In most cases, this risk is unsystematic and hence does not affect the cost of capital estimate.

3.3.2 *Dividend Discount Model Approach*

Earlier we used the Gordon growth model to develop an estimate of the equity risk premium for use in the CAPM. We can also use the Gordon growth model directly to obtain an estimate of the cost of equity. To review, the dividend discount model in general states that the intrinsic value of a share of stock is the present value of the share's expected future dividends:

$$V_0 = \sum_{t=1}^{\infty} \left(\frac{D_t}{\left(1 + r_e\right)^t} \right) = \frac{D_1}{\left(1 + r_e\right)} + \frac{D_2}{\left(1 + r_e\right)^2} + \dots$$

where

V_0 = the intrinsic value of a share
D_t = the share's dividend at the end of period t
r_e = the cost of equity

Based on Gordon's constant growth formulation, we assume dividends are expected to grow at a constant rate, g.[22] Therefore, if we assume that price reflects intrinsic value ($V_0 = P_0$), we can rewrite the valuation of the stock as

$$P_0 = \frac{D_1}{r_e - g}$$

We can then rewrite the above equation and estimate the cost of equity as we did for Equation 6 in Section 3.3.1:

$$r_e = \frac{D_1}{P_0} + g$$

Therefore, to estimate r_e, we need to estimate the dividend in the next period and the assumed constant dividend growth rate. The current stock price, P_0, is known, and the dividend of the next period, D_1, can be predicted if the company has a stable dividend policy. (The ratio D_1/P_0 may be called the forward annual dividend yield.) The challenge is estimating the growth rate.

There are at least two ways to estimate the growth rate. The first is to use a forecasted growth rate from a published source or vendor. A second is to use a relationship between the growth rate, the retention rate, and the return on equity. In this context, this is often referred to as the **sustainable growth rate** and is interpretable as the rate of dividend (and earnings) growth that can be sustained over time for a given level of return on equity, keeping the capital structure constant and without issuing additional common stock. The relationship is given in Equation 7:

$$g = \left(1 - \frac{D}{EPS}\right) ROE \tag{7}$$

where D/EPS represents the assumed stable dividend payout ratio and ROE is the historical return on equity. The term $(1 - D/EPS)$ is the company's earnings retention rate.

Consider Citigroup, Inc. Citigroup has an earnings retention rate of 59 percent. As of early January 2006, Citigroup had a forward annual dividend yield of 3.9 percent, a trailing return on equity of approximately 20 percent, but an estimated average return on equity going forward of approximately 16.6 percent. According to Equation 7, Citigroup's sustainable growth rate is 0.59(16.6 percent) = 9.79 percent. The dividend discount model estimate of the cost of equity is, therefore, 9.79 percent + 3.9 percent = 13.69 percent.

---

22 Myron J. Gordon, *The Investment, Financing, and Valuation of the Corporation*, Homewood, IL: Irwin, 1962.

3.3.3 *Bond Yield plus Risk Premium Approach*

The **bond yield plus risk premium approach** is based on the fundamental tenet in financial theory that the cost of capital of riskier cash flows is higher than that of less risky cash flows. In this approach, we sum the before-tax cost of debt, r_d, and a risk premium that captures the additional yield on a company's stock relative to its bonds. The estimate is, therefore,

$$r_e = r_d + \text{Risk premium} \tag{8}$$

The risk premium compensates for the additional risk of equity compared with debt.[23] Ideally, this risk premium is forward looking, representing the additional risk associated with the stock of the company as compared with the bonds of the same company. However, we often estimate this premium using historical spreads between bond yields and stock yields. In developed country markets, a typical risk premium added is in the range of 3 to 5 percent.

Looking again at Citigroup, as of early January 2006, the yield to maturity of the Citigroup 5.3s bonds maturing in 2016 was approximately 4.95 percent. Adding an arbitrary risk premium of 3.5 percent produces an estimate of the cost of equity of 4.95 + 3.5 = 8.45 percent. This estimate contrasts with the higher estimates of 10.72 percent, under the CAPM approach, and 13.69 percent, under the dividend discount model approach. Such disparities are not uncommon and reflect the difficulty of cost of equity estimation.

4 TOPICS IN COST OF CAPITAL ESTIMATION

When calculating a company's weighted average cost of capital (WACC), it is essential to understand the risk factors that have been considered in determining the risk-free rate, the equity risk premium, and beta to ensure a consistent calculation of WACC and avoid the double counting or omission of pertinent risk factors.

4.1 Estimating Beta and Determining a Project Beta

When the analyst uses the CAPM to estimate the cost of equity, he or she must estimate beta. The estimation of beta presents many choices as well as challenges.

One common method of estimating the company's stock beta is to use a market model regression of the company's stock returns (R_i) against market returns (R_m) over T periods:[24]

$$R_{it} = \hat{a} + \hat{b}R_{mt} \qquad t = 1, 2, \ldots T$$

where $\hat{a}$ is the estimated intercept and $\hat{b}$ is the estimated slope of the regression that is used as an estimate of beta. However, beta estimates are sensitive to the method of estimation and data used. Consider some of the issues:

▪ *Estimation period.* The estimated beta is sensitive to the length of the estimation period, with beta commonly estimated using data over two to nine years. Selection of the estimation period is a trade-off between data richness captured

---

23 This risk premium is not to be confused with the equity risk premium. The equity risk premium is the difference between the cost of equity and the *risk-free rate of interest*. The risk premium in the bond yield plus risk premium approach is the difference between the cost of equity and the *company's cost of debt*.
24 This equation is commonly referred to as the *market model* and was first introduced by Michael C. Jensen in "The Performance of Mutual Funds in the Period 1945–1964," *Journal of Finance*, Vol. 23, No. 2 (1969), pp. 389–416.

by longer estimation periods and company-specific changes that are better reflected with shorter estimation periods. In general, longer estimation periods are applied to companies with a long and stable operating history, and shorter estimation periods are used for companies that have undergone significant structural changes in the recent past (such as restructuring, recent acquisition, or divestiture) or changes in financial and operating leverage.

- *Periodicity of the return interval* (e.g., daily, weekly, or monthly). Researchers have observed smaller standard error in beta estimated using smaller return intervals, such as daily returns.[25]

- *Selection of an appropriate market index.* The choice of market index affects the estimate of beta.

- *Use of a smoothing technique.* Some analysts adjust historical betas to reflect the tendency of betas to revert to 1.[26] As an example, the expression $\beta_{i,adj} = 0.333 + 0.667\beta_i$ adjusts betas above and below 1.0 toward 1.0.

- *Adjustments for small-capitalization stocks.* Small-capitalization stocks have generally exhibited greater risks and greater returns than large-capitalization stocks over the long run. Roger Ibbotson, Paul Kaplan, and James Peterson argue that betas for small-capitalization companies be adjusted upward.[27]

Arriving at an estimated beta for publicly traded companies is generally not a problem because of the accessibility of stock return data, the ease of use of estimating beta using simple regression, and the availability of estimated betas on publicly traded companies from financial analysis vendors, such as Barra, Bloomberg, Thompson Financial's Datastream, Reuters, and Value Line. The challenge is to estimate a beta for a company that is not publicly traded or to estimate a beta for a project that is not the average or typical project of a publicly traded company. Estimating a beta in these cases requires proxying for the beta by using the information on the project or company combined with a beta of a publicly traded company.

The beta of a company or project is affected by the systematic components of business risk and by financial risk. Both of these factors affect the uncertainty of the cash flows of the company or project. The **business risk** of a company or project is the risk related to the uncertainty of revenues, referred to as **sales risk**, and to **operating risk**, which is the risk attributed to the company's operating cost structure. Sales risk is affected by the elasticity of the demand of the product, the cyclicality of the revenues, and the structure of competition in the industry. Operating risk is affected by the relative mix of fixed and variable operating costs: the greater the fixed operating costs, relative to variable operating costs, the greater the uncertainty of income and cash flows from operations.

Financial risk is the uncertainty of net income and net cash flows attributed to the use of financing that has a fixed cost, such as debt and leases. The greater the use of fixed-financing sources of capital, relative to variable sources, the greater the financial risk. In other words, a company that relies heavily on debt financing instead of equity financing is assuming a great deal of financial risk.

How does a financial analyst estimate a beta for a company or project that is not publicly traded? One common method is the **pure-play method**, which requires using a comparable publicly traded company's beta and adjusting it for financial leverage differences.

---

25 Phillip R. Daves, Michael C. Ehrhardt, and Robert A. Kunkel, "Estimating Systematic Risk: The Choice of Return Interval and Estimation Period," *Journal of Financial and Strategic Decisions*, Vol. 13, No. 1 (Spring 2000), pp. 7–13.
26 Marshall Blume, "On the Assessment of Risk," *Journal of Finance*, Vol. 26, No. 1 (March 1971), pp. 1–10.
27 Roger G. Ibbotson, Paul D. Kaplan, and James D. Peterson, "Estimates of Small Stock Betas Are Much Too Low," *Journal of Portfolio Management* (Summer 1997), pp. 104–110.

A **comparable company** is a company that has similar business risk. The reason it is referred to as the *pure-play* method is that one of the easiest ways of identifying a comparable for a project is to find a company in the same industry that is in that *single* line of business. For example, if the analyst is examining a project that involves drug stores, appropriate comparables in the United States may be Walgreens, CVS Corporation, and Rite Aid Corporation.

In estimating a beta in this way, the analyst must make adjustments to account for differing degrees of financial leverage. This requires a process of "unlevering" and "levering" the beta. The beta of the comparable is first "unlevered" by removing the effects of its financial leverage.[28] The unlevered beta is often referred to as the **asset beta** because it reflects the business risk of the assets. Once we determine the unlevered beta, we adjust it for the capital structure of the company or project that is the focus of our analysis. In other words, we "lever" the asset beta to arrive at an estimate of the equity beta for the project or company of interest.

For a given company, we can unlever its equity beta to estimate its asset beta. To do this, we must determine the relationship between a company's asset beta and its equity beta. Because the company's risk is shared between creditors and owners, we can represent the company's risk, β_{asset}, as the weighted average of the company's creditors' market risk, β_{debt}, and the market risk of the owners, β_{equity}:

$$\beta_{asset} = \beta_{debt} w_d + \beta_{equity} w_e$$

or

$$\beta_{asset} = \beta_{debt}\left(\frac{D}{D+E}\right) + \beta_{equity}\left(\frac{E}{D+E}\right)$$

where

  E = market value of equity
  D = market value of debt
  w_d = proportion of debt = $D/(D+E)$
  w_e = proportion of equity = $E/(D+E)$

But interest on debt is deducted by the company to arrive at taxable income, so the claim that creditors have on the company's assets does not cost the company the full amount but, rather, the after-tax claim; the burden of debt financing is actually less due to interest deductibility. We can represent the asset beta of a company as the weighted average of the betas of debt and equity after considering the effects of the tax-deductibility of interest:

$$\beta_{asset} = \beta_{debt}\frac{(1-t)D}{(1-t)D+E} + \beta_{equity}\frac{E}{(1-t)D+E}$$

where t is the marginal tax rate.

We generally assume that a company's debt does not have market risk, so $\beta_{debt} = 0$. This means that the returns on debt do not vary with the returns on the market, which we generally assume to be true for most large companies. If $\beta_{debt} = 0$, then[29]

---

28 The process of unlevering and levering a beta was developed by Robert S. Hamada ["The Effect of the Firm's Capital Structure on the Systematic Risk of Common Stocks," *Journal of Finance* (May 1972), pp. 435–452] and is based on the capital structure theories of Franco Modigliani and Merton Miller.

29 The first step is $\beta_{asset} = \beta_{equity}\left[\dfrac{E}{(1-t)D+E}\right]$, which we simplify to arrive at Equation 9.

$$\beta_{asset} = \beta_{equity} \left[\frac{1}{1 + \left((1 - t)\dfrac{D}{E} \right)} \right] \qquad (9)$$

Therefore, the market risk of a company's equity is affected by both the asset's market risk, β_{asset}, and a factor representing the nondiversifiable portion of the company's financial risk, $[1 + (1 - t)^D/_E)]$:

$$\beta_{equity} = \beta_{asset} \left[1 + \left((1 - t)\frac{D}{E} \right) \right] \qquad (10)$$

Suppose a company has an equity beta of 1.5, a debt-to-equity ratio of 0.4, and a marginal tax rate of 30 percent. Using Equation 9, the company's asset beta is 1.1719:

$$\beta_{asset} = 1.5 \left[\frac{1}{1 + \left((1 - 0.3)(0.4) \right)} \right] = 1.5[0.7813] = 1.1719$$

In other words, if the company did not have any debt financing, its $\beta_{asset} = \beta_{equity} = 1.1719$; however, the use of debt financing increases its β_{equity} from 1.1719 to 1.5. What would the company's equity beta be if the company's debt-to-equity ratio were 0.5 instead of 0.4? In this case, we apply Equation 10, using the debt-to-equity ratio of 0.5:

$$\beta_{equity} = 1.1719 \left[1 + \left((1 - 0.3)(0.5) \right) \right] = 1.5821$$

Therefore, the unlevering calculation produces a measure of market risk for the assets of the company—ignoring the company's capital structure. We use the levering calculation in Equation 10 to estimate the market risk of a company given a specific asset risk, marginal tax rate, and capital structure.

We can use the same unlevering and levering calculations to estimate the asset risk and equity risk for a project. We start with the equity beta of the comparable company, which is the levered beta, $\beta_{L,comparable}$, and then convert it into the equivalent asset beta for the unlevered company, $\beta_{U,comparable}$. Once we have the estimate of the unlevered beta, which is the company's asset risk, we then can use the project's capital structure and marginal tax rate to convert this asset beta into an equity beta for the project, $\beta_{L,project}$.

Estimating a Beta Using the Pure-Play Method

Step 1: Select the comparable   Determine comparable company or companies. These are companies with similar business risk.

⇩

Step 2: Estimate comparable's beta   Estimate the equity beta of the comparable company or companies.

⇩

Step 3: Unlever the comparable's beta   Unlever the beta of the comparable company or companies, removing the financial risk component of the equity beta, leaving the business risk component of the beta.

⇩

Step 4: Lever the beta for the project's financial risk   Lever the beta of the project by adjusting the asset beta for the financial risk of the project.

We begin by estimating the levered beta of the comparable company, $\beta_{L,comparable}$. Using the capital structure and tax rate of the levered company, we estimate the asset beta for the comparable company, $\beta_{U,comparable}$:

$$\beta_{U,comparable} = \frac{\beta_{L,comparable}}{\left[1 + \left(\left(1 - t_{comparable}\right)\frac{D_{comparable}}{E_{comparable}}\right)\right]} \tag{11}$$

We then consider the financial leverage of the project or company and calculate its equity risk, $\beta_{L,project}$:

$$\beta_{L,project} = \beta_{U,comparable}\left[1 + \left(\left(1 - t_{project}\right)\frac{D_{project}}{E_{project}}\right)\right] \tag{12}$$

To illustrate the use of these equations, suppose we want to evaluate a project that will be financed with debt and equity in a ratio of 0.4:1 [a debt-to-equity ratio of 0.4, corresponding to approximately 0.4/(0.4 + 1.0) = €0.286 for each euro of capital needed]. We find a comparable company operating in the same line of business as the project. The marginal tax rate for the company sponsoring the project and the comparable company is 35 percent. The comparable company has a beta of 1.2 and a debt-to-equity ratio of 0.125. The unlevered beta of the comparable is 1.1098:

$$\beta_{U,comparable} = \frac{1.2}{\left[1 + \left(\left(1 - 0.35\right)0.125\right)\right]} = 1.1098$$

The levered beta for the project is 1.3983:

$$\beta_{L,project} = 1.1098\left[1 + \left(\left(1 - 0.35\right)0.4\right)\right] = 1.3983$$

We then use the 1.3983 as the beta in our CAPM estimate of the component cost of equity for the project and, combined with the cost of debt in a weighted average, provide an estimate of the cost of capital for the project.[30]

EXAMPLE 9

Inferring an Asset Beta

Suppose that the beta of a publicly traded company's stock is 1.3 and that the market value of equity and debt are, respectively, C$540 million and C$720 million. If the marginal tax rate of this company is 40 percent, what is the asset beta of this company?

Solution:

$$\beta_U = \frac{1.3}{\left[1 + \left(\left(1 - 0.4\right)\frac{720}{540}\right)\right]} = 0.72$$

---

30 In this example, the weights are w_d = 0.4/1.4 = 0.2857 and w_e = 1/1.4 = 0.7143.

EXAMPLE 10

Calculating a Beta Using the Pure-Play Method

Raymond Cordier is the business development manager of Aerotechnique S.A., a private Belgian subcontractor of aerospace parts. Although Aerotechnique is not listed on the Belgian stock exchange, Cordier needs to evaluate the levered beta for the company. He has access to the following information:

- The average levered and average unlevered betas for the group of comparable companies operating in different European countries are 1.6 and 1.0, respectively.
- Aerotechnique's debt-to-equity ratio, based on market values, is 1.4.
- Aerotechnique's corporate tax rate is 34 percent.

Solution:

The beta for Aerotechnique is estimated on the basis of the average unlevered beta extracted from the group of comparable companies. On that basis, and applying the financing structure of Aerotechnique, the estimated beta for Aerotechnique is

$$\beta_{Aerotechnique} = 1.0\Big[1 + \big((1 - 0.34)(1.4)\big)\Big] = 1.924$$

EXAMPLE 11

Estimating the Weighted Average Cost of Capital

Georg Schrempp is the CFO of Bayern Chemicals KgaA, a large German manufacturer of industrial, commercial, and consumer chemical products. Bayern Chemicals is privately owned, and its shares are not listed on an exchange. The CFO has appointed Markus Meier, CFA, of Crystal Clear Valuation Advisors, a third-party valuator, to perform a stand-alone valuation of Bayern Chemicals. Meier had access to the following information to calculate Bayern Chemicals' weighted average cost of capital:

- The nominal risk-free rate is represented by the yield on the long-term 10-year German bund, which at the valuation date was 4.5 percent.
- The average long-term historical equity risk premium in Germany is assumed at 5.7 percent.[31]
- Bayern Chemicals' corporate tax rate is 38 percent.
- Bayern Chemicals' target debt-to-equity ratio is 0.7. Bayern is operating at its target debt-to-equity ratio.
- Bayern Chemicals' cost of debt has an estimated spread of 225 basis points over the 10-year bund.
- Table 2 supplies additional information on comparables for Bayern Chemicals.

---

31 Dimson, Marsh, and Staunton, *op. cit.*

| Table 2 | Information on Comparables |

Comparable Companies	Country	Tax Rate (%)	Market Capitalization in Millions	Net Debt in Millions	D/E	Beta
British Chemicals Ltd.	U.K.	30.0	4,500	6,000	1.33	1.45
Compagnie Petrochimique S.A.	France	30.3	9,300	8,700	0.94	0.75
Rotterdam Chemie N.V.	Netherlands	30.5	7,000	7,900	1.13	1.05
Average					1.13	1.08

Based only on the information given, calculate Bayern Chemicals' WACC.

Solution:

To calculate the cost of equity, the first step is to "unlever" the betas of the comparable companies and calculate an average for a company with business risk similar to the average of these companies:

Comparable Companies	Unlevered Beta
British Chemicals Ltd.	0.75
Compagnie Petrochimique S.A.	0.45
Rotterdam Chemie N.V.	0.59
Average*	0.60

*An analyst must apply judgment and experience to determine a representative average for the comparable companies. This example uses a simple average, but in some situations a weighted average based on some factor such as market capitalization may be more appropriate.

Levering the average unlevered beta for the peer group average, applying Bayern Chemicals' target debt-to-equity ratio and marginal tax rate, results in a beta of 0.86:

$$\beta_{\text{Bayern Chemical}} = 0.60\{1 + [(1 - 0.38)0.7]\} = 0.86$$

The cost of equity of Bayern Chemicals (r_e) can be calculated as follows:

$$r_e = 4.5 \text{ percent} + (0.86)(5.7 \text{ percent}) = 9.4 \text{ percent}$$

The weights for the cost of equity and cost of debt may be calculated as follows:

$$w_d = \frac{D/E}{\left(\frac{D}{E} + 1\right)} = \frac{0.7}{1.7} = 0.41$$

$$w_e = 1 - w_d = 1 - 0.41 = 0.59$$

The before-tax cost of debt of Bayern Chemicals (r_d) is 6.75 percent:

$$r_d = 4.5 \text{ percent} + 2.25 \text{ percent} = 6.75 \text{ percent}$$

As a result, Bayern Chemicals' WACC is 7.27 percent:

$$\begin{aligned} \text{WACC} &= \left[(0.41)(0.0675)(1 - 0.38)\right] + \left[(0.59)(0.094)\right] \\ &= 0.0726 \text{ or } 7.26 \text{ percent} \end{aligned}$$

4.2 Country Risk

The use of a stock's beta to capture the country risks of a project is well supported in empirical studies that examine developed nations. However, beta does not appear to adequately capture country risk for companies in developing nations.[32] A common approach for dealing with this problem is to adjust the cost of equity estimated using the CAPM by adding a country spread to the market risk premium.[33] The country spread is also referred to as a country risk premium.

Perhaps the simplest estimate of the country spread is the **sovereign yield spread**, which is the difference between the government bond yield in that country, denominated in the currency of a developed country, and the Treasury bond yield on a similar maturity bond in the developed country.[34] However, this approach may be too coarse for the purposes of risk premium estimation.

Another approach is to calculate the country risk premium as the product of the sovereign yield spread and the ratio of the volatility of the developing country equity market to that of the sovereign bond market denominated in terms of the currency of a developed country:[35]

$$\text{Country equity premium} = \text{Sovereign yield spread} \left[\frac{\begin{array}{c}\text{Annualized standard deviation} \\ \text{of equity index}\end{array}}{\begin{array}{c}\text{Annualized standard deviation of the} \\ \text{sovereign bond market in terms} \\ \text{of the developed market currency}\end{array}} \right] \qquad (13)$$

The logic of this calculation is that the sovereign yield spread captures the general risk of the country, which is then adjusted for the volatility of the stock market relative to the bond market. This country risk premium is then used in addition to the equity premium estimated for a project in a developed country. Therefore, if the equity risk premium for a project in a developed country is 4.5 percent and the country risk premium is 3 percent, the total equity risk premium used in the CAPM estimation is 7.5 percent. If the appropriate beta is 1.2 and the risk-free rate of interest is 4 percent, the cost of equity is

$$\text{Cost of equity} = 0.04 + 1.2(0.045 + 0.03) = 0.13 \text{ or } 13 \text{ percent}$$

---

32 Campbell R. Harvey, "The International Cost of Capital and Risk Calculator," Duke University working paper (July 2001).

33 Adding the country spread to the market risk premium for a developing country and then multiplying this sum by the market risk of the project is making the assumption that the country risk premium varies according to market risk. An alternative method calculates the cost of equity as the sum of three terms: 1) the risk-free rate of interest, 2) the product of the beta and the developed market risk premium, and 3) the country risk premium. This latter method assumes that the country risk premium is the same, regardless of the project's market risk.

34 Jorge O. Mariscal and Rafaelina M. Lee, "The Valuation of Mexican Stocks: An Extension of the Capital Asset Pricing Model," New York: Goldman Sachs (1993).

35 Aswath Damodaran, "Estimating Equity Risk Premiums," New York University working paper (1999) and Aswath Damodaran, "Measuring Company Exposure to Country Risk: Theory and Practice," New York University working paper (September 2003).

EXAMPLE 12

Estimating the Country Risk Premium

Miles Avenaugh, an analyst with the Global Company, is estimating a country risk premium to include in his estimate of the cost of equity capital for Global's investment in Argentina. Avenaugh has researched yields in Argentina and observed that the Argentinean government's 10-year bond is 9.5 percent. A similar maturity U.S. Treasury bond has a yield of 4.5 percent. The annualized standard deviation of the Argentina Merval stock index, a market value index of stocks listed on the Buenos Aires Stock Exchange, during the most recent year is 40 percent. The annualized standard deviation of the Argentina dollar-denominated 10-year government bond over the recent period was 28 percent.

What is the estimated country risk premium for Argentina based on Avenaugh's research?

Solution:

$$\text{Country risk premium} = 0.05\left(\frac{0.40}{0.28}\right) = 0.05(1.4286) = 0.0714 \text{ or } 7.14 \text{ percent}$$

Still another approach is to use country credit ratings to estimate the expected rates of returns for countries that have credit ratings but no equity markets.[36] This method requires estimating reward to credit risk measures for a large sample of countries for which there are both credit ratings and equity markets and then applying this ratio to those countries without equity markets based on the country's credit rating.

4.3 Marginal Cost of Capital Schedule

As we noted in Section 2.3, as a company raises more funds, the costs of the different sources of capital may change, resulting in a change in the weighted average cost of capital for different levels of financing. The result is the marginal cost of capital (MCC) schedule, which we often depict in graphical form as the weighted average cost of capital for different amounts of capital raised, as we showed earlier in Figure 1.[37]

Why would the cost of capital change as more capital is raised? One source of a difference in cost depending on the amount of capital raised is that a company may have existing debt with a bond covenant that restricts the company from issuing debt with similar seniority as existing debt. Or, a **debt incurrence test** may restrict a company's ability to incur additional debt at the same seniority based on one or more financial tests or conditions. For example, if a company issues senior debt such that any additional debt at that seniority violates the debt incurrence test of an existing bond covenant, the company may have to issue less senior debt or even equity, which would have a higher cost.

Another source of increasing marginal costs of capital is a deviation from the target capital structure. In the ideal, theoretical world, a company has a target capital structure and goes to the market each period and raises capital in these proportions. However, as a practical matter, companies do not necessarily tap the market in these

---

36 Claude Erb, Campbell R. Harvey, and Tadas Viskanta, "Expected Returns and Volatility in 135 Countries," *Journal of Portfolio Management* (Spring 1996), pp. 46–58.

37 Later in this section, we will discuss cases where a company's WACC may actually decrease as additional capital is raised. For example, if a company financed solely with common equity raises additional capital via debt, then the tax advantages provided by debt will result in a lower WACC under the new capital structure. For this discussion, we are assuming that the company is already operating at or near its optimum balance of debt versus equity.

ideal proportions because of considerations for economies of scale in raising new capital and market conditions. Because of such perceived economies of scale, companies tend to issue new securities such that in any given period, it may deviate from the proportions dictated by any target or optimal capital structure. In other words, these short-run deviations are due to the "lumpiness" of security issuance. As the company experiences deviations from the target capital structure, the marginal cost of capital may increase, reflecting these deviations.

The amount of capital at which the weighted average cost of capital changes— which means that the cost of one of the sources of capital changes—is referred to as a **break point**. The reality of raising capital is that the marginal cost of capital schedule is not as smooth as we depicted in Figure 1 but, rather, is a step-up cost schedule as shown in Figure 2.

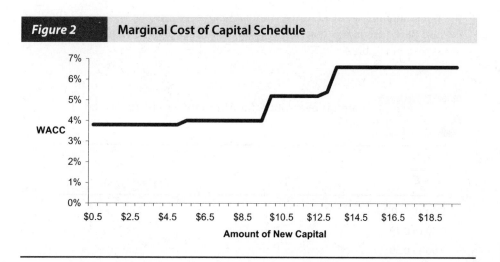

Figure 2	Marginal Cost of Capital Schedule

Consider the case of a company facing the costs of capital given in Table 3.

Table 3	Schedule of the Costs of Debt and Equity

Amount of New Debt (in Millions)	After-Tax Cost of Debt	Amount of New Equity (in Millions)	Cost of Equity
new debt ≤ €2	2.0 percent	new equity ≤ €6	5.0 percent
€2 < new debt ≤ €5	2.5 percent	€6 < new equity ≤ €8	7.0 percent
€5 < new debt	3.0 percent	€8 < new equity	9.0 percent

If the company raises capital according to its target capital structure proportions of 40 percent debt and 60 percent equity, this company faces a marginal cost of capital schedule that is upward sloping, with break points at €5 million, €10 million, €12.5 million, and €13.3 million, as depicted in Figure 2. These break points are determined from the amounts of capital at which the cost changes, calculated as

$$\text{Break point} = \frac{\text{Amount of capital at which the source's cost of capital changes}}{\text{Proportion of new capital raised from the source}} \quad \textbf{(14)}$$

For example, the first break point for debt financing is reached with €2 million/ 0.4 = €5 million of new capital raised. The first break point attributed to a change in equity cost occurs at €6 million/0.6 = €10 million. Example 13 illustrates a marginal cost of capital schedule with break points and also how the WACC figures in the choice of an optimal capital structure.

EXAMPLE 13

Marginal Cost of Capital Schedule

Alan Conlon is the CFO of Allied Canadian Breweries Ltd. He wants to determine the capital structure that will result in the lowest cost of capital for Allied. He has access to the following information:

▪ The minimum rate at which the company can borrow is the 12-month LIBOR rate plus a premium that varies with the debt-to-capital ratio $[D/(D + E)]$ as given in Table 4.

Table 4	Spreads over LIBOR for Alternative Debt-to-Capital Ratios
$\dfrac{D}{D + E}$	Spread (bps)
Less than 0.40	200
0.40 to 0.49	300
0.50 to 0.59	400
0.60 to 0.69	600
0.70 to 0.79	800
0.80 to 0.89	1,000
0.90 or higher	1,200

▪ The current 12-month LIBOR is 4.5 percent.
▪ The market risk premium is 4 percent, and unleveraged beta is 0.9.
▪ The risk-free rate is 4.25 percent.
▪ The company's tax rate is 36 percent.

1 Determine the WACC for 10 percent intervals of the debt-to-capital ratio (i.e., 0.1, 0.2, etc.) based on the information given in Table 4.

2 Recommend a target capital structure based on 10 percent intervals of the debt-to-capital ratio, recommend a target capital structure.

Solution to 1:

The WACC expressed as a function of the capital structure is shown in Table 5.

| Table 5 | | WACC for Alternative Capital Structures | | |

$\dfrac{D}{D+E}$	β	r_d (Percent)	r_e (Percent)	WACC (Percent)
0.1	0.96	6.5	8.1	7.7
0.2	1.04	6.5	8.4	7.6
0.3	1.15	6.5	8.8	7.4
0.4	1.28	7.5	9.4	7.6
0.5	1.48	8.5	10.2	7.8
0.6	1.76	10.5	11.3	8.6
0.7	2.24	12.5	13.2	9.6
0.8	3.20	14.5	17.1	10.8
0.9	6.08	16.5	28.6	12.4

Solution to 2:

The optimal capital structure is 30 percent debt; based on 10 percent intervals of the debt-to-capital ratio, this will achieve the lowest possible cost of capital.

4.4 Flotation Costs

When a company raises new capital, it generally seeks the assistance of investment bankers. Investment bankers charge the company a fee based on the size and type of offering. This fee is referred to as the **flotation cost**. In the case of debt and preferred stock, we do not usually incorporate flotation costs in the estimated cost of capital because the amount of these costs is quite small, often less than 1 percent.[38]

However, with equity issuance, the flotation costs may be substantial, so we should consider these when estimating the cost of external equity capital. For example, Inmoo Lee, Scott Lochhead, Jay Ritter, and Quanshui Zhao observe average flotation costs for new equity in the United States of 7.11 percent.[39] The flotation costs in other countries differ from the U.S. experience: Thomas Bühner and Christoph Kaserer observe flotation costs around 1.65 percent in Germany, Seth Armitage estimates an average issuance cost of 5.78 percent in the United Kingdom, and Christoph Kaserer and Fabian Steiner observe an average cost of 4.53 for Swiss capital offerings.[40] A large part of the differences in costs among these studies is likely attributed to the type of offering; cash underwritten offers, typical in the United States, are generally more expensive than rights offerings, which are common in Europe.

---

[38] We can incorporate them for these sources by simply treating the flotation costs as an outlay, hence reducing proceeds from the source.

[39] Inmoo Lee, Scott Lochhead, Jay R. Ritter, and Quanshui Zhao, "The Costs of Raising Capital," *Journal of Financial Research*, Vol. 19 (Spring, 1996), pp. 59–71.

[40] Thomas Bühner and Christoph Kaserer, "External Financing Costs and Economies of Scale in Investment Banking: The Case of Seasoned Equity Offerings in Germany," *European Financial Management*, Vol. 9 (June 2002), pp. 249; Seth Armitage, "The Direct Costs of UK Rights Issues and Open Offers, "*European Financial Management*, Vol. 6 (2000), pp. 57–68; Christoph Kaserer and Fabian Steiner, "The Cost of Raising Capital—New Evidence from Seasoned Equity Offerings in Switzerland," Technische Universität München working paper (February 2004).

Should we incorporate flotation costs into the cost of capital? There are two views on this topic. One view, which you can find often in textbooks, is to incorporate the flotation costs into the cost of capital. The other view is that flotation costs should not be included in the cost of capital but, rather, incorporated into any valuation analysis as an additional cost of the project.

Consistent with the first view, we can specify flotation costs in monetary terms, as an amount per share or as a percentage of the share price. With flotation costs in monetary terms on a per share basis, F, the cost of external equity is

$$r_e = \left(\frac{D_1}{P_0 - F}\right) + g \tag{15}$$

As a percentage applied against the price per share, the cost of external equity is

$$r_e = \left(\frac{D_1}{P_0(1 - f)}\right) + g \tag{16}$$

where f is the flotation cost as a percentage of the issue price.

Suppose a company has a current dividend of $2 per share, a current price of $40 per share, and an expected growth rate of 5 percent. The cost of internally generated equity would be 10.25 percent:

$$r_e = \left(\frac{\$2(1 + 0.05)}{\$40}\right) + 0.05 = 0.0525 + 0.05 = 0.1025, \text{ or } 10.25 \text{ percent}$$

If the flotation costs are 4 percent of the issuance, the cost of externally generated equity would be slightly higher at 10.469 percent:

$$r_e = \left(\frac{\$2(1 + 0.05)}{\$40(1 - 0.04)}\right) + 0.05 = 0.05469 + 0.05 = 0.1047, \text{ or } 10.47 \text{ percent}$$

The problem with this approach is that the flotation costs are a cash flow at the initiation of the project and affect the value of any project by reducing the initial cash flow. Adjusting the cost of capital for flotation costs is incorrect because by doing so, we are adjusting the present value of the future cash flows by a fixed percentage—in the above example, a difference of 22 basis points, which does not necessarily equate to the present value of the flotation costs.[41]

The alternative and recommended approach is to make the adjustment to the cash flows in the valuation computation. For example, consider a project that requires a €60,000 initial cash outlay and is expected to produce cash flows of €10,000 each year for 10 years. Suppose the company's marginal tax rate is 40 percent and that the before-tax cost of debt is 5 percent. Furthermore, suppose that the company's dividend next period is €1, the current price of the stock is €20, and the expected growth rate is 5 percent so that the cost of equity using the dividend discount model is (€1/€20) + 0.05 = 0.10 or 10 percent. Assume the company will finance the project with 40 percent debt and 60 percent equity. Table 6 summarizes the information on the component costs of capital.

---

41 This argument is made by John R. Ezzell and R. Burr Porter ["Flotation Costs and the Weighted Average Cost of Capital," *Journal of Financial and Quantitative Analysis*, Vol. 11, No. 3 (September 1976), pp. 403–413]. They argue that the correct treatment is to deduct flotation costs as part of the valuation as one of the initial-period cash flows.

Table 6	After-Tax Costs of Debt and Equity		
Source of Capital	Amount Raised (€)	Proportion	Marginal After-Tax Cost
Debt	24,000	0.40	0.05(1 – 0.4) = 0.03
Equity	36,000	0.60	0.10

The weighted average cost of capital is 7.2 percent calculated as 0.40(3 percent) + 0.60(10 percent). Ignoring flotation costs for the moment, the net present value (NPV) of this project is

$$\text{NPV} = €69,591 - €60,000 = €9,591$$

If the flotation costs are, say, 5 percent of the new equity capital, the flotation costs are €1,800. The net present value considering flotation costs is

$$\text{NPV} = €69,591 - €60,000 - €1,800 = €7,791$$

If flotation costs are not tax deductible, or €69,591 – €60,000 – €1,800(0.6) = €8,511, if flotation costs are tax deductible.

If, instead of considering the flotation costs as part of the cash flows, we adjust the cost of equity, the cost of capital is 7.3578 percent and the NPV is

$$\text{NPV} = €69,089 - €60,000 = €9,089$$

As you can see, we arrive at different assessments of value using these two methods.

So, if it is preferred to deduct the flotation costs as part of the net present value calculation, why do we see the adjustment in the cost of capital so often in textbooks? The first reason is that it is often difficult to identify particular financing associated with a project. Using the adjustment for the flotation costs in the cost of capital may be useful if specific project financing cannot be identified. Second, by adjusting the cost of capital for the flotation costs, it is easier to demonstrate how costs of financing a company change as a company exhausts internally generated equity (i.e., retained earnings) and switches to externally generated equity (i.e., a new stock issue).

4.5 What Do CFOs Do?

In this reading, we have introduced you to methods that may be used to estimate the cost of capital for a company or a project. What do companies actually use when making investment decisions? In a survey of a large number of U.S. company CFOs, John Graham and Campbell Harvey asked about the methods that companies actually use.[42] Their survey revealed the following:

- The most popular method for estimating the cost of equity is the capital asset pricing model.
- Few companies use the dividend cash flow model to estimate a cost of equity.
- Publicly traded companies are more likely to use the capital asset pricing model than are private companies.
- In evaluating projects, the majority use a single company cost of capital, but a large portion apply some type of risk adjustment for individual projects.

---

[42] John Graham and Campbell Harvey, "How Do CFOs Make Capital Budgeting and Capital Structure Decisions," *Journal of Applied Corporate Finance*, Vol. 15, No. 1 (Spring 2002), pp. 8–23.

The survey also reveals that the single-factor capital asset pricing model is the most popular method for estimating the cost of equity, though the next most popular methods, respectively, are average stock returns and multifactor return models. The lack of popularity of the dividend discount model indicates that this approach, which was once favored, has lost its following in practice.[43]

In a survey of publicly traded multinational European companies, Franck Bancel and Usha Mittoo provide evidence consistent with the Graham and Harvey survey.[44] They find that over 70 percent of companies use the CAPM to determine the cost of equity; this compares with the 73.5 percent of U.S. companies that use the CAPM. In a survey of both publicly traded and private European companies, Dirk Brounen, Abe de Jong, and Kees Koedijk confirm the result of Graham and Harvey that larger companies are more likely to use the more sophisticated methods, such as CAPM, in estimating the cost of equity.[45] Brounen, Jong, and Koedijk find that the popularity of the use of CAPM is less for their sample (ranging from 34 percent to 55.6 percent, depending on the country) than for the other two surveys, which may reflect the inclusion of smaller, private companies in the latter sample.

We learn from the survey evidence that the CAPM is a popular method for estimating the cost of equity capital and that it is used less by smaller, private companies. This latter result is not surprising because of the difficulty in estimating systematic risk in cases in which the company's equity is not publicly traded.

SUMMARY

In this reading, we provided an overview of the techniques used to calculate the cost of capital for companies and projects. We examined the weighted average cost of capital, discussing the methods commonly used to estimate the component costs of capital and the weights applied to these components. The international dimension of the cost of capital, as well as key factors influencing the cost of capital, were also analyzed.

▪ The weighted average cost of capital is a weighted average of the after-tax marginal costs of each source of capital: $\text{WACC} = w_d r_d (1 - t) + w_p r_p + w_e r_e$

▪ An analyst uses the WACC in valuation. For example, the WACC is used to value a project using the net present value method:

   NPV = Present value of inflows − Present value of the outflows

▪ The before-tax cost of debt is generally estimated by means of one of the two methods: yield to maturity or bond rating.

▪ The yield-to-maturity method of estimating the before-tax cost of debt uses the familiar bond valuation equation. Assuming semi-annual coupon payments, the equation is

---

43 A survey published in 1982 by Lawrence Gitman and V. Mercurio ["Cost of Capital Techniques Used by Major U.S. Firms: Survey and Analysis of Fortune's 1000," *Financial Management*, Vol. 14, No. 4 (Winter 1982), pp. 21–29] indicated that fewer than 30 percent used the CAPM model in the estimation of the cost of equity.

44 Franck Bancel and Usha Mittoo, "The Determinants of Capital Structure Choice: A Survey of European Firms," *Financial Management*, Vol. 44, No. 4 (Winter 2004).

45 Dirk Brounen, Abe de Jong, and Kees Koedijk, "Corporate Finance in Europe: Confronting Theory with Practice," *Financial Management*, Vol. 44, No. 4 (Winter 2004).

$$P_0 = \frac{PMT_1}{\left(1 + \frac{r_d}{2}\right)} + \ldots + \frac{PMT_n}{\left(1 + \frac{r_d}{2}\right)^n} + \frac{FV}{\left(1 + \frac{r_d}{2}\right)^n} = \left(\sum_{t=1}^{n} \frac{PMT_t}{\left(1 + \frac{r_d}{2}\right)^t}\right) + \frac{FV}{\left(1 + \frac{r_d}{2}\right)^n}$$

We solve for the six-month yield ($r_d/2$) and then annualize it to arrive at the before-tax cost of debt, r_d.

- Because interest payments are generally tax-deductible, the after-tax cost is the true, effective cost of debt to the company. If a current yield or bond rating is not available, such as in the case of a private company without rated debt or a project, the estimate of the cost of debt becomes more challenging.

- The cost of preferred stock is the preferred stock dividend divided by the current preferred stock price:

$$r_p = \frac{D_p}{P_p}$$

- The cost of equity is the rate of return required by a company's common stockholders. We estimate this cost using the CAPM (or its variants) or the dividend discount method.

- The CAPM is the approach most commonly used to calculate the cost of common stock. The three components needed to calculate the cost of common stock are the risk-free rate, the equity risk premium, and beta:

$$E(R_i) = R_F + \beta_i\left[E(R_M) - R_F\right]$$

- When estimating the cost of equity capital using the CAPM when we do not have publicly traded equity, we may be able to use the pure-play method in which we estimate the unlevered beta for a company with similar business risk, β_U,

$$\beta_{U,comparable} = \frac{\beta_{L,comparable}}{\left[1 + \left(\left(1 - t_{comparable}\right)\frac{D_{comparable}}{E_{comparable}}\right)\right]}$$

and then lever this beta to reflect the financial risk of the project or company:

$$\beta_{L,project} = \beta_{U,comparable}\left[1 + \left(\left(1 - t_{project}\right)\frac{D_{project}}{E_{project}}\right)\right]$$

- It is often the case that country and foreign exchange risk are diversified so that we can use the estimated β in the CAPM analysis. However, in the case in which these risks cannot be diversified away, we can adjust our measure of systematic risk by a country equity premium to reflect this nondiversified risk:

$$\text{Country equity premium} = \text{Sovereign yield spread}\left[\frac{\text{Annualized standard deviation of equity index}}{\text{Annualized standard deviation of the sovereign bond market in terms of the developed market currency}}\right]$$

- The dividend discount model approach is an alternative approach to calculating the cost of equity, whereby the cost of equity is estimated as follows:

$$r_e = \frac{D_1}{P_0} + g$$

- We can estimate the growth rate in the dividend discount model by using published forecasts of analysts or by estimating the sustainable growth rate:

$$g = \left(1 - \frac{D}{EPS}\right)ROE$$

- In estimating the cost of equity, an alternative to the CAPM and dividend discount approaches is the bond yield plus risk premium approach. In this approach, we estimate the before-tax cost of debt and add a risk premium that reflects the additional risk associated with the company's equity.

- The marginal cost of capital schedule is a graph plotting the new funds raised by a company on the x-axis and the cost of capital on the y-axis. The cost of capital is level to the point at which one of the costs of capital changes, such as when the company bumps up against a debt covenant, requiring it to use another form of capital. We calculate a break point using information on when the different sources' costs change and the proportions that the company uses when it raises additional capital:

$$\text{Break point} = \frac{\text{Amount of capital at which the source's cost of capital changes}}{\text{Proportion of new capital raised from the source}}$$

- Flotation costs are costs incurred in the process of raising additional capital. The preferred method of including these costs in the analysis is as an initial cash flow in the valuation analysis.

- Survey evidence tells us that the CAPM method is the most popular method used by companies in estimating the cost of equity. The CAPM is more popular with larger, publicly traded companies, which is understandable considering the additional analyses and assumptions required in estimating systematic risk for a private company or project.

PRACTICE PROBLEMS

1 The cost of equity is equal to the:

   A expected market return.

   B rate of return required by stockholders.

   C cost of retained earnings plus dividends.

2 Which of the following statements is correct?

   A The appropriate tax rate to use in the adjustment of the before-tax cost of debt to determine the after-tax cost of debt is the average tax rate because interest is deductible against the company's entire taxable income.

   B For a given company, the after-tax cost of debt is generally less than both the cost of preferred equity and the cost of common equity.

   C For a given company, the investment opportunity schedule is upward sloping because as a company invests more in capital projects, the returns from investing increase.

3 Using the dividend discount model, what is the cost of equity capital for Zeller Mining if the company will pay a dividend of C$2.30 next year, has a payout ratio of 30 percent, a return on equity (ROE) of 15 percent, and a stock price of C$45?

   A 9.61 percent.

   B 10.50 percent.

   C 15.61 percent.

4 Dot.Com has determined that it could issue $1,000 face value bonds with an 8 percent coupon paid semi-annually and a five-year maturity at $900 per bond. If Dot.Com's marginal tax rate is 38 percent, its after-tax cost of debt is *closest* to:

   A 6.2 percent.

   B 6.4 percent.

   C 6.6 percent.

5 The cost of debt can be determined using the yield-to-maturity and the bond rating approaches. If the bond rating approach is used, the:

   A coupon is the yield.

   B yield is based on the interest coverage ratio.

   C company is rated and the rating can be used to assess the credit default spread of the company's debt.

6 Morgan Insurance Ltd. issued a fixed-rate perpetual preferred stock three years ago and placed it privately with institutional investors. The stock was issued at $25 per share with a $1.75 dividend. If the company were to issue preferred stock today, the yield would be 6.5 percent. The stock's current value is:

   A $25.00.

   B $26.92.

   C $37.31.

7 A financial analyst at Buckco Ltd. wants to compute the company's weighted average cost of capital (WACC) using the dividend discount model. The analyst has gathered the following data:

Before-tax cost of new debt	8 percent
Tax rate	40 percent
Target debt-to-equity ratio	0.8033
Stock price	$30
Next year's dividend	$1.50
Estimated growth rate	7 percent

Buckco's WACC is *closest* to:

A   8 percent.

B   9 percent.

C   12 percent.

8   The Gearing Company has an after-tax cost of debt capital of 4 percent, a cost of preferred stock of 8 percent, a cost of equity capital of 10 percent, and a weighted average cost of capital of 7 percent. Gearing intends to maintain its current capital structure as it raises additional capital. In making its capital-budgeting decisions for the average-risk project, the relevant cost of capital is:

A   4 percent.

B   7 percent.

C   8 percent.

9   Fran McClure of Alba Advisers is estimating the cost of capital of Frontier Corporation as part of her valuation analysis of Frontier. McClure will be using this estimate, along with projected cash flows from Frontier's new projects, to estimate the effect of these new projects on the value of Frontier. McClure has gathered the following information on Frontier Corporation:

	Current Year ($)	Forecasted for Next Year ($)
Book value of debt	50	50
Market value of debt	62	63
Book value of shareholders' equity	55	58
Market value of shareholders' equity	210	220

The weights that McClure should apply in estimating Frontier's cost of capital for debt and equity are, respectively:

A $w_d = 0.200; w_e = 0.800$.

B $w_d = 0.185; w_e = 0.815$.

C $w_d = 0.223; w_e = 0.777$.

10 Wang Securities had a long-term stable debt-to-equity ratio of 0.65. Recent bank borrowing for expansion into South America raised the ratio to 0.75. The increased leverage has what effect on the asset beta and equity beta of the company?

A   The asset beta and the equity beta will both rise.

B   The asset beta will remain the same and the equity beta will rise.

C   The asset beta will remain the same and the equity beta will decline.

11 Brandon Wiene is a financial analyst covering the beverage industry. He is evaluating the impact of DEF Beverage's new product line of flavored waters. DEF currently has a debt-to-equity ratio of 0.6. The new product line would be financed with $50 million of debt and $100 million of equity. In estimating the valuation impact of this new product line on DEF's value, Wiene has estimated the equity beta and asset beta of comparable companies. In calculating the equity beta for the product line, Wiene is intending to use DEF's existing capital structure when converting the asset beta into a project beta. Which of the following statements is correct?

   A Using DEF's debt-to-equity ratio of 0.6 is appropriate in calculating the new product line's equity beta.

   B Using DEF's debt-to-equity ratio of 0.6 is not appropriate, but rather the debt-to-equity ratio of the new product, 0.5, is appropriate to use in calculating the new product line's equity beta.

   C Wiene should use the new debt-to-equity ratio of DEF that would result from the additional $50 million debt and $100 million equity in calculating the new product line's equity beta.

12 Trumpit Resorts Company currently has 1.2 million common shares of stock outstanding and the stock has a beta of 2.2. It also has $10 million face value of bonds that have five years remaining to maturity and 8 percent coupon with semi-annual payments, and are priced to yield 13.65 percent. If Trumpit issues up to $2.5 million of new bonds, the bonds will be priced at par and have a yield of 13.65 percent; if it issues bonds beyond $2.5 million, the expected yield on the entire issuance will be 16 percent. Trumpit has learned that it can issue new common stock at $10 a share. The current risk-free rate of interest is 3 percent and the expected market return is 10 percent. Trumpit's marginal tax rate is 30 percent. If Trumpit raises $7.5 million of new capital while maintaining the same debt-to-equity ratio, its weighted average cost of capital is *closest* to:

   A 14.5 percent.

   B 15.5 percent.

   C 16.5 percent.

The following information relates to Questions 13–18[1]

Jurgen Knudsen has been hired to provide industry expertise to Henrik Sandell, CFA, an analyst for a pension plan managing a global large-cap fund internally. Sandell is concerned about one of the fund's larger holdings, auto parts manufacturer Kruspa AB. Kruspa currently operates in 80 countries, with the previous year's global revenues at €5.6 billion. Recently, Kruspa's CFO announced plans for expansion into China. Sandell worries that this expansion will change the company's risk profile and wonders if he should recommend a sale of the position.

Sandell provides Knudsen with the basic information. Kruspa's global annual free cash flow to the firm is €500 million and earnings are €400 million. Sandell estimates that cash flow will level off at a 2 percent rate of growth. Sandell also estimates that Kruspa's after-tax free cash flow to the firm on the China project for next three years is, respectively, €48 million, €52 million, and €54.4 million. Kruspa recently announced

---

1 The Level I exam uses only independent questions. This minicase is intended as a learning exercise.

a dividend of €4.00 per share of stock. For the initial analysis, Sandell requests that Knudsen ignore possible currency fluctuations. He expects the Chinese plant to sell only to customers within China for the first three years. Knudsen is asked to evaluate Kruspa's planned financing of the required €100 million with a €80 public offering of 10-year debt in Sweden and the remainder with an equity offering.

Additional information:

Equity risk premium, Sweden	4.82 percent
Risk-free rate of interest, Sweden	4.25 percent
Industry debt-to-equity ratio	0.3
Market value of Kruspa's debt	€900 million
Market value of Kruspa's equity	€2.4 billion
Kruspa's equity beta	1.3
Kruspa's before-tax cost of debt	9.25 percent
China credit A2 country risk premium	1.88 percent
Corporate tax rate	37.5 percent
Interest payments each year	Level

13 Using the capital asset pricing model, Kruspa's cost of equity capital for its typical project is *closest* to:

   A   7.62 percent.

   B   10.52 percent.

   C   12.40 percent.

14 Sandell is interested in the weighted average cost of capital of Kruspa AB prior to its investing in the China project. This weighted average cost of capital (WACC) is *closest* to:

   A   7.65 percent.

   B   9.23 percent.

   C   10.17 percent.

15 In his estimation of the project's cost of capital, Sandell would like to use the asset beta of Kruspa as a base in his calculations. The estimated asset beta of Kruspa prior to the China project is *closest* to:

   A   1.053.

   B   1.110.

   C   1.327.

16 Sandell is performing a sensitivity analysis of the effect of the new project on the company's cost of capital. If the China project has the same asset risk as Kruspa, the estimated project beta for the China project, if it is financed 80 percent with debt, is *closest* to:

   A   1.300.

   B   2.635.

   C   3.686.

17 As part of the sensitivity analysis of the effect of the new project on the company's cost of capital, Sandell is estimating the cost of equity of the China project considering that the China project requires a country equity premium to capture the risk of the project. The cost of equity for the project in this case is *closest* to:

A 10.52 percent.

B 19.91 percent.

C 28.95 percent.

18 In his report, Sandell would like to discuss the sensitivity of the project's net present value to the estimation of the cost of equity. The China project's net present value calculated using the equity beta without and with the country risk premium are, respectively:

A €26 million and €24 million.

B €28 million and €25 million.

C €30 million and €27 million.

The following information relates to Questions 19–22[2]

Boris Duarte, CFA, covers initial public offerings for Zellweger Analytics, an independent research firm specializing in global small-cap equities. He has been asked to evaluate the upcoming new issue of TagOn, a U.S.-based business intelligence software company. The industry has grown at 26 percent per year for the previous three years. Large companies dominate the market, but sizable "pure-play" companies such as Relevant, Ltd., ABJ, Inc., and Opus Software Pvt. Ltd also compete. Each of these competitors is domiciled in a different country, but they all have shares of stock that trade on the U.S. NASDAQ. The debt ratio of the industry has risen slightly in recent years.

Company	Sales in Millions ($)	Market Value Equity in Millions ($)	Market Value Debt in Millions ($)	Equity Beta	Tax Rate	Share Price ($)
Relevant Ltd.	752	3,800	0.0	1.702	23 percent	42
ABJ, Inc.	843	2,150	6.5	2.800	23 percent	24
Opus Software Pvt. Ltd.	211	972	13.0	3.400	23 percent	13

Duarte uses the information from the preliminary prospectus for TagOn's initial offering. The company intends to issue 1 million new shares. In his conversation with the investment bankers for the deal, he concludes the offering price will be between $7 and $12. The current capital structure of TagOn consists of a $2.4 million five-year non-callable bond issue and 1 million common shares. Other information that Duarte has gathered:

---

2 The Level I exam uses only independent questions. This minicase is intended as a learning exercise.

Currently outstanding bonds	$2.4 million five-year bonds, coupon of 12.5 percent, with a market value of $2.156 million
Risk-free rate of interest	5.25 percent
Estimated equity risk premium	7 percent
Tax rate	23 percent

19 The asset betas for Relevant, ABJ, and Opus, respectively, are:

   A 1.70, 2.52, and 2.73.

   B 1.70, 2.79, and 3.37.

   C 1.70, 2.81, and 3.44.

20 The average asset beta for the pure players in this industry, Relevant, ABJ, and Opus, weighted by market value of equity is *closest* to:

   A 1.67.

   B 1.97.

   C 2.27.

21 Using the capital asset pricing model, the cost of equity capital for a company in this industry with a debt-to-equity ratio of 0.01, asset beta of 2.27, and a marginal tax rate of 23 percent is *closest* to:

   A 17 percent.

   B 21 percent.

   C 24 percent.

22 The marginal cost of capital for TagOn, based on an average asset beta of 2.27 for the industry and assuming that new stock can be issued at $8 per share, is *closest* to:

   A 20.5 percent.

   B 21.0 percent.

   C 21.5 percent.

23 Two years ago, a company issued $20 million in long-term bonds at par value with a coupon rate of 9 percent. The company has decided to issue an additional $20 million in bonds and expects the new issue to be priced at par value with a coupon rate of 7 percent. The company has no other debt outstanding and has a tax rate of 40 percent. To compute the company's weighted average cost of capital, the appropriate after-tax cost of debt is *closest* to:

   A 4.2%.

   B 4.8%.

   C 5.4%.

24 An analyst gathered the following information about a company and the market:

Current market price per share of common stock	$28.00
Most recent dividend per share paid on common stock (D_0)	$2.00
Expected dividend payout rate	40%
Expected return on equity (ROE)	15%
Beta for the common stock	1.3

Expected rate of return on the market portfolio	13%
Risk-free rate of return	4%

Using the discounted cash flow (DCF) approach, the cost of retained earnings for the company is *closest* to:

A   15.7%.

B   16.1%.

C   16.8%.

25   An analyst gathered the following information about a company and the market:

Current market price per share of common stock	$28.00
Most recent dividend per share paid on common stock (D_0)	$2.00
Expected dividend payout rate	40%
Expected return on equity (ROE)	15%
Beta for the common stock	1.3
Expected rate of return on the market portfolio	13%
Risk-free rate of return	4%

Using the Capital Asset Pricing Model (CAPM) approach, the cost of retained earnings for the company is *closest* to:

A   13.6%.

B   15.7%.

C   16.1%.

26   An analyst gathered the following information about a private company and its publicly traded competitor:

Comparable Companies	Tax Rate (%)	Debt/Equity	Equity Beta
Private company	30.0	1.00	N.A.
Public company	35.0	0.90	1.75

Using the pure-play method, the estimated equity beta for the private company is *closest* to:

A   1.029.

B   1.104.

C   1.877.

27   An analyst gathered the following information about the capital markets in the U.S. and in Paragon, a developing country.

Selected Market Information (%)	
Yield on U.S. 10-year Treasury bond	4.5
Yield on Paragon 10-year government bond	10.5
Annualized standard deviation of Paragon stock index	35.0
Annualized standard deviation of Paragon dollar-denominated government bond	25.0

Based on the analyst's data, the estimated country equity premium for Paragon is *closest* to:

A   4.29%.

B   6.00%.

C   8.40%.

SOLUTIONS

1 B is correct. The cost of equity is defined as the rate of return required by stockholders.

2 B is correct. Debt is generally less costly than preferred or common stock. The cost of debt is further reduced if interest expense is tax deductible.

3 C is correct. First calculate the growth rate using the sustainable growth calculation, and then calculate the cost of equity using the rearranged dividend discount model:

$g = (1 - \text{Dividend payout ratio})(\text{Return on equity}) = (1 - 0.30)(15\%) = 10.5\%$

$r_e = (D_1 / P_0) + g = (\$2.30 / \$45) + 10.50\% = 15.61\%$

4 C is correct. $FV = \$1,000$; $PMT = \$40$; $N = 10$; $PV = \$900$

Solve for i. The six-month yield, i, is 5.3149%

$\text{YTM} = 5.3149\% \times 2 = 10.62985\%$

$r_d(1 - t) = 10.62985\%(1 - 0.38) = 6.5905\%$

5 C is correct. The bond rating approach depends on knowledge of the company's rating and can be compared with yields on bonds in the public market.

6 B is correct. The company can issue preferred stock at 6.5%.

$P_p = \$1.75/0.065 = \$26.92$

7 B is correct.

Cost of equity $= D_1/P_0 + g = \$1.50 / \$30 + 7\% = 5\% + 7\% = 12\%$

$D / (D + E) = 0.8033 / 1.8033 = 0.445$

$\text{WACC} = [(0.445)(0.08)(1 - 0.4)] + [(0.555)(0.12)] = 8.8\%$

8 B is correct. The weighted average cost of capital, using weights derived from the current capital structure, is the best estimate of the cost of capital for the average-risk project of a company.

9 C is correct.

$w_d = \$63/(\$220 + 63) = 0.223$

$w_e = \$220/(\$220 + 63) = 0.777$

10 B is correct. Asset risk does not change with a higher debt-to-equity ratio. Equity risk rises with higher debt.

11 B is correct. The debt-to-equity ratio of the new product should be used when making the adjustment from the asset beta, derived from the comparables, to the equity beta of the new product.

12 B is correct.

Capital structure:

Market value of debt: $FV = \$10,000,000$, $PMT = \$400,000$, $N = 10$,

$I/YR = 13.65\%$. Solving for PV gives the answer $7,999,688.

Market value of equity: 1.2 million shares outstanding at $10 = $12,000,000

Market value of debt	$7,999,688	40%
Market value of equity	12,000,000	60%
Total capital	$19,999,688	100%

To raise $7.5 million of new capital while maintaining the same capital structure, the company would issue $7.5 million × 40% = $3.0 million in bonds, which results in a before-tax rate of 16 percent.

$r_d(1 - t) = 0.16(1 - 0.3) = 0.112$ or 11.2%

$r_e = 0.03 + 2.2 (0.10 - 0.03) = 0.184$ or 18.4%

WACC = $[0.40(0.112)] + [0.6(0.184)] = 0.0448 + 0.1104 = 0.1552$ or 15.52%

13 B is correct.

$r_e = 0.0425 + (1.3)(0.0482) = 0.1052$ or 10.52%

14 B is correct.

WACC = $[(€900/€3300) .0925 (1 - 0.375)] + [(€2400/€3300)(0.1052)] = 0.0923$ or 9.23%

15 A is correct.

Asset beta = Unlevered beta = $1.3/(1 + [(1-0.375)(€900/€2400)]) = 1.053$

16 C is correct.

Project beta = $1.053 \{1 + [(1 - 0.375)(€80/€20)]\} = 1.053 \{3.5\} = 3.686$

17 C is correct.

$r_e = 0.0425 + 3.686(0.0482 + 0.0188) = 0.2895$ or 28.95%

18 C is correct.

Cost of equity without the country risk premium:

$r_e = 0.0425 + 3.686 (0.0482) = 0.2202$ or 22.02%

Cost of equity with the country risk premium:

$r_e = 0.0425 + 3.686 (0.0482 + 0.0188) = 0.2895$ or 28.95%

Weighted average cost of capital without the country risk premium:

WACC = $[0.80 (0.0925) (1 - 0.375)] + [0.20 (0.2202)] = 0.04625 + 0.04404 = 0.09038$ or 9.03 percent

Weighted average cost of capital with the country risk premium:

WACC = $[0.80 (0.0925) (1 - 0.375)] + [0.20 (0.2895)] = 0.04625 + 0.0579 = 0.1042$ or 10.42 percent

NPV without the country risk premium:

$$NPV = \frac{€48 \text{ million}}{(1 + 0.0903)^1} + \frac{€52 \text{ million}}{(1 + 0.0903)^2} + \frac{€54.4 \text{ million}}{(1 + 0.0903)^3} - €100 \text{ million}$$

$$= €44.03 \text{ million} + 43.74 \text{ million} + 41.97 \text{ million} - €100 \text{ million}$$

$$= €29.74 \text{ million}$$

NPV with the country risk premium:

$$NPV = \frac{€48 \text{ million}}{(1 + 0.1042)^1} + \frac{€52 \text{ million}}{(1 + 0.1042)^2} + \frac{€54.4 \text{ million}}{(1 + 0.1042)^3} - €100 \text{ million}$$

$$= €43.47 \text{ million} + 42.65 \text{ million} + 40.41 \text{ million} - €100 \text{ million}$$

$$= €26.53 \text{ million}$$

19 B is correct.

Asset betas: $\beta_{equity}/[1 + (1 - t)(D/E)]$

Relevant = $1.702/[1 + (0.77)(0)] = 1.702$

ABJ = $2.8/[1 + (0.77)(0.003)] = 2.7918$

Opus = $3.4/1 + [(0.77)(0.013)] = 3.3663$

20 C is correct.

Weights are determined based on relative market values:

Pure-Play	Market Value of Equity in Millions	Proportion of Total
Relevant	$3,800	0.5490
ABJ	2,150	0.3106
Opus	972	0.1404
Total	$6,922	1.0000

Weighted average beta $(0.5490)(1.702) + (0.3106)(2.7918) + (0.1404)(3.3572)$ = 2.27.

21 B is correct.

Asset beta = 2.27

Levered beta = $2.27 \{1 + [(1 - 0.23)(0.01)]\} = 2.2875$

Cost of equity capital = $0.0525 + (2.2875)(0.07) = 0.2126$ or 21.26%

22 C is correct.

For debt: $FV = 2,400,000; PV = 2,156,000; n = 10; PMT = 150,000$

Solve for i. $i = 0.07748$. YTM = 15.5%

Before-tax cost of debt = 15.5%

Market value of equity = 1 million shares outstanding + 1 million newly issued shares = 2 million shares at $8 = $16 million

Total market capitalization = $2.156 million + $16 million = $18.156 million

Levered beta = $2.27 \{1 + [(1 - 0.23)(2.156/16)]\} = 2.27 (1.1038) = 2.5055$

Cost of equity = 0.0525 + 2.5055 (0.07) = 0.2279 or 22.79%

Debt weight = $2.156/$18.156 = 0.1187

Equity weight = $16/$18.156 = 0.8813

TagOn's MCC	= [(0.1187)(0.155)(1 − 0.23)] + [(0.8813)(0.2279)]
	= 0.01417 + 0.20083
	= 0.2150 or 21.50%

23 A is correct. The relevant cost is the marginal cost of debt. The before-tax marginal cost of debt can be estimated by the yield to maturity on a comparable outstanding. After adjusting for tax, the after-tax cost is 7(1 − 0.4) = 7(0.6) = 4.2%.

24 C is correct. The expected return is the sum of the expected dividend yield plus expected growth. The expected growth is (1 − 0.4)15% = 9%. The expected dividend yield is $2.18/$28 = 7.8%. The sum is 16.8%.

25 B is correct. Using the CAPM approach, 4% + 1.3(9%) = 15.7%.

26 C is correct. Inferring the asset beta for the public company: unlevered beta = 1.75/[1 + (1 − 0.35) (0.90)] = 1.104. Relevering to reflect the target debt ratio of the private firm: levered beta = 1.104 × [1 + (1 − 0.30) (1.00)] = 1.877.

27 C is correct. The country equity premium can be estimated as the sovereign yield spread times the volatility of the country's stock market relative to its bond market. Paragon's equity premium is (10.5% − 4.5%) × (35%/25%) = 6% × 1.4 = 8.40%.

Measures of Leverage

*by Pamela Peterson Drake, CFA, Raj Aggarwal, CFA,
Cynthia Harrington, CFA, and Adam Kobor, CFA*

LEARNING OUTCOMES

Mastery	The candidate should be able to:
☐	**a.** define and explain leverage, business risk, sales risk, operating risk, and financial risk, and classify a risk, given a description;
☐	**b.** calculate and interpret the degree of operating leverage, the degree of financial leverage, and the degree of total leverage;
☐	**c.** describe the effect of financial leverage on a company's net income and return on equity;
☐	**d.** calculate the breakeven quantity of sales and determine the company's net income at various sales levels;
☐	**e.** calculate and interpret the operating breakeven quantity of sales.

INTRODUCTION

1

This reading presents elementary topics in leverage. **Leverage** is the use of fixed costs in a company's cost structure. Fixed costs that are operating costs (such as depreciation or rent) create operating leverage. Fixed costs that are financial costs (such as interest expense) create financial leverage.

Analysts refer to the use of fixed costs as leverage because fixed costs act as a fulcrum for the company's earnings. Leverage can magnify earnings both up and down. The profits of highly leveraged companies might soar with small upturns in revenue. But the reverse is also true: Small downturns in revenue may lead to losses.

Analysts need to understand a company's use of leverage for three main reasons. First, the degree of leverage is an important component in assessing a company's risk and return characteristics. Second, analysts may be able to discern information about a company's business and future prospects from management's decisions about the use of operating and financial leverage. Knowing how to interpret these signals also helps the analyst evaluate the quality of management's decisions. Third, the valuation of a company requires forecasting future cash flows and assessing the risk associated with those cash flows. Understanding a company's use of leverage should help in forecasting cash flows and in selecting an appropriate discount rate for finding their present value.

The reading is organized as follows: Section 2 introduces leverage and defines important terms. Section 3 illustrates and discusses measures of operating leverage and financial leverage, which combine to define a measure of total leverage that gauges the sensitivity of net income to a given percent change in units sold. This section also covers breakeven points in using leverage and corporate reorganization (a possible consequence of using leverage inappropriately). A summary and practice problems conclude this reading.

2 LEVERAGE

Leverage increases the volatility of a company's earnings and cash flows and increases the risk of lending to or owning a company. Additionally, the valuation of a company and its equity is affected by the degree of leverage: The greater a company's leverage, the greater its risk and, hence, the greater the discount rate that should be applied in its valuation. Further, highly leveraged (levered) companies have a greater chance of incurring significant losses during downturns, thus accelerating conditions that lead to financial distress and bankruptcy.

Consider the simple example of two companies, Impulse Robotics, Inc., and Malvey Aerospace, Inc. These companies have the following performance for the period of study:[1]

Exhibit 1	Impulse Robotics and Malvey Aerospace	
	Impulse Robotics	**Malvey Aerospace**
Revenues	$1,000,000	$1,000,000
Operating costs	700,000	750,000
Operating income	$300,000	$250,000
Financing expense	100,000	50,000
Net income	$200,000	$200,000

These companies have the same net income, but are they identical in terms of operating and financial characteristics? Would we appraise these two companies at the same value? Not necessarily.

The risk associated with future earnings and cash flows of a company are affected by the company's cost structure. The **cost structure** of a company is the mix of variable and fixed costs. **Variable costs** fluctuate with the level of production and sales. Some examples of variable costs are the cost of goods purchased for resale, costs of materials or supplies, shipping charges, delivery charges, wages for hourly employees, sales commissions, and sales or production bonuses. **Fixed costs** are expenses that are the same regardless of the production and sales of the company. These costs include depreciation, rent, interest on debt, insurance, and wages for salaried employees.

---

1 We are ignoring taxes for this example, but when taxes are included, the general conclusions remain the same.

Suppose that the cost structures of the companies differ in the manner shown in Exhibit 2.

Exhibit 2	Impulse Robotics and Malvey Aerospace	
	Impulse Robotics	**Malvey Aerospace**
Number of units produced and sold	100,000	100,000
Sales price per unit	$10	$10
Variable cost per unit	$2	$6
Fixed operating cost	$500,000	$150,000
Fixed financing expense	$100,000	$50,000

The risk associated with these companies is different, although, as we saw in Exhibit 1, they have the same net income. They have different operating and financing cost structures, resulting in differing volatility of net income.

For example, if the number of units produced and sold is different from 100,000, the net income of the two companies diverges. If 50,000 units are produced and sold, Impulse Robotics has a loss of $200,000 and Malvey Aerospace has $0 earnings. If, on the other hand, the number of units produced and sold is 200,000, Impulse Robotics earns $1 million whereas Malvey Aerospace earns $600,000. In other words, the variability in net income is greater for Impulse Robotics, which has higher fixed costs in terms of both fixed operating costs and fixed financing costs.

Impulse Robotics' cost structure results in more leverage than that of Malvey Aerospace. We can see this effect when we plot the net income of each company against the number of units produced and sold, as in Exhibit 3. The greater leverage of Impulse Robotics is reflected in the greater slope of the line representing net income. This means that as the number of units sold changes, Impulse Robotics experiences a greater change in net income than does Malvey Aerospace for the same change in units sold.

Exhibit 3	Net Income for Different Numbers of Units Produced and Sold

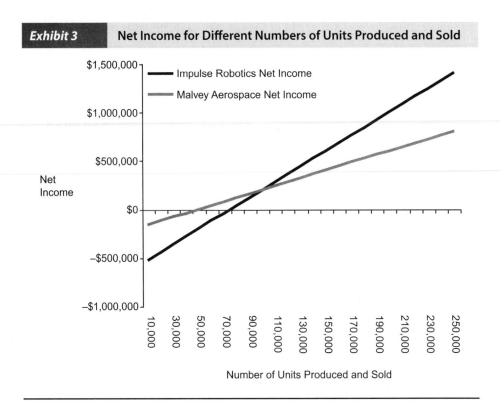

Companies that have more fixed costs relative to variable costs in their cost structures have greater variation in net income as revenues fluctuate and, hence, more risk.

3   BUSINESS RISK AND FINANCIAL RISK

Risk arises from both the operating and financing activities of a company. In the following, we address how that happens and the measures available to the analyst to gauge the risk in each case.

3.1 Business Risk and Its Components

Business risk is the risk associated with operating earnings. Operating earnings are risky because total revenues are risky, as are the costs of producing revenues. Revenues are affected by a large number of factors, including economic conditions, industry dynamics (including the actions of competitors), government regulation, and demographics. Therefore, prices of the company's goods or services or the quantity of sales may be different from what is expected. We refer to the uncertainty with respect to the price and quantity of goods and services as **sales risk**.

Operating risk is the risk attributed to the operating cost structure, in particular the use of fixed costs in operations. The greater the fixed operating costs relative to variable operating costs, the greater the operating risk. Business risk is therefore the combination of sales risk and operating risk. Companies that operate in the same line of business generally have similar business risk.

3.2 Sales Risk

Consider Impulse Robotics once again. Suppose that the forecasted number of units produced and sold in the next period is 100,000 but that the standard deviation of the number of units sold is 20,000. And suppose the price that the units sell for is expected to be $10 per unit but the standard deviation is $2. Contrast this situation with that of a company named Tolley Aerospace, Inc., which has the same cost structure but a standard deviation of units sold of 40,000 and a price standard deviation of $4.

If we assume, for simplicity's sake, that the fixed operating costs are known with certainty and that the units sold and price per unit follow a normal distribution, we can see the impact of the different risks on the operating income of the two companies through a simulation; the results are shown in Exhibit 4. Here, we see the differing distributions of operating income that result from the distributions of units sold and price per unit. So, even if the companies have the same cost structure, differing *sales risk* affects the potential variability of the company's profitability. In our example, Tolley Aerospace has a wider distribution of likely outcomes in terms of operating profit. This greater volatility in operating earnings means that Tolley Aerospace has more sales risk than Impulse Robotics.

Exhibit 4	Operating Income Simulations for Impulse Robotics and Tolley Aerospace

Panel A: Impulse Robotics

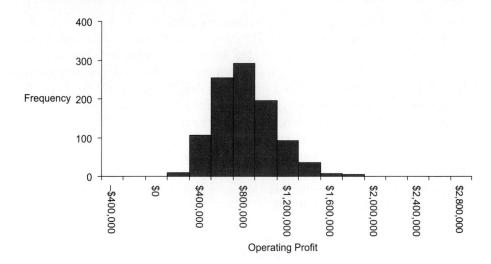

(continued)

| Exhibit 4 | (Continued) |

Panel B: Tolley Aerospace

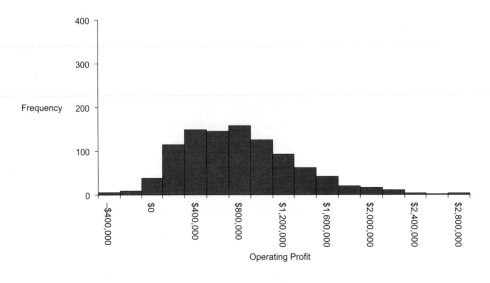

3.3 Operating Risk

The greater the fixed component of costs, the more difficult it is for a company to adjust its operating costs to changes in sales. The mixture of fixed and variable costs depends largely on the type of business. Even within the same line of business, companies can vary their fixed and variable costs to some degree. We refer to the risk arising from the mix of fixed and variable costs as **operating risk**. The greater the fixed operating costs relative to variable operating costs, the greater the operating risk.

Next, we look at how operating risk affects the variability of cash flows. A concept taught in microeconomics is **elasticity**, which is simply a measure of the sensitivity of changes in one item to changes in another. We can apply this concept to examine how sensitive a company's operating income is to changes in demand, as measured by unit sales. We will calculate the operating income elasticity, which we refer to as the **degree of operating leverage** (DOL). DOL is a quantitative measure of operating risk as it was defined earlier.

The degree of operating leverage is the ratio of the percentage change in operating income to the percentage change in units sold. We will simplify things and assume that the company sells all that it produces in the same period. Then,

$$\text{DOL} = \frac{\text{Percentage change in operating income}}{\text{Percentage change in units sold}} \tag{1}$$

For example, if DOL at a given level of unit sales is 2.0, a 5 percent increase in unit sales from that level would be expected to result in a (2.0)(5%) = 10 percent increase in operating income. As illustrated later in relation to Exhibit 6, a company's DOL is dependent on the level of unit sales being considered.

Returning to Impulse Robotics, the price per unit is $10, the variable cost per unit is $2, and the total fixed operating costs are $500,000. If Impulse Robotics' output changes from 100,000 units to 110,000 units—an increase of 10 percent in the number of units sold—operating income changes from $300,000 to $380,000:[2]

Exhibit 5	**Operating Leverage of Impulse Robotics**			

Item	Selling 100,000 Units	Selling 110,000 Units	Percentage Change
Revenues	$1,000,000	$1,100,000	+10.00
Less variable costs	200,000	220,000	+10.00
Less fixed costs	500,000	500,000	0.00
Operating income	$300,000	$380,000	+26.67

Operating income increases by 26.67 percent when units sold increases by 10 percent. What if the number of units *decreases* by 10 percent, from 100,000 to 90,000? Operating income is $220,000, representing a *decline* of 26.67 percent.

What is happening is that for a 1 percent change in units sold, the operating income changes by 2.67 times that percentage, in the same direction. If units sold increases by 10 percent, operating income increases by 26.7 percent; if units sold decreased by 20 percent, operating income would decrease by 53.3 percent.

We can represent the degree of operating leverage as given in Equation 1 in terms of the basic elements of the price per unit, variable cost per unit, number of units sold, and fixed operating costs. Operating income is revenue minus total operating costs (with variable and fixed cost components):

$$\begin{array}{l} \text{Operating} \\ \text{income} \end{array} = \left[\left(\begin{array}{c} \text{Price} \\ \text{per unit} \end{array} \right) \left(\begin{array}{c} \text{Number of} \\ \text{units sold} \end{array} \right) \right]$$
$$- \left[\left(\begin{array}{c} \text{Variable cost} \\ \text{per unit} \end{array} \right) \left(\begin{array}{c} \text{Number of} \\ \text{units sold} \end{array} \right) \right] - \left[\begin{array}{c} \text{Fixed operating} \\ \text{costs} \end{array} \right]$$

or

$$\begin{array}{l} \text{Operating} \\ \text{income} \end{array} = \left(\begin{array}{c} \text{Number of} \\ \text{units sold} \end{array} \right) \underbrace{\left[\left(\begin{array}{c} \text{Price} \\ \text{per unit} \end{array} \right) - \left(\begin{array}{c} \text{Variable cost} \\ \text{per unit} \end{array} \right) \right]}_{\text{Contribution margin}} - \left[\begin{array}{c} \text{Fixed operating} \\ \text{costs} \end{array} \right]$$

The **per unit contribution margin** is the amount that each unit sold contributes to covering fixed costs—that is, the difference between the price per unit and the variable cost per unit. That difference multiplied by the quantity sold is the **contribution margin**, which equals revenue minus variable costs.

How much does operating income change when the number of units sold changes? Fixed costs do not change; therefore, operating income changes by the contribution margin. The percentage change in operating income for a given change in units sold simplifies to

---

2 We provide the variable and fixed operating costs for our sample companies used in this reading to illustrate the leverage and breakeven concepts. In reality, however, the financial analyst does not have these breakdowns but rather is faced with interpreting reported account values that often combine variable and fixed costs and costs for different product lines.

$$DOL = \frac{Q(P-V)}{Q(P-V)-F}$$

(2)

where Q is the number of units, P is the price per unit, V is the variable operating cost per unit, and F is the fixed operating cost. Therefore, $P - V$ is the per unit contribution margin and $Q(P - V)$ is the contribution margin.

Applying the formula for DOL using the data for Impulse Robotics, we can calculate the sensitivity to change in units sold from 100,000 units:

$$\text{DOL@} \atop 100{,}000\,\text{units} = \frac{100{,}000(\$10 - \$2)}{100{,}000(\$10 - \$2) - \$500{,}000} = 2.67$$

A DOL of 2.67 means that a 1 percent change in units sold results in a 1% × 2.67 = 2.67% change in operating income; a DOL of 5 means that a 1 percent change in units sold results in a 5 percent change in operating income, and so on.

Why do we specify that the DOL is at a particular quantity sold (in this case, 100,000 units)? Because the DOL is different at different numbers of units produced and sold. For example, at 200,000 units,

$$\text{DOL@} \atop 200{,}000\,\text{units} = \frac{200{,}000(\$10 - \$2)}{200{,}000(\$10 - \$2) - \$500{,}000} = 1.45$$

We can see the sensitivity of the DOL for different numbers of units produced and sold in Exhibit 6. When operating profit is negative, the DOL is negative. At positions just below and just above the point where operating income is $0, operating income is at its most sensitive on a percentage basis to changes in units produced and sold. At the point at which operating income is $0 (at 62,500 units produced and sold in this example), the DOL is undefined because the denominator in the DOL calculation is $0. After this point, the DOL gradually declines as more units are produced and sold.

Exhibit 6	Impulse Robotics' Degree of Operating Leverage for Different Number of Units Produced and Sold

$P = \$10$; $V = \$2$; $F = \$500{,}000$

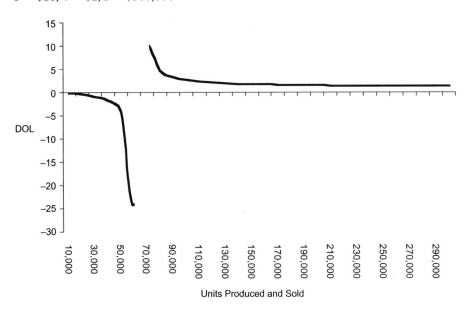

Units Produced and Sold

We will now look at a similar situation in which the company has shifted some of the operating costs away from fixed costs and into variable costs. Malvey Aerospace has a unit sales price of $10, a variable cost of $6 a unit, and $150,000 in fixed costs. A change in units sold from 100,000 to 110,000 (a 10 percent change) changes operating profit from $250,000 to $290,000, or 16 percent. The DOL in this case is 1.6:

$$\text{DOL @ } 100,000\,\text{units} = \frac{100,000(\$10 - \$6)}{100,000(\$10 - \$6) - \$150,000} = 1.6$$

and the change in operating income is 16 percent:

$$\begin{array}{c}\text{Percentage change} \\ \text{in operating income}\end{array} = (\text{DOL})\left(\begin{array}{c}\text{Percentage change} \\ \text{in units sold}\end{array}\right) = (1.6)(10\%) = 16\%$$

We can see the difference in leverage in the case of Impulse Robotics and Malvey Aerospace companies in Exhibit 7. In Panel A, we see that Impulse Robotics has higher operating income than Malvey Aerospace when both companies produce and sell more than 87,500 units, but lower operating income than Malvey when both companies produce and sell less than 87,500 units.[3]

Exhibit 7	Profitability and the DOL for Impulse Robotics and Malvey Aerospace

Impulse Robotics: $P = \$10$; $V = \$2$; $F = \$500,000$
Malvey Aerospace: $P = \$10$; $V = \$6$; $F = \$150,000$

Panel A: Operating Income and Number of Units Produced and Sold

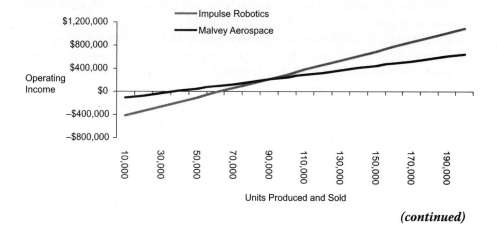

(continued)

---

3 We can calculate the number of units that produce the same operating income for these two companies by equating the operating incomes and solving for the number of units. Let X be the number of units. The X at which Malvey Aerospace and Impulse Robotics generate the same operating income is the X that solves the following: $10X - 2X - 500,000 = 10X - 6X - 150,000$; that is, $X = 87,500$.

| Exhibit 7 | (Continued) |

Panel B: Degree of Operating Leverage (DOL)

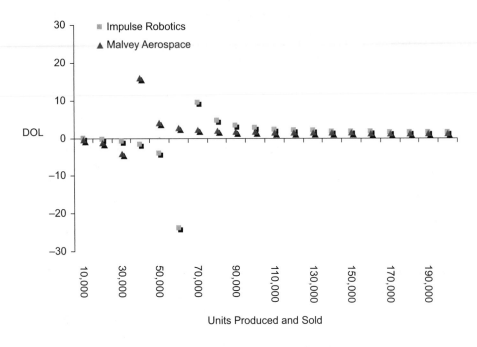

This example confirms what we saw earlier in our reasoning of fixed and variable costs: The greater the use of fixed, relative to variable, operating costs, the more sensitive operating income is to changes in units sold and, therefore, the more operating risk. Impulse Robotics has more operating risk because it has more operating leverage. However, as Panel B of Exhibit 7 shows, the degrees of operating leverage are similar for the two companies for larger numbers of units produced and sold.

Both sales risk and operating risk influence a company's business risk. And both sales risk and operating risk are determined in large part by the type of business the company is in. But management has more opportunity to manage and control operating risk than sales risk.

Suppose a company is deciding which equipment to buy to produce a particular product. The sales risk is the same no matter what equipment is chosen to produce the product. But the available equipment may differ in terms of the fixed and variable operating costs of producing the product. Financial analysts need to consider how the operating cost structure of a company affects the company's risk.

EXAMPLE 1

Calculating the Degree of Operating Leverage

Arnaud Kenigswald is analyzing the potential impact of an improving economy on earnings at Global Auto, one of the world's largest car manufacturers. Global is headquartered in Berlin. Two Global Auto divisions manufacture passenger cars and produce combined revenues of €93 billion. Kenigswald projects that sales will improve by 10 percent due to increased demand for cars. He wants to see how Global's earnings might respond given that level of increase in sales. He first looks at the degree of leverage at Global, starting with operating leverage.

Global sold 6 million passenger cars in 2009. The average price per car was €24,000, fixed costs associated with passenger car production total €15 billion per year, and variable costs per car are €14,000. What is the degree of operating leverage of Global Auto?

Solution:

$$\text{DOL @ 6 million units} = \frac{6 \text{ million } (€24{,}000 - €14{,}000)}{6 \text{ million } (€24{,}000 - €14{,}000) - €15 \text{ billion}} = 1.333$$

For a 10 percent increase in cars sold, operating income increases by 1.333 × 10% = 13.33%.

Industries that tend to have high operating leverage are those that invest up front to produce a product but spend relatively little on making and distributing it. Software developers and pharmaceutical companies fit this description. Alternatively, retailers have low operating leverage because much of the cost of goods sold is variable.

Because most companies produce more than one product, the ratio of variable to fixed costs is difficult to obtain. We can get an idea of the operating leverage of a company by looking at changes in operating income in relation to changes in sales for the entire company. This relation can be estimated by regressing changes in operating income (the variable to be explained) on changes in sales (the explanatory variable) over a recent time period.[4] Although this approach does not provide a precise measure of operating risk, it can help provide a general idea of the amount of operating leverage present. For example, compare the relation between operating earnings and revenues for Abbott Laboratories, a pharmaceutical company, and Wal-Mart Stores, a discount retailer, as shown in Exhibit 8. Note that the slope of the least-squares regression line is greater for Abbott (with a slope coefficient of 0.1488) than for Wal-Mart (with a slope coefficient of 0.0574). (A visual comparison of slopes should not be relied upon because the scales of the x- and y-axes are different in diagrams for the two regressions.) We can see that operating earnings are more sensitive to changes in revenues for the higher-operating-leveraged Abbott Laboratories as compared to the lower-operating-leveraged Wal-Mart Stores.

Exhibit 8	Relation between Operating Earnings and Revenues

Panel A: Abbott Laboratories Operating Earnings and Revenues, 1990–2004

Estimated regression: Operating earnings = $754.77 + 0.1488 Revenues
$R^2 = 66.25\%$

(continued)

---

4 A least-squares regression is a procedure for finding the best-fitting line (called the least squares regression line) through a set of data points by minimizing the squared deviations from the line.

Exhibit 8	(Continued)

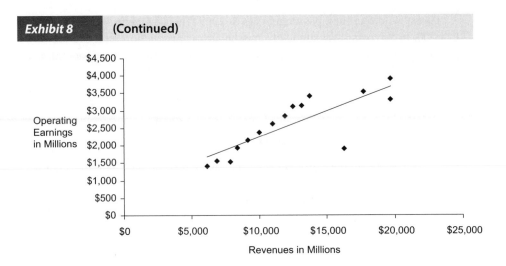

Panel B: Wal-Mart Stores Operating Earnings and Revenues, 1990–2004

Estimated regression: Operating earnings = $152.762 + 0.0574 Revenues
R^2 = 99.38%

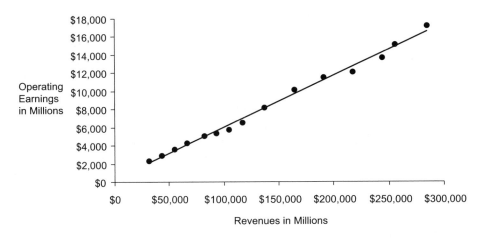

Sources: Abbott Laboratories 10-K filings and Wal-Mart Stores 10-K filings, various years.

3.4 Financial Risk

We can expand on the concept of risk to accommodate the perspective of owning a security. A security represents a claim on the income and assets of a business; therefore, the risk of the security goes beyond the variability of operating earnings to include how the cash flows from those earnings are distributed among the claimants—the creditors and owners of the business. The risk of a security is therefore affected by both business risk and financial risk.

Financial risk is the risk associated with how a company finances its operations. If a company finances with debt, it is legally obligated to pay the amounts that make up its debts when due. By taking on fixed obligations, such as debt and long-term leases, the company increases its financial risk. If a company finances its business with common equity, generated either from operations (retained earnings) or from issuing new common shares, it does not incur fixed obligations. The more fixed-cost financial obligations (e.g., debt) incurred by the company, the greater its financial risk.

We can quantify this risk in the same way we did for operating risk, looking at the sensitivity of the cash flows available to owners when operating income changes. This sensitivity, which we refer to as the **degree of financial leverage** (DFL), is

$$DFL = \frac{\text{Percentage change in net income}}{\text{Percentage change in operating income}} \qquad (3)$$

For example, if DFL at a given level of operating income is 1.1, a 5 percent increase in operating income would be expected to result in a (1.1)(5%) = 5.5 percent increase in net income. A company's DFL is dependent on the level of operating income being considered.

Net income is equal to operating income, less interest and taxes.[5] If operating income changes, how does net income change? Consider Impulse Robotics. Suppose the interest payments are $100,000 and, for simplicity, the tax rate is 0 percent: If operating income changes from $300,000 to $360,000, net income changes from $200,000 to $260,000:

Exhibit 9	Financial Risk of Impulse Robotics (1)		
	Operating Income of $300,000	**Operating Income of $360,000**	**Percentage Change**
Operating income	$300,000	$360,000	+20
Less interest	100,000	100,000	0
Net income	$200,000	$260,000	+30

A 20 percent increase in operating income increases net income by $60,000, or 30 percent. What if the fixed financial costs are $150,000? A 20 percent change in operating income results in a 40 percent change in the net income, from $150,000 to $210,000:

Exhibit 10	Financial Risk of Impulse Robotics (2)		
	Operating Income of $300,000	**Operating Income of $360,000**	**Percentage Change**
Operating income	$300,000	$360,000	+20
Less interest	150,000	150,000	0
Net income	$150,000	$210,000	+40

---

5 More complex entities than we have been using for our examples may also need to account for other income (losses) and extraordinary income (losses) together with operating income as the basis for earnings before interest and taxes.

Using more debt financing, which results in higher fixed costs, increases the sensitivity of net income to changes in operating income. We can represent the sensitivity of net income to a change in operating income, continuing the notation from before and including the fixed financial cost, C, and the tax rate, t, as

$$\text{DFL} = \frac{\left[Q(P-V)-F\right](1-t)}{\left[Q(P-V)-F-C\right](1-t)} = \frac{\left[Q(P-V)-F\right]}{\left[Q(P-V)-F-C\right]} \tag{4}$$

As you can see in Equation 4, the factor that adjusts for taxes, $(1-t)$, cancels out of the equation. In other words, the DFL is not affected by the tax rate.

In the case in which operating income is $300,000 and fixed financing costs are $100,000, the degree of financial leverage is

$$\text{DFL @ } \$300,000 \text{ operating income} = \frac{\$300,000}{\$300,000 - \$100,000} = 1.5$$

If, instead, fixed financial costs are $150,000, the DFL is equal to 2.0:

$$\text{DFL @ } \$300,000 \text{ operating income} = \frac{\$300,000}{\$300,000 - \$150,000} = 2.0$$

Again, we need to qualify our degree of leverage by the level of operating income because DFL is different at different levels of operating income.

The greater the use of financing sources that require fixed obligations, such as interest, the greater the sensitivity of net income to changes in operating income.

EXAMPLE 2

Calculating the Degree of Financial Leverage

Global Auto also employs debt financing. If Global can borrow at 8 percent, the interest cost is €40 billion. What is the degree of financial leverage of Global Auto if 6 million cars are produced and sold?

Solution:

At 6 million cars produced and sold, operating income = €45 billion. Therefore:

$$\text{DFL @ } €45 \text{ billion operating income} = \frac{€45 \text{ billion}}{€45 \text{ billion} - €40 \text{ billion}} = 9.0$$

For every 1 percent change in operating income, net income changes 9 percent due to financial leverage.

Unlike operating leverage, the degree of financial leverage is most often a choice by the company's management. Whereas operating costs are very similar among companies in the same industry, competitors may decide on differing capital structures.

Companies with relatively high ratios of tangible assets to total assets may be able to use higher degrees of financial leverage than companies with relatively low ratios because the claim on the tangible assets that lenders would have in the event of a default may make lenders more confident in extending larger amounts of credit. In general, businesses with plants, land, and equipment that can be used to collateralize borrowings and businesses whose revenues have below-average business cycle sensitivity may be able to use more financial leverage than businesses without such assets and with relatively high business cycle sensitivity.

Using financial leverage generally increases the variability of return on equity (net income divided by shareholders' equity). In addition, its use by a profitable company may increase the level of return on equity. Example 3 illustrates both effects.

EXAMPLE 3

The Leveraging Role of Debt

Consider the Capital Company, which is expected to generate $1,500,000 in revenues and $500,000 in operating earnings next year. Currently, the Capital Company does not use debt financing and has assets of $2,000,000.

Suppose Capital were to change its capital structure, buying back $1,000,000 of stock and issuing $1,000,000 in debt. If we assume that interest on debt is 5 percent and income is taxed at a rate of 30 percent, what is the effect of debt financing on Capital's net income and return on equity if operating earnings may vary as much as 40 percent from expected earnings?

| Exhibit 11 | Return on Equity of Capital Company | | |

No Debt (Shareholders' Equity = $2 million)	Expected Operating Earnings, Less 40%	Expected Operating Earnings	Expected Operating Earnings, Plus 40%
Earnings before interest and taxes	$300,000	$500,000	$700,000
Interest expense	0	0	0
Earnings before taxes	$300,000	$500,000	$700,000
Taxes	90,000	150,000	210,000
Net income	$210,000	$350,000	$490,000
Return on equity[1]	10.5%	17.5%	24.5%

Debt to Total Assets = 50%; (Shareholders' Equity = $1 million)	Expected Operating Earnings, Less 40%	Expected Operating Earnings	Expected Operating Earnings, Plus 40%
Earnings before interest and taxes	$300,000	$500,000	$700,000
Interest expense	50,000	50,000	50,000
Earnings before taxes	$250,000	$450,000	$650,000
Taxes	75,000	135,000	195,000
Net income	$175,000	$315,000	$455,000
Return on equity	17.5%	31.5%	45.5%

[1]Recall that ROE is calculated as net income/shareholders' equity.

Depicting a broader array of capital structures and operating earnings, ranging from an operating loss of $500,000 to operating earnings of $2,000,000, Exhibit 12 shows the effect of leverage on the return on equity for Capital Company:

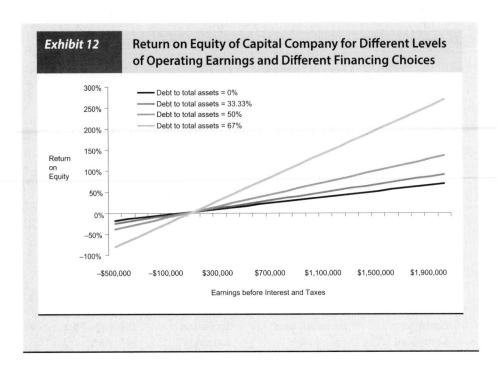

Exhibit 12 Return on Equity of Capital Company for Different Levels of Operating Earnings and Different Financing Choices

Business is generally an uncertain venture. Changes in the macroeconomic and competitive environments that influence sales and profitability are typically difficult to discern and forecast. The larger the proportion of debt in the financing mix of a business, the greater is the chance that it will face default. Similarly, the greater the proportion of debt in the capital structure, the more earnings are magnified upward in improving economic times. The bottom line? Financial leverage tends to increase the risk of ownership for shareholders.

3.5 Total Leverage

The degree of operating leverage gives us an idea of the sensitivity of operating income to changes in revenues. And the degree of financial leverage gives us an idea of the sensitivity of net income to changes in operating income. But often we are concerned about the combined effect of both operating leverage and financial leverage. Owners are concerned about the combined effect because both factors contribute to the risk associated with their future cash flows. And financial managers, making decisions intended to maximize owners' wealth, need to be concerned with how investment decisions (which affect the operating cost structure) and financing decisions (which affect the capital structure) affect lenders' and owners' risk.

Look back at the example of Impulse Robotics. The sensitivity of owners' cash flow to a given change in units sold is affected by both operating and financial leverage. Consider using 100,000 units as the base number produced and sold. A 10 percent increase in units sold results in a 27 percent increase in operating income and a 40 percent increase in net income; a like decrease in units sold results in a similar decrease in operating income and net income.

Exhibit 13	Total Leverage of Impulse Robotics		
	Units Produced and Sold:		
	90,000	**100,000**	**110,000**
Revenues	$900,000	$1,000,000	$1,100,000
Less variable costs	180,000	200,000	220,000
Less fixed costs	500,000	500,000	500,000
Operating income	$220,000	$300,000	$380,000
Less interest	100,000	100,000	100,000
Net income	$120,000	$200,000	$280,000
Relative to 100,000 units produced and sold			
Percentage change in units sold	−10%		+10%
Percentage change in operating profit	−27%		+27%
Percentage change in net income	−40%		+40%

Combining a company's degree of operating leverage with its degree of financial leverage results in the **degree of total leverage** (DTL), a measure of the sensitivity of net income to changes in the number of units produced and sold. We again make the simplifying assumption that a company sells all that it produces in the same period:

$$DTL = \frac{\text{Percentage change in net income}}{\text{Percentage change in the number of units sold}} \qquad (5)$$

or

$$DTL = \underbrace{\frac{Q(P-V)}{Q(P-V)-F}}_{DOL} \times \underbrace{\frac{[Q(P-V)-F]}{[Q(P-V)-F-C]}}_{DFL} \qquad (6)$$

$$= \frac{Q(P-V)}{Q(P-V)-F-C}$$

Suppose

Number of units sold	=	Q	=	100,000
Price per unit	=	P	=	$10
Variable cost per unit	=	V	=	$2
Fixed operating cost	=	F	=	$500,000
Fixed financing cost	=	C	=	$100,000

Then,

$$DTL = \frac{100,000(\$10 - \$2)}{100,000(\$10 - \$2) - \$500,000 - \$100,000} = 4.0$$

which we could also have determined by multiplying the DOL, 2.67, by the DFL, 1.5. This means that a 1 percent increase in units sold will result in a 4 percent increase in net income; a 50 percent increase in units produced and sold results in a 200 percent increase in net income; a 5 percent decline in units sold results in a 20 percent decline in income to owners; and so on.

Because the DOL is relative to the base number of units produced and sold and the DFL is relative to the base level of operating earnings, DTL is different depending on the number of units produced and sold. We can see the DOL, DFL, and DTL for Impulse Robotics for different numbers of units produced and sold, beginning at the number of units for which the degrees are positive, in Exhibit 14.

Exhibit 14	DOL, DFL, and DTL for Different Numbers of Units Produced and Sold

$P = \$10$, $V = \$2$, $F = \$500,000$, $C = \$100,000$

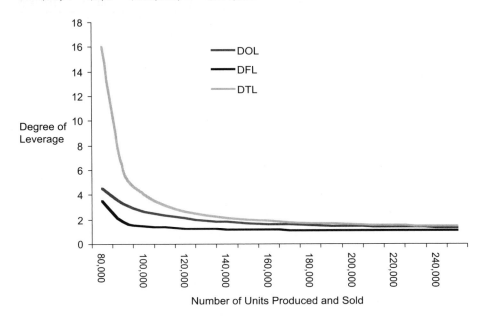

In the case of operating leverage, the fixed operating costs act as a fulcrum. The greater the proportion of operating costs that are fixed, the more sensitive operating income is to changes in sales. In the case of financial leverage, the fixed financial costs, such as interest, act as a fulcrum. The greater the proportion of financing with fixed cost sources, such as debt, the more sensitive cash flows available to owners are to changes in operating income. Combining the effects of both types of leverage, we see that fixed operating and financial costs together increase the sensitivity of earnings to owners.

EXAMPLE 4

Calculating the Degree of Total Leverage

Continuing from Example 2, Global Auto's total leverage is

$$\frac{\text{DTL @}}{\text{6 million units}} = \frac{\text{DOL @}}{\text{6 million units}} \times \frac{\text{DFL @}}{\text{€45 billion operating income}}$$

$$\frac{\text{DTL @}}{\text{6 million units}} = \frac{6 \text{ million}(\text{€24,000} - \text{€14,000})}{6 \text{ million}(\text{€24,000} - \text{€14,000}) - \text{€15 billion}}$$
$$\times \frac{\text{€45 billion}}{\text{€45 billion} - \text{€40 billion}}$$

$$\frac{\text{DTL @}}{\text{6 million units}} = 1.333 \times 9.0 = 12$$

Given Global Auto's operating and financial leverage, a 1 percent change in unit sales changes net income by 12 percent.

3.6 Breakeven Points and Operating Breakeven Points

Looking back at Exhibit 3, we see that there is a number of units at which the company goes from being unprofitable to being profitable—that is, the number of units at which the net income is zero. This number is referred to as the breakeven point. The **breakeven point**, Q_{BE}, is the number of units produced and sold at which the company's net income is zero—the point at which revenues are equal to costs.

Plotting revenues and total costs against the number of units produced and sold, as in Exhibit 15, indicates that the breakeven is at 75,000 units. At this number of units produced and sold, revenues are equal to costs and, hence, profit is zero.

Exhibit 15	Impulse Robotics Breakeven

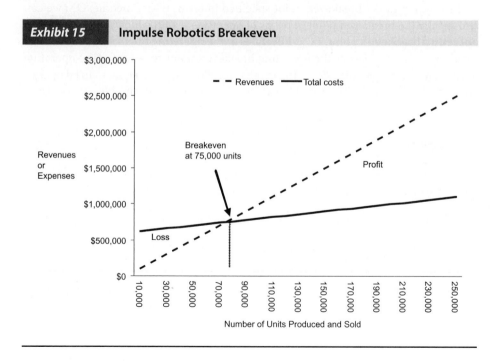

We can calculate this breakeven point for Impulse Robotics and Malvey Aerospace. Consider that net income is zero when the revenues are equal to the expenses. We can represent this equality of revenues and costs (summing variable operating costs, fixed operating costs, and fixed financing costs) by the following equation:

$$PQ = VQ + F + C$$

where

P = the price per unit
Q = the number of units produced and sold
V = the variable cost per unit
F = the fixed operating costs
C = the fixed financial cost

Therefore,

$$PQ_{BE} = VQ_{BE} + F + C$$

and the breakeven number of units, Q_{BE}, is[6]

$$Q_{BE} = \frac{F + C}{P - V} \tag{7}$$

In the case of Impulse Robotics and Malvey Aerospace, Impulse Robotics has a higher breakeven point. Using numbers taken from Exhibit 2:

$$\text{Impulse Robotics: } Q_{BE} = \frac{\$500,000 + \$100,000}{\$10 - \$2} = 75,000 \text{ units}$$

$$\text{Malvey Aerospace: } Q_{BE} = \frac{\$150,000 + \$50,000}{\$10 - \$6} = 50,000 \text{ units}$$

This means that Impulse Robotics must produce and sell more units to achieve a profit. So, while the higher-leveraged Impulse Robotics has a greater breakeven point relative to Malvey Aerospace, the profit that Impulse Robotics generates beyond this breakeven point is greater than that of Malvey Aerospace. Therefore, leverage has its rewards in terms of potentially greater profit, but it also increases risk.

In addition to the breakeven point specified in terms of net income, Q_{BE}, we can also specify the breakeven point in terms of operating profit, which we refer to as the **operating breakeven** point, Q_{OBE}. Revenues at the operating breakeven point are set equal to operating costs at the operating breakeven point to solve for the operating breakeven number of units, Q_{OBE}. The expression shows Q_{OBE} as equal to fixed operating costs divided by the difference between price per unit and variable cost per unit:

$$PQ_{OBE} = VQ_{OBE} + F$$

$$Q_{OBE} = \frac{F}{P - V}$$

For the two companies in our example, Impulse Robotics and Malvey Aerospace, the operating breakevens are 62,500 and 37,500 units, respectively:

$$\text{Impulse Robotics: } Q_{OBE} = \frac{\$500,000}{\$10 - \$2} = 62,500 \text{ units}$$

$$\text{Malvey Aerospace: } Q_{OBE} = \frac{\$150,000}{\$10 - \$6} = 37,500 \text{ units}$$

Impulse Robotics has a higher operating breakeven point in terms of the number of units produced and sold.

---

[6] You will notice that we did not consider taxes in our calculation of the breakeven point. This is because at the point of breakeven, taxable income is zero.

EXAMPLE 5

Calculating Operating Breakeven and Breakeven Points

Continuing with his analysis, Kenigswald considers the effect of a possible downturn on Global Auto's earnings. He divides the fixed costs of €15 billion by the per unit contribution margin:

$$Q_{OBE} = \frac{€15 \text{ billion}}{€24,000 - €14,000} = 1,500,000 \text{ cars}$$

The operating breakeven for Global is 1,500,000 cars, or €36 billion in revenues. We calculate the breakeven point by dividing fixed operating costs, plus interest costs, by the contribution margin:

$$Q_{BE} = \frac{€15 \text{ billion} + €40 \text{ billion}}{€24,000 - €14,000} = \frac{€55 \text{ billion}}{€10,000} = 5,500,000 \text{ cars}$$

Considering the degree of total leverage, Global's breakeven is 5.5 million cars, or revenues of €132 billion.

We can verify these calculations by constructing an income statement for the breakeven sales (in € billions):

	1,500,000 Cars	5,500,000 Cars
Revenues (= P x Q)	€36	€132
Variable operating costs (= $V \times Q$)	21	77
Fixed operating costs (F)	15	15
Operating income	€ 0	€ 40
Fixed financial costs (C)	40	40
Net income	−€40	€ 0

As business expands or contracts beyond or below breakeven points, fixed costs do not change. The breakeven points for companies with low operating and financial leverage are less important than those for companies with high leverage. Companies with greater total leverage must generate more revenue to cover fixed operating and financing costs. The farther unit sales are from the breakeven point for high-leverage companies, the greater the magnifying effect of this leverage.

3.7 The Risks of Creditors and Owners

As we discussed earlier, business risk refers to the effect of economic conditions as well as the level of operating leverage. Uncertainty about demand, output prices, and costs are among the many factors that affect business risk. When conditions change for any of these factors, companies with higher business risk experience more volatile earnings. Financial risk is the additional risk that results from the use of debt and preferred stock. The degree of financial risk grows with greater use of debt. Who bears this risk?

The risk for providers of equity and debt capital differs because of the relative rights and responsibilities associated with the use of borrowed money in a business. Lenders have a prior claim on assets relative to shareholders, so they have greater security. In return for lending money to a business, lenders require the payment of interest and principal when due. These contractual payments to lenders must be made regardless of the profitability of the business. A business must satisfy these claims in a timely fashion or face the pain of bankruptcy should it default. In return for their higher priority in claims, lenders get predefined yet limited returns.

In contrast, equity providers claim whatever is left over after all expenses, including debt service, have been paid. So, unlike the fixed and known commitments to the lenders, what is left over for the owners may be a great deal or may be nothing. In exchange for this risk, providers of equity capital exercise the decision-making power over the business, including the right to hire, guide, and if necessary, fire managers. In public companies, ownership rights are usually exercised through an elected board of directors. They undertake the decisions over what portion of the business's earnings should be paid out as dividends for common shareholders.

Legal codes in most countries provide for these rights, as well as conditions for companies to file for bankruptcy (with reference to businesses, often called insolvency). A number of bankruptcy codes provide in some form for two categories of bankruptcies. One form provides for a temporary protection from creditors so that a viable business may reorganize. In the United States, the U.S. Bankruptcy Code sets the terms for the form of negotiated **reorganization** of a company's capital structure that allows it to remain a going concern in Chapter 11.[7] For businesses that are not viable, the second form of bankruptcy process allows for the orderly satisfaction of the creditors' claims. In the United States, this form of bankruptcy is referred to as **liquidation**.[8] Whereas both types of bankruptcy lead to major dislocations in the rights and privileges of owners, lenders, employees, and managers, it is in this latter category of bankruptcy that the original business ceases to exist.

The difference between a company that reorganizes and emerges from bankruptcy and one that is liquidated is often the difference between operating and financial leverage. Companies with high operating leverage have less flexibility in making changes, and bankruptcy protection does little to help reduce operating costs. Companies with high financial leverage use bankruptcy laws and protection to change their capital structure and, once the restructuring is complete, can emerge as ongoing concerns.

EXAMPLE 6

Chapter 11 Reorganization and Owens Corning

The world's largest manufacturer of glass fiber insulation, Owens Corning Corporation of Toledo, Ohio, filed for Chapter 11 bankruptcy on 5 October 2000, as it faced growing asbestos liability claims. With revenues exceeding $6 billion per year, Owens Corning was one of the largest corporations ever afforded bankruptcy protection by the U.S. courts.

From 1952 to 1972, Owens Corning produced an asbestos-containing high-temperature pipe coating called Kaylo, and at the time of its bankruptcy filing, it had received more than 460,000 asbestos personal injury claims and had paid or agreed to pay more than $5 billion for asbestos-related awards and settlements, legal expenses, and claims processing fees. While the company had assets of $7 billion and liabilities of $5.7 billion, the trust fund it set aside to pay those claims appeared inadequate.

---

7 U.S. Code, Title 11—Bankruptcy, Chapter 11—Reorganization. Companies filing for bankruptcy under this code are referred to as having filed for Chapter 11 bankruptcy.
8 U.S. Code, Title 11—Bankruptcy, Chapter 7—Liquidation.

The company's stock traded at between $15 and $25 per share in the year prior to the announcement; the price fell to $1 per share when Owens Corning declared bankruptcy and admitted that it had been overwhelmed by the asbestos liabilities.

EXAMPLE 7

Chapter 7 and Webvan Do Not Deliver

Since the peak of the NASDAQ in March of 2000, many technology companies have found either that they cannot raise enough capital to implement their business plans or that they have an untenable business plan. Some have simply shut their doors and gone out of business, while others have filed for bankruptcy. Either way, these companies have left many unsatisfied creditors.

For example, Webvan.com was a start-up company in the late 1990s that raised over $1.2 billion in equity, $375 million of which came from an IPO in November 1999. It had very ambitious business plans to build a series of warehouses and deliver groceries to fulfill customer orders placed over the internet. Webvan.com, however, faced a number of challenges, including a downturn in the economy, and quickly ran through its capital.

Webvan.com filed for Chapter 11 bankruptcy protection in July 2001 and reported that it owed $106 million to creditors. By the time it began liquidation under Chapter 7 in January 2002, it reported that the value of its liquidated assets totaled only $25 million, leaving its creditors to receive pennies on the dollar and its investors to receive little or nothing for their $1.2 billion investment in the company.

Whereas the ability to file for bankruptcy is important to the economy, the goal of most investors is to avoid ownership of companies that are heading toward this extreme step, as well as to be able to evaluate opportunities among companies already in bankruptcy. Under both Chapter 7 and Chapter 11, providers of equity capital generally lose all value during the bankruptcy. On the other hand, debtholders typically receive at least a portion of their capital, but the payments of principal and interest are delayed during the period of bankruptcy protection.

SUMMARY

In this reading, we have reviewed the fundamentals of business risk, financial risk, and measures of leverage.

- Leverage is the use of fixed costs in a company's cost structure. Business risk is the risk associated with operating earnings and reflects both sales risk (uncertainty with respect to the price and quantity of sales) and operating risk (the risk related to the use of fixed costs in operations). Financial risk is the risk associated with how a company finances its operations (i.e., the split between equity and debt financing of the business).

- The degree of operating leverage (DOL) is the ratio of the percentage change in operating income to the percentage change in units sold. We can use the following formula to measure the degree of operating leverage:

$$DOL = \frac{Q(P-V)}{Q(P-V)-F}$$

- The degree of financial leverage (DFL) is the percentage change in net income for a one percent change in operating income. We can use the following formula to measure the degree of financial leverage:

$$DFL = \frac{[Q(P-V)-F](1-t)}{[Q(P-V)-F-C](1-t)} = \frac{[Q(P-V)-F]}{[Q(P-V)-F-C]}$$

- The degree of total leverage (DTL) is a measure of the sensitivity of net income to changes in unit sales, which is equivalent to DTL = DOL × DFL.

- The breakeven point, Q_{BE}, is the number of units produced and sold at which the company's net income is zero, which we calculate as

$$Q_{BE} = \frac{F+C}{P-V}$$

- The operating breakeven point, Q_{OBE}, is the number of units produced and sold at which the company's operating income is zero, which we calculate as

$$Q_{OBE} = \frac{F}{P-V}$$

PRACTICE PROBLEMS

1 If two companies have identical unit sales volume and operating risk, they are *most likely* to also have identical:

A sales risk.

B business risk.

C sensitivity of operating earnings to changes in the number of units produced and sold.

2 Degree of operating leverage is *best* described as a measure of the sensitivity of:

A net earnings to changes in sales.

B fixed operating costs to changes in variable costs.

C operating earnings to changes in the number of units produced and sold.

3 The Fulcrum Company produces decorative swivel platforms for home televisions. If Fulcrum produces 40 million units, it estimates that it can sell them for $100 each. Variable production costs are $65 per unit and fixed production costs are $1.05 billion. Which of the following statements is *most accurate*? Holding all else constant, the Fulcrum Company would:

A generate positive operating income if unit sales were 25 million.

B have less operating leverage if fixed production costs were 10 percent greater than $1.05 billion.

C generate 20 percent more operating income if unit sales were 5 percent greater than 40 million.

4 The business risk of a particular company is *most accurately* measured by the company's:

A debt-to-equity ratio.

B efficiency in using assets to generate sales.

C operating leverage and level of uncertainty about demand, output prices, and competition.

5 Consider two companies that operate in the same line of business and have the same degree of operating leverage: the Basic Company and the Grundlegend Company. The Basic Company and the Grundlegend Company have, respectively, no debt and 50 percent debt in their capital structure. Which of the following statements is *most accurate*? Compared to the Basic Company, the Grundlegend Company has:

A a lower sensitivity of net income to changes in unit sales.

B the same sensitivity of operating income to changes in unit sales.

C the same sensitivity of net income to changes in operating income.

6 Myundia Motors now sells 1 million units at ¥3,529 per unit. Fixed operating costs are ¥1,290 million and variable operating costs are ¥1,500 per unit. If the company pays ¥410 million in interest, the levels of sales at the operating breakeven and breakeven points are, respectively:

A ¥1,500,000,000 and ¥2,257,612,900.

B ¥2,243,671,760 and ¥2,956,776,737.

C ¥2,975,148,800 and ¥3,529,000,000.

7   Juan Alavanca is evaluating the risk of two companies in the machinery industry: The Gearing Company and Hebelkraft, Inc. Alavanca used the latest fiscal year's financial statements and interviews with managers of the respective companies to gather the following information:

	The Gearing Company	Hebelkraft, Inc.
Number of units produced and sold	1 million	1.5 million
Sales price per unit	$200	$200
Variable cost per unit	$120	$100
Fixed operating cost	$40 million	$90 million
Fixed financing expense	$20 million	$20 million

Based on this information, the breakeven points for The Gearing Company and Hebelkraft, Inc. are:

A   0.75 million and 1.1 million units, respectively.

B   1 million and 1.5 million units, respectively.

C   1.5 million and 0.75 million units, respectively.

The following information relates to Questions 8–16[1]

Mary Benn, CFA, is a financial analyst for Twin Fields Investments, located in Storrs, Connecticut, U.S.A. She has been asked by her supervisor, Bill Cho, to examine two small Japanese cell phone component manufacturers: 4G, Inc. and Qphone Corp. Cho indicates that his clients are most interested in the use of leverage by 4G and Qphone. Benn states, "I will have to specifically analyze each company's respective business risk, sales risk, operating risk, and financial risk." "Fine, I'll check back with you shortly," Cho, answers.

Benn begins her analysis by examining the sales prospects of the two firms. The results of her sales analysis appear in Exhibit 1. She also expects very little price variability for these cell phones. She next gathers more data on these two companies to assist her analysis of their operating and financial risk.

When Cho inquires as to her progress Benn responds, "I have calculated Qphone's degree of operating leverage (DOL) and degree of financial leverage (DFL) at Qphone's 2009 level of unit sales. I have also calculated Qphone's breakeven level for unit sales. I will have 4G's leverage results shortly."

Cho responds, "Good, I will call a meeting of some potential investors for tomorrow. Please help me explain these concepts to them, and the differences in use of leverage by these two companies. In preparation for the meeting, I have a number of questions":

- "You mentioned business risk; what is included in that?"

- "How would you classify the risk due to the varying mix of variable and fixed costs?"

---

1 Developed by Philip Fanara, CFA.

- "Could you conduct an analysis and tell me how the two companies will fare relative to each other in terms of net income if their unit sales increased by 10 percent above their 2009 unit sales levels?"
- "Finally, what would be an accurate verbal description of the degree of total leverage?"

The relevant data for analysis of 4G is contained in Exhibit 2, and Benn's analysis of the Qphone data appears in Exhibit 3:

Exhibit 1	Benn's Unit Sales Estimates for 4G, Inc. and Qphone Corp.		
Company	2009 Unit Sales	Standard Deviation of Unit Sales	2010 Expected Unit Sales Growth Rate (%)
4G, Inc.	1,000,000	25,000	15
Qphone Corp.	1,500,000	10,000	15

Exhibit 2	Sales, Cost, and Expense Data for 4G, Inc. (At Unit Sales of 1,000,000)
Number of units produced and sold	1,000,000
Sales price per unit	¥108
Variable cost per unit	¥72
Fixed operating cost	¥22,500,000
Fixed financing expense	¥9,000,000

Exhibit 3	Benn's Analysis of Qphone (At Unit Sales of 1,500,000)
Degree of operating leverage	1.40
Degree of financial leverage	1.15
Breakeven quantity (units)	571,429

8 Based on Benn's analysis, 4G's sales risk relative to Qphone's is *most likely* to be:
   A lower.
   B equal.
   C higher.

9 What is the *most appropriate* response to Cho's question regarding the components of business risk?
   A Sales risk and financial risk.
   B Operating risk and sales risk.

    C   Financial risk and operating risk.

10 The *most appropriate* response to Cho's question regarding the classification of risk arising from the mixture of variable and fixed costs is:

    A   sales risk.

    B   financial risk.

    C   operating risk.

11 Based on the information in Exhibit 2, the degree of operating leverage (DOL) of 4G, Inc., at unit sales of 1,000,000, is *closest* to:

    A   1.60.

    B   2.67.

    C   3.20.

12 Based on the information in Exhibit 2, 4G, Inc.'s degree of financial leverage (DFL), at unit sales of 1,000,000, is *closest* to:

    A   1.33.

    B   2.67.

    C   3.00.

13 Based on the information in Exhibit 1 and Exhibit 3, Qphone's expected percentage change in operating income for 2010 is *closest* to:

    A   17.25%.

    B   21.00%.

    C   24.30%.

14 4G's breakeven quantity of unit sales is *closest* to:

    A   437,500 units.

    B   625,000 units.

    C   875,000 units.

15 In response to Cho's question regarding an increase in unit sales above 2009 unit sales levels, it is *most likely* that 4G's net income will increase at:

    A   a slower rate than Qphone's.

    B   the same rate as Qphone's.

    C   a faster rate than Qphone's.

16 The *most appropriate* response to Cho's question regarding a description of the degree of total leverage is that degree of total leverage is:

    A   the percentage change in net income divided by the percentage change in units sold.

    B   the percentage change in operating income divided by the percentage change in units sold.

    C   the percentage change in net income divided by the percentage change in operating income.

SOLUTIONS

1 C is correct. The companies' degree of operating leverage should be the same, consistent with C. Sales risk refers to the uncertainty of the number of units produced and sold and the price at which units are sold. Business risk is the joint effect of sales risk and operating risk.

2 C is correct. The degree of operating leverage is the elasticity of operating earnings with respect to the number of units produced and sold. As an elasticity, the degree of operating leverage measures the sensitivity of operating earnings to a change in the number of units produced and sold.

3 C is correct. Because DOL is 4, if unit sales increase by 5 percent, Fulcrum's operating earnings are expected to increase by 4 × 5% = 20%. The calculation for DOL is:

$$DOL = \frac{(40 \text{ million})(\$100 - \$65)}{\left[(40 \text{ million})(\$100 - \$65)\right] - \$1.05 \text{ billion}}$$

$$= \frac{\$1.400 \text{ billion}}{\$1.400 \text{ billion} - \$1.05 \text{ billion}} = \frac{\$1.4}{\$0.35} = 4$$

4 C is correct. Business risk reflects operating leverage and factors that affect sales (such as those given).

5 B is correct. Grundlegend's degree of operating leverage is the same as Basic Company's, whereas Grundlegend's degree of total leverage and degree of financial leverage are higher.

6 B is correct.

$$\text{Operating breakeven units} = \frac{¥1,290 \text{ million}}{\left(¥3,529 - ¥1,500\right)} = 635,781.173 \text{ units}$$

$$\text{Operating breakeven sales} = ¥3,529 \times 635,781.173 \text{ units} = ¥2,243,671,760$$

or

$$\text{Operating breakeven sales} = \frac{¥1,290 \text{ million}}{1 - \left(¥1,500/¥3,529\right)} = ¥2,243,671,760$$

$$\text{Total breakeven} = \frac{¥1,290 \text{ million} + ¥410 \text{ million}}{\left(¥3,529 - ¥1,500\right)} = \frac{¥1,700 \text{ million}}{¥2,029}$$

$$= 837,851.1582 \text{ units}$$

$$\text{Breakeven sales} = ¥3,529 \times 837,851.1582 \text{ units} = ¥2,956,776,737$$

or

$$\text{Breakeven sales} = \frac{¥1,700 \text{ million}}{1 - \left(¥1,500/¥3,529\right)} = ¥2,956,776,737$$

7 A is correct. For The Gearing Company,

$$Q_{BE} = \frac{F + C}{P - V} = \frac{\$40 \text{ million} + \$20 \text{ million}}{\$200 - \$120} = 750,000$$

For Hebelkraft, Inc.,

$$Q_{BE} = \frac{F + C}{P - V} = \frac{\$90 \text{ million} + \$20 \text{ million}}{\$200 - \$100} = 1,100,000$$

8 C is correct. Sales risk is defined as uncertainty with respect to the price or quantity of goods and services sold. 4G has a higher standard deviation of unit sales than Qphone; in addition, 4G's standard deviation of unit sales stated as a fraction of its level of unit sales, at 25,000/1,000,000 = 0.025, is greater than the comparable ratio for Qphone, 10,000/1,500,000 = 0.0067.

9 B is correct. Business risk is associated with operating earnings. Operating earnings are affected by sales risk (uncertainty with respect to price and quantity), and operating risk (the operating cost structure and the level of fixed costs).

10 C is correct. Operating risk refers to the risk arising from the mix of fixed and variable costs.

11 B is correct. $DOL = \dfrac{Q(P-V)}{Q(P-V)-F}$

$$DOL @ \atop 1,000,000 \text{ units} = \frac{1,000,000(¥108 - ¥72)}{1,000,000(¥108 - ¥72) - ¥22,500,000} = 2.67$$

12 C is correct. Degree of financial leverage is

$$DFL = \frac{\left[Q(P-V)-F\right]}{\left[Q(P-V)-F-C\right]}$$
$$= \frac{1,000,000(¥108-¥72)-¥22,500,000}{1,000,000(¥108-¥72)-¥22,500,000-¥9,000,000} = 3.00$$

13 B is correct. The degree of operating leverage of Qphone is 1.4. The percentage change in operating income is equal to the DOL times the percentage change in units sold, therefore:

$$\text{Percentage change in operating income} = (DOL)\left(\text{Percentage change in units sold}\right) = (1.4)(15\%) = 21\%$$

14 C is correct. The breakeven quantity is computed

$$Q_{BE} = \frac{F+C}{P-V} = \frac{(¥22,500,000 + ¥9,000,000)}{(¥108 - ¥72)} = 875,000$$

15 C is correct. 4G, Inc.'s degree of total leverage can be shown to equal 8, whereas Qphone Corp.'s degree of total leverage is only DOL × DFL = 1.4 × 1.15 = 1.61. Therefore, a 10 percent increase in unit sales will mean an 80 percent increase in net income for 4G, but only a 16.1 percent increase in net income for Qphone Corp. The calculation for 4G, Inc.'s DTL is

$$DTL = \frac{Q(P-V)}{Q(P-V)-F-C}$$
$$= \frac{1,000,000(¥108-¥72)}{1,000,000(¥108-¥72)-¥22,500,000-¥9,000,000} = 8.00$$

16 A is correct. Degree of total leverage is defined as the percentage change in net income divided by the percentage change in units sold.

Dividends and Share Repurchases: Basics

by George H. Troughton, CFA, and Gregory Noronha, CFA

LEARNING OUTCOMES

Mastery	The candidate should be able to:
☐	a. describe regular cash dividends, extra dividends, stock dividends, stock splits, and reverse stock splits, including their expected effect on shareholders' wealth and a company's financial ratios;
☐	b. describe dividend payment chronology, including the significance of declaration, holder-of-record, ex-dividend, and payment dates;
☐	c. compare share repurchase methods;
☐	d. calculate and compare the effect of a share repurchase on earnings per share when 1) the repurchase is financed with the company's excess cash and 2) the company uses debt to finance the repurchase;
☐	e. calculate the effect of a share repurchase on book value per share;
☐	f. explain why a cash dividend and a share repurchase of the same amount are equivalent in terms of the effect on shareholders' wealth, all else being equal.

INTRODUCTION

1

This reading covers the features and characteristics of dividends and share repurchases, the two ways a company can distribute cash to its shareholders. A **dividend** is a distribution paid to shareholders based on the number of shares owned. Dividends are declared by a corporation's board of directors, whose actions may require approval by shareholders (e.g., in most of Europe in general, and in China) or may not require such approval (e.g., in the United States). In contrast to the payment of interest and principal on a bond by its issuer, the payment of dividends is discretionary rather than a legal obligation and may be limited by legal statutes (e.g., in relation to not impairing such accounting quantities as stated capital) and by debt contract provisions

CFA Institute gratefully acknowledges the contributions of Catherine E. Clark, CFA, as co-author of a prior version of this reading.

(to protect more senior interests). Interest and dividends in many jurisdictions are subject to different tax treatment at the corporate level. Interest on debt is usually tax deductible on a corporate tax return, whereas dividends are not. Dividends are taxed a second time in some jurisdictions at the shareholder level. Dividends may also be taxed differently from capital gains. In this reading, we focus on dividends on common shares (as opposed to preferred shares) and on publicly traded companies. (Synonyms for *common shares* include *ordinary shares* and *common stock*; for brevity, the reading often uses *shares* or *stock* to refer to such securities.) Taken together, cash dividends and the value of shares repurchased in any given year constitute a company's **payout** for the year. A company's **payout policy** is the set of principles guiding payouts.

Dividends and share repurchases concern analysts because, as distributions to shareholders, they affect investment returns and financial ratios. When share price volatility is high, investors sometimes forget the importance of dividends as a source of return. From its inception at year-end 1969 to the end of 2008, the gross total return on the MSCI EAFE Index was 9.7 percent compounded annually with dividends reinvested, as compared with 6.7 percent on the basis of price alone.[1] The contribution of dividends to total return for large-cap U.S. stocks over the 1926–2008 period is even more formidable. From the inception of the Ibbotson U.S. large-cap data at the beginning of 1926, the total compound annual return with dividends reinvested from the beginning of 1926 to the end of 2008 was 9.6 percent, as compared with 5.3 percent on the basis of price alone.[2] Dividends also may provide important information about future company performance and investment returns. Analysts should strive to become familiar with all investment-relevant aspects of dividends and share repurchases.

The reading is organized as follows: Section 2 describes how cash and stock dividends are paid and the mechanics of stock splits. Section 3 describes the chronology of dividend payment procedures, including record date, ex-dividend date, and payment date. Section 4 presents share repurchases, including their income statement and balance sheet effects and equivalence to cash dividends (making certain assumptions). Section 5 offers concluding remarks, and a summary and practice problems complete the reading.

2   DIVIDENDS: FORMS

Companies can pay dividends in a number of ways. Cash dividends can be distributed to shareholders through regular, extra (also called special or irregular), or liquidating dividends. Other forms of dividends include stock dividends and stock splits. In this section, we will explore the different forms that dividends can take and their impact on both the shareholder and the issuing company.

2.1 Regular Cash Dividends

Many companies choose to distribute cash to their shareholders on a regular schedule. The customary frequency of payment, however, may vary among markets. In the United States and Canada, most companies that pay dividends choose a quarterly schedule of payments, whereas in Europe and Japan, the most common choice is to pay

---

1 See www.mscibarra.com. Gross return is in U.S. dollars and before withholding taxes. Gross return is used to make the MSCI returns comparable to Ibbotson returns.
2 See *2009 Ibbotson SBBI Classic Yearbook* (Chicago: Morningstar, 2009):59. The first monographs of SBBI containing the Ibbotson return data were published by the Institute of Chartered Financial Analysts in 1977, 1979, and 1982.

dividends twice a year (i.e., semiannually). Elsewhere in Asia, companies often favor paying dividends once a year (i.e., annually). Exhibit 1 summarizes typical dividend payment schedules for selected markets.

Exhibit 1	Geographic Differences in Frequency of Payment of Cash Dividends
Market	**Most Common Frequency**
United States and Canada	Quarterly
Europe	Semiannually
Japan	Semiannually
China	Annually
Thailand	Annually

Source: Author's survey of CFA charterholders (June 2009).

Most companies that pay cash dividends strive to maintain or increase their dividends. A record of consistent dividends over a long period of time is important to many companies and shareholders because such a record is widely interpreted as evidence of consistent profitability. At a minimum, most dividend-paying companies strive not to reduce dividends when they are experiencing transitory problems, whereas some companies seek to consistently increase the dividend so as to indicate to investors that their shares are of high investment quality.

Regular dividends, and especially increasing regular dividends, also signal to investors that their company is growing and will share profits with their shareholders. Perhaps more importantly, management can use dividend announcements to communicate confidence in their company's future. Consistent with that, an increase in the regular dividend (especially if it is unexpected) often has a positive effect on share price.

2.1.1 Dividend Reinvestment Plans (DRPs)

In some world markets, companies are permitted[3] to have in place a system that allows shareholders to automatically reinvest all or a portion of cash dividends from a company in additional shares of the company. Such a dividend reinvestment plan is referred to as a DRP (pronounced "drip" and therefore often represented also as "DRIP"). Shareholders wishing to participate in a DRP must so indicate to the entity administering it. The three types of DRPs are distinguished by the company's source of shares for dividend reinvestment:[4]

- **open-market DRPs** in which the company purchases shares in the open market to acquire the additional shares credited to plan participants;

---

3 In some cases, after registering the plan with or gaining approval of the plan from local securities regulators.
4 See He (2009) for more details.

- **new-issue DRPs** (also referred to as **scrip dividend schemes** in the United Kingdom[5]) in which the company meets the need for additional shares by issuing them instead of purchasing them; and

- plans that are permitted to obtain shares through either open-market purchases or new share issuance.

A company may have several advantages in offering such plans. They may encourage a diverse shareholder base by providing small shareholders an easy means to accumulate additional shares. They may stimulate long-term investment in the company by encouraging shareholders to build loyalty to the company. New-issue DRPs allow the company to raise new equity capital without the flotation costs associated with secondary equity issuance using investment bankers. The potential advantages to the shareholder include the facts that such plans allow the accumulation of shares using cost averaging and that they are a cost-effective means for small shareholders to make additional investments in the company. Participating shareholders typically have no transaction costs in obtaining the additional shares through a DRP. Some companies, typically new-issue DRPs, offer the additional benefit to DRP participants of purchasing shares at a discount (usually 2–5 percent) to the market price. Note that such discounts dilute the holdings of shareholders who do not participate in the DRP.

A disadvantage to the shareholder is the extra record keeping involved in jurisdictions in which capital gains are taxed. Shares purchased through such plans change the average cost basis for capital gains tax purposes. If the share price for the reinvested dividend is higher (lower) than the original purchase price, reinvesting the dividend will increase (decrease) the average cost basis. Either way, detailed records must be kept to accurately compute gains or losses when shares are sold. A further perceived disadvantage to the shareholder is that cash dividends are fully taxed in the year received even when reinvested, which means the shareholder is paying tax on cash not actually received. For these reasons, use of such plans may be especially appropriate in a tax-deferred account (in which current investment earnings are not taxed), such as certain types of retirement accounts.

2.2 Extra or Special (Irregular) Dividends

An **extra dividend** or **special dividend**, also known as an irregular dividend, is a dividend paid by a company that does not pay dividends on a regular schedule, or a dividend that supplements regular cash dividends with an extra payment. These extra dividend payments may be brought about by special circumstances. For example, in 2004, Microsoft Corporation had a huge amount of excess cash and paid a $3.08 cash dividend when the stock price was $30.

Companies, particularly in cyclical industries, have sometimes chosen to use special dividends as a means of distributing more earnings only during strong earnings years. During economic downturns, when earnings are low or negative, cash that might otherwise be used for dividends is conserved. For example, a company may choose to declare a small regular dividend and then, when operating results are good, declare an extra dividend at the end of the year. Prior to the recession that began in 2008, which led to the suspension[6] of all Ford Motor Company and General Motors common dividends, Ford and GM often declared moderate regular quarterly dividends and used an "extra dividend" at the end of the year in particularly good earnings years.

---

5 For a detailed description of one such plan, see www.hsbc.com/1/2/investor-relations/dividends/scrip-dividend. Sometimes a contrast is drawn between "scrip dividend schemes" and "dividend repurchase plans" in which the latter term is understood to be only what the text describes as "open-market dividend reinvestment plans."

6 Suspension occurs when a company stops paying any cash dividends.

Example 1 concerns a company with a stated policy regarding the payment of extra dividends. In the example, the **dividend payout ratio** refers to common share cash dividends divided by net income available to common shares over the same time period.

EXAMPLE 1

TeliaSonera's Dividend Policy

TeliaSonera AB (OMX AB: TLSN) is the leading provider of telecommunication services in Sweden and Finland, with an important presence in other Nordic and Baltic markets. The company is headquartered in Stockholm, Sweden, and TLSN's shares trade on the Swedish and Finnish stock exchanges. TLSN's financial data are reported in Swedish kronor (SEK). In October 2007, TLSN's board of directors modified its dividend policy, stating:

> The company shall target a solid investment grade long-term credit rating (A– to BBB+) to secure the company's strategically important financial flexibility for investments in future growth, both organically and by acquisitions. The ordinary dividend shall be at least 40 percent of net income attributable to shareholders of the parent company. In addition, excess capital shall be returned to shareholders, after the Board of Directors has taken into consideration the company's cash at hand, cash flow projections and investment plans in a medium term perspective, as well as capital market conditions.

> *Source*: www.teliasonera.com/investor_relations/share_data/dividend.

Selected TLSN Financial per Share Data

	2008	2007
Shares outstanding	4,490.5 million	4,490.5 million
Earnings per share	SEK4.23	SEK3.94
Cash dividends per share	SEK1.80	SEK4.00

Source: www.teliasonera.com/investor_relations.

1 Calculate the cash dividend payout ratio for 2008 and 2007.

2 Assuming the board's new dividend policy became effective in 2008, calculate the amount of the annual ordinary dividend on the basis of TLSN's minimum payout policy in 2008 and the amount that could be considered an extra dividend.

Solution to 1:

With the same number of shares outstanding, the dividend payout ratio on a per share basis is dividends per share divided by earnings per share.

For 2008: SEK1.80/SEK4.23 = 42.6%

For 2007: SEK4.00/SEK3.94 = 101.5%

> **Solution to 2:**
>
> Under a policy of 40 percent of earnings, the minimum amount of dividends would be SEK4.23 × 0.40 = SEK1.69, and the amount of the extra dividend would then be SEK1.80 − SEK1.69 = SEK0.11.

2.3 Liquidating Dividends

A dividend may be referred to as a **liquidating dividend** when a company:

- goes out of business and the net assets of the company (after all liabilities have been paid) are distributed to shareholders;

- sells a portion of its business for cash and the proceeds are distributed to shareholders; or

- pays a dividend that exceeds its accumulated retained earnings (impairs stated capital).

2.4 Stock Dividends

Stock dividends are a non-cash form of dividends. With a **stock dividend** (also known as a **bonus issue of shares**), the company distributes additional shares (typically 2–10 percent of the shares then outstanding) of its common stock to shareholders instead of cash. Although the shareholder's total cost basis remains the same, the cost per share held is reduced. For example, if a shareholder owns 100 shares with a purchase price of $10 per share, the total cost basis would be $1,000. After a 5 percent stock dividend, the shareholder would own 105 shares of stock at a total cost of $1,000. However, the cost per share would decline to $9.52 ($1,000/105).

Superficially, the stock dividend might seem an improvement on the cash dividend from both the shareholders' and the company's point of view. Each shareholder ends up with more shares, which did not have to be paid for, and the company did not have to spend any actual money issuing a dividend. Furthermore, stock dividends are generally not taxable to shareholders because a stock dividend merely divides the "pie" (the market value of shareholders' equity) into smaller pieces. The stock dividend, however, does not affect the shareholder's proportionate ownership in the company (because other shareholders receive the same proportionate increase in shares); nor does it change the value of each shareholder's ownership position (because the increase in the number of shares held is accompanied by an offsetting decrease in earnings per share, and other measures of value per share, resulting from the greater number of shares outstanding).

The second point is illustrated in Exhibit 2, which shows the impact of a 3 percent stock dividend to a shareholder who owns 10 percent of a company with a market value of $20 million. As one can see, the market value of the shareholder's wealth does not change, assuming an unchanged **price to earnings ratio** (the ratio of share price, P, to earnings per share, E, or P/E). That assumption is reasonable because a stock dividend does not alter a company's asset base or earning power. (As the reader will see shortly, the same is true of a stock split.) In effect, the total market value of the company is unaffected by the stock dividend because the decrease in the share price is exactly offset by the increase in the number of shares outstanding.

Exhibit 2	Illustration of the Effect of a Stock Dividend	
	Before Dividend	**After Dividend**
Shares outstanding	1,000,000	1,030,000
Earnings per share	$1.00	$0.97 (1,000,000/1,030,000)
Stock price	$20.00	$19.4175 (20 × 0.9709)
P/E	20	20
Total market value	$20 million	$20 million (1,030,000 × $19.4175)
Shares owned	100,000 (10% × 1,000,000)	103,000 (10% × 1,030,000)
Ownership value	$2,000,000 (100,000 × $20)	$2,000,000 (103,000 × $19.4175)

Note: The exhibit shows intermediate results rounded to four decimal places, but final results are based on carrying intermediate results at full precision.

The propensity to pay stock dividends varies by market. Stock dividends are very commonly used in China, for example. Some 78 percent of the companies in the Shanghai A-share Index paid stock dividends in 2009 according to Bloomberg data, whereas an additional 7 percent of A-shares had a stock split.

Companies that regularly pay stock dividends see some advantages to this form of dividend payment. From the company's point of view, more shares outstanding broaden the shareholder base. With more shares outstanding, there is a higher probability that more individual shareholders will own the stock—almost always a plus for companies. A traditional belief is that a lower stock price will attract more investors, all else equal. U.S. companies often view the optimal share price range as $20 to $80. For a growing company, a systematic stock dividend will be more likely to keep the stock in the "optimal" range. For example, Tootsie Roll Industries (NYSE: TR) has issued a 3 percent stock dividend every year since 1966 in addition to its regular quarterly cash dividend.[7] When the company pays the same dividend rate on the new shares as it did on the old shares, a shareholder's dividend income increases, but the company could have accomplished the same result by increasing the cash dividend.

From a company's perspective, the key difference between a stock dividend and a cash dividend is that a cash dividend affects a company's capital structure, whereas a stock dividend has no economic impact on a company. Cash dividends reduce assets (because cash is being paid out) and shareholders' equity (by reducing retained earnings). All else equal, liquidity ratios, such as the cash ratio (cash and short-term marketable securities divided by current liabilities) and current ratio (current assets divided by current liabilities), should decrease (reflecting the reduction in cash). Financial leverage ratios, such as the debt-to-equity ratio (total debt divided by total shareholders' equity) and debt-to-assets ratio (total debt divided by total assets), should also increase. Stock dividends, on the other hand, do not affect assets or shareholders' equity. Although retained earnings are reduced by the value of the stock dividends paid (i.e., by the number of shares issued × price per share), contributed capital increases by the same amount (i.e., the value of the shares issued). As a result, total shareholders' equity does not change. Neither stock dividends nor stock splits (which are discussed in the next section) should affect liquidity ratios or financial leverage ratios.

---

7 It should be noted that Tootsie Roll follows a practice of increasing its cash dividend as well as paying a stock dividend.

2.5 Stock Splits

Stock splits are similar to stock dividends in that they have no economic effect on the company and the shareholders' total cost basis does not change. For example, if a company announces a two-for-one stock split, each shareholder will be issued an additional share for each share currently owned. Thus, a shareholder will have twice as many shares after the split as before the split. Therefore, earnings per share (and all other per share data) will decline by half, leaving the P/E and equity market value unchanged. Assuming the corporation maintains the same dividend payout ratio[8] as before the split, **dividend yield** (annual dividends per share divided by share price) will also be unchanged. Apart from the effect of any information or benefit that investors perceive a stock split to convey, stock splits (like stock dividends) should be neutral in their effect on shareholders' wealth.

Although two-for-one and three-for-one stock splits are the most common, unusual splits, such as five-for-four or seven-for-three, sometimes occur. It is important for each shareholder to recognize that their wealth is not changed by the stock split (just as it was not changed for a stock dividend, all else equal). Exhibit 3 shows an example of a two-for-one split and its impact on stock price, earnings per share, dividends per share, dividend payout ratio, dividend yield, P/E, and market value.

Exhibit 3	Before and After a Two-for-One Stock Split	
	Before Split	**After Split**
Number of shares outstanding	4 million	8 million
Stock price	€40.00	€20.00 (€40/2)
Earnings per share	€1.50	€0.75 (€1.50/2)
Dividends per share	€0.50	€0.25 (€0.50/2)
Dividend payout ratio	1/3	1/3
Dividend yield	1.25%	1.25% (€0.25/€20.00)
P/E	26.7	26.7 (€20.00/€0.75)
Market value of company	€160 million	€160 million (€20.00 × 8 million)

As can be seen, a two-for-one stock split is basically the same as a 100 percent stock dividend because all per share data have been reduced by 50 percent. The only difference is in the accounting treatment: Although both stock dividends and stock splits have no effect on total shareholders' equity, a stock dividend is accounted for as a transfer of retained earnings to contributed capital. A stock split, however, does not affect any of the balances in shareholder equity accounts.

A company may announce a stock split at any time. Typically, a split is announced after a period in which the stock price has risen. Many investors view the announcement of a stock split as a positive sign pointing to future stock price increases. More often, however, announced stock splits merely recognize that the stock has risen enough to justify a stock split to return the stock price to a lower, more marketable price range.

Several of the largest companies in the world (as measured by market value) had stock splits or large stock dividends in the mid-2000s. For example, Total SA (France) had a two-for-one split in 2006, Proctor & Gamble (United States) had a two-for-one

---

8 The **dividend payout ratio** is dividends declared during a fiscal year divided by net income available for common shares for the same fiscal year.

split in 2004, and Unilever PLC (United Kingdom) had an 80 percent stock dividend in 2006. In each of these cases, the stock split or the stock dividend came after a significant rise in stock price but was not, in and of itself, a meaningful predictor of future price action.

Much less common than stock splits are reverse stock splits. A **reverse stock split** increases the share price and reduces the number of shares outstanding—again, with no effect on the market value of a company's equity or on shareholders' total cost basis. Just as a high stock price might lead a company to consider a stock split, so too a low stock price may lead a company to consider a reverse stock split. The objective of a reverse stock split is to increase the price of the stock to a higher, more marketable range. As reported in *Barron's*, companies execute reverse splits "to attract institutional investors and mutual funds that often shy from buying stocks trading below \$5."[9] Reverse stock splits are perhaps most common for companies in, or coming out of, financial distress. As part of its government-aided recapitalization, shareholders of American International Group (NYSE: AIG), a global financial insurance company, approved a 1-for-20 reverse stock split effective 1 July 2009. On 30 June 2009, AIG shares closed at US\$1.16, which implies a post-reverse-split price of about US\$23.[10] KIT digital, a Dubai, UAE-based global provider of internet-protocol-based video enhancement technology, announced a 1-for-35 reverse split effective 6 March 2009 in order to meet minimum share price listing criteria on NASDAQ Global Markets.

Reverse splits are less common in Asia. For example, reverse stock splits were not permitted in Japan under Corporation Law until 2001.

EXAMPLE 2

Citigroup Announces a Planned Reverse Split

In March 2009, Citigroup, a major U.S.-based global bank, was in severe financial distress and required significant U.S. government investment. Citigroup announced it would seek shareholder approval for up to a 1-for-30 reverse split. At that time, the stock was perilously close to the \$1 a share minimum price required for continued listing on the NYSE. In July 2009, the reverse split had not yet taken place, but the shares were trading at \$2.90.

1 If the reverse split were to take place when the share price was \$2.90 on the day before the ex-dividend date, find the expected stock price after a 1-for-30 split, all other factors remaining unchanged.

2 Comment on the following statement: "Shareholder wealth is negatively affected by a reverse stock split."

Solution to 1:

If the stock was \$2.90 before the reverse split, for every 30 shares, a shareholder would have 1 share priced at 30 × \$2.90 = \$87.

Solution to 2:

The statement is not generally correct. Considering the reverse split on its own, the market capitalization of the common equity would be unchanged. If the reverse split was interpreted as a good decision (e.g., because the company will be able to retain the advantages of being listed on the NYSE), the market

---

9 Sears (2009), p. M10. Furthermore, some brokerages do not permit clients to buy stocks on margin (i.e., with money lent by the brokerage) if the stocks are trading at less than \$5 per share.
10 The *Wall Street Journal* (2 July 2009):C5.

capitalization might increase. But other factors—such as continued deterioration of its loan and derivative portfolios, or more required government investment leading to further common share dilution—could drive down the share's value.

3 DIVIDENDS: PAYMENT CHRONOLOGY

In the previous section, we saw that dividends can take several forms. Once a company's board of directors votes to pay a dividend, a fairly standard dividend chronology is set in motion. The following sections describe dividend payment chronology. Although payment chronology has some differences across world markets, declaration dates, ex-dividend dates, and record dates are common on global exchanges.

3.1 Declaration Date

The first date on the time line is the **declaration date**, the day that the corporation issues a statement declaring a specific dividend. Whether it is a regular, irregular, special, liquidating, or stock dividend, a dividend begins with a company's board of directors authorizing its payment. In China and several European countries, company shareholders must approve the payment. In Japan, the requirement of shareholder approval of dividend payments was abolished in 2006.

On the declaration date, the company will also announce the holder-of-record date and the payment date. Company websites, as well as some financial websites, post dividends declared, as well as record and payment dates.

3.2 Ex-Dividend Date

After the declaration date, the next pertinent date is the **ex-dividend date** (also referred to as the **ex-date**). In most global markets, the ex-date is two business days before the holder-of-record date, but in Hong Kong it is one business day. The amount of time between the ex-date and the holder-of record date is linked to the trade settlement cycle of the particular exchange on which the shares are listed for trading.[11] The ex-date is the first date that a share trades without (i.e., "ex") the dividend. Investors who own shares on the ex-date or who purchase shares on the business day before the ex-date will receive the dividend. For example, if the ex-date is Monday, shares must be purchased by Friday (assuming that is a business day rather than a holiday on which markets are closed) to receive the dividend (most global markets are not open on Saturday and Sunday). The ex-dividend trading day is often designated in the share price tables of business publications with an x in the volume column. This indicates that the monetary value of the upcoming dividend has been subtracted from the previous day's closing price. For example, if a share closes at $20 on Friday (the day before the ex-date) and the upcoming dividend is $0.25, then on Monday (the ex-date), all other things being equal, the shares will begin trading at $19.75. If it closes at $20 on Monday, the gain will be $0.25 for the day, even though the closing price is the same as it was the previous Friday.

[11] In most of the world's equity markets, trades settle three business days after the trade date ("$T + 3$ settlement"), so a trade two business days before the record date settles one day too late for the buyer in the trade to be recorded as an owner. The Hong Kong Stock Exchange, however, has $T + 2$ settlement, so the ex-date is one business day before the record date.

3.3 Holder-of-Record Date

The **holder-of-record date** (also called the **owner-of-record date, shareholder-of-record date, record date, date of record,** or **date of book closure**) is typically two business days after the ex-dividend date. It is the date that a shareholder listed in the corporation's records will be deemed to have ownership of the shares for purposes of receiving the upcoming dividend. Although the ex-date is determined by the security exchange on which the shares are listed, the holder-of-record date is determined by the corporation.

3.4 Payment Date

The final pertinent date in the dividend chronology is the **payment date** (also called the **payable date**). It is the day that the company actually mails out (or, more recently, electronically transfers) the dividend payment. As discussed earlier, the company states the payment date when the dividend declaration is made. Unlike other pertinent dates, such as the ex-date and record date which occur only on business days, the payment date can occur on a weekend or holiday. For example, a company may list its payment dates as 15 March, 15 June, 15 September, and 15 December, even though some of those dates will inevitably fall on a Saturday, Sunday, or holiday.

3.5 Interval between Key Dates in the Dividend Payment Chronology

The time between the ex-date and the record date is fixed (generally at two business days), but the time between the other pertinent dates is determined by each company and can vary substantially. For example, record dates typically occur anywhere from a week to a month after the declaration date but can occur later for less common irregular dividends, special dividends, liquidating dividends, and stock dividends. Similarly, the time between the record date and the payment date is typically anywhere from a few days to a month or more. Most companies follow a fairly set routine for their regular cash dividends, whether quarterly, semiannual, or annual. Some business publications, such as *The Value Line Investment Survey*, include in their individual company reports the approximate date of a company's next dividend meeting, the ex-date, and the payment date. Example 3 deals with a typical dividend chronology time line.

EXAMPLE 3

NYSE Euronext Dividend Payment Time Line

On 1 May 2009, NYSE Euronext (NYSE Euronext: NYX), the largest global stock exchange, announced in both Paris and New York City its annual dividend of US$1.20, payable on a quarterly basis. The first quarterly dividend of $1.20/4 = $0.30 was payable on 30 June. The record date on the interim payment was 15 June, and the ex-dividend date was fixed at 11 June. Note that 11 June 2009 was a Thursday, so the second business day after the ex-day was Monday, 15 June 2009. Shareholders could elect to be paid in U.S. dollars or in euros on the basis of exchange rates on the payment date. Draw a time line for the upcoming NYSE Euronext quarterly dividend.

Solution:

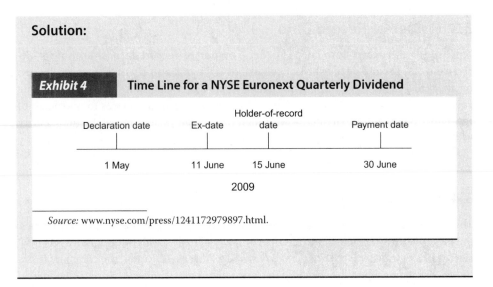

| Exhibit 4 | Time Line for a NYSE Euronext Quarterly Dividend |

Source: www.nyse.com/press/1241172979897.html.

EXAMPLE 4

Capturing Dividends

In mid-2009, Paul Desroches, a France-based investor, is considering investment in the shares of Paris-headquartered Total SA (Euronext Paris: FP), one of the world's largest integrated oil companies and a major chemical manufacturer. Total pays a cash dividend twice a year, so the amount of the semiannual cash dividend is significant: almost a 3 percent cash dividend yield per six-month period, or 6 percent annually, based on current share prices. Desroches reasons that Total's high dividend yield is particularly attractive in the 2009 context of low yields on short-term investment-grade bonds. Desroches decides to buy Total shares on the last possible trading day he can to receive an announced dividend. He explains to a colleague, "It would be like buying a bond on the last day of a six-month period without having to pay the seller accrued interest yet receiving the interest for the entire six months."

On 15 May 2009, Total reported that shareholders had adopted the board of directors' resolution to pay a dividend of €1.14 per share in May 2009. The relevant dates are

Ex-Date	Tuesday, 19 May
Payment Date	Monday, 22 June

Using only the above information and ignoring taxes and any tax effects, address the following:

1 Assuming all of Desroches's assumptions are correct, what is the last date he could buy the stock and still receive the dividend?

2 If Total closed at €38.39 a share on the last day Desroches was entitled to the dividend, what is the likely opening price on the next day assuming all other factors are unchanged?

3 Critique Desroches's statement.

Solution to 1:

The day before the ex-date, or 18 May.

Solution to 2:

The likely opening price on 19 May is €38.39 minus the dividend of €1.14, or €37.25.[12]

Solution to 3:

Assuming other factors do not change overnight and ignoring taxes, Desroches's wealth position would be the same whether he bought the stock the day before the ex-date or on the ex-date. If he bought on 18 May, he would pay €38.39 but have a €1.14 dividend receivable on 22 May, so his effective cost would be €38.39 minus €1.14 or €37.25—the same as the estimated opening price the next trading day. Desroches's statement did not take account of the expected ex-dividend date drop in stock price.

SHARE REPURCHASES

4

A **share repurchase** (or **buyback**) is a transaction in which a company buys back its own shares. Unlike stock dividends and stock splits, share repurchases use corporate cash. Hence, share repurchases can be viewed as an alternative to cash dividends. Shares that have been issued and subsequently repurchased are classified as **treasury shares** (**treasury stock**) or in some jurisdictions canceled; in either case they are not then considered for dividends, voting, or computing earnings per share.[13]

In contrast to the case of cash dividends, usage or growth in usage of share repurchases has historically required enabling regulation. In the United Kingdom, share repurchases became legal in 1981. They were never explicitly illegal in the United States[14] but usage became substantial only subsequent to U.S. Securities and Exchange Commission rule 10b–18 in 1982. (That rule protected repurchasing companies from charges of share manipulation if repurchases were conducted consistent with the terms of the rule.) Other markets in continental Europe and Asia have undertaken enabling regulation relatively recently (e.g., 1995 for Japan, 1998 for Germany and Singapore, 1999 for India and Norway, 2000 for Denmark and Sweden).[15] Share repurchases in many markets remain subject to more restrictions than in the United States. Restrictions include requiring shareholder approval of share repurchase programs, limiting the percent of share repurchases to a certain fraction (often 10 percent) of outstanding shares, allowable repurchase mechanisms, and other restrictions serving to protect creditors.[16]

Share repurchases growth can be measured in relation to cash dividends. For the United States, in the early 1980s, cash dividends were approximately five times greater than the market value of share repurchases. In the late 1990s and again in the first decade of the 21st century, the value of share repurchases often exceeded the value of cash dividends in the United States.[17] In many other markets, such as Canada, the United Kingdom, Germany, France, Hong Kong, and Korea, use of share repurchases is becoming increasingly common.

---

12 An advanced point outside the scope of this reading is that tax effects may cause share price to drop by an amount that is different from the amount of the dividend on the ex-date.
13 Across different markets, regulations differ on the permissible treatment of shares that have been repurchased.
14 See Grullon and Michaely (2002).
15 Sabri (2003).
16 See Vermaelen (2005, p. 31).
17 Brealey, Myers, and Marcus (2007, p. 432).

In general, when an amount of share repurchases is authorized, the company is not strictly committed to carrying through with repurchasing shares. This situation contrasts with the declaration of dividends, where that action does commit the company to pay the dividends. Another contrast with cash dividends is that whereas cash dividends are distributed to shareholders proportionally to their ownership percentage, share repurchases in general do not distribute cash in such a proportionate manner. For example, if repurchases are executed by a company via buy orders in the open market, cash is effectively being received by only those shareholders with concurrent sell orders.

Among the reasons that corporations have given for engaging in share repurchases are the following:

- to communicate that management perceives shares in the company to be undervalued in the marketplace or more generally to support share prices—this motivation was the most frequently mentioned by U.S. chief financial officers in one survey;[18]

- flexibility in distributing cash to shareholders—share repurchases permit the company's management flexibility as to amount and timing and are not perceived as establishing an expectation that a level of repurchase activity will continue in the future;

- tax efficiency in distributing cash, in markets in which the tax rate on cash dividends exceeds the tax rate on capital gains; and

- to absorb increases in shares outstanding resulting from the exercise of employee stock options.

Other motivations for a share repurchase are also possible. For example, share repurchase might merely reflect that the corporation has accumulated more cash than it has profitable uses for and does not want to pay an extra cash dividend.

The next section presents the means by which a company may execute a share repurchase program.

4.1 Share Repurchase Methods

Following are the four main ways that companies repurchase shares, listed in order of importance.

1 **Buy in the open market.** This method of share repurchase is the most common, with the company buying its own shares as conditions warrant in the open market. The open market share repurchase method gives the company maximum flexibility. Open market repurchases are the most flexible option for a company because there is no legal obligation to undertake or complete the repurchase program—a company may not follow through with an announced program for various reasons, such as unexpected cash needs for liquidity, acquisitions, or capital expenditures. In the United States, open market transactions do not require shareholder approval. Because shareholder approval is required in Europe, Vermaelen (2005) suggested that all companies have such authorization in place in case the opportunity to buy back undervalued shares occurs in the future.[19] Authorizations to repurchase stock can last for years. In many shareholders' minds, the announcement of a repurchase policy provides support

---

18 See Brav, Graham, Harvey, and Michaely (2005).
19 See Vermaelen, *ibid.* p. 8.

for the share price. If the share repurchases are competently timed to minimize price impact and to exploit perceived undervaluation in the marketplace, this method is also relatively cost effective.

2 **Buy back a fixed number of shares at a fixed price.** Sometimes a company will make a **fixed price tender offer** to repurchase a specific number of shares at a fixed price that is typically at a premium to the current market price. For example, in Australia, if a stock is selling at A\$37 a share, a company might offer to buy back 5 million shares from current shareholders at A\$40. If shareholders are willing to sell more than 5 million shares, the company will typically buy back a pro rata amount from each shareholder. By setting a fixed date, such as 30 days in the future, a fixed price tender offer can be accomplished quickly.

3 **Dutch Auction.** A Dutch auction is also a tender offer to existing shareholders, but instead of specifying a fixed price for a specific number of shares, the company stipulates a range of acceptable prices. A Dutch auction uncovers the minimum price at which the company can buy back the desired number of shares with the company paying that price to all qualifying bids. For example, if the stock price is A\$37 a share, the company would offer to buy back 5 million shares in a range of A\$38 to A\$40 a share. Each shareholder would then indicate the number of shares and the lowest price at which he or she would be willing to sell. The company would then begin to qualify bids beginning with those shareholders who submitted bids at A\$38 and continue to qualify bids at higher prices until 5 million shares had been qualified. In our example, that price might be A\$39.[20] Shareholders who bid between A\$38 and A\$39, inclusive, would then be paid A\$39 per share for their shares. Like Method 2, Dutch auctions can be accomplished in a short time period.[21]

4 **Repurchase by direct negotiation.** In some markets, a company may negotiate with a major shareholder to buy back its shares, often at a premium to the market price. The company may do this to keep a large block of shares from overhanging the market (and thus acting to dampen the share price). A company may try to prevent an "activist" shareholder from gaining representation on the board of directors. In some of the more infamous cases, unsuccessful takeover attempts have ended with the company buying back the would-be suitor's shares at a premium to the market price in what is referred to as a greenmail transaction, often to the detriment of remaining shareholders.[22] Vermaelen (2005) reported, however, that 45 percent of private repurchases between 1984 and 2001 were actually made at discounts, indicating that many direct negotiation repurchases are generated by the liquidity needs of large investors who are in a weak negotiating position.

Outside the United States and Canada, almost all share repurchases occur in the open market (Method 1), and not all the methods listed may be permissible according to local regulations.[23]

---

20 Shareholders who set an A\$39 price would be subject to a pro rata amount.

21 Vermaelen (2005, p. 7).

22 **Greenmail** is the purchase, usually at a substantial premium over market price, of the accumulated shares of a hostile investor by a company that is targeted for takeover by that investor.

23 See Vermaelen (2005, p. 31).

EXAMPLE 5

BCII Considers Alternative Methods of Share Repurchase

The board of directors of British Columbia Industries, Inc. (BCII) is considering a 5 million common share repurchase program. BCII has a sizable cash and marketable securities portfolio. BCII's current stock price is C$37. The company's chief financial officer wants to accomplish the share repurchases in a cost-effective manner. Some board members want repurchases accomplished as quickly as possible, whereas other board members mention the importance of flexibility. Discuss the relative advantages of each of the following methods with respect to cost, flexibility, and speed:

1   Open market share repurchases

2   A fixed price tender offer

3   Dutch auction tender offer

Solution to 1:

Open market share repurchases give the company the most flexibility. BCII can time repurchases, making repurchases when the market prices its stock below its perceived intrinsic value. BCII can also change amounts repurchased or even not execute the repurchase program. Open market repurchases are typically made opportunistically, with cost a more important consideration than speed. Because open market repurchases can be conducted so as to minimize any effects on price and can be timed to exploit prices that are perceived to be below intrinsic value, this method is also relatively cost effective.

Solution to 2:

A fixed price tender offer can be accomplished quickly, but the company usually has to offer a premium.

Solution to 3:

Dutch auctions have become quite popular in some markets because they generally enable a company to do the buyback at a lower price than with a fixed price tender offer. For example, a fixed price tender offer for 5 million shares at C$40 would cost BCII C$200 million. If the Dutch auction were successful at C$38, the cost would be C$190 million, a savings of C$10 million. Similar to fixed price tender offers, Dutch auctions can be accomplished quickly.

4.2 Financial Statement Effects of Repurchases

Share repurchases affect both the balance sheet and income statement. Both assets and shareholders' equity decline if the repurchase is financed with cash. As a result, leverage increases. Debt ratios (leverage) will increase even more if the repurchase is financed with debt.

On the income statement, fewer shares outstanding could increase earnings per share (i.e., by reducing the denominator) depending on how and at what cost the repurchase is financed. We discuss the effects on the income statement and balance sheet in the following sections.

4.2.1 *Changes in Earnings per Share*

One rationale for share repurchases often cited by corporate financial officers and some investment analysts is that reducing the number of shares outstanding can increase earnings per share (EPS). Assuming a company's net income does not change (or even that any decline is less than proportional to the decrease in outstanding shares after the buyback), a smaller number of shares after the buyback may produce a higher EPS (because EPS is net income divided by the number of shares outstanding).

Examples 6 and 7 show changes in EPS resulting from alternative methods of financing a share repurchase.

EXAMPLE 6

Share Repurchase Using Idle Cash

Takemiya Industries, a Japanese company, has been accumulating cash in recent years with a plan of expanding in emerging Asian markets. The global recession has persuaded Takemiya's management and directors that such expansion is no longer practical, and they are considering a share repurchase using surplus cash. Takemiya has 10 million shares outstanding and its net income is ¥100 million. Takemiya's share price is ¥120. Cash not needed for operations totals ¥240 million and is invested in Japanese government short-term securities that earn virtually zero interest. For a share repurchase program of the contemplated size, Takemiya's investment bankers think the stock could be bought in the open market at a ¥20 premium to the current market price, or ¥140 a share. Calculate the impact on EPS if Takemiya uses the surplus cash to repurchase shares at ¥140 per share.[24]

Solution:

First, note that current EPS = (¥100 million net income)/(10 million shares) = ¥10.00. If Takemiya repurchases shares, net income is unchanged at ¥100 million. A share repurchase at ¥140 a share reduces share count by approximately 1.7 million shares (¥240,000,000/¥140) so that 8.3 million shares remain outstanding. Thus, after the share repurchase, EPS should be (¥100 million)/(8.3 million shares) = ¥12.00, approximately. EPS would increase by 20 percent as a result of the share repurchase. Note that EPS would increase even more if the open market purchases were accomplished at the prevailing market price without the premium.

In the absence of idle cash and equivalents, companies may fund share repurchases by using long-term debt. Example 7 shows that any increase in EPS is dependent on the company's after-tax borrowing rate on the funds used to repurchase stock.

EXAMPLE 7

Share Repurchases Using Borrowed Funds

Jensen Farms Inc. plans to borrow $12 million, which it will use to repurchase shares. The following information is given:

- Share price at time of share repurchase = $60

---

[24] Accounting principles in some countries require that the calculation of EPS in a given year be on the basis of the weighted average number of shares outstanding during the year. For purposes of illustration, we ignore that convention in our examples.

- Earnings after tax = $6.6 million
- EPS before share repurchase = $3
- Price/Earnings ratio (P/E) = $60/$3 = 20
- Earnings yield (E/P) = $3/$60 = 5%[25]
- Shares outstanding = 2.2 million
- Planned share repurchase = 200,000 shares

1 Calculate the EPS after the share repurchase, assuming the after-tax cost of borrowing is the company's customary after-tax borrowing rate of 5 percent.

2 Calculate the EPS after the share repurchase, assuming the company's borrowing rate increases to 6 percent because of the increased financial risk of borrowing the $12 million.

Solution to 1:

EPS after buyback = (Earnings – After-tax cost of funds)/Shares outstanding after buyback

= [$6.6 million – ($12 million × 0.05)]/2 million shares

= [$6.6 million – ($0.6 million)]/2 million shares

= $6.0 million/2 million shares

= $3.00

With the after-tax cost of borrowing at 5 percent, the share repurchase has no effect on the company's EPS. Note that the stock's earnings yield, the ratio of earnings per share to share price or E/P, was $3/$60 = 0.05 or 5 percent, equal to the after-tax cost of debt.

Solution to 2:

EPS after buyback = (Earnings – After-tax cost of funds)/Shares outstanding after buyback

= [$6.6 million – ($12 million × 0.06)]/2 million shares

= [$6.6 million – ($0.72 million)]/2 million shares

= $5.88 million/2 million shares

= $2.94

Note that in this case, the after-tax cost of debt, 6 percent, is greater than the 5 percent earnings yield, and a reduction in EPS resulted.

In summary, a share repurchase may increase, decrease, or have no effect on EPS. The effect depends on whether the repurchase is financed internally or externally. In the case of internal financing, a repurchase increases EPS only if the funds used for the repurchase would *not* earn their cost of capital if retained by the company.[26] In the case of external financing, the effect on EPS is positive if the earnings yield exceeds the after-tax cost of financing the repurchase. In Example 7, when the after-tax borrowing rate equaled the earnings yield of 5 percent, EPS was unchanged as a result

---

25 The E/P is the reciprocal of the price-to-earnings ratio, P/E.
26 See Cornell (2009).

of the buyback. Any after-tax borrowing rate above the earnings yield would result in a decline in EPS, whereas an after-tax borrowing rate less than the earnings yield would result in an increase in EPS.

These relationships should be viewed with caution so far as any valuation implications are concerned. Notably, to infer that an increase in EPS indicates an increase in shareholders' wealth would be incorrect. For example, the same idle cash could also be distributed as a cash dividend. Informally, if one views the total return on a stock as the sum of the dividend yield and a capital gains return, any capital gains as a result of the boost to EPS from the share repurchase may be at the expense of an offsetting loss in terms of dividend yield.

4.2.2 Changes in Book Value per Share

Price to book value per share is a popular ratio used in equity valuation. The following example shows the impact of a share repurchase on book value per share (BVPS).

EXAMPLE 8

The Effect of a Share Repurchase on Book Value per Share

The market price of both Company A's and Company B's common stock is $20 a share, and each company has 10 million shares outstanding. Both companies have announced a $5 million buyback. The only difference is that Company A has a market price per share greater than its book value per share, whereas Company B has a market price per share less than its book value per share:

- Company A has a book value of equity of $100 million and BVPS of $100 million/10 million shares = $10. *The market price per share of $20 is greater than BVPS of $10.*

- Company B has a book value of equity of $300 million and BVPS of $300 million/10 million shares = $30. *The market price per share of $20 is less than BVPS of $30.*

Both companies:

- buy back 250,000 shares at the market price per share ($5 million buyback/$20 per share = 250,000 shares), and
- are left with 9.75 million shares outstanding (10 million pre-buyback shares – 0.25 million repurchased shares = 9.75 million shares).

After the share repurchase:

- Company A's shareholders' equity at book value falls to $95 million ($100 million – $5 million), and its *book value per share decreases* from $10 to $9.74 (shareholders' equity/shares outstanding = $95 million/9.75 million shares = $9.74).

- Company B's shareholders' equity at book value falls to $295 million ($300 million – $5 million), and its *book value per share increases* from $30 to $30.26 (shareholders' equity/shares outstanding = $295 million/9.75 million = $30.26).

This example shows that when the market price per share is greater than its book value per share, BVPS will decrease after the share repurchase. When the market price per share is less than BVPS, however, BVPS will increase after a share repurchase.

4.3 Valuation Equivalence of Cash Dividends and Share Repurchases: The Baseline

A share repurchase should be viewed as equivalent to the payment of cash dividends of equal amount in terms of the effect on shareholders' wealth, all other things being equal. "All other things being equal" in this context is shorthand for assumptions that the taxation and information content of cash dividends and share repurchases do not differ. Understanding this baseline equivalence result permits more advanced analysis to explore the result's sensitivity to various modifications to the "all other things being equal" assumption. Example 9 demonstrates the claim of equivalence in the "all other things being equal" case.

EXAMPLE 9

The Equivalence of Share Repurchases and Cash Dividends

Waynesboro Chemical Industries, Inc. (WCII), has 10 million shares outstanding with a current market value of $20 per share. WCII's board of directors is considering two ways of distributing WCII's current $50 million free cash flow to equity. The first method involves paying an irregular or special cash dividend of $50 million/10 million = $5 per share. The second method involves repurchasing $50 million worth of shares. For simplicity, we make the assumptions that dividends are received when the shares go ex-dividend and that any quantity of shares can be bought at the market price of $20 per share. We also assume that the taxation and information content of cash dividends and share repurchases, if any, do not differ. How would the wealth of a shareholder be affected by WCII's choice of method in distributing the $50 million?

Solution:

Cash Dividend

After the shares go ex-dividend, a shareholder of a single share would have $5 in cash (the dividend) and a share worth $20 − $5 = $15. The ex-dividend value of $15 can be demonstrated as the market value of equity after the distribution of $50 million divided by the number of shares outstanding after the dividend payment, or [(10 million)($20) − $50 million]/10 million = $150 million/10 million = $15. (Of course, the payment of a cash dividend has no effect on the number of shares outstanding.) Total wealth from ownership of one share is, therefore, $5 + $15 = $20.

Share Repurchase

With $50 million, WCII could repurchase $50 million/$20 = 2.5 million shares. The post-repurchase share price would be unchanged at $20, which can be calculated as the market value of equity after the $50 million share repurchase divided by the shares outstanding after the share repurchase, or [(10 million) ($20) − $50 million]/(10 million − 2.5 million) = $150 million/7.5 million = $20. Total wealth from ownership of one share is, therefore, $20—exactly the same as in the case of a cash dividend. Whether the shareholder actually sold the share back to WCII in the share repurchase is irrelevant for a shareholder's wealth: If the share was sold, $20 in cash would be realized; if the share was not sold, its market value of $20 would count equally toward the shareholder's wealth.

The theme of Example 9 is that a company should not expect to create or destroy shareholder wealth merely by its method of distributing money to shareholders (i.e., by share repurchases as opposed to cash dividends).[27] Example 10 illustrates that if a company repurchases shares from an individual shareholder at a negotiated price representing a premium over the market price, the remaining shareholders' wealth is reduced.

EXAMPLE 10

Direct Negotiation: A Share Repurchase That Transfers Wealth

Florida Citrus (FC) common shares sell at $20, and there are 10 million shares outstanding. Management becomes aware that Kirk Parent recently purchased a major position in its outstanding shares with the intention of influencing the business operations of FC in ways the current board does not approve. An adviser to the board has suggested approaching Parent privately with an offer to buy back $50 million worth of shares from him at $25 per share, which is a $5 premium over the current market price. The board of FC declines to do so because of the effect of such a repurchase on FC's other shareholders. Determine the effect of the proposed share repurchase on the wealth of shareholders other than Parent.

Solution:

With $50 million, FC could repurchase $50 million/$25 = 2 million shares from Parent. The post-repurchase share price would be $18.75, which can be calculated as the market value of equity after the $50 million share repurchase divided by the shares outstanding after the share repurchase, or [(10 million)($20) − $50 million]/(10 million − 2 million) = $150 million/8 million = $18.75. Shareholders other than Parent would lose $20 − $18.75 = $1.25 for each share owned. Although this share repurchase would conserve total wealth (including Parent's), it effectively transfers wealth to Parent from the other shareholders.

CONCLUDING REMARKS

5

The question of the valuation implications of share repurchases and dividends is of great interest to investors but outside the scope of the current reading. Many investors and corporate managers, however, believe that share repurchases have, on average, a net positive effect on shareholder value. Vermaelen (2005) reviewed major studies and found that share repurchase announcements are accompanied by significant positive excess returns both around the announcement date and for the next two years—and in some studies, five years. An explanation consistent with that finding is that managements tend to buy back their stock when it is undervalued in the marketplace and issue stock when it is overvalued.

Likewise, dividend initiations and unexpected increases in dividends are frequently associated with positive excess returns. The most common explanation relates to the information that dividends may be perceived to carry because management and the board of directors are presumed to know more than outsiders about a company's

27 Oded and Michel (2008) lend support to the argument of value neutrality. Using a simulation, as well as the example of Exxon Mobil, they find that no difference exists in shareholder wealth over a period of years, regardless of whether a company used its cash to repurchase shares, pay dividends, or hoard the cash.

finances and opportunities. Investors may share the view of one money manager that "dividends are a wonderful gauge for management's confidence in forward-looking profitability."[28] Empirical support exists for the notion that managements justifiably feel more confident about their company's future when they pay a cash dividend for the first time. In a study of U.S. equities, Healy and Palepu (1988) found that company earnings increased by an average of 43 percent in the year of dividend initiation and 164 percent in the subsequent four years. Furthermore, the announcement of the initiation of a regular cash dividend was accompanied by an excess return of 4 percent on average. One possible reason might be that cash dividends broaden the potential market for a company's shares. Some institutional investors are governed by bylaws that require them to invest only in dividend-paying shares. The observations in Example 11 support these ideas.

EXAMPLE 11

Information in Dividend Initiations

A   Oracle Corporation, a leading business software maker, initiated a $0.05 quarterly dividend in May 2009. Oracle's annual $0.20 dividend amounts to about $1 billion, a relatively small amount compared with operating cash flow of $8 billion and another $9 billion in cash and cash-equivalent assets on its balance sheet at the end of fiscal year 2009. An analyst who follows Oracle for institutional investors saw the Oracle announcement as a signal that the company is well positioned to ride out the downturn and also gain market share.[29]

B   In mid-2009, Paris-based Groupe Eurotunnel announced its first ever dividend after it completed a debt restructuring and received insurance proceeds resulting from a fire that had closed the Channel Tunnel. In a 2 June 2009 press release, Eurotunnel's CEO said that this "marked a turning point for the company as its business has returned to the realm of normality" as the company anticipated a return to profitability.

SUMMARY

A company's cash dividend payments and share repurchase policies, taken together, constitute its payout policy. Both entail the distribution of the company's cash to its shareholders. After management's decision on capital expenditures and how to fund those expenditures, payout policy is perhaps the most important decision sent to the board of directors for approval. In Europe and Asia, shareholders often vote on the board's recommendation. This reading has made the following points:

■   Dividends can take the form of regular or irregular cash payments, stock dividends, or stock splits. Only cash dividends are payments to shareholders. Stock dividends and splits merely carve equity into smaller pieces and do not create

---

28 Robert Arnott, quoted in the *New York Times* (3 May 2009):BU7.
29 The *Wall Street Journal* (19 March 2009):B1.

wealth for shareholders. Reverse stock splits usually occur after a stock has dropped to a very low price and do not affect shareholder wealth—they represent cosmetic repackaging of shareholder equity.

- Regular cash dividends—unlike irregular cash dividends, stock splits, and stock dividends—represent a commitment to pay cash to stockholders on a quarterly, semiannual, or annual basis.

- The key dates for cash dividends, stock dividends, and stock splits are the declaration date, the ex-date, the shareholder-of-record date, and the payment date. Share price will reflect the amount of the cash payment (or shares in the case of a stock dividend or split) on the ex-date.

- Share repurchases, or buybacks, most often occur in the open market. Alternatively, tender offers occur at a fixed price or at a price range through a Dutch auction. Shareholders who do not tender increase their relative position in the company. Direct negotiations with major shareholders to get them out of the company are less common because they could destroy value for remaining stockholders.

- Share repurchases made with excess cash have the potential to increase earnings per share, whereas share repurchases made with borrowed funds can increase, decrease, or not affect earnings per share, depending on the after-tax borrowing rate.

- A share repurchase is equivalent to the payment of a cash dividend of equal amount in its effect on shareholders' wealth, all other things being equal.

- If the buyback market price is greater (less) than the book value, the book value will decline (increase).

- Announcement of a share repurchase is sometimes accompanied by positive excess returns in the market when the market price is viewed as reflecting management's view that the stock is undervalued, and earnings per share can increase as a result of fewer shares outstanding.

- Initiation of regular cash dividends can also have a positive impact on share value. Management is seen as having enough confidence in the future to make a commitment to pay out cash to shareholders. In addition, some institutional, as well as individual, shareholders see regular cash dividend payments as a measure of investment quality.

REFERENCES

Brav, Alon, John Graham, Campbell Harvey, and Roni Michaely. 2005. "Payout Policy in the 21st Century." *Journal of Financial Economics*, vol. 77, no. 3:483–527.

Brealey, Richard, Stewart Myers, and Alan Marcus. 2007. *Fundamentals of Corporate Finance*. New York: McGraw-Hill Irwin.

Cornell, Bradford. 2009. "Stock Repurchases and Dividends: Trade-offs and Trends." *Dividends and Dividend Policy*, H. Kent Baker, ed. Hoboken, NJ: John Wiley & Sons.

Grullon, Gustavo, and Roni Michaely. 2002. "Dividends, Share Repurchases, and the Substitution Hypothesis." *Journal of Finance*, vol. 57, no. 4:1649–1684.

He, Wei. 2009. "Dividend Reinvestment Plans." In *Dividends and Dividend Policy*. Edited by H. Kent Baker. Hoboken, NJ: John Wiley & Sons.

Healy, P., and K. Palepu. 1988. "Earnings Information Conveyed by Dividend Initiations and Omissions." *Journal of Financial Economics*, vol. 21, no. 2:149–175.

Oded, Jacob, and Allen Michel. 2008. "Stock Repurchases and the EPS Enhancement Fallacy." *Financial Analysts Journal*, vol. 64, no. 4:62–75.

Sabri, Nidal Rashid. 2003. "Using Treasury 'Repurchase' Shares to Stabilize Stock Markets." *International Journal of Business*, Vol. 8, No. 4.

Sears, Steven M. 2009. "The Fortunes of Reversals." Barron's (3 August): M10.

Vermaelen, Theo. 2005. *Share Repurchases*. Hanover, MA: Now Publishers.

PRACTICE PROBLEMS

1 The payment of a 10 percent stock dividend by a company will result in an increase in that company's:

   A   current ratio.

   B   financial leverage.

   C   contributed capital.

2 If a company's common shares trade at relatively very low prices, that company would be *most likely* to consider the use of a:

   A   stock split.

   B   stock dividend.

   C   reverse stock split.

3 In a recent presentation, Doug Pearce made two statements about dividends:

   Statement 1   "A stock dividend will increase share price, all other things being equal."

   Statement 2   "One practical concern with a stock split is that it will reduce the company's price-to-earnings ratio."

  Are Pearce's two statements about the effects of the stock dividend and stock split correct?

   A   No for both statements.

   B   Yes for Statement 1 and no for Statement 2.

   C   No for Statement 1 and yes for Statement 2.

4 All other things being equal, the payment of an internally financed cash dividend is *most likely* to result in:

   A   a lower current ratio.

   B   a higher current ratio.

   C   the same current ratio.

5 The calendar dates in Column 1 are potentially significant dates in a typical dividend chronology. Column 2 lists descriptions of these potentially significant dates (in random order).

Column 1	Column 2
Friday, 10 June	A. Holder-of-record date
Thursday, 23 June	B. Declaration date
Friday, 24 June	C. Payment date
Tuesday, 28 June	D. Ex-dividend date
Sunday, 10 July	E. Last day shares trade with the right to receive the dividend

Match the significance of these typical dividend chronology dates by placing the correct letter of the description by the appropriate date. Use the template for your answer.

Dividend Chronology

Friday, 10 June	_____
Thursday, 23 June	_____
Friday, 24 June	_____
Tuesday, 28 June	_____
Sunday, 10 July	_____

---

6 Mary Young intends to take a position in Megasoft Industries once Megasoft begins paying dividends. A dividend of C\$4 is payable by Megasoft on 2 December. The ex-dividend date for the dividend is 10 November, and the holder-of-record date is 12 November. What is the last possible date for Young to purchase her shares if she wants to receive the dividend?

A 9 November.

B 10 November.

C 12 November.

7 Aiken Instruments (AIK) has recently declared a regular quarterly dividend of \$0.50, payable on 12 November, with an ex-dividend date of 28 October. Which date below would be the holder-of-record date assuming all the days listed are business days and that trades settle three business days after the trade date?

A 27 October.

B 30 October.

C 11 November.

8 A company has 1 million shares outstanding and earnings are £2 million. The company decides to use £10 million in idle cash to repurchase shares in the open market. The company's shares are trading at £50 per share. If the company uses the entire £10 million of idle cash to repurchase shares at the market price, the company's earnings per share will be *closest* to:

A £2.00.

B £2.30.

C £2.50.

9 Devon Ltd. common shares sell at \$40 a share and their estimated price-to-earnings ratio (P/E) is 32. If Devon borrows funds to repurchase shares at its after-tax cost of debt of 5 percent, its EPS is *most likely* to:

A increase.

B decrease.

C remain the same.

10 A company can borrow funds at an after-tax cost of 4.5 percent. The company's stock price is \$40 per share, earnings per share is \$2.00, and the company has 15 million shares outstanding. If the company borrows just enough to repurchase 2 million shares of stock at the prevailing market price, that company's earnings per share is *most likely* to:

A increase.

B decrease.

C remain the same.

11 Crozet Corporation plans to borrow just enough money to repurchase 100,000 shares. The following information relates to the share repurchase:

Shares outstanding before buyback	3.1 million
Earnings per share before buyback	$4.00
Share price at time of buyback	$50
After-tax cost of borrowing	6%

Crozet's earnings per share after the buyback will be *closest* to:

A $4.03.

B $4.10.

C $4.23.

12 A company with 20 million shares outstanding decides to repurchase 2 million shares at the prevailing market price of €30 per share. At the time of the buyback, the company reports total assets of €850 million and total liabilities of €250 million. As a result of the buyback, that company's book value per share will *most likely*:

A increase.

B decrease.

C remain the same.

13 An analyst gathered the following information about a company:

Number of shares outstanding	10 million
Earnings per share	$2.00
P/E	20
Book value per share	$30

If the company repurchases 1 million shares at the prevailing market price, the resulting book value per share will be *closest* to:

A $26.

B $27.

C $29.

14 If a company's objective is to support its stock price in the event of a market downturn, it would be advised to authorize:

A an open market share repurchase plan to be executed over the next five years.

B a tender offer share repurchase at a fixed price effective in 30 days.

C a Dutch auction tender offer effective in 30 days.

15 A company has positive free cash flow and is considering whether to use the entire amount of that free cash flow to pay a special cash dividend or to repurchase shares at the prevailing market price. Shareholders' wealth under the two options will be equivalent unless the:

A company's book value per share is less than the prevailing market price.

B company's book value per share is greater than the prevailing market price.

C   tax consequences and/or information content for each alternative is different.

16 Assume that a company is based in a country that has no taxes on dividends or capital gains. The company is considering either paying a special dividend or repurchasing its own shares. Shareholders of the company would have:

A   greater wealth if the company paid a special cash dividend.

B   greater wealth if the company repurchased its shares.

C   the same wealth under either a cash dividend or share repurchase program.

SOLUTIONS

1 C is correct. A stock dividend is accounted for as a transfer of retained earnings to contributed capital.

2 C is correct. A reverse stock split would increase the price per share of the stock to a higher, more marketable range that could possibly increase the number of investors who would consider buying the stock.

3 A is correct. Both statements are incorrect. A stock dividend will decrease the price per share, all other things being equal. A stock split will reduce the price and earnings per share proportionately, leaving the price-to-earnings ratio the same.

4 A is correct. By reducing corporate cash, a cash dividend reduces the current ratio, whereas a stock dividend (whatever the size) has no effect on the current ratio.

5 The typical dividend chronology is:

Friday, 10 June	B. The declaration date is the day that the corporation issues a statement declaring a dividend.
Thursday, 23 June	E. The last day shares trade with the right to receive the dividend is the day before the ex-dividend date.
Friday, 24 June	D. The ex-dividend date is the first day that the stock trades "ex" (i.e., without) the dividend. If the stock is bought on the ex-dividend date, the seller (not the buyer) will receive the dividend.
Tuesday, 28 June	A. The holder-of-record date is the date that the company uses to document which shareholders will receive the dividend.
Sunday, 10 July	C. The payment date is the date that the company sends out its dividend checks.

6 A is correct. To receive the dividend, one must purchase before the ex-dividend date.

7 B is correct. The holder-of-record date, 30 October, is two business days after the ex-dividend date, 28 October.

8 C is correct. At the current market price, the company can repurchase 200,000 shares (£10 million/£50 = 200,000 shares). The company would have 800,000 shares outstanding after the repurchase (1 million shares – 200,000 shares = 800,000 shares).

EPS before the buyback is £2.00 (£2 million/1 million shares = £2.00). Total earnings after the buyback are the same because the company uses idle (non-earning) cash to purchase the shares, but the number of shares outstanding is reduced to 800,000. EPS increases to £2.50 (£2 million/ 800,000 shares = £2.50).

9 B is correct. If the P/E is 32, the earnings-to-price ratio (earnings yield or E/P) is 1/32 = 3.125 percent. When the cost of capital is greater than the earnings yield, earnings dilution will result from the buyback.

10 A is correct. The company's earnings yield (E/P) is $2/$40 = 0.05. When the earnings yield is greater than the after-tax cost of borrowed funds, EPS will increase if shares are repurchased using borrowed funds.

11 A is correct.

> Total earnings before buyback: $4.00 × 3,100,000 shares = $12,400,000
>
> Total amount of borrowing: $50 × 100,000 shares = $5,000,000
>
> After-tax cost of borrowing the amount of funds needed: $5,000,000 × 0.06 = $300,000
>
> Number of shares outstanding after buyback: 3,100,000 − 100,000 = 3,000,000
>
> EPS after buyback: ($12,400,000 − $300,000)/3,000,000 shares = $4.03

The P/E before the buyback is $50/$4 = 12.5; thus, the E/P is 8 percent. The after-tax cost of debt is 6 percent; therefore, EPS will increase.

12 C is correct. The company's book value before the buyback is €850 million in assets − €250 million in liabilities = €600 million. Book value per share is €600 million/20 million = €30 per share. The buyback will reduce equity by 2 million shares at the prevailing market price of €30 per share. The book value of equity will be reduced to €600 million − €60 million = €540 million, and the number of shares will be reduced to 18 million; €540 million/18 million = €30 book value per share. If the prevailing market price is equal to the book value per share at the time of the buyback, book value per share is unchanged.

13 C is correct. The prevailing market price is $2.00(20) = $40.00 per share; thus, the buyback would reduce equity by $40 million. Book value of equity before the buyback is $300 million. Book value of equity after the buyback would be $300 million − $40 million = $260 million. The number of shares outstanding after the buyback would be 9 million. Thus, book value per share after the buyback would be $260 million/9 million = $28.89.

14 A is correct. Of the three methods, only an authorized open market share repurchase plan allows the company the flexibility to time share repurchases to coincide with share price declines.

15 C is correct. For the two options to be equivalent with respect to shareholders' wealth, the amount of cash distributed, the taxation, and the information content must be the same for both options.

16 C is correct. When there are no taxes, there are no tax differences between dividends and capital gains. All other things being equal, the effect on shareholder wealth of a dividend and a share repurchase should be the same.

Working Capital Management

by Edgar A. Norton, Jr., CFA, Kenneth L. Parkinson, and Pamela Peterson Drake, CFA

LEARNING OUTCOMES

Mastery	The candidate should be able to:
☐	**a.** describe primary and secondary sources of liquidity and factors that influence a company's liquidity position;
☐	**b.** compare a company's liquidity measures with those of peer companies;
☐	**c.** evaluate working capital effectiveness of a company based on its operating and cash conversion cycles, and compare the company's effectiveness with that of peer companies;
☐	**d.** describe how different types of cash flows affect a company's net daily cash position;
☐	**e.** calculate and interpret comparable yields on various securities, compare portfolio returns against a standard benchmark, and evaluate a company's short-term investment policy guidelines;
☐	**f.** evaluate a company's management of accounts receivable, inventory, and accounts payable over time and compared to peer companies;
☐	**g.** evaluate the choices of short-term funding available to a company and recommend a financing method.

INTRODUCTION

1

The focus of this reading is on the short-term aspects of corporate finance activities collectively referred to as **working capital management**. The goal of effective working capital management is to ensure that a company has adequate ready access to the funds necessary for day-to-day operating expenses, while at the same time making sure that the company's assets are invested in the most productive way. Achieving this goal requires a balancing of concerns. Insufficient access to cash could ultimately lead to severe restructuring of a company by selling off assets, reorganization via bankruptcy proceedings, or final liquidation of the company. On the other hand, excessive investment in cash and liquid assets may not be the best use of company resources.

Effective working capital management encompasses several aspects of short-term finance: maintaining adequate levels of cash, converting short-term assets (i.e., accounts receivable and inventory) into cash, and controlling outgoing payments to vendors, employees, and others. To do this successfully, companies invest short-term funds in working capital portfolios of short-dated, highly liquid securities, or they maintain credit reserves in the form of bank lines of credit or access to financing by issuing commercial paper or other money market instruments.

Working capital management is a broad-based function. Effective execution requires managing and coordinating several tasks within the company, including managing short-term investments, granting credit to customers and collecting on this credit, managing inventory, and managing payables. Effective working capital management also requires reliable cash forecasts, as well as current and accurate information on transactions and bank balances.

Both internal and external factors influence working capital needs; we summarize them in Exhibit 1.

Exhibit 1	Internal and External Factors That Affect Working Capital Needs
Internal Factors	**External Factors**
▪ Company size and growth rates	▪ Banking services
▪ Organizational structure	▪ Interest rates
▪ Sophistication of working capital management	▪ New technologies and new products
▪ Borrowing and investing positions/activities/ capacities	▪ The economy
	▪ Competitors

The scope of working capital management includes transactions, relations, analyses, and focus:

- Transactions include payments for trade, financing, and investment.

- Relations with financial institutions and trading partners must be maintained to ensure that the transactions work effectively.

- Analyses of working capital management activities are required so that appropriate strategies can be formulated and implemented.

- Focus requires that organizations of all sizes today must have a global viewpoint with strong emphasis on liquidity.

In this reading, we examine the different types of working capital and the management issues associated with each. We also look at methods of evaluating the effectiveness of working capital management.

MANGAGING AND MEASURING LIQUIDITY

Liquidity is the extent to which a company is able to meet its short-term obligations using assets that can be readily transformed into cash. When we evaluate the liquidity of an asset, we focus on two dimensions: the type of asset and the speed at which the asset can be converted to cash, either by sale or financing. Unlike many aspects of corporate finance, corporate liquidity management does not involve a great deal of theory or generally accepted principles. For companies that have the luxury of large excesses of cash, liquidity is typically taken for granted, and the focus is on putting the excess liquidity to its most productive use. On the other hand, when a company faces tighter financial situations, it is important to have effective liquidity management to ensure solvency. Unfortunately, this recognition comes too late for some companies, with bankruptcy and possible liquidation representing the company's final choice.

2.1 Defining Liquidity Management

Liquidity management refers to the ability of an organization to generate cash when and where it is needed. Liquidity refers to the resources available for an entity to tap into cash balances and to convert other assets or extend other liabilities into cash for use in keeping the entity solvent (i.e., being able to pay bills and continue in operation). For the most part, we associate liquidity with short-term assets and liabilities, yet longer-term assets can be converted into cash to provide liquidity. In addition, longer-term liabilities can also be renegotiated to reduce the drain on cash, thereby providing liquidity by preserving the limited supply of cash. Of course, the last two methods may come at a price as they tend to reduce the company's overall financial strength.

The challenges of managing liquidity include developing, implementing, and maintaining a liquidity policy. To do this effectively, a company must manage all of its key sources of liquidity efficiently. These key sources may vary from company to company, but they generally include the primary sources of liquidity, such as cash balances, and secondary sources of liquidity, such as selling assets.

2.1.1 *Primary Sources of Liquidity*

Primary sources of liquidity represent the most readily accessible resources available. They may be held as cash or as near-cash securities. Primary sources include:

- Ready cash balances, which is cash available in bank accounts, resulting from payment collections, investment income, liquidation of near-cash securities (i.e., those with maturities of less than 90 days), and other cash flows.

- Short-term funds, which may include items such as trade credit, bank lines of credit, and short-term investment portfolios.

- Cash flow management, which is the company's effectiveness in its cash management system and practices, and the degree of decentralization of the collections or payments processes. The more decentralized the system of collections, for example, the more likely the company will be to have cash tied up in the system and not available for use.

These sources represent liquidity that is typical for most companies. They represent funds that are readily accessible at relatively low cost.

2.1.2 *Secondary Sources of Liquidity*

The main difference between the primary and secondary sources of liquidity is that using a primary source is not likely to affect the normal operations of the company, whereas using a secondary source may result in a change in the company's financial and operating positions. Secondary sources include:

- negotiating debt contracts, relieving pressures from high interest payments or principal repayments;

- liquidating assets, which depends on the degree to which short-term and/or long-term assets can be liquidated and converted into cash without substantial loss in value; and

- filing for bankruptcy protection and reorganization.

Use of secondary sources may signal a company's deteriorating financial health and provide liquidity at a high price—the cost of giving up a company asset to produce emergency cash. The last source, reorganization through bankruptcy, may also be considered a liquidity tool because a company under bankruptcy protection that generates operating cash will be liquid and generally able to continue business operations until a restructuring has been devised and approved.

2.1.3 *Drags and Pulls on Liquidity*

Cash flow transactions—that is, cash receipts and disbursements—have significant effects on a company's liquidity position. We refer to these effects as drags and pulls on liquidity. A **drag on liquidity** is when receipts lag, creating pressure from the decreased available funds; a **pull on liquidity** is when disbursements are paid too quickly or trade credit availability is limited, requiring companies to expend funds before they receive funds from sales that could cover the liability.

Major drags on receipts involve pressures from credit management and deterioration in other assets and include:

- *Uncollected receivables.* The longer these are outstanding, the greater the risk that they will not be collected at all. They are indicated by the large number of days of receivables and high levels of bad debt expenses. Just as the drags on receipts may cause increased pressures on working capital, pulls on outgoing payments may have similar effects.

- *Obsolete inventory.* If inventory stands unused for long periods, it may be an indication that it is no longer usable. Slow inventory turnover ratios can also indicate obsolete inventory. Once identified, obsolete inventory should be attended to as soon as possible in order to minimize storage and other costs.

- *Tight credit.* When economic conditions make capital scarcer, short-term debt becomes more expensive to arrange and use. Attempting to smooth out peak borrowings can help blunt the impact of tight credit as can improving the company's collections.

In many cases, drags may be alleviated by stricter enforcement of credit and collection practices.[1]

---

[1] In a recent survey of CFOs, companies have become more efficient in working capital management, with U.S. companies in 2005 reducing their investment in working capital by 2.5 percent from 2004 levels and European companies reducing their investment by 3.3 percent (REL 2005 CFO Survey, www.relconsult.com).

However, managing the cash outflows may be as important as managing the inflows. If suppliers and other vendors who offer credit terms perceive a weakened financial position or are unfamiliar with a company, they may restrict payment terms so much that the company's liquidity reserves are stretched thin. Major pulls on payments include:

- *Making payments early.* By paying vendors, employees, or others before the due dates, companies forgo the use of funds. Effective payment management means not making early payments. Payables managers typically hold payments until they can be made by the due date.

- *Reduced credit limits.* If a company has a history of making late payments, suppliers may cut the amount of credit they will allow to be outstanding at any time, which can squeeze the company's liquidity. Some companies try to extend payment periods as long as possible, disregarding the possible impact of reduced credit limits.

- *Limits on short-term lines of credit.* If a company's bank reduces the line of credit it offers the company, a liquidity squeeze may result. Credit line restrictions may be government-mandated, market-related, or simply company-specific. Many companies try to avert this situation by establishing credit lines far in excess of what they are likely to need. This "over-banking" approach is often commonplace in emerging economies or even in more-developed countries where the banking system is not sound and the economy is shaky.

- *Low liquidity positions.* Many companies face chronic liquidity shortages, often because of their particular industry or from their weaker financial position. The major remedy for this situation is, of course, to improve the company's financial position, or else the company will be heavily affected by interest rates and credit availability. Most companies facing this situation have to deal with secured borrowing to obtain any working capital funds. Therefore, it is important for these companies to identify assets that can be used to help support the company's short-term borrowing activities.

It is critical that these drags and pulls be identified as soon as possible, often when they have not yet happened or have just arisen.

2.2 Measuring Liquidity

Liquidity contributes to a company's credit-worthiness. **Credit-worthiness** is the perceived ability of the borrower to pay what is owed on the borrowing in a timely manner and represents the ability of a company to withstand adverse impacts on its cash flows. Credit-worthiness allows the company to obtain lower borrowing costs and better terms for trade credit and contributes to the company's investment flexibility, enabling it to exploit profitable opportunities.

The less liquid the company, the greater the risk it will suffer financial distress or, in the extreme case, insolvency or bankruptcy. Because debt obligations are paid with cash, the company's cash flows ultimately determine solvency. The immediate source of funds for paying bills is cash on hand, proceeds from the sale of marketable securities, or the collection of accounts receivable. Additional liquidity also comes from inventory that can be sold and thus converted into cash either directly through cash sales or indirectly through credit sales (i.e., accounts receivable).

There is, however, some point at which a company may have too much invested in low- and non-earning assets. Cash, marketable securities, accounts receivable, and inventory represent a company's liquidity. However, these investments are low earning relative to the long-term, capital investment opportunities that companies may have available.

Various financial ratios can be used to assess a company's liquidity as well as its management of assets over time. Here we will look at some of these ratios in a little more detail.

We calculate **liquidity ratios** to measure a company's ability to meet short-term obligations to creditors as they mature or come due. This form of liquidity analysis focuses on the relationship between current assets and current liabilities and the rapidity with which receivables and inventory can be converted into cash during normal business operations.

In short-term financial management, a great deal of emphasis is placed on the levels of and changes in current assets and liabilities. The two most common measurements are the current ratio and the quick ratio. The **current ratio** is the ratio of current assets to current liabilities:

$$\text{Current ratio} = \frac{\text{Current assets}}{\text{Current liabilities}}$$

The **quick ratio** (also known as the **acid-test ratio**) is the ratio of the quick assets to current liabilities. **Quick assets** are those assets that can be most readily converted to cash. In most situations, the least liquid of the current assets is inventory. Hence, we typically exclude inventory when calculating the quick ratio:

$$\text{Quick ratio} = \frac{\text{Cash} + \text{Short-term marketable investments} + \text{Receivables}}{\text{Current liabilities}}$$

The greater the current ratio or the quick ratio (that is, the greater the potential ability to cover current liabilities), the higher a company's liquidity. Whether a given current or quick ratio is good or bad, however, depends on a number of factors, including the trend in these ratios, the comparability of these ratios with competitors, and the available opportunities in more-profitable, long-lived, capital investments.

In addition to looking at the relations among these balance sheet accounts, we can also form ratios that measure how well key current assets are managed over time. The key ratios for asset management are turnover ratios. For example, the **accounts receivable turnover** is the ratio of sales on credit to the average balance in accounts receivable:[2]

$$\text{Accounts receivable turnover} = \frac{\text{Credit sales}}{\text{Average receivables}}$$

This ratio is a measure of how many times, on average, accounts receivable are created by credit sales and collected on during the fiscal period. As another example, the **inventory turnover** is the ratio of the cost of goods sold to the balance in inventory:

$$\text{Inventory turnover} = \frac{\text{Cost of goods sold}}{\text{Average inventory}}$$

This ratio is a measure of how many times, on average, inventory is created or acquired and sold during the fiscal period.

Another perspective on the activity within the current accounts is to estimate the number of days of the current asset or liability that are on hand. For example, the **number of days of receivables**, also referred to as the **day's sales outstanding** and **days in receivables**, gives us an idea of the management of the extension and collection of credit to customers:

---

2 You will notice that we use credit sales instead of total revenue; the difference lies in the context. Within the context of working capital management, the corporate financial analyst would have access to details regarding the company's credit versus cash sales. For some companies, sales may be for cash or be some combination of cash sales and credit sales. For the analyst who is looking at the company without benefit of internal information regarding how much of sales is in the form of credit sales, an approximation is generally used based on industry norms for credit practices.

$$\text{Number of days of receivables} = \frac{\text{Accounts receivable}}{\text{Average day's sales on credit}}$$
$$= \frac{\text{Accounts receivable}}{\text{Sales on credit}/365}$$

For example, if this number of days is 35.5, this tells us that it takes, on average, 35.5 days to collect on the credit accounts. Whether this is good or bad depends on credit terms that are offered to customers and the relation between sales and the extension of credit, which is often dictated by industry customs and competitive pressures.

The **number of days of inventory** gives us an indication of how well the inventory acquisition, process, and distribution is managed:

$$\text{Number of days of inventory} = \frac{\text{Inventory}}{\text{Average day's cost of goods sold}}$$
$$= \frac{\text{Inventory}}{\text{Cost of goods sold}/365}$$

The number of days of inventory, also known as the average inventory period, day's sales in ending inventory, and the inventory holding period, is the length of time, on average, that the inventory remains within the company during the fiscal period. We expect variation in the number of days of inventory among industries because of differences in the production cycle of different types of inventory. For example, we expect a grocery store to have a lower number of days of inventory than, say, an aircraft manufacturer.

We can also look at the disbursement side of cash flows with the **number of days of payables**, which provides a measure of how long it takes the company to pay its own suppliers:

$$\text{Number of days of payables} = \frac{\text{Accounts payable}}{\text{Average day's purchases}} = \frac{\text{Accounts payable}}{\text{Purchases}/365}$$

The number of days of payables is also referred to as the day's payables outstanding and the average days payable. Purchases are not an item on published financial statements, so if you are evaluating a company's payables, you can estimate the purchases by using what you know about the company's cost of goods sold and beginning and ending balances in inventory.[3]

Each of these turnover ratios and numbers of days helps tell a story of how the company is managing its liquid assets. Like all ratios, the numbers themselves do not indicate much, but when we put these together with trends, information on the company's profitability, and information about competitors, we develop a good understanding of a company's performance.[4]

Some of the major applications of this type of analysis include performance evaluation, monitoring, credit-worthiness, and financial projections. But ratios are useful only when they can be compared. The comparison should be done in two ways— comparisons over time for the same company and over time for the company compared with its peer group. Peer groups can include competitors from the same industries as the company as well as other companies with comparable size and financial situations.

---

3 We know that Beginning inventory + Purchases – Cost of goods sold = Ending inventory. Therefore, if we know the inventory balances (from the balance sheet) and the cost of goods sold (from the income statement), we can determine the purchases: Purchases = Cost of goods sold + Ending inventory – Beginning inventory.
4 For example, if we see a small number of days of inventory, it could mean that the company is managing its production very efficiently or it could mean that the company is at significant risk of a shortage of inventory. We don't know more until we look at what is needed or usual for companies in the industry, trends in turnover for the company, and the company's profitability in relation to the number of days of inventory.

Consider Wal-Mart Stores, Inc. We can see the change in the current ratio and quick ratio over the fiscal years 1992 through 2005 in Exhibit 2, Panel A. Here, we see that the current ratio has declined, yet the quick ratio has increased slightly. We can see what is driving these trends in Panel B of this exhibit. One driver is the efficiency in the management of inventory, which results in holding on to inventory fewer days, as indicated by the downward trend in the number of days of inventory. Putting it in perspective, this trend may be because of, in part, the product shift when Wal-Mart Stores increased its presence in the grocery line of business. Another driver is the increasing number of days of payables, which means that company is taking longer to pay what it owes suppliers.

Exhibit 2	Liquidity Analysis of Wal-Mart Stores

Panel A: Current and Quick Ratios, 1992–2005

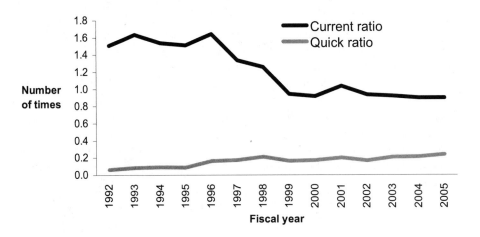

Panel B: Number of Days of Inventory and Number of Days of Payables

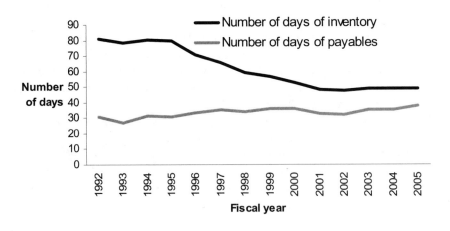

Source: Wal-Mart Stores, Inc., 10-K filings, various years.

Comparing Wal-Mart with Target Inc. and Kohl's in the 2005 fiscal year, as shown in Exhibit 3, we see differences among these three competitors. These differences may be explained, in part, by the different product mixes (e.g., Wal- Mart has more sales from grocery lines than the others), as well as different inventory management systems and different inventory suppliers. The different need for liquidity may also be explained, in part, by the different operating cycles of the companies.

Exhibit 3	Liquidity Ratios among Discount Retailers		

	Company		
Ratio for 2005 Fiscal Year	Wal-Mart	Target	Kohl's
Current ratio	0.9	1.5	2.4
Quick ratio	0.2	0.9	1.2
Number of days of inventory	48.9	61.0	94.5
Number of days of payables	38.1	64.7	33.9

Source: Company 10-K filings with Securities and Exchange Commission for fiscal year 2005.

EXAMPLE 1

Measuring Liquidity

Given the following ratios, how well has the company been managing its liquidity for the past two years?

	Current Year		Past Year	
Ratio	Company	Industry	Company	Industry
Current ratio	1.9	2.5	1.1	2.3
Quick ratio	0.7	1.0	0.4	0.9
Number of days of receivables	39.0	34.0	44.0	32.5
Number of days of inventory	41.0	30.3	45.0	27.4
Number of days of payables	34.3	36.0	29.4	35.5

Solution:

The ratios should be compared in two ways—over time (there would typically be more than two years' worth of data) and against the industry averages. In all ratios shown here, the current year shows improvement over the previous year in terms of increased liquidity. In each case, however, the company remains behind the industry average in terms of liquidity. A brief snapshot such as this example could be the starting point to initiate or encourage more improvements with the goal of reaching or beating the industry standards.

We can combine the number of days of inventory, number of days of receivables, and number of days of payables to get a sense of the company's operating cycle and net operating cycle. The **operating cycle** is a measure of the time needed to convert raw materials into cash from a sale. It consists of the number of days of inventory and the number of days of receivables:

$$\text{Operating cycle} = \frac{\text{Number of days}}{\text{of inventory}} + \frac{\text{Number of days}}{\text{of receivables}}$$

The operating cycle does not take everything into account, however, because the available cash flow is increased by deferring payment to suppliers. This deferral is considered in the **net operating cycle**, also called the **cash conversion cycle**. The net operating cycle is a measure of the time from paying suppliers for materials to collecting cash from the subsequent sale of goods produced from these supplies. It consists of the operating cycle minus the number of days of payables:

$$\text{Net operating cycle} = \frac{\text{Number of days}}{\text{of inventory}} + \frac{\text{Number of days}}{\text{of receivables}} - \frac{\text{Number of days}}{\text{of payables}}$$

In general, the shorter these cycles the greater a company's cash-generating ability and the less its need for liquid assets or outside finance. For many companies, the cash conversion cycle represents a period of time that requires financing—that is, the company offsets some of the financing need by deferring payments through payables terms, but the remainder must be financed.

3　MANAGING THE CASH POSITION

Although the mix or magnitude of data items may change from day to day, the goal is the same: ensuring that the net cash position is not negative. Ideally, the company's daily cash inflows and outflows would be equal, but this is rarely the case. Without the reliability of matching these flows, companies must take other steps to ensure that the flows net out each day. Most companies try to avoid negative balances because the cost of garnering daily funds by issuing debt or by drawing on bank overdraft facilities is very costly, although the cost of maintaining a small short-term investment portfolio, in terms of an opportunity cost, is regarded as an acceptable cost of doing business.

In addition, it is difficult to borrow the exact amount needed, so many companies borrow a little extra to be safe and invest any small excesses overnight at lower rates than if they could invest them earlier or in securities with higher rates. To manage the cash position effectively, the treasury function, which is usually responsible for this activity, must gather information from various sources at all times during the day, making decisions based on the latest information.

Several critical factors help determine how a company can establish an efficient cash flow system. In most cases, the central treasury function may not be able to dictate how the company collects from customers or pays its vendors. What it can do, however, is use the best services and techniques associated with the company's payment configuration.

As an example of a typical cycle of cash management information that occurs daily, consider the process outlined in Exhibit 4. This hypothetical schedule shows how important it is to have an efficient, smooth-flowing information system that can meet the time requirements.

Exhibit 4	An Example of the Daily Cycle of Cash Management

Information from bank reporting systems is gathered and analyzed.　*Morning*

↓

The cash manager receives information from company sources.

↓

Exhibit 4	(Continued)

The cash manager receives updates from the company's bank(s) on current-day transactions.

↓

The cash management staff is arranging short-term investments and/or loans, as necessary, through broker–dealers from their banks or investment banks.

↓

The cash management staff makes funds transfers.   *Midday*

↓

The cash movements for the day are completed or are scheduled for completion, and the company's cash position is finalized.

↓

Necessary paperwork for all transactions is completed. Also, the   *Close of the* running cash worksheet is updated and set for the next business day.   *business day*

3.1 Forecasting Short-Term Cash Flows

Forecasting cash flows is necessary to allow effective management of working capital accounts. For cash forecasting to be effective, it has to be relatively precise. However, a forecast that is precise may not be *accurate*. There are many factors that are outside of the company's control, such as the general economy, unexpected raw material shortages, and changing interest rates. The uncertainty in forecasting encourages companies to maintain some minimum level of cash on hand as a buffer.

3.1.1 *Minimum Cash Balances*

Most companies want a cash buffer as protection from unexpected cash needs or to provide the financial flexibility to take advantage of attractive opportunities, such as procuring raw material inventory at a discount. This buffer is often expressed as a minimum desired cash balance. The size of this buffer depends on several influences, including the variation in the levels of the company's cash inflows and outflows, the company's ability to access other liquidity sources, and the company's ability to access borrowing facilities with little lead time.

3.1.2 *Identifying Typical Cash Flows*

Having an accurate forecast can help a financial manager make better use of the company's financial history. Many product lines, especially those that are not in high-growth stages but rather are in steadier, mature stages, will have similar cash flows from year to year or season to season. If an extensive database has been established, it will be possible to draw reasonable projections for the current period or longer.

Even in cases of heavy growth through mergers and acquisitions, companies should try to transfer the acquired company's cash flow history to be used as a starting point for consolidating the new operation into the rest of the company. The cash manager must identify cash flow elements to build a reliable forecast. These elements are not difficult to identify in general terms, but it is much harder to define them more specifically to be able to collect data regularly.

The cash elements that comprise a total forecast vary from company to company. However, it is good practice to identify the elements that pertain to any one individual company. Exhibit 5 shows typical elements arranged as inflows and outflows. It may be more useful to try to arrange the elements in this manner—i.e., show matching elements by the direction of their flow (in or out). In most cases, a company's data elements can be arranged this way to facilitate data gathering, reviewing variances, and presenting final reports to management and other cash users or providers.

Exhibit 5	Examples of Cash Inflows and Outflows
Inflows	**Outflows**
■ Receipts from operations, broken down by operating unit, departments, etc.	■ Payables and payroll disbursements, broken down by operating unit, departments, etc.
■ Funds transfers from subsidiaries, joint ventures, third parties	■ Funds transfers to subsidiaries
■ Maturing investments	■ Investments made
■ Debt proceeds (short and long term)	■ Debt repayments
■ Other income items (interest, etc.)	■ Interest and dividend payments
■ Tax refunds	■ Tax payments

These elements should reflect real cash flows, excluding such items as depreciation or accruals that are paid at a later date (these should be included when they are to be paid).

3.1.3 *Cash Forecasting Systems*

Cash forecasting should be structured as a system in order to be effective, and to do this, several aspects of the forecast must be considered. We provide some examples of these aspects in Exhibit 6, which highlights each aspect for three different forecast horizons. In some cases, one aspect may be more important than others. For instance, if daily cash is being handled fairly easily, it may be more critical to spend time and resources to ensure that the medium-term forecasting part of the overall system is functioning at the highest levels of reliability. In addition, some factors, such as format or time horizon, should not be changed arbitrarily because change may affect their accuracy and reliability levels.

Exhibit 6	Examples of Cash Forecasting Aspects over Different Forecast Horizons		
	Short Term	**Medium Term**	**Long Term**
Data frequency	Daily/weekly for 4–6 weeks	Monthly for one year	Annually for 3–5 years
Format	Receipts and disbursements	Receipts and disbursements	Projected financial statements
Techniques	Simple projections	Projection models and averages	Statistical models
Accuracy	Very high	Moderate	Lowest
Reliability	Very high	Fairly high	Not as high
Uses	Daily cash management	Planning financial transactions	Long-range financial position

3.2 Monitoring Cash Uses and Levels

Another facet of cash forecasting is monitoring and control. Managing the cash position essentially means keeping a "running score" on daily cash flows. Monitoring daily cash flows is a key aspect of a company's cash forecasting system in that the financial manager in charge of managing the cash position must know the company's cash balance in the bank on virtually a real-time basis. However, it really is not *forecasting* as such, because most of the transactions are actually known; the challenge lies in the collection of this known information in time to do something with that information. For example, receiving information about a deposit too late to transfer the funds renders the information valueless.

To receive the appropriate information on a timely basis, information should be gathered from principal users and providers of cash, supplemented by short-term cash projections in days or even throughout the current day. The minimum level of cash available is estimated in advance, adjusted for known funds transfers, seasonality, or other factors, and is used as a **target balance** figure for each bank. Note that most companies use one major bank as their lead bank (or concentration bank) and control the balances for the bank through one main concentration account, with the target balance applied to the main account. For larger companies, more than one concentration bank is possible, but managing the cash positions in multiple concentration banks quickly makes the system complex and requires an efficient information processing system.

For most companies, it is necessary to manage a cash position with the assistance of short-term investments and borrowings. These short-term liquidity sources help counter the excesses and deficits that typically occur in a company's cash flow. The short-term investments are usually kept in a portfolio that is very liquid, with short maturities. In this way, funds are available whenever they are needed, but the company gives up the extra yield that might have been earned if the investments were made for longer periods of time or with securities with less liquidity. Short-term borrowing is for very short periods of time, but a borrower may find more economies in borrowing for regular periods, such as thirty days, to reduce the number of transactions and associated paperwork. Also, by extending the borrowing period, companies can usually obtain better rates and availabilities of funds than if they continually borrow very short maturities.

Many companies face predictable peaks and valleys in their business throughout the year. For instance, manufacturers of consumer electronics products achieve the bulk of their sales during the holiday shopping season (from late November through the end of the year), which means that they have build-up of products that are shipped well before they receive payment. Thus, they have to finance this inventory roll-out before they receive any cash. During this period, they are likely to use up most or all of the temporary excess funds they set aside or to tap into the credit lines they arranged for this purpose. When sales roll in during the busy shopping season, they use the proceeds to pay down the borrowing and then invest any excess.

Other influencing factors on a company's cash needs may be associated with non-operating activities, such as major capital expenditure programs, mergers and acquisitions, sales or disposition of company assets, and the timing of long-term financial transactions, such as bond issues, private placements of debt or equity, and equity issues.

Predicting the peak need caused by seasonality or other non-operating activities is important if the company is going to have to borrow funds to cover the need. If a company sets aside too much, it will incur excess costs that are unjustified. If it sets aside too little, it will have to pay a penalty to raise funds quickly. Either case is a costly error. A reliable forecast can help avoid this situation.

4   INVESTING SHORT-TERM FUNDS

Short-term investments represent a temporary store of funds that are not necessarily needed in a company's daily transactions. If a substantial portion of a company's working capital portfolio is not needed for short-term transactions, it should be separated from a working capital portfolio and placed in a longer-term portfolio. Such longer-term portfolios are often handled by another area or are handled by an outside money manager under the company's supervision. In this way, the risks, maturities, and portfolio management of longer-term portfolios can be managed independently of the working capital portfolio.

Short-term working capital portfolios consist of securities that are highly liquid, less risky, and shorter in maturity than other types of investment portfolios. Thus, a company's working capital portfolio may consist of short-term debt securities, such as short-term U.S. government securities and short-term bank and corporate obligations. This type of portfolio changes almost constantly, as cash is needed or more excess cash is available for investments.

4.1 Short-Term Investment Instruments

We describe examples of the major instruments for short-term investments in Exhibit 7. The relative amounts of each security can vary from one company to another, depending on the company's risk tolerance and how quickly the invested funds will be needed.

Exhibit 7	Examples of Short-Term Investment Instruments		
Instruments	**Typical Maturities**	**Features**	**Risks**
U.S. Treasury Bills (T-bills)	13, 26, and 52 weeks	■ Obligations of U.S. government (guaranteed), issued at a discount ■ Active secondary market ■ Lowest rates for traded securities	Virtually no risk
Federal agency securities	5–30 days	■ Obligations of U.S. federal agencies (e.g., Fannie Mae, Federal Home Loan Board) issued as interest-bearing ■ Slightly higher yields than T-bills	Slight liquidity risk; insignificant credit risk
Bank certificates of deposit (CDs)	14–365 days	■ Bank obligations, issued interest-bearing in $100,000 increments ■ "Yankee" CDs offer slightly higher yields	Credit and liquidity risk (depending on bank's credit)
Banker's acceptances (BAs)	30–180 days	■ Bank obligations for trade transactions (usually foreign), issued at a discount ■ Investor protected by underlying company and trade flow itself ■ Small secondary market	Credit and liquidity risk (depending on bank's credit)
Eurodollar time deposits	1–180 days	■ Time deposit with bank off-shore (outside United States, such as Bahamas) ■ Can be CD or straight time deposit (TD) ■ Interest-bearing investment ■ Small secondary market for CDs, but not TDs	Credit risk (depending on bank) Very high liquidity risk for TDs

Exhibit 7	(Continued)

Instruments	Typical Maturities	Features	Risks
Bank sweep services	1 day	■ Service offered by banks that essentially provides interest on checking account balance (usually over a minimum level) ■ Large number of sweeps are for overnight	Credit and liquidity risk (depending on bank)
Repurchase agreements (Repos)	1 day +	■ Sale of securities with the agreement of the dealer (seller) to buy them back at a future time ■ Typically over-collateralized at 102 percent ■ Often done for very short maturities (< 1 week)	Credit and liquidity risk (depending on dealer)
Commercial paper (CP)	1–270 days	■ Unsecured obligations of corporations and financial institutions, issued at discount ■ Secondary market for large issuers ■ CP issuers obtain short-term credit ratings	Credit and liquidity risk (depending on credit rating)
Mutual funds and money market mutual funds	Varies	■ Money market mutual funds commonly used by smaller businesses ■ Low yields but high liquidity for money market funds; mutual fund liquidity dependent on underlying securities in fund ■ Can be linked with bank sweep arrangement	Credit and liquidity risk (depending on fund manager)
Tax-advantaged securities	7, 28, 35, 49, and 90 days	■ Preferred stock in many forms, including adjustable rate preferred stocks (ARPs), auction rate preferred stocks (AURPs), and convertible adjustable preferred stocks (CAPs) ■ Dutch auction often used to set rate ■ Offer higher yields	Credit and liquidity risk (depending on issuer's credit)

4.1.1 Computing Yields on Short-Term Investments

Some securities, such as T-bills and banker's acceptances, are issued at a discount. Thus, the investor invests less than the face value of the security and receives the face value back at maturity. For instance, a $1 million security that pays 5 percent in interest with one month remaining to maturity would be purchased at:

$$\text{Purchase price} = \$1,000,000 - \left[(0.05)(1/12)(\$1,000,000)\right] = \$995,833.33$$

$$\text{Proceeds(face value)} = \$1,000,000$$

The difference between the purchase price and the face value, $4,166.67, is the **discount interest**.

Interest-bearing securities differ from discounted securities in that the investor pays the face amount and receives back that same face amount plus the interest on the security. For example, a 5 percent, 30-day, $1 million security would return $1 million face value plus interest earned:

$$\text{Purchase price(face value)} = \$1,000,000$$

$$\text{Proceeds} = \$1,000,000 + \left[(0.05)(1/12)(\$1,000,000)\right] = \$1,004,166.67$$

Rates on securities may be quoted as nominal rates or as yields. A **nominal rate** is a rate of interest based on the security's face value. In the previous two examples, the nominal rate in each instance was 5 percent. A **yield**, on the other hand, is the actual return on the investment if it is held to maturity. For example, if you buy the discount security for $995,833.33 and hold it for one month until it matures for $1 million, your yield on this investment is

$$\text{Yield} = \left(\frac{\$1,000,000 - 995,833.33}{995,833.33}\right)(12) = (0.004184)(12) = 5.0209\%$$

where the second factor, 12, annualizes the monthly yield of 0.4184 percent. The factor that is used to annualize the yield depends on the type of security and the traditions for quoting yields. For example, the **money market yield** is typically annualized using the ratio of 360 to the number of days to maturity:

$$\text{Money market yield} = \left(\frac{\text{Face value} - \text{Purchase price}}{\text{Purchase price}}\right)\left(\frac{360}{\text{Number of days to maturity}}\right)$$

On the other hand, the **bond equivalent yield** is typically annualized using the ratio of 365 to the number of days to maturity:

$$\text{Bond equivalent yield} = \left(\frac{\text{Face value} - \text{Purchase price}}{\text{Purchase price}}\right)\left(\frac{365}{\text{Number of days to maturity}}\right)$$

One source of confusion is that the yield on U.S. T-bills may be quoted on the basis of the discount basis or the bond equivalent basis (also referred to as the investment yield basis). The yield on a T-bill using the discount basis is calculated using the face value as the basis for the yield and then using a 360-day year:

$$\text{Discount-basis yield} = \left(\frac{\text{Face value} - \text{Purchase price}}{\text{Face value}}\right)\left(\frac{360}{\text{Number of days to maturity}}\right)$$

Although the relevant yield for investment decision purposes is the bond equivalent yield, it is important to understand the discount basis because it is often quoted in the context of these securities.

EXAMPLE 2

Computing Investment Yields

For a 91-day $100,000 U.S. T-bill sold at a discounted rate of 7.91 percent, calculate the following:

1   Money market yield.
2   Bond equivalent yield.

$$\text{Purchase price} = \$100,000 - \left[(.0791)(91/360)(\$100,000)\right]$$
$$= \$98,000.53$$

Solution to 1:

$$\text{Money market yield} = \left[1,999.47/98,000.53\right] \times \left[360/91\right] = 8.07 \text{ percent}$$

Solution to 2:

$$\text{Bond equivalent yield} = \left[1,999.47/98,000.53\right] \times \left[365/91\right] = 8.18 \text{ percent}$$

4.1.2 Investment Risks

Investors face several types of risks. We list a number of these in Exhibit 8. In this exhibit, we list the types of risk—credit, market, liquidity, and foreign exchange—and the attributes and safety measures associated with each type. The attributes describe the conditions that contribute to the type of risk, and the safety measures describe the steps that investors usually take to prevent losses from the risk. With the exception of foreign exchange risk, the key safety measures taken are to shift to "safety" (i.e., government securities, such as U.S. T-bills) or to shorten maturities so that securities will mature quicker, allowing an investor to shift funds to a safer type of security.

Exhibit 8	Types of Investment Risks and Safety Measures	
Type of Risk	**Key Attributes**	**Safety Measures**
Credit (or default)	■ Issuer may default ■ Issuer could be adversely affected by economy, market ■ Little secondary market	■ Minimize amount ■ Keep maturities short ■ Watch for "questionable" names ■ Emphasize government securities
Market (or interest rate)	■ Price or rate changes may adversely affect return ■ There is no market to sell the maturity to, or there is only a small secondary market	■ Keep maturities short ■ Keep portfolio diverse in terms of maturity, issuers
Liquidity	■ Security is difficult or impossible to (re)sell ■ Security must be held to maturity and cannot be liquidated until then	■ Stick with government securities ■ Look for good secondary market ■ Keep maturities short
Foreign exchange	■ Adverse general market movement against your currency	■ Hedge regularly ■ Keep most in your currency and domestic market (avoid foreign exchange)

4.2 Strategies

Short-term investment strategies are fairly simple because the securities in a working capital portfolio are limited in type and are much shorter in maturity than a longer-term portfolio. Most short-term investors seek "reasonable" returns and do not want to take on substantial risk. Short-term investment strategies can be grouped into two types: passive and active. A **passive strategy** is characterized by one or two decision rules for making daily investments, whereas an **active strategy** involves constant monitoring and may involve matching, mismatching, or laddering strategies.

Passive strategies are less aggressive than active ones and place top priority on safety and liquidity. Yet, passive strategies do not have to offer poor returns, especially if companies have reliable cash forecasts. Often, companies with good cash forecasts can combine a passive strategy with an active matching strategy to enhance the yield of a working capital portfolio without taking on substantially greater risks.

The major problem associated with passive strategies is complacency, which can cause the company to roll over the portfolio mechanically, with little attention paid to yields and more focus on simply reinvesting funds as they mature. Passive strategies must be monitored, and the yield from investment portfolios should be benchmarked regularly against a suitable standard, such as a T-bill with comparable maturity.

Active strategies require more daily involvement and possibly a wider choice of investments. Although investments are rolled over with an active strategy, just as they are with a passive strategy, this type of strategy calls for more shopping around, better forecasts, and a more flexible investment policy/guideline.

Active strategies can include intentional matching or mismatching the timing of cash outflows with investment maturities. A **matching strategy** is the more conservative of the two and uses many of the same investment types as are used with passive strategies. A **mismatching strategy** is riskier and requires very accurate and reliable cash forecasts. These strategies usually use securities that are more liquid, such as T-bills, so that securities can be liquidated if adverse market conditions arise. Mismatching strategies may also be accomplished using derivatives, which may pose additional risks to a company unaccustomed to buying and selling derivatives.

A **laddering strategy** is another form of active strategy, which entails scheduling maturities on a systematic basis within the investment portfolio such that investments are spread out equally over the term of the ladder. A laddering strategy falls somewhere between a matching and a passive strategy. Laddering strategies have been used effectively in managing longer-term investment portfolios, but laddering also should be an effective short-term strategy.

Managing a working capital portfolio involves handling and safeguarding assets of the company. Accordingly, companies with investment portfolios should have a formal, written policy/guideline that protects the company and the investment managers. Investment policy/guidelines should not be very lengthy, especially because they must be understood by the company's investment managers and communicated to the company's investment dealers.

Although the investment policy/guideline should be customized for an individual company, the basic structure of such a policy is provided in Exhibit 9.

Exhibit 9	Sample Format of an Investment Policy
Purpose	List and explain the reasons that the portfolio exists and also describe the general attributes of the portfolio, such as a summary of the strategy that will be used and the general types of securities that are acceptable investments.
Authorities	Identify the executives who oversee the portfolio managers who make the investments that compose the portfolio and the outside managers that could be used and how they would be managed. Also describe procedures that must be performed if the policy is not followed.
Limitations and/or restrictions	Describe, in general terms, the types of investments that should be considered for inclusion in the portfolio. The list should not consist of specific securities; it should describe the general *types* of securities, such as commercial paper, U.S. T-bills, or bank CDs. In this manner, the policy retains more flexibility than if specific issuers or securities are listed. In the latter case, the policy would require change every time an issuer was no longer issuing any securities. This section should also include any restrictions as to the relative amount of each security that is allowable in the overall portfolio. This section may also include procedures when a maximum has been exceeded or must be exceeded under special circumstances, such as when the portfolio is temporarily inflated prior to using the funds for an acquisition or other long-term use.

Exhibit 9	(Continued)
Quality	May be in a separate section or may be included with the previous one. Investments with working capital funds must be safe, so many companies include credit standards for potential investments in their policy statements. Reference may be made to long-term ratings or, more frequently, to short-term credit ratings. The ratings cited are usually those from the major rating agencies: Standard & Poor's and Moody's.
Other items	Other items are sometimes included in a policy/guideline, such as statements that require the portfolio to be included in the financial audit or that regular reports will be generated by the investment manager. Some companies also define the types of securities that are "eligible," but this does not seem necessary if the policy is well written.

EXAMPLE 3

Evaluating an Investment Policy

A sample investment policy is shown below. Review the client's investment policy, considering the basic investment policy structure shown in Exhibit 9. The average portfolio size is $100 million, with no significant peaks or valleys throughout the year. After reviewing the policy, answer the following questions:

1 Is the policy an effective one?

2 What shortcomings or potential problem areas, if any, does it have?

3 How would you change this policy, if at all?

Working Capital Portfolio Investment Policy/Guidelines

- Purpose: This is a working capital portfolio with emphasis on safety and liquidity. We will sacrifice return for either of these two goals.

- Authorities: The treasurer, with agreement from the CFO, will be in charge of managing short-term investments. Authority and control to execute can be delegated by the treasurer or CFO to another treasury manager if documented.

- Maximum maturity: Securities may not be made for longer than three (3) years.

- Types/amounts of investments permitted: no more than 10 percent of the portfolio or $50 million with any issuer, subject to the credit limitation that any eligible issuer must be rated A-1, P-1 by Standard & Poor's and Moody's.

- Repurchase agreements must be equal to, or preferably exceed, the PSA Standard Investment Agreement, which requires 102 percent collateral for repurchases.

- All investments must be held in safekeeping by XYZ Bank.

- The investment manager can execute exception transactions but must document them in writing.

Solution to 1:

The policy is fairly effective in that it tries to provide simple, understandable rules. It calls for credit quality, limits the possible position with any single issuer, accepts market standards (such as the PSA), and calls for safekeeping. It also has an exception procedure that is straightforward.

Solution to 2:

The credit ratings may be too restrictive. Many investment securities may not be rated by both S&P and Moody's, which is implied, if not stated, in the policy. Also, the 10 percent limitation apparently is to be applied to all securities. However, most investment managers do not consider securities issued by governmental agencies or the government itself to be so risky that a limitation needs to be applied.

Solution to 3:

The words "or equivalent" should be added to the credit quality of the types of investments. Also, there should be no limitation to highly rated governmental securities, such as U.S. Treasury-bills and the equivalent from the major developed countries. A credit rating reference could be applied to determine eligible governmental securities.

4.3 Evaluating Short-Term Funds Management

Tracking tools can range from simple spreadsheets to more expensive treasury workstations. If both portfolios are not too large or diversified, a spreadsheet may be sufficient to be able to compare effective yields and borrowing costs on an ongoing basis and to generate periodic performance reports.

Investment returns should be expressed as bond equivalent yields, to allow comparability among investment alternatives. In addition, the overall portfolio return should be weighted according to the currency size of the investment. We provide an abbreviated example of a portfolio report in Exhibit 10. The report provides the weighted average returns of the different investments. The yields are all calculated on a bond equivalent yield basis.

Exhibit 10	Short-Term Investment Portfolio Report				
Security/Loan	**Dealer/Bank**	**€ Amt (000)**	**Weight (%)**	**Yield (%)**	**Maturity**
U.S. T-bills	ABC Bank	23,575	39.8	3.50	90 days
Finco CP	XYZ Co.	20,084	33.9	4.65	45 days
Megabank CD	Megabank	15,560	26.3	5.05	30 days
Weighted average yield from investments				**4.30**	
Short-term benchmark rate[a]				**4.25**	

[a] Benchmark rate = independent source, such as synthetic portfolio maintained independently or rate provided by third party, such as a money manager or other empirical source (e.g., a financial institution, trade association, or central bank).

MANAGING ACCOUNTS RECEIVABLE

5

Credit accounts vary by type of customer and the industry, and granting credit involves a tradeoff between increasing sales and uncollectible accounts. There are three primary activities in accounts receivable management: granting credit and processing transactions, monitoring credit balances, and measuring performance of the credit function.

Processing accounts receivable transactions requires recording credit sales to create a record and posting customer payments—or at least monitoring the posting—to the accounts receivable account by applying the payment against the customer's outstanding credit balance. Monitoring the outstanding accounts receivable requires a regular reporting of outstanding receivable balances and notifying the collection managers of past due situations. Monitoring is an ongoing activity. Measuring the performance of the credit functions entails preparing and distributing key performance measurement reports, including an accounts receivable aging schedule and day's sales outstanding reports.

Essentially, the accounts receivable management function is a go-between for the credit manager, treasury manager, and accounting manager. This role is an important one because it can slow up the recording of payments, which may, in turn, prevent customers from purchasing more of the company's products or, worse yet, could prevent the treasury manager from depositing the check and converting the check to available funds.

The accounts receivable management function is also considered to be a derivative activity from credit granting because it helps in providing information needed by the credit management function. It depends on the source of the sale for its records, on the credit manager for additional information on the status of the accounts receivable record, and possibly on the treasury manager to establish an efficient system of getting the payment information to the accounts receivable manager for cash application (e.g., from a bank lockbox).

The goals for the accounts receivable management system include the following:

- efficient processing and maintaining accurate, up-to-date records that are available to credit managers and other interested parties as soon as possible after payments have been received;

- control of accounts receivable and ensuring that accounts receivable records are current and that no unauthorized entry into the accounts receivable file has occurred;

- collection on accounts and coordination with the treasury management function;

- coordination and notification with the credit managers frequently; and

- preparation of regular performance measurement reports.

Companies may achieve scale economies by centralizing the accounts receivable function by using a captive finance subsidiary.[5] A **captive finance subsidiary** is a wholly owned subsidiary of the company that is established to provide financing of the sales of the parent company.

---

5 As pointed out by Shehzad L. Mian and Clifford W. Smith ["Accounts Receivable Management Policy: Theory and Evidence," *Journal of Finance*, vol. 47, no. 1 (March 1992) pp. 169–200], companies that have highly variable accounts receivable (for example, from seasonality) may find the use of a captive finance subsidiary attractive because it may allow the subsidiary's debt indentures to differ from those of the parent company.

One of the challenges in accounts receivable management is monitoring receivables and collecting on accounts. Many companies resort to outsourcing the accounts receivable function, primarily to increase the collection on accounts, provide credit evaluation services, and to apply the most recent technology.[6] Also, some companies may invest in credit insurance, which reduces the risk of bad debts and shifts some of the evaluation of credit-worthiness to the insurer.

5.1 Key Elements of the Trade Credit Granting Process

Credit management is an integral part of the collection process. It sets the framework for sales in that it can restrict sales by rejecting credit or expand it by loosening acceptance criteria. It also links the collection and cash application processes and has a profound effect on the method of collection as well. In addition, credit management techniques incorporate fundamental financial analysis methods in setting credit policy, granting credit, and managing existing credit customers.

A weak, ineffective credit management function may enhance sales, but many of those sales may become bad debts. On the other hand, a strong, active credit management function can work in tandem with sales and marketing on one side and accounting and treasury on the other. To establish an effective credit management function a company must have a well-conceived strategy customized to the company's needs and reflecting the company's goals.

Credit management policies are usually established as a set of basic guidelines to be used by credit managers. A company's credit policy sets the boundaries for the credit management function. It lays out procedures as part of the policy and offers guidance for each typical situation. The policy shows the steps in the granting process and provides decision rules for specific situations. The policy can also influence the sales level by making it easy or difficult for customers to buy on credit.

Customers may start out with one type of credit account that is restrictive, such as cash on delivery, and may eventually demonstrate that they are regular payers and can be given open book credit accounts.

The major types of credit accounts include the following:

■ open book, which is the most common for company to company;

■ documentary, with or without lines of credit, most common for cross-border transactions;

■ installment credit, with regular timed payments; and

■ revolving credit.

The types of credit terms offered vary by type of customer, the relative financial strength of the customer, and the type of credit terms the competition is offering. The different forms of terms of credit other than cash, which generally implies 7 to 10 days, include the following:

■ **Ordinary terms**. Terms are set forth in a standard format—*net t* or *d/t₁ net t₂*, where t in the first example refers to the length of time a customer has to pay the invoice before becoming past due. In the second example, t_1 is the time period for taking discounts, and t_2 is the same as t in the first example. For example, *net 60* means that the full amount of the invoice is due in 60 days. Most trade credit customers will take the full 60 days. Terms of *1/10 net 30*

---

6 Martin Hall, "A/R Outsourcing: Coming of Age in the New Millennium," *Business Credit* (February 2003), pp. 1–2.

mean that the customer can take a 1 percent discount if the invoice is paid within 10 days or else pay the full amount of the invoice by 30 days from the invoice date.

- **Cash before delivery (CBD)** terms require that the amount of the invoice must be paid in advance before delivery will be scheduled. Checks must clear before any shipment is made.

- **Cash on delivery (COD)** terms require that payment must be made (usually in the form of a bank check) when the product is delivered; otherwise, no delivery will be made.

- **Bill-to-bill**. These terms require that each prior bill must be paid before new shipments are possible.

- **Monthly billing**. These terms require payment monthly. They have a different format; for example, *2/10th Prox net 30th* means that the customer can take a 2 percent discount if it pays within the first 10 days of the next month or else it must pay the full amount of the invoice by the 30th day of the next month.

Credit managers may evaluate customers' credit-worthiness using a credit scoring model. A **credit scoring model** is a statistical model used to classify borrowers according to credit-worthiness. These models were first designed for assisting in making consumer credit decisions. Major credit card issuers needed a tool they could use to make mass credit decisions. It was also used for small business loans after many larger banks discovered that their costs of reviewing and deciding whether to grant loans were such that they could not efficiently make loans of the smaller sizes required by smaller businesses. To overcome this problem, they adopted credit scoring models.

Credit scoring models offer an opportunity for a company to make fast decisions on the basis of simple data, not requiring a great deal of paperwork. The scoring models give greater weight to such factors as:

- ready cash (e.g., high checking account balances);

- organization type, with corporations rated higher than sole proprietorships or partnership; and

- being current in supplier payments, as indicated by financial services such as Dun & Bradstreet.

The models penalize the potential borrower for:

- prior late payment behavior or defaults: payment patterns are habitual;

- heavy use of personal credit cards: no reserves or reduced reserves available;

- previous *personal* bankruptcy or tax liens: carries over from person to company; and

- high-risk categories: food services, hospitality industries.

Credit scoring can also be used to predict late payers.

5.2 Managing Customers' Receipts

Cash collections systems are a function of the types of customers a company has and the methods of payment that the customers use. For instance, if a company's sales are made at retail locations, it cannot take advantage of the benefits offered by bank lockbox services. Instead, it must deal with organizing and controlling local deposits and concentrating these deposits efficiently and economically. On the other hand, if a company manufactures and sells products to other businesses, it can use a bank lockbox services to expedite processing and clearing of check payments.

We illustrate a typical network for a company with both electronic and check payments in Exhibit 11. Checks from one type of customer are directed to a bank lockbox, while electronic payments from another type of customer are transmitted via **electronic funds transfer (EFT)** through one of the available networks, such as the **Automated Clearing House (ACH)** system or the **Giro system**. The ACH system is an electronic payment network available to businesses, individuals, and financial institutions in the United States, U.S. Territories, and Canada. The Giro systems are postal-based systems in Europe and elsewhere.

Exhibit 11	Cash Collections and Concentration

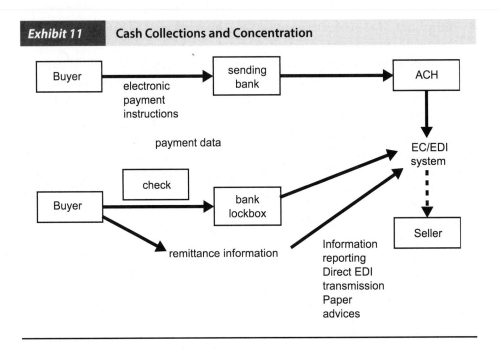

In most cases, the best practice for collections involves the establishment of a system that accelerates payments as well as their information content, such as the customer's name and identification number and which invoices are being paid. From the collecting company's point of view, the way to achieve this best practice is to establish an electronic collection network. This can apply to either retail or wholesale companies.

Retail payments can be made by credit/debit cards or electronic checks, which are converted to electronic debits or digitized images, or by direct debit. These payments clear electronically and can be facilitated through **point of sale (POS)** systems, which are systems that capture the transaction data at the physical location in which the sale is made. A **direct debit program** is an arrangement whereby the customer authorizes a debit to a demand account and is used by companies—such as utilities, telecommunications service providers, cable companies, insurance companies, and credit card companies—to collect routine payments for services.

If payments cannot be converted to electronic payments, the next best practice is to use a bank lockbox service. A **lockbox system** is coordinated with the banking institution in which customer payments are mailed to a post office box and the banking institution retrieves and deposits these payments several times a day, enabling the company to have use of the fund sooner than in a centralized system in which customer payments are sent to the company. An acceptable bank lockbox arrangement is one in which the checks deposited today are available tomorrow or the next business day. This one-day availability lays the groundwork for best practices in cash concentration.

A good performance measure for check deposits is a calculated **float factor**. The **float** in this context is the amount of money that is in transit between payments made by customers and the funds that are usable by the company. We compute the float factor by dividing the average daily deposit in dollars into the average daily float:[7]

$$\text{Float factor} = \frac{\text{Average daily float}}{\text{Average daily deposit}}$$

$$= \frac{\text{Average daily float}}{\text{Total amount of checks deposited}/\text{Number of days}}$$

This calculation gives the average number of days it took deposited checks to clear. If the float factor is very small (e.g., less than 1.0), it is probably worthwhile to investigate further to determine whether same-day wire transfers from the depository account are warranted, assuming the depository account is with a bank other than the company's lead bank. The float factor only measures how long it takes for checks to clear, not how long it takes to receive the checks, deposit them, and then have them clear. However, it is still very useful and can be computed easily for any depository accounts.

EXAMPLE 4

Calculating Float Factors

Given the following data, compute a float factor for this company bank account.

Total deposits for the month:	$3,360,900
Number of days in month:	30 days
Average daily float:	$154,040

Solution:

Average daily deposit = ($3,360,900)/30 = $112,030

Float factor = Average daily float/Average daily deposit

= $154,040/$112,030 = 1.375

Cash concentration involves two major activities: consolidating deposits and moving funds between company accounts or to outside points. The best practice for cash concentration may be different for consolidating deposits than for moving funds, depending on the timing required and the availability of the funds being transferred.

For bank lockbox concentration, assuming that the checks clear in one business day (on average), the concentration technique of choice is the electronic funds transfer method. In this method, bank lockbox personnel call in the deposit via a reporting service or directly to the concentration bank. The concentration bank creates an electronic funds transfer debit that clears overnight, giving the company available funds in its concentration account. This system can be set up to run with or without intervention by the company's cash manager. In most cases, the best practice does not involve any intervention.

Electronic funds transfers offer distinct advantages to companies that use them for concentration of funds. First, they are substantially cheaper than the alternative, the wire transfer. In addition, they are reliable in that the transfer can be made part

---

7 We determine the average daily float from an analysis of cash accounts.

of a routine that can be performed daily without exception. Even small payments that would not be economical to transfer out by wire can be transferred economically by electronic funds transfer.

5.3 Evaluating Accounts Receivable Management

There are numerous ways of measuring accounts receivable performance. Most of them deal with how effectively outstanding accounts receivable items can be converted into cash. Measures can be derived from general financial reports as well as more detailed internal financial records.

Many measures, such as number of days of receivables, can be calculated easily from financial statements. The standard number of days of receivables evaluates the total receivables outstanding but does not consider the age distribution within this outstanding balance.

5.3.1 Accounts Receivable Aging Schedule

One key report that accounts receivable managers should use is the **aging schedule**, which is a breakdown of the accounts into categories of days outstanding. We provide an example of an aging schedule in Exhibit 12, Panel A. As you can see in this example, the report shows the total sales and receivables for each reporting period (typically 30 days). It is handier to convert the aging schedule to percentages, as we show in this exhibit. Note that in the exhibit, it is easy to spot a change in April's aging: Accounts receivable have not been collected and converted to cash as rapidly as in previous months. In this case, the April change should be scrutinized. For example, the extension of credit terms may have been increased as part of a special program. This change could also signal a change in payments by the company's customers.

Exhibit 12	An Accounts Receivable Aging Schedule

Panel A: The Aging Schedule

($ Millions)	January	February	March	April
Sales	530	450	560	680
Total accounts receivable	600	560	650	720
Current (1–30 days old)	330	290	360	280
1–30 days past due	90	120	160	250
31–60 days past due	80	60	60	110
61–90 days past due	70	50	40	50
>90 days past due	30	40	30	30

Aging Expressed as Percent	January	February	March	April
Current (1–30 days old)	55.0	51.8	55.4	38.9
1–30 days past due	15.0	21.4	24.6	34.7
31–60 days past due	13.3	10.7	9.2	15.3
61–90 days past due	11.7	8.9	6.2	6.9
>90 days past due	5.0	7.1	4.6	4.2

Exhibit 12	(Continued)

Panel B: Calculation of the Weighted Average Collection Period

	March			April		
Aging Group	Collection Days[a]	Weight[b] (%)	Weighted Days[c]	Collection Days	Weight (%)	Weighted Days
Current (1–30 days)	20	55.4	11.1	29	38.9	11.3
31–60 days	48	24.6	11.8	55	34.7	19.1
61–90 days	80	9.2	7.4	88	15.3	13.5
91–120 days	110	6.2	6.8	115	6.9	7.9
121+ days	130	4.6	6.0	145	4.2	6.1
Weighted average collection days[d]			43.0			57.9

[a] The average days for collecting receivables in each grouping.
[b] The weighting from the aging schedule.
[c] This figure, expressed in days, is the product of the previous two columns.
[d] The sum of each grouping's product equals the overall days.

5.3.2 The Number of Days of Receivables

The number of days of receivables gives us the overall picture of accounts receivable collection. We can compare the number of days with the credit policy to give us an idea of how well the company is collecting on its accounts, relative to the terms that it grants credit. But we can take this a step further by calculating a weighted average of the collection period, or weighted average day's sales outstanding. By focusing on the time it takes to collect receivables, the weighted average collection period is a good measure of how long it is taking to collect from the company's customers regardless of the sales level or the changes in sales.

The calculation of the weighted average collection period requires data on the number of days it takes to collect accounts of each age grouping. For example, we could group receivables in regular increments, such as 30-day periods, and then weight the collection period in each group by the monetary amount of accounts in the group.

Using the data provided in Exhibit 12, Panel A, it is possible to compute number of days of receivables for March and April, as shown in Panel B of this exhibit. As you can see in this example, we can get a better idea of why the number of days of receivables changed from one month to the next. The weighted average collection days increased from March to April, primarily because of the large representation in receivable accounts in the 31–60 and 61–90 day ranges, which made up only 24.6 percent + 9.2 percent = 33.8 percent of accounts in March, but 50 percent of accounts in April.

The primary drawback to this measure is that it requires more information than number of days of receivables, and this information is not readily available, especially for comparisons among companies.

6 MANAGING INVENTORY

The primary goal for an inventory system is to maintain the level of inventory so that production management and sales management can make and sell the company's products without more than necessary invested in this asset. Like cash and accounts receivable management, inventory management involves balancing: having sufficient inventory, but not too much.

Inventory is a current asset that is created by purchasing, paid by accounts payable, and funded by the treasury. The investment in inventory does not produce cash until it is sold or otherwise disposed of. Excessive levels of inventory can possibly overstate the value of inventory because the more that is on hand, the greater the potential for obsolete inventory, which can be sold off, but at a discount. Shortages of inventory result in lost sales.

The amount of inventory that a company holds or feels it has to hold creates a financial requirement for the company. If the company's product lines are more diverse or if its production processes are more involved in using inventory to make final products and then store the products, the company may have a significant financial investment in inventory.

The investment in inventory has been quite staggering for many companies, which has caused them to look for new inventory management techniques. New techniques in inventory control, aided by improved technology, have enabled substantial reduction of the inventory levels a company must maintain and still be able to make products and have them available for sale as needed. For instance, newer just-in-time approaches to inventory management have lowered required inventory balances and cemented major trading partner relationships.

The motives for holding inventory, which dictate how much inventory will be held and, in turn, how much working capital will be tied up in inventory, are very similar to the need for holding cash. The major motives include the transactions motive, the precautionary motives, and the speculative motive.

The **transactions motive** reflects the need for inventory as part of the routine production–sales cycle. Inventory need is equal to the planned manufacturing activity, and the approach to inventory will be dictated by the manufacturing plan.

Precautionary stocks also may be desirable to avoid any **stock-out losses**, which are profits lost from not having sufficient inventory on hand to satisfy demand. Managing inventory well means keeping extra inventory, especially if it could become obsolete quickly, at a minimum. To do this, a company must have a reliable forecast and a flexible inventory approach. In addition, many companies that do not have a reliable forecast maintain a reserve as a precaution for shortfalls in the plan. Of course, how much stock is determined by the lead time for additional inventory purchases, the length of time it takes to deliver final products to the market, and how much can be spent on extra inventory.

In certain industries, managers may acquire inventory for speculative reasons, such as ensuring the availability and pricing of inventory. Inventory managers working together with purchasing managers can benefit from out-of-the-ordinary purchases. For instance, if a publisher is certain that paper costs will be increasing for the next year, it can buy more paper in the current year and store it for future use. This decision assumes that the storage costs are not greater than the savings.

Companies usually attempt to strike a balance in managing their inventory levels. Overinvestment can result in liquidity squeezes or related problems with an increase in debt without an increase in cash. Overinvestment can also lead to the misuse of facilities as more storage is required for the built-up inventory. Having large amounts of inventory on hand can result in losses from shrinkage, spoilage, and so on. Finally, overinvestment can reduce the company's competitiveness as it may not be able to match pricing because of its large inventory costs.

On the other hand, underinvestment in inventory can create problems from losing customers who could not purchase a product, or gaining their ill-will from long delays in delivery. Plant shutdowns and expensive special runs can also be costly. Finally, a risk with underinvestment is the company's inability to avoid price increases by suppliers.

6.1 Approaches to Managing Levels of Inventory

To control inventory costs, a company should adopt the appropriate approach for its inventory. The two basic approaches are the economic order quantity and just-in-time.

Many companies use the classical approach, **economic order quantity–reorder point (EOQ–ROP)**, at least for some portion of their inventory. This method is based on expected demand and the predictability of demand, and it requires determining the level of inventory at which new inventory is ordered. This ordering point is determined based on the costs of ordering and carrying inventory, such that the total cost associated with inventory is minimized. The demand and lead times determine the inventory level. For EOQ–ROP to work well, there must be a reliable short-term forecast. Often, a company may use EOQ–ROP for smaller items that have low unit costs.

Use of the EOQ–ROP method may involve safety stocks and anticipation stocks. A **safety stock** is a level of inventory beyond anticipated needs that provides a cushion in the event that it takes longer to replenish inventory than expected or in the case of greater than expected demand. A company may consider the number of days of inventory on hand and the lead time in replenishing stock in determining the appropriate level of the safety stock. An **anticipation stock** is inventory in excess of that needed for anticipated demand, which may fluctuate with the company's sales or production seasonality. We illustrate the EOQ–ROP method in Exhibit 13.

Exhibit 13	EOQ–ROP Inventory Method

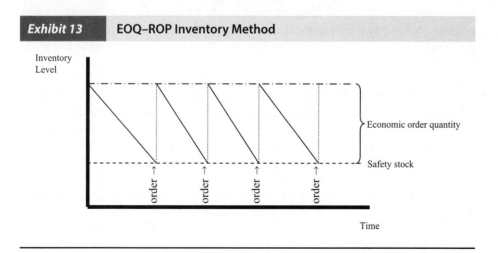

The **just-in-time (JIT) method** is a system that minimizes in-process inventory stocks—raw materials and in production—by evaluating the entire system of the delivery of materials and production. Materials are ordered, for example, at a point at which current stocks of material reach a reorder point, a point determined primarily by historical demand. Materials or **manufacturing resource planning (MRP)** systems incorporate production planning into inventory management. The analysis of production and materials needed for production are incorporated into an analysis that provides both a materials acquisition schedule and a production schedule. Combining the JIT and MRP methods can provide a broader base for integrating inventory into the company's supply chain management and effectively reduce inventory levels.[8]

In most instances, companies will have several types of inventory that can be managed effectively using one or more of these approaches. Obviously, a company should select the method that allows the most cost-beneficial investment in inventory.

6.2 Inventory Costs

There are several component costs of inventory. Some components represent opportunity costs, whereas others may be real costs. The component costs include:

- *Ordering.* Procurement or replenishment costs, both of which may be fixed or variable. These costs depend on the number of orders placed. Examples: freight, labor and handling, paperwork, machine setup.

- *Carrying.* Financing and holding costs, which are opportunity or real costs. These costs depend on average inventory levels and the type of goods. Examples: storage, capital costs, obsolescence, insurance, and taxes.

- *Stock-out.* Opportunity or real costs, which are affected by level of inventory, item mix, processing time versus term of sale. These costs might vary greatly depending on how they are estimated. Examples: lost sales, back-order costs, substitution costs.

- *Policy.* Costs of gathering data and general operating costs, which may be real costs or "soft" costs. These costs depend on inventory mix and complexity. Examples: data processing, labor charges, overtime, training.

6.3 Evaluating Inventory Management

The most common way to measure the company's investment in inventory and evaluate its inventory management is to compute the inventory turnover ratio and the number of days of inventory. The inventory turnover is a rough measure, but it is simple to calculate and compare with other standards or past history. Inventory turnover will vary among industries, as you can see in Exhibit 14, which provides a calculated inventory turnover and number of days of inventory for various industries.

Further, the inventory turnover may differ among companies within an industry because of different product mixes. For example, in fiscal year 2005, Wal-Mart Stores had an inventory turnover of 7.5 times compared with Target's 5.7 times. This difference may be because of Wal-Mart's greater foothold in the higher turnover grocery business, as compared with Target.

Although the analysis of trends is important, care should be taken when interpreting changes. For example, a decrease in the inventory turnover may mean that more inventory is on hand and is not moving through manufacturing and being sold. On the other hand, a decrease in inventory turnover may indicate a change in the company's product mix, or it may mean that the company is reducing its risk of inventory stock-outs.

---

8 More-recent innovations have integrated cash management and inventory management. For example, the moment a customer orders and pays for a computer with Dell Corporation, the production process begins. This efficiency results in a negative operating cycle; that is, Dell Corporation is collecting on accounts as it invests in the inventory production. Because it uses trade credit for its supplies, it has little need for working capital.

	Inventory Turnover (Times)	Number of Days of Inventory
Exhibit 14 Inventory Turnover and Number of Days of Inventory for U.S. Corporations in Different Industries, 2002		
Industry		
Apparel manufacturing	4.9	74.0
Chemical manufacturing	5.7	64.4
Electronics and appliances stores	7.3	50.2
Food manufacturing	8.1	44.9
Food, beverage, and liquor stores	11.2	32.7
Machinery manufacturing	5.6	65.2
Mining	10.4	35.2
Motor vehicle dealers and parts dealers	5.6	65.2
Paper manufacturing	6.8	53.8
Transportation equipment manufacturing	9.7	37.7

Source: Statistics of Income, 2002, Corporation Returns with Net Income, Table 7, www.irs.gov.

EXAMPLE 5

Financial Impact of Inventory Methods

If a company's inventory turnover ratio is 6.1 times (annually) and the industry average number of days of inventory is 52 days, how does the company compare with the industry average?

Solution:

Convert the turnover ratio to a number of days of inventory:

Number of days of inventory = 365/Inventory turnover

$$= 365/6.1 = 59.84 \text{days}$$

Comparing this answer with the industry average, 52.0 days, it appears that the company's inventory turnover is slower than the industry average.

MANAGING ACCOUNTS PAYABLE   **7**

Accounts payable are amounts due suppliers of goods and services that have not been paid. They arise from **trade credit**, which is a spontaneous form of credit in which a purchaser of the goods or service is, effectively, financing its purchase by delaying the date on which payment is made. Trade credit may involve a delay of payment, with a discount for early payment. The terms of the latter form of credit are generally stated in the discount form: A discount from the purchase price is allowed if payment is received within a specified number of days; otherwise the full amount is due by a specified date. For example, the terms "2/10, net 30" indicate that a 2 percent discount is available if the account is paid within 10 days; otherwise the full amount is due by the 30th day. The terms will differ among industries, influenced by tradition within the industry, terms of competitors, and current interest rates.

A key working capital link is the purchasing–inventory–payables process. This process is concerned with the procurement of goods—finished or not—that become the company's items for sale. Handled efficiently, the process minimizes excess funds "in the pipeline." Handled inefficiently, the process can create a severe drain on a company's liquidity, tying up funds and reducing the company's financial reserves.

Inefficiencies may arise in managing purchasing, inventory, and payables. Each area has to be organized and efficiently linked with the other areas. Purchasing can often influence how payments are to be made and the terms of credit. Here again, purchasing management needs to be kept informed as to the types of payment mechanisms the company can handle to avoid agreeing with suppliers to make payments in a medium that the company does not yet support.

The effective management of accounts payable is an important working capital management activity because inefficient payables management may result in opportunity costs from payments made too early, lost opportunities to take advantage of trade discounts, and failure to use the benefits of technologies offered by e-commerce and other web-based activities.

Accounts payable is the final step in the procurement cycle because it combines the paperwork, approvals, and disbursements of funds. An effective accounts payable function helps integrate the components of the cycle and does not require the uneconomical outlay of the company's funds until the outlay is due.

A company may not believe that it needs a formal guideline or policy to manage the function well. However, there must be some method to ensure that payables practices are organized, consistent, and cost-effective. For example, if payables management is decentralized and more than one operating entity deals with the same supplier, the credit terms offered to each entity should be the same unless there are special circumstances, such as volume constraints, that warrant different terms. To handle payables effectively, a company needs rules to ensure that company assets are not being depleted unnecessarily.

There are several factors that a company should consider as guidelines for effectively managing its accounts payable, including:

- *Financial organization's centralization.* The degree to which the company's core financial function is centralized or decentralized affects how tightly payables can be controlled.

- *Number, size, and location of vendors.* The composition of the company's supply chain and how dependent the company is on its trading partners (and vice versa) determines how sophisticated a payables system it needs.

- *Trade credit and cost of borrowing or alternative cost.* The importance of credit to the company and its ability to evaluate trade credit opportunities, such as trade discounts, encourages standardized payables procedures and enhanced information management throughout the company.

- *Control of disbursement float.* Many companies still pay suppliers by check and create **disbursement float**—the amount of time between check issuance and a check's clearing back against the company's account. This float has value to many companies because it allows them to use their funds longer than if they had to fund their checking account on the day the checks were mailed.

- *Inventory management.* Newer inventory control techniques, such as MRP and JIT, increase the number of payments that must be processed by accounts payable. Many older systems cannot accommodate this extra volume, so newer management techniques and systems are required.

- *E-commerce and electronic data interchange (EDI).* Global developments to use the internet and other direct connections between customer and supplier are revolutionizing the supply chain for many companies. Because payments for many of these activities should be considered as part of the overall process, many companies have determined that paying electronically offers a more efficient, cost-effective alternative to checks, which only are more valuable when the disbursement float value is large and interest rates (which provide value to float) are also high.

Stretching payables, also known as pushing on payables when it stretches beyond the due date, is sometimes done by corporate cash managers and other financial managers.[9] Stretching payables is taking advantage of vendor grace periods. The evaluation of payables stretching opportunities is fairly straightforward. The number of additional days that payments can be extended or stretched is determined and valued by applying the company's opportunity cost for the additional days times the amount of the payable.

For example, if a payable that averaged $100,000 can be stretched for an additional seven days, the company gains an additional seven days' use of the funds. This opportunity can be valued by multiplying the amount, $100,000, by the company's opportunity cost for short-term funds. For example, if the company's estimated cost for short-term funds is 8 percent annually (0.02191 percent daily), then the value of stretching a $100,000 payment for seven days is $153.42. The values for each opportunity (throughout a year's activity) can be valued in this way to determine the overall benefit, which can then be weighed against the costs (both financial and nonfinancial ones).

There are basically two countering forces: paying too early is costly unless the company can take advantage of discounts, and paying late affects the company's perceived credit-worthiness.

7.1 The Economics of Taking a Trade Discount

One key activity that companies should review from time to time is the evaluation of trade discounts. Trade discounts should be evaluated using the formula shown below, which computes the implicit rate (of return) that is represented by the trade discount offer; that is, it is the equivalent return to the customer of an alternative investment.

The implicit rate is calculated as follows:

$$\text{Cost of trade credit} = \left(1 + \frac{\text{Discount}}{1 - \text{Discount}}\right)^{\left(365 \Big/ \substack{\text{Number of days} \\ \text{beyond discount period}}\right)} - 1$$

The cost of funds during the discount period is 0 percent, so it is beneficial for the customer to pay close to the end of the discount period. Once the discount period ends, the cost of the credit to the customer jumps up and then declines as the net day is approached. For example, if the terms are 2/10, net 30, which means that there is a 2 percent discount for paying within 10 days and the net amount is due by the 30th day, the cost of trade credit is 109 percent if the credit is paid on the 20th day, but it is only 44.6 percent if paid on the 30th day.

If the customer's cost of funds or short-term investment rate is less than the calculated rate, the discount offers a better return or incremental return over the company's short-term borrowing rate.

---

9 Keep in mind that stretching payments beyond their due dates might be considered unethical and may draw retaliation from suppliers in the form of tighter credit terms in the future.

EXAMPLE 6

Evaluating Trade Discounts

Compute the cost of trade credit if terms are 1/10, net 30 and the account is paid on:

- the 20th day, and
- the 30th day.

Solution:

$$\text{Cost of trade credit if paid on day 20} = \left(1 + \frac{0.01}{1 - 0.01}\right)^{(365/10)} - 1$$
$$= 44.32 \text{ percent}$$

$$\text{Cost of trade credit if paid on day 30} = \left(1 + \frac{0.01}{1 - 0.01}\right)^{(365/20)} - 1$$
$$= 20.13 \text{ percent}$$

As you can see, the cost of the credits is much lower when the company pays on the net day than any day prior to the net day.

7.2 Managing Cash Disbursements

Handling cash disbursements effectively is a common goal for most companies. To accomplish this, companies use best practices that include the ability to delay funding bank accounts until the day checks clear, to erect safeguards against check fraud, to pay electronically when it is cost-effective to do so, and to manage bank charges for disbursement services. Best practices in cash disbursements, like check collections, depend on the nature of the payments—i.e., whether they are made electronically or by check.

Banks offer controlled disbursement services to optimize the funding of checks on the same day they clear against the company's account. When combined with a positive pay service, which provides a filter against check fraud, this method provides the best practice in handling paper-based (check) disbursements.

7.3 Evaluating Accounts Payable Management

The number of days of payables, which is also referred to as the average age of payables, is a useful measure in evaluating a company's credit extension and collection.

If the accounts payable balance from the company's balance sheet is €450 million and the amount of purchases is €4,100 million, the number of days of payables is

$$\text{Number of days of payables} = \frac{\text{Accounts payable}}{\text{Average day's purchases}} = \frac{450}{4100 / 365}$$
$$= 40.06 \text{ days}$$

Comparing the number of days of payables with the credit terms under which credit was granted to the company is important; paying sooner than necessary is costly in terms of the cost of credit, and paying later than the net day is costly in terms of relations with suppliers.

In some cases, treasurers will manage the company's payables closely, comparing the number of days of payables with the number of days of inventory because in some industries these two numbers of days are similar to one another.

MANAGING SHORT-TERM FINANCING

8

An overall short-term financial strategy should focus on ensuring that the company maintains a sound liquidity position. It should also reflect the degree of risk the company believes can be managed without affecting the company's stability. It is common to consider short-term financial strategies as applying mostly to investments. However, they should include other financial activities as well. In many cases, a company will only be an investor or borrower, but it is common for large multinational corporations to have both short-term investments and short-term borrowing.

A short-term policy should include guidelines for managing investment, borrowing, foreign exchange, and risk management activities and should encompass all the company's operations, including foreign subsidiaries and other domestic subsidiaries that are self-financing. These guidelines accomplish several things.

Too often companies do not explore their options sufficiently, and as a result, they do not take advantage of cost savings that some forms of borrowing offer. This lack of awareness usually indicates that a company's treasurer may not be familiar with the common forms of short-term borrowing and has not factored them into an effective borrowing strategy.

8.1 Sources of Short-Term Financing

The main types of short-term borrowing alternatives that borrowers should consider include bank sources as well as money market sources. The main types of bank short-term borrowing include uncommitted and committed bank lines of credit and revolving credit agreements ("revolvers"). The latter two types can be unsecured or secured, depending on the company's financial strength and the general credit situation, which may vary from country to country. Two of these types—uncommitted lines and revolvers—are more common in the United States, whereas regular lines are more common in other parts of the world. We provide examples of several types of short-term borrowing options in Exhibit 15, with bank sources in Panel A of this exhibit and nonbank sources in Panel B. In this exhibit, we provide the primary features for each type of borrowing, including the typical users, source(s) for the alternative, the base rate for computing interest, type of compensation required, and any other comments.

| **Exhibit 15** | **Short-Term Financing Instruments** |

Panel A: Bank Sources

Source/Type	Users	Rate Base	Compensation	Other
Uncommitted line	Large corporations		None	Mainly in U.S.; limited reliability
Regular line	All sizes	Prime (U.S.) or base rate (other countries), money market, LIBOR +	Commitment fee	Common everywhere
Overdraft line	All sizes		Commitment fee	Mainly outside U.S.

(continued)

Exhibit 15	(Continued)

Panel A (Continued)

Source/Type	Users	Rate Base	Compensation	Other
Revolving credit agreement	Larger corporations		Commitment fee+ extra fees	Strongest form (primarily in U.S.)
Collateralized loan	Small, weak borrowers	Base +	Collateral	Common everywhere
Discounted receivables	Large companies	Varies	Extra fees	More overseas, but some in U.S.
Banker's acceptances	International companies	Spread over commercial paper	None	Small volume
Factoring	Smaller	Prime + +	Service fees	Special industries

Panel B: Nonbank Sources

Source/Type	Users	Rate Base	Compensation	Other
Nonbank finance companies	Small, weak borrowers	Prime + + +	Service fees	Weak credits
Commercial paper	Largest corporations	Money market sets rate	Backup line of credit, commissions +	Lowest rates for short-term funds

Uncommitted lines of credit are, as the name suggests, the weakest form of bank borrowing. A bank may offer an uncommitted line of credit for an extended period of time, but it reserves the right to refuse to honor any request for use of the line. In other words, an uncommitted line is very unstable and is only as good as the bank's desire to offer it. Therefore, companies should not rely very much on uncommitted lines. In fact, banks will not "officially" acknowledge that an uncommitted line is usable, which means that uncommitted lines cannot be shown as a financial reserve in a footnote to the company's financial statements. The primary attraction of uncommitted lines is that they do not require any compensation other than interest.

Committed lines of credit are the form of bank line of credit that most companies refer to as regular lines of credit. They are stronger than uncommitted because of the bank's formal commitment, which can be verified through an acknowledgment letter as part of the annual financial audit and can be footnoted in the company's annual report. These lines of credit are in effect for 364 days (one day short of a full year). This effectively makes sure that they are short-term liabilities, usually classified as notes payable or the equivalent, on the financial statements.

Regular lines are unsecured and are pre-payable without any penalties. The borrowing rate is a negotiated item. The most common interest rates negotiated are borrowing at the bank's prime rate or at a money market rate plus a spread. The most common money market rate is an offshore rate—the **London Interbank Offered Rate** (LIBOR), which is a Eurodollar rate—plus a spread. The spread varies depending on the borrower's credit-worthiness. Regular lines, unlike uncommitted lines, require compensation, usually in the form of a commitment fee. The fee is typically a fractional percent (e.g., ½ percent) of the full amount or the unused amount of the line, depending on bank–company negotiations.

Revolving credit agreements, which are often referred to as revolvers, are the strongest form of short-term bank borrowing facilities. They have formal legal agreements that define the aspects of the agreement. These agreements are similar to regular lines with respect to borrowing rates, compensation, and being unsecured. Revolvers differ in that they are in effect for multiple years (e.g., 3–5 years) and may have optional medium-term loan features. In addition, they are often done for much larger amounts than a regular line, and these larger amounts are spread out among more than one bank.

For companies with weak financial positions, such as those facing financial distress or that have deteriorated profitability, and many smaller companies that do not have sufficient capital, banks or other lenders (see nonbank sources in Exhibit 15) require that the company (or individual for much smaller companies) provide collateral in the form of an asset, such as a fixed asset that the company owns or high-quality receivables and inventory. These assets are pledged against the loans, and banks or other lenders file a lien against them with the state in which the loan is made. This lien becomes part of the borrower's financial record and is shown on its credit report.

8.2 Short-Term Borrowing Approaches

Given the various forms of short-term borrowing, it is essential that a borrower have a planned strategy before getting stuck in an uneconomical situation. Many borrowing companies spend too little time establishing a sound strategy for their short-term borrowing beyond making sure that they are able to borrow at all, from any source.

The major objectives of a short-term borrowing strategy include the following:

- Ensuring that there is sufficient capacity to handle peak cash needs.
- Maintaining sufficient sources of credit to be able to fund ongoing cash needs.
- Ensuring that rates obtained are cost-effective and do not substantially exceed market averages.

In addition, there are several factors that borrowers should consider as part of their short-term borrowing strategies, including the following:

- *Size and credit-worthiness.* There is no doubt that the size of the borrower dictates the options available. Larger companies can take advantage of economies of scale to access commercial paper, banker's acceptances, and so on. The size of the borrower often reflects a manufacturing company's need for short-term financing. The size of lender is also an important criterion, as larger banks have higher house or legal lending limits. Credit-worthiness of the borrower will determine the rate, compensation, or even whether the loan will be made at all.

- *Sufficient access.* Borrowers should diversify to have adequate alternatives and not be too reliant on one lender or form of lending if the amount of their lending is very large. Even so, it is typical for borrowers to use one alternative primarily, but often with more than one provider. Borrowers should be ready to go to other sources and know how to. Borrowers should not stay too long with just one source or with lowest rates. Many borrowers are usually prepared to trade off rates (somewhat) for certainty.

- *Flexibility of borrowing options.* Flexibility means the ability to manage maturities efficiently; that is, there should not be any "big" days, when significant amounts of loans mature. To do this successfully, borrowers need active maturity management, awareness of the market conditions (e.g., knowing when the market or certain maturities should be avoided), and the ability to prepay loans when unexpected cash receipts happen.

Borrowing strategies, like investment strategies, can be either passive or active. Passive strategies usually involve minimal activity with one source or type of borrowing and with little (if any) planning. This "take what you can get" strategy is often reactive in responding to immediate needs or "panic attacks." Passive strategies are characterized by steady, often routine rollovers of borrowings for the same amount of funds each time, without much comparison shopping. Passive strategies may also arise when borrowing is restricted, such as instances where borrowers are limited to one or two lenders by agreement (e.g., in a secured loan arrangement).

Active strategies are usually more flexible, reflecting planning, reliable forecasting, and seeking the best deal. With active strategies, borrowers are more in control and do not fall into the rollover "trap" that is possible with passive strategies.

Many active strategies are matching strategies. Matching borrowing strategies function in a manner similar to matching investment strategies—loans are scheduled to mature when large cash receipts are expected. These receipts can pay back the loan, so the company does not have to invest the funds at potentially lower rates than the borrowing cost, thereby creating unnecessary costs.

8.3 Asset-Based Loans

Many companies that do not have the credit quality sufficient to qualify for unsecured bank loans may borrow from financial institutions by arranging for a secured loan, where the loan is secured using assets of the company. These secured loans are often referred to as **asset-based loans**. Often the assets used in short-term secured loans are the current assets of receivables and inventory. Unlike the collateral that may be used in longer-term borrowing, asset-based loans secured by accounts receivable and inventory present a challenge for the lender because the cash flows from accounts receivable depend on the amount and timing of collections and are influenced by the business risk of the company and its customers.

Lenders of these short-term asset-based loans are protected by the existence of the collateral and by provisions in the law that may provide them with a blanket lien on current and future assets of the company. The downside of a blanket lien is that even if the asset-based loan was secured by, say, accounts receivable, the lender may have a legal interest in other assets of the company until the loan is repaid.

Besides using working capital as the security for a loan, a company can use other means to generate cash flow from these working capital accounts. For example, a company can use its accounts receivable to generate cash flow through the **assignment of accounts receivable**, which is the use of these receivables as collateral for a loan, or a company can **factor** its accounts receivable, which is selling the receivables to the factor. In an assignment arrangement, the company remains responsible for the collection of the accounts, whereas in a factoring arrangement the company is shifting the credit granting and collection process to the factor. The cost of this credit depends on the credit quality of the accounts and the costs of collection.

Like accounts receivables, inventory may be a source of cash flow through the use of the inventory as collateral, with different types of arrangements possible:

- An **inventory blanket lien**, in which the lender has a claim on some or all of the company's inventory, but the company can sell the inventory in the ordinary course of business.

- A **trust receipt arrangement**, in which the lender requires the company to certify that the goods are segregated and held in trust, with proceeds of any sale remitted to the lender immediately.

- A **warehouse receipt arrangement** is similar to the trust receipt arrangement, but there is a third party (i.e., a warehouse company) that supervises the inventory.

The cost of asset-based loans security by inventory depends on the length of time it takes to sell the goods.

8.4 Computing the Costs of Borrowing

In carrying out a sound short-term borrowing strategy, one of the key decisions is selecting the most cost-effective form of short-term loan. However, this selection is often not a simple task, because each of the major forms has to be adjusted to be on a common basis for comparability. The fundamental rule is to compute the total cost of the form of borrowing and divide that number by the total amount of loan you received (i.e., net proceeds), adjusted for any discounting or compensating balances.

For example, in the case of a line of credit that requires a commitment fee,[10] the cost of the line of credit is

$$\text{Cost} = \frac{\text{Interest} + \text{Commitment fee}}{\text{Loan amount}}$$

On the other hand, if the interest rate is stated as "all inclusive" such that the amount borrowed includes the interest, as may be the case in a banker's acceptance, the interest is compared with the net proceeds when determining the cost:

$$\text{Cost} = \frac{\text{Interest}}{\text{Net proceeds}} = \frac{\text{Interest}}{\text{Loan amount} - \text{Interest}}$$

If there are dealer's fees and other fees, the expenses beyond the interest must be considered when determining the cost. For example, if a borrowing involves a dealer's fee and a backup fee and is quoted as all inclusive, the cost is

$$\text{Cost} = \frac{\text{Interest} + \text{Dealer's commission} + \text{Backup costs}}{\text{Loan amount} - \text{Interest}}$$

The key is to compare the interest and fees paid with the net proceeds of the loan. If the loan is for a period less than a year, then we annualize accordingly.

EXAMPLE 7

Computing the Effective Cost of Short-Term Borrowing Alternatives

You are asked to select one of the following choices as the best offer for borrowing $5,000,000 for one month:

1 Drawing down on a line of credit at 6.5 percent with a 1/2 percent commitment fee on the full amount. **Note:** One-twelfth of the cost of the commitment fee (which gives an option to borrow any time during the year) is allocated to the first month.

2 A banker's acceptance at 6.75 percent, an all-inclusive rate.

3 Commercial paper at 6.15 percent with a dealer's commission of 1/8 percent and a backup line cost of 1/4 percent, both of which would be assessed on the $5 million of commercial paper issued.

Solution:

Line of credit cost:

---

10 A commitment fee is a fee paid to the lender in return for the legal commitment to lend funds in the future.

$$\text{Line cost} = \frac{\text{Interest} + \text{Commitment fee}}{\text{Usable loan amount}} \times 12$$

$$= \frac{(0.065 \times \$5,000,000 \times 1/12) + (0.005 \times \$5,000,000 \times 1/12)}{\$5,000,000} \times 12$$

$$= \frac{\$27,083.33 + 2,083.33}{\$5,000,000} \times 12 = 0.07 \text{ or } 7 \text{ percent}$$

Banker's acceptance cost:

$$\text{BA cost} = \frac{\text{Interest}}{\text{Net proceeds}} \times 12$$

$$= \frac{0.0675 \times \$5,000,000 \times 1/12}{\$5,000,000 - (0.0675 \times \$5,000,000 \times 1/12)} \times 12$$

$$= \frac{\$28,125}{\$4,971,875} \times 12 = 0.0679 \text{ or } 6.79 \text{ percent}$$

Commercial paper cost (quoted as nominal rate at a discount):

CP cost

$$= \frac{\text{Interest} + \text{Dealer's commissions} + \text{Backup costs}}{\text{Net proceeds}} \times 12$$

$$= \frac{(0.0615 \times \$5,000,000 \times 1/12) + (0.00125 \times \$5,000,000 \times 1/12) + (0.0025 \times \$5,000,000 \times 1/12)}{\$5,000,000 - (0.0615 \times \$5,000,000 \times 1/12)} \times 12$$

$$= \frac{\$25,625 + 520.83 + 1041.67}{\$5,000,000 - 25,625} \times 12 = 0.0656 \text{ or } 6.56 \text{ percent}$$

We have simplified this cost analysis by assuming a loan for one month, using a factor of 1/12 to determine the interest and a factor of 12 to annualize. For specific arrangements for which the cost is determined using a 365-day or 360-day year, the appropriate adjustment would be required.

As the results show, the commercial paper alternative comes out with the lowest effective cost, and the line of credit has the highest effective cost. The commitment fee that was payable on the full line added more additional costs than the additional fees and discounting effects added in the other two options.

Line cost	7.00 percent
Banker's acceptance cost	6.79 percent
Commercial paper cost	6.56 percent

SUMMARY

In this reading, we considered a key aspect of financial management: the management of a company's working capital. This aspect of finance is a critical one in that it ensures, if done effectively, that the company will stay solvent and remain in business. If done improperly, the results can be disastrous for the company.

Working capital management covers a wide range of activities, most of which are focused on or involve the company's cash levels. Competing uses for the company's cash, which is often a scarce resource, create the need for an efficient method of handling the short-term financing of company activities.

Major points that were covered in this reading:

- Understanding how to evaluate a company's liquidity position.
- Calculating and interpreting operating and cash conversion cycles.
- Evaluating overall working capital effectiveness of a company and comparing it with other peer companies.
- Identifying the components of a cash forecast to be able to prepare a short-term (i.e., up to one year) cash forecast.
- Understanding the common types of short-term investments, and computing comparable yields on securities.
- Measuring the performance of a company's accounts receivable function.
- Measuring the financial performance of a company's inventory management function.
- Measuring the performance of a company's accounts payable function.
- Evaluating the short-term financing choices available to a company and recommending a financing method.

Working capital management is an integral part of the financial management of a company because many short-term activities have effects on long-term financial decisions. Having an effective short-term financial strategy, for example, allows a company to plan ahead with the confidence that its short-term concerns are being handled properly. Perhaps unlike other areas of finance, short-term finance has more qualitative features, making each company's case somewhat different from another's. This unique nature, combined with the short time frame associated with this aspect of finance, makes short-term finance a dynamic, challenging activity.

PRACTICE PROBLEMS

1   Suppose a company has a current ratio of 2.5 times and a quick ratio of 1.5 times. If the company's current liabilities are €100 million, the amount of inventory is *closest* to:

    A   €50 million.

    B   €100 million.

    C   €150 million.

2   Given the following financial statement data, calculate the operating cycle for this company.

	In Millions ($)
Credit sales	25,000
Cost of goods sold	20,000
Accounts receivable	2,500
Inventory—Beginning balance	2,000
Inventory—Ending balance	2,300
Accounts payable	1,700

The operating cycle for this company is *closest* to:

    A   42.0 days.

    B   47.9 days.

    C   78.5 days.

3   Given the following financial statement data, calculate the net operating cycle for this company.

	In Millions ($)
Credit sales	40,000
Cost of goods sold	30,000
Accounts receivable	3,000
Inventory—Beginning balance	1,500
Inventory—Ending balance	2,000
Accounts payable	4,000

The net operating cycle of this company is *closest* to:

    A   3.8 days.

    B   24.3 days.

    C   51.7 days.

4   The bond equivalent yield for a 182-day U.S. Treasury bill that has a price of $9,725 per $10,000 face value is *closest* to:

    A   5.44%.

B 5.53%.

C 5.67%.

5   A company increasing its credit terms for customers from 1/10, net 30 to 1/10, net 60 will *most likely* experience:

A   an increase in cash on hand.

B   a higher level of uncollectible accounts.

C   an increase in the average collection period.

6   Suppose a company uses trade credit with the terms of 2/10, net 50. If the company pays its account on the 50th day, the effective borrowing cost of skipping the discount on day 10 is *closest* to:

A   14.9%.

B   15.0%.

C   20.2%.

7   William Jones is evaluating three possible means of borrowing $1 million for one month:

● Drawing down on a line of credit at 7.2 percent with a 1/2 percent commitment fee on the full amount with no compensating balances.

● A banker's acceptance at 7.1 percent, an all-inclusive rate.

● Commercial paper at 6.9 percent with a dealer's commission of 1/4 percent and a backup line cost of 1/3 percent, both of which would be assessed on the $1 million of commercial paper issued.

Which of these forms of borrowing results in the lowest cost of credit?

A   Line of credit.

B   Banker's acceptance.

C   Commercial paper.

The following information relates to Questions 8–12

Mary Gonzales is evaluating companies in the office supply industry and has compiled the following information:

| Company | 20X1 | | 20X2 | |
	Credit Sales ($)	Average Receivables Balance ($)	Credit Sales ($)	Average Receivables Balance ($)
A	5.0 million	1.0 million	6.0 million	1.2 million
B	3.0 million	1.2 million	4.0 million	1.5 million
C	2.5 million	0.8 million	3.0 million	1.0 million
D	0.5 million	0.1 million	0.6 million	0.2 million
Industry	25.0 million	5.0 million	28.0 million	5.4 million

8   Which of the companies had the highest number of days of receivables for the year 20X1?

    A   Company A.

    B   Company B.

    C   Company C.

9 Which of the companies has the lowest accounts receivable turnover in the year 20X2?

    A   Company A.

    B   Company B.

    C   Company D.

10 The industry average receivables collection period:

    A   increased from 20X1 to 20X2.

    B   decreased from 20X1 to 20X2.

    C   did not change from 20X1 to 20X2.

11 Which of the companies reduced the average time it took to collect on accounts receivable from 20X1 to 20X2?

    A   Company B.

    B   Company C.

    C   Company D.

12 Mary determined that Company A had an operating cycle of 100 days in 20X2, whereas Company D had an operating cycle of 145 days for the same fiscal year. This means that:

    A   Company D's inventory turnover is less than that of Company A.

    B   Company D's inventory turnover is greater than that of Company A.

    C   Company D's cash conversion cycle is shorter than that of Company A.

SOLUTIONS

1 B is correct.

Current ratio = Current assets/Current Liabilities = Current assets/ €100 million = 2.5

Therefore, current assets = €250 million

Quick ratio = (Current assets – Inventory)/ Current Liabilities = (€250 million – Inventory)/€100 million = 1.5

Therefore, Inventory = **€100 million**

2 C is correct.

Number of days of inventory = $2,300/($20,000/365) = 41.975 days

Number of days of receivables = $2,500/($25,000/365) = 36.5 days

Operating cycle = 41.975 + 36.5 days = **78.475 days**

Note: The net operating cycle is 47.9 days.

Purchases = $20,000 + $2,300 – $2,000 = $20,300

Number of days of payables = $1,700/($20,300/365) = 30.567 days

The net operating cycle is 78.475 – 30.567 = 47.908 days

3 A is correct.

Number of days of inventory = $2,000/($30,000/365) = 24.333 days

Number of days of receivables = $3,000/($40,000/365) = 27.375 days

Operating cycle = 24.333 + 27.375 days = 51.708 days

Purchases = $30,000 + $2,000 – $1,500 = $30,500

Number of days of payables = $4,000/($30,500/365) = 47.869 days

The net operating cycle is 51.708 – 47.869 = **3.839 days**

4 C is correct.

Bond equivalent yield = [($10,000 – 9,725)/$9,725] × (365/182) = **5.671 percent**

5 C is correct. A higher level of uncollectible accounts may occur, but a longer average collection period will certainly occur.

6 C is correct.

$$\text{Cost} = \left(1 + \frac{0.02}{0.98}\right)^{365/40} - 1 = 20.24 \text{ percent}$$

7 B is correct.

$$\text{Line cost} = \frac{\text{Interest} + \text{Commitment fee}}{\text{Net Proceed}} \times 12$$

$$= \frac{(0.072 \times \$1,000,000 \times 1/12) + (0.005 \times \$1,000,000 \times 1/12)}{\$1,000,000} \times 12$$

$$= \frac{\$6,000 + 416.67}{\$1,000,000} \times 12 = 0.077 \text{ or } 7.7 \text{ percent}$$

$$\text{Banker's acceptance cost} = \frac{\text{Interest}}{\text{Net Proceed}} \times 12$$

$$= \frac{(0.071 \times \$1,000,000 \times 1/12)}{\$1,000,000 - (0.071 \times \$1,000,000 \times 1/12)} \times 12$$

$$= \frac{\$5,916.67}{\$994,083.33} \times 12 = 0.0714 \text{ or } 7.14 \text{ percent}$$

$$\text{Commercial paper cost} = \frac{\text{Interest} + \text{Dealer's commission} + \text{Backup costs}}{\text{Net proceed}} \times 12$$

$$= \frac{(0.069 \times \$1,000,000 \times 1/12) + (0.0025 \times \$1,000,000 \times 1/12) + (0.003333 \times \$1,000,000 \times 1/12)}{\$1,000,000 - (0.069 \times \$1,000,000 \times 1/12)} \times 1/12$$

$$= \frac{\$5,750 + 208.33 + 277.78}{\$1,000,000 - 5,750} \times 12 = 0.0753 \text{ or } 7.53 \text{ percent}$$

8   B is correct.

Company A: $1.0 million/($5.0 million/365) = 73.0 days

Company B: $1.2 million/($3.0 million/365) = 146.0 days

Company C: $0.8 million/($2.5 million/365) = 116.8 days

Company D: $0.1 million/($0.5 million/365) = 73.0 days

9   B is correct.

Company A: $6.0 million/$1.2 million = 5.00

Company B: $4.0 million/$1.5 million = 2.67

Company C: $3.0 million/$1.0 million = 3.00

Company D: $0.6 million/$0.2 million = 3.00

10   B is correct.

20X1: 73 days

20X2: 70.393

Note: If the number of days decreased from 20X1 to 20X2, the receivable turnover increased.

11   A is correct.

Company B increased its accounts receivable (A/R) turnover and reduced its number of days of receivables between 20X1 and 20X2.

Company	20X1		20X2	
	A/R Turnover	Number of Days of Receivables	A/R Turnover	Number of Days of Receivables
A	5.000	73.000	5.000	73.000
B	2.500	146.000	2.667	136.875
C	3.125	116.800	3.000	121.667
D	5.000	73.000	3.000	121.667

12 B is correct.

Company A number of days of inventory = 100 − 73 = 27 days

Company D number of days of inventory = 145 − 121.67 = 23.33 days

Company A's turnover = 365/27 = 13.5 times

Company D's inventory turnover = 365/23.3 = 15.6 times

The Corporate Governance of Listed Companies: A Manual for Investors

by Kurt Schacht, CFA, James C. Allen, CFA, and Matthew Orsagh, CFA, CIPM

LEARNING OUTCOMES

Mastery	The candidate should be able to:
☐	**a.** define corporate governance;
☐	**b.** describe practices related to board and committee independence, experience, compensation, external consultants, and frequency of elections, and determine whether they are supportive of shareowner protection;
☐	**c.** describe board independence and explain the importance of independent board members in corporate governance;
☐	**d.** identify factors that an analyst should consider when evaluating the qualifications of board members;
☐	**e.** describe responsibilities of the audit, compensation, and nominations committees and identify factors an investor should consider when evaluating the quality of each committee;
☐	**f.** explain provisions that should be included in a strong corporate code of ethics;
☐	**g.** evaluate, from a shareowner's perspective, company policies related to voting rules, shareowner sponsored proposals, common stock classes, and takeover defenses.

INTRODUCTION

The past decade of business around the world has highlighted the role that corporate governance practices play in maintaining viable entities and safeguarding investors' interests. The governance failures at Enron Corporation, Worldcom, Parmalat, and others in the early 2000s and the more recent troubles at the Bear Stearns Companies, Lehman Brothers Holdings, and Northern Rock illustrate the risks posed by corporate governance breakdowns. The global governance problems in the early part of this decade were characterized by a lack of transparency and internal controls. Many have pointed to inadequate risk management systems and to remuneration systems discon-nected from the long-term strategic interests of the company as the main governance issues of the recent financial crises. In both cases, a lack of understanding of the risks being taken and a lack of overall industry expertise by boards played a crucial role. Losses of trillions of dollars of investors' capital around the world illustrated that the existing set of corporate checks and balances on insiders' activities have not protected shareowners from the misplaced priorities of board members, the manipulation and misappropriation of company resources by management, or the misunderstanding of risk (or failure to adequately measure risk) by management and other groups that exercised significant influence over a company's affairs.

It was with the goal of educating and empowering the investor that this manual was first produced. It endeavors to provide investors a way of assessing a company's corporate governance policies and the associated risks.[1]

Since the first edition of this manual in 2005, many countries, industry groups, and constituencies have proposed or created new or amended corporate governance codes in response to the wide-ranging effects of recent corporate failures on global markets. Many of these codes established internal controls or set an ethical tone that focused on investors' interests. Although these government-mandated and voluntary industry codes helped restore a degree of investor confidence in the markets, they provided only part of the answer. As we have witnessed in subsequent years, inves-tors also must take the initiative to evaluate the presence—or absence—of corporate governance safeguards, as well as corporate cultures, at the companies in which they invest. In many cases such initiatives were not adequately taken, and governance safeguards were not effectively installed at a number of institutions—mainly financial institutions—which contributed to the crisis that has enveloped the global financial system, destroying trillions of dollars of public company market capitalization and dealing another serious blow to investor confidence in the integrity of the markets.

Therefore, the CFA Institute Centre for Financial Market Integrity, through the work of its Global Corporate Governance Task Force, has updated the original manual. We hope that all interested parties—existing shareowners, analysts, and investors—can use this information as part of their analysis of a company and make decisions about investing in that company, in light of their particular investment perspectives, objectives, and risk-tolerance levels.

The manual does not provide a set of best practices, nor does it take positions on the best corporate governance structures for investors. Instead, its purpose is to alert investors to the primary corporate governance issues and risks affecting companies and to highlight some of the factors they should consider when making investment decisions.

Issuers of financial securities may also find this manual useful as a reference tool for determining what corporate governance issues are important to investors. We hope that this manual will raise awareness of the governance standards within the investment community.

The Importance of Corporate Governance to Investors

The most effective and productive corporate governance structures rely on active and prudent shareowner engagement. Benjamin Graham and David Dodd recognized the direct correlation between active ownership and strong governance as early as the 1930s, advising that:

---

1 See these and other publications related to corporate governance issues at www.cfainstitute.org: *The Compensation of Senior Executives at Listed Companies; Environmental, Social, and Governance Factors at Listed Companies; Shareowner Rights across the Markets.*

> *The choice of a common stock is a single act, its ownership is a continuing process. Certainly there is just as much reason to exercise care and judgment in being a shareholder as in becoming one.*[2]

A number of studies published in recent years reinforce the link between good corporate governance and strong profitability and investment performance. For example, a joint study by Institutional Shareholder Services (ISS) and Georgia State University[3] found that the best-governed companies—as measured by the ISS Corporate Governance Quotient—had mean returns on investment and equity that were, respectively, 18.7 percent and 23.8 percent better than those of poorly governed companies during the year reviewed.[4] Research carried out by employees of the California Public Employees Retirement System (CalPERS) on the effects of the system's Focus List suggests that efforts by investment funds to improve the governance of companies that are considered poorly governed also produce returns in excess of market performance.[5] For this reason, one would expect investors to reward companies that have superior governance with higher valuations. Indeed, a study of U.S. markets by Paul Gompers of Harvard University and colleagues from Harvard and the University of Pennsylvania[6] found that portfolios of companies with strong shareowner-rights protections outperformed portfolios of companies with weaker protections by 8.5 percent per year. A similar study in Europe found annual disparities of 3.0 percent.[7]

Academics and investors have continued to probe the link between corporate governance and performance. Some recent studies delve into specialized areas of corporate governance and performance, such as the effects of hedge fund activism targeting companies in need of improved corporate governance.[8] Some studies have found that the mixed results previously found in determining the link between governance and performance may have something to do with the difficulty of defining exactly what constitutes good corporate governance at a level that is measurable by researchers and investors.[9]

This search for the link between governance and performance is not limited to developed markets. Even before the collapse of Enron, Amar Gill, an analyst at Credit Lyonnais Securities Asia Group, found that investors in emerging markets

---

2 Benjamin Graham and David Dodd, *Security Analysis*, 6th ed. (New York: McGraw Hill, 2009):540.

3 Lawrence D. Brown and Marcus Caylor, "Corporate Governance Study: The Correlation between Corporate Governance and Company Performance" (Institutional Shareholder Services, 2004).

4 See also Sanjai Bhagat and Brian J. Bolton, "Corporate Governance and Firm Performance," working paper (June 2007).

5 Mark Anson, Ted White, and Ho Ho, "Good Corporate Governance Works: More Evidence from CalPERS," *Journal of Asset Management* (February 2004). Also see "The Shareholder Wealth Effects of CalPERS' Focus List" by the same authors, published in the *Journal of Applied Corporate Finance* (Winter 2003):8–17. The authors found that between 1992 and 2002, publication of the CalPERS Focus List, which identifies underperforming companies, and efforts to improve the corporate governance of companies on that list generated one-year average cumulative excess returns of 59.4 percent. Cumulative excess return was defined as the cumulative "return earned over and above the risk-adjusted return required for each public corporation."

6 Paul A. Gompers, Joy L. Ishii, and Andrew Metrick, "Corporate Governance and Equity Prices," *Quarterly Journal of Economics* (revised January 2009). The authors compared the investment performance of some 1,500 U.S.-listed companies with a corporate governance index that the authors constructed from 24 distinct governance rules. Also see Lucian Bebchuk, Alma Cohen, and Allen Ferrell, "What Matters in Corporate Governance," *Review of Financial Studies* (February 2009).

7 Rob Bauer and Nadja Guenster, "Good Corporate Governance Pays Off!" research report (2003). This study used Deminor ratings of corporate governance as the basis for determining which companies perform better on the stock market relative to corporate governance quality.

8 Alon Brav, Wei Jiang, Randall S. Thomas, and Frank Partnoy, "Hedge Fund Activism, Corporate Governance and Firm Performance," *Journal of Finance* (May 2008).

9 David F. Larker, Scott A. Richardson, and A. Irem Tuna, "Corporate Governance, Accounting Outcomes, and Organizational Performance," *Accounting Review* (October 2007).

overwhelmingly prefer companies with good governance.[10] Of the 100 largest emerging market companies CLSA Group followed, those with the best governance—based on management discipline, transparency, independence, accountability, responsibility, fairness, and social responsibility—generated five-year returns well above average.[11] CLSA Group continues to focus research on corporate governance in emerging markets because its clients are investors that believe strong corporate governance can add value in the markets in which they invest.

Studies linking corporate governance to performance (and attempting to disprove the link of governance to performance) are continually being published. Recently, in the wake of the crisis in global markets, a number of authors have tried to look back and, using corporate governance practices as a lens through which to evaluate a company's practices, draw lessons from the governance failures of past years. These authors urge investors to ask pertinent governance questions of the companies in which they invest.[12]

We believe good corporate governance leads to better results for companies and for investors. Corporate governance, therefore, is a factor that investors cannot ignore but should consider in seeking the best possible results for themselves and their clients.

DEFINITIONS

In this manual, we have used the following definitions:

Corporate Governance

Corporate governance is the system of internal controls and procedures by which individual companies are managed. It provides a framework that defines the rights, roles, and responsibilities of various groups—management, board, controlling shareowners, and minority or noncontrolling shareowners—within an organization.

At its core, corporate governance is the arrangement of checks, balances, and incentives a company needs in order to minimize and manage the conflicting interests between insiders and external shareowners. Its purpose is to prevent one group from expropriating the cash flows and assets of one or more other groups.

In general, good corporate governance practices seek to ensure that:

- board members act in the best interests of shareowners, although in some jurisdictions, good corporate governance is tied to the interests of a broader *stakeholder* group (e.g., labor groups, society at large);

- the company acts in a lawful and ethical manner in its dealings with all stakeholders and their representatives;

- all shareowners have a right to participate in the governance of the company and receive fair treatment from the board and management and all rights of shareowners and other stakeholders are clearly delineated and communicated;

---

10 Amar Gill, "Corporate Governance in Emerging Markets—Saints and Sinners: Who's Got Religion?" Credit Lyonnais Securities Asia (April 2001). Gill points out that CLSA assigned corporate governance ratings to 495 companies in 25 markets.
11 The five-year returns reported by Gill amounted to 930 percent for the well-governed large-cap companies in emerging markets, versus the total average return of 388 percent for large-cap companies in emerging markets during that period.
12 See, for example, Julie Hudson, "Corporate Governance and Capital Markets," UBS (2008).

- the board and its committees are structured to act independently from management and individuals or entities that have control over management and other nonshareowner groups;

- appropriate controls and procedures are in place covering management's activities in running the day-to-day operations of the company;

- the company's governance activities, as well as its operating and financial activities, are consistently reported to shareowners in a fair, accurate, timely, reliable, relevant, complete, and verifiable manner.

How well a company achieves these goals depends in large part on 1) the adequacy of the company's corporate governance structure and 2) the strength of the shareowner's voice in corporate governance matters through shareowner voting rights. This manual focuses on these two areas as the way to evaluate the corporate governance practices of companies.

Independence

A number of national corporate governance codes and stock exchange–based rules prescribe factors to consider in determining the independence of board and board committee members. Each company, each code of corporate governance, and each market will have its own definition of independence, so investors need to be able to define independence and its importance for themselves. Generally, to be considered independent, a board member must not have a material business or other relationship with the following individuals or groups:

- the company or its subsidiaries or members of its group, including former employees and executives and their family members;

- individuals, groups, or other entities that can exert significant influence on the company's management, such as controlling individuals, controlling families, or governments;

- executive managers, including family members;

- company advisers (including external auditors) and their families;

- any entity that has a cross-directorship relationship with the company.

Shareowners also need to understand how other relationships a director may have with a company may compromise his/her independence. Shareowners should understand whether directors

- have recently had material business relationships with a company, or

- represent a company with substantial voting rights in the company in question.

Board Members

The term "board member" (which in some jurisdictions is termed "director") in this manual refers to all individuals who sit on the board (defined below), including executive board members, independent board members, and nonindependent board members.

Executive Board Members

This term refers to the members of executive management. In a *unitary* board (or "committee system"), executive board members also serve as members of the board. In a "two-tiered" board, these individuals are part of only the management board. These individuals are not considered independent.

Independent Board Members

An independent board member is an individual who meets the qualifications listed under "independence."

Nonindependent Board Members

Individuals in this category may represent interests that conflict with those of the majority of shareowners. This category may include board members who are affiliated with individuals or entities that have control over management, who are part of a cross-directorship arrangement with another listed company, or who are representatives of labor organizations.

Shareowners should also be cognizant of any individual, government entity, or organization that may qualify as a "shadow director"—namely, any holder of a controlling share of the company who is not a named director but who has a great deal of influence over management and the board. These individuals may be large stakeholders, sovereign wealth funds, governments, or other interested parties who may have motivations that are different from those of shareowners.

Board

The term "board" in this manual refers to a "supervisory" type of board (or "board of corporate auditors" in Japan) in countries with the two-tiered board structure. In countries that use a unitary board, the term refers to the board of directors. In most jurisdictions, corporate structures take the form of one or the other of these types, but in some countries, such as France and Japan, companies have the option of choosing which of the two structures to use.

Two-Tiered (Dual) Board

Common in some parts of Europe—Germany, the Netherlands, Austria, and Denmark—the two-tiered board structure has two elements, the management board and the supervisory board:

Management Board

The management board consists exclusively of executive managers. It is charged, in consultation with the supervisory board, with running the company on a daily basis and setting the corporate strategy for the company. Its members do *not* sit on the company's supervisory board.

Supervisory Board

The supervisory board is charged with overseeing and advising the company's management board.

Corporate Auditors System

In Japan, the two-tiered board structure is called the "corporate auditors system" and is used by most large Japanese companies. The system includes 1) directors who are elected by shareowners and are responsible for business decisions and 2) a board consisting of corporate auditors, including at least one full-time corporate auditor. At least half the members of the board of corporate auditors must be outside auditors. These corporate auditors are elected separately by shareowners and are charged with auditing the performance of the board.

Unitary Board

In a unitary board structure, the board may include executive, nonexecutive, and independent board members. The board oversees and advises management and helps set corporate strategy, although in many jurisdictions, it does not engage in corporate decision making except in such matters as mergers, acquisitions, divestitures, and sale of the company. Jurisdictions increasingly require independent board members to constitute at least a majority of the board.

Committee System

The committee system is most often used in unitary board structures to delegate specific tasks to committees of the board, such as audit, nominations, and compensation committees—all of which must have at least three members, and a majority of them must be either independent board members or nonexecutive board members. Committees are asked to look at particular matters in more detail than the whole board, but responsibility for decision making remains with the board as a whole.

Company

The "company" as used here is the corporate organization in which the shareowners have an ownership position and in which investors are considering an investment.

Investors

This term refers to all individuals or institutions considering investment opportunities in shares and other securities of the company.

Shareowners

The term "shareowners," unlike the term "investors," refers only to those individuals, institutions, or entities that own shares of common or ordinary stock in the company in question.

SUMMARY OF CORPORATE GOVERNANCE CONSIDERATIONS

The Board

Investors and Shareowners should:

- *determine whether a company's board has, at a minimum, a majority of independent board members;*
- *determine whether board members have the qualifications the company needs for the challenges it faces;*
- *determine whether the board and its committees have budgetary authority to hire independent third-party consultants without having to receive approval from management;*
- *determine whether board members are elected annually or whether the company has adopted an election process that staggers board member elections;*

- *investigate whether the company engages in outside business relationships (related-party transactions) with management, board members, or individuals associated with management or board members for goods and services on behalf of the company;*
- *determine whether the board has established a committee of independent board members, including those with recent and relevant experience in finance and accounting, to oversee the audit of the company's financial reports;*
- *determine whether the company has a committee of independent board members charged with setting executive remuneration/compensation;*
- *determine whether the company has a nominations committee of independent board members that is responsible for recruiting board members;*
- *determine whether the board has other committees that are responsible for overseeing management's activities in select areas, such as corporate governance, mergers and acquisitions, legal matters, risk management, and environmental health and safety issues;*
- *evaluate the communications the board has with shareowners and the ability shareowners have to meet with the board.*

Management

Investors and Shareowners should:

- *determine whether the company has adopted a code of ethics and whether the company's actions indicate a commitment to an appropriate ethical framework;*
- *determine whether the company permits insiders (management or board members) or their family members to use company assets for personal reasons;*
- *analyze both the amounts paid to key executives for managing the company's affairs and the manner in which compensation is provided to determine whether the compensation paid to its executives 1) is commensurate with the executives' responsibilities and performance and 2) provides appropriate incentives;*
- *inquire into the size, purpose, means of financing, and duration of share-repurchase programs and price-stabilization efforts;*
- *evaluate the level of communications that management has with shareowners and the ability shareowners have to meet with the management;*
- *determine whether management has adequately communicated its long-term strategic plans to investors and shareowners;*
- *determine whether the incentive structures of management are aligned with the interests of shareowners and are tied to the execution of the long-term strategic plan, or whether they may encourage undue risk-taking that may be harmful to the interests of shareowners;*

- *determine whether management adequately understands and communicates how nonfinancial key performance indicators and the environmental, social, and governance-related risks and opportunities are being handled by the company;*

- *determine whether the company communicates and discloses management's financial and nonfinancial performance in a consistent and transparent manner.*

Shareowner Rights

Investors and Shareowners should:

- *examine the company's ownership structure to determine whether it has different classes of common shares that separate the voting rights of those shares from their economic value;*

- *determine whether the company permits shareowners to vote their shares prior to scheduled meetings of shareowners regardless of whether the shareowners are able to attend the meetings in person;*

- *determine whether shareowners are able to cast confidential votes;*

- *determine whether shareowners are allowed to cast the cumulative number of votes allotted to their shares for one or a limited number of board nominees ("cumulative voting");*

- *determine whether shareowners have the right to approve changes to corporate structures and policies that may alter the relationship between shareowners and the company;*

- *determine whether the board must receive shareowner approval for important decisions, such as adoption of a poison pill and some merger agreements, and whether a simple majority or super-majority vote is required;*

- *determine whether shareowners are allowed to elect directors according to a "majority voting" standard;*

- *determine whether shareowners have either a binding or advisory "say on pay" concerning management remuneration;*

- *determine whether shareowners enjoy preemption rights that guard against dilutive instruments such as new share issuances or convertible securities;*

- *determine whether and in what circumstances shareowners are permitted to recommend director nominees to the board or place their own nominees on the proxy ballot;*

- *determine whether and in what circumstances shareowners may submit proposals for consideration at the company's annual general meeting;*

- *determine whether the board and management are required to implement proposals that shareowners approve;*

- *determine whether the corporate governance code and other legal statutes of the jurisdiction in which the company is headquartered permit shareowners to take legal action or seek regulatory action to protect and enforce their ownership rights;*

- *carefully evaluate the structure of an existing or proposed takeover defense and analyze how it could affect the value of shares in a normal market environment and in the event of a takeover bid;*
- *understand that the actions of other shareowners are governance issues they need to consider with the same degree of interest as they do the actions of the board and management.*

THE BOARD

Board members have a duty to make decisions based on what ultimately is best for the long-term interests of shareowners. There has been much discussion in recent years about the needs for boards and management to balance the short-term operations of a company with a long-term sustainable strategic outlook.[13] Although shareowners with a short holding period may indeed be interested in corporate governance, long-term shareowners (those that hold shares for years) are more likely to incorporate corporate governance factors into their investment analyses. The reason is that governance aspects often affect company value over a long time frame. To act in the best interests of shareowners, board members need a combination of four things: independence, experience, resources, and accurate information about the company's financial and operating position.

First: A board should be composed of at least a majority of independent board members with the autonomy to act independently from management. Rather than simply voting with management, board members should bring with them a commitment to take an unbiased approach in making decisions that will benefit the company and shareowners.

Second: Board members who have appropriate experience and expertise relevant to the company's business are best able to evaluate what is in the best interests of shareowners. Depending on the nature of the business, specialized expertise by at least some board members may be required.

Third: Internal mechanisms are needed to support the independent work of the board. Such mechanisms include the authority to hire the external auditor and other outside consultants without management's intervention or approval. This mechanism alone provides the board with the ability to obtain expert help in specialized areas, helps it to circumvent potential areas of conflict with management, and overall, helps preserve the integrity of the board's independent oversight function.

Fourth: Directors must have access to complete and accurate information about the financial position of the company and its underlying value drivers to enable them to steer the company in the best long-term interests of shareowners.

All of these points and how investors can evaluate them are discussed in more detail in the following subsections.

Board Independence

Investors should determine whether a company's board has, at a minimum, a majority of independent board members.

---

13 See *Breaking the Short-Term Cycle*, Charlottesville, VA: CFA Institute Centre (July 2006): www.cfapubs. org/loi/ccb.

What Is Independence?   Independence, as it relates to board members, refers to the degree to which they are not biased or otherwise controlled by company management or other groups who exert control over management. Factors to consider in determining whether a board member meets this definition are provided in the "Definitions" section of the "Introduction" to this manual.

Implications for Investors   A board that is not predominantly independent, or a committee that is not completely independent, may be more likely than independent individuals to make decisions that unfairly or improperly benefit the interests of management and those who have influence over management. These decisions may also be detrimental to the long-term interests of shareowners.

Things to Consider   Investors should determine whether

- independent board members constitute, at a minimum, a majority of the board. A board with this makeup is more likely to limit undue influence of management over the affairs of the board;

- independent board members are meeting regularly without management present—ideally at least annually—and routinely reporting on their activities to shareowners. Such meetings permit board members to discuss issues facing the company without influence from executive board members;

- the board chair also holds the title of chief executive. Combining the two positions may give undue influence to executive board members and impair the ability and willingness of board members to exercise their independent judgment. Several national corporate governance codes require the separation of these two positions. Many jurisdictions consider the separation of the chair and CEO positions a best practice because it ensures that the board agenda is set by an independent voice uninfluenced by the CEO;

- independent board members have a lead member if the board chair is not independent. Some companies have kept the combined chair/CEO format but have named a "lead independent director" as a compromise. In such cases, shareowners must determine whether the lead director is able to set or influence the board agenda and is truly a chief spokesperson for shareowners;

- the board chair is a former chief executive of the company. If so, this arrangement could impair the board's ability to act independently of undue management influence and in the best interests of shareowners. Such a situation also increases the risk that the chair may hamper efforts to undo the mistakes made by him/her as chief executive;

- members of the board are aligned with a company supplier or customer or are aligned with a manager or adviser to the company's share-option or pension plan. In some cases, a company with a large number of suppliers, customers, and advisers may need to nominate individuals to the board who are aligned with these entities to ensure that it has the expertise it needs to make reasoned decisions. In such instance, investors should determine whether such board members recuse themselves on issues that may create a conflict.

Where to find information about the independence of the board and its committees: In most jurisdictions, companies disclose the names, credentials, and company affiliations of existing board members either in their annual reports to shareowners or in their annual proxy statements to shareowners. Companies often devote a special section in their annual reports to a discussion of the issues confronted by the board and board committees during the previous year. In addition, the websites of many listed companies provide information about board members' independence.

Some specialty research providers focus exclusively on corporate governance issues and are a good source for such information as director independence and shareowner rights.

Board Member Qualifications and Ability to Serve as Shareowner Representative

Investors should determine whether board members have the qualifications the company needs for the challenges it faces.

Implications for Investors   Investors should assess whether individual board members have the knowledge and experience that is required to advise management in light of the particularities of the company, its businesses, and the competitive environment. Board members who lack the skills, knowledge, or expertise to conduct a meaningful review of the company's activities are more likely to defer to management when making decisions. Such reliance on management threatens the duty of board members to consider shareowner interests first. Moreover, having board members who are not capable of in-depth evaluation of the issues affecting the company's business could threaten the company's overall performance. (See also the subsection "Nominations Committee" in this section.)

Things to Consider   Among the factors investors should consider when analyzing board members' qualifications[14] are whether the board members

- are able to make informed decisions about the company's future with regard to finance, accounting, business, and law;
- are able to act with care and competence as a result of relevant expertise or understanding of
  - the principal technologies, products, or services offered in the company's business,
  - financial operations,
  - legal matters,
  - accounting,
  - auditing,
  - strategic planning, and
  - the risks—financial risks and operational risks—that the company assumes as part of its business operations;
- have made public statements that can provide an indication of their ethical perspectives;
- have had legal or regulatory problems as a result of working for or serving on the board of another company;
- have experience serving on other boards, particularly with companies known for having good corporate governance practices;
- serve on boards for a number of other companies, which constrains the time needed to serve effectively on each board;[15]
- regularly attend board and committee meetings;

---

14 The factors to consider are drawn from the CFA Institute textbook for the CFA Program titled *Corporate Finance*.

15 Some corporate governance codes, including the code in Pakistan, put a limit on the number of company boards on which individuals may participate. In Pakistan, the limit is 10 board mandates for a board member.

- have committed to the needs of shareowners—for example, by making significant investments in the company or by avoiding situations or businesses that could create a conflict of interest with his/her position as a board member;

- have the background, expertise, and knowledge in specific areas needed by the board;

- have served individually on the board for more than 10 years. Such long-term participation may enhance the individual board member's knowledge of the company, but it also may cause the board member to develop a cooperative relationship with management that could impair his/her willingness to act in the best interests of shareowners.

Investors should also consider whether

- the board and its committees have performed peer- or self-assessments and, if available, any information relating to these assessments. This review will help investors determine whether the board has the competence and independence to respond to the competitive and financial challenges facing the company;

- the board requires ongoing training or continuing education for directors on particular committees so that those directors may properly execute their duties. An example would be training in enterprise risk management or valuing derivatives for the audit committee of a large financial firm.

Where to find information about the qualifications of board members: Many listed companies post the names and qualifications of board members on their websites. In regions where this is not the practice, companies typically provide information about their board members in the annual reports to shareowners and, where applicable, in their annual proxy statements.

In many countries, companies report on the number of board and board committee meetings, as well as attendance by individual board members, in their annual reports, on their websites, or where applicable, in their annual corporate governance reports.

Some corporate governance codes in Australia, Canada, and the European Union require listed companies to disclose in their annual reports whether they failed to comply with the codes' provisions and why they did not comply.

The European Union has adopted a European Commission recommendation that the boards of listed companies annually discuss their internal organizations, their procedures, and the extent to which their self-assessments have led to material changes.

In the United States, companies typically list the names and qualifications of board members in annual proxy statements and on their websites. The nominations committees also include their reports concerning members and activities in the annual proxy statements.

In Pakistan, auditors are required to certify that a company has complied with the country's Code of Corporate Governance.

Authority to Hire External Consultants

Investors should determine whether the board and its committees have budgetary authority to hire independent third-party consultants without having to receive approval from management.

Implications for Investors   This authority ensures that the board will receive specialized advice on technical decisions that could affect shareowner value.

Independent board members typically have limited time to devote to their board duties. Consequently, board members need support in gathering and analyzing the large amount of information relevant to managing and overseeing the company.

The board and its committees often need specialized and independent advice as they consider various corporate issues and risks, such as compensation; proposed mergers and acquisitions; legal, regulatory, and financial matters; and reputational concerns. The ability to hire external consultants without first having to seek management's approval provides the board with an independent means of receiving advice uninfluenced by management's interests. Remember, however, that responsibilities for decisions taken on the advice of consultants ultimately belong to the board.

Things to Consider   Among other issues, investors should determine whether

- at relevant periods in the past, the board hired external financial consultants to help it consider mergers, acquisitions, divestitures, or risk management issues;
- the nominations committee has used external advisers in the past to recruit qualified nominees for management or for the board;
- the remuneration committee has hired external advisers in the past to help determine appropriate compensation for key executives.

Where to find information about the authority of the board to hire external consultants: The three most likely places to find information relating to the board's authority to hire external consultants are the corporate governance section of the company's annual report, the annual corporate governance report to shareowners, and the corporate governance section of the company's website.

Other possible places to find this kind of information include the company's articles of organization or by-laws, national corporate governance codes, stock exchange-mandated corporate governance requirements, and third-party corporate governance reports.

Other Board Issues

Board Member Terms and Board Composition

Investors should determine whether board members are elected annually or whether the company has adopted an election process that staggers board member elections.

Reasons for Reviewing Board Member Terms   Investors need to understand the mechanisms that provide, limit, or eliminate altogether their ability to exercise their rights to vote on individual board members.

Implications for Investors   Companies that prevent shareowners from approving or rejecting board members on an annual basis limit shareowners' ability to change the board's composition when, for example, board members fail to act on behalf of shareowners and also limit their ability to elect individuals with needed expertise in response to a change in company strategy.

Things to Consider   When reviewing a company's policy for the election of board members, investors should consider whether

- shareowners elect board members every year or for staggered multiple-year terms (producing what is known as a "staggered" or "classified" board). An annually elected board may provide more flexibility to nominate new board members to meet changes in the marketplace, if needed, than a staggered board. On the one hand, staggered boards may also be used as antitakeover devices.[16] On the other hand, a staggered board may provide better continuity of board expertise. In Japan, shareowners of a company that uses a corporate auditors system elect board members for two-year terms and elect members of the corporate auditors board for four-year terms. Shareowners of a company using a committees system elect board members every year;

■ the board has filled a vacancy for the remainder of a board member's term without receiving shareowner approval at the next annual general meeting;

■ the board is the appropriate size for the circumstances of the company. A large board may have difficulty coordinating its members' views, be slow to act, and defer more frequently to the chief executive. A small board may lack depth of experience and counsel and may not be able to adequately spread the workload among its members to operate effectively.

Where to find information about the mechanisms related to board terms and composition: In most cases, the best place to find information about the election of board members is in the notice of the company's annual general meeting. In the United States and Canada, this information is typically part of the annual proxy statement to shareowners. Investors should check also the company's by-laws and articles of organization to determine whether management and the board are permitted to fill vacancies without shareowner approval.

Related-Party Transactions

Investors should investigate whether the company engages in outside business relationships (related-party transactions) with management, board members, or individuals associated with management or board members for goods and services on behalf of the company.[17]

Reasons for Reviewing the Company's Policies on Related-Party Transactions As they relate to board members, policies that cover related-party transactions attempt to ensure the independence of board members by discouraging them from engaging in the following practices, among others:

■ receiving consultancy fees for work performed on behalf of the company, and

■ receiving finders' fees for bringing merger, acquisition, or corporate sale partners to the company's attention.

Implications for Investors Receiving personal benefits from the company for which board members are supposed to make independent decisions poses an inherent conflict of interest if the benefits fall outside the role of a board member. Limitations on such transactions, through either the company's ethical code or its board policies, reduce the likelihood that management can use company resources to sway board members' allegiance away from shareowners.

---

16 See, especially, Lucian A. Bebchuk, John C. Coates IV, and Guhan Subramanian, "The Powerful Antitakeover Force of Staggered Boards: Theory, Evidence, and Policy," *Stanford Law Review* (2002). The authors conclude that the ballot-box route to a takeover is illusory for a company with an effective staggered board because, in part, a bidder must foster interest and votes during two elections spread at least 14 months apart.

17 For more on related-party transactions in Hong Kong, see *Related-Party Transactions: Cautionary Tales for Investors in Asia*, Charlottesville, VA: CFA Institute Centre (January 2009): www.cfapubs.org/loi/ccb.

Things to Consider   When reviewing a company's policies regarding related-party transactions, investors should determine whether

- the company has a policy for reviewing and approving related-party transactions. If the company has such a policy, consider whether interested directors (directors with financial interests in the transaction) are allowed to approve such transactions;

- the company's ethical code or the board's policies and procedures limit the circumstances in which insiders, including board members and those associated with them, can accept remuneration or in-kind benefits from the company for consulting or other services outside the scope of their positions as board members. The intent of such provisions is not only to discourage actions that could compromise board members' independence but also to discourage the company from entering into contracts that may not provide the best value to the company and its shareowners;

- the company has disclosed any material related-party transactions or commercial relationships with existing board members or board nominees (see also the discussion of this issue in the preceding section titled "Board Independence");

- board members or executive officers have lent, leased, or otherwise provided property or equipment to the company;

- the company has paid board members finders' fees for their roles in acquisitions or other significant company transactions;

- the company has provided to board members in-kind benefits/perquisites—e.g., the personal use of company facilities or resources, company donations to personal charities.

Where to find information about related-party transactions: The annual reports of companies in many countries include a discussion of insider transactions and fees paid to board members and controlling shareowners, often under the heading of "Related-Party Transactions."

In the United States and Canada, listed companies are required to provide information relating to dealings with insiders in the annual proxy statement, often under the heading of "Related-Party Transactions."

Investors also should look for any disclosures of related-party transactions in the prospectus of a company preceding a public offering of securities. This document should inform investors about transactions that permit insiders to purchase shares at a discount prior to an offering at a higher price.

Board Committees

In this section, we consider separately the audit committee, the remuneration or compensation committee, the nominations committee, and other committees.

Audit Committee

Investors should determine whether the board has established a committee of independent board members, including those with recent and relevant experience in finance and accounting, to oversee the audit of the company's financial reports.

The Purpose of the Audit Committee   The audit committee's primary objective is to ensure that the financial information reported by the company to shareowners is complete, accurate, reliable, relevant, and timely. To this end, the audit committee is responsible for hiring and supervising the independent external auditors and ensuring that

- the external auditors' priorities are aligned with the best interests of shareowners,
- the auditor is independent of management influences,
- the information included in the financial reports to shareowners is complete, accurate, reliable, relevant, verifiable, and timely,
- the financial statements are prepared in accordance with generally accepted accounting principles (GAAP) or international accounting standards (IAS) and regulatory disclosure requirements in the company's jurisdiction,
- the audit is conducted in accordance with generally accepted auditing standards (GAAS),
- all conflicts of interest between the external auditor and the company are resolved in favor of the shareowners, and
- the independent auditors have authority over the audit of the entire group, including foreign subsidiaries and affiliated companies.

Implications for Investors   If the independence of the audit committee is compromised, there could be doubts about the integrity of the financial reporting process and about the credibility of the company's financial statements. Misrepresentations of, or other distortions about, the company's performance and financial condition ultimately could have a detrimental effect on the company's share valuation.

Things to Consider   Investors should determine whether

- all of the board members serving on the audit committee are independent;
- any of the board members serving on the audit committee are considered financial experts;[18]
- the board submits the appointment of the external auditors to a vote of shareowners;
- the audit committee has the authority to approve or reject other proposed non-audit engagements with the external audit firm. This conclusion should be based on a review of the committee's report on the services received from and fees paid to the external audit firm. Investors also should determine whether the audit committee has policies relating to any fees paid by the company to the external auditor for non-audit consulting services and for resolving these types of potential conflicts of interest. Such non-audit fees may influence the auditors in a way that leads them to resolve conflicts regarding financial reporting issues in favor of management rather than for the benefit of shareowners;

---

18 Under U.S. SEC rules developed in response to the Sarbanes-Oxley Act of 2002, a financial expert is a director who (1) understands GAAP and financial statements; (2) can assess the application of GAAP for estimates, accruals, and reserves; (3) has prepared, audited, analyzed, or evaluated financial statements similar to those of the company or has experience supervising those who performed these functions; (4) understands internal controls and financial reporting procedures; and (5) understands audit committee functions. Directors may acquire these attributes through education and experience as (or by supervising) a principal financial officer, principal accounting officer, controller, public accountant, or auditor; by overseeing or assessing companies or public accountants in the preparation, auditing, or evaluation of financial statements; or from other relevant experience. See the SEC document at www.sec.gov/rules/final/33-8177.htm, under "Audit Committee Financial Experts."

- the company has procedures and provisions ensuring that the internal auditor reports directly to the audit committee in the case of concerns regarding the accuracy or integrity of the financial reports or accounting practices. Similarly, the audit committee should have unimpeded access to the internal auditor;

- there were any discussions between the committee and the external auditors resulting in a change in the financial reports as a result of questionable interpretations of accounting rules, fraud, or other accounting problems and whether the company has fired its external auditors as a result of such issues;

- the committee controls the audit budget to enable it to address unanticipated or complex issues;

- the company has signed any agreement with the auditor limiting the auditor's liability in the event of negligence, breach of duty, or breach of trust;

- the committee undergoes or is required to undergo periodic training to stay educated about current financial issues.

Where to find information about the audit committee:

Australia   Companies listed on the Australian Securities Exchange are required to disclose in their annual reports if they have *not* complied with the exchange's recommendations relating to the audit committee, together with an explanation of why they did not comply.

Canada   Companies listed on the Toronto Stock Exchange are required to disclose in their annual reports whether

- they have an audit committee,

- its members are nonexecutive,

- the board has defined its roles and responsibilities,

- it communicates directly with internal and external auditors, and

- it is responsible for overseeing management reporting and internal control systems.

European Union   All listed companies in the EU must have an audit committee or "body carrying out equivalent functions." The committee has to have at least one independent member—although most national codes set a higher standard—and at least one member with "competence in accounting and/or auditing." The audit committee is also required to report on the company's system of internal controls in the annual director's report.

United States   Companies must disclose whether they have at least one financial expert on their audit committees and the name of at least one of the committee's financial experts. They also must disclose whether the named board members are independent. If they disclose that they do not have at least one financial expert, they must explain why.

Companies also must disclose the following in their annual proxy statements:

- whether they have a standing audit committee and, if so, the name of each committee member, the number of meetings held, and a description of the functions performed by the committee;

- whether the board has adopted a written charter for the audit committee. If so, the company must include a copy of the charter as an appendix to the proxy statement at least once every three years. If this information is available, investors will most likely find it on the company's website;

- if the company's shares are quoted on the NASDAQ or the American or New York stock exchanges, whether the audit committee members are independent as defined in the applicable listing standards (together with certain information regarding any audit committee member who is not independent);

- whether the audit committee has reviewed and discussed the audited financial reports with management and the independent auditors and whether the auditors made appropriate disclosures regarding their independence;

- a statement by the audit committee about whether it recommended to the board that the audited financial statements be included in the annual report.

In some U.S. jurisdictions, the audit committee is the primary committee responsible for assessing and mitigating the risks a company faces. If the audit committee is charged with such a responsibility, shareowners need to determine whether the committee reviews all of the risks a company faces, including credit, market, fiduciary, liquidity, reputation, operational, strategic, and technology risks.

Remuneration/Compensation Committee

Investors should determine whether the company has a committee of independent board members charged with setting executive remuneration/compensation.[19]

The Purpose of the Remuneration/Compensation Committee   The remuneration committee is responsible for ensuring that compensation and other awards encourage executive managers to act in ways that enhance the company's long-term profitability and value. It is also responsible for ensuring that the remuneration packages offered to management are commensurate with the level of responsibilities of the executives and appropriate in light of the company's performance. The committee can further these goals by

- including only independent board members on the committee,[20]

- linking executive compensation to the long-term profitability of the company and long-term increases in share value relative to competitors and other comparably situated companies,

- eliminating any potential conflicts of interests between the compensation committee and the company by, for instance, using only independent compensation consultants who report solely to the committee,

- communicating regularly with the company's shareowners about compensation philosophy and how it complements the company's strategic goals,

- establishing clear mechanisms in compensation packages for recouping incentive pay from management if the money was earned through fraud,

- developing clear (that is, "plain language") explanations of compensation philosophy and policies that are periodically communicated to all shareowners, and

- making sure that compensation committee members (or the board if the board sets compensation) understand all components of executive pay packages and are aware of what final payments may be made to executives in both best-case and worst-case scenarios.

---

19 For more on executive compensation in Asia, see *It Pays to Disclose: Bridging the Information Gap in Executive-Compensation Disclosures in Asia*, Charlottesville, VA: CFA Institute Centre (March 2008), and *The Compensation of Senior Executives at Listed Companies: A Manual for Investors*, Charlottesville, VA: CFA Institute Centre (December 2007): www.cfapubs.org/loi/ccb.
20 See a discussion of the independence of committees, particularly in Japan, in the earlier discussion titled "Audit Committee."

Implications for Investors   The existence of the committee and its independence from executive management bias help to ensure that the rewards and incentives offered to management are consistent with the best long-term interests of shareowners. Committees that lack independence may be overly pressured by management to award compensation that is excessive when compared with other comparably situated companies or to provide incentives for actions that boost short-term share prices at the expense of long-term profitability and value.

Things to Consider   As part of their analyses relating to this committee, investors should determine whether

- the overall composition of the compensation packages offered to senior management is appropriate;
- the committee adequately articulates its compensation philosophy, policies, and procedures to shareowners;
- executive compensation is linked to the long-term profitability of the company and long-term increases in share value relative to competitors and comparable companies. Shareowners should also determine whether incentive structures encourage management to take excessive risks in the short term that may prove detrimental to the company's long-term viability;
- compensation packages contain clear mechanisms for recouping incentive pay from management if it was earned through fraud or other activities deemed detrimental to the company's sustainable performance or viability;
- the compensation committee members understand all components of executive pay packages and are aware of what final payment may be made to executives in best-case and worst-case scenarios;
- members of the committee regularly attended meetings during the previous year;
- the company has provided detailed information to shareowners in public documents relating to the compensation paid during the previous year to the company's five highest paid executives and its board members. Investors also should review any disclosures about the major components and amounts paid to these individuals. Some jurisdictions require companies to provide only summary information about the compensation of senior managers and the board;
- the terms and conditions of options granted to management and employees are disclosed and whether the terms are reasonable;
- the company intends to issue newly registered shares to fulfill its share-based remuneration obligations or it intends to settle these options with shares repurchased in the open market;
- the company and the board are required to receive shareowner approval for any share-based remuneration plans. Such plans affect the number of shares outstanding and, consequently, current shareowners' ownership interests, as well as the basis on which earnings per share are reported and the market valuations of the company's securities;
- the board receives variable remuneration instruments, such as stock options or restricted stock, and whether such awards adequately align the interests of the board with those of shareowners;
- senior executives from other companies who have cross-directorship links with the company are members of the committee. Executive remuneration is often based on compensation of similarly positioned individuals at other companies, and if the committee has individuals who could benefit directly from reciprocal

decisions on remuneration, those decisions may not be in the best interests of the company's shareowners (also see the earlier discussion titled "Board Independence");

- whether potential conflicts of interest exist between the compensation committee and the company. One way of avoiding such conflicts is to use only independent compensation consultants who report solely to the committee.[21]

Where to find information about the remuneration/compensation committee:

Australia Companies that list on the Australian Securities Exchange are required to disclose in their annual reports if they did not comply with the exchange's recommendations for remuneration committees and provide an explanation of why they did not comply.

Canada The Toronto Stock Exchange requires TSE-listed companies to report in their annual reports or their management information and proxy circulars whether they have a compensation committee and, if so, whether it is composed of independent or nonexecutive board members and whether a majority are independent. New rules that came into force for annual reports after 31 December 2008, not unlike the SEC rules, require disclosure of total compensation in a "compensation disclosure & analysis" section.[22]

United Kingdom Listed U.K. companies are required to report in their annual reports on the frequency of and attendance by members at remuneration committee meetings. These companies also must disclose the responsibilities delegated to the committee.

United States Listed U.S. companies report in their annual proxy statements on whether they have a standing compensation committee. These reports also include names of committee members, summaries of compensation strategies, and the policies and procedures of the committee.

Nominations Committee

Investors should determine whether the company has a nominations committee of independent board members that is responsible for recruiting board members.

The Purpose of the Nominations Committee The nominations committee is responsible for

- recruiting new board members with appropriate qualities and experience in light of the company's business needs,
- regularly examining the performance, independence, skills, and expertise of existing board members to determine whether they meet the current and future needs of the company and the board,
- creating nominations policies and procedures, and
- preparing for the succession of executive management and the board.

Implications for Investors The slate of candidates offered by this committee will determine whether the board ultimately works for the benefit of shareowners. It is important for this committee to remain independent[23] to ensure that it recruits individuals

---

21 For more discussion on this topic, see *The Compensation of Senior Executives at Listed Companies: A Manual for Investors*, Charlottesville, VA: CFA Institute Centre (December 2007): www.cfapubs.org/loi/ccb.
22 See the amendments to National Instrument 51-102, Continuous Disclosure Obligations, at www.osc.gov.on.ca/Regulation/Rulemaking/Current/Part5/rule_20081231_51-102_unofficial-consolidated.pdf.
23 See the discussion of the independence of committees, particularly in Japan, under the earlier discussion in the "Audit Committee."

who can and will work on behalf of shareowners and to ensure that the performance assessment of current board members is fair and appropriate. (See also the section "Board Member Qualifications and Ability to Serve as Shareowner Representative.")

Things to Consider   Investors may have to review company reports over several years to adequately assess whether this committee has recruited board members who act in the interests of shareowners. They also should review the following:

- the criteria for new board members;
- the composition, background, and areas of expertise of existing board members and whether new nominees complement the board's current portfolio of talents;
- how the committee finds potential new board members. Among the considerations is whether the committee engages in a search for candidates, such as by using an executive search firm, or whether its members rely on the advice of management or other board members;
- the attendance records of board members at regular and special meetings;
- whether the company has a succession plan for executive management in the event of unforeseen circumstances, such as the sudden incapacitation of the chief operating or finance officers. Investors should examine the information provided by the company about the plan and determine who is expected to lead and implement it;
- the report of the committee, including any discussion of its actions and decisions during the previous year (including the number of meetings held, attendance by committee members, and the committee's policies and procedures).

Where to find information about the nominations committee: The annual reports of companies in many countries include a general discussion of the actions taken by the committee during the previous year. Moreover, the websites of many listed companies describe the activities and members of the committee and, in some countries, provide information about the committee's charter.

The annual reports of companies listed in some countries, such as Australia and the United Kingdom, are required to disclose and explain when a company fails to comply with applicable nominations committee rules.

The corporate governance report, if there is one, often includes an explanation of the company's nominations process and whether the company has a specially designated nominations committee.

In some jurisdictions, such as the United States, investors should look in the annual proxy statement to shareowners for indications about the work of this committee, including the name of each committee member and the number of meetings held.

Other Board Committees

Investors should determine whether the board has other committees that are responsible for overseeing management's activities in certain areas, such as corporate governance, mergers and acquisitions, legal matters, risk management, and environmental health and safety issues.

Implications for Investors   Because "other" committees are not covered by national corporate governance codes or exchange-mandated guidelines in the manner that audit, remuneration, or nominations committees are, they are more likely to have members who are part of executive management. Consequently, these committees may not, and possibly need not, achieve the levels of independence expected of the audit, nominations, and remuneration committees.

Depending on each committee's purpose, committees created by the board can provide additional insight into the goals, focus, and strategies of the company. For example, a committee dedicated to risk management may consider the identification and quantification of financial and operational risks faced by the company and determine its optimal risk exposure. In the wake of the recent global financial crisis, risk management committees—especially those at financial institutions—have heightened profiles and have taken on responsibilities now seen as important as those of other, traditionally more recognizable board committees (audit and compensation committees, for example). Risk management committees around the globe are now charged with a thorough review of the company's financial risks, such as leverage, counterparty risks, and exposure concentrations.

Things to Consider   Investors should understand the amount of risk management and risk measurement expertise present on a committee charged with managing and measuring a company's risk profile.

Where to find information about other board committees: As in the case with the audit, compensation, and nominations committees, investors have four primary places to look for information about special-purpose committees—namely, the annual reports to shareowners; the annual corporate governance report, where available; the websites of listed companies; jurisdictions such as the United States and Canada, the annual proxy statement to shareowners; and on the websites of listed companies.

Board Communications with Shareowners

Investors should evaluate the communications the board has with shareowners and the ability shareowners have to meet with the board.

Implications for Investors   A corporate board does not have the time or resources to meet with all shareowners, but it should be open to talking with shareowners who hold a significant stake in the company or represent important stakeholders so that it can properly address legitimate investor concerns. A board should not breach its fiduciary duty to all shareowners by acting in the interests of a minority shareowner to the detriment of the company and shareowners as a whole or by disclosing material information to one group of shareowners while withholding it from others. A board should take care to establish ways for shareowners to communicate their concerns to the board in a way that helps the board understand legitimate concerns of shareowners that may not have been addressed by the board.

Things to Consider   Most jurisdictions do not set out formal rules governing the interaction of boards and shareowners; therefore, the culture of board-shareowner interaction and collegiality will vary from market to market. Also, because of a lack of time and resources, a board is likely to meet with only institutional shareowners that have significant holdings in the company. Information technology not available in past decades may, however, allow owners of smaller amounts of shares to communicate their concerns with the board, although face-to-face meetings between a board and individual investors are rare. Shareowners should consider whether they have a direct line to the board chair or lead independent director.

Where to find information about board communications: A company's corporate governance documents and websites will likely detail ways in which shareowners may communicate with the board if such communications are available. Institutional investors and analysts who meet with boards are likely to reach a board through its company investor relations contact, its corporate secretary, or a preexisting personal relationship with a member of the board.

MANAGEMENT

Although the board, in consultation with management, helps set the strategic, ethical, and financial course for a company, investors ultimately must rely on management to implement that course. Management also has the responsibility to communicate to directors, investors, and the public about the company's performance, financial condition, and any changes in strategy or corporate initiatives in a complete, effective, and timely manner.

Investors are generally familiar with the reports that management issues with regard to a company's financial performance and condition. They may not be aware of other sources of information, however, that may provide insight into the corporate culture or the company's governance practices. The company's code of ethics, corporate governance principles, compensation policies, share-repurchase and price-stabilization programs, takeover defenses, and approach to shareowner communication—all provide valuable insights into whether management's focus is on maximizing shareowner value.

To help investors understand management's role and responsibilities in corporate governance matters, the following section provides a general discussion of company codes of ethics and corporate culture, followed by specific discussions of aspects of corporate transparency.

Implementation of Code of Ethics

Investors should determine whether the company has adopted a code of ethics and whether the company's actions indicate a commitment to an appropriate ethical framework.

The Purpose of a Code of Ethics   A company's code of ethics sets standards for ethical conduct that are based on basic principles of integrity, trust, and honesty. It provides personnel with a framework for behavior while they are conducting the company's business and guidance for addressing conflicts of interest. In effect, it represents a part of the company's risk management policies, which are intended to prevent company representatives from engaging in practices that could harm the company, its products, or shareowners.

Implications for Investors   Reported breaches of ethics in a company often result in regulatory sanctions, fines, management turnover, and unwanted negative media coverage, all of which can adversely affect the company's performance. Adoption of and adherence to an appropriate corporate code of ethics indicates a commitment on the part of management to establish and maintain ethical practices. The existence of such a code may also be a mitigating factor in regulatory actions when breaches do occur.

Things to Consider   As part of their analyses of the company's ethical climate, investors should determine whether the company

- gives the board access to relevant corporate information in a timely and comprehensive manner;
- has an ethical code and whether that code prohibits any practice that would provide advantages to company insiders that are not also offered to shareowners. For example, a code might prohibit the company from offering shares at discounted prices to management, board members, and other insiders prior to a public offering of securities to prevent dilution of the value and interests of those who buy at the public offering price;
- has an ethical code that the company promotes internally and requires training for employees on compliance with the code;

- has designated someone who is responsible for corporate ethics;

- has an ethical code that provides waivers from its prohibitions to certain levels of management and the reasons why;

- has waived any of its code's provisions during recent periods and why;

- is in compliance with the corporate governance code of the country where it is located or the governance requirements of the stock exchange that lists its securities. Typically, companies must disclose whether they have failed to adhere to such codes and, if so, give reasons for the failure. In some cases, noncompliance may result in fines or sanctions by regulators. The company also may face informal sanctions, such as product boycotting by customers or political groups;

- regularly performs an audit of its ethical/governance policies and procedures to make improvements.

Where to find information about a company's code of ethics and other ethical matters: Companies with ethical codes typically post them on their public websites, in their annual reports to shareowners, or in countries that require them, in their annual corporate governance reports.[24]

The annual reports of companies listed in some countries, such as Australia, disclose when and why a company failed to meet applicable governance standards regarding the creation and implementation of a code of conduct.

Investors may check on the requirements of a country's national corporate governance code or exchange-mandated governance requirements.

Personal Use of Company Assets

Investors should determine whether the company permits insiders (management or board members) or their family members to use company assets for personal reasons.

Reasons for Reviewing the Company's Policies on the Personal Use of Company Assets   As they relate to insiders, policies that limit or prohibit the use of company assets by insiders attempt to ensure that resources are used in the most efficient and productive manner for the purpose of generating returns for the company and all of its shareowners. Such policies and procedures also seek to preserve the independence of board members by attempting to prevent the conflicts of interest that may result when board members or their families use company assets.

Implications for Investors   When insiders—management, board members, or their families—use company assets for personal reasons, those resources are not available for investment in productive and income-generating activities. Such use also creates conflicts of interest for board members.

Things to Consider   When reviewing a company's policies regarding the personal use of company assets, investors should determine whether the company

- has an ethical code or policies and procedures that place limits on the ability of insiders to use company assets for personal benefit;

- has lent or donated cash or other resources to insiders, their families, or other related parties;

---

24 Proposed rules in Canada will not require codes to be filed with the securities regulators but will require only summaries of those codes and a description of where they can be obtained.

- has purchased property or other assets, such as houses or airplanes, for the personal use of management, board members, or their family members;

- has leased assets, such as dwellings or transportation vehicles, to management, board members, or their family members and whether the terms of such contracts are appropriate in light of market conditions.

Where to find information about insider transactions: Investors may find information about loans to company executives, board members, or their families in the "Related-Party Transactions" section of a company's annual report, its annual corporate governance report, an annual proxy statement to shareowners, or its website. Investors also should review the prospectus of a company preceding a public offering of securities for any related-party transactions. This document should inform investors about transactions that permit insiders to purchase shares at a discount prior to an offering at a higher price.

Corporate Transparency

In this section, we review aspects of executive compensation, share-repurchase and price stabilization plans, and management communications with shareowners

Executive Compensation

Investors should analyze both the amounts paid to key executives for managing the company's affairs and the manner in which compensation is provided to determine whether compensation paid to the company's executives 1) is commensurate with the executives' responsibilities and performance and 2) provides appropriate incentives.

Reasons for Reviewing Executive Compensation Disclosures   Disclosures of how much, in what manner, and on what basis executive management is paid shed light on a board's stewardship of shareowner assets. Furthermore, these disclosures allow investors to evaluate whether the compensation is reasonable in light of the apparent return to the company in terms of performance.

Implications for Shareowners   The purpose of compensation is to reward managers for gains attributable directly to superior performance. An appropriately designed program should create incentives for company executives to generate sustainable value added for shareowners.

A flawed compensation program may encourage executives to make decisions that generate additional compensation for themselves through short-term gains rather than decisions that implement an appropriate strategy focused on long-term growth. A flawed program may reward managers for excessive risk-taking or broad sector- or industry-wide trends. It may also dilute the ownership positions of existing shareowners.

Compensation is often split between a basic salary and some form of bonus. Although there is no single model, best practice has moved toward (1) a bonus that reflects recent business performance against targeted indicators (e.g., "Key Performance Indicators" linked to the company's strategy) and (2) a bonus based on a long-term incentive plan (LTIP), which uses forward-looking indicators of success. The LTIP is designed to capture how well the management is positioning the company for long-term growth. In general, the salary is not performance dependent but the bonus and LTIP are.

Things to Consider   When reviewing a company's executive compensation disclosures, investors should examine the following:

- *Remuneration/compensation program.* An examination of the terms and conditions of the company's executive compensation program, together with an analysis of summaries of agreements with executives, will help investors determine whether the program rewards long-term growth or short-term increases in share value. This review should include a plain-language explanation of whether the remuneration/compensation committee uses consultants to set pay for company executives or relies on internal sources, which may be biased. Investors also should focus on whether the rewards offered to management are based on the performance of the company relative to its competitors or on some other metric.

- *Past executive compensation.* Analysis of the actual compensation paid to the company's top executives during recent years and the elements of the compensation packages offered to key employees can help shareowners determine whether the company is receiving adequate returns for the investment it has made in management and whether remuneration is aligned with shareowner interests. For example, the mix between fixed and variable compensation can indicate management's risk appetite.

- *Whether compensation is variable or performance based.* Investors should determine whether the compensation package is linked (throughout a normal business cycle) to the long-term profitability and share-price performance of the company relative to its competitors and peers. Best practices include disclosure of the targets the board uses to determine incentive-based compensation (both the bonus and LTIP). Key questions investors should ask include the following:
  - Is performance measured relative to peers, and are these peers the right comparison group?
  - Do targets require adequate stretching by executives in the current economic climate?
  - Are targets clearly linked to the company's strategy?
  - Is performance measured over a reasonable time frame, ideally through a complete business cycle?
  - Does performance measurement take account of risk taken?

- *Use of external consultants.* Investors should determine whether the remuneration/compensation committee uses consultants to set pay for company executives or whether it relies on internal sources, which may be biased.

- *Share-based compensation terms.* Examination of the terms of this type of remuneration program, including the total shares offered to key executives and other employees, should alert investors to how the program can affect shares outstanding, dilution of shareowner interests, and share values. Investors also should determine whether the company seeks shareowner approval for creation or amendments to such plans (see the upcoming section "Shareowner Rights" for other issues that may require a vote of shareowners).

- *Stock-option expensing.* Compensation, regardless of whether it is paid in cash, shares, or share options, involves payment for services received and should appear as an expense on the income statement. International Financial Reporting Standards (IFRS) and U.S. GAAP both require companies to expense stock option grants.[25]

---

25 This requirement is applicable for U.S.-listed companies with fiscal years that end after 15 June 2005.

- *Option repricing.* Investors should remain aware of efforts by the company to reprice downward the strike prices of stock options previously granted. Changes in the strike price remove the incentives the original options created for management, and thus reduce the link of long-term profitability and performance of the company with management remuneration.

- *Equity award vesting schedules.* Shareowners need to determine whether options, restricted stock, and other equity-based awards vest immediately, which may engender a short-term mindset, or vest over a series of years, which may better align the interests of management with those of shareowners.

- *Supplemental executive retirement plans (SERPs).* Many companies have established SERPs or other retirement plans for their executives that provide benefits above and beyond those covered in the company's ordinary retirement plans. Investors should understand the details of supplemental plans to determine what company resources are and will be devoted to these plans over the life of an executive's contract.

- *Perquisites.* Shareowners should understand the nonfinancial benefits given to executives and the outlays of company resources that are behind such benefits. Perquisites include automobiles, personal use of corporate aircraft, security systems, executive dining rooms, legal/tax/financial consulting services, and low-interest-rate loans.

- *Share ownership by management.* Investors should determine whether members of management have share holdings other than those related to stock option grants. Such holdings should align the interests of company executives with those of shareowners.

- *The company's peer group.* Shareowners should note whether the peer group that is used to benchmark the company's performance is disclosed by the company. If so, shareowners then need to determine whether this peer group is appropriate. Also important is whether the peer group has been relatively stable over the years. A compensation red flag may be raised if a peer group is not appropriate for comparison or is frequently changing.[26]

- *Claw-back provisions.* Investors need to understand whether the company has provisions for the return of money by managers in clear cases of fraud.

Where to find information about executive compensation: In many jurisdictions, companies report information about executive compensation in their annual reports. In some cases, disclosures about amounts paid to individual executives is voluntary, although accounting standards setters and securities regulators are increasingly making such disclosures compulsory.

In the United States and Canada, executive compensation strategies and reports of actual compensation paid to key executives are included in the company's annual proxy statement to shareowners.

Investors also may find such information posted on companies' websites.

Share-Repurchase and Price-Stabilization Programs

Shareowners should inquire into the size, purpose, means of financing, and duration of share-repurchase programs and price-stabilization efforts.

---

[26] See also *The Compensation of Senior Executives at Listed Companies: A Manual for Investors*, Charlottesville, VA: CFA Institute Centre (December 2007): www.cfapubs.org/loi/ccb.

Reasons for Reviewing Disclosures of Share-Repurchase and Price-Stabilization Programs   A company may use a share-repurchase program to buy its own shares that are already trading on a public stock exchange. In a stabilization program, the company has its investment bankers buy and sell shares following a public offering of shares as a means of reducing the price volatility of the shares.

Implications for Investors   Buying shares on the open market can have a positive effect on share values by reducing the number of shares available and increasing the value for the remaining shares outstanding. Price-stabilization programs may reduce the volatility of a security's price following an offering and permit the market to achieve a balance between buyers and sellers, but such programs may provide insiders with an opportunity to trade at a higher price in anticipation that the share price will decline or buy at a lower price in anticipation of future price gains.

Things to Consider   When reviewing share-repurchase and price-stabilization programs, investors should determine the following:

- *The intention of the program.* Investors should determine whether the board intends to use repurchased shares (1) to reduce the number of shares outstanding in order to increase long-term valuations, (2) to fund the future exercise of management share options, or (3) to prevent a hostile takeover. Depending on the perspective of the investor, the program may enhance or hurt long-term share value. Fixed-income investors, for example, may view the use of cash to repurchase shares as detrimental to the ability of the company to repay its outstanding debts.[27] Equity investors, in contrast, may see such actions as beneficial to their valuations.

- *The size and financing of the program.* This information, together with disclosures about whether the company plans to use internally generated cash from operations or issue debt to finance the purchases, can help equity investors determine how the program will affect the value of the company's shares.

In addition, investors should review the following:

- *Regular updates on the program's progress.* In particular, investors should review the prices at which open-market purchases of shares were made, the number of shares purchased, cumulative amounts of shares repurchased to date, and the average price paid to date. This information should help investors anticipate completion of the program and how that may affect share value. It also should help investors determine whether the program is proceeding as planned or exceeding original intentions for scope and cost.

- *Disclosures relating to stabilization activities.* Investors should determine prior to investing in a public offering of securities whether the company intends to use such stabilization services and should subsequently review updates about the number of shares purchased and sold under the program, the average price paid and received, and when the activities concluded. This information will indicate whether the company and its advisers acted as proposed or whether they engaged in unintended or undisclosed activities.

Where to find information about share-repurchase and price-stabilization programs: The annual and interim reports of a company will in most cases provide the information relating to a share-repurchase program. The prospectus for an offering

---

27 Bond indentures may require that the company repay outstanding debt securities or receive a waiver from bondholders prior to launching a share-repurchase program.

should include initial information relating to stabilization activities. Annual and interim financial reports should provide final information about the activities of stabilization programs.

Investors should look to the prospectus of an offering to determine whether at the time of the offering the company intended to use agents to perform price stabilization services following the issuance of the securities.

Of particular interest are poststabilization disclosures. In the European Union, companies are required by the Market Abuse Directive to disclose (1) whether stabilization activities were undertaken and, if so, (2) the dates the program began and ended, and (3) the range of prices at which such activities were conducted. The ultimate disclosures will come from either the issuer or the lead underwriter.

The SEC currently does not require poststabilization disclosures like those of the EU, although it is considering implementation of such a policy.[28] Currently, NASDAQ requires market makers to attach a special symbol to an order for this purpose; other exchanges require underwriters to notify the exchange and provide disclosure to the recipient of the bid that such bids are part of a stabilization program.

Poststabilization disclosures in many other jurisdictions are required to be made only to the company and the exchange.

Management Communications with Shareowners

Investors should evaluate the level of communications that management has with shareowners and the ability shareowners have to speak with management.

Implications for Investors   As was the case when discussing board–shareowner communications, investors need to understand that corporate management does not have the time or resources to meet with all shareowners, but as was the case with the board, management also should be open to listening to shareowners who hold a significant stake in the company or represent important stakeholders in order to properly address legitimate investor concerns. Management must not give information to certain shareowners that is not given to all shareowners, but management should be open to suggestions and concerns of their shareowners.

Things to Consider   Most large companies employ in-house investor relations teams or outsourced investor relations professionals to handle communications between management and individual shareowners. These avenues are probably the best way for investors to communicate with management. There is rarely a direct avenue for individual shareowners to contact management outside an annual meeting.

To engender the kind of communications they want from management, shareowners should

- encourage companies to provide frequent and meaningful communications about strategy and long-term vision, including transparent financial reporting that reflects a company's progress toward its strategic goals; and

- encourage the inclusion of statements concerning long-term corporate strategy in all company communications.

---

28 See "Amendments to Regulation M: Anti-Manipulation Rules Concerning Securities Offerings; Proposed Rule," *Federal Register*, vol. 69, no. 242 (17 December 2004):75782, under the third question: "Should the Commission consider, in addition to the proposed disclosure, revising Rule 104 to require a general notification to the market (*e.g.*, through a press release, a website posting, or an administrative message sent over the Tape) that [the] activity has commenced (and another notification when [the activity] has ceased)?"

Where to find information about management communications: Much of the communication management has with shareowners comes through prescribed avenues, such as the company's annual report, annual meetings, earnings press releases, earnings conference calls, and conference presentations.

Institutional investors and analysts who meet with management are more likely than individual investors to reach management through a company investor relations contact, corporate secretary, or preexisting personal relationship with a member of management.

SHAREOWNER RIGHTS

The value of a financial security is determined not only by its claim on the company's future earnings but also by the rights associated with that security. Among the rights associated with shares of common stock are the right to elect board members and the right to vote on matters that may affect the value of shareowner holdings, such as mergers or acquisitions. Other rights may include the right to apply the cumulative votes of one's shares to one or a limited number of board nominees, the ability to nominate persons to the board, or the right to propose changes to company operations.

Shareowners may not have all these rights in all cases, nor will they always find it easy to exercise those rights that *are* accessible. For example, companies in some regions can restrict voting to only those owners who are present at scheduled meetings of shareowners. Companies may also be able to prevent shareowners—in return for exercising their vote—from trading for a designated period prior to the annual general meeting. In other cases, individuals and institutions cannot confidentially cast their votes. In still other cases, founding-family members or government shareowners may exercise disproportionate influence over the companies' affairs through the ownership of special classes of shares that grant them super voting rights.

Shareowners may have the power to remedy situations in certain cases, but such remedies are not universal. Local laws and regulations also may provide legal or regulatory redress.

Such issues are of interest not only to equity investors but also to investors interested in fixed-income investments—for example, companies that grant super voting rights to a certain class of stock and shareowners historically use debt financing more than equity financing to fund investments in new business opportunities.[29] Such a strategy may raise the financial risk of a company and, ultimately, increase the possibility of default.

Investors should recognize what specific rights are attached to the securities they are considering and factor that information into any investment decisions. Doing so may avoid situations that result in reduced valuations and poor investment performance. Shareowner-rights standards and the legal and regulatory environments that underpin those rights vary from market to market. Therefore, shareowners must seek out information to understand their rights in each market.[30]

Following is a discussion of issues that investors should consider in evaluating the shareowner rights of various companies.

---

29 A December 2003 study by Paul A. Gompers, Joy L. Ishii, and Andrew Metrick found that companies with two classes of common shares that separated the voting rights from the cash flow rights resulted in underinvestment and lower valuations. See Gompers et al, "Incentives vs. Control" (2003).

30 See *Shareowner Rights across the Markets: A Manual for Investors*, Charlotteville, VA: CFA Institute Centre (April 2009): www.cfapubs.org/loi/ccb.

Shareowner Voting

Companies have all kinds of rules governing the way shareowners may vote their shares. We review in this section aspects of shareowner voting about which investors should be aware: ownership structure and voting rights, proxy voting, confidential voting and vote tabulation, cumulative voting, voting for other corporate changes, and shareowner proposals.

Ownership Structure and Voting Rights

Investors should examine the company's ownership structure to determine whether it has different classes of common shares that separate the voting rights of those shares from their economic value.

Reasons for Examining the Ownership Structure of the Company　A company that assigns one vote to each share is more likely to have a board that considers and acts in the best interests of all shareowners, and the one-share/one-vote standard is considered best practice by most international corporate governance professionals. Conversely, a company with different classes of common shares in which the majority, or all, of the voting rights are given to one class of shareowners may create a situation in which the management and board are disproportionately focused on the interests of those favored shareowners. It is usually in the shareowners' best interests for cash flow rights and voting rights to be equivalent. Companies with dual classes or multiple classes of shares often have a separation of cash flow rights (to all shareowners) and voting rights (in favor of certain shareowners with higher voting rights).

Implications for Investors　Companies with dual classes of common equity could encourage potential acquirers to deal directly with those shareowners who own the shares with super voting rights. Moreover, studies have shown that companies that separate voting rights from economic rights (entitling a shareowner to a pro rata share of the earnings and residual asset value of the company) of their common shares have more difficulty raising equity capital to invest in capital improvements and product development than companies that combine those rights.

Things to Consider　When analyzing the ownership structure of a company, investors should consider whether

- there are different classes of shares and how voting rights differ between them;
- the company has safeguards in its articles of organization or by-laws that protect the rights and interests of those shareowners whose shares have inferior voting rights;
- the company was recently privatized by a government or governmental entity and whether the selling government has retained voting rights that could veto certain decisions of management and the board. If so, a government could prevent shareowners from receiving full value for their shares;
- the super voting rights granted to certain classes of shareowners have impaired the company's ability to raise equity capital for future investment. Investors may find the inferior class of shares unattractive, which could harm the company's ability to finance future growth by means other than raising debt capital and increasing leverage.[31]

---

31 See *Shareowner Rights across the Markets*, op cit.

Where to find information about whether the company has more than one class of shares: In certain jurisdictions and in certain companies, investors may find information about the different classes of shares in the annual proxy statement to shareowners. The company's website also is likely to describe the differences between shares of common stock and may provide hyperlinks to the company's articles of organization, annual and interim financial reports, prospectuses, and proxy statements.

The prospectus relating to the initial or follow-on offerings of common shares to the public is likely to include a discussion about different classes of common shares, including whether any entity or group of investors retains sufficient voting power to overrule certain management or board decisions.

The notes to the financial statements, particularly in the annual report, will likely disclose the existence of different classes of common shares.

Proxy Voting

Investors should determine whether the company permits shareowners to vote their shares prior to scheduled meetings of shareowners regardless of whether they are able to attend the meetings in person.

Reasons for Evaluating a Company's Voting Rules   The ability to vote one's shares is a fundamental right of share ownership. In some jurisdictions, shareowners may find it difficult to vote their shares, however, because the company accepts only those votes cast at its annual general meeting and does not allow shareowners the right to vote by proxy or electronically.

Implications for Investors   By making it difficult for shareowners to vote their common shares, a company limits a shareowner's ability to choose board members or otherwise express their views on initiatives that could alter the company's course.

Things to Consider   In examining whether a company permits proxy voting, investors should consider whether the company

- limits shareowners' ability to cast votes by conditioning the exercise of their right to vote on their presence at the annual general meeting;
- coordinates the timing of its annual general meeting with other companies in its region to ensure that all of them hold their meetings on the same day but in different locations. In some regions that require shareowners to attend such meetings to vote, such actions seek to prevent shareowners from attending all the meetings and, therefore, from exercising their voting rights. In Pakistan, to avoid companies bunching their annual meeting dates together and disenfranchising shareowners, companies must submit meeting dates to the securities regulator for approval;
- permits proxy voting by means of paper ballot, electronic voting, proxy voting services, or some other remote mechanism;
- is permitted under its national governance code to use share blocking, whereby the company prevents investors that wish to exercise their voting rights from trading their shares during a period prior to the annual general meeting to permit the company and various financial institutions to certify who owns the shares;
- gives shareowners enough time between the release of the proxy and the actual annual meeting to thoughtfully review any voting decisions and vote their shares. In some markets shareowners are given only days or weeks to make such voting decisions, which renders voting especially difficult for foreign investors who may not be able to vote their shares as quickly as those investors in the local market.

Where to find information about the company's proxy voting rules: Investors can look to the company's articles of organization and by-laws to determine the mechanisms shareowners can use to vote their shares. Investors can also examine the company's corporate governance statement for information about whether proxy voting is permitted.

In the United States and Canada, the proxy statement describes the mechanisms by which shareowners can cast their votes by proxy. Also, state corporation law in the United States and provincial securities legislation in Canada regulate issues relating to proxies. Consequently, investors may have to determine the locality in which a company is incorporated—typically found in the articles of incorporation—to review the proxy regulations governing the company.

Confidential Voting and Vote Tabulation

Investors should determine whether shareowners are able to cast confidential votes.

Reasons for Determining Whether Shareowners Are Able to Cast Confidential Votes   Shareowners are more likely to vote and to do so conscientiously if they are assured that board members and management will not find out how they voted.

Implications for Investors   Confidentiality of voting ensures that all votes are counted equally and that the board members and management cannot resolicit the votes of individuals and institutions who voted against the positions of these insiders until the votes are officially recorded.[32]

Things to Consider   In examining whether shareowners can vote anonymously, investors should consider whether

- the company uses a third-party entity to tabulate shareowner votes;
- the company or its third-party agent retains voting records;
- the company provides "timely disclosure" (immediate or a day or two after the vote) of annual meeting voting results;
- the vote tabulation performed by the company or its third-party agent is subject to an audit to ensure accuracy;
- shareowners are permitted to vote only if they are present at a scheduled company meeting. (See the previous section "Proxy Voting" for a discussion of this issue.)

Where to find information concerning confidentiality of voting rights: Investors should look to the company's by-laws or articles of organization to determine the procedures for counting and tabulating shareowner votes.

Cumulative Voting

Investors should determine whether shareowners are allowed to cast the cumulative number of votes allotted to their shares for one or a limited number of board nominees (which is cumulative voting).

Implications for Investors   The ability to use cumulative voting enables shareowners to vote in a manner that enhances the likelihood that their interests are represented on the board.

---

32 In the case of pooled investment funds, CFA Institute has taken the position that the funds should disclose to investors how they voted the shares of each company on behalf of the fund's beneficiaries. Such disclosures are different from disclosing those votes to management and the board, in that the investment fund is disclosing its voting record to the *beneficiaries* on whose behalf it is acting.

Things to Consider   In evaluating how a company handles cumulative voting, investors should consider whether the company has a significant minority shareowner group, such as a founding family, that might be able to use cumulative voting to elect board members who represent its specific interests at the expense of the interests of other shareowners.

Where to find information about whether a company permits cumulative voting: The articles of organization and by-laws frequently provide information about how a company regards shareowner initiatives and rights. The prospectus that a listed company must file with the local regulator will typically describe the circumstances under which shareowners can exercise their voting rights.

In the United States, investors also may look to Form 8-A, which listed companies must file with the SEC, for a description of the rights afforded a company's common shares.

Voting for Other Corporate Changes

Investors should determine whether shareowners have the right to approve changes to corporate structures and policies that may alter the relationship between shareowners and the company.

Reasons for Considering Shareowner Input on Corporate Changes   Changes to certain corporate structures have the ability to affect the value, ownership percentage, and rights associated with the company's securities. Among the issues shareowners should review is the ability of shareowners to effect changes to the following company aspects:

- articles of organization,
- by-laws,
- governance structures,
- voting rights and mechanisms,
- poison pills,
- change-in-control provisions, and
- board membership (by contesting board elections or recommending directors).

Implications for Investors   Certain changes to the company's by-laws or articles of organization can affect the shareowner's interests in the company. For example, the introduction or modification of an antitakeover mechanism might make a takeover too expensive for potential acquirers to consider, thereby denying shareowners full market value for their shares. Similarly, providing large quantities of stock options to management and employees may dilute the value of shares held by existing shareowners while redistributing company resources to insiders without shareowner approval. Shareowners should also consider whether such option grants put too much emphasis on short-term goals without regard to long-term risks.

Things to Consider   In reviewing what issues require shareowner approval, investors should determine whether shareowners

- have an opportunity to vote on the sale of their company or a substantial portion of their company to a third-party buyer. Investors also may wish to consider whether shareowners have an opportunity to vote on significant acquisitions and divestitures that could increase or reduce annual revenues by 10 percent or more;
- have the right to vote on certain aspects of executive compensation (see also the subsection "Executive Compensation" in the section "Corporate Transparency");

- have the right to vote against directors;

- have the right to approve a new antitakeover measure and whether such measures are subject to periodic review and retention by shareowners (see the subsection "Takeover Defenses" in the section "Other Shareowner-Rights Issues");

- have the ability to periodically reconsider and revote on rules that require super-majority voting to revise the company's by-laws, articles of organization, or other governance documents. Although these super-majority requirements may have been useful in making unwanted changes more difficult at a particular time in the company's development, they may not serve the same purpose in light of the company's evolution. Such provisions can make even changes overwhelmingly supported by shareowners difficult to enact;

- have the ability to vote for changes to the following company elements:
  - articles of organization,
  - by-laws,
  - governance structures, and
  - voting rights and mechanisms;

- may use their ownership of a limited number of shares to force a vote on special interests that are unrelated to the company's operations. Such actions could cause the board to make it more difficult for other shareowners to propose resolutions that are relevant to the company's operations.

Investors also should review the following issues to determine whether or in what conditions shareowners may vote on

- share-repurchase programs, particularly if their purpose is to fund share-based compensation grants (see the section "Share-Repurchase and Price-Stabilization Programs"),

- amendments, additions to, or revocation of corporate charters and by-laws, and

- issuance of new capital stock, including common shares and instruments that convert into common shares.

Where to find information about whether certain corporate changes require shareowner approval: The company will often provide information to shareowners about specific issues requiring a vote as part of the company's disclosures relating to the annual general meeting or as part of disclosures related to a special meeting of shareowners.

A company typically will provide information on which issues require shareowner approval in the company's by-laws and articles of organization. These documents will also provide information about whether management and the board can fill any vacancies without shareowner approval.

Shareowner Proposals

Shareowner proposals are generally of two types: board nominations and resolutions. In all cases of shareowner proposals, one issue is whether the proposal is binding or advisory only.

Shareowner-Sponsored Board Nominations

Investors should determine whether and in what circumstances shareowners are permitted to recommend director nominees to the board or place their own nominees on the proxy ballot.

Reasons for Determining Whether Shareowners Can Propose Board Nominees The ability to nominate one or more individuals to the board can prevent erosion of shareowner value. When a board and management fail to remedy existing problems and improve the company's financial performance, shareowners may use this power to ensure that at least one nominee is independent of the existing board and its nominations committee.

Implications for Investors If shareowners have the right to nominate board members, they have the ability to force the board or management to take steps to address shareowner concerns.

Things to Consider In evaluating whether shareowners can propose nominees to the board, investors should determine

- in what circumstances shareowners have the right to nominate board members, such as when the board ignores a shareowner initiative;
- how the company handles contested board elections. At some companies, particularly in the United States and Canada, a single vote cast in favor of a nominee is sufficient for an uncontested nominee to get elected to the board. In cases where the nominations are contested by shareowners, different rules for determining winners may apply.

Where to find information about the ability of shareowners to nominate individuals for the board: The notice of the annual general meeting will provide information related to the election of board members. Also, the articles of organization and by-laws frequently provide information about how a company regards shareowner initiatives and rights. In the United States, investors may look to the company's annual proxy statement.

Shareowner-Sponsored Resolutions

Investors should determine whether and in what circumstances shareowners may submit proposals for consideration at the company's annual general meeting.

Reasons for Determining Whether Shareowners Can Propose Corporate Initiatives Investors need to understand what they can do if the board and management fail to remedy existing problems or improve the company's financial performance. Investors also need to understand the extent to which outside institutions or individuals with specific interests or biases are able to influence company activity. The ability to propose needed changes can prevent erosion of shareowner value.

Implications for Investors The right to propose initiatives for consideration at the company's annual general meeting is one way for shareowners to send a message that they do not like the way the board and/or management is handling one or more company matters. If the proposal receives an overwhelming number of votes, it could pressure the board and management either to make the changes called for or, if they fail to do so, to justify their inaction.

Things to Consider In evaluating the ability of shareowners to propose changes for the company, investors should determine whether

- the company requires a simple majority, a two-thirds majority, or some other super-majority vote for passing a shareowner resolution. The company may require a simple majority vote to pass board- or management-sponsored initiatives;

- initiatives proposed by shareowners benefit the long-term interests of all share-owners or whether they represent the narrow interests of those making the proposals;

- any "advance notice provision" exists in the jurisdiction that would require a shareowner to give notice of a proposal a certain amount of time before an annual meeting. Often such advance notice has to do with the nomination of directors, and such notice requirements call on a shareowner to give notice of such proposals to the company months before the annual meeting.

Where to find information about shareowner authority to propose voting initiatives: A company's articles of organization and by-laws frequently provide information about how a company regards shareowner-sponsored proposals. In the United States, shareowners may look to the annual proxy statement for information about how to submit proxy initiatives.

Advisory or Binding Shareowner Proposals

Investors should determine whether the board and management are required to implement proposals that shareowners approve.

Reasons for Determining Whether Shareowner Proposals Are Binding   Unless the company is required to implement an initiative that shareowners have approved, the board and management may ignore those and other shareowner concerns.

Implications for Investors   Requirements that the board and management implement approved shareowner-sponsored initiatives could pressure the board and management to act on behalf of shareowners.

Things to Consider   When reviewing the company's rules regarding shareowner initiatives, investors should determine whether

- the company has implemented or ignored approved shareowner-sponsored proposals in the past;

- the company requires a super majority of votes to approve changes to its by-laws and articles of organization;

- national regulatory agencies have pressured companies to act on the terms of approved shareowner initiatives.

Where to find information about the enforceability of shareowner-sponsored proposals: The articles of organization and by-laws typically provide information about whether shareowner initiatives are binding and, if so, the size of the majority vote needed to enforce the measure. Investors also may look to the regulatory agency in the jurisdiction where the company is headquartered to determine whether the agency has taken steps to enforce shareowner initiatives in other cases.

Other Shareowner-Rights Issues

Issues discussed here include shareowners' legal rights, takeover defenses, and the actions of other shareowners.

Shareowner Legal Rights

Investors should determine whether the corporate governance code and other legal statutes of the jurisdiction in which the company is headquartered permit shareowners to take legal action or seek regulatory action to protect and enforce their ownership rights.

Reasons for Determining the Legal Remedies Available to Shareowners   In situations where the company has failed to fully recognize shareowner rights, shareowners may have to turn to the courts or national regulators to enforce their rights of ownership.

Things to Consider   When reviewing the local governance code and statutes regarding legal and regulatory actions, investors should determine whether

- local legal statutes permit shareowners to take derivative legal actions, which permit shareowners to initiate legal actions against management or board members on behalf of the company and, if so, what conditions must be met for them to take such actions;

- the regulator in the local jurisdiction where the company is headquartered has taken action in other cases to enforce shareowner rights or to prevent the denial of shareowner rights;

- shareowners, either individually or as a class, are permitted to take legal action or seek regulatory action to enforce fraud charges against management or the board.

Where to find information about legal and regulatory relief for shareowners: The regulator in the local market of the company's headquarters may provide information about the remedies available to shareowners in a variety of legal and regulatory matters.

Takeover Defenses

Shareowners should carefully evaluate the structure of an existing or proposed takeover defense and analyze how it could affect the value of shares in a normal market environment and in the event of a takeover bid.

Reasons for Reviewing Disclosures Relating to Takeover Defenses   Such disclosures should provide shareowners with information about the situations in which takeover defenses could be used to counter a hostile bid. Examples of takeover defenses include golden parachutes, cross-shareholdings, caps on voting rights, poison pills, and greenmail.[33]

Implications for Investors   By forcing an acquiring entity to deal directly with management and the board, takeover defenses may reduce the potential for the acquirer to succeed, even in situations that would benefit shareowners. Defenses against takeovers also may cause investors to discount the value of the company's shares in normal trading because of the conditions and barriers they create.

Things to Consider   When reviewing a company's antitakeover measures, investors should

- inquire whether the company is required to receive shareowner approval for such measures prior to implementation. Each company is likely to structure antitakeover measures differently. In some cases, investors may find that the board is permitted to implement an antitakeover measure subject to approval by shareowners within a set period of time. Others may not require shareowner approval at all;

- inquire whether the company has received any formal acquisition overtures during the past two years and whether takeover defenses were used;

---

33 Greenmail is a premium paid by the object of a hostile takeover bid to the entity making that bid in return for an agreement that the bidding entity will halt its takeover bid for a certain period.

- consider the possibility that the board and management will use the company's cash and available credit lines to pay a hostile bidder to forgo a takeover. In general, shareowners should take steps to prevent the board from carrying out such actions. If the company agrees to such payments, shareowners should review any publicly available information about the terms of such greenmail payments;

- consider whether in some cases change-in-control issues are likely to invoke the interest of a national or local government, which might then pressure the seller to change the terms of a proposed acquisition or merger. In such cases, the investor is unlikely to find specific government directives decreeing such defenses, although investors may find indications about the likelihood of such actions by examining the government's past actions relating to the company or relating to other companies in similar situations;

- consider whether change-in-control provisions will trigger large severance packages and other payments to company executives;

- understand whether the company is involved in any cross-shareholding arrangements with other companies that may function as a defense against hostile takeover bids from unwanted third parties.

Where to find information about takeover provisions: A company's articles of organization are the most likely places to find information about existing takeover defenses. Newly created antitakeover provisions may or may not require shareowner approval. In any case, the company may have to provide information to its shareowners about amendments to existing defenses.

Actions of Other Shareowners

Investors should understand that the actions of other shareowners are governance issues they need to consider with the same degree of interest as they do the actions of the board and management.

Reasons for Reviewing Disclosures Relating to Other Shareowner Actions   The actions of other shareowners may have a great deal of influence on the value of a company's shares. Activist investors or investor groups with significant stakes in companies often have the power to influence corporate decisions and sometimes to replace board members and even management. Shareowners should pay attention to the actions of the owners of large amounts of the company's shares to determine whether their actions are consistent with the creation of long-term shareowner value.

Implications for Investors   Investors may see their shareholdings diluted, may see a shareowner push for changes they do not agree would be in the best interests of the company, or may get ideas from activists about strategies that investors may want to apply at other companies in which they are invested.

Things to Consider   When reviewing the activities of other shareowners, investors should understand the motivations behind the actions of any activist investor: Are the motivations short term in nature or intended to enhance the creation of long-term value?

PRACTICE PROBLEMS

1 Cumulative voting is *best* described as:

   A a mechanism for suppressing hostile takeovers.

   B a means of offsetting the negative consequences of super-voting rights shares.

   C enhancing the likelihood that shareowners' interests are represented on the Board.

2 Which of the following is *least* consistent with good corporate governance?

   A Allowing shareowners the right to vote their shares by proxy.

   B Ensuring that a majority of the members of the audit committee are independent members of the Board.

   C Requiring a supermajority to pass shareowner resolutions and a simple majority to pass Board- or management-sponsored initiatives.

3 Regarding corporate governance, for which of the following areas of responsibility is a board committee *least likely* to be created?

   A Ethics.

   B Nominations to the Board.

   C Compensation of executive management.

4 Regarding corporate governance, which of the following is *least likely* to be part of a strong code of ethics? Provisions prohibiting the:

   A Company from using stock incentive options as a form of executive compensation.

   B use of Company airplanes for the personal benefit of Board Members, management, or their family members.

   C Company from offering shares at discounted prices to management, Board Members, and other insiders prior to a public offering of securities.

SOLUTIONS

1   C is correct. Cumulative voting enhances the likelihood that shareowner interests are represented on the Board.

2   C is correct. The ability of shareowners to propose corporate initiatives can "prevent erosion of shareowner value." However, forcing shareowner initiatives to pass by a supermajority rather than a simple majority places such initiatives at a disadvantage to Board- or management-sponsored initiatives if the latter require only a simple majority to pass.

3   A is correct. While important, ethics does not generally merit a separate Board committee and is normally a responsibility of management.

4   A is correct. A strong code of ethics would not necessarily ban the use of stock incentive options.

Portfolio Management

Study Session 12 Portfolio Management

TOPIC LEVEL LEARNING OUTCOME

The candidate should be able to explain and demonstrate the use of fundamentals of portfolio management, including return and risk measurement, and portfolio planning and construction.

12

Portfolio Management

This study session provides the critical framework and context for subsequent Level I study sessions covering equities, fixed income, derivatives, and alternative investments. Furthermore, this study session also provides a basis for the coverage of portfolio management at Levels II and III.

The first reading introduces the concept of a portfolio approach to investments. After discussing the investment needs of various types of individual and institutional investors, the reading compares the types of pooled investment management products that are available to investors. The following two readings cover portfolio risk and return measures and introduce modern portfolio theory—a quantitative framework for portfolio selection and asset pricing. The last reading focuses on the portfolio planning and construction process, including the development of an investment policy statement.

READING ASSIGNMENTS

Reading 42	Portfolio Management: An Overview by Robert M. Conroy, CFA, and Alistair Byrne, CFA
Reading 43	Portfolio Risk and Return: Part I by Vijay Singal, CFA
Reading 44	Portfolio Risk and Return: Part II by Vijay Singal, CFA
Reading 45	Basics of Portfolio Planning and Construction by Alistair Byrne, CFA, and Frank E. Smudde, CFA

Portfolio Management: An Overview

by Robert M. Conroy, CFA, and Alistair Byrne, CFA

LEARNING OUTCOMES

Mastery	The candidate should be able to:
☐	a. describe the portfolio approach to investing;
☐	b. describe types of investors and distinctive characteristics and needs of each;
☐	c. describe defined contribution and defined benefit pension plans;
☐	d. describe the steps in the portfolio management process;
☐	e. describe mutual funds and compare them with other pooled investment products.

INTRODUCTION

1

In this reading we explain why the portfolio approach is important to all types of investors in achieving their financial goals. We compare the financial needs of different types of individual and institutional investors. After we outline the steps in the portfolio management process, we compare and contrast the types of investment management products that are available to investors and how they apply to the portfolio approach.

A PORTFOLIO PERSPECTIVE ON INVESTING

2

One of the biggest challenges faced by individuals and institutions is to decide how to invest for future needs. For individuals, the goal might be to fund retirement needs. For such institutions as insurance companies, the goal is to fund future liabilities in the form of insurance claims, whereas endowments seek to provide income to meet the ongoing needs of such institutions as universities. Regardless of the ultimate goal, all face the same set of challenges that extend beyond just the choice of what asset classes to invest in. They ultimately center on formulating basic principles that determine how to think about investing. One important question is: Should we invest in individual securities, evaluating each in isolation, or should we take a portfolio approach? By "portfolio approach," we mean evaluating individual securities in relation to their contribution to the investment characteristics of the whole portfolio. In the following section, we illustrate a number of reasons why a diversified portfolio perspective is important.

2.1 Portfolio Diversification: Avoiding Disaster

Portfolio diversification helps investors avoid disastrous investment outcomes. This benefit is most convincingly illustrated by examining what may happen when individuals have *not* diversified.

We are usually not able to observe how individuals manage their personal investments. However, in the case of U.S. 401(k) individual retirement portfolios,[1] it is possible to see the results of individuals' investment decisions. When we examine their retirement portfolios, we find that some individual participants make sub-optimal investment decisions.

During the 1990s, Enron Corporation was one of the most admired corporations in the United States. A position in Enron shares returned over 27 percent per year from 1990 to September 2000, compared to 13 percent for the S&P 500 Index for the same time period.

Exhibit 1	Value of US$1 Invested from January 1990 to September 2000 Enron vs. S&P 500 Composite Index (01/01/1990 = US$1.00)

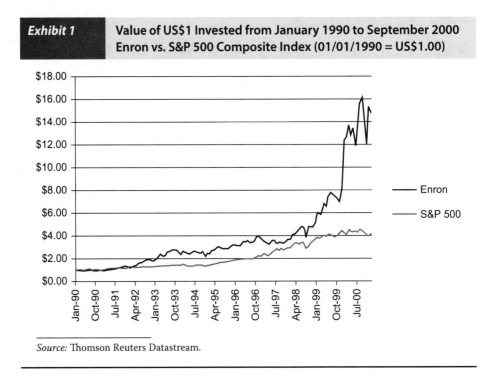

Source: Thomson Reuters Datastream.

During this time period, thousands of Enron employees participated in the company's 401(k) retirement plan. The plan allowed employees to set aside some of their earnings in a tax-deferred account. Enron participated by matching the employees' contributions. Enron made the match by depositing required amounts in the form of

---

1 In the United States, 401(k) plans are employer-sponsored individual retirement savings plans. They allow individuals to save a portion of their current income and defer taxation until the time when the savings and earnings are withdrawn. In some cases, the sponsoring firm will also make matching contributions in the form of cash or shares. Individuals within certain limits have control of the invested funds and consequently can express their preferences as to which assets to invest in.

Enron shares. Enron restricted the sale of its contributed shares until an employee turned 50 years old. In January 2001, the employees' 401(k) retirement accounts were valued at over US$2 billion, of which US$1.3 billion (or 62 percent) was in Enron shares. Although Enron restricted the sale of shares it contributed, less than US$150 million of the total of US$1.3 billion in shares had this restriction. The implication was that Enron employees continued to hold large amounts of Enron shares even though they were free to sell them and invest the proceeds in other assets.

A typical individual was Roger Bruce,[2] a 67-year-old Enron retiree who held all of his US$2 million in retirement funds in Enron shares. Unlike most stories, this one does not have a happy ending. Between January 2001 and January 2002, Enron's share price fell from about US$90 per share to zero.

Exhibit 2	Value of US$1 Invested from January 1990 to January 2002 Enron vs. S&P 500 Composite Index (1/1/1990 = US$1.00)

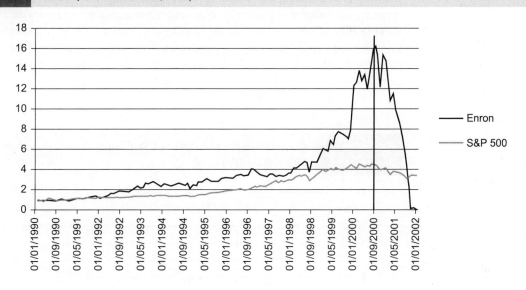

Source: Thomson Reuters Datastream.

Employees and retirees who had invested all or most of their retirement savings in Enron shares, just like Mr. Bruce, experienced financial ruin. The hard lesson that the Enron employees learned from this experience was to "not put all your eggs in one basket."[3] Unfortunately, the typical Enron employee did have most of his or her eggs in one basket. Most employees' wages and financial assets were dependent on Enron's continued viability; hence, any financial distress on Enron would have a material impact on an employee's financial health. The bankruptcy of Enron resulted in the closing of its operations, the dismissal of thousands of employees, and its shares becoming worthless. Hence, the failure of Enron was disastrous to the typical Enron employee.

Enron employees were not the only ones to be victims of over-investment in a single company's shares. Another form of pension arrangement in many corporations is the defined contribution plan, in which the employer makes periodic cash contributions to a retirement fund managed by the employees themselves instead of guaranteeing a certain pension at retirement. In the defined contribution retirement plans at Owens

---

2 Singletary (2001).
3 This expression, which most likely originated in England in the 1700s, has a timeless sense of wisdom.

Corning, Northern Telecom, Corning, and ADC Telecommunications, employees all held more than 25 percent of their assets in the company's shares during a time (March 2000 to December 2001) in which the share prices in these companies fell by almost 90 percent. The good news in this story is that the employees participating in employer-matched 401(k) plans since 2001 have significantly reduced their holdings of their employers' shares.

Thus, by taking a diversified portfolio approach, investors can spread away some of the risk. All rational investors are concerned about the risk–return trade-off of their investments. The portfolio approach provides investors with a way to reduce the risk associated with their wealth without necessarily decreasing their expected rate of return.

2.2 Portfolios: Reduce Risk

In addition to avoiding a potential disaster associated with over investing in a single security, portfolios also generally offer equivalent expected returns with lower over-all **volatility** of returns—as represented by a measure such as standard deviation. Consider this simple example: Suppose you wish to make an investment in companies listed on the Hong Kong Stock Exchange (HKSE) and you start with a sample of five companies.[4] The cumulative returns for the five companies from Q2 2004 through Q2 2008 are shown in Exhibit 3.

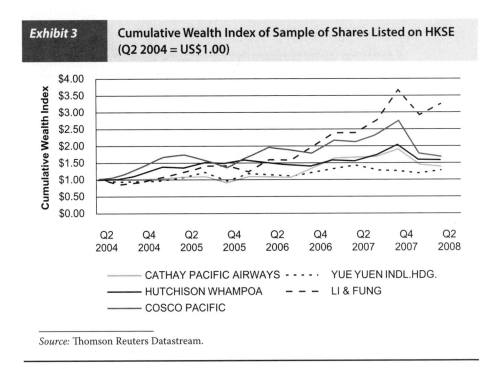

| Exhibit 3 | Cumulative Wealth Index of Sample of Shares Listed on HKSE (Q2 2004 = US$1.00) |

Source: Thomson Reuters Datastream.

The individual quarterly returns for each of the five shares are shown in Exhibit 4. The annualized means and annualized standard deviations for each are also shown.[5]

---

4 A sample of five companies from a similar industry group was arbitrarily selected for illustration purposes.
5 Mean quarterly returns are annualized by multiplying the quarterly mean by 4. Quarterly standard deviations are annualized by taking the quarterly standard deviation and multiplying it by 2.

| Exhibit 4 | Quarterly Returns (in Percent) for Sample of HKSE Listed Shares End of Q2 2004–End of Q2 2008 |

	Yue Yuen Industrial	Cathay Pacific Airways	Hutchison Whampoa	Li & Fung	COSCO Pacific	Equally Weighted Portfolio
Q3 2004	−11.1%	−2.3%	0.6%	−13.2%	−1.1%	−5.4%
Q4 2004	−0.5	−5.4	10.8	1.7	21.0	5.5
Q1 2005	5.7	6.8	19.1	13.8	15.5	12.2
Q2 2005	5.3	4.6	−2.1	16.9	12.4	7.4
Q3 2005	17.2	2.4	12.6	14.5	−7.9	7.8
Q4 2005	−17.6	−10.4	−0.9	4.4	−16.7	−8.2
Q1 2006	12.6	7.4	4.2	−10.9	15.4	5.7
Q2 2006	7.5	−0.4	−3.6	29.2	21.9	10.9
Q3 2006	−7.9	1.3	−5.1	−2.0	−1.6	−3.1
Q4 2006	8.2	27.5	0.1	26.0	−10.1	10.3
Q1 2007	18.3	24.3	16.5	22.8	25.7	21.5
Q2 2007	0.1	−2.6	−6.7	−0.4	0.3	−1.8
Q3 2007	−6.2	−4.2	16.7	11.9	11.1	5.8
Q4 2007	−8.0	17.9	−1.8	12.4	8.4	5.8
Q1 2008	3.5	−20.1	−8.5	−20.3	−31.5	−15.4
Q2 2008	2.1	−11.8	−2.6	24.2	−6.1	1.2
Mean annual return	7.3%	8.7%	12.3%	32.8%	14.2%	15.1%
Annual standard deviation	20.2%	25.4%	18.1%	29.5%	31.3%	17.9%
Diversification ratio						71.0%

Source: Thomson Reuters Datastream.

Suppose you want to invest in one of these five securities next year. There is a wide variety of risk–return trade-offs for the five shares selected. If you believe that the future will replicate the past, then choosing Li & Fung would be a good choice. For the prior four years, Li & Fung provided the best trade-off between return and risk. In other words, it provided the most return per unit of risk. However, if there is no reason to believe that the future will replicate the past, it is more likely that the risk and return on the one security selected will be more like selecting one randomly. When we randomly selected one security each quarter, we found an average annualized return of 15.1 percent and an average annualized standard deviation of 24.9 percent, which would now become your expected return and standard deviation, respectively.

Alternatively, you could invest in an equally weighted portfolio of the five shares, which means that you would invest the same dollar amount in each security for each quarter. The quarterly returns on the equally weighted portfolio are just the average of the returns of the individual shares. As reported in Exhibit 4, the equally weighted portfolio has an average return of 15.1 percent and a standard deviation of 17.9 percent. As expected, the equally weighted portfolio's return is the same as the return on the randomly selected security. However, the same does not hold true for the portfolio standard deviation. That is, the standard deviation of an equally weighted portfolio is not simply the average of the standard deviations of the individual shares. In a more advanced reading we will demonstrate in greater mathematical detail how such a portfolio offers a lower standard deviation of return than the average of its individual components due to the correlations or interactions between the individual securities.

Because the mean return is the same, a simple measure of the value of diversification is calculated as the ratio of the standard deviation of the equally weighted portfolio to the standard deviation of the randomly selected security. This ratio may be referred to as the **diversification ratio**. In this case, the equally weighted portfolio's standard deviation is approximately 71 percent of that of a security selected at random. The diversification ratio of the portfolio's standard deviation to the individual asset's standard deviation measures the risk reduction benefits of a simple portfolio construction method, equal weighting. Even though the companies were chosen from a similar industry grouping, we see significant risk reduction. An even greater portfolio effect (i.e., lower diversification ratio) could have been realized if we had chosen companies from completely different industries.

This example illustrates one of the critical ideas about portfolios: Portfolios affect risk more than returns. In the prior section portfolios helped avoid the effects of downside risk associated with investing in a single company's shares. In this section we extended the notion of risk reduction through portfolios to illustrate why individuals and institutions should hold portfolios.

2.3 Portfolios: Composition Matters for the Risk–Return Trade-off

In the previous section we compared an equally weighted portfolio to the selection of a single security. In this section we examine additional combinations of the same set of shares and observe the trade-offs between portfolio volatility of returns and expected return (for short, their risk–return trade-offs). If we select the portfolios with the best combination of risk and return (taking historical statistics as our expectations for the future), we produce the set of portfolios shown in Exhibit 5.

Exhibit 5	Optimal Portfolios for Sample of HKSE Listed Shares

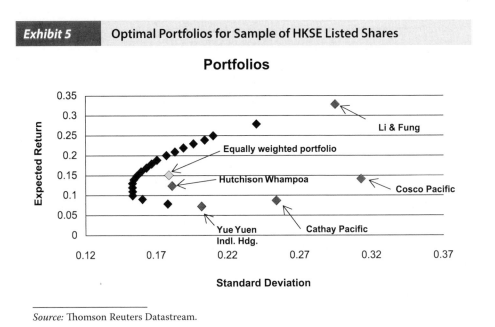

Source: Thomson Reuters Datastream.

In addition to illustrating that the diversified portfolio approach reduces risk, Exhibit 5 also shows that the composition of the portfolio matters. For example, an equally weighted portfolio (20 percent of the portfolio in each security) of the five shares has an expected return of 15.1 percent and a standard deviation of 17.9 percent. Alternatively, a portfolio with 25 percent in Yue Yuen Industrial (Holdings), 3 percent in Cathay Pacific, 52 percent in Hutchison Whampoa, 20 percent in Li & Fung, and 0 percent in COSCO Pacific produces a portfolio with an expected return of 15.1 percent and a standard deviation of 15.6 percent. Compared to a simple equally weighted portfolio, this provides an improved trade-off between risk and return because a lower level of risk was achieved for the same level of return.

2.4 Portfolios: Not Necessarily Downside Protection

A major reason that portfolios can effectively reduce risk is that combining securities whose returns do not move together provides diversification. Sometimes a subset of assets will go up in value at the same time that another will go down in value. The fact that these may offset each other creates the potential diversification benefit we attribute to portfolios. However, an important issue is that the co-movement or correlation pattern of the securities' returns in the portfolio can change in a manner unfavorable to the investor. We use historical return data from a set of global indices to show the impact of changing co-movement patterns.

When we examine the returns of a set of global equity indices over the last 15 years, we observe a reduction in the diversification benefit due to a change in the pattern of co-movements of returns. Exhibits 6 and 7 show the cumulative returns for a set of five global indices[6] for two different time periods. Comparing the first time period, from Q4 1993 through Q3 2000 (as shown in Exhibit 6), with the last time period, from Q1 2006 through Q1 2009 (as shown in Exhibit 7), we show that the degree to which these global equity indices move together has increased over time.

---

6 The S&P 500, Hang Seng, and Nikkei 500 are broad-based composite equity indices designed to measure the performance of equities in the United States, Hong Kong, and Japan. MSCI stands for Morgan Stanley Capital International. EAFE refers to developed markets in Europe, Australasia, and the Far East. AC indicates all countries, and EM is emerging markets. All index returns are in U.S. dollars.

Exhibit 6	Returns to Global Equity Indices Q4 1993–Q3 2000

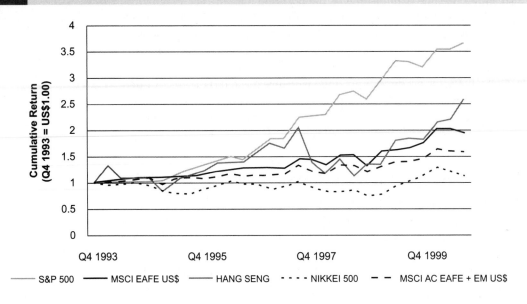

Source: Thomson Reuters Datastream.

Exhibit 7	Returns to Global Equity Indices Q1 2006–Q1 2009

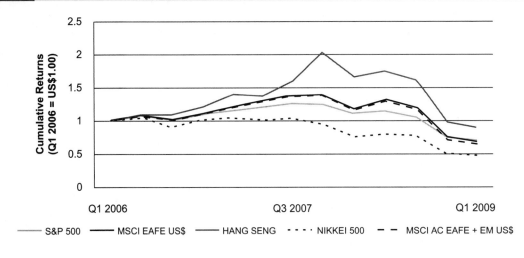

Source: Thomson Reuters Datastream.

The latter part of the second time period, from Q4 2007 to Q1 2009, was a period of dramatic declines in global share prices. Exhibit 8 shows the mean annual returns and standard deviation of returns for this time period.

| Exhibit 8 | Returns to Global Equity Indices |

Global Index	Q4 1993–Q3 2000		Q1 2006–Q1 2009		Q4 2007–Q1 2009	
	Mean	Stand. Dev.	Mean	Stand. Dev.	Mean	Stand. Dev.
S&P 500	20.5%	13.9%	−6.3%	21.1%	−40.6%	23.6%
MSCI EAFE US$	10.9	14.2	−3.5	29.4	−48.0	35.9
Hang Seng	20.4	35.0	5.1	34.2	−53.8	34.0
Nikkei 500	3.3	18.0	−13.8	27.6	−48.0	30.0
MSCI AC EAFE + EM US$	7.6	13.2	−4.9	30.9	−52.0	37.5
Randomly selected index	12.6%	18.9%	−4.7%	28.6%	−48.5%	32.2%
Equally weighted portfolio	12.6%	14.2%	−4.7%	27.4%	−48.5%	32.0%
Diversification ratio		75.1%		95.8%		99.4%

Source: Thomson Reuters Datastream.

During the period Q4 2007 through Q1 2009, the average return for the equally weighted portfolio, including dividends, was −48.5 percent. Other than reducing the risk of earning the return of the worst performing market, the diversification benefits were small. Exhibit 9 shows the cumulative quarterly returns of each of the five indices over this time period. All of the indices declined in unison. The lesson is that although portfolio diversification generally does reduce risk, it does not necessarily provide the same level of risk reduction during times of severe market turmoil as it does when the economy and markets are operating 'normally'. In fact, if the economy or markets fail totally (which has happened numerous times around the world), then diversification is a false promise. In the face of a worldwide contagion, diversification was ineffective, as illustrated at the end of 2008.

| Exhibit 9 | Return to Global Equity Indices Q4 2007–Q1 2009 |

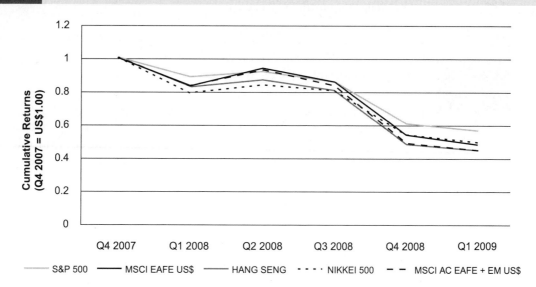

Source: Thomson Reuters Datastream.

Portfolios are *most likely* to provide:

A risk reduction.

B risk elimination.

C downside protection.

Solution:

A is correct. Combining assets into a portfolio should reduce the portfolio's volatility. However, the portfolio approach does not necessarily provide downside protection or eliminate all risk.

2.5 Portfolios: The Emergence of Modern Portfolio Theory

The concept of diversification has been around for a long time and has a great deal of intuitive appeal. However, the actual theory underlying this basic concept and its application to investments only emerged in 1952 with the publication of Harry Markowitz's classic article on portfolio selection.[7] The article provided the foundation for what is now known as **modern portfolio theory** (MPT). The main conclusion of MPT is that investors should not only hold portfolios but should also focus on how individual securities in the portfolios are related to one another. In addition to the diversification benefits of portfolios to investors, the work of William Sharpe (1964), John Lintner (1965), and Jack Treynor (1961) demonstrated the role that portfolios play in determining the appropriate individual asset risk premium (i.e., the return in excess of the risk-free return expected by investors as compensation for the asset's risk). According to capital market theory, the priced risk of an individual security is affected by holding it in a well-diversified portfolio. The early research provided the insight that an asset's risk should be measured in relation to the remaining systematic or non-diversifiable risk, which should be the only risk that affects the asset's price. This view of risk is the basis of the capital asset pricing model, or CAPM, which is discussed in greater detail in other readings. Although MPT has limitations, the concepts and intuitions illustrated in the theory continue to be the foundation of knowledge for portfolio managers.

3

INVESTMENT CLIENTS

Portfolio managers are employed or contracted by a wide variety of investment clients. We can group the clients into categories based on their distinctive characteristics and needs. Our initial distinction is between management of the private wealth of individual investors and investment management for institutional investors.

3.1 Individual Investors

Individual investors have a variety of motives for investing and constructing portfolios. Short-term goals can include providing for children's education, saving for a major purchase (such as a vehicle or a house), or starting a business. The retirement goal—investing to provide for an income in retirement—is a major part of the investment

---

7 Markowitz (1952).

planning of most individuals. Many employees of public and private companies invest for retirement through a **defined contribution pension plan** (DC plan). A DC plan is a pension plan in which contributions rather than benefits are specified, such as 401(k) plans in the United States, group personal pension schemes in the United Kingdom, and superannuation plans in Australia. Individuals will invest part of their wages while working, expecting to draw on the accumulated funds to provide income during retirement or to transfer some of their wealth to their heirs. The key to a DC plan is that the employee accepts the investment risk and is responsible for ensuring that there are enough funds in the plan to meet their needs upon retirement.

Some individuals will be investing for growth and will therefore seek assets that have the potential for capital gains. Others, such as retirees, may need to draw an income from their assets and may therefore choose to invest in fixed-income and dividend-paying shares. The investment needs of individuals will depend in part on their broader financial circumstances, such as their employment prospects and whether or not they own their own residence. They may also need to consider such issues as building up a cash reserve and the purchase of appropriate insurance policies before undertaking longer-term investments.

3.2 Institutional Investors

There are many different types of institutional investors. Examples include defined benefit pensions plans, university endowments, charitable foundations, banks, insurance companies, investment companies, and sovereign wealth funds (SWFs). Institutional investors are major participants in the investment markets. Exhibit 10 shows the relative size and growth rates of the key categories across the Organisation for Economic Co-operation and Development (OECD) countries. Investment funds are the largest category, with insurance companies and pension funds not far behind. The relative importance of these categories does vary significantly across the individual OECD countries.

Exhibit 10	Institutional Assets (in US$ billions) 1995 to 2005

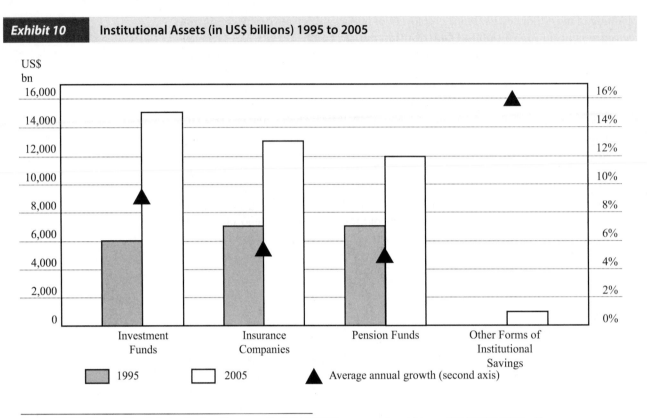

Source: OECD, "Recent Trends in Institutional Investors Statistics" (2008): www.oecd.org/dataoecd/53/49/42143444.pdf.

3.2.1 Defined Benefit Pension Plans

In a **defined benefit pension plan** (DB plan), an employer has an obligation to pay a certain annual amount to its employees when they retire. In other words, the future benefit is defined because the DB plan requires the plan sponsor to specify the obligation stated in terms of the retirement income benefits owed to participants. DB plans need to invest the assets that will provide cash flows that match the timing of the future pension payments (i.e., liabilities). Plans are committed to paying pensions to members, and the assets of these plans are there to fund those payments. Plan managers need to ensure that sufficient assets will be available to pay pension benefits as they come due. The plan may have an indefinitely long time horizon if new plan members are being admitted or a finite time horizon if the plan has been closed to new members. Even a plan closed to new members may still have a time horizon of 70 or 80 years. For example, a plan member aged 25 may not retire for another 40 years and may live 30 years in retirement. Hence, pension plans can be considered long-term investors. In some cases, the plan managers attempt to match the fund's assets to its liabilities by, for example, investing in bonds that will produce cash flows corresponding to expected future pension payments. There may be many different investment philosophies for pension plans, depending on funded status and other variables.

3.2.2 Endowments and Foundations

University endowments are established to provide continuing financial support to a university and its students (e.g., scholarships). Endowments vary in size (assets under management), but many are major investors. It is common for U.S. universities to have large endowments, but it is somewhat less common elsewhere in the world. Exhibit 11 shows the top ten U.S. university endowments by assets as of the end of

2008. In terms of non-U.S. examples, the University of Oxford, United Kingdom, and its various colleges were estimated to have a total endowment of £4.8 billion as of 2004 and the University of Cambridge, United Kingdom, and its colleges, £5.3 billion. These were by far the largest endowments in the United Kingdom. The third largest, University of Edinburgh, was £156 million.[8] The French business school INSEAD's endowment was valued at €105 million as of 2008.[9]

Exhibit 11	Top Ten U.S. University Endowments by Asset Value		
Rank	**Institution**	**State**	**Endowment Funds 2008 (US$000)**
1	Harvard University	MA	$36,556,284
2	Yale University	CT	22,869,700
3	Stanford University	CA	17,200,000
4	Princeton University	NJ	16,349,329
5	University of Texas System	TX	16,111,184
6	Massachusetts Institute of Technology	MA	10,068,800
7	University of Michigan	MI	7,571,904
8	Northwestern University	IL	7,243,948
9	Columbia University	NY	7,146,806
10	Texas A&M University System and foundations	TX	6,659,352

Source: NACUBO, "2008 NACUBO Endowment Study" (January 2009): www.nacubo.org/Research/ NACUBO_Endowment_Study.html.

Charitable foundations invest donations made to them for the purpose of funding grants that are consistent with the charitable foundation's objectives. Similar to university endowments, many charitable foundations are substantial investors. Exhibit 12 lists U.S. grant-making foundations ranked by the market value of their assets based on the most current audited financial data in the Foundation Center's database as of 5 February 2009. Again, large foundations are most common in the United States, but they also exist elsewhere. For example, the Wellcome Trust is a U.K.-based medical charity that had approximately £13 billion of assets as of 2008.[10] The Li Ka Shing Foundation is a Hong Kong-based education and medical charity with grants, sponsorships, and commitments amounting to HK$10.7 billion.

Exhibit 12	Top Ten U.S. Foundation Endowments by Asset Value	
Rank	**Foundation**	**Assets (US$000)**	**As of Fiscal Year-End Date**
1	Bill & Melinda Gates Foundation	$38,921,022	12/31/07
2	J. Paul Getty Trust	11,187,007	06/30/07

(continued)

---

8 Acharya and Dimson (2007).
9 See www.insead.com/campaign/endowment/index.cfm.
10 See www.wellcome.ac.uk/Investments/History-and-objectives/index.htm.

Exhibit 12	(Continued)		
Rank	**Foundation**	**Assets (US$000)**	**As of Fiscal Year-End Date**
3	Ford Foundation	11,045,128	09/30/08
4	Robert Wood Johnson Foundation	10,722,296	12/31/07
5	William and Flora Hewlett Foundation	9,284,917	12/31/07
6	W.K. Kellogg Foundation	8,402,996	08/31/07
7	Lilly Endowment	7,734,860	12/31/07
8	John D. and Catherine T. MacArthur Foundation	7,052,165	12/31/07
9	David and Lucile Packard Foundation	6,594,540	12/31/07
10	Andrew W. Mellon Foundation	6,539,865	12/31/07

Source: Foundation Center (2009): http://foundationcenter.org.

A typical investment objective of an endowment or a foundation is to maintain the real (inflation-adjusted) capital value of the fund while generating income to fund the objectives of the institution. Most foundations and endowments are established with the intent of having perpetual lives. Example 1 describes the US$22 billion Yale University endowment's approach to balancing short-term spending needs with ensuring that future generations also benefit from the endowment, and it also shows the £13 billion Wellcome Trust's approach. The investment approach undertaken considers the objectives and constraints of the institution (for example, no tobacco investments for a medical endowment).

EXAMPLE 1

Spending Rules

The following examples of spending rules are from the Yale University endowment (in the United States) and from the Wellcome Trust (in the United Kingdom).

Yale University Endowment

The spending rule is at the heart of fiscal discipline for an endowed institution. Spending policies define an institution's compromise between the conflicting goals of providing substantial support for current operations and preserving purchasing power of Endowment assets. The spending rule must be clearly defined and consistently applied for the concept of budget balance to have meaning.

Yale's policy is designed to meet two competing objectives. The first goal is to release substantial current income to the operating budget in a stable stream, since large fluctuations in revenues are difficult to accommodate through changes in University activities or programs. The second goal is to protect the value of Endowment assets against inflation, allowing programs to be supported at today's level far into the future.

Yale's spending rule attempts to achieve these two objectives by using a long-term spending rate of 5.25 percent combined with a smoothing rule that adjusts spending gradually to changes in Endowment market value. The amount released under the spending rule is based on a weighted average of prior spending adjusted for inflation (80 percent weight) and an amount determined by applying the target rate to the current Endowment market value (20 percent weight) with an adjustment factor based on inflation and the expected growth of the Endowment net of spending.

("2007 Yale Endowment Annual Report" (p.15): [www.yale.edu/investments/Yale_Endowment_07.pdf]).

Wellcome Trust

Our overall investment objective is to generate 6 percent real return over the long term. This is to provide for real increases in annual expenditure while preserving at least the Trust's capital base in real terms in order to balance the needs of both current and future beneficiaries. We use this absolute return strategy because it aligns asset allocation with funding requirements and it provides a competitive framework in which to judge individual investments.

(Wellcome Trust, "History and Objectives: Investment Goals" [www.wellcome.ac.uk/Investments/History-and-objectives/index.htm])

3.2.3 Banks

Banks typically accept deposits and extend loans. In some cases, banks need to invest their excess reserves, (i.e., when deposits have not been used to make loans). The investments of excess reserves need to be conservative, emphasizing fixed-income and money market instruments rather than equities and other riskier assets. In some countries, including the United States, there are legal restrictions on banks owning equity investments.[11] In addition to low risk, the investments also need to be relatively liquid so that they can be sold quickly if depositors wish to withdraw their funds. The bank's objective is to earn a return on its reserves that exceeds the rate of interest it pays on its deposits.

3.2.4 Insurance Companies

Insurance companies receive premiums for the policies they write, and they need to invest these premiums in a manner that will allow them to pay claims. Similar to banks, such investments need to be relatively conservative given the necessity of paying claims when due. Life insurance companies and non-life insurance companies (for example, auto and home insurance) differ in their purpose and objectives and hence in their investment time horizons. Life insurance companies have longer time horizons than non-life insurance companies as a result of different expectations of when payments will be required under policies.

3.2.5 Investment Companies

Investment companies that manage mutual funds are also institutional investors. The mutual fund is a collective financial institution in which investors pool their capital to have it invested by a professional manager. The investors own shares or units in the fund. For many investment managers, the mutual fund is, in effect, their client. However, mutual funds are slightly different in that they can also be considered a financial product. For many individual investors, the mutual fund is an efficient means to benefit from portfolio diversification and the skill of a professional manager. The

---

11 See, for example, www.minneapolisfed.org/publications_papers/pub_display.cfm?id=3518.

mutual fund is likely to invest in a particular category of investments, such as U.S. small capitalization equities. Mutual funds may also have certain limits and restrictions that apply to their investments, either as set by regulation and law or as decided by the board of directors of the investment company. We will revisit these investment vehicles in greater detail when we discuss pooled investments in Section 5.

3.2.6 *Sovereign Wealth Funds*

Sovereign wealth funds (SWFs) are government-owned investment funds, of which many are very sizable. For example, the largest SWF, managed by Abu Dhabi Investment Authority, is funded with oil revenues that amounted to US$627 billion[12] as of March 2009. Exhibit 13 provides a listing of the top 10 sovereign wealth funds as of March 2009.

Exhibit 13	Sovereign Wealth Funds by Asset Value		
Fund	**Assets as of March 2009 (US$ bns)**	**Inception Date**	**Country**
Abu Dhabi Investment Authority	$627	1976	Abu Dhabi, UAE
SAMA Foreign Holdings	431	n/a	Saudi Arabia
SAFE Investment Company	347	n/a	People's Republic of China
Norwegian Government Pension Fund-Global	326	1990	Norway
Government of Singapore Investment Corporation	248	1981	Singapore
National Welfare Fund	220	2008	Russia
Kuwait Investment Authority	203	1953	Kuwait
China Investment Corporation	190	2007	People's Republic of China
Hong Kong Monetary Authority Investment Portfolio	173	1998	People's Republic of China
Temasek Holdings	85	1974	Singapore
Total of top 10 SWFs	$2,850		
Total of all SWFs	$3,582		

Source: SWF Institute (www.swfinstitute.org).

Some funds have been established to invest revenues from finite natural resources (e.g., oil) for the benefit of future generations of citizens. Others manage foreign exchange reserves or other assets of the state. Some funds are quite transparent in nature—disclosing their investment returns and their investment holdings—whereas relatively little is known about the investment operations of others.

Exhibit 14 summarizes how investment needs vary across client groups. In some cases, generalizations are possible. In others, needs vary by client.

---

12 SWF Institute (www.Swfinstitute.org/funds.php).

Exhibit 14	Summary of Investment Needs by Client Type			
Client	**Time Horizon**	**Risk Tolerance**	**Income Needs**	**Liquidity Needs**
Individual investors	Varies by individual	Varies by individual	Varies by individual	Varies by individual
Defined benefit pension plans	Typically long term	Typically quite high	High for mature funds; low for growing funds	Typically quite low
Endowments and foundations	Very long term	Typically high	To meet spending commitments	Typically quite low
Banks	Short term	Quite low	To pay interest on deposits and operational expenses	High to meet repayment of deposits
Insurance companies	Short term for property and casualty; long term for life insurance companies	Typically quite low	Typically low	High to meet claims
Investment companies	Varies by fund	Varies by fund	Varies by fund	High to meet redemptions

STEPS IN THE PORTFOLIO MANAGEMENT PROCESS

4

In the previous section we discussed the different types of investment management clients and the distinctive characteristics and needs of each. The following steps in the investment process are critical in the establishment and management of a client's investment portfolio.

- The Planning Step
  - Understanding the client's needs
  - Preparation of an investment policy statement (IPS)
- The Execution Step
  - Asset allocation
  - Security analysis
  - Portfolio construction
- The Feedback Step
  - Portfolio monitoring and rebalancing
  - Performance measurement and reporting

4.1 Step One: The Planning Step

The first step in the investment process is to understand the client's needs (objectives and constraints) and develop an **investment policy statement** (IPS). A portfolio manager is unlikely to achieve appropriate results for a client without a prior understanding of the client's needs. The IPS is a written planning document that describes the client's investment objectives and the constraints that apply to the client's portfolio. The IPS may state a benchmark—such as a particular rate of return or the performance of a particular market index—that can be used in the feedback stage to assess the performance of the investments and whether objectives have been met. The IPS should be reviewed and updated regularly (for example, either every three years or when a major change in a client's objectives, constraints, or circumstances occurs).

4.2 Step Two: The Execution Step

The next step is for the portfolio manager to construct a suitable portfolio based on the IPS of the client. The portfolio execution step consists of first deciding on a target asset allocation, which determines the weighting of asset classes to be included in the portfolio. This step is followed by the analysis, selection, and purchase of individual investment securities.

4.2.1 Asset Allocation

The next step in the process is to assess the risk and return characteristics of the available investments. The analyst forms economic and capital market expectations that can be used to form a proposed allocation of asset classes suitable for the client. Decisions that need to be made in the **asset allocation** of the portfolio include the distribution between equities, fixed-income securities, and cash; sub-asset classes, such as corporate and government bonds; and geographical weightings within asset classes. Alternative assets—such as real estate, commodities, hedge funds, and private equity—may also be included.

Economists and market strategists may set the top down view on economic conditions and broad market trends. The returns on various asset classes are likely to be affected by economic conditions; for example, equities may do well when economic growth has been unexpectedly strong whereas bonds may do poorly if inflation increases. The economists and strategists will attempt to forecast these conditions.

Top down—A **top-down analysis** begins with consideration of macroeconomic conditions. Based on the current and forecasted economic environment, analysts evaluate markets and industries with the purpose of investing in those that are expected to perform well. Finally, specific companies within these industries are considered for investment.

Bottom up—Rather than emphasizing economic cycles or industry analysis, a **bottom-up analysis** focuses on company-specific circumstances, such as management quality and business prospects. It is less concerned with broad economic trends than is the case for top-down analysis, but instead focuses on company specifics.

4.2.2 Security Analysis

The top-down view can be combined with the bottom-up insights of security analysts who are responsible for identifying attractive investments in particular market sectors. They will use their detailed knowledge of the companies and industries they cover to assess the expected level and risk of the cash flows that each security will produce. This knowledge allows the analysts to assign a valuation to the security and identify preferred investments.

4.2.3 Portfolio Construction

The portfolio manager will then construct the portfolio, taking account of the target asset allocation, security analysis, and the client's requirements as set out in the IPS. A key objective will be to achieve the benefits of diversification (i.e., to avoid putting all the eggs in one basket). Decisions need to be taken on asset class weightings, sector weightings within an asset class, and the selection and weighting of individual securities or assets. The relative importance of these decisions on portfolio performance depends at least in part on the investment strategy selected; for example, consider an investor that actively adjusts asset sector weights in relation to forecasts of sector performance and one who does not. Although all decisions have an effect on portfolio performance, the asset allocation decision is commonly viewed as having the greatest impact.

Exhibit 15 shows the broad portfolio weights of the endowment funds of Yale University and the University of Virginia as of June 2008. As you can see, the portfolios have a heavy emphasis on such alternative assets as hedge funds, private equity, and real estate—Yale University particularly so.

Exhibit 15	Endowment Portfolio Weights, June 2008	
Asset Class	**Yale University Endowment**	**University of Virginia Endowment**
Public equity	25.3%	53.6%
Fixed income	4.0	15.0
Private equity	20.2	19.6
Real assets (e.g., real estate)	29.3	10.1
Absolute return (e.g., hedge funds)	25.1	8.1
Cash	−3.9	−6.5
Portfolio value	US$22.9bn	US$5.1bn

Note: The negative cash position indicates that at the point the figures were taken, the funds had net borrowing rather than net cash.

Sources: "2008 Yale Endowment Annual Report" (p. 2): www.yale.edu/investments/Yale_Endowment_08.pdf; "University of Virginia Investment Management Company Annual Report 2008" (p. 16): http://uvm-web.eservices.virginia.edu/public/reports/FinancialStatements_2008.pdf.

Risk management is an important part of the portfolio construction process. The client's risk tolerance will be set out in the IPS, and the portfolio manager must make sure the portfolio is consistent with it. As noted above, the manager will take a diversified portfolio perspective: What is important is not the risk of any single investment, but rather how all the investments perform as a portfolio.

The endowments shown above are relatively risk tolerant investors. Contrast the asset allocation of the endowment funds with the portfolio mix of the insurance companies shown in Exhibit 16. You will notice that the majority of the insurance assets are invested in fixed-income investments, typically of high quality. Note that the Yale University portfolio has only 4 percent invested in fixed income, with the remainder invested in such growth assets as equity, real estate, and hedge funds. This allocation is in sharp contrast to the Massachusetts Mutual Life Insurance Company (MassMutual) portfolio, which is over 80 percent invested in bonds, mortgages, loans, and cash—reflecting the differing risk tolerance and constraints (life insurers face regulatory constraints on their investments).

Exhibit 16	Insurance Company Portfolios, December 2008[13]	
Asset Classes	**MassMutual Portfolio**	**MetLife Portfolio**
Bonds	56.4%	58.7%
Preferred and common shares	2.2	1.0
Mortgages	15.1	15.9
Real estate	1.3	2.4
Policy loans	10.6	3.0
Partnerships	6.4	1.9
Other assets	4.5	5.3
Cash	3.5	11.8

Note: MetLife is the Metropolitan Life Insurance Company.
Sources: "MassMutual Financial Group 2008 Annual Report" (p. 26): www.massmutual.com/mmfg/docs/annual_report/index.html, "MetLife 2008 Annual Report" (p. 83): http://investor.metlife.com/phoenix.zhtml?c=121171&p=irol-reportsannual.

The portfolio construction phase also involves trading. Once the portfolio manager has decided which securities to buy and in what amounts, the securities must be purchased. In many investment firms, the portfolio manager will pass the trades to a buy-side trader—a colleague who specializes in securities trading—who will contact a stockbroker or dealer to have the trades executed.

Sell-side firm—A broker or dealer that sells securities to and provides independent investment research and recommendations to investment management companies.

Buy-side firm—Investment management companies and other investors that use the services of brokers or dealers (i.e., the clients of the sell-side firms).

4.3 Step Three: The Feedback Step

Finally, the feedback step assists the portfolio manager in rebalancing the portfolio due to a change in, for example, market conditions or the circumstances of the client.

4.3.1 Portfolio Monitoring and Rebalancing

Once the portfolio has been constructed, it needs to be monitored and reviewed and the composition revised as the security analysis changes because of changes in security prices and changes in fundamental factors. When security and asset weightings have

---

13 Asset class definitions: Bonds—Debt instruments of corporations and governments as well as various types of mortgage- and asset-backed securities; Preferred and Common Shares—Investments in preferred and common equities; Mortgages—Mortgage loans secured by various types of commercial property as well as residential mortgage whole loan pools; Real Estate—Investments in real estate; Policy Loans—Loans by policyholders that are secured by insurance and annuity contracts; Partnerships—Investments in partnerships and limited liability companies; Cash—Cash, short-term investments, receivables for securities, and derivatives. Cash equivalents have short maturities (less than one year) or are highly liquid and able to be readily sold.

drifted from the intended levels as a result of market movements, some rebalancing may be required. The portfolio may also need to be revised if it becomes apparent that the client's needs or circumstances have changed.

4.3.2 *Performance Measurement and Reporting*

Finally, the performance of the portfolio must be measured, which will include assessing whether the client's objectives have been met. For example, the investor will wish to know whether the return requirement has been achieved and how the portfolio has performed relative to any benchmark that has been set. Analysis of performance may suggest that the client's objectives need to be reviewed and perhaps changes made to the IPS. As we will discuss in the next section, there are numerous investment products that clients can use to meet their investment needs. Many of these products are diversified portfolios that an investor can purchase.

POOLED INVESTMENTS

5

The challenge faced by all investors is finding the right set of investment products to meet their needs. Just as there are many different types of investment management clients, there is a diverse set of investment products available to investors. These vary from a simple brokerage account in which the individual creates her own portfolio by assembling individual securities, to large institutions that hire individual portfolio managers for all or part of their investment management needs. Although the array of products is staggering, there are some general categories of pooled investment products that represent the full range of what is available. At one end are mutual funds and exchange traded funds in which investors can participate with a small initial investment. At the other end are hedge funds and private equity funds, which might require a minimum investment of US$1 million or more. In this context, the amount of funds that an individual or institution can commit to a particular product has a significant impact on which products are available. Exhibit 17 provides a general breakdown of what investment products are available to investors based on investable funds.

Exhibit 17	Investment Products by Minimum Investment	
■ Mutual funds ■ Exchange traded funds	■ Mutual funds ■ Exchange traded funds ■ Separately managed accounts	■ Mutual funds ■ Exchange traded funds ■ Separately managed accounts ■ Hedge funds ■ Private equity funds
As little as US$50	US$100,000	US$1,000,000 +

5.1 Mutual Funds

Rather than assemble a portfolio on their own, individual investors and institutions can turn over the selection and management of their investment portfolio to a third party. One alternative is a **mutual fund**. This type of fund is a comingled investment pool in which investors in the fund each have a pro-rata claim on the income and value of the fund. The value of a mutual fund is referred to as the "net asset value." It is computed on a daily based on the closing price of the securities in the portfolio.

At the end of the third quarter of 2008,[14] the Investment Company Institute reported over 48,000 mutual funds in over 23 countries with a total net asset value of approximately US$20 trillion. Exhibit 18 shows the breakdown of mutual fund assets across the major regions of the world as of the end of 2007.

Exhibit 18	Global Allocation of Mutual Fund Assets: 2007

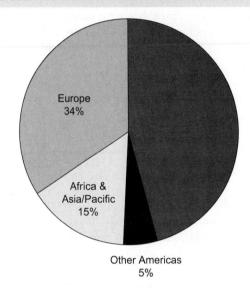

Source: 2008 Investment Company Fact Book, 48th ed. (p. 20): (www.ici.org/pdf/2008_factbook. pdf).

Mutual funds are one of the most important investment vehicles for individuals and institutions. The best way to understand how a mutual fund works is to consider a simple example. Suppose that an investment firm wishes to start a mutual fund with a target amount of US$10 million. It is able to reach this goal through investments from five individuals and two institutions. The investment of each is as follows:

Investor	Amount Invested (US$)	Percent of Total	Number of Shares
Individuals			
A	$1.0 million	10%	10,000
B	1.0	10	10,000
C	0.5	5	5,000
D	2.0	20	20,000
E	0.5	5	5,000
Institutions			
X	2.0	20	20,000
Y	3.0	30	30,000
Totals	**$10.0 million**	**100%**	**100,000**

---

14 Investment Company Institute (2009b).

Based on the US$10 million value (net asset value), the investment firm sets a total of 100,000 shares at an initial value of US$100 per share (US$10 million/100,000 = US$100). The investment firm will appoint a portfolio manager to be responsible for the investment of the US$10 million. Going forward, the total value of the fund or net asset value will depend on the value of the assets in the portfolio.

The fund can be set up as an open-end fund or a closed-end fund. If it is an **open-end fund**, it will accept new investment money and issue additional shares at a value equal to the net asset value of the fund at the time of investment. For example, assume that at a later date the net asset value of the fund increases to US$12.0 million and the new net asset value per share is US$120. A new investor, F, wishes to invest US$0.96 million in the fund. If the total value of the assets in the fund is now US$12 million or US$120 per share, in order to accommodate the new investment the fund would create 8,000 (US$0.96 million/US$120) new shares. After this investment, the net asset value of the fund would be US$12.96 million and there would be a total of 108,000 shares.

Funds can also be withdrawn at the net asset value per share. Suppose on the same day Investor E wishes to withdraw all her shares in the mutual fund. To accommodate this withdrawal, the fund will have to liquidate US$0.6 million in assets to retire 5,000 shares at a net asset value of US$120 per share (US$0.6 million/US$120). The combination of the inflow and outflow on the same day would be as follows:

Type	Investment (US$)	Shares
Inflow (Investor F buys)	$960,000	8,000
Outflow (Investor E sells)	−$600,000	−5,000
Net	$360,000	3,000

The net of the inflows and outflows on that day would be US$360,000 of new funds to be invested and 3,000 new shares created. However, the number of shares held and the value of the shares of all remaining investors, except Investor E, would remain the same.

An alternative to setting the fund up as an open-end fund would be to create a **closed-end fund** in which no new investment money is accepted into the fund. New investors invest by buying existing shares, and investors in the fund liquidate by selling their shares to other investors. Hence, the number of outstanding shares does not change. One consequence of this fixed share base is that, unlike open-end funds in which new shares are created and sold at the current net asset value per share, closed-end funds can sell for a premium or discount to net asset value depending on the demand for the shares.

There are advantages and disadvantages to each type of fund. The open-end fund structure makes it easy to grow in size but creates pressure on the portfolio manager to manage the cash inflows and outflows. One consequence of this structure is the need to liquidate assets that the portfolio manager might not want to sell at the time to meet redemptions. Conversely, the inflows require finding new assets in which to invest. As such, open-end funds tend not to be fully invested but rather keep some cash for redemptions not covered by new investments. Closed-end funds do not have these problems, but they do have a limited ability to grow. Of the total net asset value of all U.S. mutual funds at the end of 2008 (US$9.6 trillion), only approximately 2 percent were in the form of closed-end funds.

In addition to open-end or closed-end funds, mutual funds can be classified as load or no-load funds. The primary difference between the two is whether the investor pays a sales charge (a "load") to purchase, hold, or redeem shares in the fund. In the case of the **no-load fund**, there is no fee for investing in the fund or for redemption but there is an annual fee based on a percentage of the fund's net asset value. **Load funds** are funds in which, in addition to the annual fee, a percentage fee is charged to invest in the fund and/or for redemptions from the fund. In addition, load funds are usually sold through retail brokers who receive part of the upfront fee. Overall, the number and importance of load funds has declined over time.

Mutual funds also differ in terms of the type of assets that they invest in. Broadly speaking, there are four different types of funds that are differentiated by broad asset type: stock funds (domestic and international), bond funds (taxable and non-taxable), hybrid or balanced funds (combination of stocks and bonds), and money market funds (taxable and non-taxable). The approximately US$9.6 trillion in U.S. mutual fund net asset value by asset type as of the end of 2008 is shown in Exhibit 19. A breakdown for the European mutual fund market is shown in Exhibit 20.

Exhibit 19	Mutual Funds Net Asset Value by Asset Type End of 2007 and 2008.

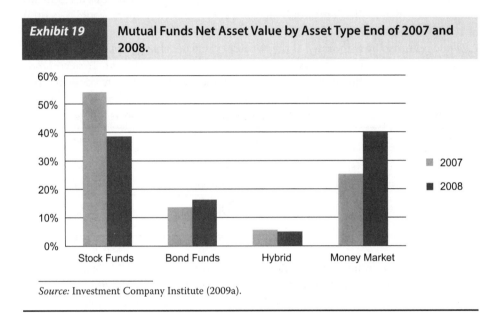

Source: Investment Company Institute (2009a).

Exhibit 20	European Mutual Fund (UCITS) Assets

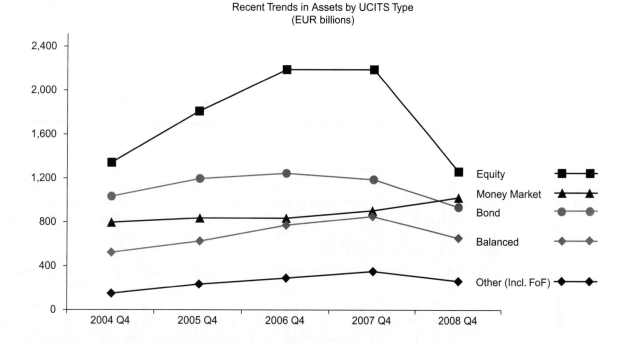

Recent Trends in Assets by UCITS Type
(EUR billions)

Note: UCITS (Undertakings for Collective Investments in Transferable Securities) are a set of regulations designed to help the European Union achieve a single funds market across Europe.

Source: EFAMA Quarterly Statistical Release No. 36 (Fourth Quarter of 2008). EFAMA is the European Fund and Asset Management Association.

Stock and money market funds make up the largest segments of the U.S. mutual fund industry. Between 2007 and 2008, however, there was a dramatic shift in the relative proportion of net asset value in stock funds and money market funds. Although there was a significant increase in the total value of assets in money market funds (24 percent, or approximately US$700 billion), the biggest change was in the value of total assets of stock funds, which fell by 43 percent or approximately US$2.8 trillion. Close to 10 percent of this drop, or US$280 billion, was the result of redemptions exceeding new investments, with the remaining of the decline attributed to the dramatic fall in share prices during 2008.[15] A similar drop in equity assets is evident in the European data.

5.2 Types of Mutual Funds

The following section introduces the major types of mutual funds differentiated by the asset type that they invest in: money market funds, bond mutual funds, stock mutual funds, and hybrid or balanced funds.

5.2.1 *Money Market Funds*

Although money market funds have been a substitute for bank savings accounts since the early 1980s, they are not insured in the same way as bank deposits. At the end of 2008, the total net asset value of U.S. money market funds was in excess of

---

15 These figures were extracted from data in Investment Company Institute (2009a).

US$3.8 trillion, with a further €1 trillion in European money market funds. In the United States, there are two basic types of money market funds: taxable and tax-free. Taxable money market funds invest in high-quality, short-term corporate debt and federal government debt. Tax-free money market funds invest in short-term state and local government debt. At the end of 2008 in the United States, there were approximately 540 taxable funds with about US$3.3 trillion in net asset value and approximately 250 tax-free money market funds with a total net asset value of about US$490 billion. From an investor's point of view, these funds are essentially cash holdings. As such, the presumption of investors is that the net asset value of a money market fund is always US$1.00 per share.

In September 2008 two large money market funds "broke the buck"; that is, the net asset value of the shares fell below US$1.00 per share. This drop in value caused investors to question the safety of money market funds and resulted in a massive outflow of funds from money market funds. This outflow continued until the U.S. Federal Reserve intervened to provide short-term insurance for some money market funds. This insurance, although similar to bank deposits, was limited in scope and time.

5.2.2 *Bond Mutual Funds*

A bond mutual fund is an investment fund consisting of a portfolio of individual bonds and, occasionally, preferred shares. The net asset value of the fund is the sum of the value of each bond in the portfolio divided by the number of shares. Investors in the mutual fund hold shares, which account for their pro-rata share or interest in the portfolio. The advantage is that an investor can invest in a bond fund for as little as US$100, which provides a stake in a diversified bond portfolio in which each individual bond may cost between US$10,000 and US$100,000. The major difference between a bond mutual fund and a money market fund is the maturity of the underlying assets. In a money market fund the maturity is as short as overnight and rarely longer than 90 days. A bond mutual fund, however, holds bonds with maturities as short as one year and as long as 30 years. Exhibit 21 illustrates the general categories of bond mutual funds.[16]

Exhibit 21	Bond Mutual Funds
Type of Bond Mutual Fund	**Securities Held**
Global	Domestic and non-domestic government, corporate, and securitized debt
Government	Government bonds and other government-affiliated bonds
Corporate	Corporate debt
High yield	Below investment-grade corporate debt
Inflation protected	Inflation-protected government debt
National tax-free bonds	National tax-free bonds (e.g., U.S. municipal bonds)

An example of a typical bond mutual fund is the T. Rowe Price Corporate Income Fund. Exhibit 22 shows the asset composition, credit quality, and maturity diversification for this bond mutual fund.

---

16 In the United States, judicial rulings on federal powers of taxation have created a distinction between (federally) taxable and (federally) tax-exempt bonds and a parallel distinction for U.S. bond mutual funds.

Exhibit 22	Asset Composition of T. Rowe Price Corporate Income Fund As of 31 March 2009

Asset Composition		Credit Quality Diversification		Maturity Diversification	
Assets	**% of Total**	**Bond Rating**[a]	**% of Total**	**Maturity (years)**	**% of Total**
U.S. corporate	78.7	AAA	7.1	0–1 year	3.7
Foreign bonds	18.4	AA	7.4	1–5 years	31.3
Cash	2.4	A	28.1	5–10 years	46.2
Other	0.5	BBB	48.8	10+ years	18.7
		BB	5.8		
		Other and not rated	0.3		
		Cash	2.4		

[a] Bond rating is from Standard & Poor's. AAA represents the highest credit quality. Bonds rated BBB and above are considered to be investment-grade bonds. Bonds rated below BBB are non-investment-grade bonds and are also known as high-yield or junk bonds.
Source: T. Rowe Price (www.troweprice.com).

5.2.3 Stock Mutual Funds

Historically, the largest types of mutual funds based on market value of assets under management are stock or equity funds. At the end of the third quarter of 2008, the worldwide investment in stock mutual funds totaled around US$8.6 trillion, with approximately US$4 trillion of that in U.S. stock mutual funds.

There are two types of stock mutual funds. The first is an actively managed fund in which the portfolio manager seeks outstanding performance through the selection of the appropriate stocks to be included in the portfolio. Passive management is followed by index funds that are very different from actively managed funds. Their goal is to match or track the performance of different indices. The first index fund was introduced in 1976 by the Vanguard Group. At the end of 2008, index funds held approximately 13 percent of the total net asset value of stock mutual funds.[17]

There are several major differences between actively managed funds and index funds. First, management fees for actively managed funds are higher than for index funds. The higher fees for actively managed funds reflect its goal to outperform an index, whereas the index fund simply aims to match the return on the index. Higher fees are required to pay for the research conducted to actively select securities. A second difference is that the level of trading in an actively managed fund is much higher than in an index fund, which has obvious tax implications. Mutual funds are required to distribute all income and capital gains realized in the portfolio, so the actively managed fund tends to have more opportunity to realize capital gains. This results in higher taxes relative to an index fund, which uses a buy-and-hold strategy. Consequently, there is less buying and selling in an index fund and less likelihood of realizing capital gains distributions.

5.2.4 Hybrid/Balanced Funds

Hybrid or balanced funds are mutual funds that invest in both bonds and shares. These types of funds represent a small fraction of the total investment in U.S. mutual funds but are more common in Europe. (See Exhibits 19 and 20.) These types of funds, however, are gaining popularity with the growth of lifecycle funds. These are funds that manage the asset mix based on a desired retirement date. For example, if an investor was 40 years old in 2008 and planned to retire at the age of 67, he could invest in a

---

17 Mamudi (2009).

mutual fund with a target date of 2035 and the fund would manage the appropriate asset mix over the next 27 years. In 2008 it might be 90 percent invested in shares and 10 percent in bonds. As time passes, however, the fund would gradually change the mix of shares and bonds to reflect the appropriate mix given the time to retirement.

5.3 Other Investment Products

In addition to mutual funds, a number of pooled investment products are increasingly popular in meeting the individual needs of clients. The following section introduces these products: exchange traded funds, separately managed accounts, hedge funds, and buyout and **venture capital funds**.

5.3.1 *Exchange Traded Funds*[18]

Exchange traded funds (ETFs) combine features of closed-end and open-end mutual funds. ETFs trade like closed-end mutual funds; however, like open-end funds, ETFs' prices track net asset value due to an innovative redemption procedure. ETFs are created by fund sponsors who determine which securities will be included in the basket of securities. To obtain the basket, the fund sponsors contact an institutional investor who deposits the securities with the fund sponsor. In return, the institutional investor receives creation units that typically represent between 50,000 and 100,000 ETF shares. These shares can then be sold to the public by the institutional investor. The institutional investor can redeem the securities held in the ETF by returning the number of shares in the original creation unit. This process prevents meaningful premiums or discounts from net asset value. Closed-end mutual funds are predominantly actively managed stock or bond funds whereas ETFs are typically index funds. The first ETF was created in the United States in 1993 and in 1999 in Europe. At the end of 2008, there were over 700 ETFs available in the United States with a total net asset value of over US$500 billion. A breakdown of the types of ETFs is shown in Exhibit 23.

The major difference between an index mutual fund and an ETF is that an investor investing in an index mutual fund buys the fund shares directly from the fund and all investments are settled at the net asset value. In the case of an ETF, however, investors buy the shares from other investors just as if they were buying or selling shares of stock. This setup includes the opportunity to short the shares or even purchase the shares on margin. The price an investor pays is based on the prevailing price at the time the transaction was made. This price may or may not be equal to the net asset value at the time, but it represents the price at that time for a willing buyer and seller. In practice, the market price of the ETF is likely to be close to the net asset value of the underlying investments.

Other main differences between an index mutual fund and an index ETF are transaction costs, transaction price, treatment of dividends, and the minimum investment amount. Expenses are lower for ETFs but, unlike mutual funds, investors do incur brokerage costs. Also as noted above, all purchases and redemptions in a mutual fund take place at the same price at the close of business. ETFs are constantly traded throughout the business day, and as such each purchase or sale takes place at the prevailing market price at that time. In the case of the ETF, dividends are paid out to the shareholders whereas index mutual funds usually reinvest the dividends. Hence, there is a direct cash flow from the ETF that is not there with the index mutual fund. Depending on the investor, this cash flow may or may not be desirable. Note that the

---

18 For more-detailed information on ETFs, see Investment Company Institute (2007) or Gastineau (2002). An additional resource for information on ETFs can be found in the American Association of Individual Investors' **AAII Journal**, which publishes an annual guide to ETFs in its October issue (see www.aaii.com/journal/index.cfm).

Exhibit 23   Types of Exchange Traded Funds (ETFs) January 2009

Type of ETF	End of 2008	Totals (in US$ millions)	Asset Class by Type of ETF as a Percentage of Assets under Management							
Broad-based equity	50.6%	$266,161	Total Market	Large Cap	Mid-Cap	Broad-Based, Other				
			7.4%	69.4%	9.4%	3.4%				
Sector	17.9%	94,101	Commodities	Consumer	Financial	Natural Resources	Real Estate	Technology	Utilities	Other Sectors
			38.0%	5.0%	16.6%	7.0%	12.8%	7.9%	4.8%	4.6%
Global/intern.	19.7%	103,713	Global	International	Regional	Single Country	Emerging Markets			
			8.8%	41.4%	5.6%	11.5%	42.3%			
Hybrid	0.0%	125	Hybrid							
			100%							
Bond	11.8%	62,185	Government Bond	Municipal Bond	Corporate Bond	International Bond				
			44.7%	3.5%	41.4%	2.4%				
Totals	100.0%	$526,285								

Source: Investment Company Institute, "Exchange-Traded Fund Assets, January 2009" (25 February 2009): http://ici.org/research/stats/etf/ci.etfs_01_09.print.

tax implications are the same with either fund type. Finally, the minimum required investment in an ETF is usually smaller. Investors can purchase as little as one share in an ETF, which is usually not the case with an index mutual fund.

ETFs are often cited as having tax advantages over index mutual funds. The advantage is not related to the dividends but rather to capital gains. As long as there is no sale of assets in either fund, no taxable capital gains would be realized by investors. It is possible, however, that because of the flow of funds into and out of index mutual funds, these funds would have a greater likelihood of generating taxable capital gains for investors. Overall, it is not clear how much of an advantage there is or if there is any advantage at all.

5.3.2 Separately Managed Accounts

A fund management service for institutions or individual investors with substantial assets is the **separately managed account** (SMA), which is also commonly referred to as a "managed account," "wrap account," or "individually managed account". An SMA is an investment portfolio managed exclusively for the benefit of an individual or institution. The account is managed by an individual investment professional to meet the specific needs of the client in relation to investment objectives, risk tolerance, and tax situation. In an SMA, the individual shares are held directly by the investor; and in return for annual fees, an individual can receive personalized investment advice.

The key difference between an SMA and a mutual fund is that the assets are owned directly by the individual. Therefore, unlike a mutual fund, the investor has control over which assets are bought and sold and the timing of the transactions. Moreover, in a mutual fund, there is no consideration given to the tax position of the individual asset. In an SMA, the transactions can take into account the specific tax needs of the investor. The main disadvantage of an SMA is that the required minimum investment is usually much higher than is the case with a mutual fund. Usually, the minimum investment is between US$100,000 and US$500,000.

Large institutions often use segregated accounts, which means their investments are held in an account on their behalf and managed by a portfolio manager or team. They can also use mutual funds. The decision on which approach to take often depends on the value of assets involved. Larger amounts of assets are more likely to be managed on a segregated basis.

5.3.3 Hedge Funds

The origin of **hedge funds**[19] can be traced back as far as 1949 to a fund managed by A.W. Jones & Co. It offered a strategy of a non-correlated offset to the "long-only" position typical of most portfolios. From this start emerged a whole new industry of hedge funds. Hedge fund strategies generally involve a significant amount of risk, driven in large measure by the liberal use of leverage and complexity. More recently, it has also involved the extensive use of derivatives.

A key difference between hedge funds and mutual funds is that the vast majority of hedge funds are exempt from many of the reporting requirements for the typical public investment company. In the United States, investment companies do not have to register with the U.S. Securities and Exchange Commission (SEC) if they have 100 or fewer investors [Section 3(c)1 of the Investment Company Act of 1940] or if the investor base is greater than 100 but less than 500 "qualified purchasers"[20] [Section 3(c)7 of the Investment Company Act of 1940]. In order to qualify for the exemption, hedge funds cannot be offered for sale to the general public; they can only be sold via

---

19 For a more comprehensive discussion of hedge funds, refer to Sihler (2004). Most of the discussion here is drawn from that document.
20 A "qualified purchaser" is an individual with over US$5 million in investment assets.

private placement. In addition, Regulation D of the Securities Act of 1933 requires that hedge funds be offered solely to "accredited investors."[21] The net effect of these regulations is that the hedge fund investor base is generally very different from that of the typical mutual fund.

From its start in 1955 to the end of 2008, the hedge fund industry has grown to over 9,200 hedge funds with approximately US$1.4 trillion in assets.[22] Not all hedge funds are the same, however. Many different strategies are employed. A few examples[23] include:

- **Convertible Arbitrage**—Buying such securities as convertible bonds that can be converted into shares at a fixed price and simultaneously selling the stock short.

- **Dedicated Short Bias**—Taking more short positions than long positions.

- **Emerging Markets**—Investing in companies in emerging markets by purchasing corporate or sovereign securities.

- **Equity Market Neutral**—Attempting to eliminate the overall market movement by going short overvalued securities and going long a nearly equal value of undervalued securities.

- **Event Driven**—Attempting to take advantage of specific company events. Event-driven strategies take advantage of transaction announcements and other one-time events.

- **Fixed-Income Arbitrage**—Attempting to profit from arbitrage opportunities in interest rate securities. When using a fixed-income arbitrage strategy, the investor assumes opposing positions in the market to take advantage of small price discrepancies while limiting interest rate risk.

- **Global Macro**—Trying to capture shifts between global economies, usually using derivatives on currencies or interest rates.

- **Long/Short**—Buying long equities that are expected to increase in value and selling short equities that are expected to decrease in value. Unlike the equity market neutral strategy, this strategy attempts to profit from market movements, not just from identifying overvalued and undervalued equities.

The list above is not all-inclusive; there are many other strategies. Hedge funds are not readily available to all investors. They require a minimum investment that is typically US$250,000 for new funds and US$1 million or more for well-established funds. In addition, they usually have restricted liquidity that could be in the form of allowing only quarterly withdrawals or having a fixed-term commitment of up to five years. Management fees are not only a fixed percentage of the funds under management; managers also collect fees based on performance. A typical arrangement would include a 1 percent to 2 percent fee on assets under management and 20 percent of the outperformance as compared to a stated benchmark.

---

21 An "accredited individual" investor must have a minimum net worth of US$1 million or a minimum individual income of US$200,000 in each of the two most recent years with the expectation of having the same income in the current year. An accredited institution must have a minimum of US$5 million in invested assets.

22 Both the number of hedge funds and the value of assets under management fell dramatically in the second half of 2008. According to Hedge Fund Research, Inc., during 2008 the total number of funds fell by 8 percent and the value of assets under management fell from approximately US$1.9 trillion to US$1.4 trillion at the end of 2008.

23 In the examples, "long" refers to owning the security and "selling short" refers to a strategy of borrowing shares and converting them to cash with the intention of repaying the shares at a later date by buying them back at a lower price. Long positions have a positive return when the price of the security increases, and short positions have a positive return when the price of the security falls.

5.3.4 *Buyout and Venture Capital Funds*

Two areas that have grown considerably over the last 15 years have been buyout and venture capital funds. Both take equity positions but in different types of companies. An essential feature of both is that they are not passive investors, and as such, they play a very active role in the management of the company. Furthermore, the equity they hold is private rather than traded on public markets. In addition, neither intends to hold the equity for the long term; from the beginning, both plan for an exit strategy that will allow them to liquidate their positions. Both venture capital funds and private equity funds operate in a manner similar to hedge funds. A minimum investment is required, there is limited liquidity during some fixed time period, and management fees are based not only on funds under management but also on the performance of the fund.

Buyout Funds The essence of a **buyout fund** is that it buys all the shares of a public company and, by holding all the shares, the company becomes private. The early **leveraged buyouts** (LBOs) of the mid-1960s through the early 1990s created the modern private equity firm. These were highly levered transactions that used the company's cash flow to pay down the debt and build the equity position. In its current form, private equity firms raise money specifically for the purpose of buying public companies, converting them to private companies, and simultaneously restructuring the company. The purchase is usually financed through a significant increase in the amount of debt issued by the company. A typical financing would include 25 percent equity and 75 percent debt in one form or another. The high level of debt is also accompanied by a restructuring of the operations of the company. The key is to increase the cash flow. Most private equity funds do not intend to hold the company for the long run because their goal is to exit the investment in three to five years either through an initial public offering (IPO) or a sale to another company. Generally, a private equity firm makes a few very large investments.

Venture Capital Funds Venture capital differs from a buyout fund in that a venture capital firm does not buy established companies but rather provides financing for companies in their start-up phase. Venture capital funds play a very active role in the management of the companies in which they invest; beyond just providing money, they provide close oversight and advice. Similar to buyout funds, venture capital funds typically have a finite investment horizon and, depending on the type of business, make the investment with the intent to exit in three to five years. These funds make a large number of small investments with the expectation that only a small number will pay off. The assumption is that the one that does pay off pays off big enough to compensate for the ones that do not pay off.

SUMMARY

- In this reading we have discussed how a portfolio approach to investing could be preferable to simply investing in individual securities.
- The problem with focusing on individual securities is that this approach may lead to the investor "putting all her eggs in one basket."
- Portfolios provide important diversification benefits, allowing risk to be reduced without necessarily affecting or compromising return.

- We have outlined the differing investment needs of various types of individual and institutional investors. Institutional clients include defined benefit pension plans, endowments and foundations, banks, insurance companies, investment companies, and sovereign wealth funds.

- Understanding the needs of your client and creating an investment policy statement represent the first steps of the portfolio management process. Those steps are followed by security analysis, portfolio construction, monitoring, and performance measurement stages.

- We also discussed the different types of investment products that investors can use to create their portfolio. These range from mutual funds, to exchange traded funds, to hedge funds, to private equity funds.

REFERENCES

Acharya, Shanta, and Elroy Dimson. 2007. *Endowment Asset Management: Investment Strategies in Oxford and Cambridge*. New York: Oxford University Press.

Gastineau, Gary L. 2002. *Exchange-Traded Funds Manual*. New York: John Wiley & Sons.

Investment Company Institute. 2007. "A Guide to Exchange-Traded Funds": (www.ici.org/investor_ed/brochures/bro_etf).

Investment Company Institute. 2009a. "Trends in Mutual Fund Investing, December 2008" (20 March).

Investment Company Institute. 2009b. "Worldwide Mutual Fund Assets and Flows, Third Quarter 2008" (5 May).

Lintner, John. 1965. "The Valuation of Risk Assets and the Selection of Risky Investments in Stock Portfolios and Capital Budgets." *Review of Economics and Statistics*, vol. 47, no. 1 (February):13–37.

Mamudi, Sam. 2009. "More Investors Ditch Market-Beating Attempts, Embrace Index Funds." *FiLife* (in partnership with the *Wall Street Journal*; 27 February): http://www.filife.com/stories/more-investors-ditch-market-beating-attempts-embrace-index-funds.

Markowitz, Harry M. 1952. "Portfolio Selection." *Journal of Finance*, vol. 7, no. 1 (March):77–91.

Sharpe, William F. 1964. "Capital Asset Prices: A Theory of Market Equilibrium under Conditions of Risk." *Journal of Finance*, vol. 19, no. 3 (September):425–442.

Sihler, William. 2004. *Introduction to Hedge Funds*. UVA-F-1529. Charlottesville, VA: Darden Business Publishing.

Singletary, Michelle. 2001. "Cautionary Tale of an Enron Employee Who Went for Broke." Seattlepi.com (10 December): http://www.seattlepi.com/money/49894_singletary10.shtml.

Treynor, J. L. 1961. "Toward a Theory of Market Value of Risky Assets." Unpublished manuscript.

PRACTICE PROBLEMS

1 Investors should use a portfolio approach to:

   A reduce risk.

   B monitor risk.

   C eliminate risk.

2 Which of the following is the *best* reason for an investor to be concerned with the composition of a portfolio?

   A Risk reduction.

   B Downside risk protection.

   C Avoidance of investment disasters.

3 With respect to the formation of portfolios, which of the following statements is *most accurate*?

   A Portfolios affect risk less than returns.

   B Portfolios affect risk more than returns.

   C Portfolios affect risk and returns equally.

4 Which of the following institutions will *on average* have the greatest need for liquidity?

   A Banks.

   B Investment companies.

   C Non-life insurance companies.

5 Which of the following institutional investors will *most likely* have the longest time horizon?

   A Defined benefit plan.

   B University endowment.

   C Life insurance company.

6 A defined benefit plan with a large number of retirees is *likely* to have a high need for

   A income.

   B liquidity.

   C insurance.

7 Which of the following institutional investors is *most likely* to manage investments in mutual funds?

   A Insurance companies.

   B Investment companies.

   C University endowments.

8 With respect to the portfolio management process, the asset allocation is determined in the:

   A planning step.

   B feedback step.

   C execution step.

These practice questions were developed by Stephen P. Huffman, CFA (University of Wisconsin, Oshkosh).

9 The planning step of the portfolio management process is *least likely* to include an assessment of the client's

 A   securities.

 B   constraints.

 C   risk tolerance.

10 With respect to the portfolio management process, the rebalancing of a portfolio's composition is *most likely* to occur in the:

 A   planning step.

 B   feedback step.

 C   execution step.

11 An analyst gathers the following information for the asset allocations of three portfolios:

Portfolio	Fixed Income (%)	Equity (%)	Alternative Assets (%)
1	25	60	15
2	60	25	15
3	15	60	25

Which of the portfolios is *most likely* appropriate for a client who has a high degree of risk tolerance?

 A   Portfolio 1.

 B   Portfolio 2.

 C   Portfolio 3.

12 Which of the following investment products is *most likely* to trade at their net asset value per share?

 A   Exchange traded funds.

 B   Open-end mutual funds.

 C   Closed-end mutual funds.

13 Which of the following financial products is *least likely* to have a capital gain distribution?

 A   Exchange traded funds.

 B   Open-end mutual funds.

 C   Closed-end mutual funds.

14 Which of the following forms of pooled investments is subject to the *least* amount of regulation?

 A   Hedge funds.

 B   Exchange traded funds.

 C   Closed-end mutual funds.

15 Which of the following pooled investments is *most likely* characterized by a few large investments?

 A   Hedge funds.

 B   Buyout funds.

 C   Venture capital funds.

SOLUTIONS

1 A is correct. Combining assets into a portfolio should reduce the portfolio's volatility. Specifically, "individuals and institutions should hold portfolios to reduce risk." As illustrated in the reading, however, risk reduction may not be as great during a period of dramatic economic change.

2 A is correct. Combining assets into a portfolio should reduce the portfolio's volatility. The portfolio approach does not necessarily provide downside protection or guarantee that the portfolio always will avoid losses.

3 B is correct. As illustrated in the reading, portfolios reduce risk more than they increase returns.

4 A is correct. The excess reserves invested by banks need to be relatively liquid. Although investment companies and non-life insurance companies have high liquidity needs, the liquidity need for banks is on average the greatest.

5 B is correct. Most foundations and endowments are established with the intent of having perpetual lives. Although defined benefit plans and life insurance companies have portfolios with a long time horizon, they are not perpetual.

6 A is correct. Income is necessary to meet the cash flow obligation to retirees. Although defined benefit plans have a need for income, the need for liquidity typically is quite low. A retiree may need life insurance; however, a defined benefit plan does not need insurance.

7 B is correct. Investment companies manage investments in mutual funds. Although endowments and insurance companies may own mutual funds, they do not issue or redeem shares of mutual funds.

8 C is correct. The client's objectives and constraints are established in the investment policy statement and are used to determine the client's target asset allocation, which occurs in the execution step of the portfolio management process.

9 A is correct. Securities are analyzed in the execution step. In the planning step, a client's objectives and constraints are used to develop the investment policy statement.

10 B is correct. Portfolio monitoring and rebalancing occurs in the feedback step of the portfolio management process.

11 C is correct. Portfolio 3 has the same equity exposure as Portfolio 1 and has a higher exposure to alternative assets, which have greater volatility (as discussed in the section of the reading comparing the endowments from Yale University and the University of Virginia).

12 B is correct. Open-end funds trade at their net asset value per share, whereas closed-end funds and exchange traded funds can trade at a premium or a discount.

13 A is correct. Exchange traded funds do not have capital gain distributions. If an investor sells shares of an ETF (or open-end mutual fund or closed-end mutual fund), the investor may have a capital gain or loss on the shares sold; however, the gain (or loss) from the sale is not a distribution.

14 A is correct. Hedge funds are currently exempt from the reporting requirements of a typical public investment company.

15 B is correct. Buyout funds or private equity firms make only a few large investments in private companies with the intent of selling the restructured companies in three to five years. Venture capital funds also have a short time horizon; however, these funds consist of many small investments in companies with the expectation that only a few will have a large payoff (and that most will fail).

Portfolio Risk and Return: Part I

by Vijay Singal, CFA

LEARNING OUTCOMES

Mastery	The candidate should be able to:
☐	**a.** calculate and interpret major return measures and describe their appropriate uses;
☐	**b.** describe characteristics of the major asset classes that investors consider in forming portfolios;
☐	**c.** calculate and interpret the mean, variance, and covariance (or correlation) of asset returns based on historical data;
☐	**d.** explain risk aversion and its implications for portfolio selection;
☐	**e.** calculate and interpret portfolio standard deviation;
☐	**f.** describe the effect on a portfolio's risk of investing in assets that are less than perfectly correlated;
☐	**g.** describe and interpret the minimum-variance and efficient frontiers of risky assets and the global minimum-variance portfolio;
☐	**h.** discuss the selection of an optimal portfolio, given an investor's utility (or risk aversion) and the capital allocation line.

INTRODUCTION

1

Construction of an optimal portfolio is an important objective for an investor. In this reading, we will explore the process of examining the risk and return characteristics of individual assets, creating all possible portfolios, selecting the most efficient portfolios, and ultimately choosing the optimal portfolio tailored to the individual in question.

During the process of constructing the optimal portfolio, several factors and investment characteristics are considered. The most important of those factors are risk and return of the individual assets under consideration. Correlations among individual assets along with risk and return are important determinants of portfolio risk. Creating a portfolio for an investor requires an understanding of the risk profile of the investor. Although we will not discuss the process of determining risk aversion for individuals or institutional investors, it is necessary to obtain such information for making an informed decision. In this reading, we will explain the broad types of investors and how their risk–return preferences can be formalized to select the optimal portfolio from among the infinite portfolios contained in the investment opportunity set.

The reading is organized as follows: Section 2 discusses the investment characteristics of assets. In particular, we show the various types of returns and risks, their computation and their applicability to the selection of appropriate assets for inclusion in a portfolio. Section 3 discusses risk aversion and how indifference curves, which incorporate individual preferences, can be constructed. The indifference curves are then applied to the selection of an optimal portfolio using two risky assets. Section 4 provides an understanding and computation of portfolio risk. The role of correlation and diversification of portfolio risk are examined in detail. Section 5 begins with the risky assets available to investors and constructs a large number of risky portfolios. It illustrates the process of narrowing the choices to an efficient set of risky portfolios before identifying the optimal risky portfolio. The risky portfolio is combined with investor risk preferences to generate the optimal risky portfolio. A summary concludes this reading.

2   INVESTMENT CHARACTERISTICS OF ASSETS

Financial assets are generally defined by their risk and return characteristics. Comparison along these two dimensions simplifies the process of selecting from millions of assets and makes financial assets substitutable. These characteristics distinguish financial assets from physical assets, which can be defined along multiple dimensions. For example, wine is characterized by its grapes, aroma, sweetness, alcohol content, and age, among other factors. The price of a television depends on picture quality, manufacturer, screen size, number and quality of speakers, and so on, none of which are similar to the characteristics for wine. Therein lies one of the biggest differences between financial and physical assets. Although financial assets are generally claims on real assets, their commonality across two dimensions (risk and return) simplifies the issue and makes them easier to value than real assets. In this section, we will compute, evaluate, and compare various measures of return and risk.

2.1 Return

Financial assets normally generate two types of return for investors. First, they may provide periodic income through cash dividends or interest payments. Second, the price of a financial asset can increase or decrease, leading to a capital gain or loss.

Certain financial assets, through design or choice, provide return through only one of these mechanisms. For example, investors in non-dividend-paying stocks, such as Google or Baidu, obtain their return from capital appreciation only. Similarly, you could also own or have a claim to assets that only generate periodic income. For example, defined benefit pension plans, retirement annuities, and reverse mortgages[1] make income payments as long as you live.

---

1 A reverse mortgage is a type of loan that allows individuals to convert part of their home equity into cash. The loan is usually disbursed in a stream of payments made to the homeowner by the lender. As long as the homeowner lives in the home, they need not be repaid during the lifetime of the homeowner. The loan, however, can be paid off at any time by the borrower not necessarily by selling the home.

You should be aware that returns reported for stock indices are sometimes misleading because most index levels only capture price appreciation and do not adjust for cash dividends unless the stock index is labeled "total return" or "net dividends reinvested." For example, as reported by Yahoo! Finance, the S&P 500 Index of U.S. stocks was at 903.25 on 31 December 2008. Similarly, Yahoo! Finance reported that the index closed on 30 July 2002 at 902.78, implying a return of close to 0 percent over the approximately six-and-a-half-year period. The results are very different, however, if the total return S&P 500 Index is considered. The index was at 1283.62 on 30 July 2002 and had risen 13.2 percent to 1452.98 on 31 December 2008, giving an annual return of 1.9 percent. The difference in the two calculations arises from the fact that index levels reported by Yahoo! Finance and other reporting agencies do not include cash dividends, which are an important part of the total return. Thus, it is important to recognize and account for income from investments.

In the following subsection, we consider various types of returns, their computation, and their application.

2.1.1 Holding Period Return

Returns can be measured over a single period or over multiple periods. Single period returns are straightforward because there is only one way to calculate them. Multiple period returns, however, can be calculated in various ways and it is important to be aware of these differences to avoid confusion.

A **holding period return** is the return earned from holding an asset for a single specified period of time. The period may be 1 day, 1 week, 1 month, 5 years, or any specified period. If the asset (bond, stock, etc.) is bought now, time $(t-1)$, at a price of 100 and sold later, say at time t, at a price of 105 with no dividends or other income, then the holding period return is 5 percent $[(105-100)/100]$. If the asset also pays an income of 2 units at time t, then the total return is 7 percent. This return can be generalized and shown as a mathematical expression:

$$R = \frac{P_t - P_{t-1} + D_t}{P_{t-1}} = \frac{P_t - P_{t-1}}{P_{t-1}} + \frac{D_t}{P_{t-1}} = \text{Capital gain} + \text{Dividend yield}$$

$$= \frac{P_T + D_T}{P_0} - 1$$

In the above expression, P is the price and D is the dividend. The subscript indicates the time of that price or dividend, $t-1$, is the beginning of the period and t is the end of the period. The following two observations are important.

- We computed a capital gain of 5 percent and a dividend yield of 2 percent in the above example. For ease of illustration, we assumed that the dividend is paid at time t. If the dividend was received any time before t, our holding period return would have been higher because we would have earned a return by putting the dividend in the bank for the remainder of the period.

- Return can be expressed in decimals (0.07), fractions (7/100), or as a percent (7%). They are all equivalent.

The holding period return can be computed for a period longer than one year. For example, you may need to compute a three-year holding period return from three annual returns. In that case, the holding period return is computed by compounding the three annual returns: $R = [(1 + R_1) \times (1 + R_2) \times (1 + R_3)] - 1$, where R_1, R_2, and R_3 are the three annual returns.

In this and succeeding parts of Section 2.1, we consider the aggregation of several single period returns.

2.1.2 Arithmetic or Mean Return

When assets have returns for multiple holding periods, it is necessary to aggregate those returns into one overall return for ease of comparison and understanding. It is also possible to compute the return for a long or an unusual holding period. Such returns, however, may be difficult to interpret. For example, a return of 455 percent earned by AstraZeneca PLC over the last 16 years (1993 to 2008) may not be meaningful unless all other returns are computed for the same period. Therefore, most holding period returns are reported as daily, monthly, or annual returns.

Aggregating returns across several holding periods becomes a challenge and can lead to different conclusions depending on the method of aggregation. The remainder of this section is designed to present various ways of computing average returns as well as discussing their applicability.

The simplest way to compute the return is to take the simple average of all holding period returns. Thus, three annual returns of −50 percent, 35 percent, and 27 percent will give us an average of 4 percent per year $= \left(\dfrac{-50\% + 35\% + 27\%}{3} \right)$. The arithmetic return is easy to compute and has known statistical properties, such as standard deviation. We can calculate the arithmetic return and its standard deviation to determine how dispersed the observations are around the mean or if the mean return is statistically different from zero.

In general, the arithmetic or mean return is denoted by $\bar{R}_i$ and given by the following equation for asset i, where R_{it} is the return in period t and T is the total number of periods:

$$\bar{R}_i = \frac{R_{i1} + R_{i2} + \ldots + R_{i,T-1} + R_{iT}}{T} = \frac{1}{T}\sum_{t=1}^{T} R_{it}$$

2.1.3 Geometric Mean Return

The arithmetic mean return is the average of the returns earned on a unit of investment at the beginning of each holding period. It assumes that the amount invested at the beginning of each period is the same, similar to the concept of calculating simple interest. However, because the base amount changes each year (the previous year's earnings needs to be added to or "compounded" to the beginning value of the investment), a holding or geometric period return may be quite different from the return implied by the arithmetic return. The geometric mean return assumes that the investment amount is not reset at the beginning of each year and, in effect, accounts for the compounding of returns. Basically, the geometric mean reflects a "buy-and-hold" strategy, whereas the arithmetic reflects a constant dollar investment at the beginning of each time period.[2]

A geometric mean return provides a more accurate representation of the growth in portfolio value over a given time period than does an arithmetic mean return. In general, the geometric mean return is denoted by $\bar{R}_{Gi}$ and given by the following equation for asset i:

---

[2] A buy-and-hold strategy assumes that the money invested initially grows or declines with time depending on whether a particular period's return is positive or negative. On the one hand, a geometric return compounds the returns and captures changes in values of the initial amount invested. On the other hand, arithmetic return assumes that we start with the same amount of money every period without compounding the return earned in a prior period.

$$\overline{R}_{Gi} = \sqrt[T]{(1 + R_{i1}) \times (1 + R_{i2}) \times ... \times (1 + R_{i,T-1}) \times (1 + R_{iT})} - 1$$

$$= \sqrt[T]{\prod_{t=1}^{T}(1 + R_{it})} - 1$$

where R_{it} is the return in period t and T is the total number of periods.

In the example in Section 2.1.2, we calculated the arithmetic mean to be 4 percent. Exhibit 1 shows the actual return for each year and the actual amount at the end of each year using actual returns. Beginning with an initial investment of €1.0000, we will have €0.8573 at the end of the three-year period as shown in the third column. Note that we compounded the returns because, unless otherwise stated, we receive return on the amount at the end of the prior year. That is, we will receive a return of 35 percent in the second year on the amount at the end of the first year, which is only €0.5000, not the initial amount of €1.0000. Let us compare the actual amount at the end of the three-year period, €0.8573, with the amount we get using an annual arithmetic mean return of 4 percent calculated above. The year-end amounts are shown in the fourth column using the arithmetic return of 4 percent. At the end of the three-year period, €1 will be worth €1.1249 (=1.0000 × 1.04³). This ending amount of €1.1249 is much larger than the actual amount of €0.8573. Clearly, the calculated arithmetic return is greater than the actual return. In general, the arithmetic return is biased upward unless the actual holding period returns are equal. The bias in arithmetic mean returns is particularly severe if holding period returns are a mix of both positive and negative returns, as in the example.

For our example and using the above formula, the geometric mean return per year is –5.0 percent, compared with an arithmetic mean return of 4.0 percent. The last column of Exhibit 1 shows that using the geometric return of –5.0 percent generates a value of €0.8574 at the end of the three-year period, which is very close to the actual value of €0.8573. The small difference in ending values is the result of a slight approximation used in computing the geometric return of –5.0 percent. Because of the effect of compounding, the geometric mean return is always less than or equal to the arithmetic mean return, $\overline{R}_{Gi} \leq \overline{R}_i$, unless there is no variation in returns, in which case they are equal.

Exhibit 1

	Actual Return for the Year (%)	Year-End Actual Amount	Year-End Amount Using Arithmetic Return of 4%	Year-End Amount Using Geometric Return of –5%
Year 0		€1.0000	€1.0000	€1.0000
Year 1	–50	0.5000	1.0400	0.9500
Year 2	35	0.6750	1.0816	0.9025
Year 3	27	0.8573	1.1249	0.8574

2.1.4 Money-Weighted Return or Internal Rate of Return

The above return computations do not account for the amount of money invested in different periods. It matters to an investor how much money was invested in each of the three years. If she had invested €10,000 in the first year, €1,000 in the second year, and €1,000 in the third year, then the return of −50 percent in the first year significantly hurts her. On the other hand, if she had invested only €100 in the first year, the effect of the −50 percent return is drastically reduced.

The **money-weighted return** accounts for the money invested and provides the investor with information on the return she earns on her actual investment. The money-weighted return and its calculation are similar to the **internal rate of return** and the yield to maturity. Just like the internal rate of return, amounts invested are cash outflows from the investor's perspective and amounts returned or withdrawn by the investor, or the money that remains at the end of an investment cycle, is a cash inflow for the investor.

The money-weighted return can be illustrated most effectively with an example. In this example, we use the actual returns from the previous example. Assume that the investor invests €100 in a mutual fund at the beginning of the first year, adds another €950 at the beginning of the second year, and withdraws €350 at the end of the second year. The cash flows are shown in Exhibit 2.

Exhibit 2

Year	1	2	3
Balance from previous year	€0	€50	€1,000
New investment by the investor (cash inflow for the mutual fund) at the start of the year	100	950	0
Net balance at the beginning of year	100	1,000	1,000
Investment return for the year	−50%	35%	27%
Investment gain (loss)	−50	350	270
Withdrawal by the investor (cash outflow for the mutual fund) at the end of the year	0	−350	0
Balance at the end of year	€50	€1,000	€1,270

The internal rate of return is the discount rate at which the sum of present values of these cash flows will equal zero. In general, the equation may be expressed as follows, where T is the number of periods, CF_t is the cash flow at time t, and IRR is the internal rate of return or the money-weighted rate of return:

$$\sum_{t=0}^{T} \frac{CF_t}{(1 + \text{IRR})^t} = 0$$

A cash flow can be positive or negative; a positive cash flow is an inflow where money flows to the investor, whereas a negative cash flow is an outflow where money flows away from the investor. We can compute the internal rate of return by using the above equation. The flows are expressed as follows, where each cash inflow or outflow occurs at the end of each year. Thus, CF_0 refers to the cash flow at the end of Year 0 or beginning of Year 1, and CF_3 refers to the cash flow at end of Year 3 or beginning of Year 4. Because cash flows are being discounted to the present—that is, end of Year 0 or beginning of Year 1—the period of discounting CF_0 is zero.

$$CF_0 = -100$$
$$CF_1 = -950$$
$$CF_2 = +350$$
$$CF_3 = +1,270$$

$$\frac{CF_0}{(1 + IRR)^0} + \frac{CF_1}{(1 + IRR)^1} + \frac{CF_2}{(1 + IRR)^2} + \frac{CF_3}{(1 + IRR)^3}$$

$$= \frac{-100}{1} + \frac{-950}{(1 + IRR)^1} + \frac{+350}{(1 + IRR)^2} + \frac{+1270}{(1 + IRR)^3} = 0$$

$$IRR = 26.11\%$$

IRR = 26.11% is the internal rate of return, or the money-weighted rate of return, which tells the investor what she earned on the actual euros invested for the entire period. This return is much greater than the arithmetic and geometric mean returns because only a small amount was invested when the mutual fund's return was −50 percent.

Although the money-weighted return is an accurate measure of what the investor actually earned on the money invested, it is limited in its applicability to other situations. For example, it does not allow for return comparison between different individuals or different investment opportunities. Two investors in the *same* mutual fund may have different money-weighted returns because they invested different amounts in different years.

2.1.5 Comparison of Returns

The previous subsections have introduced a number of return measures. The following example illustrates the computation, comparison, and applicability of each measure.

EXAMPLE 1

Computation of Returns

Ulli Lohrmann and his wife, Suzanne Lohrmann, are planning for retirement and want to compare the past performance of a few mutual funds they are considering for investment. They believe that a comparison over a five-year period would be appropriate. They are given the following information about the Rhein Valley Superior Fund that they are considering.

Year	Assets Under Management at the Beginning of Year (€)	Net Return (%)
1	30 million	15
2	45 million	−5
3	20 million	10
4	25 million	15
5	35 million	3

The Lohrmanns are interested in aggregating this information for ease of comparison with other funds.

1　Compute the holding period return for the five-year period.

2　Compute the arithmetic mean annual return.

3 Compute the geometric mean annual return. How does it compare with the arithmetic mean annual return?

4 The Lohrmanns want to earn a minimum annual return of 5 percent. Is the money-weighted annual return greater than 5 percent?

Solution to 1:

The holding period return is $R = (1+R_1)(1+R_2)(1+R_3)(1+R_4)(1+R_5) - 1 = (1.15)$ $(0.95)(1.10)(1.15)(1.03) - 1 = 0.4235 = 42.35\%$ for the five-year period.

Solution to 2:

The arithmetic mean annual return can be computed as an arithmetic mean of the returns given by this equation:

$$\bar{R}_i = \frac{15\% - 5\% + 10\% + 15\% + 3\%}{5} = 7.60\%$$

Solution to 3:

The geometric mean annual return can be computed using this equation:

$$\bar{R}_{Gi} = \sqrt[T]{(1 + R_{i1}) \times (1 + R_{i2}) \times \ldots \times (1 + R_{i,T-1}) \times (1 + R_{iT})} - 1$$

$$= \sqrt[5]{1.15 \times 0.95 \times 1.10 \times 1.15 \times 1.03} - 1$$

$$= \sqrt[5]{1.4235} - 1 = 0.0732 = 7.32\%$$

Thus, the geometric mean annual return is 7.32 percent, slightly less than the arithmetic mean return.

Solution to 4:

To calculate the money-weighted rate of return, tabulate the annual returns and investment amounts to determine the cash flows, as shown in Exhibit 3. All amounts are in millions of euros.

Exhibit 3					
Year	**1**	**2**	**3**	**4**	**5**
Balance from previous year	0	34.50	42.75	22.00	28.75
New investment by the investor (cash inflow for the Rhein fund)	30.00	10.50	0	3.00	6.25
Withdrawal by the investor (cash outflow for the Rhein fund)	0	0	−22.75	0	0
Net balance at the beginning of year	30.00	45.00	20.00	25.00	35.00
Investment return for the year	15%	−5%	10%	15%	3%
Investment gain (loss)	4.50	−2.25	2.00	3.75	1.05
Balance at the end of year	34.50	42.75	22.00	28.75	36.05

$CF_0 = -30.00$, $CF_1 = -10.50$, $CF_2 = +22.75$, $CF_3 = -3.00$, $CF_4 = -6.25$, $CF_5 = +36.05$.

For clarification, it may be appropriate to explain the notation for cash flows. Each cash inflow or outflow occurs at the end of each year. Thus, CF_0 refers to the cash flow at the end of Year 0 or beginning of Year 1, and CF_5 refers to the cash flow at end of Year 5 or beginning of Year 6. Because cash flows are being discounted to the present—that is, end of Year 0 or beginning of Year 1—the period of discounting CF_0 is zero whereas the period of discounting for CF_5 is 5 years.

To get the exact money-weighted rate of return (IRR), the following equation would be equal to zero. Instead of calculating, however, use the 5 percent return to see whether the value of the expression is positive or not. If it is positive, then the money-weighted rate of return is greater than 5 percent, because a 5 percent discount rate could not reduce the value to zero.

$$\frac{-30.00}{(1.05)^0} + \frac{-10.50}{(1.05)^1} + \frac{22.75}{(1.05)^2} + \frac{-3.00}{(1.05)^3} + \frac{-6.25}{(1.05)^4} + \frac{36.05}{(1.05)^5} = 1.1471$$

Because the value is positive, the money-weighted rate of return is greater than 5 percent. Using a financial calculator, the exact money-weighted rate of return is 5.86 percent.

2.1.6 Annualized Return

The period during which a return is earned or computed can vary and often we have to annualize a return that was calculated for a period that is shorter (or longer) than one year. You might buy a short-term treasury bill with a maturity of 3 months, or you might take a position in a futures contract that expires at the end of the next quarter. How can we compare these returns? In many cases, it is most convenient to annualize all available returns. Thus, daily, weekly, monthly, and quarterly returns are converted to an annual return. In addition, many formulas used for calculating certain values or prices may require all returns and periods to be expressed as annualized rates of return. For example, the most common version of the Black–Scholes option-pricing model requires annualized returns and periods to be in years.

To annualize any return for a period shorter than one year, the return for the period must be compounded by the number of periods in a year. A monthly return is compounded 12 times, a weekly return is compounded 52 times, and a quarterly return is compounded 4 times. Daily returns are normally compounded 365 times. For an uncommon number of days, we compound by the ratio of 365 to the number of days.

If the weekly return is 0.2 percent, then the compound annual return is computed as shown because there are 52 weeks in a year:

$$r_{annual} = \left(1 + r_{weekly}\right)^{52} - 1 = \left(1 + 0.2\%\right)^{52} - 1$$
$$= \left(1.002\right)^{52} - 1 = 0.1095 = 10.95\%$$

If the return for 15 days is 0.4 percent, the annualized return is computed assuming 365 days in a year. Thus,

$$r_{annual} = \left(1 + r_{15}\right)^{365/15} - 1 = \left(1 + 0.4\%\right)^{365/15} - 1$$
$$= \left(1.004\right)^{365/15} - 1 = 0.1020 = 10.20\%$$

A general equation to annualize returns is given, where c is the number of periods in a year. For a quarter, $c = 4$ and for a month, $c = 12$:

$$r_{annual} = \left(1 + r_{period}\right)^{c} - 1$$

How can we annualize a return when the holding period return is more than one year? For example, how do we annualize an 18-month holding period return? Because one year contains $2/3^{\text{rd}}$ of 18-month periods, $c = 2/3$ in the above equation. An 18-month return of 20 percent can be annualized, as shown:

$$r_{annual} = \left(1 + r_{18month}\right)^{2/3} - 1 = \left(1 + 0.20\right)^{2/3} - 1 = 0.1292 = 12.92\%$$

Similar expressions can be constructed when quarterly or weekly returns are needed for comparison instead of annual returns. In such cases, c is equal to the number of holding periods in a quarter or in a week. For example, assume that you want to convert daily returns to weekly returns or annual returns to weekly returns for comparison between weekly returns. For converting daily returns to weekly returns, $c = 5$, assuming that there are five trading days in a week. For converting annual returns to weekly returns, $c = 1/52$. The expressions for annual returns can then be rewritten as expressions for weekly returns, as shown:

$$r_{weekly} = \left(1 + r_{daily}\right)^{5} - 1; \; r_{weekly} = \left(1 + r_{annual}\right)^{1/52} - 1$$

One major limitation of annualizing returns is the implicit assumption that returns can be repeated precisely, that is, money can be reinvested repeatedly while earning a similar return. This type of return is not always possible. An investor may earn a return of 5 percent during a week because the market went up that week or he got lucky with his stock, but it is highly unlikely that he will earn a return of 5 percent every week for the next 51 weeks, resulting in an annualized return of 1,164.3 percent (= $1.05^{52} - 1$). Therefore, it is important to annualize short-term returns with this limitation in mind. Annualizing returns, however, allows for comparison among different assets and over different time periods.

EXAMPLE 2

Annualized Returns

London Arbitrageurs, PLC employs many analysts who devise and implement trading strategies. Mr. Brown is trying to evaluate three trading strategies that have been used for different periods of time.

▪ Keith believes that he can predict share price movements based on earnings announcements. In the last 100 days he has earned a return of 6.2 percent.

▪ Thomas has been very successful in predicting daily movements of the Australian dollar and the Japanese yen based on the carry trade. In the last 4 weeks, he has earned 2 percent after accounting for all transactions costs.

▪ Lisa follows the fashion industry and luxury retailers. She has been investing in these companies for the last 3 months. Her return is 5 percent.

Mr. Brown wants to give a prize to the best performer but is somewhat confused by the returns earned over different periods. Annualize returns in all three cases and advise Mr. Brown.

Solution:

Annualized return for Keith: $R_{Keith} = (1 + 0.062)^{365/100} - 1 = 0.2455 = 24.55\%$

Annualized return for Thomas: $R_{Thomas} = (1 + 0.02)^{52/4} - 1 = 0.2936 = 29.36\%$

Annualized return for Lisa: $R_{Lisa} = (1 + 0.05)^{4} - 1 = 0.2155 = 21.55\%$

> Thomas earned the highest return and deserves the reward, assuming the per-formance of all traders is representative of what they can achieve over the year.

2.1.7 Portfolio Return

When several individual assets are combined into a portfolio, we can compute the portfolio return as a weighted average of the returns in the portfolio. The portfolio return is simply a weighted average of the returns of the individual investments, or assets. If Asset 1 has a return of 20 percent and constitutes 25 percent of the portfolio's investment, then the contribution to the portfolio return is 5 percent (= 25% of 20%). In general, if Asset i has a return of R_i and has a weight of w_i in the portfolio, then the portfolio return, R_p, is given as:

$$R_P = \sum_{i=1}^{N} w_i R_i, \quad \sum_{i=1}^{N} w_i = 1$$

Note that the weights must add up to 1 because the assets in a portfolio, includ-ing cash, must account for 100 percent of the investment. Also, note that these are single period returns, so there are no cash flows during the period and the weights remain constant.

A two-asset portfolio is easier to work with, so we will use only two assets to illustrate most concepts. Extending the analysis to multiple assets, however, is easily achieved and covered in later sections. With only two assets in the portfolio, the port-folio return can be written as shown, where w_1 and w_2 are weights in assets 1 and 2.

$$R_p = w_1 R_1 + w_2 R_2$$

Because the portfolio consists of only two assets, the sum of the two weights should equal 100 percent. Therefore, $w_1 + w_2 = 1$ or $w_2 = (1 - w_1)$. By substituting, we can rewrite the above equation as follows:

$$R_p = w_1 R_1 + (1 - w_1) R_2$$

2.2 Other Major Return Measures and their Applications

The statistical measures of return discussed in the previous section are generally applicable across a wide range of assets and time periods. Special assets, however, such as mutual funds, and other considerations, such as taxes or inflation, may require return measures that are specific to a particular application.

Although it is not possible to consider all types of special applications, we will dis-cuss the effect of fees (gross versus net returns), taxes (pre-tax and after-tax returns), inflation (nominal and real returns), and **leverage**. Many investors use mutual funds or other external entities (i.e., investment vehicles) for investment. In those cases, funds charge management fees and expenses to the investors. Consequently, gross and net-of-fund-expense returns should also be considered. Of course, an investor may be interested in the net-of-expenses after-tax real return, which is in fact what an investor truly receives. We consider these additional return measures in the following sections.

2.2.1 Gross and Net Return

A gross return is the return earned by an asset manager prior to deductions for manage-ment expenses, custodial fees, taxes, or any other expenses that are not directly related to the generation of returns but rather related to the management and administration of an investment. These expenses are not deducted from the gross return because they may vary with the amount of assets under management or may vary because of the tax status of the investor. Trading expenses, however, such as commissions, are accounted for in (i.e., deducted from) the computation of gross return because trading expenses contribute directly to the return earned by the manager. Thus, gross return is an appropriate measure for evaluating and comparing the investment skill of asset managers because it does not include any fees related to the management and administration of an investment.

Net return is a measure of what the investment vehicle (mutual fund, etc.) has earned for the investor. Net return accounts for (i.e., deducts) all managerial and administrative expenses that reduce an investor's return. Because individual investors are most concerned about the net return (i.e., what they actually receive), small mutual funds with a limited amount of assets under management are at a disadvantage compared with the larger funds that can spread their largely fixed administrative expenses over a larger asset base. As a result, many small-sized mutual funds waive part of the expenses to keep the funds competitive.

2.2.2 Pre-tax and After-tax Nominal Return

All return measures discussed previously are pre-tax nominal returns—that is, no adjustment has been made for taxes or inflation. In general, all returns are pre-tax nominal returns unless they are otherwise designated.

Investors are concerned about the tax liability of their returns because taxes reduce the actual return that they receive. The two types of returns, capital gains (change in price) and income (such as dividends or interest), are usually taxed differently. Capital gains come in two forms: short-term capital gains and long-term capital gains. Long-term capital gains typically receive preferential tax treatment in a number of countries. Interest income is taxed as ordinary income in most countries. Dividend income may be taxed as ordinary income, may have a lower tax rate, or may be exempt from taxes depending on the country and the type of investor. The after-tax nominal return is computed as the total return minus any allowance for taxes on realized gains.[3]

Because taxes are paid on realized capital gains and income, the investment manager can minimize the tax liability by selecting appropriate securities (e.g., those subject to more favorable taxation, all other investment considerations equal) and reducing trading turnover. Therefore, many investors evaluate investment managers based on the after-tax nominal return.

2.2.3 Real Returns

A nominal return (r) consists of three components: a real risk-free return as compensation for postponing consumption (r_{rF}), inflation as compensation for loss of purchasing power (π), and a **risk premium** for assuming risk (RP). Thus, nominal return and real return can be expressed as:

$$(1 + r) = (1 + r_{rF}) \times (1 + \pi) \times (1 + RP)$$

$$(1 + r_{real}) = (1 + r_{rF}) \times (1 + RP) \text{ or}$$

$$(1 + r_{real}) = (1 + r) \div (1 + \pi)$$

Often the real risk-free return and the risk premium are combined to arrive at the real "risky" rate as given in the second equation above, simply referred to as the real return. Real returns are particularly useful in comparing returns across time periods because inflation rates may vary over time. Real returns are also useful in comparing returns among countries when returns are expressed in local currencies instead of a constant investor currency in which inflation rates vary between countries (which are usually the case). Finally, the after-tax real return is what the investor receives as compensation for postponing consumption and assuming risk after paying taxes on investment returns. As a result, the after-tax real return becomes a reliable benchmark

---

3 Bonds issued at a discount to the par value may be taxed based on accrued gains instead of realized gains.

for making investment decisions. Although it is a measure of an investor's benchmark return, it is not commonly calculated by asset managers because it is difficult to estimate a general tax component applicable to all investors. For example, the tax component depends on an investor's specific taxation rate (marginal tax rate), how long the investor holds an investment (long-term versus short-term), and the type of account the asset is held in (tax-exempt, tax-deferred, or normal).

2.2.4 Leveraged Return

In the previous calculations, we have assumed that the investor's position in an asset is equal to the total investment made by an investor using his or her own money. This section differs in that the investor creates a leveraged position. There are two ways of creating a claim on asset returns that are greater than the investment of one's own money. First, an investor may trade futures contracts in which the money required to take a position may be as little as 10 percent of the notional value of the asset. In this case, the leveraged return, the return on the investor's own money, is 10 times the actual return of the underlying security. Note that both the gains and losses are amplified by a factor of 10.

Investors can also invest more than their own money by borrowing money to purchase the asset. This approach is easily done in stocks and bonds, and very common when investing in real estate. If half (50 percent) of the money invested is borrowed, then the asset return to the investor is doubled but the investor must account for interest to be paid on borrowed money.

EXAMPLE 3

Computation of Special Returns

Let's return to Example 1. After reading this section, Mr. Lohrmann decided that he was not being fair to the fund manager by including the asset management fee and other expenses because the small size of the fund would put it at a competitive disadvantage. He learns that the fund spends a fixed amount of €500,000 every year on expenses that are unrelated to the manager's performance.

Mr. Lohrmann has become concerned that both taxes and inflation may reduce his return. Based on the current tax code, he expects to pay 20 percent tax on the return he earns from his investment. Historically, inflation has been around 2 percent and he expects the same rate of inflation to be maintained.

1 Estimate the annual gross return for the first year by adding back the fixed expenses.

2 What is the net return that investors in the Rhein Valley Superior Fund earned during the five-year period?

3 What is the after-tax net return for the first year that investors earned from the Rhein Valley Superior Fund? Assume that all gains are realized at the end of the year and the taxes are paid immediately at that time.

4 What is the anticipated after-tax real return that investors would have earned in the fifth year?

Solution to 1:

The gross return for the first year is higher by 1.67 percent (= €500,000/€30,000,000) than the investor return reported by the fund. Thus, the gross return is 16.67 percent (= 15% + 1.67%).

Solution to 2:

The investor return reported by the mutual fund is the net return of the fund after accounting for all direct and indirect expenses. The net return is also the pre-tax nominal return because it has not been adjusted for taxes or inflation. The net return for the five-year holding period was 42.35 percent.

Solution to 3:

The net return earned by investors during the first year was 15 percent. Applying a 20 percent tax rate, the after-tax return that accrues to the investors is 12 percent [= 15% − (0.20 × 15%)].

Solution to 4:

As in Part 3, the after-tax return earned by investors in the fifth year is 2.4 percent [= 3% − (0.20 × 3%)]. Inflation reduces the return by 2 percent so the after-tax real return earned by investors in the fifth year is 0.39 percent, as shown:

$$\frac{(1+2.40\%)}{(1+2.00\%)} - 1 = \frac{(1+0.0240)}{(1+0.0200)} - 1 = 1.0039 - 1 = 0.0039 = 0.39\%$$

Note that taxes are paid before adjusting for inflation.

2.3 Variance and Covariance of Returns

Having discussed the various kinds of returns in considerable detail, we now turn to measures of riskiness of those returns. Just like return, there are various kinds of risk. For now, we will consider the total risk of an asset or a portfolio of assets as measured by its standard deviation, which is the square root of variance.

2.3.1 Variance of a Single Asset

Variance, or risk, is a measure of the volatility or the dispersion of returns. Variance is measured as the average squared deviation from the mean. Higher variance suggests less predictable returns and therefore a more risky investment. The variance (σ^2) of asset returns is given by the following equation,

$$\sigma^2 = \frac{\sum_{t=1}^{T}(R_t - \mu)^2}{T}$$

where R_t is the return for period t, T is the total number of periods, and μ is the mean of T returns, assuming T is the population of returns.

If only a sample of returns is available instead of the population of returns (as is usually the case in the investment world), then the above expression underestimates the variance. The correction for *sample* variance is made by replacing the denominator with ($T − 1$), as shown next, where $\overline{R}$ is the mean return of the sample observations and s^2 is the sample variance:

$$s^2 = \frac{\sum_{t=1}^{T}(R_t - \overline{R})^2}{T-1}$$

2.3.2 Standard Deviation of an Asset

The **standard deviation** of returns of an asset is the square root of the variance of returns. The *population* standard deviation (σ) and the *sample* standard deviation (s) are given below.

$$\sigma = \sqrt{\frac{\sum_{t=1}^{T}(R_t - \mu)^2}{T}}; \quad s = \sqrt{\frac{\sum_{t=1}^{T}(R_t - \overline{R})^2}{T-1}}$$

Standard deviation is another measure of the risk of an asset, which may also be referred to as its volatility. In a later section, we will decompose this risk measure into its separate components.

2.3.3 Variance of a Portfolio of Assets

Like a portfolio's return, we can calculate a portfolio's variance. When computing the variance of portfolio returns, standard statistical methodology can be used by finding the variance of the full expression of portfolio return. Although the return of a portfolio is simply a weighted average of the returns of each security, this is not the case with the standard deviation of a portfolio (unless all securities are perfectly correlated—that is, correlation equals one). Variance can be expressed more generally for N securities in a portfolio using the notation from section 2.1.7 of this reading:

$$\sum_{i=1}^{N} w_i = 1$$

$$\sigma_P^2 = Var(R_P) = Var\left(\sum_{i=1}^{N} w_i R_i\right)$$

The right side of the equation is the variance of the weighted average returns of individual securities. Weight is a constant, but the returns are variables whose variance is shown by $Var(R_i)$. We can rewrite the equation as shown next. Because the covariance of an asset with itself is the variance of the asset, we can separate the variances from the covariances in the second equation:

$$\sigma_P^2 = \sum_{i,j=1}^{N} w_i w_j Cov(R_i, R_j)$$

$$\sigma_P^2 = \sum_{i=1}^{N} w_i^2 Var(R_i) + \sum_{i,j=1, i \neq j}^{N} w_i w_j Cov(R_i, R_j)$$

$Cov(R_i, R_j)$ is the covariance of returns, R_i and R_j, and can be expressed as the product of the correlation between the two returns ($\rho_{1,2}$) and the standard deviations of the two assets. Thus, $Cov(R_i, R_j) = \rho_{ij}\sigma_i\sigma_j$.

For a two asset portfolio, the expression for portfolio variance simplifies to the following using covariance and then using correlation:

$$\sigma_P^2 = w_1^2\sigma_1^2 + w_2^2\sigma_2^2 + 2w_1 w_2 Cov(R_1, R_2)$$

$$\sigma_P^2 = w_1^2\sigma_1^2 + w_2^2\sigma_2^2 + 2w_1 w_2 \rho_{12}\sigma_1\sigma_2$$

The standard deviation of a two asset portfolio is given by the square root of the portfolio's variance:

$$\sigma_P = \sqrt{w_1^2\sigma_1^2 + w_2^2\sigma_2^2 + 2w_1 w_2 Cov(R_1, R_2)}$$

or,

$$\sigma_P = \sqrt{w_1^2\sigma_1^2 + w_2^2\sigma_2^2 + 2w_1 w_2 \rho_{12}\sigma_1\sigma_2}$$

EXAMPLE 4

Return and Risk of a Two-Asset Portfolio

Assume that as a U.S. investor, you decide to hold a portfolio with 80 percent invested in the S&P 500 U.S. stock index and the remaining 20 percent in the MSCI Emerging Markets index. The expected return is 9.93 percent for the S&P 500 and 18.20 percent for the Emerging Markets index. The risk (standard deviation) is 16.21 percent for the S&P 500 and 33.11 percent for the Emerging Markets index. What will be the portfolio's expected return and risk given that the covariance between the S&P 500 and the Emerging Markets index is 0.5 percent or 0.0050? Note that units for covariance and variance are written as $\%^2$ when not expressed as a fraction. These are units of measure like squared feet and the numbers themselves are not actually squared.

Solution:

Portfolio return, $R_p = w_1 R_1 + (1 - w_1)R_2 = (0.80 \times 0.0993) + (0.20 \times 0.1820) = 0.1158 = 11.58\%$.

$$\text{Portfolio risk} = \sigma_P = \sqrt{w_1^2 \sigma_1^2 + w_2^2 \sigma_2^2 + 2w_1 w_2 Cov(R_1, R_2)}$$

$$\sigma_p^2 = w_{US}^2 \sigma_{US}^2 + w_{EM}^2 \sigma_{EM}^2 + 2w_{US} w_{EM} Cov_{US,EM}$$

$$\sigma_p^2 = \left(0.80^2 \times 0.1621^2\right) + \left(0.20^2 \times 0.3311^2\right)$$
$$+ \left(2 \times 0.80 \times 0.20 \times 0.0050\right)$$

$$\sigma_p^2 = 0.01682 + 0.00439 + 0.00160 = 0.02281$$

$$\sigma_p = 0.15103 = 15.10\%$$

The portfolio's expected return is 11.58 percent and the portfolio's risk is 15.10 percent. Look at this example closely. It shows that we can take the portfolio of a U.S. investor invested only in the S&P 500, combine it with a *riskier* portfolio consisting of emerging markets securities, and the return of the U.S. investor increases from 9.93 percent to 11.58 percent while the risk of the portfolio actually falls from 16.21 percent to 15.10 percent. Exhibit 4 depicts how the combination of the two assets results in a superior risk–return trade-off. Not only does the investor get a higher return, but he also gets it at a lower risk. That is the power of diversification as you will see later in this reading.

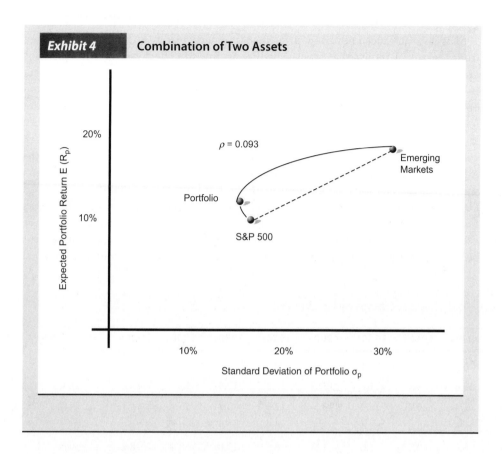

Exhibit 4   Combination of Two Assets

2.4 Historical Return and Risk

At this time, it is beneficial to look at historical risk and returns for the three main asset categories: stocks, bonds, and Treasury bills. Stocks refer to corporate ownership, bonds refer to long-term fixed-income securities, and Treasury bills refer to short-term government debt securities. Although there is generally no expectation of default on government securities, long-term government bond prices are volatile (risky) because of possible future changes in interest rates. In addition, bondholders also face the risk that inflation will reduce the purchasing power of their cash flows.

2.4.1 *Historical Mean Return and Expected Return*

Before examining historical data, it is useful to distinguish between the historical mean return and expected return, which are very different concepts but easy to confuse. Historical return is what was actually earned in the *past*, whereas expected return is what an investor anticipates to earn in the *future*.

Expected return is the nominal return that would cause the marginal investor to invest in an asset based on the real risk-free interest rate (r_{rF}), expected inflation $[E(\pi)]$, and expected risk premium for the risk of the asset $[E(RP)]$. The real risk-free interest rate is expected to be positive as compensation for postponing consumption. Similarly, the risk premium is expected to be positive in most cases.[4] The expected inflation rate is generally positive, except when the economy is in a deflationary state and prices are falling. Thus, expected return is generally positive. The relationship between the expected return and the real risk-free interest rate, inflation rate, and risk premium can be expressed by the following equation:

$$1 + E(R) = (1 + r_{rF}) \times [1 + E(\pi)] \times [1 + E(RP)]$$

---

4 There are exceptions when an asset reduces overall risk of a portfolio. We will consider those exceptions in section 4.3.

The historical mean return for investment in a particular asset, however, is obtained from the actual return that was earned by an investor. Because the investment is risky, there is no guarantee that the actual return will be equal to the expected return. In fact, it is very unlikely that the two returns are equal for a specific time period being considered. Given a long enough period of time, we can *expect* that the future (expected) return will equal the average historical return. Unfortunately, we do not know how long that period is—10 years, 50 years, or 100 years. As a practical matter, we often assume that the historical mean return is an adequate representation of the expected return, although this assumption may not be accurate. For example, Exhibit 5 shows that the historical equity returns in the last nine years (2000–2008) for large U.S. company stocks were negative whereas the expected return was nearly always positive. Nonetheless, longer-term returns (1926–2008) were positive and could be consistent with expected return. Though it is unknown if the historical mean returns accurately represent expected returns, it is an assumption that is commonly made.

Exhibit 5		Risk and Return for U.S. Asset Classes by Decade (%)								
		1930s	**1940s**	**1950s**	**1960s**	**1970s**	**1980s**	**1990s**	**2000s***	**1926–2008**
Large company stocks	Return	−0.1	9.2	19.4	7.8	5.9	17.6	18.2	−3.6	9.6
	Risk	41.6	17.5	14.1	13.1	17.2	19.4	15.9	15.0	20.6
Small company stocks	Return	1.4	20.7	16.9	15.5	11.5	15.8	15.1	4.1	11.7
	Risk	78.6	34.5	14.4	21.5	30.8	22.5	20.2	24.5	33.0
Long-term corporate bonds	Return	6.9	2.7	1.0	1.7	6.2	13.0	8.4	8.2	5.9
	Risk	5.3	1.8	4.4	4.9	8.7	14.1	6.9	11.3	8.4
Long-term government bonds	Return	4.9	3.2	−0.1	1.4	5.5	12.6	8.8	10.5	5.7
	Risk	5.3	2.8	4.6	6.0	8.7	16.0	8.9	11.7	9.4
Treasury bills	Return	0.6	0.4	1.9	3.9	6.3	8.9	4.9	3.1	3.7
	Risk	0.2	0.1	0.2	0.4	0.6	0.9	0.4	0.5	3.1
Inflation	Return	−2.0	5.4	2.2	2.5	7.4	5.1	2.9	2.5	3.0
	Risk	2.5	3.1	1.2	0.7	1.2	1.3	0.7	1.6	4.2

* Through 31 December 2008.
Note: Returns are measured as annualized geometric mean returns.
Risk is measured by annualizing monthly standard deviations.
Source: 2009 Ibbotson SBBI Classic Yearbook (Tables 2-1, 6-1, C-1 to C-7).

Going forward, be sure to distinguish between expected return and historical mean return. We will alert the reader whenever historical returns are used to estimate expected returns.

2.4.2 *Nominal Returns of Major U.S. Asset Classes*

We focus on three major asset categories in Exhibit 5: stocks, bonds, and T-bills. The mean nominal returns for U.S. asset classes are reported decade by decade since the 1930s. The total for the 1926–2008 period is in the last column. All returns are annual geometric mean returns. Large company stocks had an overall annual return of 9.6 percent during the 83-year period. The return was negative in the 1930s and 2000s, and positive in all remaining decades. The 1950s and 1990s were the best decades for large company stocks. Small company stocks fared even better. The nominal return was never negative for any decade, and had double-digit growth in all decades except two, leading to an overall 83-year annual return of 11.7 percent.

Long-term corporate bonds and long-term government bonds earned overall returns of 5.9 percent and 5.7 percent, respectively. The corporate bonds did not have a single negative decade, although government bonds recorded a negative return in the 1950s when stocks were doing extremely well. Bonds also had some excellent decades, earning double-digit returns in the 1980s and 2000s.

Treasury bills (short-term government securities) did not earn a negative return in any decade. In fact, Treasury bills earned a negative return only in 1938 (−0.02 percent) when the inflation rate was −2.78 percent. Consistently positive returns for Treasury bills are not surprising because nominal interest rates are almost never negative and the Treasury bills suffer from little interest rate or inflation risk. Since the Great Depression, there has been no deflation in any decade, although inflation rates were highly negative in 1930 (−6.03 percent), 1931 (−9.52 percent), and 1932 (−10.30 percent). Conversely, inflation rates were very high in the late 1970s and early 1980s, reaching 13.31 percent in 1979. Inflation rates have fallen since then to a negligible level of 0.09 percent in 2008. Overall, the inflation rate was 3.0 percent for the 83-year period.

2.4.3 Real Returns of Major U.S. Asset Classes

Because inflation rates can vary greatly, from −10.30 percent to +13.31 percent in the last 83 years, comparisons across various time periods is difficult and misleading using nominal returns. Therefore, it is more effective to rely on real returns. Real returns on stocks, bonds, and T-bills are reported from 1900 in Exhibits 6 and 7.

Exhibit 6	Cumulative Returns on U.S. Asset Classes in Real Terms, 1900–2011

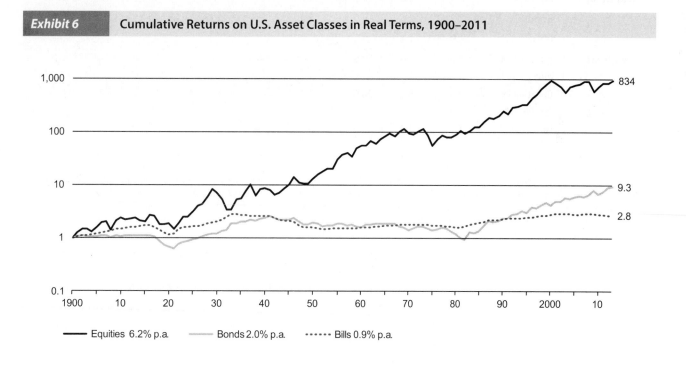

Source: E. Dimson, P. Marsh, and M. Staunton, *Credit Suisse Global Investment Returns Yearbook 2012*, Credit Suisse Research Institute (February 2009). This chart is updated annually and can be found at www.tinyurl.com/DMSsourcebook.

Exhibit 6 shows that $1 would have grown to $834 if invested in stocks, to only $9.30 if invested in bonds, and to $2.80 if invested in T-bills. The difference in growth among the three asset categories is huge, although the difference in real returns does not seem that large: 6.2 percent per year for equities compared with 2.0 percent per year for bonds. This difference represents the effect of compounding over a 112-year period.

Exhibit 7 reports both the nominal and real rates of return. As we discussed earlier and as shown in the table, geometric mean is never greater than the arithmetic mean. Our analysis of returns focuses on the geometric mean because it is a more accurate representation of returns for multiple holding periods than the arithmetic mean. We observe that the real returns for U.S. stocks are higher than the real returns for U.S. bonds, and that the real returns for bonds are higher than the real returns for U.S. T-bills.

Exhibit 7	Nominal Returns, Real Returns and Risk Premiums for Asset Classes (1900–2008)									
		United States			**World**			**World excluding U.S.**		
	Asset	GM (%)	AM (%)	SD (%)	GM (%)	AM (%)	SD (%)	GM (%)	AM (%)	SD (%)
Nominal Returns	Equities	9.2	11.1	20.2	8.4	9.8	17.3	7.9	9.7	20.1
	Bonds	5.2	5.5	8.3	4.8	5.2	8.6	4.2	5.0	13.0
	Bills	4.0	4.0	2.8	—	—	—	—	—	—
	Inflation	3.0	3.1	4.9	—	—	—	—	—	—
Real Returns	Equities	6.0	8.0	20.4	5.2	6.7	17.6	4.8	6.7	20.2
	Bonds	2.2	2.6	10.0	1.8	2.3	10.3	1.2	2.2	14.1
	Bills	1.0	1.1	4.7	—	—	—	—	—	—
Premiums	Equities vs. bills	5.0	7.0	19.9	—	—	—	—	—	—
	Equities vs. bonds	3.8	5.9	20.6	3.4	4.6	15.6	3.5	4.7	15.9
	Bonds vs. bills	1.1	1.4	7.9	—	—	—	—	—	—

Note: All returns are in percent per annum measured in US$. GM = geometric mean, AM = arithmetic mean, SD = standard deviation. "World" consists of 17 developed countries: Australia, Belgium, Canada, Denmark, France, Germany, Ireland, Italy, Japan, the Netherlands, Norway, South Africa, Spain, Sweden, Switzerland, United Kingdom, and the United States. Weighting is by each country's relative market capitalization size.
Sources: Credit Suisse Global Investment Returns Sourcebook, 2009. Compiled from tables 62, 65, and 68. T-bills and inflation rates are not available for the world and world excluding the United States.

2.4.4 *Nominal and Real Returns of Asset Classes in Major Countries*

Along with U.S. returns, returns of major asset classes for a 17-country world and the world excluding the United States are also presented in Exhibit 7. Equity returns are weighted by each country's GDP before 1968 because of a lack of reliable market capitalization data. Returns are weighted by a country's market capitalization beginning with 1968. Similarly, bond returns are defined by a 17-country bond index, except GDP is used to create the weights because equity market capitalization weighting is inappropriate for a bond index and bond market capitalizations were not readily available.

The nominal mean return for the world stock index over the last 109 years was 8.4 percent, and bonds had a nominal geometric mean return of 4.8 percent. The nominal geometric mean returns for the world excluding the United States are 7.9 percent for stocks and 4.2 percent for bonds. For both stocks and bonds, the United States has earned higher returns than the world excluding the U.S. Similarly, real returns for stocks and bonds in the United States are higher than the real returns for rest of the world. No separate information is available for Treasury bills for non-U.S. countries.

2.4.5 Risk of Major Asset Classes

Risk for major asset classes in the United States is reported for 1926–2008 in Exhibit 5, and the risk for major asset classes for the United States, the world, and the world excluding the United States are reported for 1900–2008 in Exhibit 7. Exhibit 5 shows that U.S. small company stocks had the highest risk, 33.0 percent, followed by U.S. large company stocks, 20.6 percent. Long-term government bonds and long-term corporate bonds had lower risk at 9.4 percent and 8.4 percent, with Treasury bills having the lowest risk at about 3.1 percent.

Exhibit 7 shows that the risk for world stocks is 17.3 percent and for world bonds is 8.6 percent. The world excluding the United States has risks of 20.1 percent for stocks and 13.0 percent for bonds. The effect of diversification is apparent when world risk is compared with U.S. risk and world excluding U.S. risk. Although the risk of U.S. stocks is 20.2 percent and the risk of world excluding U.S. stocks is 20.1 percent, the combination gives a risk of only 17.3 percent for world stocks. We can see a similar impact for world bonds when compared with U.S. bonds and world bonds excluding U.S. bonds. We observe a similar pattern in the risk levels of real returns.

2.4.6 Risk–Return Trade-off

The expression "risk–return trade-off" refers to the positive relationship between expected risk and return. In other words, a higher return is not possible to attain in efficient markets and over long periods of time without accepting higher risk. Expected returns should be greater for assets with greater risk.

The historical data presented above show the risk–return trade-off. Exhibit 5 shows for the United States that small company stocks had higher risk and higher return than large company stocks. Large company stocks had higher returns and higher risk than both long-term corporate bonds and government bonds. Bonds had higher returns and higher risk than Treasury bills. Uncharacteristically, however, long-term government bonds had higher total risk than long-term corporate bonds, although the returns of corporate bonds were slightly higher. These factors do not mean that long-term government bonds had greater default risk, just that they were more variable than corporate bonds during this historic period.

Turning to real returns, we find the same pattern: Higher returns were earned by assets with higher risk. Exhibit 7 reveals that the risk and return for stocks were the highest of the asset classes, and the risk and return for bonds were lower than stocks for the United States, the world, and the world excluding the United States. U.S. Treasury bills had the lowest return and lowest risk among T-bills, bonds, and stocks.

Another way of looking at the risk–return trade-off is to focus on the **risk premium**, which is the extra return investors can expect for assuming additional risk, after accounting for the nominal risk-free interest rate (includes both compensation for expected inflation and the real risk-free interest rate). Worldwide equity risk premiums reported at the bottom of Exhibit 7 show that equities outperformed bonds and bonds outperformed T-bills. Investors in equities earned a higher return than investors in T-bills because of the higher risk in stocks. Conversely, investors in T-bills cannot expect to earn as high a return as equity investors because the risk of their holdings is much lower.

A more dramatic representation of the risk–return trade-off is shown in Exhibit 6, which shows the cumulative returns of U.S. asset classes in real terms. The line representing T-bills is much less volatile than the other lines. Adjusted for inflation, the average real return on T-bills was 0.9 percent per year. The line representing bonds is more volatile than the line for T-bills but less volatile than the line representing stocks. The total return for equities including dividends and capital gains shows how $1 invested at the beginning of 1900 grows to $834, generating an annualized return of 6.2 percent in real terms.

Over long periods of time, we observe that higher risk does result in higher mean returns. Thus, it is reasonable to claim that, over the long term, market prices reward higher risk with higher returns, which is a characteristic of a risk-averse investor, a topic that we discuss in Section 3.

2.5 Other Investment Characteristics

In evaluating investments using mean (expected return) and variance (risk), we make two important assumptions. First, we assume that the returns are normally distributed because a normal distribution can be fully characterized by its mean and variance. Second, we assume that markets are not only informationally efficient but that they are also operationally efficient. To the extent that these assumptions are violated, we need to consider additional investment characteristics. These are discussed below.

2.5.1 *Distributional Characteristics*

As explained in an earlier reading, a **normal distribution** has three main characteristics: its mean and median are equal; it is completely defined by two parameters, mean and variance; and it is symmetric around its mean with:

- 68 percent of the observations within ±1σ of the mean,
- 95 percent of the observations within ±2σ of the mean, and
- 99 percent of the observations within ±3σ of the mean.

Using only mean and variance would be appropriate to evaluate investments if returns were distributed normally. Returns, however, are not normally distributed; deviations from normality occur both because the returns are skewed, which means they are not symmetric around the mean, and because the probability of extreme events is significantly greater than what a normal distribution would suggest. The latter deviation is referred to as kurtosis or fat tails in a return distribution. The next sections discuss these deviations more in-depth.

Skewness   **Skewness** refers to asymmetry of the return distribution, that is, returns are not symmetric around the mean. A distribution is said to be left skewed or negatively skewed if most of the distribution is concentrated to the right, and right skewed or positively skewed if most is concentrated to the left. Exhibit 8 shows a typical representation of negative and positive skewness, whereas Exhibit 9 demonstrates the negative skewness of stock returns by plotting a histogram of U.S. large company stock returns for 1926–2008. Stock returns are usually negatively skewed because there is a higher frequency of negative deviations from the mean, which also has the effect of overestimating standard deviation.

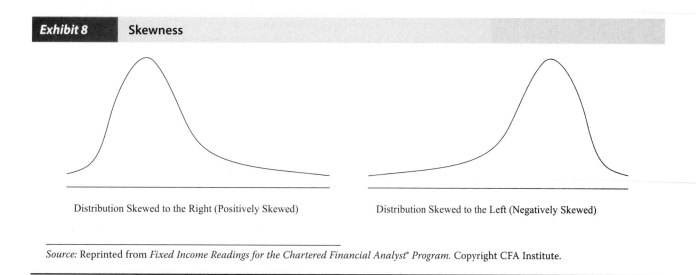

Exhibit 8   Skewness

Distribution Skewed to the Right (Positively Skewed)   Distribution Skewed to the Left (Negatively Skewed)

Source: Reprinted from *Fixed Income Readings for the Chartered Financial Analyst® Program.* Copyright CFA Institute.

Exhibit 9   Histogram of U.S. Large Company Stock Returns, 1926–2008 (Percent)

Source: 2009 Ibbotson SBBI Classic Yearbook (Table 2.2)

Kurtosis   Kurtosis refers to fat tails or higher than normal probabilities for extreme returns and has the effect of increasing an asset's risk that is not captured in a mean–variance framework, as illustrated in Exhibit 10. Investors try to evaluate the effect of kurtosis by using such statistical techniques as value at risk (VAR) and conditional tail expectations.[5] Several market participants note that the probability and the magnitude

---

5 Value at risk is a money measure of the minimum losses expected on a portfolio during a specified time period at a given level of probability. It is commonly used to measure the losses a portfolio can suffer under normal market conditions. For example, if a portfolio's one-day 10 percent VAR is £200,000, it implies that there is a 10 percent probability that the value of the portfolio will decrease by more than £200,000 over a single one-day period (under normal market conditions). This probability implies that the portfolio will experience a loss of at least £200,000 on one out of every ten days.

of extreme events is underappreciated and was a primary contributing factor to the financial crisis of 2008.[6] The higher probability of extreme negative outcomes among stock returns can also be observed in Exhibit 9.

Exhibit 10	Kurtosis

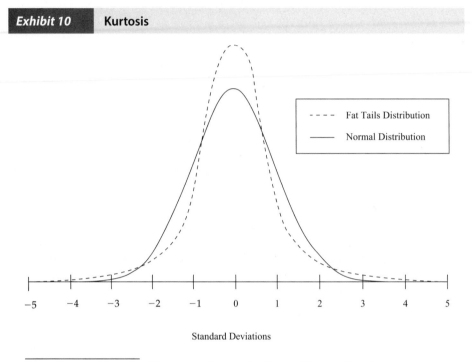

Standard Deviations

Source: Reprinted from *Fixed Income Readings for the Chartered Financial Analyst® Program.* Copyright CFA Institute.

2.5.2 *Market Characteristics*

In the previous analysis, we implicitly assumed that markets are both informationally and operationally efficient. Although informational efficiency of markets is a topic beyond the purview of this reading, we should highlight certain operational limitations of the market that affect the choice of investments. One such limitation is **liquidity**.

The cost of trading has three main components—brokerage commission, bid–ask spread, and price impact—of which liquidity affects the latter two. Brokerage commission is usually negotiable and does not constitute a large fraction of the total cost of trading except in small-sized trades. Stocks with low liquidity can have wide bid–ask spreads. The bid–ask spread, which is the difference between the buying price and the selling price, is incurred as a cost of trading a security. The larger the bid–ask spread, the higher is the cost of trading. If a $100 stock has a spread of 10 cents, the bid–ask spread is only 0.1 percent ($0.10/$100). On the other hand, if a $10 stock has a spread of 10 cents, the bid–ask spread is 1 percent. Clearly, the $10 stock is more expensive to trade and an investor will need to earn 0.9 percent extra to make up the higher cost of trading relative to the $100 stock.

Liquidity also has implications for the price impact of trade. Price impact refers to how the price moves in response to an order in the market. Small orders usually have little impact, especially for liquid stocks. For example, an order to buy 100 shares of a $100 stock with a spread of 1 cent may have no effect on the price. On the other

---

6 For example, see Bogle (2008) and Taleb (2007).

hand, an order to buy 100,000 shares may have a significant impact on the price as the buyer has to induce more and more stockholders to tender their shares. The extent of the price impact depends on the liquidity of the stock. A stock that trades millions of shares a day may be less affected than a stock that trades only a few hundred thousand shares a day. Investors, especially institutional investors managing large sums of money, must keep the liquidity of a stock in mind when making investment decisions.

Liquidity is a bigger concern in emerging markets than in developed markets because of the smaller volume of trading in those markets. Similarly, liquidity is a more important concern in corporate bond markets and especially for bonds of lower credit quality than in equity markets because an individual corporate bond issue may not trade for several days or weeks. This certainly became apparent during the global financial crisis.

There are other market-related characteristics that affect investment decisions because they might instill greater confidence in the security or might affect the costs of doing business. These include analyst coverage, availability of information, firm size, etc. These characteristics about companies and financial markets are essential components of investment decision making.

RISK AVERSION AND PORTFOLIO SELECTION $\qquad$ 3

As we have seen, stocks, bonds, and T-bills provide different levels of returns and have different levels of risk. Although investment in equities may be appropriate for one investor, another investor may not be inclined to accept the risk that accompanies a share of stock and may prefer to hold more cash. In the last section, we considered investment characteristics of assets in understanding their risk and return. In this section, we consider the characteristics of investors, both individual and institutional, in an attempt to pair the right kind of investors with the right kind of investments.

First, we discuss risk aversion and utility theory. Later we discuss their implications for portfolio selection.

3.1 The Concept of Risk Aversion

The concept of **risk aversion** is related to the behavior of individuals under uncertainty. Assume that an individual is offered two alternatives: one where he will get £50 for sure and the other is a gamble with a 50 percent chance that he gets £100 and 50 percent chance that he gets nothing. The expected value in both cases is £50, one with certainty and the other with uncertainty. What will an investor choose? There are three possibilities: an investor chooses the gamble, the investor chooses £50 with certainty, or the investor is indifferent. Let us consider each in turn. However, please understand that this is only a representative example, and a single choice does not determine the risk aversion of an investor.

Risk Seeking

If an investor chooses the gamble, then the investor is said to be risk loving or risk seeking. The gamble has an uncertain outcome, but with the same expected value as the guaranteed outcome. Thus, an investor choosing the gamble means that the investor gets extra "utility" from the uncertainty associated with the gamble. How much is that extra utility worth? Would the investor be willing to accept a smaller expected value because he gets extra utility from risk? Indeed, risk seekers will accept less return because of the risk that accompanies the gamble. For example, a risk seeker may choose a gamble with an expected value of £45 in preference to a guaranteed outcome of £50.

There is a little bit of gambling instinct in many of us. People buy lottery tickets although the expected value is less than the money they pay to buy it. Or people gamble at casinos in Macau or Las Vegas with the full knowledge that the expected return is negative, a characteristic of risk seekers. These or any other isolated actions, however, cannot be taken at face value except for compulsive gamblers.

Risk Neutral

If an investor is indifferent about the gamble or the guaranteed outcome, then the investor may be risk neutral. Risk neutrality means that the investor cares only about return and not about risk, so higher return investments are more desirable even if they come with higher risk. Many investors may exhibit characteristics of risk neutrality when the investment at stake is an insignificant part of their wealth. For example, a billionaire may be indifferent about choosing the gamble or a £50 guaranteed outcome.

Risk Averse

If an investor chooses the guaranteed outcome, he/she is said to be **risk averse** because the investor does not want to take the chance of not getting anything at all. Depending on the level of aversion to risk, an investor may be willing to accept a guaranteed outcome of £45 instead of a gamble with an expected value of £50.

In general, investors are likely to shy away from risky investments for a lower, but guaranteed return. That is why they want to minimize their risk for the same amount of return, and maximize their return for the same amount of risk. The risk–return trade-off discussed earlier is an indicator of risk aversion. A risk-neutral investor would maximize return irrespective of risk and a risk-seeking investor would maximize both risk and return.

Data presented in the last section illustrate the historically positive relationship between risk and return, which demonstrates that market prices were based on transactions and investments by risk-averse investors and reflect risk aversion. Therefore, for all practical purposes and for our future discussion, we will assume that the representative investor is a risk-averse investor. This assumption is the standard approach taken in the investment industry globally.

Risk Tolerance

Risk tolerance refers to the amount of risk an investor is willing to tolerate to achieve an investment goal. The higher the risk tolerance, the greater is the willingness to take risk. Thus, risk tolerance is negatively related to risk aversion.

3.2 Utility Theory and Indifference Curves

Continuing with our previous example, a risk-averse investor would rank the guaranteed outcome of £50 higher than the uncertain outcome with an expected value of £50. We can say that the utility that an investor or an individual derives from the guaranteed outcome of £50 is greater than the utility or satisfaction or happiness he/she derives from the alternative. In general terms, utility is a measure of relative satisfaction from consumption of various goods and services or in the case of investments, the satisfaction that an investor derives from different portfolios.

Because individuals are different in their preferences, all risk-averse individuals may not rank investment alternatives in the same manner. Consider the £50 gamble again. All risk-averse individuals will rank the guaranteed outcome of £50 higher than the gamble. What if the guaranteed outcome is only £40? Some risk-averse investors might consider £40 inadequate, others might accept it, and still others may now be indifferent about the uncertain £50 and the certain £40.

A simple implementation of utility theory allows us to quantify the rankings of investment choices using risk and return. There are several assumptions about individual behavior that we make in the definition of utility given in the equation below. We assume that investors are risk averse. They always prefer more to less (greater return to lesser return). They are able to rank different portfolios in the order of their preference and that the rankings are internally consistent. If an individual prefers X to Y and Y to Z, then he/she must prefer X to Z. This property implies that the indifference curves (see Exhibit 11) for the same individual can never touch or intersect. An example of a utility function is given below

$$U = E(r) - \frac{1}{2}A\sigma^2$$

where, U is the utility of an investment, $E(r)$ is the expected return, and σ^2 is the variance of the investment.

In the above equation, A is a measure of risk aversion, which is measured as the marginal reward that an investor requires to accept additional risk. More risk-averse investors require greater compensation for accepting additional risk. Thus, A is higher for more risk-averse individuals. As was mentioned previously, a risk-neutral investor would maximize return irrespective of risk and a risk-seeking investor would maximize both risk and return.

We can draw several conclusions from the utility function. First, utility is unbounded on both sides. It can be highly positive or highly negative. Second, higher return contributes to higher utility. Third, higher variance reduces the utility but the reduction in utility gets amplified by the risk aversion coefficient, A. Utility can always be increased, albeit marginally, by getting higher return or lower risk. Fourth, utility does not indicate or measure satisfaction. It can be useful only in ranking various investments. For example, a portfolio with a utility of 4 is not necessarily two times better than a portfolio with a utility of 2. The portfolio with a utility of 4 could increase our happiness 10 times or just marginally. But we do prefer a portfolio with a utility of 4 to a portfolio with a utility of 2. Utility cannot be compared among individuals or investors because it is a very personal concept. From a societal point of view, by the same argument, utility cannot be summed among individuals.

Let us explore the utility function further. The risk aversion coefficient, A, is greater than zero for a risk-averse investor. So any increase in risk reduces his/her utility. The risk aversion coefficient for a risk-neutral investor is 0, and changes in risk do not affect his/her utility. For a risk lover, the risk aversion coefficient is negative, creating an inverse situation so that additional risk contributes to an increase in his/her utility. Note that a risk-free asset ($\sigma^2 = 0$) generates the same utility for all individuals.

3.2.1 *Indifference Curves*

An **indifference curve** plots the combinations of risk–return pairs that an investor would accept to maintain a given level of utility (i.e., the investor is indifferent about the combinations on any one curve because they would provide the same level of overall utility). Indifference curves are thus defined in terms of a trade-off between expected rate of return and variance of the rate of return. Because an infinite number of combinations of risk and return can generate the same utility for the same investor, indifference curves are continuous at all points.

Exhibit 11	Indifference Curves for Risk-Averse Investors

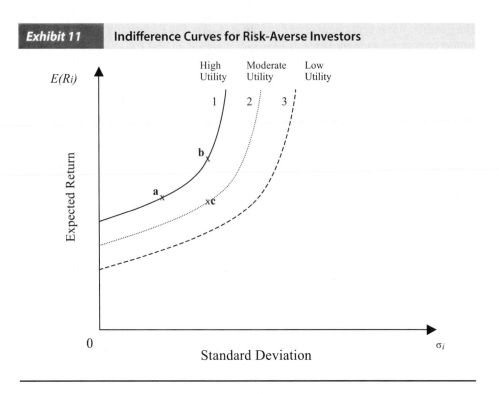

A set of indifference curves is plotted in Exhibit 11. By definition, all points on any one of the three curves have the same utility. An investor does not care whether he/she is at Point **a** or Point **b** on indifference Curve 1. Point **a** has lower risk and lower return than Point **b**, but the utility of both points is the same because the higher return at Point **b** is offset by the higher risk.

Like Curve 1, all points on Curve 2 have the same utility and an investor is indifferent about where he/she is on Curve 2. Now compare Point **c** with Point **b**. Point **c** has the same risk but significantly lower return than Point **b**, which means that the utility at Point **c** is less than the utility at Point **b**. Given that all points on Curve 1 have the same utility and all points on Curve 2 have the same utility and Point **b** has higher utility than Point **c**, Curve 1 has higher utility than Curve 2. Therefore, risk-averse investors with indifference Curves 1 and 2 will prefer Curve 1 to Curve 2. The utility of risk-averse investors always increases as you move northwest—higher return with lower risk. Because all investors prefer more utility to less, investors want to move northwest to the indifference curve with the highest utility.

The indifference curve for risk-averse investors runs from the southwest to the northeast because of the risk–return trade-off. If risk increases (going east) then it must be compensated by higher return (going north) to generate the same utility. The indifference curves are convex because of diminishing marginal utility of return (or wealth). As risk increases, an investor needs greater return to compensate for higher risk at an increasing rate (i.e., the curve gets steeper). The upward-sloping convex indifference curve has a slope coefficient closely related to the risk aversion coefficient. The greater the slope, the higher is the risk aversion of the investor as a greater increment in return is required to accept a given increase in risk.

Indifference curves for investors with different levels of risk aversion are plotted in Exhibit 12. The most risk-averse investor has an indifference curve with the greatest slope. As volatility increases, this investor demands increasingly higher returns to compensate for risk. The least risk-averse investor has an indifference curve with the least slope and so the demand for higher return as risk increases is not as acute as for the more risk-averse investor. The risk-loving investor's indifference curve, however, exhibits a negative slope, implying that the risk-lover is happy to substitute risk for return. For a risk lover, the utility increases both with higher risk and higher return. Finally, the indifference curves of risk-neutral investors are horizontal because the utility is invariant with risk.

Exhibit 12   **Indifference Curves for Various Types of Investors**

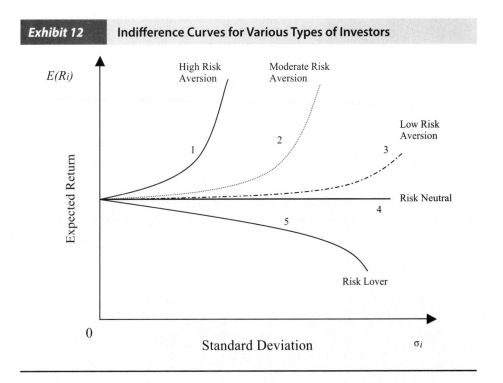

In the remaining parts of this reading, all investors are assumed to be risk averse unless stated otherwise.

EXAMPLE 5

Comparing a Gamble with a Guaranteed Outcome

Assume that you are given an investment with an expected return of 10 percent and a risk (standard deviation) of 20 percent, and your risk aversion coefficient is 3.

1   What is your utility of this investment?

2   What must be the minimum risk-free return you should earn to get the same utility?

Solution to 1:

$U = 0.10 - 0.5 \times 3 \times 0.20^2 = 0.04$.

Solution to 2:

A risk-free return's σ is zero, so the second term disappears. To get the same utility (0.04), the risk-free return must be at least 4 percent. Thus, in your mind, a risky return of 10 percent is equivalent to a risk-free return or a guaranteed outcome of 4 percent.

EXAMPLE 6

Computation of Utility

Based on investment information given below and the utility formula $U = E(r) - 0.5A\sigma^2$, answer the following questions. Returns and standard deviations are both expressed as percent per year. When using the utility formula, however, returns and standard deviations must be expressed in decimals.

Investment	Expected Return $E(r)$	Standard Deviation σ
1	12%	30%
2	15	35
3	21	40
4	24	45

1   Which investment will a risk-averse investor with a risk aversion coefficient of 4 choose?

2   Which investment will a risk-averse investor with a risk aversion coefficient of 2 choose?

3   Which investment will a risk-neutral investor choose?

4   Which investment will a risk-loving investor choose?

Solutions to 1 and 2:

The utility for risk-averse investors with $A = 4$ and $A = 2$ for each of the four investments are shown in the following table. Complete calculations for Investment 1 with $A = 4$ are as follows: $U = 0.12 - 0.5 \times 4 \times 0.30^2 = -0.06$.

Investment	Expected Return $E(r)$	Standard Deviation σ	Utility A = 4	Utility A = 2
1	12%	30%	−0.0600	0.0300
2	15	35	−0.0950	0.0275
3	21	40	−0.1100	0.0500
4	24	45	−0.1650	0.0375

The risk-averse investor with a risk aversion coefficient of 4 should choose Investment 1. The risk-averse investor with a risk aversion coefficient of 2 should choose Investment 3.

Solution to 3:

A risk-neutral investor cares only about return. In other words, his risk aversion coefficient is 0. Therefore, a risk-neutral investor will choose Investment 4 because it has the highest return.

Solution to 4:

A risk-loving investor likes both higher risk and higher return. In other words, his risk aversion coefficient is negative. Therefore, a risk-loving investor will choose Investment 4 because it has the highest return and highest risk among the four investments.

3.3 Application of Utility Theory to Portfolio Selection

The simplest application of utility theory and risk aversion is to a portfolio of two assets, a risk-free asset and a risky asset. The risk-free asset has zero risk and a return of R_f. The risky asset has a risk of σ_i (> 0) and an expected return of $E(R_i)$. Because the risky asset has risk that is greater than that of the risk-free asset, the expected return from the risky asset will be greater than the return from the risk-free asset, that is, $E(R_i) > R_f$.

We can construct a portfolio of these two assets with a portfolio expected return, $E(R_p)$, and portfolio risk, σ_p, based on sections 2.1.7 and 2.3.3. In the equations given below, w_1 is the weight in the risk-free asset and $(1 - w_1)$ is the weight in the risky asset. Because $\sigma_f = 0$ for the risk-free asset, the first and third terms in the formula for variance are zero leaving only the second term. We arrive at the last equation by taking the square root of both sides, which shows the expression for standard deviation for a portfolio of two assets when one asset is the risk-free asset:

$$E(R_p) = w_1 R_f + (1 - w_1)E(R_i)$$

$$\sigma_P^2 = w_1^2 \sigma_f^2 + (1 - w_1)^2 \sigma_i^2 + 2w_1(1 - w_1)\rho_{12}\sigma_f\sigma_i = (1 - w_1)^2 \sigma_i^2$$

$$\sigma_p = (1 - w_1)\sigma_i$$

The two-asset portfolio is drawn in Exhibit 13 by varying w_1 from 0 percent to 100 percent. The portfolio standard deviation is on the horizontal axis and the portfolio return is on the vertical axis. If only these two assets are available in the economy and the risky asset represents the market, the line in Exhibit 13 is called the **capital allocation line**. The capital allocation line represents the portfolios available to an investor. The equation for this line can be derived from the above two equations by rewriting the second equation as $w_1 = 1 - \dfrac{\sigma_p}{\sigma_i}$. Substituting the value of w_1 in the equation for expected return, we get the following equation for the capital allocation line:

$$E(R_p) = \left(1 - \frac{\sigma_p}{\sigma_i}\right)R_f + \frac{\sigma_p}{\sigma_i}E(R_i).$$

This equation can be rewritten in a more usable form:

$$E(R_p) = R_f + \frac{(E(R_i) - R_f)}{\sigma_i}\sigma_p$$

The capital allocation line has an intercept of R_f, and a slope of $\dfrac{(E(R_i) - R_f)}{\sigma_i}$, which is the additional required return for every increment in risk, and is sometimes referred to as the market price of risk.

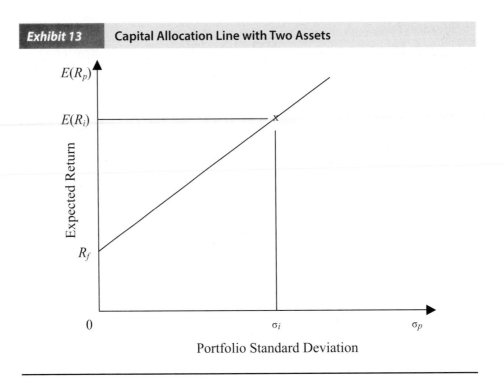

Exhibit 13 **Capital Allocation Line with Two Assets**

Because the equation is linear, the plot of the capital allocation line is a straight line. The line begins with the risk-free asset as the leftmost point with zero risk and a risk-free return, R_f. At that point, the portfolio consists of only the risk-free asset. If 100 percent is invested in the portfolio of all risky assets, however, we have a return of $E(R_i)$ with a risk of σ_i.

We can move further along the line in pursuit of higher returns by borrowing at the risk-free rate and investing the borrowed money in the portfolio of all risky assets. If 50 percent is borrowed at the risk-free rate, then $w_i = -0.50$ and 150 percent is placed in the risky asset, giving a return $= 1.50E(R_i) - 0.50R_f$, which is $> E(R_i)$ because $E(R_i) > R_f$.

The line plotted in Exhibit 13 is comprised of an unlimited number of risk–return pairs or portfolios. Which *one* of these portfolios should be chosen by an investor? The answer lies in combining indifference curves from utility theory with the capital allocation line from portfolio theory. Utility theory gives us the utility function or the indifference curves for an individual, as in Exhibit 11, and the capital allocation line gives us the set of feasible investments. Overlaying each individual's indifference curves on the capital allocation line will provide us with the optimal portfolio for that investor. Exhibit 14 illustrates this process of portfolio selection.

Exhibit 14	Portfolio Selection

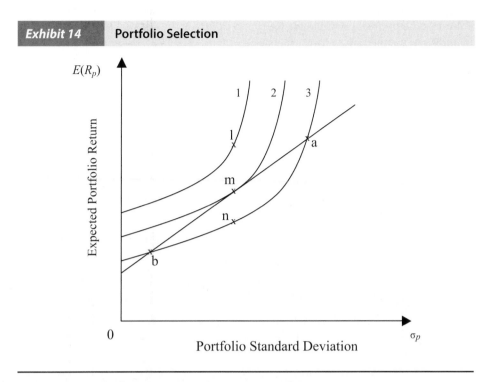

The capital allocation line consists of the set of feasible portfolios. Points under the capital allocation line may be attainable but are not preferred by any investor because the investor can get a higher return for the same risk by moving up to the capital allocation line. Points above the capital allocation line are desirable but not achievable with available assets.

Three indifference curves for the same individual are also shown in Exhibit 14. Curve 1 is above the capital allocation line, Curve 2 is tangential to the line, and Curve 3 intersects the line at two points. Curve 1 has the highest utility and Curve 3 has the lowest utility. Because Curve 1 lies completely above the capital allocation line, points on Curve 1 are not achievable with the available assets on the capital allocation line. Curve 3 intersects the capital allocation line at two Points, **a** and **b**. The investor is able to invest at either Point **a** or **b** to derive the risk–return trade-off and utility associated with Curve 3. Comparing points with the same risk, observe that Point **n** on Curve 3 has the same risk as Point **m** on Curve 2, yet Point **m** has the higher expected return. Therefore, all investors will choose Curve 2 instead of Curve 3. Curve 2 is tangential to the capital allocation line at Point **m**. Point **m** is on the capital allocation line and investable. Point **m** and the utility associated with Curve 2 is the best that the investor can do because he/she cannot move to a higher utility indifference curve. Thus, we have been able to select the optimal portfolio for the investor with indifference Curves 1, 2, and 3. Point **m**, the optimal portfolio for one investor, may not be optimal for another investor. We can follow the same process, however, for finding the optimal portfolio for other investors: the optimal portfolio is the point of tangency between the capital allocation line and the indifference curve for that investor. In other words, the optimal portfolio maximizes the return per unit of risk (as it is on the capital allocation line), and it simultaneously supplies the investor with the most satisfaction (utility).

As an illustration, Exhibit 15 shows two indifference curves for two different investors: Kelly with a risk aversion coefficient of 2 and Jane with a risk aversion coefficient of 4. The indifference curve for Kelly is to the right of the indifference curve for Jane because Kelly is less risk averse than Jane and can accept a higher amount of risk, i.e. has a higher tolerance for risk. Accordingly, their optimal portfolios are different:

Point **k** is the optimal portfolio for Kelly and Point **j** is the optimal portfolio for Jane. In addition, for the same return, the slope of Jane's curve is higher than Kelly's suggesting that Jane needs greater incremental return as compensation for accepting an additional amount of risk compared with Kelly.

Exhibit 15	Portfolio Selection for Two Investors with Various Levels of Risk Aversion

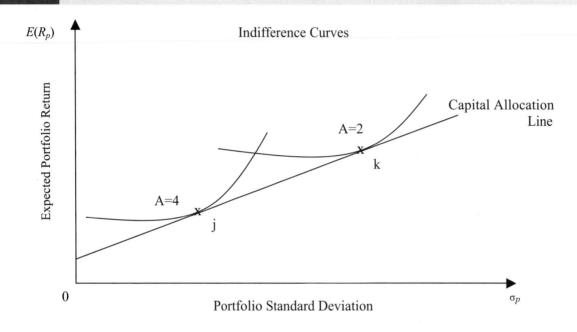

4 PORTFOLIO RISK

We have seen before that investors are risk averse and demand a higher return for a riskier investment. Therefore, ways of controlling portfolio risk without affecting return are valuable. As a precursor to managing risk, this section explains and analyzes the components of portfolio risk. In particular, it examines and describes how a portfolio consisting of assets with low correlations have the potential of reducing risk without necessarily reducing return.

4.1 Portfolio of Two Risky Assets

The return and risk of a portfolio of two assets was introduced in Section 2 of this reading. In this section, we briefly review the computation of return and extend the concept of portfolio risk and its components.

4.1.1 *Portfolio Return*

When two individual assets are combined in a portfolio, we can compute the portfolio return as a weighted average of the returns of the two assets. Consider Assets 1 and 2 with weights of 25 percent and 75 percent in a portfolio. If their returns are

20 percent and 5 percent, the weighted average return = (0.25 × 20%) + (0.75 × 5%) = 8.75%. More generally, the portfolio return can be written as below, where R_p is return of the portfolio and R_1, R_2 are returns on the two assets:

$$R_P = w_1 R_1 + (1 - w_1)R_2$$

4.1.2 Portfolio Risk

Portfolio risk or variance measures the amount of uncertainty in portfolio returns. Portfolio variance can be calculated by taking the variance of both sides of the return equation as below, where $Cov(R_1, R_2)$ is the covariance of returns, R_1 and R_2, w_1 is the weight in Asset 1, w_2 $(= 1 - w_1)$ is the weight in Asset 2, and σ_1^2, σ_2^2 are the variances of the two assets:

$$\sigma_P^2 = Var(R_P) = Var(w_1 R_1 + w_2 R_2)$$
$$= w_1^2 Var(R_1) + w_2^2 Var(R_2) + 2w_1 w_2 Cov(R_1, R_2)$$
$$= w_1^2 \sigma_1^2 + w_2^2 \sigma_2^2 + 2w_1 w_2 Cov(R_1, R_2)$$

The standard deviation, or risk, of a portfolio of two assets is given by the square root of the portfolio's variance:

$$\sigma_P = \sqrt{w_1^2 \sigma_1^2 + w_2^2 \sigma_2^2 + 2w_1 w_2 Cov(R_1, R_2)}$$

4.1.3 Covariance and Correlation

The **covariance** in the formula for portfolio standard deviation can be expanded as $Cov(R_1, R_2) = \rho_{12} \sigma_1 \sigma_2$ where ρ_{12} is the correlation between returns, R_1, R_2. Although covariance is important, it is difficult to interpret because it is unbounded on both sides. It is easier to understand the **correlation coefficient** (ρ_{12}), which is bounded but provides similar information.

Correlation is a measure of the consistency or tendency for two investments to act in a similar way. The correlation coefficient, ρ_{12}, can be positive or negative and ranges from −1 to +1. Consider three different values of the correlation coefficient:

- ρ_{12} = +1: Returns of the two assets are perfectly *positively* correlated. Assets 1 and 2 move together 100 percent of the time.

- ρ_{12} = −1: Returns of the two assets are perfectly *negatively* correlated. Assets 1 and 2 move in opposite directions 100 percent of the time.

- ρ_{12} = 0: Returns of the two assets are *uncorrelated*. Movement of Asset 1 provides no prediction regarding the movement of Asset 2.

The correlation coefficient between two assets determines the effect on portfolio risk when the two assets are combined. To see how this works, consider two different values of ρ_{12}. You will find that portfolio risk is unaffected when the two assets are perfectly correlated (ρ_{12} = +1). In other words, the portfolio's standard deviation is simply a weighted average of the standard deviations of the two assets and as such a portfolio's risk is unchanged with the addition of assets with the same risk parameters. Portfolio risk falls, however, when the two assets are not perfectly correlated (ρ_{12} < +1). Sufficiently low values of the correlation coefficient can make the portfolio riskless under certain conditions.

First, let ρ_{12} = +1

$$\sigma_p^2 = w_1^2\sigma_1^2 + w_2^2\sigma_2^2 + 2w_1w_2\rho_{12}\sigma_1\sigma_2 = w_1^2\sigma_1^2 + w_2^2\sigma_2^2 + 2w_1w_2\sigma_1\sigma_2$$

$$= (w_1\sigma_1 + w_2\sigma_2)^2$$

$$\sigma_p = w_1\sigma_1 + w_2\sigma_2$$

The first set of terms on the right side of the first equation contain the usual terms for portfolio variance. Because the correlation coefficient is equal to +1, the right side can be rewritten as a perfect square. The third row shows that portfolio risk is a weighted average of the risks of the individual assets' risks. In Subsection 4.1.1., the portfolio return was shown always to be a weighted average of returns. Because both risk and return are just weighted averages of the two assets in the portfolio there is no reduction in risk when $\rho_{12} = +1$.

Now let $\rho_{12} < +1$

The above analysis showed that portfolio risk is a weighted average of asset risks when $\rho_{12} = +1$. When $\rho_{12} < +1$, the portfolio risk is less than the weighted average of the individual assets' risks.

To show this, we begin by reproducing the general formula for portfolio risk, which is expressed by the terms to the left of the "<" sign below. The term to the right of "<" shows the portfolio risk when $\rho_{12} = +1$:

$$\sigma_p = \sqrt{w_1^2\sigma_1^2 + w_2^2\sigma_2^2 + 2w_1w_2\rho_{12}\sigma_1\sigma_2} < \sqrt{w_1^2\sigma_1^2 + w_2^2\sigma_2^2 + 2w_1w_2\sigma_1\sigma_2}$$

$$= (w_1\sigma_1 + w_2\sigma_2)$$

$$\sigma_p < (w_1\sigma_1 + w_2\sigma_2)$$

The left side is smaller than the right side because the correlation coefficient on the left side for the new portfolio is <1. Thus, the portfolio risk is less than the weighted average of risks while the portfolio return is still a weighted average of returns.

As you can see, we have achieved diversification by combining two assets that are not perfectly correlated. For an extreme case in which $\rho_{12} = -1$ (that is, the two asset returns move in opposite directions), the portfolio can be made risk free.

EXAMPLE 7

Effect of Correlation on Portfolio Risk

Two stocks have the same return and risk (standard deviation): 10 percent return with 20 percent risk. You form a portfolio with 50 percent each of Stock 1 and Stock 2 to examine the effect of correlation on risk.

1 Calculate the portfolio return and risk if the correlation is 1.0.

2 Calculate the portfolio return and risk if the correlation is 0.0.

3 Calculate the portfolio return and risk if the correlation is −1.0.

4 Compare the return and risk of portfolios with different correlations.

Solution to 1:

$$R_1 = R_2 = 10\% = 0.10; \sigma_1 = \sigma_2 = 20\% = 0.20; w_1 = w_2 = 50\%$$
$$= 0.50. \text{ } Case \text{ } 1\text{: } \rho_{12} = +1$$

$$R_p = w_1 R_1 + w_2 R_2$$

$$R_p = (0.5 \times 0.1) + (0.5 \times 0.1) = 0.10 = 10\%$$

$$\sigma_p^2 = w_1^2 \sigma_1^2 + w_2^2 \sigma_2^2 + 2w_1 w_2 \sigma_1 \sigma_2 \rho_{12}$$

$$\sigma_p^2 = (0.5^2 \times 0.2^2) + (0.5^2 \times 0.2^2) + (2 \times 0.5 \times 0.5 \times 0.2 \times 0.2 \times 1) = 0.04$$

$$\sigma_p = \sqrt{0.04} = 0.20 = 20\%$$

This equation demonstrates the earlier point that with a correlation of 1.0 the risk of the portfolio is the same as the risk of the individual assets.

Solution to 2:

$$\rho_{12} = 0$$

$$R_p = w_1 R_1 + w_2 R_2 = 0.10 = 10\%$$

$$\sigma_p^2 = w_1^2 \sigma_1^2 + w_2^2 \sigma_2^2 + 2w_1 w_2 \sigma_1 \sigma_2 \rho_{12}$$

$$\sigma_p^2 = (0.5^2 \times 0.2^2) + (0.5^2 \times 0.2^2)$$
$$+ (2 \times 0.5 \times 0.5 \times 0.2 \times 0.2 \times 0) = 0.02$$

$$\sigma_p = \sqrt{0.02} = 0.14 = 14\%$$

This equation demonstrates the earlier point that, when assets have correlations of less than 1.0, they can be combined in a portfolio that has less risk than either of the assets individually.

Solution to 3:

$$\rho_{12} = -1$$

$$R_p = w_1 R_1 + w_2 R_2 = 0.10 = 10\%$$

$$\sigma_p^2 = w_1^2 \sigma_1^2 + w_2^2 \sigma_2^2 + 2w_1 w_2 \sigma_1 \sigma_2 \rho_{12}$$

$$\sigma_p^2 = (0.5^2 \times 0.2^2) + (0.5^2 \times 0.2^2)$$
$$+ (2 \times 0.5 \times 0.5 \times 0.2 \times 0.2 \times -1) = 0$$

$$\sigma_p = 0\%$$

This equation demonstrates the earlier point that, if the correlation of assets is low enough, in this case 100 percent negative correlation or −1.00 (exactly inversely related), a portfolio can be designed that eliminates risk. The individual assets retain their risk characteristics, but the portfolio is risk free.

Solution to 4:

The expected return is 10 percent in all three cases; however, the returns will be more volatile in Case 1 and least volatile in Case 3. In the first case, there is no diversification of risk (same risk as before of 20 percent) and the return remains the same. In the second case, with a correlation coefficient of 0, we have achieved diversification of risk (risk is now 14 percent instead of 20 percent), again with the same return. In the third case with a correlation coefficient of

−1, the portfolio is risk free, although we continue to get the same return of 10 percent. This example shows the power of diversification that we expand on further in Section 4.3.

4.1.4 Relationship between Portfolio Risk and Return

The previous example illustrated the effect of correlation on portfolio risk while keeping the weights in the two assets equal and unchanged. In this section, we consider how portfolio risk and return vary with different portfolio weights and different correlations. Formulas for computation are in Subsections 4.1.1 and 4.1.2.

Asset 1 has an annual return of 7 percent and annualized risk of 12 percent, whereas Asset 2 has an annual return of 15 percent and annualized risk of 25 percent. The relationship is tabulated in Exhibit 16 for the two assets and graphically represented in Exhibit 17.

Exhibit 16	Relationship between Risk and Return				
Weight in Asset 1 (%)	**Portfolio Return**	**Portfolio Risk with Correlation of**			
		1.0	**0.5**	**0.2**	**−1.0**
0	15.0	25.0	25.0	25.0	25.0
10	14.2	23.7	23.1	22.8	21.3
20	13.4	22.4	21.3	20.6	17.6
30	12.6	21.1	19.6	18.6	13.9
40	11.8	19.8	17.9	16.6	10.2
50	11.0	18.5	16.3	14.9	6.5
60	10.2	17.2	15.0	13.4	2.8
70	9.4	15.9	13.8	12.3	0.9
80	8.6	14.6	12.9	11.7	4.6
90	7.8	13.3	12.2	11.6	8.3
100	7.0	12.0	12.0	12.0	12.0

| Exhibit 17 | Relationship between Risk and Return |

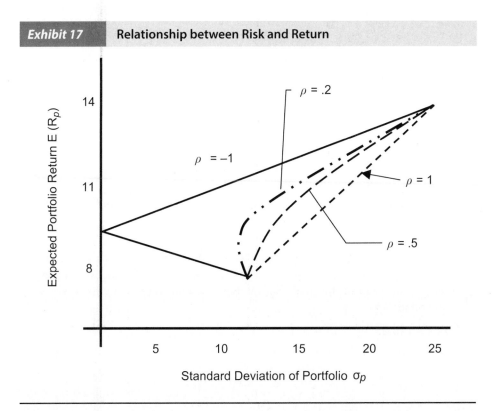

The table shows the portfolio return and risk for four correlation coefficients ranging from +1.0 to −1.0 and 11 weights ranging from 0 percent to 100 percent. The portfolio return and risk are 15 percent and 25 percent, respectively, when 0 percent is invested in Asset 1, versus 7 percent and 12 percent when 100 percent is invested in Asset 1. The portfolio return varies with weights but is unaffected by the correlation coefficient.

Portfolio risk becomes smaller with each successive decrease in the correlation coefficient, with the smallest risk when $\rho_{12} = -1$. The graph in Exhibit 17 shows that the risk–return relationship is a straight line when $\rho_{12} = +1$. As the correlation falls, the risk becomes smaller and smaller as in the table. The curvilinear nature of a portfolio of assets is recognizable in all investment opportunity sets (except at the extremes where $\rho_{12} = -1$ or $+1$).

EXAMPLE 8

Portfolio of Two Assets

An investor is considering investing in a small-cap stock fund and a general bond fund. Their returns and standard deviations are given below and the correlation between the two fund returns is 0.10.

	Expected Annual Return (%)	Standard Deviation of Returns (%)
Small-cap fund, S	19	33
Bond fund, B	8	13

1 If the investor requires a portfolio return of 12 percent, what should the proportions in each fund be?

2 What is the standard deviation of the portfolio constructed in Part 1?

Solution to 1:

We can calculate the weights by setting the portfolio return equal to 12 percent. $12\% = w_1 \times 19\% + (1 - w_1) \times 8\%$; $w_1 = 36.4\%$, $(1 - w_1) = 63.6\%$. Thus, 36.4 percent should be invested in the small-cap fund and 63.6 percent should be invested in the bond fund.

Solution to 2:

$$\sigma_p = \sqrt{w_1^2\sigma_1^2 + w_2^2\sigma_2^2 + 2w_1w_2\rho_{12}\sigma_1\sigma_2}$$
$$= \sqrt{(0.364^2 \times 0.33^2) + (0.636^2 \times 0.13^2) + (2 \times 0.364 \times 0.636 \times 0.10 \times 0.33 \times 0.13)}$$
$$= 15.23\%$$

The portfolio risk is 15.23 percent, which is much less than a weighted average of risks of 20.28% ($63.6\% \times 13\% + 36.4\% \times 33\%$).

4.2 Portfolio of Many Risky Assets

In the previous section, we discussed how the correlation between two assets can affect the risk of a portfolio and the smaller the correlation the lower is the risk. The above analysis can be extended to a portfolio with many risky assets (N). Recall the following equations from Sections 2.1.7 and 2.3.3 for portfolio return and variance:

$$E(R_p) = \sum_{i=1}^{N} w_i E(R_i), \quad \sigma_P^2 = \left(\sum_{i=1}^{N} w_i^2\sigma_i^2 + \sum_{i,j=1,i\neq j}^{N} w_iw_j Cov(i,j)\right), \quad \sum_{i=1}^{N} w_i = 1$$

To examine how a portfolio with many risky assets works and the ways in which we can reduce the risk of a portfolio, assume that the portfolio has equal weights ($1/N$) for all N assets. In addition, assume that $\bar{\sigma}^2$ and $\overline{Cov}$ are the average variance and average covariance. Given equal weights and average variance/covariance, we can rewrite the portfolio variance as below (intermediate steps are omitted to focus on the main result):

$$\sigma_P^2 = \left(\sum_{i=1}^{N} w_i^2\sigma_i^2 + \sum_{i,j=1,i\neq j}^{N} w_iw_j Cov(i,j)\right)$$
$$\sigma_P^2 = \frac{\bar{\sigma}^2}{N} + \frac{(N-1)}{N}\overline{Cov}$$

The equation in the second line shows that as N becomes large, the first term on the right side with the denominator of N becomes smaller and smaller, implying that the contribution of one asset's variance to portfolio variance gradually becomes negligible.

The second term, however, approaches the average covariance as N increases. It is reasonable to say that for portfolios with a large number of assets, covariance among the assets accounts for almost all of the portfolio's risk.

4.2.1 *Importance of Correlation in a Portfolio of Many Assets*

The analysis becomes more instructive and interesting if we assume that all assets in the portfolio have the same variance and the same correlation among assets. In that case, the portfolio risk can then be rewritten as:

$$\sigma_p = \sqrt{\frac{\sigma^2}{N} + \frac{(N-1)}{N}\rho\sigma^2}$$

The first term under the root sign becomes negligible as the number of assets in the portfolio increases leaving the second term (correlation) as the main determining factor for portfolio risk. If the assets are unrelated to one another, the portfolio can have close to zero risk. In the next section, we review these concepts to learn how portfolios can be diversified.

4.3 The Power of Diversification

Diversification is one of the most important and powerful concepts in investments. Because investors are risk averse, they are interested in reducing risk preferably without reducing return. In other cases, investors may accept a lower return if it will reduce the chance of catastrophic losses. In previous sections of this reading, you learned the importance of correlation and covariance in managing risk. This section applies those concepts to explore ways for risk diversification. We begin with a simple but intuitive example.

EXAMPLE 9

Diversification with Rain and Shine

Assume a company Beachwear rents beach equipment. The annual return from the company's operations is 20 percent in years with many sunny days but falls to 0 percent in rainy years with few sunny days. The probabilities of a sunny year and a rainy year are equal at 50 percent. Thus, the average return is 10 percent, with a 50 percent chance of 20 percent return and a 50 percent chance of 0 percent return. Because Beachwear can earn a return of 20 percent or 0 percent, its average return of 10 percent is risky.

You are excited about investing in Beachwear but do not like the risk. Having heard about diversification, you decide to add another business to the portfolio to reduce your investment risk.

- There is a snack shop on the beach that sells all the healthy food you like. You estimate that the annual return from the Snackshop is also 20 percent in years with many sunny days and 0 percent in other years. As with the Beachwear shop, the average return is 10 percent.

You decide to invest 50 percent each in Snackshop and Beachwear. The average return is still 10 percent, with 50 percent of 10 percent from Snackshop and 50 percent of 10 percent from Beachwear. In a sunny year, you would earn 20 percent (= 50% of 20% from Beachwear + 50% of 20% from Snackshop). In a rainy year, you would earn 0 percent (=50% of 0% from Beachwear + 50% of 0% from Snackshop). The results are tabulated in Exhibit 18.

Exhibit 18

Type	Company	Percent Invested	Return in Sunny Year (%)	Return in Rainy Year (%)	Average Return (%)
Single stock	Beachwear	100	20	0	10
Single stock	Snackshop	100	20	0	10
Portfolio of two stocks	Beachwear	50	20	0	10
	Snackshop	50	20	0	10
	Total	100	20	0	10

These results seem counterintuitive. You thought that by adding another business you would be able to diversify and reduce your risk, but the risk is exactly the same as before. What went wrong? Note that both businesses do well when it is sunny and both businesses do poorly when it rains. The correlation between the two businesses is +1.0. No reduction in risk occurs when the correlation is +1.0.

■ To reduce risk, you must consider a business that does well in a rainy year. You find a company that rents DVDs. DVDrental company is similar to the Beachwear company, except that its annual return is 20 percent in a rainy year and 0 percent in a sunny year, with an average return of 10 percent. DVDrental's 10 percent return is also risky just like Beachwear's return.

If you invest 50 percent each in DVDrental and Beachwear, then the average return is still 10 percent, with 50 percent of 10 percent from DVDrental and 50 percent of 10 percent from Beachwear. In a sunny year, you would earn 10 percent (= 50% of 20% from Beachwear + 50% of 0% from DVDrental). In a rainy year also, you would earn 10 percent (=50% of 0% from Beachwear + 50% of 20% from DVDrental). You have no risk because you earn 10 percent in both sunny and rainy years. Thus, by adding DVDrental to Beachwear, you have reduced (eliminated) your risk without affecting your return. The results are tabulated in Exhibit 19.

Exhibit 19

Type	Company	Percent Invested	Return in Sunny Year (%)	Return in Rainy Year (%)	Average Return (%)
Single stock	Beachwear	100	20	0	10
Single stock	DVDrental	100	0	20	10
Portfolio of two stocks	Beachwear	50	20	0	10
	DVDrental	50	0	20	10
	Total	100	10	10	10

In this case, the two businesses have a correlation of –1.0. When two businesses with a correlation of –1.0 are combined, risk can always be reduced to zero.

4.3.1 *Correlation and Risk Diversification*

Correlation is the key in diversification of risk. Notice that the returns from Beachwear and DVDRental always go in the opposite direction. If one of them does well, the other does not. Therefore, adding assets that do not behave like other assets in your portfolio is good and can reduce risk. The two companies in the above example have a correlation of −1.0.

Even when we expand the portfolio to many assets, correlation among assets remains the primary determinant of portfolio risk. Lower correlations are associated with lower risk. Unfortunately, most assets have high positive correlations. The challenge in diversifying risk is to find assets that have a correlation that is much lower than +1.0.

4.3.2 *Historical Risk and Correlation*

When we discussed asset returns in section 2.4.1, we were careful to distinguish between historical or past returns and expected or future returns because historical returns may not be a good indicator of future returns. Returns may be highly positive in one period and highly negative in another period depending on the risk of that asset. Exhibit 5 showed that returns for large U.S. company stocks were high in the 1990s but have been very low in the 2000s.

Risk for an asset class, however, does not usually change dramatically from one period to the next. Stocks have been risky even in periods of low returns. T-bills are always less risky even when they earn high returns. From Exhibit 5, we can see that risk has typically not varied much from one decade to the next, except that risk for bonds has been much higher in recent decades when compared with earlier decades. Therefore, it is not unreasonable to assume that historical risk can work as a good proxy for future risk.

As with risk, correlations are quite stable among assets of the same country. Intercountry correlations, however, have been on the rise in the last few decades as a result of globalization and the liberalization of many economies. A correlation above 0.90 is considered high because the assets do not provide much opportunity for diversification of risk, such as the correlations that exist among large U.S. company stocks on the NYSE, NASDAQ, S&P 500 Index, and Dow Jones Industrial Average. Correlations below 0.30 are considered attractive for portfolio diversification.

4.3.3 *Historical Correlation among Asset Classes*

Correlations among major U.S. asset classes and international stocks are reported in Exhibit 20 for 1970–2008. The highest correlation is between U.S. large company stocks and U.S. small company stocks at about 70 percent, whereas the correlation between U.S. large company stocks and international stocks is approximately 66 percent. Although these are the highest correlations, they still provide diversification benefits because the correlations are less than 100 percent. The correlation between international stocks and U.S. small company stocks is lower, at 49 percent. The lowest correlations are between stocks and bonds, with some correlations being negative, such as that between U.S. small company stocks and U.S. long-term government bonds. Similarly, the correlation between T-bills and stocks is close to zero and is marginally negative for international stocks.[7]

---

7 In any short period, T-bills are riskless and uncorrelated with other asset classes. For example, a 3-month U.S. Treasury bill is redeemable at its face value upon maturity irrespective of what happens to other assets. When we consider multiple periods, however, returns on T-bills may be related to other asset classes because short-term interest rates vary depending on the strength of the economy and outlook for inflation.

Exhibit 20		Correlation Among U.S. Assets and International Stocks (1970–2008)					
Series	International Stocks	U.S. Large Company Stocks	U.S. Small Company Stocks	U.S. Long-Term Corporate Bonds	U.S. Long-Term Treasury Bonds	U.S. T-Bills	U.S. Inflation
International stocks	1.00						
U.S. large company stocks	0.66	1.00					
U.S. small company stocks	0.49	0.71	1.00				
U.S. long-term corporate bonds	0.07	0.31	0.13	1.00			
U.S. long-term Treasury bonds	−0.04	0.13	−0.05	0.92	1.00		
U.S. T-bills	−0.02	0.15	0.07	0.02	0.90	1.00	
U.S. inflation	−0.09	−0.09	0.06	−0.40	−0.40	0.65	1.00

Source: 2009 Ibbotson SBBI Classic Yearbook (Table 13-5).

The low correlations between stocks and bonds are attractive for portfolio diversification. Similarly, including international securities in a portfolio can also control portfolio risk. It is not surprising that most diversified portfolios of investors contain domestic stocks, domestic bonds, foreign stocks, foreign bonds, real estate, cash, and other asset classes.

4.3.4 Avenues for Diversification

The reason for diversification is simple. By constructing a portfolio with assets that do not move together, you create a portfolio that reduces the ups and downs in the short term but continues to grow steadily in the long term. Diversification thus makes a portfolio more resilient to gyrations in financial markets.

We describe a number of approaches for diversification, some of which have been discussed previously and some of which might seem too obvious. Diversification, however, is such an important part of investing that it cannot be emphasized enough, especially when we continue to meet and see many investors who are not properly diversified.

■ *Diversify with asset classes.* Correlations among major asset classes[8] are not usually high, as can be observed from the few U.S. asset classes listed in Exhibit 20. Correlations for other asset classes and other countries are also typically low, which provides investors the opportunity to benefit from diversifying among many asset classes to achieve the biggest benefit from diversification. A partial list of asset classes includes domestic large caps, domestic small caps, growth stocks, value stocks, domestic corporate bonds, long-term domestic government bonds, domestic Treasury bills (cash), emerging market stocks, emerging market bonds, developed market stocks (i.e., developed markets excluding domestic market), developed market bonds, real estate, and gold and other commodities. In addition, industries and sectors are used to diversify portfolios. For example, energy stocks may not be well correlated with health

---

8 Major asset classes are distinguished from sub-classes, such as U.S. value stocks and U.S. growth stocks.

care stocks. The exact proportions in which these assets should be included in a portfolio depend on the risk, return, and correlation characteristics of each and the home country of the investor.

- *Diversify with index funds.* Diversifying among asset classes can become costly for small portfolios because of the number of securities required. For example, creating exposure to a single category, such as a domestic large company asset class, may require a group of at least 30 stocks. Exposure to 10 asset classes may require 300 securities, which can be expensive to trade and track. Instead, it may be effective to use exchange-traded funds or mutual funds that track the respective indices, which could bring down the costs associated with building a well-diversified portfolio. Therefore, many investors should seriously consider index mutual funds as an investment vehicle as opposed to individual securities.

- *Diversification among countries.* Countries are different because of industry focus, economic policy, and political climate. The U.S. economy produces many financial and technical services and invests a significant amount in innovative research. The Chinese and Indian economies, however, are focused on manu- facturing. Countries in the European Union are vibrant democracies whereas East Asian countries are experimenting with democracy. Thus, financial returns in one country over time are not likely to be highly correlated with returns in another country. Country returns may also be different because of different currencies. In other words, the return on a foreign investment may be different when translated to the home country's currency. Because currency returns are uncorrelated with stock returns, they may help reduce the risk of investing in a foreign country even when that country, in isolation, is a very risky emerging market from an equity investment point of view. Investment in foreign coun- tries is an essential part of a well-diversified portfolio.

- *Diversify by* not *owning your employer's stock.* Companies encourage their employees to invest in company stock through employee stock plans and retirement plans. You should evaluate investing in your company, however, just as you would evaluate any other investment. In addition, you should consider the nonfinancial investments that you have made, especially the human capi- tal you have invested in your company. Because you work for your employer, you are already heavily invested in it because your earnings depend on your employer. The level of your earnings, whether your compensation improves or whether you get a promotion, depends on how well your employer performs. If a competitor drives your employer out of the market, you will be out of a job. Additional investments in your employer will concentrate your wealth in one asset even more so and make you less diversified.

- *Evaluate each asset before adding to a portfolio.* Every time you add a security or an asset class to the portfolio, recognize that there is a cost associated with diversification. There is a cost of trading an asset as well as the cost of tracking a larger portfolio. In some cases, the securities or assets may have different names but belong to an asset class in which you already have sufficient exposure. A general rule to evaluate whether a new asset should be included to an existing portfolio is based on the following risk–return trade-off relationship:

$$E(R_{new}) = R_f + \frac{\sigma_{new}\rho_{new,p}}{\sigma_p} \times [E(R_p) - R_f]$$

where $E(R)$ is the return from the asset, R_f is the return on the risk-free asset, σ is the standard deviation, ρ is the correlation coefficient, and the subscripts *new* and *p* refer to the new stock and existing portfolio. If the new asset's risk-adjusted return benefits the portfolio, then the asset should be included. The condition can be rewritten using the Sharpe ratio on both sides of the equation as:

$$\frac{E(R_{new}) - R_f}{\sigma_{new}} > \frac{E(R_p) - R_f}{\sigma_p} \times \rho_{new,p}$$

If the Sharpe ratio of the new asset is greater than the Sharpe ratio of the current portfolio times the correlation coefficient, it is beneficial to add the new asset.

▪ *Buy insurance for risky portfolios.* It may come as a surprise, but insurance is an investment asset—just a different kind of asset. Insurance has a negative correlation with your assets and is thus very valuable. Insurance gives you a positive return when your assets lose value, but pays nothing if your assets maintain their value. Over time, insurance generates a negative average return. Many individuals, however, are willing to accept a small negative return because insurance reduces their exposure to an extreme loss. In general, it is reasonable to add an investment with a negative return if that investment significantly reduces risk (an example of a classic case of the risk–return trade-off).

Alternatively, investments with negative correlations also exist. Historically, gold has a negative correlation with stocks; however, the expected return is usually small and sometimes even negative. Investors often include gold and other commodities in their portfolios as a way of reducing their overall portfolio risk, including currency risk and inflation risk.

Buying put options is another way of reducing risk. Because put options pay when the underlying asset falls in value (negative correlation), they can protect an investor's portfolio against catastrophic losses. Of course, put options cost money, and the expected return is zero or marginally negative.

5   EFFICIENT FRONTIER AND INVESTOR'S OPTIMAL PORTFOLIO

In this section, we formalize the effect of diversification and expand the set of investments to include all available risky assets in a mean–variance framework. The addition of a risk-free asset generates an optimal risky portfolio and the capital allocation line. We can then derive an investor's optimal portfolio by overlaying the capital allocation line with the indifference curves of investors.

5.1 Investment Opportunity Set

If two assets are perfectly correlated, the risk–return opportunity set is represented by a straight line connecting those two assets. The line contains portfolios formed by changing the weight of each asset invested in the portfolio. This correlation was depicted by the straight line (with ρ = 1) in Exhibit 17. If the two assets are not perfectly correlated, the portfolio's risk is less than the weighted average risk of the components, and the portfolio formed from the two assets bulges on the left as shown by curves with the correlation coefficient (ρ) less than 1.0 in Exhibit 17. All of the points connecting the two assets are achievable (or feasible). The addition of new assets to this portfolio creates more and more portfolios that are either a linear combination of the existing portfolio and the new asset or a curvilinear combination, depending on the correlation between the existing portfolio and the new asset.

As the number of available assets increases, the number of possible combinations increases rapidly. When all investable assets are considered, and there are hundreds and thousands of them, we can construct an opportunity set of investments. The opportunity set will ordinarily span all points within a frontier because it is also possible to reach every possible point within that curve by judiciously creating a portfolio from the investable assets.

We begin with individual investable assets and gradually form portfolios that can be plotted to form a curve as shown in Exhibit 21. All points on the curve and points to the right of the curve are attainable by a combination of one or more of the investable assets. This set of points is called the investment opportunity set. Initially, the opportunity set consists of domestic assets only and is labeled as such in Exhibit 21.

Exhibit 21	Investment Opportunity Set

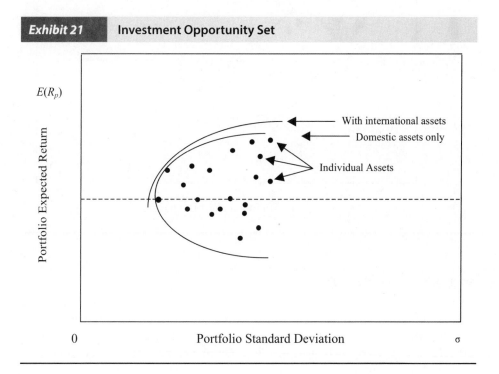

5.1.1 Addition of Asset Classes

Exhibit 21 shows the effect of adding a new asset class, such as international assets. As long as the new asset class is not perfectly correlated with the existing asset class, the investment opportunity set will expand out further to the northwest, providing a superior risk–return trade-off.

The investment opportunity set with international assets dominates the opportunity set that includes only domestic assets. Adding other asset classes will have the same impact on the opportunity set. Thus, we should continue to add asset classes until they do not further improve the risk–return trade-off. The benefits of diversification can be fully captured in this way in the construction of the investment opportunity set, and eventually in the selection of the optimal portfolio.

In the discussion that follows in this section, we will assume that *all* investable assets available to an investor are included in the investment opportunity set and no special attention needs to be paid to new asset classes or new investment opportunities.

5.2 Minimum-Variance Portfolios

The investment opportunity set consisting of all available investable sets is shown in Exhibit 22. There are a large number of portfolios available for investment, but we must choose a single optimal portfolio. In this subsection, we begin the selection process by narrowing the choice to fewer portfolios.

Exhibit 22	Minimum-Variance Frontier

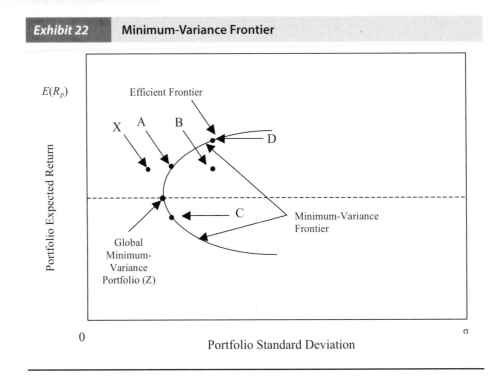

5.2.1 *Minimum-Variance Frontier*

Risk-averse investors seek to minimize risk for a given return. Consider Points A, B, and X in Exhibit 22 and assume that they are on the same horizontal line by construction. Thus, the three points have the same expected return, $E(R_1)$, as do all other points on the imaginary line connecting A, B, and X. Given a choice, an investor will choose the point with the minimum risk, which is Point X. Point X, however, is unattainable because it does not lie within the investment opportunity set. Thus, the minimum risk that we can attain for $E(R_1)$ is at Point A. Point B and all points to the right of Point A are feasible but they have higher risk. Therefore, a risk-averse investor will choose only Point A in preference to any other portfolio with the same return.

Similarly, Point C is the minimum variance point for the return earned at C. Points to the right of C have higher risk. We can extend the above analysis to all possible returns. In all cases, we find that the **minimum-variance portfolio** is the one that lies on the solid curve drawn in Exhibit 22. The entire collection of these minimum-variance portfolios is referred to as the minimum-variance frontier. The minimum-variance frontier defines the smaller set of portfolios in which investors would want to invest. Note that no risk-averse investor will choose to invest in a portfolio to the right of the minimum-variance frontier because a portfolio on the minimum-variance frontier can give the same return but at a lower risk.

5.2.2 *Global Minimum-Variance Portfolio*

The left-most point on the minimum-variance frontier is the portfolio with the minimum variance among all portfolios of risky assets, and is referred to as the **global minimum-variance portfolio**. An investor cannot hold a portfolio consisting of *risky* assets that has less risk than that of the global minimum-variance portfolio. Note the emphasis on "risky" assets. Later, the introduction of a risk-free asset will allow us to relax this constraint.

5.2.3 *Efficient Frontier of Risky Assets*

The minimum-variance frontier gives us portfolios with the minimum variance for a given return. However, investors also want to maximize return for a given risk. Observe Points A and C on the minimum-variance frontier shown in Exhibit 22. Both of them have the same risk. Given a choice, an investor will choose Portfolio A because it has a higher return. No one will choose Portfolio C. The same analysis applies to all points on the minimum-variance frontier that lie below the global minimum-variance portfolio. Thus, portfolios on the curve below the global minimum-variance portfolio and to the right of the global minimum-variance portfolio are not beneficial and are inefficient portfolios for an investor.

The curve that lies above and to the right of the global minimum-variance portfolio is referred to as the **Markowitz efficient frontier** because it contains all portfolios of risky assets that rational, risk-averse investors will choose.

An important observation that is often ignored is the slope at various points on the efficient frontier. As we move right from the global minimum-variance portfolio (Point Z) in Exhibit 22, there is an increase in risk with a concurrent increase in return. The increase in return with every unit increase in risk, however, keeps decreasing as we move from left to right because the slope continues to decrease. The slope at Point D is less than the slope at Point A, which is less than the slope at Point Z. The increase in return by moving from Point Z to Point A is the same as the increase in return by moving from Point A to Point D. It can be seen that the additional risk in moving from Point A to Point D is 3 to 4 times more than the additional risk in moving from Point Z to Point A. Thus, investors obtain decreasing increases in returns as they assume more risk.

5.3 A Risk-Free Asset and Many Risky Assets

Until now, we have only considered risky assets in which the return is risky or uncertain. Most investors, however, have access to a risk-free asset, most notably from securities issued by the government. The addition of a risk-free asset makes the investment opportunity set much richer than the investment opportunity set consisting only of risky assets.

5.3.1 *Capital Allocation Line and Optimal Risky Portfolio*

By definition, a risk-free asset has zero risk so it must lie on the y-axis in a mean-variance graph. A risk-free asset with a return of R_f is plotted in Exhibit 23. This asset can now be combined with a portfolio of risky assets. The combination of a risk-free asset with a portfolio of risky assets is a straight line, such as in Section 3.3 (see Exhibit 13). Unlike in Section 3.3, however, we have many risky portfolios to choose from instead of a single risky portfolio.

| Exhibit 23 | Optimal Risky Portfolio |

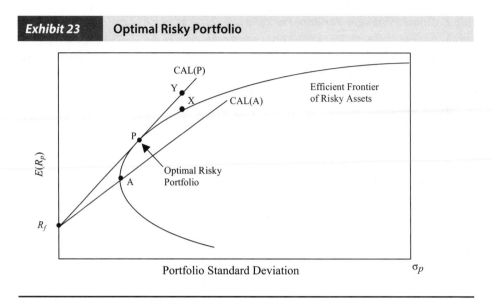

All portfolios on the efficient frontier are candidates for being combined with the risk-free asset. Two combinations are shown in Exhibit 23: one between the risk-free asset and efficient Portfolio A and the other between the risk-free asset and efficient Portfolio P. Comparing capital allocation line A and capital allocation line P reveals that there is a point on CAL(P) with a higher return and same risk for each point on CAL(A). In other words, the portfolios on CAL(P) dominate the portfolios on CAL(A). Therefore, an investor will choose CAL(P) over CAL(A). We would like to move further northwest to achieve even better portfolios. None of those portfolios, however, is attainable because they are above the efficient frontier.

What about other points on the efficient frontier? For example, Point X is on the efficient frontier and has the highest return of all risky portfolios for its risk. However, Point Y on CAL(P), achievable by leveraging Portfolio P as seen in Section 3.3, lies above Point X and has the same risk but higher return. In the same way, we can observe that not only does CAL(P) dominate CAL(A) but it also dominates the Markowitz efficient frontier of risky assets.

CAL(P) is the optimal capital allocation line and Portfolio P is the optimal risky portfolio. Thus, with the addition of the risk-free asset, we are able to narrow our selection of risky portfolios to a single optimal risky portfolio, P, which is at the tangent of CAL(P) and the efficient frontier of risky assets.

5.3.2 *The Two-Fund Separation Theorem*

The **two-fund separation theorem** states that all investors regardless of taste, risk preferences, and initial wealth will hold a combination of two portfolios or funds: a risk-free asset and an optimal portfolio of risky assets.[9]

The separation theorem allows us to divide an investor's investment problem into two distinct steps: the investment decision and the financing decision. In the first step, as in the previous analysis, the investor identifies the optimal risky portfolio. The optimal risky portfolio is selected from numerous risky portfolios without considering the investor's preferences. The investment decision at this step is based on the optimal risky portfolio's (a single portfolio) return, risk, and correlations.

---

9 In the next reading, you will learn that the optimal portfolio of risky assets is the market portfolio.

The capital allocation line connects the optimal risky portfolio and the risk-free asset. All optimal investor portfolios must be on this line. Each investor's optimal portfolio on the CAL(P) is determined in the second step. Considering each individual investor's risk preference, using indifference curves, determines the investor's allocation to the risk-free asset (lending) and to the optimal risky portfolio. Portfolios beyond the optimal risky portfolio are obtained by borrowing at the risk-free rate (i.e., buying on margin). Therefore, the individual investor's risk preference determines the amount of financing (i.e., lending to the government instead of investing in the optimal risky portfolio or borrowing to purchase additional amounts of the optimal risky portfolio).

EXAMPLE 10

Choosing the Right Portfolio

In Exhibit 24, the risk and return of the points marked are as follows:

Point	Return (%)	Risk (%)	Point (%)	Return (%)	Risk (%)
A	15	10	B	11	10
C	15	30	D	25	30
F	4	0	G (gold)	10	30
P	16	17			

Exhibit 24

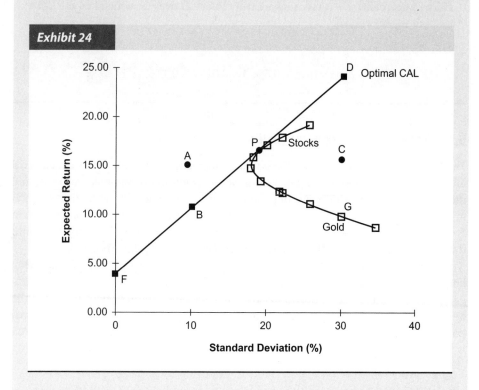

Answer the following questions with reference to the points plotted on Exhibit 24 and explain your answers. The investor is choosing one portfolio based on the graph.

1   Which of the above points is not achievable?

2   Which of these portfolios will not be chosen by a rational, risk-averse investor?

3 Which of these portfolios is most suitable for a risk-neutral investor?

4 Gold is on the inefficient part of the feasible set. Nonetheless, gold is owned by many rational investors as part of a larger portfolio. Why?

5 What is the utility of an investor at point P with a risk aversion coefficient of 3?

Solution to 1:

Portfolio A is not attainable because it lies outside the feasible set and not on the capital allocation line.

Solution to 2:

Portfolios G and C will not be chosen because D provides higher return for the same risk. G and C are the only investable points that do not lie on the capital allocation line.

Solution to 3:

Portfolio D is most suitable because a risk-neutral investor cares only about return and portfolio D provides the highest return. A = 0 in the utility formula.

Solution to 4:

Gold may be owned as part of a portfolio (not as *the* portfolio) because gold has low or negative correlation with many risky assets, such as stocks. Being part of a portfolio can thus reduce overall risk even though its standalone risk is high and return is low. Note that gold's price is not stable—its return is very risky (30 percent). Even risk seekers will choose D over G, which has the same risk but higher return.

Solution to 5:

$$U = E(r) - 0.5 \, A \, \sigma^2 = 0.16 - 0.5 \times 3 \times 0.0289 = 0.1167 = 11.67\%.$$

5.4 Optimal Investor Portfolio

The CAL(P) in Exhibits 23 and 25 contains the best possible portfolios available to investors. Each of those portfolios is a linear combination of the risk-free asset and the optimal risky portfolio. Among the available portfolios, the selection of each investor's optimal portfolio depends on the risk preferences of an investor. In Section 3, we discussed that the individual investor's risk preferences are incorporated into their indifference curves. These can be used to select the optimal portfolio.

Exhibit 25 shows an indifference curve that is tangent to the capital allocation line, CAL(P). Indifference curves with higher utility than this one lie above the capital allocation line, so their portfolios are not achievable. Indifference curves that lie below this one are not preferred because they have lower utility. Thus, the optimal portfolio for the investor with this indifference curve is portfolio C on CAL(P), which is tangent to the indifference curve.

| Exhibit 25 | Optimal Investor Portfolio |

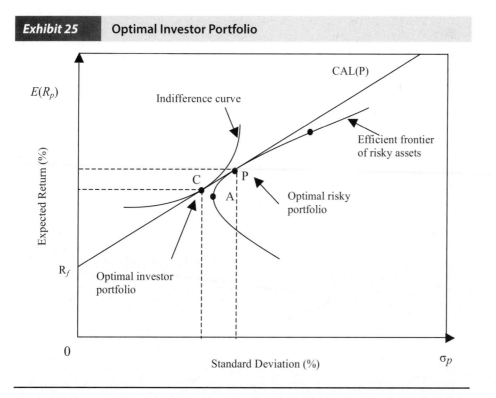

EXAMPLE 11

Comprehensive Example on Portfolio Selection

This comprehensive example reviews many concepts learned in this reading. The example begins with simple information about available assets and builds an optimal investor portfolio for the Lohrmanns.

Suppose the Lohrmanns can invest in only two risky assets, A and B. The expected return and standard deviation for asset A are 20 percent and 50 percent, and the expected return and standard deviation for asset B are 15 percent and 33 percent. The two assets have zero correlation with one another.

1 Calculate portfolio expected return and portfolio risk (standard deviation) if an investor invests 10 percent in A and the remaining 90 percent in B.

Solution to 1:

The subscript "rp" means risky portfolio.

$$R_{rp} = \left[0.10 \times 20\%\right] + \left[(1 - 0.10) \times 15\%\right] = 0.155 = 15.50\%$$

$$\sigma_{rp} = \sqrt{w_A^2\sigma_A^2 + w_B^2\sigma_B^2 + 2w_Aw_B\rho_{AB}\sigma_A\sigma_B}$$

$$= \sqrt{(0.10^2 \times 0.50^2) + (0.90^2 \times 0.33^2) + (2 \times 0.10 \times 0.90 \times 0.0 \times 0.50 \times 0.33)}$$

$$= 0.3012 = 30.12\%$$

Note that the correlation coefficient is 0, so the last term for standard deviation is zero.

2 Generalize the above calculations for portfolio return and risk by assuming an investment of w_A in Asset A and an investment of $(1 - w_A)$ in Asset B.

Solution to 2:

$$R_{rp} = w_A \times 20\% + (1 - w_A) \times 15\% = 0.05w_A + 0.15$$

$$\sigma_{rp} = \sqrt{w_A^2 \times 0.5^2 + (1 - w_A)^2 \times 0.33^2} = \sqrt{0.25w_A^2 + 0.1089(1 - 2w_A + w_A^2)}$$

$$= \sqrt{0.3589w_A^2 - 0.2178w_A + 0.1089}$$

The investment opportunity set can be constructed by using different weights in the expressions for $E(R_{rp})$ and σ_{rp} in Part 1 of this example. Exhibit 26 shows the combination of Assets A and B.

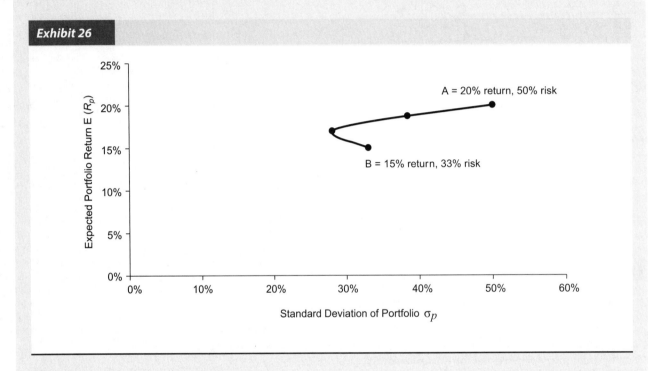

Exhibit 26

3 Now introduce a risk-free asset with a return of 3 percent. Write an equation for the capital allocation line in terms of w_A that will connect the risk-free asset to the portfolio of risky assets. (Hint: use the equation in Section 3.3 and substitute the expressions for a risky portfolio's risk and return from Part 2 above).

Solution to 3:

The equation of the line connecting the risk-free asset to the portfolio of risky assets is given below (see Section 3.3), where the subscript "rp" refers to the risky portfolio instead of "i," and the subscript "p" refers to the new portfolio of two risky assets and one risk-free asset.

$$E(R_p) = R_f + \frac{E(R_i) - R_f}{\sigma_i}\sigma_p,$$

Rewritten as

$$E(R_p) = R_f + \frac{E(R_{rp}) - R_f}{\sigma_{rp}}\sigma_p$$

$$= 0.03 + \frac{0.05w_A + 0.15 - 0.03}{\sqrt{0.3589w_A^2 - 0.2178w_A + 0.1089}}\sigma_p$$

$$= 0.03 + \frac{0.05w_A + 0.12}{\sqrt{0.3589w_A^2 - 0.2178w_A + 0.1089}}\sigma_p$$

The capital allocation line is the line that has the maximum slope because it is tangent to the curve formed by portfolios of the two risky assets. Exhibit 27 shows the capital allocation line based on a risk-free asset added to the group of assets.

Exhibit 27

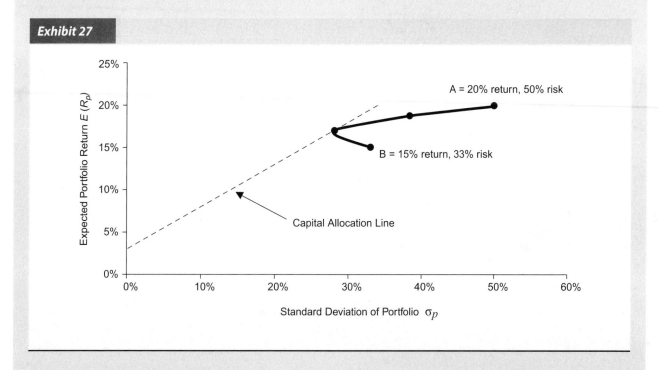

4 The slope of the capital allocation line is maximized when the weight in Asset A is 38.20 percent.[10] What is the equation for the capital allocation line using w_A of 38.20 percent?

Solution to 4:

By substituting 38.20 percent for w_A in the equation in Part 3, we get $E(R_p) = 0.03 + 0.4978\, \sigma_p$ as the capital allocation line.

5 Having created the capital allocation line, we turn to the Lohrmanns. What is the standard deviation of a portfolio that gives a 20 percent return and is on the capital allocation line? How does this portfolio compare with asset A?

Solution to 5:

Solve the equation for the capital allocation line to get the standard deviation: $0.20 = 0.03 + 0.4978\, \sigma_p$. $\sigma_p = 34.2\%$. The portfolio with a 20 percent return has the same return as Asset A but a lower standard deviation, 34.2 percent instead of 50.0 percent.

6 What is the risk of portfolios with returns of 3 percent, 9 percent, 15 percent, and 20 percent?

Solution to 6:

You can find the risk of the portfolio using the equation for the capital allocation line: $E(R_p) = 0.03 + 0.4978\, \sigma_p$.
   For a portfolio with a return of 15 percent, write $0.15 = 0.03 + 0.4978\, \sigma_p$. Solving for σ_p gives 24.1 percent. You can similarly calculate risks of other portfolios with the given returns.

---

10 You can maximize $\dfrac{0.05 w_A + 0.12}{\sqrt{0.3589 w_A^2 - 0.2178 w_A + 0.1089}}$ by taking the first derivative of the slope with respect to w_A and setting it to 0.

The risk of the portfolio for a return of 3 percent is 0.0 percent, for a return of 9 percent is 12.1 percent, for a return of 15 percent is 24.1 percent, and for a return of 20 percent is 34.2 percent. The points are plotted in Exhibit 28.

Exhibit 28

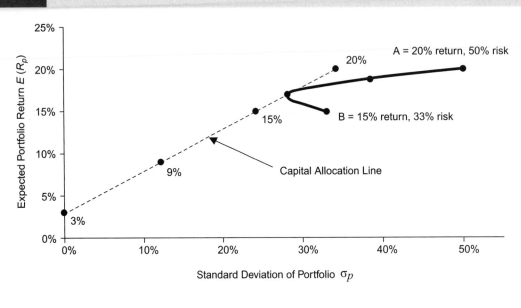

7 What is the utility that the Lohrmanns derive from a portfolio with a return of 3 percent, 9 percent, 15 percent, and 20 percent? The risk aversion coefficient for the Lohrmanns is 2.5.

Solution to 7:

To find the utility, use the utility formula with a risk aversion coefficient of 2.5:

$$\text{Utility} = E\left(R_p\right) - 0.5 \times 2.5\sigma_p^2$$

$$\text{Utility}\left(3\%\right) = 0.0300.$$

$$\text{Utility}\left(9\%\right) = 0.09 - 0.5 \times 2.5 \times 0.121^2 = +0.0717$$

$$\text{Utility}\left(15\%\right) = 0.15 - 0.5 \times 2.5 \times 0.241^2 = +0.0774$$

$$\text{Utility}\left(20\%\right) = 0.20 - 0.5 \times 2.5 \times 0.341^2 = +0.0546$$

Based on the above information, the Lohrmanns choose a portfolio with a return of 15 percent and a standard deviation of 24.1 percent because it has the highest utility: 0.0774. Finally, Exhibit 29 shows the indifference curve that is tangent to the capital allocation line to generate Lohrmanns' optimal investor portfolio.

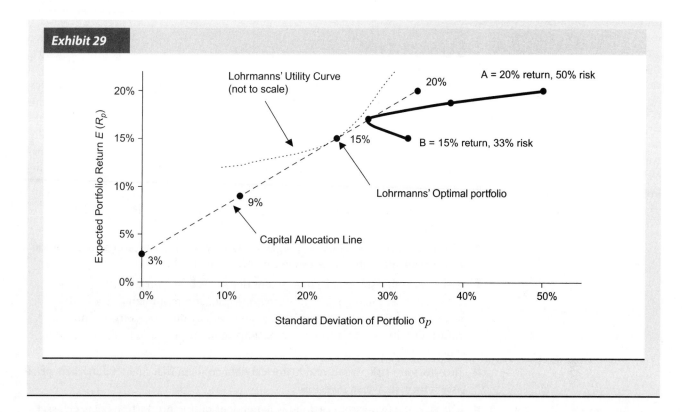

Exhibit 29

5.4.1 Investor Preferences and Optimal Portfolios

The location of an optimal investor portfolio depends on the investor's risk preferences. A highly risk-averse investor may invest a large proportion, even 100 percent, of his/her assets in the risk-free asset. The optimal portfolio in this investor's case will be located close to the y-axis. A less risk-averse investor, however, may invest a large portion of his/her wealth in the optimal risky asset. The optimal portfolio in this investor's case will lie closer to Point P in Exhibit 25.

Some less risk-averse investors (i.e., with a high risk tolerance) may wish to accept even more risk because of the chance of higher return. Such an investor may borrow money to invest more in the risky portfolio. If the investor borrows 25 percent of his wealth, he/she can invest 125 percent in the optimal risky portfolio. The optimal investor portfolio for such an investor will lie to the right of Point P on the capital allocation line.

Thus, moving from the risk-free asset along the capital allocation line, we encounter investors who are willing to accept more risk. At Point P, the investor is 100 percent invested in the optimal risky portfolio. Beyond Point P, the investor accepts even more risk by borrowing money and investing in the optimal risky portfolio.

Note that we are able to accommodate all types of investors with just two portfolios: the risk-free asset and the optimal risky portfolio. Exhibit 25 is also an illustration of the two-fund separation theorem. Portfolio P is the optimal risky portfolio that is selected without regard to investor preferences. The optimal investor portfolio is selected on the capital allocation line by overlaying the indifference curves that incorporate investor preferences.

SUMMARY

This reading provides a description and computation of investment characteristics, such as risk and return, that investors use in evaluating assets for investment. This was followed by sections about portfolio construction, selection of an optimal risky portfolio, and an understanding of risk aversion and indifference curves. Finally, the tangency point of the indifference curves with the capital allocation line allows identification of the optimal investor portfolio. Key concepts covered in the reading include the following:

▪ Holding period return is most appropriate for a single, predefined holding period.

▪ Multiperiod returns can be aggregated in many ways. Each return computation has special applications for evaluating investments.

▪ Risk-averse investors make investment decisions based on the risk–return trade-off, maximizing return for the same risk, and minimizing risk for the same return. They may be concerned, however, by deviations from a normal return distribution and from assumptions of financial markets' operational efficiency.

▪ Investors are risk averse, and historical data confirm that financial markets price assets for risk-averse investors.

▪ The risk of a two-asset portfolio is dependent on the proportions of each asset, their standard deviations and the correlation (or covariance) between the asset's returns. As the number of assets in a portfolio increases, the correlation among asset risks becomes a more important determinate of portfolio risk.

▪ Combining assets with low correlations reduces portfolio risk.

▪ The two-fund separation theorem allows us to separate decision making into two steps. In the first step, the optimal risky portfolio and the capital allocation line are identified, which are the same for all investors. In the second step, investor risk preferences enable us to find a unique optimal investor portfolio for each investor.

▪ The addition of a risk-free asset creates portfolios that are dominant to portfolios of risky assets in all cases except for the optimal risky portfolio.

By successfully understanding the content of this reading, you should be comfortable calculating an investor's optimal portfolio given the investor's risk preferences and universe of investable assets available.

REFERENCES

2009 Ibbotson Stocks, Bonds, Bills, and Inflation (SBBI) Classic Yearbook. 2009. Chicago, IL: Morningstar.

Bogle, John C. 2008. "Black Monday and Black Swans." *Financial Analysts Journal*, vol. 64, no. 2: 30–40.

Dimson, Elroy, Paul Marsh, and Mike Staunton. 2009. *Credit Suisse Global Investment Returns Sourcebook.* 2009. Zurich, Switzerland: Credit Suisse Research Institute.

Taleb, Nassim N. 2007. *The Black Swan: The Impact of the Highly Improbable.* New York: Random House Inc.

PRACTICE PROBLEMS

1 An investor purchased 100 shares of a stock for $34.50 per share at the beginning of the quarter. If the investor sold all of the shares for $30.50 per share after receiving a $51.55 dividend payment at the end of the quarter, the holding period return is *closest* to:

   A   −13.0%.

   B   −11.6%.

   C   −10.1%.

2 An analyst obtains the following annual rates of return for a mutual fund:

Year	Return (%)
2008	14
2009	−10
2010	−2

The fund's holding period return over the three-year period is *closest* to:

   A   0.18%.

   B   0.55%.

   C   0.67%.

3 An analyst observes the following annual rates of return for a hedge fund:

Year	Return (%)
2008	22
2009	−25
2010	11

The hedge fund's annual geometric mean return is *closest* to:

   A   0.52%.

   B   1.02%.

   C   2.67%.

4 Which of the following return calculating methods is *best* for evaluating the annualized returns of a buy-and-hold strategy of an investor who has made annual deposits to an account for each of the last five years?

   A   Geometric mean return.

   B   Arithmetic mean return.

   C   Money-weighted return.

5 An investor evaluating the returns of three recently formed exchange-traded funds gathers the following information:

Developed by Stephen P. Huffman, CFA (University of Wisconsin, Oshkosh). Copyright © 2011 CFA Institute.

ETF	Time Since Inception	Return Since Inception (%)
1	146 days	4.61
2	5 weeks	1.10
3	15 months	14.35

The ETF with the highest annualized rate of return is:

A ETF 1.

B ETF 2.

C ETF 3.

6 With respect to capital market theory, which of the following asset characteristics is *least likely* to impact the variance of an investor's equally weighted portfolio?

A Return on the asset.

B Standard deviation of the asset.

C Covariances of the asset with the other assets in the portfolio.

7 A portfolio manager creates the following portfolio:

Security	Security Weight (%)	Expected Standard Deviation (%)
1	30	20
2	70	12

If the correlation of returns between the two securities is 0.40, the expected standard deviation of the portfolio is *closest* to:

A 10.7%.

B 11.3%.

C 12.1%.

8 A portfolio manager creates the following portfolio:

Security	Security Weight (%)	Expected Standard Deviation (%)
1	30	20
2	70	12

If the covariance of returns between the two securities is −0.0240, the expected standard deviation of the portfolio is *closest* to:

A 2.4%.

B 7.5%.

C 9.2%.

The following information relates to Questions 9–10

A portfolio manager creates the following portfolio:

Security	Security Weight (%)	Expected Standard Deviation (%)
1	30	20
2	70	12

9   If the standard deviation of the portfolio is 14.40%, the correlation between the two securities is equal to:

A   −1.0.

B   0.0.

C   1.0.

10 If the standard deviation of the portfolio is 14.40%, the covariance between the two securities is equal to:

A   0.0006.

B   0.0240.

C   1.0000.

The following information relates to Questions 11–14

An analyst observes the following historic geometric returns:

Asset Class	Geometric Return (%)
Equities	8.0
Corporate Bonds	6.5
Treasury bills	2.5
Inflation	2.1

11 The real rate of return for equities is *closest* to:

A   5.4%.

B   5.8%.

C   5.9%.

12 The real rate of return for corporate bonds is *closest* to:

A   4.3%.

B   4.4%.

C   4.5%.

13 The risk premium for equities is *closest* to:

    A 5.4%.

    B 5.5%.

    C 5.6%.

14 The risk premium for corporate bonds is *closest* to:

    A 3.5%.

    B 3.9%.

    C 4.0%.

15 With respect to trading costs, liquidity is *least likely* to impact the:

    A stock price.

    B bid–ask spreads.

    C brokerage commissions.

16 Evidence of risk aversion is *best* illustrated by a risk–return relationship that is:

    A negative.

    B neutral.

    C positive.

17 With respect to risk-averse investors, a risk-free asset will generate a numerical utility that is:

    A the same for all individuals.

    B positive for risk-averse investors.

    C equal to zero for risk seeking investors.

18 With respect to utility theory, the most risk-averse investor will have an indifference curve with the:

    A most convexity.

    B smallest intercept value.

    C greatest slope coefficient.

19 With respect to an investor's utility function expressed as: $U = E(r) - \frac{1}{2}A\sigma^2$, which of the following values for the measure for risk aversion has the *least* amount of risk aversion?

    A −4.

    B 0.

    C 4.

The following information relates to Questions 20–23

A financial planner has created the following data to illustrate the application of utility theory to portfolio selection:

Investment	Expected Return (%)	Expected Standard Deviation (%)
1	18	2
2	19	8
3	20	15
4	18	30

20 A risk-neutral investor is *most likely* to choose:

  A Investment 1.

  B Investment 2.

  C Investment 3.

21 If an investor's utility function is expressed as $U = E(r) - \frac{1}{2}A\sigma^2$ and the measure for risk aversion has a value of –2, the risk-seeking investor is *most likely* to choose:

  A Investment 2.

  B Investment 3.

  C Investment 4.

22 If an investor's utility function is expressed as $U = E(r) - \frac{1}{2}A\sigma^2$ and the measure for risk aversion has a value of 2, the risk-averse investor is *most likely* to choose:

  A Investment 1.

  B Investment 2.

  C Investment 3.

23 If an investor's utility function is expressed as $U = E(r) - \frac{1}{2}A\sigma^2$ and the measure for risk aversion has a value of 4, the risk-averse investor is *most likely* to choose:

  A Investment 1.

  B Investment 2.

  C Investment 3.

24 With respect to the mean–variance portfolio theory, the capital allocation line, CAL, is the combination of the risk-free asset and a portfolio of all:

  A risky assets.

  B equity securities.

  C feasible investments.

25 Two individual investors with different levels of risk aversion will have optimal portfolios that are:

  A below the capital allocation line.

  B on the capital allocation line.

  C above the capital allocation line.

The following information relates to Questions 26–28

A portfolio manager creates the following portfolio:

Security	Expected Annual Return (%)	Expected Standard Deviation (%)
1	16	20
2	12	20

26 If the portfolio of the two securities has an expected return of 15%, the proportion invested in Security 1 is:

A 25%.

B 50%.

C 75%.

27 If the correlation of returns between the two securities is –0.15, the expected standard deviation of an equal-weighted portfolio is *closest* to:

A 13.04%.

B 13.60%.

C 13.87%.

28 If the two securities are uncorrelated, the expected standard deviation of an equal-weighted portfolio is *closest* to:

A 14.00%.

B 14.14%.

C 20.00%.

29 As the number of assets in an equally-weighted portfolio increases, the contribution of each individual asset's variance to the volatility of the portfolio:

A increases.

B decreases.

C remains the same.

30 With respect to an equally-weighted portfolio made up of a large number of assets, which of the following contributes the *most* to the volatility of the portfolio?

A Average variance of the individual assets.

B Standard deviation of the individual assets.

C Average covariance between all pairs of assets.

31 The correlation between assets in a two-asset portfolio increases during a market decline. If there is no change in the proportion of each asset held in the portfolio or the expected standard deviation of the individual assets, the volatility of the portfolio is *most likely* to:

A increase.

B decrease.

C remain the same.

The following information relates to Questions 32–34

An analyst has made the following return projections for each of three possible outcomes with an equal likelihood of occurrence:

Asset	Outcome 1 (%)	Outcome 2 (%)	Outcome 3 (%)	Expected Return (%)
1	12	0	6	6
2	12	6	0	6
3	0	6	12	6

32 Which pair of assets is perfectly negatively correlated?

 A Asset 1 and Asset 2.

 B Asset 1 and Asset 3.

 C Asset 2 and Asset 3.

33 If the analyst constructs two-asset portfolios that are equally-weighted, which pair of assets has the *lowest* expected standard deviation?

 A Asset 1 and Asset 2.

 B Asset 1 and Asset 3.

 C Asset 2 and Asset 3.

34 If the analyst constructs two-asset portfolios that are equally weighted, which pair of assets provides the *least* amount of risk reduction?

 A Asset 1 and Asset 2.

 B Asset 1 and Asset 3.

 C Asset 2 and Asset 3.

35 Which of the following statements is *least* accurate? The efficient frontier is the set of all attainable risky assets with the:

 A highest expected return for a given level of risk.

 B lowest amount of risk for a given level of return.

 C highest expected return relative to the risk-free rate.

36 The portfolio on the minimum-variance frontier with the lowest standard deviation is:

 A unattainable.

 B the optimal risky portfolio.

 C the global minimum-variance portfolio.

37 The set of portfolios on the minimum-variance frontier that dominates all sets of portfolios below the global minimum-variance portfolio is the:

 A capital allocation line.

 B Markowitz efficient frontier.

 C set of optimal risky portfolios.

38 The dominant capital allocation line is the combination of the risk-free asset and the:

 A optimal risky portfolio.

    B levered portfolio of risky assets.

    C global minimum-variance portfolio.

39 Compared to the efficient frontier of risky assets, the dominant capital allocation line has higher rates of return for levels of risk greater than the optimal risky portfolio because of the investor's ability to:

    A lend at the risk-free rate.

    B borrow at the risk-free rate.

    C purchase the risk-free asset.

40 With respect to the mean–variance theory, the optimal portfolio is determined by each individual investor's:

    A risk-free rate.

    B borrowing rate.

    C risk preference.

SOLUTIONS

1 C is correct. −10.1% is the holding period return, which is calculated as: $(3{,}050 − 3{,}450 + 51.55)/3{,}450$, which is comprised of a dividend yield of $1.49\% = 51.55/(3{,}450)$ and a capital loss yield of $−11.59\% = −400/(3{,}450)$.

2 B is correct. $[(1 + 0.14)(1 − 0.10)(1 − 0.02)] − 1 = 0.0055 = 0.55\%$.

3 A is correct. $[(1 + 0.22)(1 − 0.25)(1 + 0.11)]^{(1/3)} − 1 = 1.0157^{(1/3)} − 1 = 0.0052 = 0.52\%$

4 A is correct. The geometric mean return compounds the returns instead of the amount invested.

5 B is correct. The annualized rate of return for ETF 2 is $12.05\% = (1.0110^{52/5}) − 1$, which is greater than the annualized rate of ETF 1, $11.93\% = (1.0461^{365/146}) − 1$, and ETF 3, $11.32\% = (1.1435^{12/15}) − 1$. Despite having the lowest value for the periodic rate, ETF 2 has the highest annualized rate of return because of the reinvestment rate assumption and the compounding of the periodic rate.

6 A is correct. The asset's returns are not used to calculate the portfolio's variance [only the assets' weights, standard deviations (or variances), and covariances (or correlations) are used].

7 C is correct.

$$\sigma_{port} = \sqrt{w_1^2\sigma_1^2 + w_2^2\sigma_2^2 + 2w_1w_2\rho_{1,2}\sigma_1\sigma_2}$$
$$= \sqrt{(0.3)^2(20\%)^2 + (0.7)^2(12\%)^2 + 2(0.3)(0.7)(0.40)(20\%)(12\%)}$$
$$= (0.3600\% + 0.7056\% + 0.4032\%)^{0.5} = (1.4688\%)^{0.5} = 12.11\%.$$

8 A is correct.

$$\sigma_{port} = \sqrt{w_1^2\sigma_1^2 + w_2^2\sigma_2^2 + 2w_1w_2 Cov(R_1 R_2)}$$
$$= \sqrt{(0.3)^2(20\%)^2 + (0.7)^2(12\%)^2 + 2(0.3)(0.7)(−0.0240)}$$
$$= (0.3600\% + 0.7056\% − 1.008\%)^{0.5} = (0.0576\%)^{0.5} = 2.40\%.$$

9 C is correct. A portfolio standard deviation of 14.40% is the weighted average, which is possible only if the correlation between the securities is equal to 1.0.

10 B is correct. A portfolio standard deviation of 14.40% is the weighted average, which is possible only if the correlation between the securities is equal to 1.0. If the correlation coefficient is equal to 1.0, then the covariance must equal 0.0240, calculated as: $Cov(R_1,R_2) = \rho_{12}\sigma_1\sigma_2 = (1.0)(20\%)(12\%) = 2.40\% = 0.0240$.

11 B is correct. $(1 + 0.080)/(1 + 0.0210) = 5.8\%$

12 A is correct. $(1 + 0.065)/(1 + 0.0210) = 4.3\%$

13 A is correct. $(1 + 0.080)/(1 + 0.0250) = 5.4\%$

14 B is correct. $(1 + 0.0650)/(1 + 0.0250) = 3.9\%$

15 C is correct. Brokerage commissions are negotiated with the brokerage firm. A security's liquidity impacts the operational efficiency of trading costs. Specifically, liquidity impacts the bid−ask spread and can impact the stock price (if the ability to sell the stock is impaired by the uncertainty associated with being able to sell the stock).

16 C is correct. Historical data over long periods of time indicate that there exists a positive risk–return relationship, which is a reflection of an investor's risk aversion.

17 A is correct. A risk-free asset has a variance of zero and is not dependent on whether the investor is risk neutral, risk seeking or risk averse. That is, given that the utility function of an investment is expressed as $U = E(r) - \frac{1}{2}A\sigma^2$, where A is the measure of risk aversion, then the sign of A is irrelevant if the variance is zero (like that of a risk-free asset).

18 C is correct. The most risk-averse investor has the indifference curve with the greatest slope.

19 A is correct. A negative value in the given utility function indicates that the investor is a risk seeker.

20 C is correct. Investment 3 has the highest rate of return. Risk is irrelevant to a risk-neutral investor, who would have a measure of risk aversion equal to 0. Given the utility function, the risk-neutral investor would obtain the greatest amount of utility from Investment 3.

Investment	Expected Return (%)	Expected Standard Deviation (%)	Utility A = 0
1	18	2	0.1800
2	19	8	0.1900
3	20	15	0.2000
4	18	30	0.1800

21 C is correct. Investment 4 provides the highest utility value (0.2700) for a risk-seeking investor, who has a measure of risk aversion equal to –2.

Investment	Expected Return (%)	Expected Standard Deviation (%)	Utility A = –2
1	18	2	0.1804
2	19	8	0.1964
3	20	15	0.2225
4	18	30	0.2700

22 B is correct. Investment 2 provides the highest utility value (0.1836) for a risk-averse investor who has a measure of risk aversion equal to 2.

Investment	Expected Return (%)	Expected Standard Deviation (%)	Utility A = 2
1	18	2	0.1796
2	19	8	0.1836
3	20	15	0.1775
4	18	30	0.0900

23 A is correct. Investment 1 provides the highest utility value (0.1792) for a risk-averse investor who has a measure of risk aversion equal to 4.

Investment	Expected Return (%)	Expected Standard Deviation (%)	Utility A = 4
1	18	2	0.1792
2	19	8	0.1772
3	20	15	0.1550
4	18	30	0.0000

24 A is correct. The CAL is the combination of the risk-free asset with zero risk and the portfolio of all risky assets that provides for the set of feasible investments. Allowing for borrowing at the risk-free rate and investing in the portfolio of all risky assets provides for attainable portfolios that dominate risky assets below the CAL.

25 B is correct. The CAL represents the set of all feasible investments. Each investor's indifference curve determines the optimal combination of the risk-free asset and the portfolio of all risky assets, which must lie on the CAL.

26 C is correct.

$$R_p = w_1 \times R_1 + \left(1 - w_1\right) \times R_2$$
$$R_p = w_1 \times 16\% + \left(1 - w_1\right) \times 12\%$$
$$15\% = 0.75\left(16\%\right) + 0.25\left(12\%\right)$$

27 A is correct.

$$\sigma_{port} = \sqrt{w_1^2 \sigma_1^2 + w_2^2 \sigma_2^2 + 2w_1 w_2 \rho_{1,2} \sigma_1 \sigma_2}$$
$$= \sqrt{(0.5)^2 (20\%)^2 + (0.5)^2 (20\%)^2 + 2(0.5)(0.5)(-0.15)(20\%)(20\%)}$$
$$= \left(1.0000\% + 1.0000\% - 0.3000\%\right)^{0.5} = \left(1.7000\%\right)^{0.5} = 13.04\%$$

28 B is correct.

$$\sigma_{port} = \sqrt{w_1^2 \sigma_1^2 + w_2^2 \sigma_2^2 + 2w_1 w_2 \rho_{1,2} \sigma_1 \sigma_2}$$
$$= \sqrt{(0.5)^2 (20\%)^2 + (0.5)^2 (20\%)^2 + 2(0.5)(0.5)(0.00)(20\%)(20\%)}$$
$$= \left(1.0000\% + 1.0000\% + 0.0000\%\right)^{0.5} = \left(2.0000\%\right)^{0.5} = 14.14\%$$

29 B is correct. The contribution of each individual asset's variance (or standard deviation) to the portfolio's volatility decreases as the number of assets in the equally weighted portfolio increases. The contribution of the co-movement measures between the assets increases (i.e., covariance and correlation) as the number of assets in the equally weighted portfolio increases. The following equation for the variance of an equally weighted portfolio illustrates these points: $\sigma_p^2 = \dfrac{\overline{\sigma}^2}{N} + \dfrac{N-1}{N}\overline{COV} = \dfrac{\overline{\sigma}^2}{N} + \dfrac{N-1}{N}\overline{\rho}\overline{\sigma}^2$.

30 C is correct. The co-movement measures between the assets increases (i.e., covariance and correlation) as the number of assets in the equally weighted portfolio increases. The contribution of each individual asset's variance (or standard deviation) to the portfolio's volatility decreases as the number of assets in the equally weighted portfolio increases. The following equation for the variance of an equally weighted portfolio illustrates these points:

$$\sigma_p^2 = \frac{\overline{\sigma}^2}{N} + \frac{N-1}{N}\overline{COV} = \frac{\overline{\sigma}^2}{N} + \frac{N-1}{N}\overline{\rho}\,\overline{\sigma}^2.$$

31 A is correct. Higher correlations will produce less diversification benefits provided that the other components of the portfolio standard deviation do not change (i.e., the weights and standard deviations of the individual assets).

32 C is correct. Asset 2 and Asset 3 have returns that are the same for Outcome 2, but the exact opposite returns for Outcome 1 and Outcome 3; therefore, because they move in opposite directions at the same magnitude, they are perfectly negatively correlated.

33 C is correct. An equally weighted portfolio of Asset 2 and Asset 3 will have the lowest portfolio standard deviation, because for each outcome, the portfolio has the same expected return (they are perfectly negatively correlated).

34 A is correct. An equally weighted portfolio of Asset 1 and Asset 2 has the highest level of volatility of the three pairs. All three pairs have the same expected return; however, the portfolio of Asset 1 and Asset 2 provides the least amount of risk reduction.

35 C is correct. The minimum-variance frontier does not account for the risk-free rate. The minimum-variance frontier is the set of all attainable risky assets with the highest expected return for a given level of risk or the lowest amount of risk for a given level of return.

36 C is correct. The global minimum-variance portfolio is the portfolio on the minimum-variance frontier with the lowest standard deviation. Although the portfolio is attainable, when the risk-free asset is considered, the global minimum-variance portfolio is not the optimal risky portfolio.

37 B is correct. The Markowitz efficient frontier has higher rates of return for a given level of risk. With respect to the minimum-variance portfolio, the Markowitz efficient frontier is the set of portfolios above the global minimum-variance portfolio that dominates the portfolios below the global minimum-variance portfolio.

38 A is correct. The use of leverage and the combination of a risk-free asset and the optimal risky asset will dominate the efficient frontier of risky assets (the Markowitz efficient frontier).

39 B is correct. The CAL dominates the efficient frontier at all points except for the optimal risky portfolio. The ability of the investor to purchase additional amounts of the optimal risky portfolio by borrowing (i.e., buying on margin) at the risk-free rate makes higher rates of return for levels of risk greater than the optimal risky asset possible.

40 C is correct. Each individual investor's optimal mix of the risk-free asset and the optimal risky asset is determined by the investor's risk preference.

Portfolio Risk and Return: Part II

by Vijay Singal, CFA

LEARNING OUTCOMES

Mastery	The candidate should be able to:
☐	a. describe the implications of combining a risk-free asset with a portfolio of risky assets;
☐	b. explain the capital allocation line (CAL) and the capital market line (CML);
☐	c. explain systematic and nonsystematic risk, including why an investor should not expect to receive additional return for bearing nonsystematic risk;
☐	d. explain return generating models (including the market model) and their uses;
☐	e. calculate and interpret beta;
☐	f. explain the capital asset pricing model (CAPM), including its assumptions, and the security market line (SML);
☐	g. calculate and interpret the expected return of an asset using the CAPM;
☐	h. describe and demonstrate applications of the CAPM and the SML.

INTRODUCTION

1

Our objective in this reading is to identify the optimal risky portfolio for all investors by using the capital asset pricing model (CAPM). The foundation of this reading is the computation of risk and return of a portfolio and the role that correlation plays in diversifying portfolio risk and arriving at the efficient frontier. The efficient frontier and the capital allocation line consist of portfolios that are generally acceptable to all investors. By combining an investor's individual indifference curves with the market-determined capital allocation line, we are able to illustrate that the only optimal risky portfolio for an investor is the portfolio of all risky assets (i.e., the market).

Additionally, we discuss the capital market line, a special case of the capital allocation line that is used for passive investor portfolios. We also differentiate between systematic and nonsystematic risk, and explain why investors are compensated for bearing systematic risk but receive no compensation for bearing nonsystematic risk. We discuss in detail the CAPM, which is a simple model for estimating asset returns based only on the asset's systematic risk. Finally, we illustrate how the CAPM allows security selection to build an optimal portfolio for an investor by changing the asset mix beyond a passive market portfolio.

The reading is organized as follows. In Section 2, we discuss the consequences of combining a risk-free asset with the market portfolio and provide an interpretation of the capital market line. Section 3 decomposes total risk into systematic and nonsystematic risk and discusses the characteristics of and differences between the two kinds of risk. We also introduce return-generating models, including the single-index model, and illustrate the calculation of beta by using formulas and graphically by using the security characteristic line. In Section 4, we introduce the capital asset pricing model and the security market line. We discuss many applications of the CAPM and the SML throughout the reading, including the use of expected return in making capital budgeting decisions, the evaluation of portfolios using the CAPM's risk-adjusted return as the benchmark, security selection, and determining whether adding a new security to the current portfolio is appropriate. Our focus on the CAPM does not suggest that the CAPM is the only viable asset pricing model. Although the CAPM is an excellent starting point, more advanced readings expand on these discussions and extend the analysis to other models that account for multiple explanatory factors. A preview of a number of these models is given in Section 5, and a summary and practice problems conclude the reading.

2 CAPITAL MARKET THEORY

You have learned how to combine a risk-free asset with one risky asset and with many risky assets to create a capital allocation line. In this section, we will expand our discussion of multiple risky assets and consider a special case of the capital allocation line, called the capital market line. While discussing the capital market line, we will define the market and its role in passive portfolio management. Using these concepts, we will illustrate how leveraged portfolios can enhance both risk and return.

2.1 Portfolio of Risk-Free and Risky Assets

Although investors desire an asset that produces the highest return and carries the lowest risk, such an asset does not exist. As the risk–return capital market theory illustrates, one must assume higher risk in order to earn a higher return. We can improve an investor's portfolio, however, by expanding the opportunity set of risky assets because this allows the investor to choose a superior mix of assets.

Similarly, an investor's portfolio improves if a risk-free asset is added to the mix. In other words, a combination of the risk-free asset and a risky asset can result in a better risk–return trade-off than an investment in only one type of asset because the risk-free asset has zero correlation with the risky asset. The combination is called the **capital allocation line** (and is depicted in Exhibit 2). Superimposing an investor's indifference curves on the capital allocation line will lead to the optimal investor portfolio.

Investors with different levels of risk aversion will choose different portfolios. Highly risk-averse investors choose to invest most of their wealth in the risk-free asset and earn low returns because they are not willing to assume higher levels of risk. Less risk-averse investors, in contrast, invest more of their wealth in the risky asset, which is expected to yield a higher return. Obviously, the higher return cannot come without higher risk, but the less risk-averse investor is willing to accept the additional risk.

2.1.1 *Combining a Risk-Free Asset with a Portfolio of Risky Assets*

We can extend the analysis of one risky asset to a portfolio of risky assets. For convenience, assume that the portfolio contains all available risky assets,[1] although an investor may not wish to include all of these assets in the portfolio because of the investor's specific preferences. If an asset is not included in the portfolio, its weight will be zero. The risk–return characteristics of a portfolio of N risky assets are given by the following equations:

$$E(R_p) = \sum_{i=1}^{N} w_i E(R_i), \ \ \sigma_p^2 = \left(\sum_{i=1,j=1}^{N} w_i w_j \mathrm{Cov}(i,j) \right), \text{ and } \sum_{i=1}^{N} w_i = 1$$

The expected return on the portfolio, $E(R_p)$, is the weighted average of the expected returns of individual assets, where w_i is the fractional weight in asset i and R_i is the expected return of asset i. The risk of the portfolio (σ_p), however, depends on the weights of the individual assets, the risk of the individual assets, and their interrelationships. The **covariance** between assets i and j, $\mathrm{Cov}(i, j)$, is a statistical measure of the interrelationship between each pair of assets in the portfolio and can be expressed as follows, where ρ_{ij} is the **correlation** between assets i and j and σ_i is the risk of asset i:

$$\mathrm{Cov}(i,j) = \rho_{ij}\sigma_i\sigma_j$$

Note from the equation below that the correlation of an asset with itself is 1; therefore:

$$\mathrm{Cov}(i,i) = \rho_{ii}\sigma_i\sigma_i = \sigma_i^2$$

By substituting the above expressions for covariance, we can rewrite the portfolio variance equation as

$$\sigma_p^2 = \left(\sum_{i=1}^{N} w_i^2 \sigma_i^2 + \sum_{i,j=1,i\neq j}^{N} w_i w_j \rho_{ij}\sigma_i\sigma_j \right)$$

The suggestion that portfolios have lower risk than the assets they contain may seem counterintuitive. These portfolios can be constructed, however, as long as the assets in the portfolio are not perfectly correlated. As an illustration of the effect of asset weights on portfolio characteristics, consider a simple two-asset portfolio with zero weights in all other assets. Assume that Asset 1 has a return of 10 percent and a standard deviation (risk) of 20 percent. Asset 2 has a return of 5 percent and a standard deviation (risk) of 10 percent. Furthermore, the correlation between the two assets is zero. Exhibit 1 shows risks and returns for Portfolio X with a weight of 25 percent in Asset 1 and 75 percent in Asset 2, Portfolio Y with a weight of 50 percent in each of the two assets, and Portfolio Z with a weight of 75 percent in Asset 1 and 25 percent in Asset 2.

---

1 N risky assets.

Exhibit 1	Portfolio Risk and Return			
Portfolio	**Weight in Asset 1 (%)**	**Weight in Asset 2 (%)**	**Portfolio Return (%)**	**Portfolio Standard Deviation (%)**
X	25.0	75.0	6.25	9.01
Y	50.0	50.0	7.50	11.18
Z	75.0	25.0	8.75	15.21
Return	10.0	5.0		
Standard deviation	20.0	10.0		
Correlation between Assets 1 and 2		0.0		

From this example we observe that the three portfolios are quite different in terms of their risk and return. Portfolio X has a 6.25 percent return and only 9.01 percent standard deviation, whereas the standard deviation of Portfolio Z is more than two-thirds higher (15.21 percent), although the return is only slightly more than one-third higher (8.75 percent). These portfolios may become even more dissimilar as other assets are added to the mix.

Consider three portfolios of risky assets, A, B, and C, as in Exhibit 2, that may have been presented to a representative investor by three different investment advisers. Each portfolio is combined with the risk-free asset to create three capital allocation lines, CAL(A), CAL(B), and CAL(C). The exhibit shows that Portfolio C is superior to the other two portfolios because it has a greater expected return for any given level of risk. As a result, an investor will choose the portfolio that lies on the capital allocation line for Portfolio C. The combination of the risk-free asset and the risky Portfolio C that is selected for an investor depends on the investor's degree of risk aversion.

Exhibit 2   **Risk-Free Asset and Portfolio of Risky Assets**

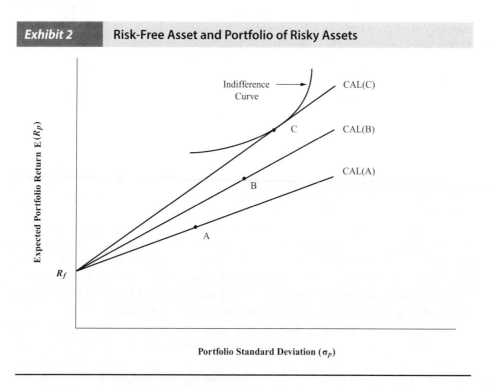

2.1.2 Does a Unique Optimal Risky Portfolio Exist?

We assume that all investors have the same economic expectation and thus have the same expectations of prices, cash flows, and other investment characteristics. This assumption is referred to as **homogeneity of expectations**. Given these investment characteristics, everyone goes through the same calculations and should arrive at the same optimal risky portfolio. Therefore, assuming homogeneous expectations, only one optimal portfolio exists. If investors have different expectations, however, they might arrive at different optimal risky portfolios. To illustrate, we begin with an expression for the price of an asset:

$$P = \sum_{t=0}^{T} \frac{CF_t}{(1 + r_t)^t}$$

where CF_t is the cash flow at the end of period t and r_t is the discount rate or the required rate of return for that asset for period t. Period t refers to all periods beginning from now until the asset ceases to exist at the end of time T. Because the current time is the end of period 0, which is the same as the beginning of period 1, there are $(T + 1)$ cash flows and $(T + 1)$ required rates of return. These conditions are based on the assumption that a cash flow, such as an initial investment, can occur now ($t = 0$). Ordinarily, however, CF_0 is zero.

We use the formula for the price of an asset to estimate the intrinsic value of an asset. For ease of reference, assume that the asset we are valuing is a share of HSBC Holdings (parent of HSBC Bank), a British company that also trades on the Hong Kong Stock Exchange. In the case of corporate stock, there is no expiration date, so T could be extremely large, meaning we will need to estimate a large number of cash flows and rates of return. Fortunately, the denominator reduces the importance of distant cash flows, so it may be sufficient to estimate, say, 20 annual cash flows and 20 rates of returns. How much will HSBC earn next year and the year after next? What will the banking sector look like in five years' time? Different analysts and investors will have their own estimates that may be quite different from one another. Also, as we delve further into the future, more serious issues in estimating future revenue, expenses, and growth rates arise. Therefore, to assume that cash flow estimates for HSBC will vary among these investors is reasonable. In addition to the numerator (cash flows), it is also necessary to estimate the denominator, the required rates of return. We know that riskier companies will require higher returns because risk and return are positively correlated. HSBC stock is riskier than a risk-free asset, but by how much? And what should the compensation for that additional risk be? Again, it is evident that different analysts will view the riskiness of HSBC differently and, therefore, arrive at different required rates of return.

HSBC closed at HK$89.40 on 31 December 2009 on the Hong Kong Stock Exchange. The traded price represents the value that a marginal investor attaches to a share of HSBC, say, corresponding to Analyst A's expectation. Analyst B may think that the price should be HK$50, however, and Analyst C may think that the price should be HK$150. Given a current price of HK$89.40, the expected returns of HSBC are quite different for the three analysts. Analyst B, who believes the price should be HK$50, concludes that HSBC is overvalued and may assign a weight of zero to HSBC in the recommended portfolio even though the market capitalization of HSBC is in excess of HK$1 trillion. In contrast, Analyst C, with a valuation of HK$150, thinks HSBC is undervalued and will significantly overweight HSBC in a portfolio.

Our discussion illustrates that analysts can arrive at different valuations that necessitate the assignment of different asset weights in a portfolio. Given the existence of many asset classes and numerous assets in each asset class, one can visualize that each investor will have his or her own optimal risky portfolio depending on his or her assumptions underlying the valuation computations. Therefore, market participants will have their own and possibly different optimal risky portfolios.

If investors have different valuations of assets, then the construction of a unique optimal risky portfolio is not possible. If we make a simplifying assumption of homogeneity in investor expectations, we will have a single optimal risky portfolio as previously mentioned. Even if investors have different expectations, market prices are a proxy of what the marginal, informed investor expects, and the market portfolio becomes the base case, the benchmark, or the reference portfolio that other portfolios can be judged against. For HSBC, the market price is HK$89.40 per share and the market capitalization is HK$1.08 trillion. In constructing the market portfolio, HSBC's weight in the market portfolio will be equal to its market value divided by the value of all other assets included in the market portfolio.

2.2 The Capital Market Line

In the previous section, we discussed how the risk-free asset could be combined with a risky portfolio to create a capital allocation line. In this section, we discuss a specific CAL that uses the market portfolio as the optimal risky portfolio and is known as the capital market line. We also discuss the significance of the market portfolio and applications of the capital market line.

2.2.1 *Passive and Active Portfolios*

In the above subsection, we arrived at three possible valuations for each share of HSBC: HK$50, HK$89.40, and HK$150. Which one is correct?

If the market is an **informationally efficient market**, the price in the market, HK$89.40, is an unbiased estimate of all future discounted cash flows (recall the formula for the price of an asset). In other words, the price aggregates and reflects all information that is publicly available, and investors cannot expect to earn a return that is greater than the required rate of return for that asset. If, however, the price reflects all publicly available information and there is no way to outperform the market, then there is little point in investing time and money in evaluating HSBC to arrive at your price using your own estimates of cash flows and rates of return.

In that case, a simple and convenient approach to investing is to rely on the prices set by the market. Portfolios that are based on the assumption of unbiased market prices are referred to as passive portfolios. Passive portfolios most commonly replicate and track market indices, which are passively constructed on the basis of market prices and market capitalizations. Examples of market indices are the S&P 500 Index, the Nikkei 300, and the CAC 40. Passive portfolios based on market indices are called index funds and generally have low costs because no significant effort is expended in valuing securities that are included in an index.

In contrast to passive investors' reliance on market prices and index funds, active investors may not rely on market valuations. They have more confidence in their own ability to estimate cash flows, growth rates, and discount rates. Based on these estimates, they value assets and determine whether an asset is fairly valued. In an actively managed portfolio, assets that are undervalued, or have a chance of offering above-normal returns, will have a positive weight (i.e., overweight compared to the market weight in the benchmark index), whereas other assets will have a zero weight, or even a negative weight if short selling is permitted (i.e., some assets will be underweighted compared with the market weight in the benchmark index). This style of investing is called active investment management, and the portfolios are referred to as active portfolios. Most open-end mutual funds and hedge funds practice active investment management, and most analysts believe that active investing adds value. Whether these analysts are right or wrong is the subject of continuing debate.

2.2.2 What Is the "Market"?

In the previous discussion, we referred to the "market" on numerous occasions without actually defining the market. The optimal risky portfolio and the capital market line depend on the definition of the market. So what is the market?

Theoretically, the **market** includes all risky assets or anything that has value, which includes stocks, bonds, real estate, and even human capital. Not all assets are tradable, however, and not all tradable assets are investable. For example, the Taj Mahal in India is an asset but is not a tradable asset. Similarly, human capital is an asset that is not tradable. Moreover, assets may be tradable but not investable because of restrictions placed on certain kinds of investors. For example, all stocks listed on the Shanghai Stock Exchange are tradable. Class A shares, however, are available only to domestic investors, whereas Class B shares are available to both domestic and foreign investors. For investors not domiciled in China, Class A shares are not investable—that is, they are not available for investment.

If we consider all stocks, bonds, real estate assets, commodities, etc., probably hundreds of thousands of assets are tradable and investable. The "market" should contain as many assets as possible; we emphasize the word "possible" because it is not practical to include all assets in a single risky portfolio. Even though advancements in technology and interconnected markets have made it much easier to span the major equity markets, we are still not able to easily invest in other kinds of assets like bonds and real estate except in the most developed countries.

For the rest of this reading, we will define the "market" quite narrowly because it is practical and convenient to do so. Typically, a local or regional stock market index is used as a proxy for the market because of active trading in stocks and because a local or regional market is most visible to the local investors. For our purposes, we will use the S&P 500 Index as the market's proxy. The S&P 500 is commonly used by analysts as a benchmark for market performance throughout the United States. It contains 500 of the largest stocks that are domiciled in the United States, and these stocks are weighted by their market capitalization (price times the number of outstanding shares).

The stocks in the S&P 500 account for approximately 80 percent of the total equity market capitalization in the United States, and because the U.S. stock markets represent about 32 percent of the world markets, the S&P 500 represents roughly

25 percent of worldwide publicly traded equity. Our definition of the market does not include non-U.S. stock markets, bond markets, real estate, and many other asset classes, and therefore, "market" return and the "market" risk premium refer to U.S. equity return and the U.S. equity risk premium, respectively. The use of this proxy, however, is sufficient for our discussion, and is relatively easy to expand to include other tradable assets.

2.2.3 *The Capital Market Line (CML)*

A capital allocation line includes all possible combinations of the risk-free asset and any risky portfolio. The **capital market line** is a special case of the capital allocation line, where the risky portfolio is the market portfolio. The risk-free asset is a debt security with no default risk, no inflation risk, no liquidity risk, no interest rate risk, and no risk of any other kind. U.S. Treasury bills are usually used as a proxy of the risk-free return, R_f.

The S&P 500 is a proxy of the market portfolio, which is the optimal risky portfolio. Therefore, the expected return on the risky portfolio is the expected market return, expressed as $E(R_m)$. The capital market line is shown in Exhibit 3, where the standard deviation (σ_p), or total risk, is on the *x*-axis and expected portfolio return, $E(R_p)$, is on the *y*-axis. Graphically, the market portfolio is the point on the Markowitz efficient frontier where a line from the risk-free asset is tangent to the Markowitz efficient frontier. All points on the interior of the Markowitz efficient frontier are inefficient portfolios in that they provide the same level of return with a higher level of risk or a lower level of return with the same amount of risk. When plotted together, the point at which the CML is tangent to the Markowitz efficient frontier is the optimal combination of risky and risk-free assets, on the basis of market prices and market capitalizations. The optimal risky portfolio is the market portfolio.

Exhibit 3	Capital Market Line

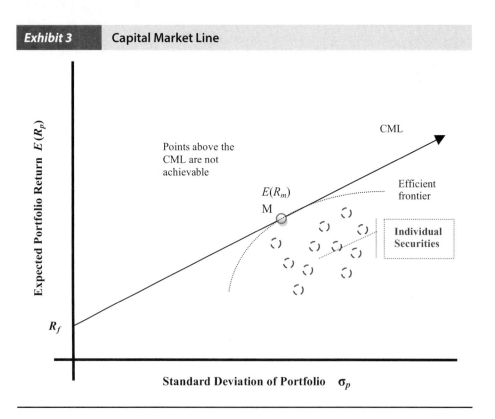

The CML's intercept on the y-axis is the risk-free return (R_f) because that is the return associated with zero risk. The CML passes through the point represented by the market return, $E(R_m)$. With respect to capital market theory, any point above the CML is not achievable and any point below the CML is dominated by and inferior to any point on the CML.

Note that we identify the CML and CAL as lines even though they are a combination of two assets. Unlike a combination of two risky assets, which is usually not a straight line, a combination of the risk-free asset and a risky portfolio is a straight line, as illustrated below by computing the combination's risk and return.

Risk and return characteristics of the portfolio represented by the CML can be computed by using the return and risk expressions for a two-asset portfolio:

$$E(R_p) = w_1 R_f + (1 - w_1)E(R_m),$$

and

$$\sigma_p = \sqrt{w_1^2 \sigma_f^2 + (1 - w_1)^2 \sigma_m^2 + 2w_1(1 - w_1)\text{Cov}(R_f, R_m)}$$

The proportion invested in the risk-free asset is given by w_1, and the balance is invested in the market portfolio, $(1 - w_1)$. The risk of the risk-free asset is given by σ_f, the risk of the market is given by σ_m, the risk of the portfolio is given by σ_p, and the covariance between the risk-free asset and the market portfolio is represented by $\text{Cov}(R_f, R_m)$.

By definition, the standard deviation of the risk-free asset is zero. Because its risk is zero, the risk-free asset does not co-vary or move with any other asset. Therefore, its covariance with all other assets, including the market portfolio, is zero, making the first and third terms under the square root sign zero. As a result, the portfolio return and portfolio standard deviation can be simplified and rewritten as:

$$E(R_p) = w_1 R_f + (1 - w_1)E(R_m),$$

and

$$\sigma_p = (1 - w_1)\sigma_m$$

By substitution, we can express $E(R_p)$ in terms of σ_p. Substituting for w_1, we get:

$$E(R_p) = R_f + \left(\frac{E(R_m) - R_f}{\sigma_m}\right) \times \sigma_p$$

Note that the expression is in the form of a line, $y = a + bx$. The y-intercept is the risk-free rate, and the slope of the line referred to as the market price of risk is $[E(R_m) - R_f]/\sigma_m$. The CML has a positive slope because the market's risky return is larger than the risk-free return. As the amount of the total investment devoted to the market increases—that is, as we move up the line—both standard deviation (risk) and expected return increase.

EXAMPLE 1

Risk and Return on the CML

Mr. Miles is a first time investor and wants to build a portfolio using only U.S. T-bills and an index fund that closely tracks the S&P 500 Index. The T-bills have a return of 5 percent. The S&P 500 has a standard deviation of 20 percent and an expected return of 15 percent.

1 Draw the CML and mark the points where the investment in the market is 0 percent, 25 percent, 75 percent, and 100 percent.

2 Mr. Miles is also interested in determining the exact risk and return at each point.

Solution to 1:

We calculate the equation for the CML as $E(R_p) = 5\% + 0.50 \times \sigma_p$ by substituting the given information into the general CML equation. The intercept of the line is 5 percent, and its slope is 0.50. We can draw the CML by arbitrarily taking any two points on the line that satisfy the above equation.

Alternatively, the CML can be drawn by connecting the risk-free return of 5 percent on the y-axis with the market portfolio at (20 percent, 15 percent). The CML is shown in Exhibit 4.

Exhibit 4	Risk and Return on the CML

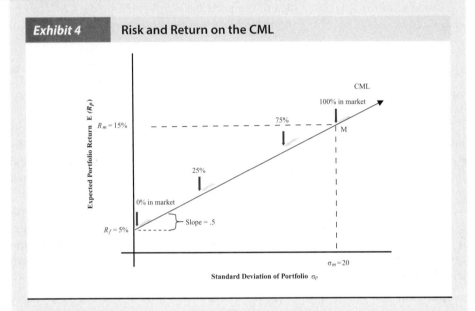

Solution to 2:

Return with 0 percent invested in the market = 5 percent, which is the risk-free return.

Standard deviation with 0 percent invested in the market = 0 percent because T-bills are not risky.

Return with 25 percent invested in the market = $(0.75 \times 5\%) + (0.25 \times 15\%) = 7.5\%$.

Standard deviation with 25 percent invested in the market = $0.25 \times 20\% = 5\%$.

Return with 75 percent invested in the market = $(0.25 \times 5\%) + (0.75 \times 15\%) = 12.50\%$.

Standard deviation with 75 percent invested in the market = $0.75 \times 20\% = 15\%$.

Return with 100 percent invested in the market = 15 percent, which is the return on the S&P 500.

Standard deviation with 100 percent invested in the market = 20 percent, which is the risk of the S&P 500.

2.2.4 *Leveraged Portfolios*

In the previous example, Mr. Miles evaluated an investment of between 0 percent and 100 percent in the market and the balance in T-bills. The line connecting R_f and M (market portfolio) in Exhibit 4 illustrates these portfolios with their respective levels of investment. At R_f, an investor is investing all of his or her wealth into risk-free securities, which is equivalent to lending 100 percent at the risk-free rate. At Point M he or she is holding the market portfolio and not lending any money at the risk-free rate. The combinations of the risk-free asset and the market portfolio, which may be achieved by the points between these two limits, are termed "lending" portfolios. In effect, the investor is lending part of his or her wealth at the risk-free rate.

If Mr. Miles is willing to take more risk, he may be able to move to the right of the market portfolio (Point M in Exhibit 4) by borrowing money and purchasing more of Portfolio M. Assume that he is able to borrow money at the same risk-free rate of interest, R_f, at which he can invest. He can then supplement his available wealth with borrowed money and construct a borrowing portfolio. If the straight line joining R_f and M is extended to the right of Point M, this extended section of the line represents borrowing portfolios. As one moves further to the right of Point M, an increasing amount of borrowed money is being invested in the market. This means that there is *negative* investment in the risk-free asset, which is referred to as a *leveraged position* in the risky portfolio. The particular point chosen on the CML will depend on the individual's utility function, which, in turn, will be determined by his risk and return preferences.

EXAMPLE 2

Risk and Return of a Leveraged Portfolio with Equal Lending and Borrowing Rates

Mr. Miles decides to set aside a small part of his wealth for investment in a portfolio that has greater risk than his previous investments because he anticipates that the overall market will generate attractive returns in the future. He assumes that he can borrow money at 5 percent and achieve the same return on the S&P 500 as before: an expected return of 15 percent with a standard deviation of 20 percent.

Calculate his expected risk and return if he borrows 25 percent, 50 percent, and 100 percent of his initial investment amount.

Solution:

The leveraged portfolio's standard deviation and return can be calculated in the same manner as before with the following equations:

$$E(R_p) = w_1 R_f + (1 - w_1)E(R_m)$$

and

$$\sigma_p = (1 - w_1)\sigma_m$$

The proportion invested in T-bills becomes negative instead of positive because Mr. Miles is borrowing money. If 25 percent of the initial investment is borrowed, $w_1 = -0.25$, and $(1 - w_1) = 1.25$, etc.

Return with −25 percent invested in T-bills = (−0.25 × 5%) + (1.25 × 15%) = 17.5%.

Standard deviation with −25 percent invested in T-bills = 1.25 × 20% = 25%.

Return with −50 percent invested in T-bills = (−0.50 × 5%) + (1.50 × 15%) = 20.0%.

Standard deviation with −50 percent invested in T-bills = 1.50 × 20% = 30%.

Return with −100 percent invested in T-bills = (−1.00 × 5%) + (2.00 × 15%) = 25.0%.

Standard deviation with −100 percent invested in T-bills = 2.00 × 20% = 40%.

Note that negative investment (borrowing) in the risk-free asset provides a higher expected return for the portfolio but that higher return is also associated with higher risk.

Leveraged Portfolios with Different Lending and Borrowing Rates   Although we assumed that Mr. Miles can borrow at the same rate as the U.S. government, it is more likely that he will have to pay a higher interest rate than the government because his ability to repay is not as certain as that of the government. Now consider that although Mr. Miles can invest (lend) at R_f, he can borrow at only R_b, a rate that is higher than the risk-free rate.

With different lending and borrowing rates, the CML will no longer be a single straight line. The line will have a slope of $[E(R_m) - R_f]/\sigma_m$ between Points R_f and M, where the lending rate is R_f, but will have a smaller slope of $[E(R_m) - R_b]/\sigma_m$ at points to the right of M, where the borrowing rate is R_b. Exhibit 5 illustrates the CML with different lending and borrowing rates.

Exhibit 5	CML with Different Lending and Borrowing Rates

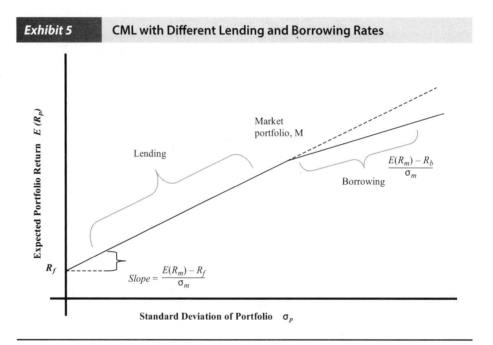

The equations for the two lines are given below.

$$w_1 \geq 0 : E(R_p) = R_f + \left(\frac{E(R_m) - R_f}{\sigma_m} \right) \times \sigma_p$$

and

$$w_1 < 0 : E(R_p) = R_b + \left(\frac{E(R_m) - R_b}{\sigma_m} \right) \times \sigma_p$$

The first equation is for the line where the investment in the risk-free asset is zero or positive—that is, at M or to the left of M in Exhibit 5. The second equation is for the line where borrowing, or negative investment in the risk-free asset, occurs. Note that the only difference between the two equations is in the interest rates used for borrowing and lending.

All passive portfolios will lie on the kinked CML, although the investment in the risk-free asset may be positive (lending), zero (no lending or borrowing), or negative (borrowing). Leverage allows less risk-averse investors to increase the amount of risk they take by borrowing money and investing more than 100 percent in the passive portfolio.

EXAMPLE 3

Leveraged Portfolio with Different Lending and Borrowing Rates

Mr. Miles approaches his broker to borrow money against securities held in his portfolio. Even though Mr. Miles' loan will be secured by the securities in his portfolio, the broker's rate for lending to customers is 7 percent. Assuming a risk-free rate of 5 percent and a market return of 15 percent with a standard deviation of 20 percent, estimate Mr. Miles' expected return and risk if he invests 25 percent and 75 percent in the risk-free asset and if he decides to borrow 25 percent and 75 percent of his initial investment and invest the money in the market.

Solution:

The unleveraged portfolio's standard deviation and return are calculated using the same equations as before:

$$E(R_p) = w_1 R_f + (1 - w_1)E(R_m),$$

and

$$\sigma_p = (1 - w_1)\sigma_m$$

The results are unchanged. The slope of the line for the unleveraged portfolio is 0.50, just as before:

Return with 25 percent invested in the market = $(0.75 \times 5\%) + (0.25 \times 15\%)$ = 7.5%.

Standard deviation with 25 percent invested in the market = $0.25 \times 20\%$ = 5%.

Return with 75 percent invested in the market = $(0.25 \times 5\%) + (0.75 \times 15\%)$ = 12.5%.

Standard deviation with 75 percent invested in the market = $0.75 \times 20\%$ = 15%.

For the leveraged portfolio, everything remains the same except that R_f is replaced with R_b.

$$E(R_p) = w_1 R_b + (1 - w_1)E(R_m),$$

and

$$\sigma_p = (1 - w_1)\sigma_m.$$

Return with −25 percent invested in T-bills = $(-0.25 \times 7\%) + (1.25 \times 15\%)$ = 17.0%.

Standard deviation with −25 percent invested in T-bills = $1.25 \times 20\%$ = 25%.

Return with −75 percent invested in T-bills = $(-0.75 \times 7\%) + (1.75 \times 15\%)$ = 21.0%.

Standard deviation with −75 percent invested in T-bills = $1.75 \times 20\%$ = 35%.

The risk and return of the leveraged portfolio is higher than that of the unleveraged portfolio. As Mr. Miles borrows more money to invest in the market, the expected return increases but so does the standard deviation of the portfolio. The slope of the line for the leveraged portfolio is 0.40, compared with 0.50 for the unleveraged portfolio, which means that for every 1 percent increase in risk, the investor gets a 0.40 percent increase in expected return in the leveraged part of the portfolio, compared with a 0.50 percent increase in expected return in the unleveraged part of the portfolio. Only investors who are less risk averse will choose leveraged portfolios.

3　PRICING OF RISK AND COMPUTATION OF EXPECTED RETURN

In constructing a portfolio, it is important to understand the concept of correlation and how less than perfect correlation can diversify the risk of a portfolio. As a consequence, the risk of an asset held alone may be greater than the risk of that same asset when it is part of a portfolio. Because the risk of an asset varies from one environment to another, which kind of risk should an investor consider and how should that risk be priced? This section addresses the question of pricing of risk by decomposing the total risk of a security or a portfolio into systematic and nonsystematic risk. The meaning of these risks, how they are computed, and their relevance to the pricing of assets are also discussed.

3.1　Systematic Risk and Nonsystematic Risk

Systematic risk, also known as non-diversifiable or market risk, is the risk that affects the entire market or economy. In contrast, nonsystematic risk is the risk that pertains to a single company or industry and is also known as company-specific, industry-specific, diversifiable, or idiosyncratic risk.

Systematic risk is risk that cannot be avoided and is inherent in the overall market. It is non-diversifiable because it includes risk factors that are innate within the market and affect the market as a whole. Examples of factors that constitute systematic risk include interest rates, inflation, economic cycles, political uncertainty, and widespread natural disasters. These events affect the entire market, and there is no way to avoid their effect. Systematic risk can be magnified through selection or by using leverage, or diminished by including securities that have a low correlation with the portfolio, assuming they are not already part of the portfolio.

Nonsystematic risk is risk that is local or limited to a particular asset or industry that need not affect assets outside of that asset class. Examples of nonsystematic risk could include the failure of a drug trial, major oil discoveries, or an airliner crash. All these events will directly affect their respective companies and possibly industries, but have no effect on assets that are far removed from these industries. Investors are capable of avoiding nonsystematic risk through diversification by forming a portfolio of assets that are not highly correlated with one another.

We will derive expressions for each kind of risk later in this reading. You will see that the sum of systematic variance and nonsystematic variance equals the total variance of the security or portfolio:

Total variance = Systematic variance + Nonsystematic variance

Although the equality relationship is between variances, you will find frequent references to total risk as the sum of systematic risk and nonsystematic risk. In those cases, the statements refer to variance, not standard deviation.

3.1.1 *Pricing of Risk*

Pricing or valuing an asset is equivalent to estimating its expected rate of return. If an asset has a known terminal value, such as the face value of a bond, then a lower current price implies a higher future return and a higher current price implies a lower future return. The relationship between price and return can also be observed in the valuation expression shown in Section 2.1.2. Therefore, we will occasionally use price and return interchangeably when discussing the price of risk.

Consider an asset with both systematic and nonsystematic risk. Assume that both kinds of risk are priced—that is, you receive a return for both systematic risk and non-systematic risk. What will you do? Realizing that nonsystematic risk can be diversified away, you would buy assets that have a large amount of nonsystematic risk. Once you have bought those assets with nonsystematic risk, you would diversify, or reduce that risk, by including other assets that are not highly correlated. In the process, you will minimize nonsystematic risk and eventually eliminate it altogether from your portfolio. Now, you would have a diversified portfolio with only systematic risk, yet you would be compensated for nonsystematic risk that you no longer have. Just like everyone else, you would have an incentive to take on more and more diversifiable risk because you are compensated for it even though you can get rid of it. The demand for diversifiable risk will keep increasing until its price becomes infinite and its expected return falls to zero. This means that our initial assumption of a non-zero return for diversifiable risk was incorrect and that the correct assumption is zero return for diversifiable risk. Therefore, we can assume that in an efficient market, no incremental reward can be earned for taking on diversifiable risk.

In the previous exercise we illustrated why investors should not be compensated for taking on nonsystematic risk. Therefore, investors who have nonsystematic risk must diversify it away by investing in many industries, many countries, and many asset classes. Because future returns are unknown and it is not possible to pick only winners, diversification helps in offsetting poor returns in one asset class by garnering good returns in another asset class, thereby reducing the overall risk of the portfolio. In contrast, investors must be compensated for accepting systematic risk because that risk cannot be diversified away. If investors do not receive a return commensurate with the amount of systematic risk they are taking, they will refuse to accept systematic risk.

In summary, systematic or non-diversifiable risk is priced and investors are compensated for holding assets or portfolios based only on that investment's systematic risk. Investors do not receive any return for accepting nonsystematic or diversifiable risk. Therefore, it is in the interest of risk-averse investors to hold only well-diversified portfolios.

EXAMPLE 4

Systematic and Nonsystematic Risk

1. Describe the systematic and nonsystematic risk components of the following assets:

   A. A risk-free asset, such as a three-month Treasury bill

   B. The market portfolio, such as the S&P 500, with total risk of 20 percent

2. Consider two assets, A and B. Asset A has total risk of 30 percent, half of which is nonsystematic risk. Asset B has total risk of 17 percent, all of which is systematic risk. Which asset should have a higher expected rate of return?

Solution to 1A:

By definition, a risk-free asset has no risk. Therefore, a risk-free asset has zero systematic risk and zero nonsystematic risk.

Solution to 1B:

As we mentioned earlier, a market portfolio is a diversified portfolio, one in which no more risk can be diversified away. We have also described it as an efficient portfolio. Therefore, a market portfolio does not contain any nonsystematic risk. All of its total risk, 20 percent, is systematic risk.

Solution to 2:

The amount of systematic risk in Asset A is 15 percent, and the amount of systematic risk in Asset B is 17 percent. Because only systematic risk is priced or receives a return, the expected rate of return must be higher for Asset B.

3.2 Calculation and Interpretation of Beta

As previously mentioned, in order to form the market portfolio, you should combine all available assets. Knowledge of the correlations among those assets allows us to estimate portfolio risk. You also learned that a fully diversified portfolio will include all asset classes and essentially all assets in those asset classes. The work required for construction of the market portfolio is formidable. For example, for a portfolio of 1,000 assets, we will need 1,000 return estimates, 1,000 standard deviation estimates, and 499,500 ($1,000 \times 999 \div 2$) correlations. Other related questions that arise with this analysis are whether we really need all 1,000 assets and what happens if there are errors in these estimates.

An alternate method of constructing an optimal portfolio is simpler and easier to implement. An investor begins with a known portfolio, such as the S&P 500, and then adds other assets one at a time on the basis of the asset's standard deviation, expected return, and impact on the portfolio's risk and return. This process continues until the addition of another asset does not have a significant impact on the performance of the portfolio. The process requires only estimates of systematic risk for each asset because investors will not be compensated for nonsystematic risk. Expected returns can be calculated by using return-generating models, as we will discuss in this section. In addition to using return-generating models, we will also decompose total variance into systematic variance and nonsystematic variance and establish a formal relationship between systematic risk and return. In the next section, we will expand on this discussion and introduce the CAPM as the preferred return-generating model.

3.2.1 *Return-Generating Models*

A **return-generating model** is a model that can provide an estimate of the expected return of a security given certain parameters. If systematic risk is the only relevant parameter for return, then the return-generating model will estimate the expected return for any asset given the level of systematic risk.

As with any model, the quality of estimates of expected return will depend on the quality of input estimates and the accuracy of the model. Because it is difficult to decide which factors are appropriate for generating returns, the most general form of a return-generating model is a multi-factor model. A **multi-factor model** allows more than one variable to be considered in estimating returns and can be built using different kinds of factors, such as macroeconomic, fundamental, and statistical factors.

Macroeconomic factor models use economic factors that are correlated with security returns. These factors may include economic growth, the interest rate, the inflation rate, productivity, employment, and consumer confidence. Past relationships with returns are estimated to obtain parameter estimates, which are, in turn, used for computing expected returns. Fundamental factor models analyze and use relationships between security returns and the company's underlying fundamentals, such as, for example, earnings, earnings growth, cash flow generation, investment in research, advertising, and number of patents. Finally, in a statistical factor model, historical and cross-sectional return data are analyzed to identify factors that explain variance or covariance in observed returns. These statistical factors, however, may or may not have an economic or fundamental connection to returns. For example, the conference to which the American football Super Bowl winner belongs, whether the American Football Conference or the National Football Conference, may be a factor in U.S. stock returns, but no obvious economic connection seems to exist between the winner's conference and U.S. stock returns. Moreover, data mining may generate many spurious factors that are devoid of any economic meaning. Because of this limitation, analysts prefer the macroeconomic and fundamental factor models for specifying and estimating return-generating models.

A general return-generating model is expressed in the following manner:

$$E(R_i) - R_f = \sum_{j=1}^{k} \beta_{ij} E(F_j) = \beta_{i1}[E(R_m) - R_f] + \sum_{j=2}^{k} \beta_{ij} E(F_j)$$

The model has k factors, $E(F_1), E(F_2), \ldots E(F_k)$. The coefficients, β_{ij}, are called factor weights or factor loadings associated with each factor. The left-hand side of the model has excess return, or return over the risk-free rate. The right-hand side provides the risk factors that would generate the return or premium required to assume that risk. We have separated out one factor, $E(R_m)$, which represents the market return. All models contain return on the market portfolio as a key factor.

Three-Factor and Four-Factor Models   Eugene Fama and Kenneth French[2] suggested that a return-generating model for stock returns should include relative size of the company and relative book-to-market value of the company in addition to beta. Fama and French found that past returns could be explained better with their model than with other models available at that time, most notably, the capital asset pricing model. Mark Carhart (1997) extended the Fama and French model by adding another factor: momentum, defined as relative past stock returns. We will discuss these models further in Section 5.3.2.

The Single-Index Model   The simplest form of a return-generating model is a single-factor linear model, in which only one factor is considered. The most common implementation is a single-index model, which uses the market factor in the following form: $E(R_i) - R_f = \beta_i[E(R_m) - R_f]$.

Although the single-index model is simple, it fits nicely with the capital market line. Recall that the CML is linear, with an intercept of R_f and a slope of $[E(R_m) - R_f]/\sigma_m$. We can rewrite the CML by moving the intercept to the left-hand side of the equation, rearranging the terms, and generalizing the subscript from p to i, for any security:

$$E(R_i) - R_f = \left(\frac{\sigma_i}{\sigma_m}\right)[E(R_m) - R_f]$$

The factor loading or factor weight, σ_i/σ_m, refers to the ratio of total security risk to total market risk. To obtain a better understanding of factor loading and to illustrate that the CML reduces to a single-index model, we decompose total risk into its components.

---

2 Fama and French (1992).

3.2.2 *Decomposition of Total Risk for a Single-Index Model*

With the introduction of return-generating models, particularly the single-index model, we are able to decompose total variance into systematic and nonsystematic variances. Instead of using expected returns in the single index, let us use realized returns. The difference between expected returns and realized returns is attributable to non-market changes, as an error term, e_i, in the second equation below:

$$E(R_i) - R_f = \beta_i[E(R_m) - R_f]$$

and

$$R_i - R_f = \beta_i(R_m - R_f) + e_i$$

The variance of realized returns can be expressed in the equation below (note that R_f is a constant). We can further drop the covariance term in this equation because, by definition, any non-market return is uncorrelated with the market. Thus, we are able to decompose total variance into systematic and nonsystematic variances in the second equation below:

$$\sigma_i^2 = \beta_i^2 \sigma_m^2 + \sigma_e^2 + 2\text{Cov}(R_m, e_i)$$

Total variance = Systematic variance + Nonsystematic variance, which can be written as

$$\sigma_i^2 = \beta_i^2 \sigma_m^2 + \sigma_e^2$$

Total risk can be expressed as

$$\sigma_i = \sqrt{\beta_i^2 \sigma_m^2 + \sigma_e^2}$$

Because nonsystematic risk is zero for well-diversified portfolios, such as the market portfolio, the total risk of a market portfolio and other similar portfolios is only systematic risk, which is $\beta_i \sigma_m$. We can now return to the CML discussed in the previous subsection and replace σ_i with $\beta_i \sigma_m$ because the CML assumes that the market is a diversified portfolio. By making this substitution for the above equation, we get the following single-index model:

$$E(R_i) - R_f = \left(\frac{\sigma_i}{\sigma_m}\right) \times \left[E(R_m) - R_f\right] = \left(\frac{\beta_i \sigma_m}{\sigma_m}\right) \times [E(R_m) - R_f],$$

$$E(R_i) - R_f = \beta_i[E(R_m) - R_f]$$

Thus, the CML, which is only for well-diversified portfolios, is fully consistent with a single-index model.

In this section, you have learned how to decompose total variance into systematic and nonsystematic variances and how the CML is the same as a single-index model for diversified portfolios.

3.2.3 *Return-Generating Models: The Market Model*

The most common implementation of a single-index model is the **market model**, in which the market return is the single factor or single index. In principle, the market model and the single-index model are similar. The difference is that the market model is easier to work with and is normally used for estimating beta risk and computing abnormal returns. The market model is

$$R_i = \alpha_i + \beta_i R_m + e_i$$

To be consistent with the previous section, $\alpha_i = R_f(1 - \beta)$. The intercept, α_i, and slope coefficient, β_i, can be estimated by using historical security and market returns. These parameter estimates are then used to predict company-specific returns that a security may earn in a future period. Assume that a regression of Wal-Mart's historical daily returns on S&P 500 daily returns gives an α_i of 0.0001 and a β_i of 0.9. Thus,

Wal-Mart's expected daily return $= 0.0001 + 0.90 \times R_m$. If on a given day the market rises by 1 percent and Wal-Mart's stock rises by 2 percent, then Wal-Mart's company-specific return (e_i) for that day $= R_i - E(R_i) = R_i - (\alpha_i + \beta_i R_m) = 0.02 - (0.0001 + 0.90 \times 0.01) = 0.0109$, or 1.09%. In other words, Wal-Mart earned an abnormal return of 1.09 percent on that day.

3.2.4 *Calculation and Interpretation of Beta*

We begin with the single-index model introduced in Section 3.2.2 using realized returns and rewrite it as

$$R_i = (1 - \beta_i)R_f + \beta_i \times R_m + e_i$$

Because systematic risk depends on the correlation between the asset and the market, we can arrive at a measure of systematic risk from the covariance between R_i and R_m, where R_i is defined using the above equation. Note that the risk-free rate is a constant, so the first term in R_i drops out.

$$\begin{aligned} \mathrm{Cov}(R_i, R_m) &= \mathrm{Cov}(\beta_i \times R_m + e_i, R_m) \\ &= \beta_i \mathrm{Cov}(R_m, R_m) + \mathrm{Cov}(e_i, R_m) \\ &= \beta_i \sigma_m^2 + 0 \end{aligned}$$

The first term is beta multiplied by the variance of R_m. Because the error term is uncorrelated with the market, the second term drops out. Then, we can rewrite the equation in terms of beta as follows:

$$\beta_i = \frac{\mathrm{Cov}(R_i, R_m)}{\sigma_m^2} = \frac{\rho_{i,m}\sigma_i\sigma_m}{\sigma_m^2} = \frac{\rho_{i,m}\sigma_i}{\sigma_m}$$

The above formula shows the expression for beta, β_i, which is similar to the factor loading in the single-index model presented in Section 3.2.1. For example, if the correlation between an asset and the market is 0.70 and the asset and market have standard deviations of return of 0.25 and 0.15, respectively, the asset's beta would be $(0.70)(0.25)/0.15 = 1.17$. If the asset's covariance with the market and market variance were given as 0.026250 and 0.02250, respectively, the calculation would be $0.026250/0.02250 = 1.17$. The beta in the market model includes an adjustment for the correlation between asset i and the market because the market model covers all assets whereas the CML works only for fully diversified portfolios.

As shown in the above equation, **beta** is a measure of how sensitive an asset's return is to the market as a whole and is calculated as the covariance of the return on i and the return on the market divided by the variance of the market return; that expression is equivalent to the product of the asset's correlation with the market with a ratio of standard deviations of return (i.e., the ratio of the asset's standard deviation to the market's). As we have shown, beta captures an asset's systematic risk, or the portion of an asset's risk that cannot be eliminated by diversification. The variances and correlations required for the calculation of beta are usually based on historical returns.

A positive beta indicates that the return of an asset follows the general market trend, whereas a negative beta shows that the return of an asset generally follows a trend that is opposite to that of the market. In other words, a positive beta indicates that the return of an asset moves in the same direction of the market, whereas a negative beta indicates that the return of an asset moves in the opposite direction of the market. A risk-free asset's beta is zero because its covariance with other assets is zero. In other words, a beta of zero indicates that the asset's return has no correlation with movements in the market. The market's beta can be calculated by substituting σ_m for σ_i in the numerator. Also, any asset's correlation with itself is 1, so the beta of the market is 1:

$$\beta_i = \frac{\rho_{i,m}\sigma_i}{\sigma_m} = \frac{\rho_{m,m}\sigma_m}{\sigma_m} = 1$$

Because the market's beta is 1, the average beta of stocks in the market, by definition, is 1. In terms of correlation, most stocks, especially in developed markets, tend to be highly correlated with the market, with correlations in excess of 0.70. Some U.S. broad market indices, such as the S&P 500, the Dow Jones 30, and the NASDAQ 100, have even higher correlations that are in excess of 0.90. The correlations among different sectors are also high, which shows that companies have similar reactions to the same economic and market changes. As a consequence and as a practical matter, finding assets that have a consistently negative beta because of the market's broad effects on all assets is unusual.

EXAMPLE 5

Calculation of Beta

Assuming that the risk (standard deviation) of the market is 25 percent, calculate the beta for the following assets:

1 A short-term U.S. Treasury bill.

2 Gold, which has a standard deviation equal to the standard deviation of the market but a zero correlation with the market.

3 A new emerging market that is not currently included in the definition of "market"—the emerging market's standard deviation is 60 percent, and the correlation with the market is −0.1.

4 An initial public offering or new issue of stock with a standard deviation of 40 percent and a correlation with the market of 0.7 (IPOs are usually very risky but have a relatively low correlation with the market).

We use the formula for beta in answering the above questions: $\beta_i = \dfrac{\rho_{i,m}\sigma_i}{\sigma_m}$

Solution to 1:

By definition, a short-term U.S. Treasury bill has zero risk. Therefore, its beta is zero.

Solution to 2:

Because the correlation of gold with the market is zero, its beta is zero.

Solution to 3:

Beta of the emerging market is −0.1 × 0.60 ÷ 0.25 = −0.24.

Solution to 4:

Beta of the initial public offering is 0.7 × 0.40 ÷ 0.25 = 1.12.

3.2.5 Estimation of Beta

An alternative and more practical approach is to estimate beta directly by using the market model described above. The market model, $R_i = \alpha_i + \beta_i R_m + e_i$, is estimated by using regression analysis, which is a statistical process that evaluates the relationship between a given variable (the dependent variable) and one or more other (independent) variables. Historical security returns (R_i) and historical market returns (R_m) are inputs used for estimating the two parameters α_i and β_i.

Regression analysis is similar to plotting all combinations of the asset's return and the market return (R_i, R_m) and then drawing a line through all points such that it minimizes the sum of squared linear deviations from the line. Exhibit 6 illustrates the market model and the estimated parameters. The intercept, α_i (sometimes referred to as the constant), and the slope term, β_i, are all that is needed to define the security characteristic line and obtain beta estimates.

Exhibit 6	Beta Estimation Using a Plot of Security and Market Returns

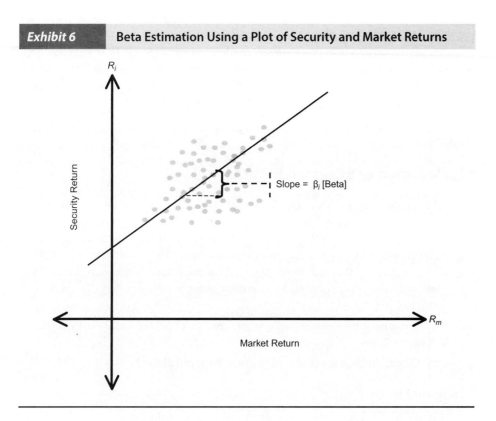

Although beta estimates are important for forecasting future levels of risk, there is much concern about their accuracy. In general, shorter periods of estimation (e.g., 12 months) represent betas that are closer to the asset's current level of systematic risk. Shorter period beta estimates, however, are also less accurate than beta estimates measured over three to five years because they may be affected by special events in that short period. Although longer period beta estimates are more accurate, they may be a poor representation of future expectations, especially if major changes in the asset have occurred. Therefore, it is necessary to recognize that estimates of beta, whether obtained through calculation or regression analysis, may or may not represent current or future levels of an asset's systematic risk.

3.2.6 Beta and Expected Return

Although the single-index model, also called the **capital asset pricing model** (CAPM), will be discussed in greater detail in the next section, we will use the CAPM in this section to estimate returns, given asset betas. The CAPM is usually written with the risk-free rate on the right-hand side:

$$E(R_i) = R_f + \beta_i[E(R_m) - R_f]$$

The model shows that the primary determinant of expected return for a security is its beta, or how well the security correlates with the market. The higher the beta of an asset, the higher its expected return will be. Assets with a beta greater than 1 have an expected return that is higher than the market return, whereas assets with a beta of less than 1 have an expected return that is less than the market return.

In certain cases, assets may require a return less than the risk-free return. For example, if an asset's beta is negative, the required return will be less than the risk-free rate. When combined with the market, the asset reduces the risk of the overall portfolio, which makes the asset very valuable. Insurance is one such asset. Insurance gives a positive return when the insured's wealth is reduced because of a catastrophic loss. In the absence of such a loss or when the insured's wealth is growing, the insured is required to pay an insurance premium. Thus, insurance has a negative beta and a negative expected return, but helps in reducing overall risk.

EXAMPLE 6

Calculation of Expected Return

1 Alpha Natural Resources (ANR), a coal producer, buys a large but privately held coal producer in China. As a result of the cross-border acquisition of a private company, ANR's standard deviation of returns is reduced from 50 percent to 30 percent and its correlation with the market falls from 0.95 to 0.75. Assume that the standard deviation and return of the market remain unchanged at 25 percent and 10 percent, respectively, and that the risk-free rate is 3 percent.

   A Calculate the beta of ANR stock and its expected return before the acquisition.

   B Calculate the expected return after the acquisition.

Solution to 1A:

Using the formula for β_i, we can calculate β_i and then the return.

$$\beta_i = \frac{\rho_{i,m}\sigma_i}{\sigma_m} = \frac{0.95 \times 0.50}{0.25} = 1.90$$

$$E(R_i) = R_f + \beta_i[E(R_m) - R_f] = 0.03 + 1.90 \times (0.10 - 0.03) = 0.163 = 16.3\%$$

Solution to 1B:

We follow the same procedure but with the after-acquisition correlation and risk.

$$\beta_i = \frac{\rho_{i,m}\sigma_i}{\sigma_m} = \frac{0.75 \times 0.30}{0.25} = 0.90$$

$$E(R_i) = R_f + \beta_i[E(R_m) - R_f] = 0.03 + 0.90 \times (0.10 - 0.03) = 0.093 = 9.3\%$$

The market risk premium is 7 percent (10% − 3%). As the beta changes, the change in the security's expected return is the market risk premium multiplied by the change in beta. In this scenario, ANR's beta decreased by 1.0, so the new expected return for ANR is 7 percentage points lower.

2 Mr. Miles observes the strong demand for iPods and iPhones and wants to invest in Apple stock. Unfortunately, Mr. Miles doesn't know the return he should expect from his investment. He has been given a risk-free rate of 3 percent, a market return of 10 percent, and Apple's beta of 1.5.

A Calculate Apple's expected return.

B An analyst looking at the same information decides that the past performance of Apple is not representative of its future performance. He decides that, given the increase in Apple's market capitalization, Apple acts much more like the market than before and thinks Apple's beta should be closer to 1.1. What is the analyst's expected return for Apple stock?

Solution to 2A:

$$E(R_i) = R_f + \beta_i[E(R_m) - R_f] = 0.03 + 1.5 \times (0.10 - 0.03) = 0.135 = 13.5\%$$

Solution to 2B:

$$E(R_i) = R_f + \beta_i[E(R_m) - R_f] = 0.03 + 1.1 \times (0.10 - 0.03) = 0.107 = 10.7\%$$

This example illustrates the lack of connection between estimation of past returns and projection into the future. Investors should be aware of the limitations of using past returns for estimating future returns.

THE CAPITAL ASSET PRICING MODEL

4

The capital asset pricing model is one of the most significant innovations in portfolio theory. The model is simple, yet powerful; is intuitive, yet profound; and uses only one factor, yet is broadly applicable. The CAPM was introduced independently by William Sharpe, John Lintner, Jack Treynor, and Jan Mossin and builds on Harry Markowitz's earlier work on diversification and modern portfolio theory.[3] The model provides a linear expected return–beta relationship that precisely determines the expected return given the beta of an asset. In doing so, it makes the transition from total risk to systematic risk, the primary determinant of expected return. Recall the following equation:

$$E(R_i) = R_f + \beta_i[E(R_m) - R_f]$$

The CAPM asserts that the expected returns of assets vary only by their systematic risk as measured by beta. Two assets with the same beta will have the same expected return irrespective of the nature of those assets. Given the relationship between risk and return, all assets are defined only by their beta risk, which we will explain as the assumptions are described.

In the remainder of this section, we will examine the assumptions made in arriving at the CAPM and the limitations those assumptions entail. Second, we will implement the CAPM through the security market line to price any portfolio or asset, both efficient and inefficient. Finally, we will discuss ways in which the CAPM can be applied to investments, valuation, and capital budgeting.

---

3 See, for example, Markowitz (1952), Sharpe (1964), Lintner (1965a, 1965b), Treynor (1961, 1962), and Mossin (1966).

4.1 Assumptions of the CAPM

Similar to all other models, the CAPM ignores many of the complexities of financial markets by making simplifying assumptions. These assumptions allow us to gain important insights into how assets are priced without complicating the analysis. Once the basic relationships are established, we can relax the assumptions and examine how our insights need to be altered. Some of these assumptions are constraining, whereas others are benign. And other assumptions affect only a particular set of assets or only marginally affect the hypothesized relationships.

1 *Investors are risk-averse, utility-maximizing, rational individuals.*

Risk aversion means that investors expect to be compensated for accepting risk. Note that the assumption does not require investors to have the same degree of risk aversion; it only requires that they are averse to risk. Utility maximization implies that investors want higher returns, not lower returns, and that investors always want more wealth (i.e., investors are never satisfied). Investors are understood to be rational in that they correctly evaluate and analyze available information to arrive at rational decisions. Although rational investors may use the same information to arrive at different estimates of expected risk and expected returns, homogeneity among investors (see Assumption 4) requires that investors be rational individuals.

Risk aversion and utility maximization are generally accepted as reflecting a realistic view of the world. Yet, rationality among investors has been questioned because investors may allow their personal biases and experiences to disrupt their decision making, resulting in suboptimal investments. Nonetheless, the model's results are unaffected by such irrational behavior as long as it does not affect prices in a significant manner (i.e., the trades of irrational investors cancel each other or are dominated by the trades of rational investors).

2 *Markets are frictionless, including no transaction costs and no taxes.*

Frictionless markets allow us to abstract the analysis from the operational characteristics of markets. In doing so, we do not allow the risk–return relationship to be affected by, for example, the trading volume on the New York Stock Exchange or the difference between buying and selling prices. Specifically, frictionless markets do not have transaction costs, taxes, or any costs or restrictions on short selling. We also assume that borrowing and lending at the risk-free rate is possible.

The transaction costs of many large institutions are negligible, and many institutions do not pay taxes. Even the presence of non-zero transaction costs, taxes, or the inability to borrow at the risk-free rate does not materially affect the general conclusions of the CAPM. Costs of short selling[4] or restrictions on short selling, however, can introduce an upward bias in asset prices, potentially jeopardizing important conclusions of the CAPM.

3 *Investors plan for the same single holding period.*

The CAPM is a single-period model, and all investor decisions are made on the basis of that one period. The assumption of a single period is applied for convenience because working with multi-period models is more difficult. A single-period model, however, does not allow learning to occur, and bad decisions can

---

4 Short selling shares involves selling shares that you do not own. Because you do not own the shares, you (or your broker) must borrow the shares before you can short sell. You sell the borrowed shares in the market hoping that you will be able to return the borrowed shares by buying them later in the market at a lower price. Brokerage houses and securities lenders lend shares to you to sell in return for a portion (or all) of the interest earned on the cash you receive for the shares that are short sold.

persist. In addition, maximizing utility at the end of a multi-period horizon may require decisions in certain periods that may seem suboptimal when examined from a single-period perspective. Nonetheless, the single holding period does not severely limit the applicability of the CAPM to multi-period settings.

4 *Investors have homogeneous expectations or beliefs.*

This assumption means that all investors analyze securities in the same way using the same probability distributions and the same inputs for future cash flows. In addition, given that they are rational individuals, the investors will arrive at the same valuations. Because their valuations of all assets are identical, they will generate the same optimal risky portfolio, which we call the market portfolio.

The assumption of homogeneous beliefs can be relaxed as long as the differences in expectations do not generate significantly different optimal risky portfolios.

5 *All investments are infinitely divisible.*

This assumption implies that an individual can invest as little or as much as he or she wishes in an asset. This supposition allows the model to rely on continuous functions rather than on discrete jump functions. The assumption is made for convenience only and has an inconsequential impact on the conclusions of the model.

6 *Investors are price takers.*

The CAPM assumes that there are many investors and that no investor is large enough to influence prices. Thus, investors are price takers, and we assume that security prices are unaffected by investor trades. This assumption is generally true because even though investors may be able to affect prices of small stocks, those stocks are not large enough to affect the primary results of the CAPM.

The main objective of these assumptions is to create a marginal investor who rationally chooses a mean–variance-efficient portfolio in a predictable fashion. We assume away any inefficiency in the market from both operational and informational perspectives. Although some of these assumptions may seem unrealistic, relaxing most of them will have only a minor influence on the model and its results. Moreover, the CAPM, with all its limitations and weaknesses, provides a benchmark for comparison and for generating initial return estimates.

4.2 The Security Market Line

In this subsection, we apply the CAPM to the pricing of securities. The **security market line** (SML) is a graphical representation of the capital asset pricing model with beta on the x-axis and expected return on the y-axis. Using the same concept as the capital market line, the SML intersects the y-axis at the risk-free rate of return, and the slope of this line is the market risk premium, $R_m - R_f$. Recall that the capital allocation line (CAL) and the capital market line (CML) do not apply to all securities or assets but only to efficient portfolios. In contrast, the security market line applies to any security, efficient or not. The difference occurs because the CAL and the CML use the total risk of the asset rather than its systematic risk. Because only systematic risk is priced and the CAL and the CML are based on total risk, the CAL and the CML can only be applied to those assets whose total risk is equal to systematic risk. Total risk and systematic risk are equal only for efficient portfolios because those portfolios have no diversifiable risk remaining. We are able to relax the requirement of efficient portfolios for the SML because the CAPM, which forms the basis for the SML, prices a security based only on its systematic risk, not its total risk.

Exhibit 7 is a graphical representation of the CAPM, the security market line. As shown earlier in this reading, the beta of the market is 1 (*x*-axis) and the market earns an expected return of R_m (*y*-axis). Using this line, it is possible to calculate the expected return of an asset. The next example illustrates the beta and return calculations.

Exhibit 7	**The Security Market Line**

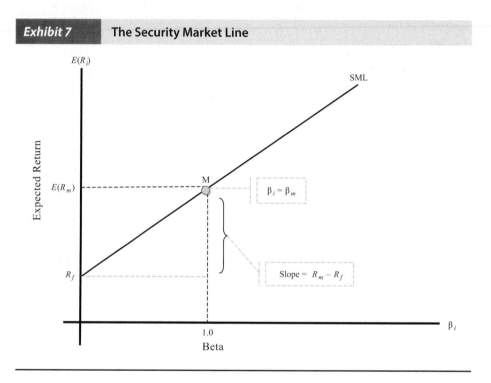

EXAMPLE 7

Security Market Line and Expected Return

1 Suppose the risk-free rate is 3 percent, the expected return on the market portfolio is 13 percent, and its standard deviation is 23 percent. An Indian company, Bajaj Auto, has a standard deviation of 50 percent but is uncorrelated with the market. Calculate Bajaj Auto's beta and expected return.

2 Suppose the risk-free rate is 3 percent, the expected return on the market portfolio is 13 percent, and its standard deviation is 23 percent. A German company, Mueller Metals, has a standard deviation of 50 percent and a correlation of 0.65 with the market. Calculate Mueller Metal's beta and expected return.

Solution to 1:

Using the formula for β_i, we can calculate β_i and then the return.

$$\beta_i = \frac{\rho_{i,m}\sigma_i}{\sigma_m} = \frac{0.0 \times 0.50}{0.23} = 0$$

$$E(R_i) = R_f + \beta_i[E(R_m) - R_f] = 0.03 + 0 \times (0.13 - 0.03) = 0.03 = 3.0\%$$

Because of its zero correlation with the market portfolio, Bajaj Auto's beta is zero. Because the beta is zero, the expected return for Bajaj Auto is the risk-free rate, which is 3 percent.

Solution to 2:

Using the formula for β_i, we can calculate β_i and then the return.

$$\beta_i = \frac{\rho_{i,m}\sigma_i}{\sigma_m} = \frac{0.65 \times 0.50}{0.23} = 1.41$$

$$E(R_i) = R_f + \beta_i[E(R_m) - R_f] = 0.03 + 1.41 \times (0.13 - 0.03) = 0.171 = 17.1\%$$

Because of the high degree of correlation with the market, the beta for Mueller Metals is 1.41 and the expected return is 17.1 percent. Because Mueller Metals has systematic risk that is greater than that of the market, it has an expected return that exceeds the expected return of the market.

4.2.1 Portfolio Beta

As we stated above, the security market line applies to all securities. But what about a combination of securities, such as a portfolio? Consider two securities, 1 and 2, with a weight of w_i in Security 1 and the balance in Security 2. The return for the two securities and return of the portfolio can be written as:

$$E(R_1) = R_f + \beta_1[E(R_m) - R_f]$$
$$E(R_2) = R_f + \beta_2[E(R_m) - R_f]$$
$$E(R_p) = w_1 E(R_1) + w_2 E(R_2)$$
$$= w_1 R_f + w_1\beta_1[E(R_m) - R_f] + w_2 R_f + w_2\beta_2[E(R_m) - R_f]$$
$$= R_f + (w_1\beta_1 + w_2\beta_2)[E(R_m) - R_f]$$

The last equation gives the expression for the portfolio's expected return. From this equation, we can conclude that the portfolio's beta = $w_1\beta_1 + w_2\beta_2$. In general, the portfolio beta is a weighted sum of the betas of the component securities and is given by:

$$\beta_p = \sum_{i=1}^{n} w_i\beta_i; \sum_{i=1}^{n} w_i = 1$$

The portfolio's return given by the CAPM is

$$E(R_p) = R_f + \beta_p[E(R_m) - R_f]$$

This equation shows that a linear relationship exists between the expected return of a portfolio and the systematic risk of the portfolio as measured by β_p.

EXAMPLE 8

Portfolio Beta and Return

You invest 20 percent of your money in the risk-free asset, 30 percent in the market portfolio, and 50 percent in RedHat, a U.S. stock that has a beta of 2.0. Given that the risk-free rate is 4 percent and the market return is 16 percent, what are the portfolio's beta and expected return?

Solution:

The beta of the risk-free asset = 0, the beta of the market = 1, and the beta of RedHat is 2.0. The portfolio beta is

$$\beta_p = w_1\beta_1 + w_2\beta_2 + w_3\beta_3 = (0.20 \times 0.0) + (0.30 \times 1.0) + (0.50 \times 2.0) = 1.30$$

$$E(R_i) = R_f + \beta_i[E(R_m) - R_f] = 0.04 + 1.30 \times (0.16 - 0.04) = 0.196 = 19.6\%$$

The portfolio beta is 1.30, and its expected return is 19.6 percent.

Alternate Method:

Another method for calculating the portfolio's return is to calculate individual security returns and then use the portfolio return formula (i.e., weighted average of security returns) to calculate the overall portfolio return.

Return of the risk-free asset = 4 percent; return of the market = 16 percent

RedHat's return based on its beta = $0.04 + 2.0 \times (0.16 - 0.04) = 0.28$

Portfolio return = $(0.20 \times 0.04) + (0.30 \times 0.16) + (0.50 \times 0.28) = 0.196 = 19.6\%$

Not surprisingly, the portfolio return is 19.6 percent, as calculated in the first method.

4.3 Applications of the CAPM

The CAPM offers powerful and intuitively appealing predictions about risk and the relationship between risk and return. The CAPM is not only important from a theoretical perspective but is also used extensively in practice. In this section, we will discuss some common applications of the model. When applying these tools to different scenarios, it is important to understand that the CAPM and the SML are functions that give an indication of what the return in the market *should* be, given a certain level of risk. The actual return may be quite different from the expected return.

Applications of the CAPM include estimates of the expected return for capital budgeting, comparison of the actual return of a portfolio or portfolio manager with the CAPM return for performance appraisal, and the analysis of alternate return estimates and the CAPM returns as the basis for security selection. The applications are discussed in more detail in this section.

4.3.1 *Estimate of Expected Return*

Given an asset's systematic risk, the expected return can be calculated using the CAPM. Recall that the price of an asset is the sum of all future cash flows discounted at the required rate of return, where the discount rate or the required rate of return is commensurate with the asset's risk. The expected rate of return obtained from the CAPM is normally the first estimate that investors use for valuing assets, such as stocks, bonds, real estate, and other similar assets. The required rate of return from the CAPM is also used for capital budgeting and determining the economic feasibility of projects. Again, recall that when computing the net present value of a project, investments and net revenues are considered cash flows and are discounted at the required rate of return. The required rate of return, based on the project's risk, is calculated using the CAPM.

Because risk and return underlie almost all aspects of investment decision making, it is not surprising that the CAPM is used for estimating expected return in many scenarios. Other examples include calculating the cost of capital for regulated companies by regulatory commissions and setting fair insurance premiums. The next example shows an application of the CAPM to capital budgeting.

EXAMPLE 9

Application of the CAPM to Capital Budgeting

GlaxoSmithKline Plc is examining the economic feasibility of developing a new medicine. The initial investment in Year 1 is $500 million. The investment in Year 2 is $200 million. There is a 50 percent chance that the medicine will be developed and will be successful. If that happens, GlaxoSmithKline must spend another $100 million in Year 3, but its income from the project in Year 3 will be $500 million, not including the third-year investment. In Years 4, 5, and 6, it will earn $400 million a year if the medicine is successful. At the end of Year 6, it intends to sell all rights to the medicine for $600 million. If the medicine is unsuccessful, none of GlaxoSmithKline's investments can be salvaged. Assume that the market return is 12 percent, the risk-free rate is 2 percent, and the beta risk of the project is 2.3. All cash flows occur at the end of each year.

1 Calculate the annual cash flows using the probability of success.

2 Calculate the expected return.

3 Calculate the net present value.

Solution to 1:

There is a 50 percent chance that the cash flows in Years 3–6 will occur. Taking that into account, the annual cash flows are:

Year 1: –$500 million (outflow)

Year 2: –$200 million (outflow)

Year 3: 50% of –$100 million (outflow) + 50% of $500 million = $200 million

Year 4: 50% of $400 million = $200 million

Year 5: 50% of $400 million = $200 million

Year 6: 50% of $400 million + 50% of $600 million = $500 million

Solution to 2:

The expected or required return for the project can be calculated using the CAPM, which is = $0.02 + 2.3 \times (0.12 - 0.02) = 0.25$.

Solution to 3:

The net present value is the discounted value of all cash flows:

$$NPV = \sum_{t=0}^{T} \frac{CF_t}{(1 + r_t)^t}$$

$$= \frac{-500}{(1 + 0.25)} + \frac{-200}{(1 + 0.25)^2} + \frac{200}{(1 + 0.25)^3} + \frac{200}{(1 + 0.25)^4}$$

$$+ \frac{200}{(1 + 0.25)^5} + \frac{500}{(1 + 0.25)^6}$$

$$= -400 - 128 + 102.40 + 81.92 + 65.54 + 131.07 = -147.07.$$

Because the net present value is negative (–$147.07 million), the project should not be accepted by GlaxoSmithKline.

4.3.2 *Portfolio Performance Evaluation*

Institutional money managers, pension fund managers, and mutual fund managers manage large amounts of money for other people. Are they doing a good job? How does their performance compare with a passively managed portfolio—that is, one in which the investor holds just the market portfolio? Evaluating the performance of a portfolio is of interest to all investors and money managers. Because active management costs significantly more than passive management, we expect active managers to perform better than passive managers or at least to cover the difference in expenses. For example, Fidelity's passively managed Spartan 500 Index fund has an expense ratio of only 0.10 percent whereas Fidelity's actively managed Contrafund has an expense ratio of 0.94 percent. Investors need a method for determining whether the manager of the Contrafund is worth the extra 0.84 percent in expenses.

In this reading, **performance evaluation** is based only on the CAPM. However, it is easy to extend this analysis to multi-factor models that may include industry or other special factors. Four ratios are commonly used in performance evaluation.

Sharpe and Treynor Ratios　　Performance has two components, risk and return. Although return maximization is a laudable objective, comparing just the return of a portfolio with that of the market is not sufficient. Because investors are risk averse, they will require compensation for higher risk in the form of higher returns. A commonly used measure of performance is the **Sharpe ratio**, which is defined as the portfolio's risk premium divided by its risk:

$$\text{Sharpe ratio} = \frac{R_p - R_f}{\sigma_p}$$

Recalling the CAL from earlier in the reading, one can see that the Sharpe ratio, also called the reward-to-variability ratio, is simply the slope of the capital allocation line; the greater the slope, the better the asset. Note, however, that the ratio uses the *total risk* of the portfolio, not its systematic risk. The use of total risk is appropriate if the portfolio is an investor's total portfolio—that is, the investor does not own any other assets. Sharpe ratios of the market and other portfolios can also be calculated in a similar manner. The portfolio with the highest Sharpe ratio has the best performance, and the one with the lowest Sharpe ratio has the worst performance, provided that the numerator is positive for all comparison portfolios. If the numerator is negative, the ratio will be less negative for riskier portfolios, resulting in incorrect rankings.

The Sharpe ratio, however, suffers from two limitations. First, it uses total risk as a measure of risk when only systematic risk is priced. Second, the ratio itself (e.g., 0.2 or 0.3) is not informative. To rank portfolios, the Sharpe ratio of one portfolio must be compared with the Sharpe ratio of another portfolio. Nonetheless, the ease of computation makes the Sharpe ratio a popular tool.

The **Treynor ratio** is a simple extension of the Sharpe ratio and resolves the Sharpe ratio's first limitation by substituting beta risk for total risk. The Treynor ratio is

$$\text{Treynor ratio} = \frac{R_p - R_f}{\beta_p}$$

Just like the Sharpe ratio, the numerators must be positive for the Treynor ratio to give meaningful results. In addition, the Treynor ratio does not work for negative-beta assets—that is, the denominator must also be positive for obtaining correct estimates and rankings. Although both the Sharpe and Treynor ratios allow for ranking of portfolios, neither ratio gives any information about the economic significance of differences in performance. For example, assume the Sharpe ratio of one portfolio is 0.75 and the Sharpe ratio for another portfolio is 0.80. The second portfolio is superior, but is that difference meaningful? In addition, we do not know whether either of the portfolios is better than the passive market portfolio. The remaining two measures, M^2 and Jensen's alpha, attempt to address that problem by comparing portfolios while also providing information about the extent of the overperformance or underperformance.

M-Squared (M^2) M^2 was created by Franco Modigliani and his granddaughter, Leah Modigliani—hence the name M-squared. M^2 is an extension of the Sharpe ratio in that it is based on *total risk*, not beta risk. The idea behind the measure is to create a portfolio (P') that mimics the risk of a market portfolio—that is, the mimicking portfolio (P') alters the weights in Portfolio P and the risk-free asset until Portfolio P' has the same total risk as the market (i.e., $\sigma_p = \sigma_m$). Because the risks of the mimicking portfolio and the market portfolio are the same, we can obtain the return on the mimicking portfolio and directly compare it with the market return. The weight in Portfolio P, w_p, that makes the risks equal can be calculated as follows:

$$\sigma_{p'} = w_p\sigma_p + (1 - w_p)\sigma_{Rf} = \sigma_m = w_p\sigma_p, \text{ which gives}$$

$$w_p = \frac{\sigma_m}{\sigma_p}$$

Because the correlation between the market and the risk-free asset is zero, we get w_p as the weight invested in Portfolio P and the balance invested in the risk-free asset. The risk-adjusted return for the mimicking portfolio is:

$$R_{p'} = w_p R_p + (1 - w_p)R_f = \left(\frac{\sigma_m}{\sigma_p}\right)R_p + \left(1 - \frac{\sigma_m}{\sigma_p}\right)R_f$$

$$= R_f + \left(\frac{\sigma_m}{\sigma_p}\right)\left(R_p - R_f\right) = R_f + \sigma_m\left(\frac{R_p - R_f}{\sigma_p}\right)$$

The return of the mimicking portfolio based on excess returns is $(R_p - R_f)\frac{\sigma_m}{\sigma_p}$.[5] The difference in the return of the mimicking portfolio and the market return is M^2, which can be expressed as a formula:

$$M^2 = (R_p - R_f)\frac{\sigma_m}{\sigma_p} - (R_m - R_f)$$

M^2 gives us rankings that are identical to those of the Sharpe ratio. They are easier to interpret, however, because they are in percentage terms. A portfolio that matches the performance of the market will have an M^2 of zero, whereas a portfolio that outperforms the market will have an M^2 that is positive. By using M^2, we are not only able to determine the rank of a portfolio but also which, if any, of our portfolios beat the market on a risk-adjusted basis.

Jensen's Alpha   Like the Treynor ratio, Jensen's alpha is based on systematic risk. We can measure a portfolio's systematic risk by estimating the market model, which is done by regressing the portfolio's daily return on the market's daily return. The coefficient on the market return is an estimate of the beta risk of the portfolio (see Section 3.2.5 for more details). We can calculate the risk-adjusted return of the portfolio using the beta of the portfolio and the CAPM. The difference between the actual portfolio return and the calculated risk-adjusted return is a measure of the portfolio's performance relative to the market portfolio and is called Jensen's alpha. By definition, α_m of the market is zero. Jensen's alpha is also the vertical distance from the SML measuring the excess return for the same risk as that of the market and is given by

---

5 Note that the last term within parentheses on the right-hand side of the previous equation is the Sharpe ratio.

$$\alpha_p = R_p - [R_f + \beta_p(R_m - R_f)]$$

If the period is long, it may contain different risk-free rates, in which case R_f represents the average risk-free rate. Furthermore, the returns in the equation are all realized, actual returns. The sign of α_p indicates whether the portfolio has outperformed the market. If α_p is positive, then the portfolio has outperformed the market; if α_p is negative, the portfolio has underperformed the market. Jensen's alpha is commonly used for evaluating most institutional managers, pension funds, and mutual funds. Values of alpha can be used to rank different managers and the performance of their portfolios, as well as the magnitude of underperformance or overperformance. For example, if a portfolio's alpha is 2 percent and another portfolio's alpha is 5 percent, the second portfolio has outperformed the first portfolio by 3 percentage points and the market by 5 percentage points. Jensen's alpha is the maximum amount that you should be willing to pay the manager to manage your money.

EXAMPLE 10

Portfolio Performance Evaluation

A British pension fund has employed three investment managers, each of whom is responsible for investing in one-third of all asset classes so that the pension fund has a well-diversified portfolio. Information about the managers is given below.

Manager	Return	σ	β
X	10%	20%	1.1
Y	11	10	0.7
Z	12	25	0.6
Market (M)	9	19	
Risk-free rate (R_f)	3		

Calculate the expected return, Sharpe ratio, Treynor ratio, M^2, and Jensen's alpha. Analyze your results and plot the returns and betas of these portfolios.

Solution:

In each case, the calculations are shown only for Manager X. All answers are tabulated below. Note that the β of the market is 1 and the σ and β of the risk-free rate are both zero.

$$Expected\ return:\ E(R_X) = R_f + \beta_X\left[E(R_m) - R_f\right] = 0.03 + 1.10$$
$$\times (0.09 - 0.03) = 0.096 = 9.6\%$$

$$Sharpe\ ratio = \frac{R_X - R_f}{\sigma_X} = \frac{0.10 - 0.03}{0.20} = 0.35$$

$$Treynor\ ratio = \frac{R_X - R_f}{\beta_X} = \frac{0.10 - 0.03}{1.1} = 0.064$$

$$M^2 = (R_X - R_f)\frac{\sigma_m}{\sigma_X} - (R_m - R_f) = (0.10 - 0.03)\frac{0.19}{0.20}$$
$$- (0.09 - 0.03) = 0.0065 = 0.65\%$$

$$\alpha_X = R_X - \left[R_f + \beta_X(R_m - R_f)\right] = 0.10 - (0.03 + 1.1 \times 0.06)$$
$$= 0.004 = 0.40\%$$

Exhibit 8	Measures of Portfolio Performance Evaluation							
Manager	R_i	σ_i	β_i	$E(R_i)$	Sharpe Ratio	Treynor Ratio	M^2	α_i
X	10.0%	20.0%	1.10	9.6%	0.35	0.064	0.65%	0.40%
Y	11.0	10.0	0.70	7.2	0.80	0.114	9.20	3.80
Z	12.0	25.0	0.60	6.6	0.36	0.150	0.84	5.40
M	9.0	19.0	1.00	9.0	0.32	0.060	0.00	0.00
R_f	3.0	0.0	0.00	3.0	–	–	–	0.00

Let us begin with an analysis of the risk-free asset. Because the risk-free asset has zero risk and a beta of zero, calculating the Sharpe ratio, Treynor ratio, or M^2 is not possible because they all require the portfolio risk in the denominator. The risk-free asset's alpha, however, is zero. Turning to the market portfolio, we see that the absolute measures of performance, the Sharpe ratio and the Treynor ratio, are positive for the market portfolio. These ratios are positive as long as the portfolio earns a return that is in excess of that of the risk-free asset. M^2 and α_i are performance measures relative to the market, so they are both equal to zero for the market portfolio.

All three managers have Sharpe and Treynor ratios greater than those of the market, and all three managers' M^2 and α_i are positive; therefore, the pension fund should be satisfied with their performance. Among the three managers, Manager X has the worst performance, irrespective of whether total risk or systematic risk is considered for measuring performance. The relative rankings are depicted in Exhibit 9.

Exhibit 9	Ranking of Portfolios by Performance Measure			
Rank	Sharpe Ratio	Treynor Ratio	M^2	α_i
1	Y	Z	Y	Z
2	Z	Y	Z	Y
3	X	X	X	X
4	M	M	M	M
5	–	–	–	R_f

Comparing Y and Z, we can observe that Y performs much better than Z when total risk is considered. Y has a Sharpe ratio of 0.80, compared with a Sharpe ratio of 0.36 for Z. Similarly, M^2 is higher for Y (9.20 percent) than for Z (0.84 percent). In contrast, when systematic risk is used, Z outperforms Y. The Treynor ratio is higher for Z (0.150) than for Y (0.114), and Jensen's alpha is also higher for Z (5.40 percent) than for Y (3.80 percent), which indicates that Y has done a better job of generating excess return relative to systematic risk than Y because Z has diversified away more of the nonsystematic risk than Y.

Exhibit 10 confirms these observations in that all three managers outperform the benchmark because all three points lie above the SML. Among the three portfolios, Z performs the best when we consider risk-adjusted returns because it is the point in Exhibit 10 that is located northwest relative to the portfolios X and Y.

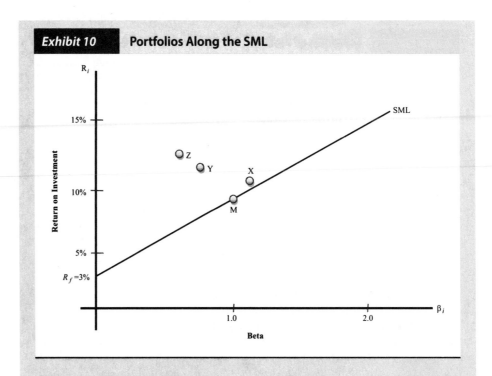

Exhibit 10   **Portfolios Along the SML**

When do we use total risk performance measures like the Sharpe ratio and M^2, and when do we use beta risk performance measures like the Treynor ratio and Jensen's alpha? Total risk is relevant for an investor when he or she holds a portfolio that is not fully diversified, which is not a desirable portfolio. In such cases, the Sharpe ratio and M^2 are appropriate performance measures. Thus, if the pension fund were to choose only one fund manager to manage all its assets, it should choose Manager Y. Performance measures relative to beta risk—Treynor ratio and Jensen's alpha—are relevant when the investor holds a well-diversified portfolio with negligible diversifiable risk. In other words, if the pension fund is well diversified and only the systematic risk of the portfolio matters, the fund should choose Manager Z.

The measures of performance evaluation assume that the benchmark market portfolio is the correct portfolio. As a result, an error in the benchmark may cause the results to be misleading. For example, evaluating a real estate fund against the S&P 500 is incorrect because real estate has different characteristics than equity. In addition to errors in benchmarking, errors could occur in the measurement of risk and return of the market portfolio and the portfolios being evaluated. Finally, many estimates are based on historical data. Any projections based on such estimates assume that this level of performance will continue in the future.

4.3.3 Security Characteristic Line

Similar to the SML, we can draw a **security characteristic line** (SCL) for a security. The SCL is a plot of the excess return of the security on the excess return of the market. In Exhibit 11, Jensen's alpha is the intercept and the beta is the slope. The equation of the line can be obtained by rearranging the terms in the expression for Jensen's alpha and replacing the subscript p with i:

$$R_i - R_f = \alpha_i + \beta_i(R_m - R_f)$$

As an example, the SCL is drawn in Exhibit 11 using Manager X's portfolio from Exhibit 8. The security characteristic line can also be estimated by regressing the excess security return, $R_i - R_f$, on the excess market return, $R_m - R_f$.

Exhibit 11	The Security Characteristic Line

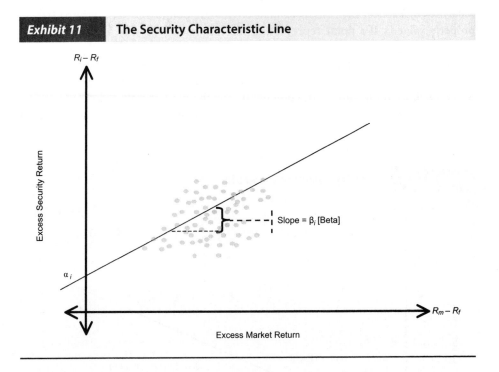

4.3.4 *Security Selection*

When discussing the CAPM, we assumed that investors have homogeneous expectations and are rational, risk-averse, utility-maximizing investors. With these assumptions, we were able to state that all investors assign the same value to all assets and, therefore, have the same optimal risky portfolio, which is the market portfolio. In other words, we assumed that there is commonality among beliefs about an asset's future cash flows and the required rate of return. Given the required rate of return, we can discount the future cash flows of the asset to arrive at its current value, or price, which is agreed upon by all or most investors.

In this section, we introduce heterogeneity in beliefs of investors. Because investors are price takers, it is assumed that such heterogeneity does not significantly affect the market price of an asset. The difference in beliefs can relate to future cash flows, the systematic risk of the asset, or both. Because the current price of an asset is the discounted value of the future cash flows, the difference in beliefs could result in an investor-estimated price that is different from the CAPM-calculated price. The CAPM-calculated price is the current market price because it reflects the beliefs of all other investors in the market. If the investor-estimated current price is higher (lower) than the market price, the asset is considered undervalued (overvalued). Therefore, the CAPM is an effective tool for determining whether an asset is undervalued or overvalued and whether an investor should buy or sell the asset.

Although portfolio performance evaluation is backward looking and security selection is forward looking, we can apply the concepts of portfolio evaluation to security selection. The best measure to apply is Jensen's alpha because it uses systematic risk and is meaningful even on an absolute basis. A positive Jensen's alpha indicates a superior security, whereas a negative Jensen's alpha indicates a security that is likely to underperform the market when adjusted for risk.

Another way of presenting the same information is with the security market line. Potential investors can plot a security's expected return and beta against the SML and use this relationship to decide whether the security is overvalued or undervalued in the market.[6] Exhibit 12 shows a number of securities along with the SML. All securities that reflect the consensus market view are points directly on the SML (i.e., properly valued). If a point representing the estimated return of an asset is above the SML (Points A and C), the asset has a low level of risk relative to the amount of expected return and would be a good choice for investment. In contrast, if the point representing a particular asset is below the SML (Point B), the stock is considered overvalued. Its return does not compensate for the level of risk and should not be considered for investment. Of course, a short position in Asset B can be taken if short selling is permitted.

Exhibit 12	Security Selection Using SML

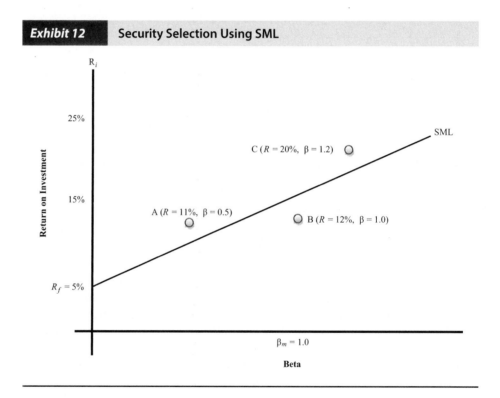

4.3.5 Constructing a Portfolio

Based on the CAPM, investors should hold a combination of the risk-free asset and the market portfolio. The true market portfolio consists of a large number of securities, and an investor would have to own all of them in order to be completely diversified. Because owning all existing securities is not practical, in this section, we will consider an alternate method of constructing a portfolio that may not require a large number of securities and will still be sufficiently diversified. Exhibit 13 shows the reduction in risk as we add more and more securities to a portfolio. As can be seen from the exhibit, much of the nonsystematic risk can be diversified away in as few as 30 securities. These securities, however, should be randomly selected and represent different

---

6 In this reading, we do not consider transaction costs, which are important whenever deviations from a passive portfolio are considered. Thus, the magnitude of undervaluation or overvaluation should be considered in relation to transaction costs prior to making an investment decision.

asset classes for the portfolio to effectively diversify risk. Otherwise, one may be better off using an index (e.g., the S&P 500 for a diversified large-cap equity portfolio and other indices for other asset classes).

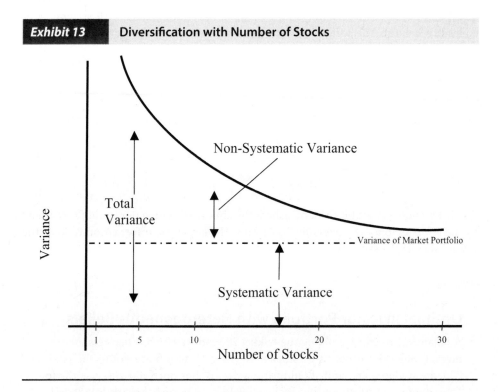

| Exhibit 13 | Diversification with Number of Stocks |

Let's begin constructing the optimal portfolio with a portfolio of securities like the S&P 500. Although the S&P 500 is a portfolio of 500 securities, it is a good starting point because it is readily available as a single security for trading. In contrast, it represents only the large corporations that are traded on the U.S. stock markets and, therefore, does not encompass the global market entirely. Because the S&P 500 is the base portfolio, however, we treat it is as the market for the CAPM.

Any security not included in the S&P 500 can be evaluated to determine whether it should be integrated into the portfolio. That decision is based on the α_i of the security, which is calculated using the CAPM with the S&P 500 as the market portfolio. Note that security i may not necessarily be priced incorrectly for it to have a non-zero α_i; α_i can be positive merely because it is not well correlated with the S&P 500 and its return is sufficient for the amount of systematic risk it contains. For example, assume a new stock market, ABC, opens to foreign investors only and is being considered for inclusion in the portfolio. We estimate ABC's model parameters relative to the S&P 500 and find an α_i of approximately 3 percent, with a β_i of 0.60. Because α_i is positive, ABC should be added to the portfolio. Securities with a significantly negative α_i may be short sold to maximize risk-adjusted return. For convenience, however, we will assume that negative positions are not permitted in the portfolio.

In addition to the securities that are correctly priced but enter the portfolio because of their risk–return superiority, securities already in the portfolio (S&P 500) may be undervalued or overvalued based on investor expectations that are incongruent with the market. Securities in the S&P 500 that are overvalued (negative α_i) should be dropped from the S&P 500 portfolio, if it is possible to exclude individual securities, and positions in securities in the S&P 500 that are undervalued (positive α_i) should be increased.

This brings us to the next question: What should the relative weight of securities in the portfolio be? Because we are concerned with maximizing risk-adjusted return, securities with a higher α_i should have a higher weight, and securities with greater nonsystematic risk should be given less weight in the portfolio. A complete analysis of portfolio optimization is beyond the scope of this reading, but the following principles are helpful. The weight in each nonmarket security should be proportional to $\dfrac{\alpha_i}{\sigma_{ei}^2}$, where the denominator is the nonsystematic variance of security i. The total

weight of nonmarket securities in the portfolio is proportional to $\dfrac{\sum\limits_{i=1}^{N} w_i \alpha_i}{\sum\limits_{i=1}^{N} w_i^2 \sigma_{ei}^2}$. The weight

in the market portfolio is a function of $\dfrac{E(R_m)}{\sigma_m^2}$. The information ratio, $\dfrac{\alpha_i}{\sigma_{ei}}$ (i.e., alpha divided by nonsystematic risk), measures the abnormal return per unit of risk added by the security to a well-diversified portfolio. The larger the information ratio is, the more valuable the security.

EXAMPLE 11

Optimal Investor Portfolio with Heterogeneous Beliefs

A Japanese investor is holding the Nikkei 225 index, which is her version of the market. She thinks that three stocks, P, Q, and R, which are not in the Nikkei 225, are undervalued and should form a part of her portfolio. She has the following information about the stocks, the Nikkei 225, and the risk-free rate (the information is given as expected return, standard deviation, and beta):

P: 15%, 30%, 1.5

Q: 18%, 25%, 1.2

R: 16%, 23%, 1.1

Nikkei 225: 12%, 18%, 1.0

Risk-free rate: 2%, 0%, 0.0

1 Calculate Jensen's alpha for P, Q, and R.

2 Calculate nonsystematic variance for P, Q, and R.

3 Should any of the three stocks be included in the portfolio? If so, which stock should have the highest weight in the portfolio?

Solution to 1:

Stock P's α: $R_i - [R_f + \beta_i(R_m - R_f)] = 0.15 - (0.02 + 1.5 \times 0.10) = -0.02$

Stock Q's α: $R_i - [R_f + \beta_i(R_m - R_f)] = 0.18 - (0.02 + 1.2 \times 0.10) = 0.04$

Stock R's α: $R_i - [R_f + \beta_i(R_m - R_f)] = 0.16 - (0.02 + 1.1 \times 0.10) = 0.03$

Solution to 2:

Total variance = Systematic variance + Nonsystematic variance. From Section 3.2.2, we write the equation as $\sigma_{ei}^2 = \sigma_i^2 - \beta_i^2 \sigma_m^2$.

Stock P's nonsystematic variance = $(0.30 \times 0.30) - (1.5 \times 1.5 \times 0.18 \times 0.18) = 0.09 - 0.0729 = 0.0171$

Stock Q's nonsystematic variance = $(0.25 \times 0.25) - (1.2 \times 1.2 \times 0.18 \times 0.18) = 0.0625 - 0.0467 = 0.0158$

Stock R's nonsystematic variance = $(0.23 \times 0.23) - (1.1 \times 1.1 \times 0.18 \times 0.18) = 0.0529 - 0.0392 = 0.0137$

Solution to 3:

Stock P has a negative α and should not be included in the portfolio, unless a negative position can be assumed through short selling. Stocks Q and R have a positive α; therefore, they should be included in the portfolio with positive weights.

The relative weight of Q is $0.04/0.0158 = 2.53$.

The relative weight of R is $0.03/0.0137 = 2.19$.

Stock Q will have the largest weight among the nonmarket securities to be added to the portfolio. In relative terms, the weight of Q will be 15.5 percent greater than the weight of R $(2.53/2.19 = 1.155)$. As the number of securities increases, the analysis becomes more complex. However, the contribution of each additional security toward improvement in the risk–return trade-off will decrease and eventually disappear, resulting in a well-diversified portfolio.

BEYOND THE CAPITAL ASSET PRICING MODEL

5

In general, return-generating models allow us to estimate an asset's return given its characteristics, where the asset characteristics required for estimating the return are specified in the model. Estimating an asset's return is important for investment decision making. These models are also important as a benchmark for evaluating portfolio, security, or manager performance. The return-generating models were briefly introduced in Section 3.2.1, and one of those models, the capital asset pricing model, was discussed in detail in Section 4.

The purpose of this section is to make readers aware that, although the CAPM is an important concept and model, the CAPM is not the only return-generating model. In this section, we revisit and highlight the limitations of the CAPM and preview return-generating models that address some of those limitations.

5.1 The CAPM

The CAPM is a model that simplifies a complex investment environment and allows investors to understand the relationship between risk and return. Although the CAPM affords us this insight, its assumptions can be constraining and unrealistic, as mentioned in Section 5.2. In Section 5.3, we discuss other models that have been developed along with their own limitations.

5.2 Limitations of the CAPM

The CAPM is subject to theoretical and practical limitations. Theoretical limitations are inherent in the structure of the model, whereas practical limitations are those that arise in implementing the model.

5.2.1 *Theoretical Limitations of the CAPM*

■ Single-factor model: Only systematic risk or beta risk is priced in the CAPM. Thus, the CAPM states that no other investment characteristics should be considered in estimating returns. As a consequence, it is prescriptive and easy to understand and apply, although it is very restrictive and inflexible.

■ Single-period model: The CAPM is a single-period model that does not consider multi-period implications or investment objectives of future periods, which can lead to myopic and suboptimal investment decisions. For example, it may be optimal to default on interest payments in the current period to maximize current returns, but the consequences may be negative in the next period. A single-period model like the CAPM is unable to capture factors that vary over time and span several periods.

5.2.2 *Practical Limitations of the CAPM*

In addition to the theoretical limitations, implementation of the CAPM raises several practical concerns, some of which are listed below.

■ Market portfolio: The true market portfolio according to the CAPM includes all assets, financial and nonfinancial, which means that it also includes many assets that are not investable, such as human capital and assets in closed economies. Richard Roll[7] noted that one reason the CAPM is not testable is that the true market portfolio is unobservable.

■ Proxy for a market portfolio: In the absence of a true market portfolio, market participants generally use proxies. These proxies, however, vary among analysts, the country of the investor, etc. and generate different return estimates for the same asset, which is impermissible in the CAPM.

■ Estimation of beta risk: A long history of returns (three to five years) is required to estimate beta risk. The historical state of the company, however, may not be an accurate representation of the current or future state of the company. More generally, the CAPM is an *ex ante* model, yet it is usually applied using *ex post* data. In addition, using different periods for estimation results in different estimates of beta. For example, a three-year beta is unlikely to be the same as a five-year beta, and a beta estimated with daily returns is unlikely to be the same as the beta estimated with monthly returns. Thus, we are likely to estimate different returns for the same asset depending on the estimate of beta risk used in the model.

■ The CAPM is a poor predictor of returns: If the CAPM is a good model, its estimate of asset returns should be closely associated with realized returns. However, empirical support for the CAPM is weak.[8] In other words, tests of the CAPM show that asset returns are not determined only by systematic risk. Poor predictability of returns when using the CAPM is a serious limitation because return-generating models are used to estimate future returns.

■ Homogeneity in investor expectations: The CAPM assumes that homogeneity exists in investor expectations for the model to generate a single optimal risky portfolio (the market) and a single security market line. Without this assumption, there will be numerous optimal risky portfolios and numerous security market lines. Clearly, investors can process the same information in a rational manner and arrive at different optimal risky portfolios.

---

7 Roll (1977).
8 See, for example, Fama and French (1992).

5.3 Extensions to the CAPM

Given the limitations of the CAPM, it is not surprising that other models have been proposed to address some of these limitations. These new models are not without limitations of their own, which we will mention while discussing the models. We divide the models into two categories and provide one example of each type.

5.3.1 Theoretical Models

Theoretical models are based on the same principle as the CAPM but expand the number of risk factors. The best example of a theoretical model is the arbitrage pricing theory (APT), which was developed by Stephen Ross.[9] Like the CAPM, APT proposes a linear relationship between expected return and risk:

$$E(R_p) = R_F + \lambda_1 \beta_{p,1} + \dots + \lambda_K \beta_{p,K}$$

where

$E(R_p)$ = the expected return of portfolio p

R_F = the risk-free rate

λ_j = the risk premium (expected return in excess of the risk-free rate) for factor j

$\beta_{p,j}$ = the sensitivity of the portfolio to factor j

K = the number of risk factors

Unlike the CAPM, however, APT allows numerous risk factors—as many as are relevant to a particular asset. Moreover, other than the risk-free rate, the risk factors need not be common and may vary from one asset to another. A no-arbitrage condition in asset markets is used to determine the risk factors and estimate betas for the risk factors.

Although it is theoretically elegant, flexible, and superior to the CAPM, APT is not commonly used in practice because it does not specify any of the risk factors and it becomes difficult to identify risk factors and estimate betas for each asset in a portfolio. So from a practical standpoint, the CAPM is preferred to APT.

5.3.2 Practical Models

If beta risk in the CAPM does not explain returns, which factors do? Practical models seek to answer this question through extensive research. As mentioned in Section 3.2.1, the best example of such a model is the four-factor model proposed by Fama and French (1992) and Carhart (1997).

Based on an analysis of the relationship between past returns and a variety of different factors, Fama and French (1992) proposed that three factors seem to explain asset returns better than just systematic risk. Those three factors are relative size, relative book-to-market value, and beta of the asset. With Carhart's (1997) addition of relative past stock returns, the model can be written as follows:

$$E(R_{it}) = \alpha_i + \beta_{i,MKT} MKT_t + \beta_{i,SMB} SMB_t + \beta_{i,HML} HML_t + \beta_{i,UMD} UMD_t$$

where

$E(R_i)$ = the return on an asset in excess of the one-month T-bill return

MKT = the excess return on the market portfolio

SMB = the difference in returns between small-capitalization stocks and large-capitalization stocks (size)

---

9 Ross (1976).

      HML = the difference in returns between high-book-to-market stocks and low-book-to-market stocks (value versus growth)

      UMD = the difference in returns of the prior year's winners and losers (momentum)

Historical analysis shows that the coefficient on *MKT* is not significantly different from zero, which implies that stock return is unrelated to the market. The factors that explain stock returns are size (smaller companies outperform larger companies), book-to-market ratio (value companies outperform glamour companies), and momentum (past winners outperform past losers).

The four-factor model has been found to predict asset returns much better than the CAPM and is extensively used in estimating returns for *U.S. stocks*. Note the emphasis on U.S. stocks; because these factors were estimated for U.S. stocks, they have worked well for U.S. stocks over the last several years.

Three observations are in order. First, no strong economic arguments exist for the three additional risk factors. Second, the four-factor model does not necessarily apply to other assets or assets in other countries, and third, there is no expectation that the model will continue to work well in the future.

5.4 The CAPM and Beyond

The CAPM has limitations and, more importantly, is ineffective in modeling asset returns. However, it is a simple model that allows us to estimate returns and evaluate performance. The newer models provide alternatives to the CAPM, although they are not necessarily better in all situations or practical in their application in the real world.

SUMMARY

In this reading, we discussed the capital asset pricing model in detail and covered related topics such as the capital market line. The reading began with an interpretation of the CML, uses of the market portfolio as a passive management strategy, and leveraging of the market portfolio to obtain a higher expected return. Next, we discussed systematic and nonsystematic risk and why one should not expect to be compensated for taking on nonsystematic risk. The discussion of systematic and nonsystematic risk was followed by an introduction to beta and return-generating models. This broad topic was then broken down into a discussion of the CAPM and, more specifically, the relationship between beta and expected return. The final section included applications of the CAPM to capital budgeting, portfolio performance evaluation, and security selection. The highlights of the reading are as follows.

- The capital market line is a special case of the capital allocation line, where the efficient portfolio is the market portfolio.

- Obtaining a unique optimal risky portfolio is not possible if investors are permitted to have heterogeneous beliefs because such beliefs will result in heterogeneous asset prices.

- Investors can leverage their portfolios by borrowing money and investing in the market.

- Systematic risk is the risk that affects the entire market or economy and is not diversifiable.

- Nonsystematic risk is local and can be diversified away by combining assets with low correlations.

- Beta risk, or systematic risk, is priced and earns a return, whereas nonsystematic risk is not priced.

- The expected return of an asset depends on its beta risk and can be computed using the CAPM, which is given by $E(R_i) = R_f + \beta_i[E(R_m) - R_f]$.

- The security market line is an implementation of the CAPM and applies to all securities, whether they are efficient or not.

- Expected return from the CAPM can be used for making capital budgeting decisions.

- Portfolios can be evaluated by several CAPM-based measures, such as the Sharpe ratio, the Treynor ratio, M^2, and Jensen's alpha.

- The SML can assist in security selection and optimal portfolio construction.

By successfully understanding the content of this reading, you should feel comfortable decomposing total variance into systematic and nonsystematic variance, analyzing beta risk, using the CAPM, and evaluating portfolios and individual securities.

REFERENCES

Carhart, Mark. 1997. "On Persistence in Mutual Fund Performance." *Journal of Finance*, vol. 52, no. 1:57–82.

Fama, Eugene, and Kenneth French. 1992. "The Cross-Section of Expected Stock Returns." *Journal of Finance*, vol. 47, no. 2:427–466.

Lintner, John. 1965a. "Security Prices, Risk, and Maximal Gains from Diversification." *Journal of Finance*, vol. 20, no. 4:587–615.

Lintner, John. 1965b. "The Valuation of Risk Assets and the Selection of Risky Investments in Stock Portfolios and Capital Budgets." *Review of Economics and Statistics*, vol. 47, no. 1:13–37.

Markowitz, Harry. 1952. "Portfolio Selection." *Journal of Finance*, vol. 7, no. 1:77–91.

Mossin, Jan. 1966. "Equilibrium in a Capital Asset Market." *Econometrica*, vol. 34, no. 4:768–783.

Roll, Richard. 1977. "A Critique of the Asset Pricing Theory's Tests Part I: On Past and Potential Testability of the Theory." *Journal of Financial Economics*, vol. 4, no. 2:129–176.

Ross, Stephen A. 1976. "The Arbitrage Theory of Capital Asset Pricing." *Journal of Economic Theory*, vol. 13, no. 3:341–360.

Sharpe, William F. 1964. "Capital Asset Prices: A Theory Of Market Equilibrium under Conditions of Risk." *Journal of Finance*, vol. 19, no. 3:425–442.

Treynor, Jack L. 1961. *Market Value, Time, and Risk*. Unpublished manuscript.

Treynor, Jack L. 1962. *Toward a Theory of Market Value of Risky Assets*. Unpublished manuscript.

PRACTICE PROBLEMS

1 The line depicting the risk and return of portfolio combinations of a risk-free asset and any risky asset is the:

A security market line.

B capital allocation line.

C security characteristic line.

2 The portfolio of a risk-free asset and a risky asset has a better risk-return trade-off than investing in only one asset type because the correlation between the risk-free asset and the risky asset is equal to:

A −1.0.

B 0.0.

C 1.0.

3 With respect to capital market theory, an investor's optimal portfolio is the combination of a risk-free asset and a risky asset with the highest:

A expected return.

B indifference curve.

C capital allocation line slope.

4 Highly risk-averse investors will *most likely* invest the majority of their wealth in:

A risky assets.

B risk-free assets.

C the optimal risky portfolio.

5 The capital market line, CML, is the graph of the risk and return of portfolio combinations consisting of the risk-free asset and:

A any risky portfolio.

B the market portfolio.

C the leveraged portfolio.

6 Which of the following statements *most accurately* defines the market portfolio in capital market theory? The market portfolio consists of all:

A risky assets.

B tradable assets.

C investable assets.

7 With respect to capital market theory, the optimal risky portfolio:

A is the market portfolio.

B has the highest expected return.

C has the lowest expected variance.

8 Relative to portfolios on the CML, any portfolio that plots above the CML is considered:

A inferior.

B inefficient.

C unachievable.

Practice questions were developed by Stephen P. Huffman, CFA (University of Wisconsin, Oshkosh).

9 A portfolio on the capital market line with returns greater than the returns on the market portfolio represents a(n):

   A lending portfolio.

   B borrowing portfolio.

   C unachievable portfolio.

10 With respect to the capital market line, a portfolio on the CML with returns less than the returns on the market portfolio represents a(n):

   A lending portfolio.

   B borrowing portfolio.

   C unachievable portfolio.

11 Which of the following types of risk is *most likely* avoided by forming a diversified portfolio?

   A Total risk.

   B Systematic risk.

   C Nonsystematic risk.

12 Which of the following events is *most likely* an example of nonsystematic risk?

   A A decline in interest rates.

   B The resignation of chief executive officer.

   C An increase in the value of the U.S. dollar.

13 With respect to the pricing of risk in capital market theory, which of the following statements is *most accurate*?

   A All risk is priced.

   B Systematic risk is priced.

   C Nonsystematic risk is priced.

14 The sum of an asset's systematic variance and its nonsystematic variance of returns is equal to the asset's:

   A beta.

   B total risk.

   C total variance.

15 With respect to return-generating models, the intercept term of the market model is the asset's estimated:

   A beta.

   B alpha.

   C variance.

16 With respect to return-generating models, the slope term of the market model is an estimate of the asset's:

   A total risk.

   B systematic risk.

   C nonsystematic risk.

17 With respect to return-generating models, which of the following statements is *most accurate*? Return-generating models are used to directly estimate the:

   A expected return of a security.

   B weights of securities in a portfolio.

   C parameters of the capital market line.

The following information relates to Questions 18–20

An analyst gathers the following information:

Security	Expected Annual Return (%)	Expected Standard Deviation (%)	Correlation between Security and the Market
Security 1	11	25	0.6
Security 2	11	20	0.7
Security 3	14	20	0.8
Market	10	15	1.0

18 Which security has the *highest* total risk?

  A   Security 1.

  B   Security 2.

  C   Security 3.

19 Which security has the *highest* beta measure?

  A   Security 1.

  B   Security 2.

  C   Security 3.

20 Which security has the *least* amount of market risk?

  A   Security 1.

  B   Security 2.

  C   Security 3.

21 With respect to capital market theory, the average beta of all assets in the market is:

  A   less than 1.0.

  B   equal to 1.0.

  C   greater than 1.0.

22 The slope of the security characteristic line is an asset's:

  A   beta.

  B   excess return.

  C   risk premium.

23 The graph of the capital asset pricing model is the:

  A   capital market line.

  B   security market line.

  C   security characteristic line.

24 With respect to capital market theory, correctly priced individual assets can be plotted on the:

  A   capital market line.

  B   security market line.

  C   capital allocation line.

25 With respect to the capital asset pricing model, the primary determinant of expected return of an individual asset is the:

  A asset's beta.

  B market risk premium.

  C asset's standard deviation.

26 With respect to the capital asset pricing model, which of the following values of beta for an asset is *most likely* to have an expected return for the asset that is less than the risk-free rate?

  A −0.5

  B 0.0

  C 0.5

27 With respect to the capital asset pricing model, the market risk premium is:

  A less than the excess market return.

  B equal to the excess market return.

  C greater than the excess market return.

The following information relates to Questions 28–31

An analyst gathers the following information:

Security	Expected Standard Deviation (%)	Beta
Security 1	25	1.50
Security 2	15	1.40
Security 3	20	1.60

28 With respect to the capital asset pricing model, if the expected market risk premium is 6% and the risk-free rate is 3%, the expected return for Security 1 is *closest* to:

  A 9.0%.

  B 12.0%.

  C 13.5%.

29 With respect to the capital asset pricing model, if expected return for Security 2 is equal to 11.4% and the risk-free rate is 3%, the expected return for the market is *closest* to:

  A 8.4%.

  B 9.0%.

  C 10.3%.

30 With respect to the capital asset pricing model, if the expected market risk premium is 6% the security with the *highest* expected return is:

  A Security 1.

  B Security 2.

  C Security 3.

31 With respect to the capital asset pricing model, a decline in the expected market return will have the *greatest* impact on the expected return of:

  A Security 1.

  B Security 2.

  C Security 3.

32 Which of the following performance measures is consistent with the CAPM?

  A *M*-squared.

  B Sharpe ratio.

  C Jensen's alpha.

33 Which of the following performance measures does *not* require the measure to be compared to another value?

  A Sharpe ratio.

  B Treynor ratio.

  C Jensen's alpha.

34 Which of the following performance measures is *most* appropriate for an investor who is *not* fully diversified?

  A *M*-squared.

  B Treynor ratio.

  C Jensen's alpha.

35 Analysts who have estimated returns of an asset to be greater than the expected returns generated by the capital asset pricing model should consider the asset to be:

  A overvalued.

  B undervalued.

  C properly valued.

36 With respect to capital market theory, which of the following statements *best* describes the effect of the homogeneity assumption? Because all investors have the same economic expectations of future cash flows for all assets, investors will invest in:

  A the same optimal risky portfolio.

  B the Standard and Poor's 500 Index.

  C assets with the same amount of risk.

37 With respect to capital market theory, which of the following assumptions allows for the existence of the market portfolio? All investors:

  A are price takers.

  B have homogeneous expectations.

  C plan for the same, single holding period.

38 The intercept of the best fit line formed by plotting the excess returns of a manager's portfolio on the excess returns of the market is *best* described as Jensen's:

  A beta.

  B ratio.

  C alpha.

39 Portfolio managers who are maximizing risk-adjusted returns will seek to invest *more* in securities with:

  A lower values of Jensen's alpha.

    B   values of Jensen's alpha equal to 0.

    C   higher values of Jensen's alpha.

40 Portfolio managers, who are maximizing risk-adjusted returns, will seek to invest *less* in securities with:

    A   lower values for nonsystematic variance.

    B   values of nonsystematic variance equal to 0.

    C   higher values for nonsystematic variance.

SOLUTIONS

1 B is correct. The capital allocation line, CAL, is a combination of the risk-free asset and a risky asset (or a portfolio of risky assets). The combination of the risk-free asset and the market portfolio is a special case of the CAL, which is the capital market line, CML.

2 B is correct. A portfolio of the risk-free asset and a risky asset or a portfolio of risky assets can result in a better risk-return tradeoff than an investment in only one type of an asset, because the risk-free asset has zero correlation with the risky asset.

3 B is correct. Investors will have different optimal portfolios depending on their indifference curves. The optimal portfolio for each investor is the one with highest utility; that is, where the CAL is tangent to the individual investor's highest possible indifference curve.

4 B is correct. Although the optimal risky portfolio is the market portfolio, highly risk-averse investors choose to invest most of their wealth in the risk-free asset.

5 B is correct. Although the capital allocation line includes all possible combinations of the risk-free asset and any risky portfolio, the capital market line is a special case of the capital allocation line, which uses the market portfolio as the optimal risky portfolio.

6 A is correct. The market includes all risky assets, or anything that has value; however, not all assets are tradable, and not all tradable assets are investable.

7 A is correct. The optimal risky portfolio is the market portfolio. Capital market theory assumes that investors have homogeneous expectations, which means that all investors analyze securities in the same way and are rational. That is, investors use the same probability distributions, use the same inputs for future cash flows, and arrive at the same valuations. Because their valuations of all assets are identical, all investors will invest in the same optimal risky portfolio (i.e., the market portfolio).

8 C is correct. Theoretically, any point above the CML is not achievable and any point below the CML is dominated by and inferior to any point on the CML.

9 B is correct. As one moves further to the right of point M on the capital market line, an increasing amount of borrowed money is being invested in the market portfolio. This means that there is negative investment in the risk-free asset, which is referred to as a leveraged position in the risky portfolio.

10 A is correct. The combinations of the risk-free asset and the market portfolio on the CML where returns are less than the returns on the market portfolio are termed 'lending' portfolios.

11 C is correct. Investors are capable of avoiding nonsystematic risk by forming a portfolio of assets that are not highly correlated with one another, thereby reducing total risk and being exposed only to systematic risk.

12 B is correct. Nonsystematic risk is specific to a firm, whereas systematic risk affects the entire economy.

13 B is correct. Only systematic risk is priced. Investors do not receive any return for accepting nonsystematic or diversifiable risk.

14 C is correct. The sum of systematic variance and nonsystematic variance equals the total variance of the asset. References to total risk as the sum of systematic risk and nonsystematic risk refer to variance, not to risk.

15 B is correct. In the market model, $R_i = \alpha_i + \beta_i R_m + e_i$, the intercept, α_i, and slope coefficient, β_i, are estimated using historical security and market returns.

16 B is correct. In the market model, $R_i = \alpha_i + \beta_i R_m + e_i$, the slope coefficient, β_i, is an estimate of the asset's systematic or market risk.

17 A is correct. In the market model, $R_i = \alpha_i + \beta_i R_m + e_i$, the intercept, α_i, and slope coefficient, β_i, are estimated using historical security and market returns. These parameter estimates then are used to predict firm-specific returns that a security may earn in a future period.

18 A is correct. Security 1 has the highest total variance; $0.0625 = 0.25^2$ compared to Security 2 and Security 3 with a total variance of 0.0400.

19 C is correct. Security 3 has the highest beta value; $1.07 = \dfrac{\rho_{3,m}\sigma_3}{\sigma_m} = \dfrac{(0.80)(20\%)}{15\%}$ compared to Security 1 and Security 2 with beta values of 1.00 and 0.93, respectively.

20 B is correct. Security 2 has the lowest beta value; $.93 = \dfrac{\rho_{2,m}\sigma_2}{\sigma_m} = \dfrac{(0.70)(20\%)}{15\%}$ compared to Security 1 and 3 with beta values of 1.00 and 1.07, respectively.

21 B is correct. The average beta of all assets in the market, by definition, is equal to 1.0.

22 A is correct. The security characteristic line is a plot of the excess return of the security on the excess return of the market. In such a graph, Jensen's alpha is the intercept and the beta is the slope.

23 B is correct. The security market line (SML) is a graphical representation of the capital asset pricing model, with beta risk on the x-axis and expected return on the y-axis.

24 B is correct. The security market line applies to any security, efficient or not. The CAL and the CML use the total risk of the asset (or portfolio of assets) rather than its systematic risk, which is the only risk that is priced.

25 A is correct. The CAPM shows that the primary determinant of expected return for an individual asset is its beta, or how well the asset correlates with the market.

26 A is correct. If an asset's beta is negative, the required return will be less than the risk-free rate in the CAPM. When combined with a positive market return, the asset reduces the risk of the overall portfolio, which makes the asset very valuable. Insurance is an example of a negative beta asset.

27 B is correct. In the CAPM, the market risk premium is the difference between the return on the market and the risk-free rate, which is the same as the return in excess of the market return.

28 B is correct. The expected return of Security 1, using the CAPM, is 12.0% = 3% + 1.5(6%); $E(R_i) = R_f + \beta_i(E(R_m) - R_f)$.

29 B is correct. The expected risk premium for Security 2 is 8.4%, (11.4% – 3%), indicates that the expected market risk premium is 6%; therefore, since the risk-free rate is 3% the expected rate of return for the market is 9%. That is, using the CAPM, $E(R_i) = R_f + \beta_i(E(R_m) - R_f)$, 11.4% = 3% + 1.4(X%), where X% = (11.4% – 3%)/1.4 = 6.0% = market risk premium.

30 C is correct. Security 3 has the highest beta; thus, regardless of the value for the risk-free rate, Security 3 will have the highest expected return:

$$E(R_i) = R_f + \beta_i(E(R_m) - R_f)$$

31 C is correct. Security 3 has the highest beta; thus, regardless of the risk-free rate the expected return of Security 3 will be most sensitive to a change in the expected market return.

32 C is correct. Jensen's alpha adjusts for systematic risk, and M-squared and the Sharpe Ratio adjust for total risk.

33 C is correct. The sign of Jensen's alpha indicates whether or not the portfolio has outperformed the market. If alpha is positive, the portfolio has outperformed the market; if alpha is negative, the portfolio has underperformed the market.

34 A is the correct. M-squared adjusts for risk using standard deviation (i.e., total risk).

35 B is correct. If the estimated return of an asset is above the SML (the expected return), the asset has a lower level of risk relative to the amount of expected return and would be a good choice for investment (i.e., undervalued).

36 A is correct. The homogeneity assumption refers to all investors having the same economic expectation of future cash flows. If all investors have the same expectations, then all investors should invest in the same optimal risky portfolio, therefore implying the existence of only one optimal portfolio (i.e., the market portfolio).

37 B is correct. The homogeneous expectations assumption means that all investors analyze securities in the same way and are rational. That is, they use the same probability distributions, use the same inputs for future cash flows, and arrive at the same valuations. Because their valuation of all assets is identical, they will generate the same optimal risky portfolio, which is the market portfolio.

38 C is correct. This is because of the plot of the excess return of the security on the excess return of the market. In such a graph, Jensen's alpha is the intercept and the beta is the slope.

39 C is correct. Since managers are concerned with maximizing risk-adjusted returns, securities with a higher value of Jensen's alpha, α_i, should have a higher weight.

40 C is correct. Since managers are concerned with maximizing risk-adjusted returns, securities with greater nonsystematic risk should be given less weight in the portfolio.

Basics of Portfolio Planning and Construction

by Alistair Byrne, CFA, and Frank E. Smudde, CFA

LEARNING OUTCOMES

Mastery	The candidate should be able to:
☐	**a.** describe the reasons for a written investment policy statement (IPS);
☐	**b.** describe the major components of an IPS;
☐	**c.** describe risk and return objectives and how they may be developed for a client;
☐	**d.** distinguish between the willingness and the ability (capacity) to take risk in analyzing an investor's financial risk tolerance;
☐	**e.** describe the investment constraints of liquidity, time horizon, tax concerns, legal and regulatory factors, and unique circumstances and their implications for the choice of portfolio assets;
☐	**f.** explain the specification of asset classes in relation to asset allocation;
☐	**g.** discuss the principles of portfolio construction and the role of asset allocation in relation to the IPS.

INTRODUCTION

1

To build a suitable portfolio for a client, investment advisers should first seek to understand the client's investment goals, resources, circumstances, and constraints. Investors can be categorized into broad groups based on shared characteristics with respect to these factors (e.g., various types of individual investors and institutional investors). Even investors within a given type, however, will invariably have a number of distinctive requirements. In this reading, we consider in detail the planning for investment success based on an individualized understanding of the client.

This reading is organized as follows: Section 2 discusses the investment policy statement, a written document that captures the client's investment objectives and the constraints. Section 3 discusses the portfolio construction process, including the first step of specifying a strategic asset allocation for the client. A summary and practice problems conclude the reading.

2   PORTFOLIO PLANNING

Portfolio planning can be defined as a program developed in advance of constructing a portfolio that is expected to satisfy the client's investment objectives. The written document governing this process is the investment policy statement (IPS).

2.1 The Investment Policy Statement

The IPS is the starting point of the portfolio management process. Without a full understanding of the client's situation and requirements, it is unlikely that successful results will be achieved. "Success" can be defined as a client achieving his or her important investment goals using means that he or she is comfortable with (in terms of risks taken and other concerns). The IPS essentially communicates a plan for achieving investment success.

The IPS will be developed following a fact finding discussion with the client. This fact finding discussion can include the use of a questionnaire designed to articulate the client's risk tolerance as well as specific circumstances. In the case of institutional clients, the fact finding may involve asset–liability management studies, identification of liquidity needs, and a wide range of tax and legal considerations.

The IPS can take a variety of forms. A typical format will include the client's investment objectives and the constraints that apply to the client's portfolio.

The client's objectives are specified in terms of risk tolerance and return requirements. These must be consistent with each other: a client is unlikely to be able to find a portfolio that offers a relatively high expected return without taking on a relatively high level of risk.

The constraints section covers factors that need to be taken into account when constructing a portfolio for the client that meets the objectives. The typical constraint categories are liquidity requirements, time horizon, regulatory requirements, tax status, and unique needs. The constraints may be internal (i.e., set by the client), or external (i.e., set by law or regulation). These are discussed in detail below.

Having a well constructed IPS for all clients should be standard procedure for a portfolio manager. The portfolio manager should have the IPS close at hand and be able to refer to it to assess the suitability of a particular investment for the client. In some cases, the need for the IPS goes beyond simply being a matter of standard procedure. In some countries, the IPS (or an equivalent document) is a legal or regulatory requirement. For example, U.K. pension schemes must have a statement of investment principles under the Pensions Act 1995 (Section 35), and this statement is in essence an IPS. The U.K. Financial Services Authority also has requirements for investment firms to "know their customers." The European Union's Markets in Financial Instruments Directive ("MiFID") requires firms to assign clients to categories, such as professional clients and retail clients.

In the case of an institution, such as a pension plan or university endowment, the IPS may set out the governance arrangements that apply to the investment funds. For example, this information could cover the investment committee's approach to appointing and reviewing investment managers for the portfolio, and the discretion that those managers have. The IPS could also set out the institution's approach to corporate governance, in terms of how it will approach the use of shareholder voting rights and other forms of engagement with corporate management.

The IPS should be reviewed on a regular basis to ensure that it remains consistent with the client's circumstances and requirements. For example, the U.K. Pensions Regulator suggests that a pension scheme's statements of investment principles—a form of IPS—should be reviewed at least every three years. The IPS should also be reviewed if the manager becomes aware of a material change in the client's circumstances, or on the initiative of the client when his or her objectives, time horizon, or liquidity needs change.

2.2 Major Components of an IPS

There is no single standard format for an IPS. Many IPS, however, include the following sections:

- *Introduction*. This section describes the client.

- *Statement of Purpose*. This section states the purpose of the IPS.

- *Statement of Duties and Responsibilities*. This section details the duties and responsibilities of the client, the custodian of the client's assets, and the investment managers.

- *Procedures*. This section explains the steps to take to keep the IPS current and the procedures to follow to respond to various contingencies.

- *Investment Objectives*. This section explains the client's objectives in investing.

- *Investment Constraints*. This section presents the factors that constrain the client in seeking to achieve the investment objectives.

- *Investment Guidelines*. This section provides information about how policy should be executed (e.g., on the permissible use of leverage and derivatives) and on specific types of assets excluded from investment, if any.

- *Evaluation and Review*. This section provides guidance on obtaining feedback on investment results.

- *Appendices*: (A) Strategic Asset Allocation (B) Rebalancing Policy. Many investors specify a strategic asset allocation (SAA), also known as the policy portfolio, which is the baseline allocation of portfolio assets to asset classes in view of the investor's investment objectives and the investor's policy with respect to rebalancing asset class weights.

The sections that are most closely linked to the client's distinctive needs, and probably the most important from a planning perspective, are those dealing with investment objectives and constraints. An IPS focusing on these two elements has been called an IPS in an "objectives and constraints" format.

In the following sections, we discuss the investment objectives and constraints format of an IPS beginning with risk and return objectives. We follow a tradition of CFA Institute presentations in discussing risk objectives first. The process of developing the IPS is the basic mechanism for evaluating and trying to improve an investor's overall expected return–risk stance. In a portfolio context, "investors have learned to appreciate that their objective is not to manage reward but to control and manage risk."[1] Stated another way, return objectives and expectations must be tailored to be consistent with risk objectives. The risk and return objectives must also be consistent with the constraints that apply to the portfolio.

---

1 Maginn and Tuttle (1983), p. 23.

2.2.1 *Risk Objectives*

When constructing a portfolio for a client, it is important to ensure that the risk of the portfolio is suitable for the client. The IPS should state clearly the risk tolerance of the client.

Risk objectives are specifications for portfolio risk that reflect the risk tolerance of the client. Quantitative risk objectives can be absolute or relative or a combination of the two.

Examples of an absolute risk objective would be a desire not to suffer any loss of capital or not to lose more than a given percent of capital in any 12-month period. Note that these objectives are not related to investment market performance, good or bad, and are absolute in the sense of being self-standing. The fulfillment of such objectives could be achieved by not taking any risk; for example, by investing in an insured bank certificate of deposit at a credit-worthy bank. If investments in risky assets are undertaken, however, such statements would need to be restated as a probability statement to be operational (i.e., practically useful). For example, the desire not to lose more than 4 percent of capital in any 12-month period might be restated as an objective that with 95 percent probability the portfolio not lose more than 4 percent in any 12-month period. Measures of absolute risk include the variance or standard deviation of returns and value at risk.[2]

Some clients may choose to express relative risk objectives, which relate risk relative to one or more benchmarks perceived to represent appropriate risk standards. For example, investments in large-cap U.K. equities could be benchmarked to an equity market index, such as the FTSE 100 Index. The S&P 500 Index could be used as a benchmark for large-cap U.S. equities, or for investments with cash-like characteristics, the benchmark could be an interest rate such as LIBOR or a Treasury bill rate. For risk relative to a benchmark, the relevant measure is tracking risk, or tracking error.[3]

For institutional clients, the benchmark may be linked to some form of liability the institution has. For example, a pension plan must meet the pension payments as they come due and the risk objective will be to minimize the probability that it will fail to do so. (A related return objective might be to outperform the discount rate used in finding the present value of liabilities over a multi-year time horizon.)

When a policy portfolio (that is, a specified set of long-term asset class weightings) is used, the risk objective may be expressed as a desire for the portfolio return to be within a band of plus or minus X percent of the benchmark return calculated by assigning an index or benchmark to represent each asset class present in the policy portfolio. Again, this objective has to be interpreted as a statement of probability; for example, a 95 percent probability that the portfolio return will be within X percent of the benchmark return over a stated time period. Example 1 reviews this material.

EXAMPLE 1

Types of Risk Objectives

A Japanese institutional investor has a portfolio valued at ¥10 billion. The investor expresses his first risk objective as a desire not to lose more than ¥1 billion in the coming 12-month period. The investor specifies a second risk objective of achieving returns within 4 percent of the return to the TOPIX stock market index, which is the investor's benchmark. Based on this information, address the following:

---

2 Value at risk is a money measure of the minimum value of losses expected during a specified time period at a given level of probability.

3 Tracking risk (sometimes called **tracking error**) is the standard deviation of the differences between a portfolio's returns and its benchmark's returns.

1 **A** Characterize the first risk objective as absolute or relative.

B Give an example of how the risk objective could be restated in a practical manner.

2 **A** Characterize the second risk objective as absolute or relative.

B Identify a measure for quantifying the risk objective.

Solutions to 1:

A This is an absolute risk objective.

B This risk objective could be restated in a practical manner by specifying that the 12-month 95 percent value at risk of the portfolio must not be more than ¥1 billion.

Solutions to 2:

A This is a relative risk objective.

B This risk objective could be quantified using the tracking risk as a measure. For example, assuming returns follow a normal distribution, an expected tracking risk of 2 percent would imply a return within 4 percent of the index return approximately 95 percent of the time. Remember that tracking risk is stated as a one standard deviation measure.

A client's overall risk tolerance is a function of the client's ability to bear (accept) risk and his or her "risk attitude," which might be considered as the client's willingness to take risk. For ease of expression, from this point on we will refer to ability to bear risk and willingness to take risk as the two components of risk tolerance. Above average ability to bear risk and above average willingness to take risk imply above average risk tolerance. Below average ability to bear risk and below average willingness to take risk imply below average risk tolerance.

The ability to bear risk is measured mainly in terms of objective factors, such as time horizon, expected income, and the level of wealth relative to liabilities. For example, an investor with a 20-year time horizon can be considered to have a greater ability to bear risk, other things being equal, than an investor with a 2-year horizon. This difference is because over 20 years there is more scope for losses to be recovered or other adjustments to circumstances to be made than there is over 2 years.

Similarly, an investor whose assets are comfortably in excess of their liabilities has more ability to bear risk than an investor whose wealth and expected future expenditure are more closely balanced. For example, a wealthy individual who can sustain a comfortable lifestyle after a very substantial investment loss has a relatively high ability to bear risk. A pension plan that has a large surplus of assets over liabilities has a relatively high ability to bear risk.

Risk attitude, or willingness to take risk, is a more subjective factor based on the client's psychology and perhaps also his or her current circumstances. Although the list of factors that are related to an individual's risk attitude remains open to debate, it is believed that some psychological factors, such as personality type, self-esteem, and inclination to independent thinking, are correlated with risk attitude. Some individuals are comfortable taking financial and investment risk, whereas others find it distressing. Although there is no single agreed-upon method for measuring risk tolerance, a willingness to take risk may be gauged by discussing risk with the client or by asking the client to complete a psychometric questionnaire. For example, financial planning academic John Grable and collaborators have developed 13-item and 5-item risk attitude questionnaires that have undergone some level of technical validation. The five-item questionnaire is shown in Exhibit 1.

Exhibit 1	**A Five-Item Risk Assessment Instrument**

1 Investing is too difficult to understand.

   a Strongly agree

   b Tend to agree

   c Tend to disagree

   d Strongly disagree

2 I am more comfortable putting my money in a bank account than in the stock market.

   a Strongly agree

   b Tend to agree

   c Tend to disagree

   d Strongly disagree

3 When I think of the word "risk" the term "loss" comes to mind immediately.

   a Strongly agree

   b Tend to agree

   c Tend to disagree

   d Strongly disagree

4 Making money in stocks and bonds is based on luck.

   a Strongly agree

   b Tend to agree

   c Tend to disagree

   d Strongly disagree

5 In terms of investing, safety is more important than returns.

   a Strongly agree

   b Tend to agree

   c Tend to disagree

   d Strongly disagree

Source: Grable and Joo (2004).

The responses, a), b), c), and d), are coded 1, 2, 3, and 4, respectively, and summed. The lowest score is 5 and the highest score is 20, with higher scores indicating greater risk tolerance. For two random samples drawn from the faculty and staff of large U.S. universities (n = 406), the mean score was 12.86 with a standard deviation of 3.01 and a median score of 13.

Note that a question, such as the first one in Exhibit 1, indicates that risk attitude may be associated with non-psychological factors (such as level of financial knowledge and understanding and decision-making style) as well as psychological factors.

The adviser needs to examine whether a client's ability to accept risk is consistent with the client's willingness to take risk. For example, a wealthy investor with a 20-year time horizon, who is thus able to take risk, may also be comfortable taking risk; in this case the factors are consistent. If the wealthy investor has a low willingness to take risk, there would be a conflict.

In the institutional context, there could also be conflict between ability and willingness to take risk. In addition, different stakeholders within the institution may take different views. For example, the trustees of a well-funded pension plan may desire a low-risk approach to safeguard the funding of the scheme and beneficiaries of the scheme may take a similar view. The sponsor, however, may wish a higher-risk/higher-return approach in an attempt to reduce future funding costs. When a trustee bears a fiduciary responsibility to pension beneficiaries and the interests of the pension sponsor and the pension beneficiaries conflict, the trustee should act in the best interests of the beneficiaries.

When ability to take risk and willingness to take risk are consistent, the investment adviser's task is the simplest. When ability to take risk is below average and willingness to take risk is above average, the investor's risk tolerance should be assessed as below average overall. When ability to take risk is above average but willingness is below average, the portfolio manager or adviser may seek to counsel the client and explain the conflict and its implications. For example, the adviser could outline the reasons why the client is considered to have a high ability to take risk and explain the likely consequences, in terms of reduced expected return, of not taking risk. The investment adviser, however, should not aim to change a client's willingness to take risk that is not a result of a miscalculation or misperception. Modification of elements of personality is not within the purview of the investment adviser's role. The prudent approach is to reach a conclusion about risk tolerance consistent with the lower of the two factors (ability and willingness) and to document the decisions made.

Example 2 is the first of a set that follows the analysis of a private wealth management client through the preparation of the major elements of an IPS.

EXAMPLE 2

The Case of Henri Gascon: Risk Tolerance

Henri Gascon is an energy trader who works for a major French oil company based in Paris. He is 30-years old and married with one son, aged 5. Gascon has decided that it is time to review his financial situation and consults a financial adviser. The financial adviser notes the following aspects of Gascon's situation:

- Gascon's annual salary of €250,000 is more than sufficient to cover the family's outgoings.

- Gascon owns his apartment outright and has €1,000,000 of savings.

- Gascon perceives that his job is reasonably secure.

- Gascon has a good knowledge of financial matters and is confident that equity markets will deliver positive returns over the longer term.

- In the risk tolerance questionnaire, Gascon strongly disagrees with the statements that "making money in stocks and bonds is based on luck" and that "in terms of investing, safety is more important than returns."

- Gascon expects that most of his savings will be used to fund his retirement, which he hopes to start at age 50.

Based only on the information given, which of the following statements is *most* accurate?

A Gascon has a low ability to take risk, but a high willingness to take risk.

B Gascon has a high ability to take risk, but a low willingness to take risk.

C Gascon has a high ability to take risk, and a high willingness to take risk.

Solution:

C is correct. Gascon has a high income relative to outgoings, a high level of assets, a secure job, and a time horizon of 20 years. This information suggests a high *ability* to take risk. At the same time, Gascon is knowledgeable and confident about financial markets and responds to the questionnaire with answers that suggest risk tolerance. This result suggests he also has a high *willingness* to take risk.

EXAMPLE 3

The Case of Jacques Gascon: Risk Tolerance

Henri Gascon is so pleased with the services provided by the financial adviser, that he suggests to his brother Jacques that he should also consult the adviser. Jacques thinks it is a good idea. Jacques is a self-employed computer consultant also based in Paris. He is 40-years old and divorced with four children, aged between 12 and 16. The financial adviser notes the following aspects of Jacques' situation:

- Jacques' consultancy earnings average €40,000 per annum, but are quite volatile.

- Jacques is required to pay €10,000 per year to his ex-wife and children.

- Jacques has a mortgage on his apartment of €100,000 and €10,000 of savings.

- Jacques has a good knowledge of financial matters and expects that equity markets will deliver very high returns over the longer term.

- In the risk tolerance questionnaire, Jacques strongly disagrees with the statements "I am more comfortable putting my money in a bank account than in the stock market" and "When I think of the word "risk" the term "loss" comes to mind immediately."

- Jacques expects that most of his savings will be required to support his children at university.

Based on the above information, which statement is correct?

A Jacques has a low ability to take risk, but a high willingness to take risk.

B Jacques has a high ability to take risk, but a low willingness to take risk.

C Jacques has a high ability to take risk, and a high willingness to take risk.

Solution:

A is correct. Jacques does not have a particularly high income, his income is unstable, and he has reasonably high outgoings for his mortgage and maintenance payments. His investment time horizon is approximately two to six years given the ages of his children and his desire to support them at university. This finely balanced financial situation and short time horizon suggests a low ability to take risk. In contrast, his expectations for financial market returns and risk tolerance questionnaire answers suggest a high willingness to take risk. The financial adviser may wish to explain to Jacques how finely balanced his financial situation is and suggest that, despite his desire to take more risk, a relatively cautious portfolio might be the most appropriate approach to take.

2.2.2 Return Objectives

A client's return objectives can be stated in a number of ways. Similar to risk objectives, return objectives may be stated on an absolute or a relative basis.

As an example of an absolute objective, the client may want to achieve a particular percentage rate of return, for example, X percent. This could be a nominal rate of return or be expressed in real (inflation-adjusted) terms.

Alternatively, the return objective can be stated on a relative basis, for example, relative to a benchmark return. The benchmark could be an equity market index, such as the S&P 500 or the FTSE 100, or a cash rate of interest such as LIBOR. LIBOR might be appropriate when the investor has some liability that is linked to that rate; for example, a bank that has a particular cost of funding linked to LIBOR. A relative return objective might be stated as, for example, a desire to outperform the benchmark index by one percentage point per year.

Some institutions also set their return objective relative to a peer group or universe of managers; for example, an endowment aiming for a return that is in the top 50 percent of returns of similar institutions, or a private equity mandate aiming for returns in the top quartile among the private equity universe. This objective can be problematic when limited information is known about the investment strategies or the returns calculation methodology being used by peers, and we must bear in mind the impossibility of *all* institutions being "above average." Furthermore, a good benchmark should be investable—that is, able to be replicated by the investor—and a peer benchmark typically does not meet that criterion.

In each case, the return requirement can be stated before or after fees. Care should be taken that the fee basis used is clear and understood by both the manager and client. The return can also be stated on either a pre- or post-tax basis when the investor is required to pay tax. For a taxable investor, the baseline is to state and analyze returns on an after-tax basis.

The return objective could be a required return—that is, the amount the investor needs to earn to meet a particular future goal—such as a certain level of retirement income.

The manager or adviser must ensure that the return objective is realistic. Care should be taken that client and manager are in agreement on whether the return objective is nominal (which is more convenient for measurement purposes) or real (i.e., inflation-adjusted, which usually relates better to the objective). It must be consistent with the client's risk objective (high expected returns are unlikely to be possible without high levels of risk) and also with the current economic and market environment. For example, 15 percent nominal returns might be possible when inflation is 10 percent, but will be unlikely when inflation is 3 percent.

When a client has unrealistic return expectations, the manager or adviser will need to counsel them about what is achievable in the current market environment and within the client's tolerance for risk.

EXAMPLE 4

The Case of Henri Gascon: Return Objectives

Having assessed his risk tolerance, Henri Gascon now begins to discuss his retirement income needs with the financial adviser. He wishes to retire at age 50, which is 20 years from now. His salary meets current and expected future expenditure requirements, but he does not expect to be able to make any additional pension contributions to his fund. Gascon sets aside €100,000 of his savings as an emergency fund to be held in cash. The remaining €900,000 is invested for his retirement.

Gascon estimates that a before-tax amount of €2,000,000 in today's money will be sufficient to fund his retirement income needs. The financial adviser expects inflation to average 2 percent per year over the next 20 years. Pension fund contributions and pension fund returns in France are exempt from tax, but pension fund distributions are taxable upon retirement.

1   Which of the following is closest to the amount of money Gascon will have to accumulate in nominal terms by his retirement date to meet his retirement income objective (i.e., expressed in money of the day in 20 years)?

    A   €900,000.

    B   €2,000,000.

    C   €3,000,000.

2   Which of the following is closest to the annual rate of return that Gascon must earn on his pension portfolio to meet his retirement income objective?

    A   2.0%.

    B   6.2%.

    C   8.1%.

Solution to 1:

C is correct. At 2 percent annual inflation, €2,000,000 in today's money equates to €2,971,895 in 20 years measured in money of the day [$2m \times (1+2\%)^{20}$].

Solution to 2:

B is correct. €900,000 growing at 6.2 percent per year for 20 years will accumulate to €2,997,318, which is just above the required amount. [The solution of 6.2 percent comes from €2,997,318/€900,000 = $(1+X)^{20}$, where X is the required rate of return.]

In the following sections, we analyze five major types of constraints on portfolio selection: liquidity, time horizon, tax concerns, legal and regulatory factors, and unique circumstances.

2.2.3 Liquidity

The IPS should state what the likely requirements are to withdraw funds from the portfolio. Examples for an individual investor would be outlays for covering healthcare payments or tuition fees. For institutions, it could be spending rules and requirements for endowment funds, the existence of claims coming due in the case of property and casualty insurance, or benefit payments for pension funds and life insurance companies.

When the client does have such a requirement, the manager should allocate part of the portfolio to cover the liability. This part of the portfolio will be invested in assets that are liquid—that is, easily converted to cash—and low risk at the point in time the liquidity need is actually present (e.g., a bond maturing at the time when private education expenses will be incurred), so that their value is known with reasonable certainty. For example, the asset allocation in the insurance portfolios of Finnish insurer Sampo (see Exhibit 2) shows a large allocation to fixed-income investments, some of which are either highly liquid or have a short maturity. These investments enable the company, in the case of property and casualty insurance, to pay out on potentially "lumpy" claims of which the timing is unpredictable, and in the case of life insurance, to pay out on life benefits, the size and timing of which are more predictable and can therefore be matched with the maturity profile of the fixed-income portfolio.

Exhibit 2	**Asset Allocation of Sampo**

Panel A: Allocation of Investment Assets, Sampo Group, 31 December 2008

Sampo Group €16,502 Million

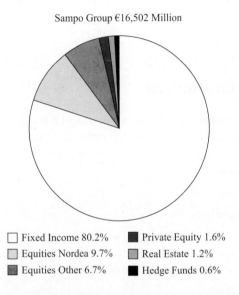

☐ Fixed Income 80.2%   ■ Private Equity 1.6%

☐ Equities Nordea 9.7%   ■ Real Estate 1.2%

■ Equities Other 6.7%   ■ Hedge Funds 0.6%

Panel B: Fixed-Income Investments by Type of Instrument, Sampo Group, 31 December 2008

Sampo Group €13,214 Million

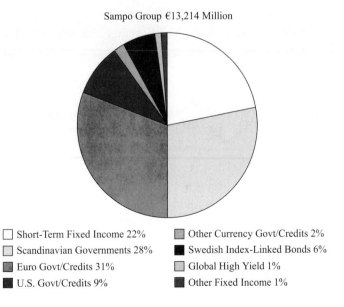

☐ Short-Term Fixed Income 22%   ▨ Other Currency Govt/Credits 2%

☐ Scandinavian Governments 28%   ■ Swedish Index-Linked Bonds 6%

▨ Euro Govt/Credits 31%   ☐ Global High Yield 1%

■ U.S. Govt/Credits 9%   ■ Other Fixed Income 1%

Source: Sampo Group, 2008 Annual Report, pp. 59–61.

2.2.4 *Time Horizon*

The IPS should state the time horizon over which the investor is investing. It may be the period over which the portfolio is accumulating before any assets need to be withdrawn; it could also be the period until the client's circumstances are likely to change. For example, a 50-year old pension plan investor hoping to retire at age 60 has a 10-year horizon. The portfolio may not be liquidated at age 60, but its structure may need to change, for example, as the investor begins to draw an income from the fund.

The time horizon of the investor will affect the nature of investments used in the portfolio. Illiquid or risky investments may be unsuitable for an investor with a short time horizon because the investor may not have enough time to recover from investment losses, for example. Such investments, however, may be suitable for an investor with a longer horizon, especially if the risky investments are expected to have higher returns.

EXAMPLE 5

Investment Time Horizon

1 Frank Johnson is investing for retirement and has a 20-year horizon. He has an average risk tolerance. Which investment is likely to be the *least* suitable for a major allocation in Johnson's portfolio?

   A Listed equities.

   B Private equity.

   C U.S. Treasury bills.

2 Al Smith has to pay a large tax bill in six months and wants to invest the money in the meantime. Which investment is likely to be the *least* suitable for a major allocation in Smith's portfolio?

   A Listed equities.

   B Private equity.

   C U.S. Treasury bills.

Solution to 1:

C is correct. With a 20-year horizon and average risk tolerance, Johnson can accept the additional risk of listed equities and private equity compared with U.S. Treasury bills.

Solution to 2:

B is correct. Private equity is risky, has no public market, and is the least liquid among the assets mentioned.

2.2.5 *Tax Concerns*

Tax status varies among investors. Some investors will be subject to taxation on investment returns and some will not. For example, in many countries returns to pension funds are exempt from tax. Some investors will face various rates of tax on income (dividends and interest payments) than they do on capital gains (associated with increases in asset prices). Typically, when there is a differential, income is taxed more highly than gains. Gains may be subject to a lower rate of tax or part or all of the gain may be exempt from taxation. Furthermore, income may be taxed as it is earned, whereas gains may be taxed when they are realized. Hence, in such cases there is a time value of money benefit in the deferment of taxation of gains relative to income.

In many cases, the portfolio should reflect the tax status of the client. For example, a taxable investor may wish to hold a portfolio that emphasizes capital gains and receives little income. A taxable investor based in the United States is also likely to consider including U.S. municipal bonds ("munis") in his or her portfolio because interest income from munis, unlike from treasuries and corporate bonds, is exempt from taxes. A tax-exempt investor, such as a pension fund, will be relatively indifferent to the form of returns.

2.2.6 *Legal and Regulatory Factors*

The IPS should state any legal and regulatory restrictions that constrain how the portfolio is invested.

In some countries, such institutional investors as pension funds are subject to restrictions on the composition of the portfolio. For example, there may be a limit on the proportion of equities or other risky assets in the portfolio, or on the proportion of the portfolio that may be invested overseas. The United States has no limits on pension fund asset allocation but some countries do, examples of which are shown in Exhibit 3. Pension funds also often face restrictions on the percentage of assets that can be invested in securities issued by the plan sponsor, so called **self-investment limits**.

Exhibit 3	Examples of Pension Fund Investment Restrictions				
Country	**Listed Equity**	**Real Estate**	**Government Bonds**	**Corporate Bonds**	**Foreign Assets**
Switzerland	50%	50%	No limits	No limits	30%
Russia	65%	Not allowed	No limits	80%	10%
Japan	No limits	Not permitted	No limits	No limits	No limits
India	Minimum 25 percent in central government bonds; minimum 15 percent in state government bonds; minimum 30 percent invested in bonds of public sector enterprises				

Source: OECD "Survey of Investment Regulations of Pension Funds," July 2008.

When an individual has access to material nonpublic information about a particular security, this situation may also form a constraint. For example, the directors of a public company may need to refrain from trading the company's stock at certain points of the year before financial results are published. The IPS should note this constraint so that the portfolio manager does not inadvertently trade the stock on the client's behalf.

2.2.7 *Unique Circumstances*

This section of the IPS should cover any other aspect of the client's circumstances that is likely to have a material impact on the composition of the portfolio. A client may have considerations derived from his or her religion or ethical values that could constrain investment choices. For instance, a Muslim investor seeking compliance with Shari'a (the Islamic law) will avoid investing in businesses and financial instruments inconsistent with Shari'a, such as casinos and bonds, because Shari'a prohibits gambling and lending money on interest. Similarly, a Christian investor may wish to avoid investments that he or she believes are inconsistent with their faith.

Whether rooted in religious beliefs or not, a client may have personal objections to certain products (e.g., pornography, weapons, tobacco, gambling) or practices (e.g., environmental impact of business activities, human impact of government policies, labour standards), which could lead to the exclusion of certain companies, countries, or types of securities (e.g., interest-bearing debt) from the investable universe as well as the client's benchmark. Such considerations are often referred to as ESG (environmental, social, governance), and investing in accordance with such considerations is referred to as SRI (socially responsible investing).

EXAMPLE 6

Ethical Preferences

The £3 billion F&C Stewardship Growth Fund is designed for investors who wish to have ethical and environmental principles applied to the selection of their investments. The fund's managers apply both positive (characteristics to be emphasized in the portfolio) and negative (characteristics to be avoided in the portfolio) screening criteria:

Positive Criteria

- Supplies the basic necessities of life (e.g., healthy food, housing, clothing, water, energy, communication, healthcare, public transport, safety, personal finance, education)
- Offers product choices for ethical and sustainable lifestyles (e.g. fair trade, organic)
- Improves quality of life through the responsible use of new technologies
- Shows good environmental management
- Actively addresses climate change (e.g., renewable energy, energy efficiency)
- Promotes and protects human rights
- Supports good employment practices
- Provides a positive impact on local communities
- Maintains good relations with customers and suppliers
- Applies effective anti-corruption controls
- Uses transparent communication

Negative Criteria

- Tobacco production
- Alcohol production
- Gambling
- Pornography or violent material
- Manufacture and sale of weapons
- Unnecessary exploitation of animals
- Nuclear power generation
- Poor environmental practices
- Human rights abuses
- Poor relations with employees, customers or suppliers

Source: Excerpted from F&C documents; www.fandc.com/new/Advisor/Default.aspx?ID=79620.

When the portfolio represents only part of the client's total wealth, there may be aspects or portions of wealth not under the control of the manager that have implications for the portfolio. For example, an employee of a public company whose labour income and retirement income provision are reliant on that company and who may have substantial investment exposure to the company through employee share options and stock holdings, may decide that his or her portfolio should not invest additional amounts in that stock. An entrepreneur may be reluctant to see his or her portfolio invested in the shares of competing businesses or in any business that has risk exposures aligned with his or her entrepreneurial venture.

A client's income may rely on a particular industry or asset class. Appropriate diversification requires that industry or asset class to be de-emphasized in the client's investments. For example, a stockbroker should consider having a relatively low weighting in equities, as his skills and thus income-generating ability are worth less when equities do not perform well. Employees should similarly be wary of having concentrated share positions in the equity of the company they work for. If the employer encounters difficulties, not only may the employee lose his or her job, but their investment portfolio could also suffer a significant loss of value.

2.3 Gathering Client Information

As noted above, it is important for portfolio managers and investment advisers to know their clients. For example, Dutch securities industry practice requires financial intermediaries to undertake substantial fact finding. This is required not only in the case of full service wealth management or in the context of an IPS, but also in "lighter" forms of financial intermediation, such as advisory relationships (in which clients make investment decisions after consultation with their investment adviser or broker) or execution-only relationships (in which the client makes his investment decisions independently).

An exercise in fact finding about the customer should take place at the beginning of the client relationship. This will involve gathering information about the client's circumstances as well as discussing the client's objectives and requirements.

Important data to gather from a client should cover family and employment situation as well as financial information. If the client is an individual, it may also be necessary to know about the situation and requirements of the client's spouse or other family members. The health of the client and his or her dependents is also relevant information. In an institutional relationship, it will be important to know about key stakeholders in the organization and what their perspective and requirements are. Information gathering may be done in an informal way or may involve structured interviews or questionnaires or analysis of data. Many advisers will capture data electronically and use special systems that record data and produce customized reports.

Good record keeping is very important, and may be crucial in a case in which any aspect of the client relationship comes into dispute at a later stage.

EXAMPLE 7

Henri Gascon: Description of Constraints

Henri Gascon continues to discuss his investment requirements with the financial adviser. The financial adviser begins to draft the constraints section of the IPS.

Gascon expects that he will continue to work for the oil company and that his relatively high income will continue for the foreseeable future. Gascon and his wife do not plan to have any additional children, but expect that their son will go to a university at age 18. They expect that their son's education costs can be met out of their salary income.

Gascon's emergency reserve of €100,000 is considered to be sufficient as a reserve for unforeseen expenditures and emergencies. His retirement savings of €900,000 has been contributed to his defined-contribution pension plan account to fund his retirement. Under French regulation, pension fund contributions are paid from gross income (i.e., income prior to deduction of tax) and pension fund returns are exempt from tax, but pension payments from a fund to retirees are taxed as income to the retiree.

With respect to Gascon's retirement savings portfolio, refer back to Example 2 as needed and address the following:

1 As concerns liquidity,

   A a maximum of 50 percent of the portfolio should be invested in liquid assets.

   B the portfolio should be invested entirely in liquid assets because of high spending needs.

   C the portfolio has no need for liquidity because there are no short-term spending requirements.

2 The investment time horizon is *closest* to:

   A 5 years.

   B 20 years.

   C 40 years.

3 As concerns taxation, the portfolio:

   A should emphasize capital gains because income is taxable.

   B should emphasize income because capital gains are taxable.

   C is tax exempt and thus indifferent between income and capital gains.

4 The principle legal and regulatory factors applying to the portfolio are:

   A U.S. Securities laws.

   B European banking laws.

   C French pension fund regulations.

5 As concerns unique needs, the portfolio should:

   A have a high weighting in oil and other commodity stocks.

   B be invested only in responsible and sustainable investments.

   C not have significant exposure to oil and other commodity stocks.

Solution to 1:

C is correct. The assets are for retirement use, which is 20 years away. Any short-term spending needs will be met from other assets or income.

Solution to 2:

B is correct. The relevant time horizon is to the retirement date, which is 20 years away. The assets may not be liquidated at that point, but a restructuring of the portfolio is to be expected as Gascon starts to draw an income from it.

Solution to 3:

C is correct. Because no tax is paid in the pension fund, it does not matter whether returns come in the form of income or capital gains.

Solution to 4:

C is correct. The management of the portfolio will have to comply with any rules relating the French pension funds.

Solution to 5:

C is correct. Gascon's human capital (i.e., future labour income) is affected by the prospects of the oil industry. If his portfolio has significant exposure to oil stocks, he would be increasing a risk exposure he already has.

Example 8, the final one based on Henri Gascon, shows how the information obtained from the fact-finding exercises might be incorporated into the objectives and constraints section of an IPS.

EXAMPLE 8

Henri Gascon: Outline of an IPS

Following is a simplified excerpt from the IPS the adviser prepares for Henri Gascon, covering objectives and constraints.

Risk Objectives:

- The portfolio may take on relatively high amounts of risk in seeking to meet the return requirements. With a 20-year time horizon and significant assets and income, the client has an above average ability to take risk. The client is a knowledgeable investor, with an above average willingness to take risk. Hence, the client's risk tolerance is above average, explaining the above portfolio risk objective.

- The portfolio should be well diversified with respect to asset classes and concentration of positions within an asset class. Although the client has above average risk tolerance, his investment assets should be diversified to control the risk of catastrophic loss.

Return Objectives:

The portfolio's long-term return requirement is 6.2 percent per year, in nominal terms and net of fees, to meet the client's retirement income goal.

Constraints:

- *Liquidity*: The portfolio consists of pension fund assets and there is no need for liquidity in the short to medium term.

- *Time Horizon*: The portfolio will be invested with a 20-year time horizon. The client intends to retire in 20 years, at which time an income will be drawn from the portfolio.

- *Tax Status*: Under French law, contributions to the fund are made gross of tax and returns in the fund are tax-free. Hence, the client is indifferent between income and capital gains in the fund.

- *Legal and Regulatory Factors*: The management of the portfolio must comply with French pension fund regulations.

- *Unique Needs*: The client is an executive in the oil industry. The portfolio should strive to minimize additional exposures to oil and related stocks.

3　PORTFOLIO CONSTRUCTION

Once the IPS has been compiled, the investment manager can construct a suitable portfolio. Strategic asset allocation is a traditional focus of the first steps in portfolio construction. The strategic asset allocation is stated in terms of percent allocations to asset classes. An **asset class** is a category of assets that have similar characteristics, attributes, and risk–return relationships. The **strategic asset allocation** (SAA) is the set of exposures to IPS-permissible asset classes that is expected to achieve the client's long-term objectives given the client's investment constraints.

The focus on the SAA is the result of a number of important investment principles. One principle is that a portfolio's systematic risk accounts for most of its change in value over the long term. **Systematic risk** is risk related to the economic system (e.g., risk related to business cycle) that cannot be eliminated by holding a diversified portfolio. This risk is different from the particular risks of individual securities, which may be avoided by holding other securities with offsetting risks. A second principle is that the returns to groups of similar assets (e.g., long-term debt claims) predictably reflect exposures to certain sets of systematic factors (e.g., for the debt claims, unexpected changes in the inflation rate). Thus, the SAA is a means of providing the investor with exposure to the systematic risks of asset classes in proportions that meet the risk and return objectives.

The process of formulating a strategic asset allocation is based on the IPS, already discussed, and capital market expectations, introduced in Section 3.1. How to make the strategic asset allocation operational with a rebalancing policy and a translation into actual investment portfolios will be described in Section 3.3. Section 3.4 lists some alternatives to the approach chosen and describes some portfolio construction techniques.

3.1　Capital Market Expectations

Capital market expectations are the investor's expectations concerning the risk and return prospects of asset classes, however broadly or narrowly the investor defines those asset classes.[4] When associated with the client's investment objectives, the result is the strategic asset allocation that is expected to allow the client to achieve his or her investment objectives (at least under normal capital market conditions).

Traditionally, capital market expectations are quantified in terms of asset class expected returns, standard deviation of returns, and correlations among pairs of asset classes. Formally, the expected return of an asset class consists of the risk-free rate and one or more risk premium(s) associated with the asset class. Expected returns are in practice developed in a variety of ways, including the use of historical estimates, economic analysis, and various kinds of valuation models. Standard deviations and correlation estimates are frequently based on historical data.

3.2　The Strategic Asset Allocation

Traditionally, investors have distinguished cash, equities, bonds, and real estate as the major asset classes. In recent years, this list has been expanded with private equity, hedge funds, and commodities. In addition, such assets as art and intellectual property rights may be considered asset classes for those investors prepared to take a more

---

4 For an in-depth discussion of this topic see Calverley, Meder, Singer, and Staub (2007).

innovative approach and to accept some illiquidity. Combining such new asset classes as well as hedge funds and private equity under the header "alternative investments" has become accepted practice.

As the strategic asset allocation is built up by asset classes, the decision about how to define those asset classes is an important one. Defining the asset classes also determines the extent to which the investor controls the risk and return characteristics of the eventual investment portfolio. For example, separating bonds into government bonds and corporate bonds, and then further separating corporate bonds into investment grade and non-investment grade (high yield) and government bonds into domestic and foreign government bonds, creates four bond categories for which risk–return expectations can be expressed and correlations with other asset classes (and, in an asset–liability management context, with the liabilities) can be estimated. An asset allocator who wants to explicitly consider the risk–return characteristics of those bond categories in the strategic asset allocation may choose to treat them as distinct asset classes. Similarly, in equities some investors distinguish between emerging market and developed market equities, between domestic and international equities, or between large-cap and small-cap equities. In some regulatory environments for institutional investors, asset class definitions are mandatory, thereby forcing asset allocators to articulate risk–return expectations (and apply risk management) on the asset classes specified.

When defining asset classes, a number of criteria apply. Intuitively, an asset class should contain relatively homogeneous assets while providing diversification relative to other asset classes. In statistical terms, risk and return expectations should be similar and paired correlations of assets should be relatively high within an asset class but should be lower versus assets in other asset classes.[5] Also, the asset classes, while being mutually exclusive, should add up to a sufficient approximation of the relevant investable universe. Applying these criteria ensures that the strategic asset allocation process has considered all available investment alternatives.

EXAMPLE 9

Specifying Asset Classes

The strategic asset allocations of many institutional investors make a distinction between domestic equities and international equities, or between developed market equities and emerging market equities. Often, equities are separated into different market capitalization brackets, resulting, for example, in an asset class such as domestic small-cap equity.

The correlation matrix in Exhibit 4 shows the paired correlations between different equity asset classes and other asset classes. These correlations are measured over 10 years of monthly returns through February 2009. In addition, the exhibit shows the annualized volatility of monthly returns.

---

5 A technically precise characterization other than one in terms of pairwise correlations is given by Kritzman (1999).

Exhibit 4		Asset Class Correlation Matrix										
	A	**B**	**C**	**D**	**E**	**F**	**G**	**H**	**I**	**J**	**K**	**L**
A. MSCI Europe	1.00	0.77	0.95	0.97	0.88	0.20	0.59	−0.08	−0.35	0.10	−0.29	0.01
B. MSCI Emerging Markets	0.77	1.00	0.82	0.83	0.76	0.35	0.63	0.18	−.25	0.22	−0.20	0.11
C. MSCI World	0.95	0.82	1.00	0.96	0.97	0.25	0.69	0.00	−0.31	0.18	−0.27	0.06
D. MSCI EAFE	0.97	0.83	0.96	1.00	0.88	0.27	0.65	−0.01	−0.34	0.15	−0.29	0.05
E. MSCI U.S.	0.88	0.76	0.97	0.88	1.00	0.20	0.70	−0.01	−0.27	0.18	−0.24	0.06
F. Commodities	0.20	0.35	0.25	0.27	0.20	1.00	0.27	0.25	−0.04	0.14	−0.07	0.14
G. Real Estate	0.59	0.63	0.69	0.65	0.70	0.27	1.00	0.18	−0.01	0.40	0.02	0.32
H. Gold	−0.08	0.18	0.00	−0.01	−0.01	0.25	0.18	1.00	0.21	0.30	0.12	0.14
I. U.S. Treasuries	−0.35	−0.25	−0.31	−0.34	−0.27	−0.04	−0.01	0.21	1.00	0.67	0.78	0.55
J. U.S. Investment Grade	0.10	0.22	0.18	0.15	0.18	0.14	0.40	0.30	0.67	1.00	0.61	0.79
K. European Government Bonds	−0.29	−0.20	−0.27	−0.29	−0.24	−0.07	0.02	0.12	0.78	0.61	1.00	0.83
L. European Investment Grade Corporates	0.01	0.11	0.06	0.05	0.06	0.14	0.32	0.14	0.55	0.79	0.83	1.00
Annualized Volatility	16.6%	20.7%	15.0%	15.4%	15.7%	25.4%	18.9%	16.6%	5.0%	6.0%	3.1%	3.2%

Data based on monthly returns in local currencies from January 1999 to February 2009. Commodities, Real Estate, and Gold in USD. *Source*: MSCI, NAREIT, Barclays Capital, Standard and Poor's.

Based only on the information given, address the following:

1 Contrast the correlations between equity asset classes with the correlations between equity asset classes and European government bonds.

2 Which equity asset class is most sharply distinguished from MSCI Europe?

Solution to 1:

The matrix reveals very strong correlation between the equity asset classes (MSCI Europe, MSCI Emerging Markets, MSCI EAFE, and MSCI U.S.). For example, the correlation between European equities and U.S. equities is 0.88. The correlation of equities with bonds, however, is much lower. For example, both asset classes have a similar negative correlation with European government bonds (−0.29 and −0.24, respectively). It is worth noting, however, that correlations can vary through time, and the values shown may be specific to the sample period used. In this particular case, extreme market conditions in 2008 resulted in negative correlations between equities and bonds.

Solution to 2:

Correlations of emerging market equities with other categories of equities are 0.76 or higher, whereas all groupings of equities share similar correlations with commodities (between 0.20 and 0.35), gold (between −0.08 and 0.18), and real estate (between 0.59 and 0.70). These high-paired correlations between equity asset classes, combined with the similarity of the correlations between any of these asset classes and non-equity asset classes, suggests that defining the equity asset class more narrowly has limited added value in providing diversification. The case for treatment as a separate asset class can best be made for emerging markets stocks, which usually have the lowest correlation of all equity asset classes with other asset classes and have a volatility of returns far in excess of the other equity groupings.

Using correlation as a metric, Example 9 tends to indicate that only emerging markets were well differentiated from European equities. So, why do investors still often subdivide equities? Apart from any regulatory reasons, one explanation might be that this decomposition into smaller asset classes corresponds to the way the asset allocation is structured in portfolios. Many investment managers have expertise exclusively in specific areas of the market, such as emerging market equities, U.S. small-cap equity, or international investment-grade credit. Bringing the asset class definitions of the asset allocation in line with investment products actually available in the market may simplify matters from an organizational perspective.

The risk–return profile of the strategic asset allocation depends on the expected returns and risks of the individual asset classes, as well as the correlation between those asset classes. In general, adding assets classes with low correlation improves the risk–return trade-off (more return for similar risk), as long as the stand-alone risk of such asset classes does not exceed its diversification effect. Typically, the strategic asset allocation for risk-averse investors will have a large weight in government bonds and cash, whereas those with more willingness and ability to take risk will have more of their assets in risky asset classes, such as equities and many types of alternative investments.

EXAMPLE 10

Objective of a Strategic Asset Allocation

ABP is a pension fund with approximately 2.6 million members. It manages a defined-benefit scheme for civil servants in the Netherlands, and its goal is to pay out a "real" pension (i.e., one that will increase through time in line with consumer price inflation). With €173 billion under management at the end of 2008, ABP is one of the world's largest pension funds. It decides on its asset allocation in an investment plan that is reviewed every three years. The asset class terminology used by ABP is distinctive.[6] Exhibit 5 shows ABP's SAA under the plan for 2007–2009.

Exhibit 5	Strategic Asset Allocation for ABP
Real assets	
Equities, developed countries	27%
Equities, emerging markets	5
Convertible bonds	2
	(continued)

---

6 ABP defines an asset class category called "real assets," which contains asset classes (not fixed-income securities) that are expected to perform well in times of inflation, but considered a major risk. The use of the term "real assets" differs from the use elsewhere in the CFA curriculum. The term "innovation" refers to alternative investments that are relatively new to ABP's portfolio. An example of such an investment is music rights. "Infrastructure" is investments in non-public equity of infrastructure projects such as toll roads. Inflation-linked bonds are fixed-income securities of which the payout depends on a measure of inflation in the issuing country. Some major issuers of such bonds are the United States, the United Kingdom, and France.

Exhibit 5	(Continued)	
Real assets		
Private Equity	5	
Hedge Funds	5	
Commodities	3	
Real estate	9	
Infrastructure	2	
Innovation	2	
Total real assets	*60%*	
Fixed income securities		
Inflation-linked bonds	7%	
Government bonds	10	
Corporate bonds	23	
Total fixed income securities	*40%*	
Total	100%	

1   Discuss the way the asset classes have been defined.

2   How does the asset allocation relate to the pension fund's ambition to pay out a real (i.e., inflation-adjusted) pension?

Solution to 1:

The asset allocation is fairly narrow in its definition of alternative asset classes, whereas the traditional asset classes, such as bonds and equities, are defined quite broadly. It appears that allocations within the broader groupings of government bonds, credits, and equities (developed and emerging) are not made on the strategic level.

Solution to 2:

This asset allocation seems to reflect an attempt to control the risk of inflation: only 33 percent of the strategic asset allocation is in nominal bonds, whereas 7 percent is in inflation-linked bonds and 60 percent in "real" assets (assets believed to have a positive correlation with inflation and, therefore, hedging inflation to some degree).

A strategic asset allocation results from combining the constraints and objectives articulated in the IPS and long-term capital market expectations regarding the asset classes. The strategic asset allocation or policy portfolio will subsequently be implemented into real portfolios. Exhibit 6 illustrates conceptually how investment objectives and constraints and long-term capital market expectations combine into a policy portfolio.

| Exhibit 6 | Strategic Asset Allocation Process |

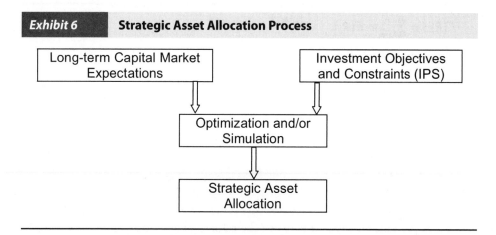

In some frameworks used in practice, the asset allocation is an integral part of the investment policy statement. This presentation, however, keeps the asset allocation separate from the investment policy statement because clients' investment objectives and constraints qualitatively differ in nature from capital market expectations, thus requiring different types of analysis, different sources of information, and different review cycles.

How will capital market expectations and investment objectives and constraints eventually translate into a strategic asset allocation? In general, investors choosing from a range of asset allocations with similar returns would prefer those with lower risk. Choosing from allocations with similar levels of risk, investors would prefer those with the highest return. Formally, investors' risk and return objectives can be described as a utility function, in which utility increases with higher expected returns and lower risk. The assumption that expected utility is increasing in expected return and decreasing in variance of return could yield an expected utility equation, such as that shown in Equation 1.[7]

$$U_p = E\left(R_p\right) - \lambda \sigma_p^2 \qquad (1)$$

where

U_p = the investor's expected utility from the portfolio
$E(R_p)$ = the expected return of the portfolio
σ_p = the standard deviation of returns of the portfolio
λ = a measure of the investor's risk aversion

This utility function expresses a positive relationship between utility and expected portfolio return (i.e., higher expected return increases utility, all else equal) and a negative relationship between utility and volatility of portfolio return as measured by the variance of portfolio returns. The stronger the negative relationship, the greater the investor's risk aversion. The portfolio is understood to represent a particular asset allocation. The asset allocation providing the highest expected utility is the one that is optimal for the investor given his or her risk aversion.

For different values of U_p, a line can be plotted that links those combinations of risk and expected return that produces that level of utility: an indifference curve. An investor would attain equal utility from all risk/return combinations on that curve.

Capital market expectations, specified in asset classes' expected returns, standard deviations of return, and correlations, translate into an efficient frontier of portfolios. A multi-asset class portfolio's expected return is given by

---

7 Sharpe, Chen, Pinto, and McLeavey (2007).

$$E(R_P) = \sum_{i=1}^{n} w_i E(R_i) \qquad \text{(2)}$$

where w_i equals the weight of asset class i in the portfolio, and its risk is given by

$$\sigma_p = \sqrt{\sum_{i=1}^{n}\sum_{j=1}^{n} w_{p,i} w_{p,j} \text{Cov}(R_i, R_j)} \qquad \text{(3)}$$

The covariance between the returns on asset classes i and j is given by the product of the correlation between the two asset classes and their standard deviations of return:

$$\text{Cov}(R_i, R_j) = \rho_{i,j} \sigma_i \sigma_j \qquad \text{(4)}$$

where

$\text{Cov}(R_i, R_j)$ = the covariance between the return of asset classes i and j

$\rho_{i,j}$ = the correlation between the returns of asset classes i and j

The resulting portfolios can be represented as a scatter of dots in a chart depicting their risk and expected return. As a portfolio's risk is a positive function of the risk of its assets and the correlations among them, a portfolio consisting of lowly correlated risky assets has lower risk than one with similarly risky assets with high correlation. It is therefore possible to construct different portfolios with equal expected returns but with different levels of risk. The line that connects those portfolios with the minimal risk for each level of expected return (above that of the minimum variance portfolio) is the efficient frontier. Clearly, the efficient frontier will move "upward" as more lowly correlated assets with sufficient expected return are added to the mix because it lowers the risk in the portfolios. Similarly, when return expectations increase for asset classes while volatility and correlation assumptions remain unchanged, the efficient frontier will move upward because each portfolio is able to generate higher returns for the same level of risk.

Both the efficient frontier and a range of indifference curves can be plotted in the risk–return space. In Exhibit 7, the dark curves that are concave from below represent efficient frontiers associated with different assumed expected returns. The lighter colored curves are indifference curves. The point where the efficient frontier intersects with the indifference curve with the highest utility attainable (i.e., the point of tangency) represents the optimal asset allocation for the client/investor. In Exhibit 7, efficient frontier 1 has a point of tangency with indifference curve 1. Higher levels of utility, such as those associated with indifference curve 0, can apparently not be reached with the assets underlying the efficient frontier. It is clear that when capital market expectations change, this change moves the efficient frontier away from its original location. In the chart, this movement is illustrated by efficient frontier 2, which incorporates different capital market expectations. This new efficient frontier has a point of tangency with indifference curve 2, which is associated with a lower level of expected utility. Because the point of tangency represents the strategic asset allocation, it implies the asset allocation should be adjusted. Similarly, should investment objectives or constraints change, the indifference curves will change their shape and location. This change will again move the point of tangency, and hence change the asset allocation.

Exhibit 7	Strategic Asset Allocation Efficient Frontier

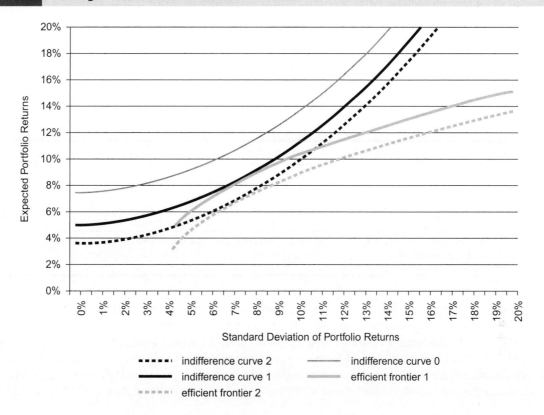

This framework describes how investor objectives and capital market expectations should theoretically be reconciled. It will, however, not be the exact procedure that in practice will be followed. First, an IPS does not necessarily translate the client's investment objectives and constraint into a utility function. Rather, an IPS gives threshold levels for risk and expected return, combined with a number of additional constraints that cannot be captured in this model. Second, the model illustrated is a single-period model, whereas in practice, the constraints from the IPS will make it more appropriate to use multi-period models. Multi-period problems can be more effectively addressed using simulation.

EXAMPLE 11

Approaching a SAA for a Private Investor

Rainer Gottschalk recently sold his local home construction company in the south of Germany to a large homebuilder with a nationwide reach. Upon selling his company, he accepted a job as regional manager for that nationwide homebuilder. He is now considering his and his family's financial future. He looks forward to his new job, where he likes his new role, and which provides him with income to fulfill his family's short-term and medium-term liquidity needs. He feels strongly that he should not invest the proceeds of the sale of his company in real estate because his income already depends on the state of the real estate market. He consults a financial adviser from his bank about how to invest his money to retire in good wealth in 20 years.

The IPS they develop suggests a return objective of 6 percent, with a standard deviation of 12 percent. The bank's asset management division provides Gottschalk and his adviser with the following data (Exhibit 8) on market expectations.

Exhibit 8	Risk, Return, and Correlation Estimates					

	Expected Return (%)	Standard Deviation (%)	Correlation Matrix		
			European Equities	Emerging Mkt. Equities	European Govt. Bonds
European equities	8.40	24	1.00	0.86	−0.07
Emerging market equities	9.20	28	0.86	1.00	−0.07
European government bonds	3.50	7	−0.07	−0.07	1.00

Note: Standard deviation and correlation calculated over the period March 1999–December 2008. All data in unhedged euros.
Sources: Barclay's, MSCI, Bloomberg.

To illustrate the possibilities, the adviser presents Gottschalk with the following plot (Exhibit 9), in which the points forming the shaded curve outline the risk–return characteristics of the portfolios that can be constructed out of the three assets. An imaginary line linking the points with the lowest standard deviation for each attainable level of return would be the efficient frontier. The two straight lines show the risk and return objectives. Gottschalk should aim for portfolios that offer an expected return of at least 6 percent (the straight horizontal line or above) and a standard deviation of return of 12 percent or lower (the straight vertical line to the left).

| Exhibit 9 | Efficient Frontier |

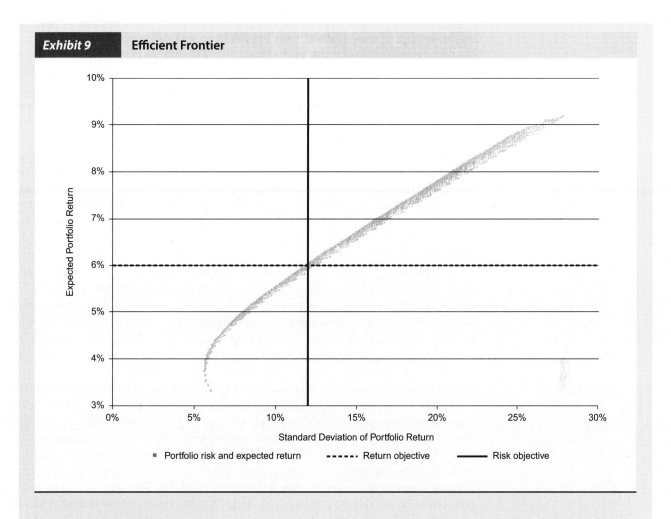

Exhibit 9 shows that a portfolio on the efficient frontier satisfies the two objectives. This portfolio consists of 28 percent European stocks, 20 percent emerging market equities, and 52 percent government bonds and gives a 6 percent expected return and a 12 percent standard deviation. This combination is what the adviser recommends to Gottschalk as his strategic asset allocation.

3.3 Steps Toward an Actual Portfolio

The strategic asset allocation in itself does not yet represent an actual investment portfolio. It is the first step in implementing an investment strategy. For quantitatively oriented portfolio managers, the next step is often risk budgeting.

As used in this reading, **risk budgeting** is the process of deciding on the amount of risk to assume in a portfolio (the overall risk budget), and subdividing that risk over the sources of investment return (e.g., strategic asset allocation, tactical asset allocation, and security selection).[8] Because the decision about the amount of risk to be taken is made in constructing the IPS, at this stage we are concerned about the subdivision of that risk.

Apart from the exposures to systematic risk factors specified in the strategic asset allocation, the returns of an investment strategy depend on two other sources: tactical asset allocation and security selection. **Tactical asset allocation** is the decision to deliberately deviate from the policy exposures to systematic risk factors (i.e., the

---

8 Some writers use risk budgeting to refer to allocating an amount or budget of tracking risk to active portfolio managers on a given asset class. See Waring, Whitney, Pirone, Castille (2000).

policy weights of asset classes) with the intent to add value based on forecasts of the near-term returns of those asset classes. For instance, an investor may decide to temporarily invest more of the portfolio in equities than the SAA prescribes if the investor anticipates that equities will deliver a higher return over the short term than other asset classes. **Security selection** is an attempt to generate higher returns than the asset class benchmark by selecting securities with a higher expected return. For example, an investment manager may decide to add more IBM stock in his portfolio than the weight in his equity benchmark if he expects this stock to do better than the benchmark. To fund this purchase, he may sell another stock expected to do worse than either the benchmark or IBM. Obviously, deciding to deviate from policy weights or to select securities aiming to beat the benchmark creates additional uncertainty about returns. This risk is over and above the risk inherent in the policy portfolio. Hence, an investment policy should set risk limits and desired payoffs for each of these three activities.

Risk budgeting implies that the portfolio manager has to choose, for every asset class, whether to deploy security selection as a return generator. This choice is generally referred to as the choice between active or passive management. Contrary to strategic asset allocation, where exposures to sources of systematic risk are selected and sized, security selection is not rewarded with a long-run payoff to risk. Security selection is a zero-sum game: All investors in an asset class are competing with each to identify a typically limited number of assets that are misvalued. In total, the gross returns of all market participants average out to the market return (the reward for taking systematic risk). This implies that the average active investor will match the market return, and that one investor's gain versus the market return is the other investor's loss versus the market return. However, because active managers tend to trade more and have to pay people (including themselves) to generate investment ideas or information leading to such ideas, the average active manager will underperform the market, net of costs. This does not imply, however, that there are no skillful investment managers who, with some consistency, beat their benchmarks. Neither does it imply that all passive managers will be able to match the benchmark. The higher the turnover of an index, the more trading costs a passive manager will incur, making the task of effectively mimicking an index more difficult.

The likelihood of adding a significant amount of value from security selection depends on the skills of the manager and the informational efficiency of the market for the asset class his skill relates to. The more efficient an asset class or a subset of that asset class (such as a regional stock, bond, or real estate market or a size category within the stock market), the more skillful an asset manager has to be to add value. Broadly speaking, an efficient market is a market in which prices, on average, very quickly reflect newly available information. That requires a sizeable participation of mean–variance optimizing investors, acting on rational expectations, using the same or similar pricing models, and having equal opportunities to access relevant information. Clearly, the market for U.S. large-capitalization equities would be quite efficient. By contrast, some regional bond and equity markets do not have the technical and regulatory systems for information dissemination that are sufficient to serve all investors on a timely basis. Skilled managers should be able to exploit the resulting inefficiencies.

Sometimes, however, the choice between active and passive management is actually made implicitly when the asset class is included in the asset allocation. The markets for some assets—such as those for non-listed real estate, art, and infrastructure assets—are so illiquid that it is very difficult to buy a diversified exposure. As a result, there is no way of taking exposure to the asset class without engaging in security selection.

As the portfolio is constructed and its value changes with the returns of the asset classes and securities in which it is invested, the weights of the asset classes will gradually deviate from the policy weights in the strategic asset allocation. This process is referred to as drift. Periodically, or when a certain threshold deviation from the policy weight (the bandwidth) has been breached, the portfolio should be rebalanced back to the policy weights. The set of rules that guide the process of restoring the portfolio's original exposures to systematic risk factors is known as the **rebalancing policy**. Even absent a formal risk budget, formulating a rebalancing policy is an important element of risk management.

EXAMPLE 12

Strategic Asset Allocation for a European charity

A European charity has an asset allocation at the beginning of the year consisting of the asset classes and weights shown in Exhibit 10:

Exhibit 10   Asset Allocation of a European Charity (Beginning of Year)

Asset Class	Policy Weight	Corridor (+/–)	Upper Limit	Lower Limit
European equities	30.0%	2.0%	32.0%	28.0%
International equities	15.0	2.0	17.0	13.0
European government bonds	20.0	2.0	22.0	18.0
Corporate bonds	20.0	2.0	22.0	18.0
Cash and money market instruments	15.0	2.0	17.0	13.0
Total	100.0			

As Exhibit 10 reveals, the charity has a policy that the asset class weights cannot deviate from the policy weights by more than 2 percent (the corridor). The resulting upper and lower limits for the asset class weights are shown in the rightmost columns of the table. There are two reasons for asset class actual weights to deviate from policy weights: by deliberate choice (tactical asset allocation or market timing) and as a result of divergence of the returns of the different asset classes (drift). In this example, the asset class weights start the year exactly in line with policy weights.

After half a year, the investment portfolio is as shown in Exhibit 11.

Exhibit 11   Asset Allocation for a European Charity (6 Months Later)

Asset Class	Policy Weight	Corridor (+/–)	Upper Limit	Lower Limit	Period Return	Ending Weight
European equities	30.0%	2.0%	32.0%	28.0%	15.0%	32.4%
International equities	15.0	2.0	17.0	13.0	10.0	15.5
European government bonds	20.0	2.0	22.0	18.0	0.5	18.9
Corporate bonds	20.0	2.0	22.0	18.0	1.5	19.1
Cash and money market instruments	15.0	2.0	17.0	13.0	1.0	14.2
Total	100.0%				6.6%	100.0%

1   Discuss the returns of the portfolio and comment on the main asset weight changes.

Solution to 1:

The investment portfolio generated a return calculated on beginning (policy) weights of 6.55 percent or 6.6 percent (= 0.30 × 15% + 0.15 × 10% + 0.20 × 0.5% + 0.20 × 1.5% + 0.15 × 1.0%), mainly driven by a strong equity market. Bond returns were more subdued, leading to considerable drift in asset class weights. In particular, the European equity weight breached the upper limit of its allowed actual weight.

The investment committee decides against reducing European equities back to policy weight and adding to the fixed income and cash investments toward policy weights. Although this rebalancing would be prudent, the committee decides to engage in tactical asset allocation based on the view that this market will continue to be strong over the course of the year. It decides to just bring European equities back to within its bandwidth (a 32 percent portfolio weight) and add the proceeds to cash. Exhibit 12 shows the outcome after another half year.

Exhibit 12   Asset Allocation for a European Charity (an Additional 6 Months Later)

Asset Class	Policy Weight	Starting Weight	Corridor (+/−)	Upper Limit	Lower Limit	Period Return	Ending Weight
European equities	30.0%	32.0%	2.0%	32.0%	28.0%	−9.0%	29.7%
International equities	15.0	15.5	2.0	17.0	13.0	−6.0	14.9
European government bonds	20.0	18.9	2.0	22.0	18.0	4.0	20.0
Corporate bonds	20.0	19.1	2.0	22.0	18.0	4.0	20.2
Cash and money market instruments	15.0	14.6	2.0	17.0	13.0	2.0	15.2
Total	100.0%					−2.0%	100.0%

The prior decision not to rebalance to policy weights did not have a positive result. Contrary to the expectations of the investment committee, both European and international equities performed poorly while bonds recovered. The return of the portfolio was −2.0 percent.

2 How much of this return can be attributed to tactical asset allocation?

Solution to 2:

Because tactical asset allocation is the deliberate decision to deviate from policy weights, the return contribution from tactical asset allocation is equal to the difference between the actual return, and the return that would have been made if the asset class weights were equal to the policy weights. Exhibit 13 shows the difference to be −0.30 percent.

Exhibit 13   Returns to Tactical Asset Allocation

Asset Class	Policy Weight I	Starting Weight II	Weights Difference III (= II − I)	Period Return IV	TAA Contribution V (= III × IV)
European equities	30.0%	32.0%	2.0%	−9.0%	−0.18%
International equities	15.0	15.5	0.5	−6.0	−0.03
European government bonds	20.0	18.9	−1.1	4.0	−0.05
Corporate bonds	20.0	19.1	−0.9	4.0	−0.04

Exhibit 13	(Continued)				
Asset Class	Policy Weight I	Starting Weight II	Weights Difference III (= II − I)	Period Return IV	TAA Contribution V (= III × IV)
Cash and money market instruments	15.0	14.6	−0.4	2.0	−0.01
Total	100.0%			−2.0%	−0.30%

The process of executing an investment strategy continues with selecting the appropriate manager(s) for each asset class and allocating funds to them. The investment portfolio management process is then well into the execution stage.

The investment managers' performance will be monitored, as well as the results of the strategic asset allocation. When asset class weights move outside their corridors, money is transferred from the asset classes that have become too large compared with the SAA to those that fall short. Managers as well as the strategic asset allocation will be reviewed on the basis of the outcome of the monitoring process. In addition, capital market expectations may change, as may the circumstances and objectives of the client. These changes could result in an adjustment of the strategic asset allocation.

3.4 Additional Portfolio Organizing Principles

The top-down oriented framework laid out in earlier paragraphs is quite general. Other models of portfolio organization are also used in practice, and these are described briefly here. In addition, this section introduces some portfolio construction concepts in use to better capture the value of active management.

According to some practitioners, a top-down investment process as described earlier has two drawbacks. They both result from the fact that in a top-down process, a multitude of specialist managers may work for the same client within the same asset class. Each of these managers will manage risk versus the client's benchmark, and because these benchmarks may be similar to or overlapping with those of other managers, the aggregate of all the portfolios within one asset class may be less active than was intended. The resulting investment portfolio may underutilize its risk budget. Another drawback is that as the investment managers each engage in trading over the full extent (including the benchmark exposure) of their portfolio, the aggregate of all portfolios may not be efficient from a capital gains tax point of view. More trading results in more capital gains being realized, increasing the tax bill at the end of the year. To circumvent these issues, the core–satellite approach was developed. In this approach, a majority of the portfolio is invested on a passive or low active risk basis (usually a combination of a bond portfolio and an equity portfolio) while a minority of the assets is managed aggressively in smaller "satellite" portfolios. The aim of the satellite portfolios is to generate a high active return with little regard for benchmark exposure, whereas the core is managed with low turnover to capture the long-term systematic risk premium of its assets on a tax-optimal basis. The aggressive management in satellites can be executed with the objective of market timing (in which case tactical asset tilts are executed through long–short positions in asset class indices or derivatives), as well as security selection (in which case, highly active security selection vehicles act as satellites). A drawback of the core–satellite approach is that the assignment of asset class monies to actual portfolio managers—with their various expected alphas, risk surrounding those alphas, and correlations between those alphas—can be seen as an optimization process in its own right. The outcome of that process is not necessarily consistent with a core–satellite structure (Waring and Siegel, 2003).

SUMMARY

In this reading, we have discussed construction of a client's investment policy statement, including discussion of risk and return objectives and the various constraints that will apply to the portfolio. We have also discussed the portfolio construction process, with emphasis on the strategic asset allocation decisions that must be made.

- The IPS is the starting point of the portfolio management process. Without a full understanding of the client's situation and requirements, it is unlikely that successful results will be achieved.

- The IPS can take a variety of forms. A typical format will include the client's investment objectives and also list the constraints that apply to the client's portfolio.

- The client's objectives are specified in terms of risk tolerance and return requirements.

- The constraints section covers factors that need to be considered when constructing a portfolio for the client that meets the objectives. The typical constraint categories are liquidity requirements, time horizon, regulatory requirements, tax status, and unique needs.

- Risk objectives are specifications for portfolio risk that reflect the risk tolerance of the client. Quantitative risk objectives can be absolute or relative or a combination of the two.

- The client's overall risk tolerance is a function of the client's ability to accept risk and their "risk attitude," which can be considered the client's willingness to take risk.

- The client's return objectives can be stated on an absolute or a relative basis. As an example of an absolute objective, the client may want to achieve a particular percentage rate of return. Alternatively, the return objective can be stated on a relative basis, for example, relative to a benchmark return.

- The liquidity section of the IPS should state what the client's requirements are to draw cash from the portfolio.

- The time horizon section of the IPS should state the time horizon over which the investor is investing. This horizon may be the period during which the portfolio is accumulating before any assets need to be withdrawn.

- Tax status varies among investors and a client's tax status should be stated in the IPS.

- The IPS should state any legal or regulatory restrictions that constrain the investment of the portfolio.

- The unique circumstances section of the IPS should cover any other aspect of a client's circumstances that is likely to have a material impact on the composition of the portfolio; for example, any religious or ethical preferences.

- Asset classes are the building blocks of an asset allocation. An asset class is a category of assets that have similar characteristics, attributes, and risk–return relationships. Traditionally, investors have distinguished cash, equities, bonds, and real estate as the major asset classes.

- A strategic asset allocation results from combining the constraints and objectives articulated in the IPS and capital market expectations regarding the asset classes.

- As time goes on, a client's asset allocation will drift from the target allocation, and the amount of allowable drift as well as a rebalancing policy should be formalized.

- In addition to taking systematic risk, an investment committee may choose to take tactical asset allocation risk or security selection risk. The amount of return attributable to these decisions can be measured.

REFERENCES

Calverley, John P., Alan M. Meder, Brian D. Singer, and Renato Staub. 2007. "Capital Market Expectations." *Managing Investment Portfolios; A Dynamic Process.* 3rd ed. New York: Wiley.

Grable, John E., and Soo-Hyun Joo. 2004. "Environmental and Biopsychosocial Factors Associated with Financial Risk Tolerance." *Financial Counseling and Planning*, vol. 15, no. 1: 73–82.

Kritzman, Mark. 1999. "Toward Defining an Asset Class." *Journal of Alternative Investments*, vol. 2, no. 1: 79–82.

Maginn, John L., and Donald L. Tuttle. 1983. "The Portfolio Management Process and its Dynamics." *Managing Investment Portfolios: A Dynamic Process.* Boston: Warren, Gorham & Lamont.

Sharpe, William F., Peng Chen, Jerald E. Pinto, and Dennis W. McLeavey. 2007. "Asset Allocation." *Managing Investment Portfolios: A Dynamic Process.* 3rd ed. New York: Wiley.

Waring, M. Barton, and Laurence B. Siegel. 2003. "The Dimensions of Active Management." *Journal of Portfolio Management*, vol. 29, no. 3: 35–51.

Waring, M. Barton, Duane Whitney, John Pirone, and Charles Castille. 2000. "Optimizing Manager Structure and Budgeting Manager Risk." *Journal of Portfolio Management*, vol. 26, no. 3: 90–104.

PRACTICE PROBLEMS

1 Which of the following is *least* important as a reason for a written investment policy statement (IPS)?

   A The IPS may be required by regulation.

   B Having a written IPS is part of best practice for a portfolio manager.

   C Having a written IPS ensures the client's risk and return objectives can be achieved.

2 Which of the following *best* describes the underlying rationale for a written investment policy statement (IPS)?

   A A written IPS communicates a plan for trying to achieve investment success.

   B A written IPS provides investment managers with a ready defense against client lawsuits.

   C A written IPS allows investment managers to instruct clients about the proper use and purpose of investments.

3 A written investment policy statement (IPS) is *most* likely to succeed if:

   A it is created by a software program to assure consistent quality.

   B it is a collaborative effort of the client and the portfolio manager.

   C it reflects the investment philosophy of the portfolio manager.

4 The section of the investment policy statement (IPS) that provides information about how policy may be executed, including investment constraints, is *best* described as the:

   A *Investment Objectives.*

   B *Investment Guidelines.*

   C *Statement of Duties and Responsibilities.*

5 Which of the following is *least* likely to be placed in the appendices to an investment policy statement (IPS)?

   A *Rebalancing Policy.*

   B *Strategic Asset Allocation.*

   C *Statement of Duties and Responsibilities.*

6 Which of the following typical topics in an investment policy statement (IPS) is *most* closely linked to the client's "distinctive needs"?

   A *Procedures.*

   B *Investment Guidelines.*

   C *Statement of Duties and Responsibilities.*

7 An investment policy statement that includes a return objective of outperforming the FTSE 100 by 120 basis points is *best* characterized as having a(n):

   A relative return objective.

   B absolute return objective.

   C arbitrage-based return objective.

8 Risk assessment questionnaires for investment management clients are *most* useful in measuring:

   A value at risk.

   B   ability to take risk.

   C   willingness to take risk.

9   Which of the following is *best* characterized as a relative risk objective?

   A   Value at risk for the fund will not exceed US$3 million.

   B   The fund will not underperform the DAX by more than 250 basis points.

   C   The fund will not lose more than €2.5 million in the coming 12-month period.

10   In preparing an investment policy statement, which of the following is *most* difficult to quantify?

   A   Time horizon.

   B   Ability to accept risk.

   C   Willingness to accept risk.

11   After interviewing a client in order to prepare a written investment policy statement (IPS), you have established the following:

- The client has earnings that vary dramatically between £30,000 and £70,000 (pre-tax) depending on weather patterns in Britain.

- In three of the previous five years, the after-tax income of the client has been less than £20,000.

- The client's mother is dependent on her son (the client) for approximately £9,000 per year support.

- The client's own subsistence needs are approximately £12,000 per year.

- The client has more than 10 years experience trading investments including commodity futures, stock options, and selling stock short.

- The client's responses to a standard risk assessment questionnaire suggest he has above average risk tolerance.

The client is *best* described as having a:

   A   low ability to take risk, but a high willingness to take risk.

   B   high ability to take risk, but a low willingness to take risk.

   C   high ability to take risk and a high willingness to take risk.

12   After interviewing a client in order to prepare a written investment policy statement (IPS), you have established the following:

- The client has earnings that have exceeded €120,000 (pre-tax) each year for the past five years.

- She has no dependents.

- The client's subsistence needs are approximately €45,000 per year.

- The client states that she feels uncomfortable with her lack of understanding of securities markets.

- All of the client's current savings are invested in short-term securities guaranteed by an agency of her national government.

- The client's responses to a standard risk assessment questionnaire suggest she has low risk tolerance.

The client is *best* described as having a:

   A   low ability to take risk, but a high willingness to take risk.

   B   high ability to take risk, but a low willingness to take risk.

   C   high ability to take risk and a high willingness to take risk.

13 A client who is a 34-year old widow with two healthy young children (aged 5 and 7) has asked you to help her form an investment policy statement. She has been employed as an administrative assistant in a bureau of her national government for the previous 12 years. She has two primary financial goals—her retirement and providing for the college education of her children. This client's time horizon is *best* described as being:

　A　long term.

　B　short term.

　C　medium term.

14 The timing of payouts for property and casualty insurers is unpredictable ("lumpy") in comparison with the timing of payouts for life insurance companies. Therefore, in general, property and casualty insurers have:

　A　lower liquidity needs than life insurance companies.

　B　greater liquidity needs than life insurance companies.

　C　a higher return objective than life insurance companies.

15 A client who is a director of a publicly listed corporation is required by law to refrain from trading that company's stock at certain points of the year when disclosure of financial results are pending. In preparing a written investment policy statement (IPS) for this client, this restriction on trading:

　A　is irrelevant to the IPS.

　B　should be included in the IPS.

　C　makes it illegal for the portfolio manager to work with this client.

16 Consider the pairwise correlations of monthly returns of the following asset classes:

	Brazilian Equities	East Asian Equities	European Equities	U.S. Equities
Brazilian equities	1.00	0.70	0.85	0.76
East Asian equities	0.70	1.00	0.91	0.88
European equities	0.85	0.91	1.00	0.90
U.S. equities	0.76	0.88	0.90	1.00

Based solely on the information in the above table, which equity asset class is *most* sharply distinguished from U.S. equities?

　A　Brazilian equities.

　B　European equities.

　C　East Asian equities.

17 Returns on asset classes are *best* described as being a function of:

　A　the failure of arbitrage.

　B　exposure to the idiosyncratic risks of those asset classes.

　C　exposure to sets of systematic factors relevant to those asset classes.

18 In defining asset classes as part of the strategic asset allocation decision, pairwise correlations within asset classes should generally be:

　A　equal to correlations among asset classes.

　B　lower than correlations among asset classes.

　C　higher than correlations among asset classes.

19 Tactical asset allocation is *best* described as:

   A attempts to exploit arbitrage possibilities among asset classes.

   B the decision to deliberately deviate from the policy portfolio.

   C selecting asset classes with the desired exposures to sources of systematic risk in an investment portfolio.

20 Investing the majority of the portfolio on a passive or low active risk basis while a minority of the assets is managed aggressively in smaller portfolios is *best* described as:

   A the core–satellite approach.

   B a top-down investment policy.

   C a delta-neutral hedge approach.

SOLUTIONS

1 C is correct. Depending on circumstances, a written IPS or its equivalent may be required by law or regulation and a written IPS is certainly consistent with best practices. The mere fact that a written IPS is prepared for a client, however, does not *ensure* that risk and return objectives will in fact be achieved.

2 A is correct. A written IPS is best seen as a communication instrument allowing clients and portfolio managers to mutually establish investment objectives and constraints.

3 B is correct. A written IPS, to be successful, must incorporate a full understanding of the client's situation and requirements. As stated in the reading, "The IPS will be developed following a fact finding discussion with the client."

4 B is correct. The major components of an IPS are listed in Section 2.2 of the reading. *Investment Guidelines* are described as the section that provides information about how policy may be executed, including investment constraints. *Statement of Duties and Responsibilities* "detail[s] the duties and responsibilities of the client, the custodian of the client's assets, the investment managers, and so forth." *Investment Objectives* is "a section explaining the client's objectives in investing."

5 C is correct. The major components of an IPS are listed in Section 2.2 of the reading. Strategic Asset Allocation (also known as the policy portfolio) and Rebalancing Policy are often included as appendices to the IPS. The *Statement of Duties and Responsibilities*, however, is an integral part of the IPS and is unlikely to be placed in an appendix.

6 B is correct. According to the reading, "The sections of an IPS that are most closely linked to the client's distinctive needs are those dealing with investment objectives and constraints." *Investment Guidelines* "[provide] information about how policy may be executed, including investment constraints." *Procedures* "[detail] the steps to be taken to keep the IPS current and the procedures to follow to respond to various contingencies." *Statement of Duties and Responsibilities* "detail[s] the duties and responsibilities of the client, the custodian of the client's assets, the investment managers, and so forth."

7 A is correct. Because the return objective specifies a target return *relative to* the FTSE 100 Index, the objective is best described as a relative return objective.

8 C is correct. Risk attitude is a subjective factor and measuring risk attitude is difficult. Oftentimes, investment managers use psychometric questionnaires, such as those developed by Grable and Joo (2004), to assess a client's willingness to take risk.

9 B is correct. The reference to the DAX marks this response as a relative risk objective. Value at risk establishes a minimum value of loss expected during a specified time period at a given level of probability. A statement of maximum allowed absolute loss (€2.5 million) is an absolute risk objective.

10 C is correct. Measuring willingness to take risk (risk tolerance, risk aversion) is an exercise in applied psychology. Instruments attempting to measure risk attitudes exist, but they are clearly less objective than measurements of ability to take risk. Ability to take risk is based on relatively objective traits such as expected income, time horizon, and existing wealth relative to liabilities.

11 A is correct. The volatility of the client's income and the significant support needs for his mother and himself suggest that the client has a low ability to take risk. The client's trading experience and his responses to the risk assessment questionnaire indicate that the client has an above average willingness to take risk.

12 B is correct. On the one hand, the client has a stable, high income and no dependents. On the other hand, she exhibits above average risk aversion. Her ability to take risk is high, but her willingness to take risk is low.

13 A is correct. The client's financial objectives are long term. Her stable employment indicates that her immediate liquidity needs are modest. The children will not go to college until 10 or more years later. Her time horizon is best described as being long term.

14 B is correct. The unpredictable nature of property and casualty (P&C) claims forces P&C insurers to allocate a substantial proportion of their investments into liquid, short maturity assets. This need for liquidity also forces P&C companies to accept investments with relatively low expected returns. Liquidity is of less concern to life insurance companies given the greater predictability of life insurance payouts.

15 B is correct. When a client has a restriction in trading, such as this obligation to refrain from trading, the IPS "should note this constraint so that the portfolio manager does not inadvertently trade the stock on the client's behalf."

16 A is correct. The correlation between U.S. equities and Brazilian equities is 0.76. The correlations between U.S. equities and East Asian equities and the correlation between U.S. equities and European equities both exceed 0.76. Lower correlations indicate a greater degree of separation between asset classes. Therefore, using solely the data given in the table, returns on Brazilian equities are most sharply distinguished from returns on U.S. equities.

17 C is correct. Strategic asset allocation depends on several principles. As stated in the reading, "One principle is that a portfolio's systematic risk accounts for most of its change in value over the long run." A second principle is that, "the returns to groups of like assets… predictably reflect exposures to certain sets of systematic factors." This latter principle establishes that returns on asset classes primarily reflect the systematic risks of the classes.

18 C is correct. As the reading states, "an asset class should contain homogeneous assets… paired correlations of securities would be high within an asset class, but should be lower versus securities in other asset classes."

19 B is correct. Tactical asset allocation allows actual asset allocation to deviate from that of the strategic asset allocation (policy portfolio) of the IPS. Tactical asset allocation attempts to take advantage of temporary dislocations from the market conditions and assumptions that drove the policy portfolio decision.

20 A is correct. The core–satellite approach to constructing portfolios is defined as "investing the majority of the portfolio on a passive or low active risk basis while a minority of the assets is managed aggressively in smaller portfolios."

Glossary

A priori probability A probability based on logical analysis rather than on observation or personal judgment.

Abnormal profit Equal to accounting profit less the implicit opportunity costs not included in total accounting costs; the difference between total revenue (TR) and total cost (TC).

Abnormal return The amount by which a security's actual return differs from its expected return, given the security's risk and the market's return.

Absolute advantage A country's ability to produce a good or service at a lower absolute cost than its trading partner.

Absolute dispersion The amount of variability present without comparison to any reference point or benchmark.

Absolute frequency The number of observations in a given interval (for grouped data).

Accelerated book build An offering of securities by an investment bank acting as principal that is accomplished in only one or two days.

Accelerated methods Depreciation methods that allocate a relatively large proportion of the cost of an asset to the early years of the asset's useful life.

Account With the accounting systems, a formal record of increases and decreases in a specific asset, liability, component of owners' equity, revenue, or expense.

Accounting (or explicit) costs Payments to non-owner parties for services or resources they supply to the firm.

Accounting loss When accounting profit is negative.

Accounting profit Income as reported on the income statement, in accordance with prevailing accounting standards, before the provisions for income tax expense. Also called *income before taxes* or *pretax income*.

Accounts payable Amounts that a business owes to its vendors for goods and services that were purchased from them but which have not yet been paid.

Accounts receivable Amounts customers owe the company for products that have been sold as well as amounts that may be due from suppliers (such as for returns of merchandise). Also called *commercial receivables* or *trade receivables*.

Accounts receivable turnover Ratio of sales on credit to the average balance in accounts receivable.

Accrued expenses Liabilities related to expenses that have been incurred but not yet paid as of the end of an accounting period—an example of an accrued expense is rent that has been incurred but not yet paid, resulting in a liability "rent payable." Also called *accrued liabilities*.

Accrued interest Interest earned but not yet paid.

Accrued revenue Revenue that has been earned but not yet billed to customers as of the end of an accounting period.

Accumulated depreciation An offset to property, plant, and equipment (PPE) reflecting the amount of the cost of PPE that has been allocated to current and previous accounting periods.

Acid-test ratio A stringent measure of liquidity that indicates a company's ability to satisfy current liabilities with its most liquid assets, calculated as (cash + short-term marketable investments + receivables) divided by current liabilities.

Acquisition method A method of accounting for a business combination where the acquirer is required to measure each identifiable asset and liability at fair value. This method was the result of a joint project of the IASB and FASB aiming at convergence in standards for the accounting of business combinations.

Action lag Delay from policy decisions to implementation.

Active investment An approach to investing in which the investor seeks to outperform a given benchmark.

Active return The return on a portfolio minus the return on the portfolio's benchmark.

Active strategy In reference to short-term cash management, an investment strategy characterized by monitoring and attempting to capitalize on market conditions to optimize the risk and return relationship of short-term investments.

Activity ratio The ratio of the labor force to total population of working age. Also called *participation ratio*.

Activity ratios Ratios that measure how efficiently a company performs day-to-day tasks, such as the collection of receivables and management of inventory. Also called *asset utilization ratios* or *operating efficiency ratios*.

Add-on interest A procedure for determining the interest on a bond or loan in which the interest is added onto the face value of a contract.

Add-on rates Bank certificates of deposit, repos, and indices such as Libor and Euribor are quoted on an add-on rate basis (bond equivalent yield basis).

Addition rule for probabilities A principle stating that the probability that A or B occurs (both occur) equals the probability that A occurs, plus the probability that B occurs, minus the probability that both A and B occur.

Agency bonds See *quasi-government bond*.

Aggregate demand The quantity of goods and services that households, businesses, government, and foreign customers want to buy at any given level of prices.

Aggregate demand curve Inverse relationship between the price level and real output.

Aggregate income The value of all the payments earned by the suppliers of factors used in the production of goods and services.

Aggregate output The value of all the goods and services produced in a specified period of time.

Aggregate supply The quantity of goods and services producers are willing to supply at any given level of price.

Aggregate supply curve The level of domestic output that companies will produce at each price level.

Aging schedule A breakdown of accounts into categories of days outstanding.

All-or-nothing (AON) orders An order that includes the instruction to trade only if the trade fills the entire quantity (size) specified.

Allocationally efficient Said of a market, a financial system, or an economy that promotes the allocation of resources to their highest value uses.

Allowance for bad debts An offset to accounts receivable for the amount of accounts receivable that are estimated to be uncollectible.

Alternative investment markets Market for investments other than traditional securities investments (i.e., traditional common and preferred shares and traditional fixed income instruments). The term usually encompasses direct and indirect investment in real estate (including timberland and farmland) and commodities (including precious metals); hedge funds, private equity, and other investments requiring specialized due diligence.

Alternative trading systems Trading venues that function like exchanges but that do not exercise regulatory authority over their subscribers except with respect to the conduct of the subscribers' trading in their trading systems. Also called *electronic communications networks* or *multilateral trading facilities*.

American depository receipt A U.S. dollar-denominated security that trades like a common share on U.S. exchanges.

American depository share The underlying shares on which American depository receipts are based. They trade in the issuing company's domestic market.

American option An option that can be exercised at any time until its expiration date.

American-style Said of an option contract that can be exercised at any time up to the option's expiration date.

Amortisation The process of allocating the cost of intangible long-term assets having a finite useful life to accounting periods; the allocation of the amount of a bond premium or discount to the periods remaining until bond maturity.

Amortised cost The historical cost (initially recognised cost) of an asset, adjusted for amortisation and impairment.

Amortizing bond Bond with a payment schedule that calls for periodic payments of interest and repayments of principal.

Annual percentage rate The cost of borrowing expressed as a yearly rate.

Annuity A finite set of level sequential cash flows.

Annuity due An annuity having a first cash flow that is paid immediately.

Anticipation stock Excess inventory that is held in anticipation of increased demand, often because of seasonal patterns of demand.

Antidilutive With reference to a transaction or a security, one that would increase earnings per share (EPS) or result in EPS higher than the company's basic EPS—antidilutive securities are not included in the calculation of diluted EPS.

Arbitrage 1) The simultaneous purchase of an undervalued asset or portfolio and sale of an overvalued but equivalent asset or portfolio, in order to obtain a riskless profit on the price differential. Taking advantage of a market inefficiency in a risk-free manner. 2) The condition in a financial market in which equivalent assets or combinations of assets sell for two different prices, creating an opportunity to profit at no risk with no commitment of money. In a well-functioning financial market, few arbitrage opportunities are possible. 3) A risk-free operation that earns an expected positive net profit but requires no net investment of money.

Arbitrageurs Traders who engage in arbitrage. See *arbitrage*.

Arc elasticity An elasticity based on two points, in contrast with (point) elasticity. With reference to price elasticity, the percentage change in quantity demanded divided by the percentage change in price between two points for price.

Arithmetic mean The sum of the observations divided by the number of observations.

Arms index A flow of funds indicator applied to a broad stock market index to measure the relative extent to which money is moving into or out of rising and declining stocks.

Ascending price auction An auction in which an auctioneer calls out prices for a single item and potential buyers bid directly against each other, with each subsequent bid being higher than the previous one.

Asian call option A European-style option with a value at maturity equal to the difference between the stock price at maturity and the average stock price during the life of the option, or $0, whichever is greater.

Ask The price at which a dealer or trader is willing to sell an asset, typically qualified by a maximum quantity (ask size). See *offer*.

Ask size The maximum quantity of an asset that pertains to a specific ask price from a trader. For example, if the ask for a share issue is $30 for a size of 1,000 shares, the trader is offering to sell at $30 up to 1,000 shares.

Asset allocation The process of determining how investment funds should be distributed among asset classes.

Asset beta The unlevered beta; reflects the business risk of the assets; the asset's systematic risk.

Asset class A group of assets that have similar characteristics, attributes, and risk/return relationships.

Asset swap Converts the periodic fixed coupon of a specific bond to a Libor plus or minus a spread.

Asset utilization ratios Ratios that measure how efficiently a company performs day-to-day tasks, such as the collection of receivables and management of inventory.

Asset-based loan A loan that is secured with company assets.

Asset-based valuation models Valuation based on estimates of the market value of a company's assets.

Assets Resources controlled by an enterprise as a result of past events and from which future economic benefits to the enterprise are expected to flow.

Assignment of accounts receivable The use of accounts receivable as collateral for a loan.

At the money An option in which the underlying's price equals the exercise price.

Auction A type of bond issuing mechanism often used for sovereign bonds that involves bidding.

Autarkic price The price of a good or service in an autarkic economy.

Autarky A state in which a country does not trade with other countries.

Automated Clearing House (ACH) An electronic payment network available to businesses, individuals, and financial institutions in the United States, U.S. Territories, and Canada.

Automatic stabilizer A countercyclical factor that automatically comes into play as an economy slows and unemployment rises.

Available-for-sale Debt and equity securities not classified as either held-to-maturity or held-for-trading securities. The investor is willing to sell but not actively planning to sell. In general, available-for-sale securities are reported at fair value on the balance sheet.

Average fixed cost Total fixed cost divided by quantity.

Average product Measures the productivity of inputs on average and is calculated by dividing total product by the total number of units for a given input that is used to generate that output.

Average revenue Quantity sold divided into total revenue.

Average total cost Total costs divided by quantity.

Average variable cost Total variable cost divided by quantity.

Back simulation Another term for the historical method of estimating VAR. This term is somewhat misleading in that the method involves not a *simulation* of the past but rather what *actually happened* in the past, sometimes adjusted to reflect the fact that a different portfolio may have existed in the past than is planned for the future.

Back-testing With reference to portfolio strategies, the application of a strategy's portfolio selection rules to historical data to assess what would have been the strategy's historical performance.

Backup lines of credit A type of credit enhancement provided by a bank to an issuer of commercial paper to ensure that the issuer will have access to sufficient liquidity to repay maturing commercial paper if issuing new paper is not a viable option.

Balance of payments A double-entry bookkeeping system that summarizes a country's economic transactions with the rest of the world for a particular period of time, typically a calendar quarter or year.

Balance of trade deficit When the domestic economy is spending more on foreign goods and services than foreign economies are spending on domestic goods and services.

Balance sheet The financial statement that presents an entity's current financial position by disclosing resources the entity controls (its assets) and the claims on those resources (its liabilities and equity claims), as of a particular point in time (the date of the balance sheet). Also called *statement of financial position* or *statement of financial condition*.

Balance sheet ratios Financial ratios involving balance sheet items only.

Balanced With respect to a government budget, one in which spending and revenues (taxes) are equal.

Balloon payment Large payment required at maturity to retire a bond's outstanding principal amount.

Bank discount basis A quoting convention that annualizes, on a 360-day year, the discount as a percentage of face value.

Bar chart A price chart with four bits of data for each time interval—the high, low, opening, and closing prices. A vertical line connects the high and low. A cross-hatch left indicates the opening price and a cross-hatch right indicates the close.

Barter economy An economy where economic agents as house-holds, corporations, and governments "pay" for goods and services with another good or service.

Base rates The reference rate on which a bank bases lending rates to all other customers.

Basic EPS Net earnings available to common shareholders (i.e., net income minus preferred dividends) divided by the weighted average number of common shares outstanding.

Basis point Used in stating yield spreads, one basis point equals one-hundredth of a percentage point, or 0.01%.

Basket of listed depository receipts An exchange-traded fund (ETF) that represents a portfolio of depository receipts.

Bearer bonds Bonds for which ownership is not recorded; only the clearing system knows who the bond owner is.

Behavioral equations With respect to demand and supply, equations that model the behavior of buyers and sellers.

Behavioral finance A field of finance that examines the psychological variables that affect and often distort the investment decision making of investors, analysts, and portfolio managers.

Behind the market Said of prices specified in orders that are worse than the best current price; e.g., for a limit buy order, a limit price below the best bid.

Benchmark A comparison portfolio; a point of reference or comparison.

Benchmark issue The latest sovereign bond issue for a given maturity. It serves as a benchmark against which to compare bonds that have the same features but that are issued by another type of issuer.

Benchmark rate Typically the yield-to-maturity on a government bond having the same, or close to the same, time-to-maturity.

Benchmark spread The yield spread over a specific benchmark, usually measured in basis points.

Bermuda-style Said of an option contract that can be exercised on specified dates up to the option's expiration date.

Bernoulli random variable A random variable having the outcomes 0 and 1.

Bernoulli trial An experiment that can produce one of two outcomes.

Best bid The highest bid in the market.

Best effort offering An offering of a security using an investment bank in which the investment bank, as agent for the issuer, promises to use its best efforts to sell the offering but does not guarantee that a specific amount will be sold.

Best offer The lowest offer (ask price) in the market.

Beta A measure of systematic risk that is based on the covariance of an asset's or portfolio's return with the return of the overall market.

Bid The price at which a dealer or trader is willing to buy an asset, typically qualified by a maximum quantity.

Bid size The maximum quantity of an asset that pertains to a specific bid price from a trader.

Bid–ask spread The difference between the prices at which dealers will buy from a customer (bid) and sell to a customer (offer or ask). It is often used as an indicator of liquidity.

Bid–offer spread The difference between the prices at which dealers will buy from a customer (bid) and sell to a customer (offer or ask). It is often used as an indicator of liquidity.

Bilateral loan A loan from a single lender to a single borrower.

Binomial model A model for pricing options in which the underlying price can move to only one of two possible new prices.

Binomial random variable The number of successes in n Bernoulli trials for which the probability of success is constant for all trials and the trials are independent.

Binomial tree The graphical representation of a model of asset price dynamics in which, at each period, the asset moves up with probability p or down with probability $(1 - p)$.

Block brokers A broker (agent) that provides brokerage services for large-size trades.

Blue chip Widely held large market capitalization companies that are considered financially sound and are leaders in their respective industry or local stock market.

Bollinger Bands A price-based technical analysis indicator consisting of a moving average plus a higher line representing the moving average plus a set number of standard deviations from average price (for the same number of periods as used to calculate the moving average) and a lower line that is a moving average minus the same number of standard deviations.

Bond Contractual agreement between the issuer and the bondholders.

Bond equivalent yield   A calculation of yield that is annualized using the ratio of 365 to the number of days to maturity. Bond equivalent yield allows for the restatement and comparison of securities with different compounding periods.

Bond indenture   The governing legal credit agreement, typically incorporated by reference in the prospectus.

Bond market vigilantes   Bond market participants who might reduce their demand for long-term bonds, thus pushing up their yields.

Bond option   An option in which the underlying is a bond; primarily traded in over-the-counter markets.

Bond yield plus risk premium approach   An estimate of the cost of common equity that is produced by summing the before-tax cost of debt and a risk premium that captures the additional yield on a company's stock relative to its bonds. The additional yield is often estimated using historical spreads between bond yields and stock yields.

Bonus issue of shares   A type of dividend in which a company distributes additional shares of its common stock to shareholders instead of cash.

Book building   Investment bankers' process of compiling a "book" or list of indications of interest to buy part of an offering.

Book value   The net amount shown for an asset or liability on the balance sheet; book value may also refer to the company's excess of total assets over total liabilities. Also called *carrying value*.

Boom   An expansionary phase characterized by economic growth "testing the limits" of the economy.

Bottom-up analysis   With reference to investment selection processes, an approach that involves selection from all securities within a specified investment universe, i.e., without prior narrowing of the universe on the basis of macroeconomic or overall market considerations.

Break point   In the context of the weighted average cost of capital (WACC), a break point is the amount of capital at which the cost of one or more of the sources of capital changes, leading to a change in the WACC.

Breakeven point   The number of units produced and sold at which the company's net income is zero (revenues = total costs); in the case of perfect competition, the quantity where price, average revenue, and marginal revenue equal average total cost.

Bridge financing   Interim financing that provides funds until permanent financing can be arranged.

Broad money   Encompasses narrow money plus the entire range of liquid assets that can be used to make purchases.

Broker   1) An agent who executes orders to buy or sell securities on behalf of a client in exchange for a commission. 2) See *futures commission merchants*.

Brokered market   A market in which brokers arrange trades among their clients.

Broker–dealer   A financial intermediary (often a company) that may function as a principal (dealer) or as an agent (broker) depending on the type of trade.

Budget constraint   A constraint on spending or investment imposed by wealth or income.

Budget surplus/deficit   The difference between government revenue and expenditure for a stated fixed period of time.

Business risk   The risk associated with operating earnings. Operating earnings are uncertain because total revenues and many of the expenditures contributed to produce those revenues are uncertain.

Buy-side firm   An investment management company or other investor that uses the services of brokers or dealers (i.e., the client of the sell side firms).

Buyback   A transaction in which a company buys back its own shares. Unlike stock dividends and stock splits, share repurchases use corporate cash.

Buyout fund   A fund that buys all the shares of a public company so that, in effect, the company becomes private.

CBOE Volatility Index   A measure of near-term market volatility as conveyed by S&P 500 stock index option prices.

CD equivalent yield   A yield on a basis comparable to the quoted yield on an interest-bearing money market instrument that pays interest on a 360-day basis; the annualized holding period yield, assuming a 360-day year.

Call   An option that gives the holder the right to buy an underlying asset from another party at a fixed price over a specific period of time.

Call market   A market in which trades occur only at a particular time and place (i.e., when the market is called).

Call money rate   The interest rate that buyers pay for their margin loan.

Call option   An option that gives the holder the right to buy an underlying asset from another party at a fixed price over a specific period of time.

Call protection   The time during which the issuer of the bond is not allowed to exercise the call option.

Callable bond   A bond containing an embedded call option that gives the issuer the right to buy the bond back from the investor at specified prices on pre-determined dates.

Callable common shares   Shares that give the issuing company the option (or right), but not the obligation, to buy back the shares from investors at a call price that is specified when the shares are originally issued.

Candlestick chart   A price chart with four bits of data for each time interval. A candle indicates the opening and closing price for the interval. The body of the candle is shaded if the opening price was higher than the closing price, and the body is clear if the opening price was lower than the closing price. Vertical lines known as wicks or shadows extend from the top and bottom of the candle to indicate the high and the low prices for the interval.

Cannibalization   Cannibalization occurs when an investment takes customers and sales away from another part of the company.

Cap   1) A contract on an interest rate, whereby at periodic payment dates, the writer of the cap pays the difference between the market interest rate and a specified cap rate if, and only if, this difference is positive. This is equivalent to a stream of call options on the interest rate. 2) A combination of interest rate call options designed to hedge a borrower against rate increases on a floating-rate loan.

Capacity   The ability of the borrower to make its debt payments on time.

Capital account   A component of the balance of payments account that measures transfers of capital.

Capital allocation line   (CAL) A graph line that describes the combinations of expected return and standard deviation of return available to an investor from combining the optimal portfolio of risky assets with the risk-free asset.

Capital asset pricing model   (CAPM) An equation describing the expected return on any asset (or portfolio) as a linear function of its beta relative to the market portfolio.

Capital budgeting   The allocation of funds to relatively long-range projects or investments.

Capital consumption allowance A measure of the wear and tear (depreciation) of the capital stock that occurs in the production of goods and services.

Capital deepening investment Increases the stock of capital relative to labor.

Capital expenditure Expenditure on physical capital (fixed assets).

Capital market expectations An investor's expectations concerning the risk and return prospects of asset classes.

Capital market line (CML) The line with an intercept point equal to the risk-free rate that is tangent to the efficient frontier of risky assets; represents the efficient frontier when a risk-free asset is available for investment.

Capital market securities Securities with maturities at issuance longer than one year.

Capital markets Financial markets that trade securities of longer duration, such as bonds and equities.

Capital rationing A capital rationing environment assumes that the company has a fixed amount of funds to invest.

Capital restrictions Controls placed on foreigners' ability to own domestic assets and/or domestic residents' ability to own foreign assets.

Capital stock The accumulated amount of buildings, machinery, and equipment used to produce goods and services.

Capital structure The mix of debt and equity that a company uses to finance its business; a company's specific mixture of long-term financing.

Capital-indexed bonds Type of index-linked bond. The coupon rate is fixed but is applied to a principal amount that increases in line with increases in the index during the bond's life.

Caplet Each component call option in a cap.

Captive finance subsidiary A wholly-owned subsidiary of a company that is established to provide financing of the sales of the parent company.

Carrying amount The amount at which an asset or liability is valued according to accounting principles.

Carrying value The net amount shown for an asset or liability on the balance sheet; book value may also refer to the company's excess of total assets over total liabilities. For a bond, the purchase price plus (or minus) the amortized amount of the discount (or premium).

Cartel Participants in collusive agreements that are made openly and formally.

Cash In accounting contexts, cash on hand (e.g., petty cash and cash not yet deposited to the bank) and demand deposits held in banks and similar accounts that can be used in payment of obligations.

Cash conversion cycle A financial metric that measures the length of time required for a company to convert cash invested in its operations to cash received as a result of its operations; equal to days of inventory on hand + days of sales outstanding – number of days of payables. Also called *net operating cycle*.

Cash equivalents Very liquid short-term investments, usually maturing in 90 days or less.

Cash flow additivity principle The principle that dollar amounts indexed at the same point in time are additive.

Cash flow from operating activities The net amount of cash provided from operating activities.

Cash flow from operations The net amount of cash provided from operating activities.

Cash flow yield The internal rate of return on a series of cash flows.

Cash market securities Money market securities settled on a "same day" or "cash settlement" basis.

Cash markets See *spot markets*.

Cash prices See *spot prices*.

Cash settlement A procedure used in certain derivative transactions that specifies that the long and short parties engage in the equivalent cash value of a delivery transaction.

Cash-settled forwards See *non-deliverable forwards*.

Central bank funds market The market in which deposit-taking banks that have an excess reserve with their national central bank can loan money to banks that need funds for maturities ranging from overnight to one year. Called the Federal or Fed funds market in the United States.

Central bank funds rates Interest rates at which central bank funds are bought (borrowed) and sold (lent) for maturities ranging from overnight to one year. Called Federal or Fed funds rates in the United States.

Central banks The dominant bank in a country, usually with official or semi-official governmental status.

Certificate of deposit An instrument that represents a specified amount of funds on deposit with a bank for a specified maturity and interest rate. It is issued in small or large denominations, and can be negotiable or non-negotiable.

Change in polarity principle A tenet of technical analysis that once a support level is breached, it becomes a resistance level. The same holds true for resistance levels; once breached, they become support levels.

Change in quantity supplied A movement along a given supply curve.

Change in supply A shift in the supply curve.

Change of control put A covenant giving bondholders the right to require the issuer to buy back their debt, often at par or at some small premium to par value, in the event that the borrower is acquired.

Character The quality of a debt issuer's management.

Chart of accounts A list of accounts used in an entity's accounting system.

Cheapest-to-deliver bond A bond in which the amount received for delivering the bond is largest compared with the amount paid in the market for the bond.

Classified balance sheet A balance sheet organized so as to group together the various assets and liabilities into subcategories (e.g., current and noncurrent).

Clawback A requirement that the GP return any funds distributed as incentive fees until the LPs have received back their initial investment and a percentage of the total profit.

Clearing The process by which the exchange verifies the execution of a transaction and records the participants' identities.

Clearing instructions Instructions that indicate how to arrange the final settlement ("clearing") of a trade.

Clearinghouse An entity associated with a futures market that acts as middleman between the contracting parties and guarantees to each party the performance of the other.

Closed economy An economy that does not trade with other countries; an *autarkic economy*.

Closed-end fund A mutual fund in which no new investment money is accepted. New investors invest by buying existing shares, and investors in the fund liquidate by selling their shares to other investors.

Coefficient of variation (CV) The ratio of a set of observations' standard deviation to the observations' mean value.

Coincident economic indicators Turning points that are usually close to those of the overall economy; they are believed to have value for identifying the economy's present state.

Collateral The quality and value of the assets supporting an issuer's indebtedness.

Collateral trust bonds Bonds secured by securities such as common shares, other bonds, or other financial assets.

Collateralized bond obligations A structured asset-backed security that is collateralized by a pool of bonds.

Collateralized debt obligations A securitized pool of fixed-income assets.

Collateralized loan obligations A structured asset-backed security that is collateralized by a pool of loans.

Collateralized mortgage obligation (CMO) A structured asset-backed security that is collateralized by a pool of mortgages.

Collaterals Assets or financial guarantees underlying a debt obligation above and beyond the issuer's promise to pay.

Combination A listing in which the order of the listed items does not matter.

Commercial paper A short-term, negotiable, unsecured promissory note that represents a debt obligation of the issuer.

Commercial receivables Amounts customers owe the company for products that have been sold as well as amounts that may be due from suppliers (such as for returns of merchandise). Also called *trade receivables* or *accounts receivable*.

Committed capital The amount that the limited partners have agreed to provide to the private equity fund.

Committed lines of credit A bank commitment to extend credit up to a pre-specified amount; the commitment is considered a short-term liability and is usually in effect for 364 days (one day short of a full year).

Commodity swap A swap in which the underlying is a commodity such as oil, gold, or an agricultural product.

Common market Level of economic integration that incorporates all aspects of the customs union and extends it by allowing free movement of factors of production among members.

Common shares A type of security that represent an ownership interest in a company.

Common stock See *common shares*.

Common value auction An auction in which the item being auctioned has the same value to each auction participant, although participants may be uncertain as to what that value is.

Common-size analysis The restatement of financial statement items using a common denominator or reference item that allows one to identify trends and major differences; an example is an income statement in which all items are expressed as a percent of revenue.

Company analysis Analysis of an individual company.

Comparable company A company that has similar business risk; usually in the same industry and preferably with a single line of business.

Comparative advantage A country's ability to produce a good or service at a lower relative cost, or opportunity cost, than its trading partner.

Competitive strategy A company's plans for responding to the threats and opportunities presented by the external environment.

Complements Said of goods which tend to be used together; technically, two goods whose cross-price elasticity of demand is negative.

Complete markets Informally, markets in which the variety of distinct securities traded is so broad that any desired payoff in a future state-of-the-world is achievable.

Complete preferences The assumption that a consumer is able to make a comparison between any two possible bundles of goods.

Completed contract A method of revenue recognition in which the company does not recognize any revenue until the contract is completed; used particularly in long-term construction contracts.

Component cost of capital The rate of return required by suppliers of capital for an individual source of a company's funding, such as debt or equity.

Compounding The process of accumulating interest on interest.

Comprehensive income The change in equity of a business enterprise during a period from nonowner sources; includes all changes in equity during a period except those resulting from investments by owners and distributions to owners; comprehensive income equals net income plus other comprehensive income.

Conditional expected value The expected value of a stated event given that another event has occurred.

Conditional probability The probability of an event given (conditioned on) another event.

Conditional variances The variance of one variable, given the outcome of another.

Consistent With reference to estimators, describes an estimator for which the probability of estimates close to the value of the population parameter increases as sample size increases.

Conspicuous consumption Consumption of high status goods, such as a luxury automobile or a very expensive piece of jewelry.

Constant returns to scale The characteristic of constant per-unit costs in the presence of increased production.

Constant-cost industry When firms in the industry experience no change in resource costs and output prices over the long run.

Constant-yield price trajectory A graph that illustrates the change in the price of a fixed-income bond over time assuming no change in yield-to-maturity. The trajectory shows the "pull to par" effect on the price of a bond trading at a premium or a discount to par value.

Constituent securities With respect to an index, the individual securities within an index.

Consumer choice theory The theory relating consumer demand curves to consumer preferences.

Consumer surplus The difference between the value that a consumer places on units purchased and the amount of money that was required to pay for them.

Consumption The purchase of final goods and services by individuals.

Consumption basket A specific combination of the goods and services that a consumer wants to consume.

Consumption bundle A specific combination of the goods and services that a consumer wants to consume.

Contingency provision Clause in a legal document that allows for some action if a specific event or circumstance occurs.

Contingent claims Derivatives in which the payoffs occur if a specific event occurs; generally referred to as options.

Contingent convertible bonds Bonds that automatically convert into equity if a specific event or circumstance occurs, such as the issuer's equity capital falling below the minimum requirement set by the regulators. Also called *CoCos*.

Continuation patterns A type of pattern used in technical analysis to predict the resumption of a market trend that was in place prior to the formation of a pattern.

Continuous random variable A random variable for which the range of possible outcomes is the real line (all real numbers between $-\infty$ and $+\infty$ or some subset of the real line).

Continuous time Time thought of as advancing in extremely small increments.

Continuous trading market A market in which trades can be arranged and executed any time the market is open.

Continuously compounded return The natural logarithm of 1 plus the holding period return, or equivalently, the natural logarithm of the ending price over the beginning price.

Contra account An account that offsets another account.

Contraction The period of a business cycle after the peak and before the trough; often called a *recession* or, if exceptionally severe, called a *depression*.

Contractionary Tending to cause the real economy to contract.

Contractionary fiscal policy A fiscal policy that has the objective to make the real economy contract.

Contracts for differences See *non-deliverable forwards*.

Contribution margin The amount available for fixed costs and profit after paying variable costs; revenue minus variable costs.

Conventional bond See *plain vanilla bond*.

Conventional cash flow A conventional cash flow pattern is one with an initial outflow followed by a series of inflows.

Convergence The tendency for differences in output per capita across countries to diminish over time; in technical analysis, a term that describes the case when an indicator moves in the same manner as the security being analyzed.

Conversion factor An adjustment used to facilitate delivery on bond futures contracts in which any of a number of bonds with different characteristics are eligible for delivery.

Conversion price For a convertible bond, the price per share at which the bond can be converted into shares.

Conversion ratio For a convertible bond, the number of common shares that each bond can be converted into.

Conversion value For a convertible bond, the current share price multiplied by the conversion ratio.

Convertible bond Bond that gives the bondholder the right to exchange the bond for a specified number of common shares in the issuing company.

Convertible preference shares A type of equity security that entitles shareholders to convert their shares into a specified number of common shares.

Convexity adjustment For a bond, one half of the annual or approximate convexity statistic multiplied by the change in the yield-to-maturity squared.

Core inflation The inflation rate calculated based on a price index of goods and services except food and energy.

Correlation A number between −1 and +1 that measures the comovement (linear association) between two random variables.

Correlation coefficient A number between −1 and +1 that measures the consistency or tendency for two investments to act in a similar way. It is used to determine the effect on portfolio risk when two assets are combined.

Cost averaging The periodic investment of a fixed amount of money.

Cost of capital The rate of return that suppliers of capital require as compensation for their contribution of capital.

Cost of debt The cost of debt financing to a company, such as when it issues a bond or takes out a bank loan.

Cost of goods sold For a given period, equal to beginning inventory minus ending inventory plus the cost of goods acquired or produced during the period.

Cost of preferred stock The cost to a company of issuing preferred stock; the dividend yield that a company must commit to pay preferred stockholders.

Cost recovery method A method of revenue recognition in which the seller does not report any profit until the cash amounts paid by the buyer—including principal and interest on any financing from the seller—are greater than all the seller's costs for the merchandise sold.

Cost structure The mix of a company's variable costs and fixed costs.

Cost-push Type of inflation in which rising costs, usually wages, compel businesses to raise prices generally.

Counterparty risk The risk that the other party to a contract will fail to honor the terms of the contract.

Cournot assumption Assumption in which each firm determines its profit-maximizing production level assuming that the other firms' output will not change.

Covariance A measure of the co-movement (linear association) between two random variables.

Covariance matrix A matrix or square array whose entries are covariances; also known as a variance–covariance matrix.

Covenants The terms and conditions of lending agreements that the issuer must comply with; they specify the actions that an issuer is obligated to perform (affirmative covenant) or prohibited from performing (negative covenant).

Covered bond Debt obligation secured by a segregated pool of assets called the cover pool. The issuer must maintain the value of the cover pool. In the event of default, bondholders have recourse against both the issuer and the cover pool.

Covered call An option strategy involving the holding of an asset and sale of a call on the asset.

Credit With respect to double-entry accounting, a credit records increases in liability, owners' equity, and revenue accounts or decreases in asset accounts; with respect to borrowing, the willingness and ability of the borrower to make promised payments on the borrowing.

Credit analysis The evaluation of credit risk; the evaluation of the creditworthiness of a borrower or counterparty.

Credit curve A curve showing the relationship between time to maturity and yield spread for an issuer with comparable bonds of various maturities outstanding, usually upward sloping.

Credit default swap (CDS) A type of credit derivative in which one party, the credit protection buyer who is seeking credit protection against a third party, makes a series of regularly scheduled payments to the other party, the credit protection seller. The seller makes no payments until a credit event occurs.

Credit derivatives A contract in which one party has the right to claim a payment from another party in the event that a specific credit event occurs over the life of the contract.

Credit enhancements Provisions that may be used to reduce the credit risk of a bond issue.

Credit migration risk The risk that a bond issuer's creditworthiness deteriorates, or migrates lower, leading investors to believe the risk of default is higher. Also called *downgrade risk*.

Credit risk The risk of loss caused by a counterparty's or debtor's failure to make a promised payment. Also called *default risk*.

Credit scoring model A statistical model used to classify borrowers according to creditworthiness.

Credit spread option An option on the yield spread on a bond.

Credit-linked coupon bond Bond for which the coupon changes when the bond's credit rating changes.

Credit-linked note Fixed-income security in which the holder of the security has the right to withhold payment of the full amount due at maturity if a credit event occurs.

Credit-worthiness The perceived ability of the borrower to pay what is owed on the borrowing in a timely manner; it represents the ability of a company to withstand adverse impacts on its cash flows.

Cross-default provisions Provisions whereby events of default such as non-payment of interest on one bond trigger default on all outstanding debt; implies the same default probability for all issues.

Cross-price elasticity of demand The percent change in quantity demanded for a given small change in the price of another good; the responsiveness of the demand for Product A that is associated with the change in price of Product B.

Cross-sectional analysis Analysis that involves comparisons across individuals in a group over a given time period or at a given point in time.

Cross-sectional data Observations over individual units at a point in time, as opposed to time-series data.

Crossing networks Trading systems that match buyers and sellers who are willing to trade at prices obtained from other markets.

Crowding out The thesis that government borrowing may divert private sector investment from taking place.

Cumulative distribution function A function giving the probability that a random variable is less than or equal to a specified value.

Cumulative preference shares Preference shares for which any dividends that are not paid accrue and must be paid in full before dividends on common shares can be paid.

Cumulative relative frequency For data grouped into intervals, the fraction of total observations that are less than the value of the upper limit of a stated interval.

Cumulative voting Voting that allows shareholders to direct their total voting rights to specific candidates, as opposed to having to allocate their voting rights evenly among all candidates.

Currencies Monies issued by national monetary authorities.

Currency option An option that allows the holder to buy (if a call) or sell (if a put) an underlying currency at a fixed exercise rate, expressed as an exchange rate.

Currency option bonds Bonds that give the bondholder the right to choose the currency in which he or she wants to receive interest payments and principal repayments.

Currency swap A swap in which each party makes interest payments to the other in different currencies.

Current account A component of the balance of payments account that measures the flow of goods and services.

Current assets (or liquid assets) Assets that are expected to be consumed or converted into cash in the near future, typically one year or less.

Current cost With reference to assets, the amount of cash or cash equivalents that would have to be paid to buy the same or an equivalent asset today; with reference to liabilities, the undiscounted amount of cash or cash equivalents that would be required to settle the obligation today.

Current government spending With respect to government expenditures, spending on goods and services that are provided on a regular, recurring basis including health, education, and defense.

Current liabilities Short-term obligations, such as accounts payable, wages payable, or accrued liabilities, that are expected to be settled in the near future, typically one year or less.

Current ratio A liquidity ratio calculated as current assets divided by current liabilities.

Current yield The sum of the coupon payments received over the year divided by the flat price; also called the *income* or *interest yield* or *running yield*.

Curve duration The sensitivity of the bond price (or the market value of a financial asset or liability) with respect to a benchmark yield curve.

Customs union Extends the free trade area (FTA) by not only allowing free movement of goods and services among members, but also creating a common trade policy against nonmembers.

Cyclical See *cyclical companies*.

Cyclical companies Companies with sales and profits that regularly expand and contract with the business cycle or state of economy.

Daily settlement See *mark to market* and *marking to market*.

Dark pools Alternative trading systems that do not display the orders that their clients send to them.

Data mining The practice of determining a model by extensive searching through a dataset for statistically significant patterns. Also called *data snooping*.

Data snooping See *data mining*.

Date of book closure The date that a shareholder listed on the corporation's books will be deemed to have ownership of the shares for purposes of receiving an upcoming dividend; two business days after the ex-dividend date.

Date of record The date that a shareholder listed on the corporation's books will be deemed to have ownership of the shares for purposes of receiving an upcoming dividend; two business days after the ex-dividend date.

Day order An order that is good for the day on which it is submitted. If it has not been filled by the close of business, the order expires unfilled.

Day trader A trader holding a position open somewhat longer than a scalper but closing all positions at the end of the day.

Days in receivables Estimate of the average number of days it takes to collect on credit accounts.

Days of inventory on hand (DOH) An activity ratio equal to the number of days in the period divided by inventory turnover over the period.

Day's sales outstanding Estimate of the average number of days it takes to collect on credit accounts.

Dead cross A technical analysis term that describes a situation where a short-term moving average crosses from above a longer-term moving average to below it; this movement is considered bearish.

Deadweight loss A net loss of total (consumer and producer) surplus.

Dealers A financial intermediary that acts as a principal in trades.

Dealing securities Securities held by banks or other financial intermediaries for trading purposes.

Debentures Type of bond that can be secured or unsecured.

Debit   With respect to double-entry accounting, a debit records increases of asset and expense accounts or decreases in liability and owners' equity accounts.

Debt incurrence test   A financial covenant made in conjunction with existing debt that restricts a company's ability to incur additional debt at the same seniority based on one or more financial tests or conditions.

Debt-rating approach   A method for estimating a company's before-tax cost of debt based upon the yield on comparably rated bonds for maturities that closely match that of the company's existing debt.

Debt-to-assets ratio   A solvency ratio calculated as total debt divided by total assets.

Debt-to-capital ratio   A solvency ratio calculated as total debt divided by total debt plus total shareholders' equity.

Debt-to-equity ratio   A solvency ratio calculated as total debt divided by total shareholders' equity.

Declaration date   The day that the corporation issues a statement declaring a specific dividend.

Decreasing returns to scale   Increase in cost per unit resulting from increased production.

Decreasing-cost industry   An industry in which per-unit costs and output prices are lower when industry output is increased in the long run.

Deductible temporary differences   Temporary differences that result in a reduction of or deduction from taxable income in a future period when the balance sheet item is recovered or settled.

Deep-in-the-money   Options that are far in-the-money.

Deep-out-of-the-money   Options that are far out-of-the-money.

Default probability   The probability that a borrower defaults or fails to meet its obligation to make full and timely payments of principal and interest, according to the terms of the debt security. Also called *default risk*.

Default risk   The probability that a borrower defaults or fails to meet its obligation to make full and timely payments of principal and interest, according to the terms of the debt security. Also called *default probability*.

Default risk premium   An extra return that compensates investors for the possibility that the borrower will fail to make a promised payment at the contracted time and in the contracted amount.

Defensive companies   Companies with sales and profits that have little sensitivity to the business cycle or state of the economy.

Defensive interval ratio   A liquidity ratio that estimates the number of days that an entity could meet cash needs from liquid assets; calculated as (cash + short-term marketable investments + receivables) divided by daily cash expenditures.

Deferred coupon bond   Bond that pays no coupons for its first few years but then pays a higher coupon than it otherwise normally would for the remainder of its life. Also called *split coupon bond*.

Deferred income   A liability account for money that has been collected for goods or services that have not yet been delivered; payment received in advance of providing a good or service.

Deferred revenue   A liability account for money that has been collected for goods or services that have not yet been delivered; payment received in advance of providing a good or service.

Deferred tax assets   A balance sheet asset that arises when an excess amount is paid for income taxes relative to accounting profit. The taxable income is higher than accounting profit and income tax payable exceeds tax expense. The company expects to recover the difference during the course of future operations when tax expense exceeds income tax payable.

Deferred tax liabilities   A balance sheet liability that arises when a deficit amount is paid for income taxes relative to accounting profit. The taxable income is less than the accounting profit and income tax payable is less than tax expense. The company expects to eliminate the liability over the course of future operations when income tax payable exceeds tax expense.

Defined benefit pension plans   Plan in which the company promises to pay a certain annual amount (defined benefit) to the employee after retirement. The company bears the investment risk of the plan assets.

Defined contribution pension plans   Individual accounts to which an employee and typically the employer makes contributions, generally on a tax-advantaged basis. The amounts of contributions are defined at the outset, but the future value of the benefit is unknown. The employee bears the investment risk of the plan assets.

Deflation   Negative inflation.

Degree of confidence   The probability that a confidence interval includes the unknown population parameter.

Degree of financial leverage   (DFL) The ratio of the percentage change in net income to the percentage change in operating income; the sensitivity of the cash flows available to owners when operating income changes.

Degree of operating leverage   (DOL) The ratio of the percentage change in operating income to the percentage change in units sold; the sensitivity of operating income to changes in units sold.

Degree of total leverage   The ratio of the percentage change in net income to the percentage change in units sold; the sensitivity of the cash flows to owners to changes in the number of units produced and sold.

Degrees of freedom (df)   The number of independent observations used.

Delivery   A process used in a deliverable forward contract in which the long pays the agreed-upon price to the short, which in turn delivers the underlying asset to the long.

Delivery option   The feature of a futures contract giving the short the right to make decisions about what, when, and where to deliver.

Delta   The relationship between the option price and the underlying price, which reflects the sensitivity of the price of the option to changes in the price of the underlying.

Demand   The willingness and ability of consumers to purchase a given amount of a good or service at a given price.

Demand and supply analysis   The study of how buyers and sellers interact to determine transaction prices and quantities.

Demand curve   Graph of the inverse demand function.

Demand function   A relationship that expresses the quantity demanded of a good or service as a function of own-price and possibly other variables.

Demand shock   A typically unexpected disturbance to demand, such as an unexpected interruption in trade or transportation.

Demand-pull Type of inflation in which increasing demand raises prices generally, which then are reflected in a business's costs as workers demand wage hikes to catch up with the rising cost of living.

Dependent With reference to events, the property that the probability of one event occurring depends on (is related to) the occurrence of another event.

Depository bank A bank that raises funds from depositors and other investors and lends it to borrowers.

Depository institutions Commercial banks, savings and loan banks, credit unions, and similar institutions that raise funds from depositors and other investors and lend it to borrowers.

Depository receipt A security that trades like an ordinary share on a local exchange and represents an economic interest in a foreign company.

Depreciation The process of systematically allocating the cost of long-lived (tangible) assets to the periods during which the assets are expected to provide economic benefits.

Depression See *contraction*.

Derivative pricing rule A pricing rule used by crossing networks in which a price is taken (derived) from the price that is current in the asset's primary market.

Derivatives A financial instrument whose value depends on the value of some underlying asset or factor (e.g., a stock price, an interest rate, or exchange rate).

Descending price auction An auction in which the auctioneer begins at a high price, then lowers the called price in increments until there is a willing buyer for the item being auctioned.

Descriptive statistics The study of how data can be summarized effectively.

Development capital Minority equity investments in more mature companies that are looking for capital to expand or restructure operations, enter new markets, or finance major acquisitions.

Diffuse prior The assumption of equal prior probabilities.

Diffusion index Reflects the proportion of the index's components that are moving in a pattern consistent with the overall index.

Diluted EPS The EPS that would result if all dilutive securities were converted into common shares.

Diluted shares The number of shares that would be outstanding if all potentially dilutive claims on common shares (e.g., convertible debt, convertible preferred stock, and employee stock options) were exercised.

Diminishing balance method An accelerated depreciation method, i.e., one that allocates a relatively large proportion of the cost of an asset to the early years of the asset's useful life.

Diminishing marginal productivity Describes a state in which each additional unit of input produces less output than previously.

Direct debit program An arrangement whereby a customer authorizes a debit to a demand account; typically used by companies to collect routine payments for services.

Direct format With reference to the cash flow statement, a format for the presentation of the statement in which cash flow from operating activities is shown as operating cash receipts less operating cash disbursements. Also called *direct method*.

Direct method See *direct format*.

Direct taxes Taxes levied directly on income, wealth, and corporate profits.

Direct write-off method An approach to recognizing credit losses on customer receivables in which the company waits until such time as a customer has defaulted and only then recognizes the loss.

Disbursement float The amount of time between check issuance and a check's clearing back against the company's account.

Discount To reduce the value of a future payment in allowance for how far away it is in time; to calculate the present value of some future amount. Also, the amount by which an instrument is priced below its face (par) value.

Discount interest A procedure for determining the interest on a loan or bond in which the interest is deducted from the face value in advance.

Discount margin See *required margin*.

Discount rates In general, the interest rate used to calculate a present value. In the money market, however, discount rate is a specific type of quoted rate.

Discounted cash flow models Valuation models that estimate the intrinsic value of a security as the present value of the future benefits expected to be received from the security.

Discouraged worker A person who has stopped looking for a job or has given up seeking employment.

Discrete random variable A random variable that can take on at most a countable number of possible values.

Discriminatory pricing rule A pricing rule used in continuous markets in which the limit price of the order or quote that first arrived determines the trade price.

Diseconomies of scale Increase in cost per unit resulting from increased production.

Dispersion The variability around the central tendency.

Display size The size of an order displayed to public view.

Distressed investing Investing in securities of companies in financial difficulties. Private equity funds typically buy the debt of mature companies in financial difficulties.

Divergence In technical analysis, a term that describes the case when an indicator moves differently from the security being analyzed.

Diversification ratio The ratio of the standard deviation of an equally weighted portfolio to the standard deviation of a randomly selected security.

Dividend A distribution paid to shareholders based on the number of shares owned.

Dividend discount model (DDM) A present value model that estimates the intrinsic value of an equity share based on the present value of its expected future dividends.

Dividend discount model based approach An approach for estimating a country's equity risk premium. The market rate of return is estimated as the sum of the dividend yield and the growth rate in dividends for a market index. Subtracting the risk-free rate of return from the estimated market return produces an estimate for the equity risk premium.

Dividend payout ratio The ratio of cash dividends paid to earnings for a period.

Dividend yield Annual dividends per share divided by share price.

Divisor A number (denominator) used to determine the value of a price return index. It is initially chosen at the inception of an index and subsequently adjusted by the index provider, as necessary, to avoid changes in the index value that are unrelated to changes in the prices of its constituent securities.

Domestic content provisions   Stipulate that some percentage of the value added or components used in production should be of domestic origin.

Double bottoms   In technical analysis, a reversal pattern that is formed when the price reaches a low, rebounds, and then sells off back to the first low level; used to predict a change from a downtrend to an uptrend.

Double coincidence of wants   A prerequisite to barter trades, in particular that both economic agents in the transaction want what the other is selling.

Double declining balance depreciation   An accelerated depreciation method that involves depreciating the asset at double the straight-line rate. This rate is multiplied by the book value of the asset at the beginning of the period (a declining balance) to calculate depreciation expense.

Double top   In technical analysis, a reversal pattern that is formed when an uptrend reverses twice at roughly the same high price level; used to predict a change from an uptrend to a downtrend.

Double-entry accounting   The accounting system of recording transactions in which every recorded transaction affects at least two accounts so as to keep the basic accounting equation (assets = liabilities + owners' equity) in balance.

Down transition probability   The probability that an asset's value moves down in a model of asset price dynamics.

Downgrade risk   The risk that a bond issuer's creditworthiness deteriorates, or migrates lower, leading investors to believe the risk of default is higher. Also called *credit migration risk.*

Drag on liquidity   When receipts lag, creating pressure from the decreased available funds.

Drawdown   A reduction in net asset value (NAV).

DuPont analysis   An approach to decomposing return on investment, e.g., return on equity, as the product of other financial ratios.

Dual-currency bonds   Bonds that make coupon payments in one currency and pay the par value at maturity in another currency.

Duration gap   A bond's Macaulay duration minus the investment horizon.

Dutch Book theorem   A result in probability theory stating that inconsistent probabilities create profit opportunities.

Dutch auction   An auction in which the auctioneer begins at a high price, then lowers the called price in increments until there is a willing buyer for the item being auctioned.

Earnings per share   The amount of income earned during a period per share of common stock.

Earnings surprise   The portion of a company's earnings that is unanticipated by investors and, according to the efficient market hypothesis, merits a price adjustment.

Economic costs   All the remuneration needed to keep a productive resource in its current employment or to acquire the resource for productive use; the sum of total accounting costs and implicit opportunity costs.

Economic indicator   A variable that provides information on the state of the overall economy.

Economic loss   The amount by which accounting profit is less than normal profit.

Economic order quantity–reorder point (EOQ–ROP)   An approach to managing inventory based on expected demand and the predictability of demand; the ordering point for new inventory is determined based on the costs of ordering and carrying inventory, such that the total cost associated with inventory is minimized.

Economic profit   Equal to accounting profit less the implicit opportunity costs not included in total accounting costs; the difference between total revenue (TR) and total cost (TC). Also called *abnormal profit* or *supernormal profit.*

Economic rent   The surplus value that results when a particular resource or good is fixed in supply and market price is higher than what is required to bring the resource or good onto the market and sustain its use.

Economic stabilization   Reduction of the magnitude of economic fluctuations.

Economic union   Incorporates all aspects of a common market and in addition requires common economic institutions and coordination of economic policies among members.

Economics   The study of the production, distribution, and consumption of goods and services; the principles of the allocation of scarce resources among competing uses. Economics is divided into two broad areas of study: macroeconomics and microeconomics.

Economies of scale   Reduction in cost per unit resulting from increased production.

Effective annual rate   The amount by which a unit of currency will grow in a year with interest on interest included.

Effective annual yield (EAY)   An annualized return that accounts for the effect of interest on interest; EAY is computed by compounding 1 plus the holding period yield forward to one year, then subtracting 1.

Effective convexity   A *curve convexity* statistic that measures the secondary effect of a change in a benchmark yield curve on a bond's price.

Effective duration   The sensitivity of a bond's price to a change in a benchmark yield curve.

Efficient market   A market in which asset prices reflect new information quickly and rationally.

Elastic   Said of a good or service when the magnitude of elasticity is greater than one.

Elasticity   The percentage change in one variable for a percentage change in another variable; a measure of how sensitive one variable is to a change in the value of another variable.

Elasticity of supply   A measure of the sensitivity of quantity supplied to a change in price.

Electronic communications networks   See *alternative trading systems.*

Electronic funds transfer (EFT)   The use of computer networks to conduct financial transactions electronically.

Elliott wave theory   A technical analysis theory that claims that the market follows regular, repeated waves or cycles.

Embedded option   Contingency provisions that provide the issuer or the bondholders the right, but not the obligation, to take action. These options are not part of the security and cannot be traded separately.

Empirical probability   The probability of an event estimated as a relative frequency of occurrence.

Employed   The number of people with a job.

Endogenous variables   Variables whose equilibrium values are determined within the model being considered.

Enterprise value   A measure of a company's total market value from which the value of cash and short-term investments have been subtracted.

Equal weighting   An index weighting method in which an equal weight is assigned to each constituent security at inception.

Equilibrium condition   A condition necessary for the forces within a system to be in balance.

Equipment trust certificates   Bonds secured by specific types of equipment or physical assets.

Equity   Assets less liabilities; the residual interest in the assets after subtracting the liabilities.

Equity forward   A contract calling for the purchase of an individual stock, a stock portfolio, or a stock index at a later date at an agreed-upon price.

Equity options   Options on individual stocks; also known as stock options.

Equity risk premium   The expected return on equities minus the risk-free rate; the premium that investors demand for investing in equities.

Equity swap   A swap transaction in which at least one cash flow is tied to the return to an equity portfolio position, often an equity index.

Equity-linked note   Type of index-linked bond for which the final payment is based on the return of an equity index.

Estimate   The particular value calculated from sample observations using an estimator.

Estimation   With reference to statistical inference, the subdivision dealing with estimating the value of a population parameter.

Estimator   An estimation formula; the formula used to compute the sample mean and other sample statistics are examples of estimators.

Eurobonds   Type of bond issued internationally, outside the jurisdiction of the country in whose currency the bond is denominated.

Eurodollar   A dollar deposited outside the United States.

European option   An option that can only be exercised on its expiration date.

European-style   Said of an option contract that can only be exercised on the option's expiration date.

Event   Any outcome or specified set of outcomes of a random variable.

Ex-date   The first date that a share trades without (i.e. "ex") the dividend.

Ex-dividend date   The first date that a share trades without (i.e. "ex") the dividend.

Excess kurtosis   Degree of peakedness (fatness of tails) in excess of the peakedness of the normal distribution.

Excess supply   A condition in which the quantity ready to be supplied is greater than the quantity demanded.

Exchange for physicals (EFP)   A permissible delivery procedure used by futures market participants, in which the long and short arrange a delivery procedure other than the normal procedures stipulated by the futures exchange.

Exchanges   Places where traders can meet to arrange their trades.

Execution instructions   Instructions that indicate how to fill an order.

Exercise   The process of using an option to buy or sell the underlying.

Exercise price   The fixed price at which an option holder can buy or sell the underlying. Also called *strike price*, *striking price*, or *strike*.

Exercise rate   The fixed rate at which the holder of an interest rate option can buy or sell the underlying.

Exercise value   The value obtained if an option is exercised based on current conditions.

Exercising the option   The process of using an option to buy or sell the underlying.

Exhaustive   Covering or containing all possible outcomes.

Exogenous variables   Variables whose equilibrium values are determined outside of the model being considered.

Expansion   The period of a business cycle after its lowest point and before its highest point.

Expansionary   Tending to cause the real economy to grow.

Expansionary fiscal policy   Fiscal policy aimed at achieving real economic growth.

Expected inflation   The level of inflation that economic agents expect in the future.

Expected loss   Default probability times Loss severity given default.

Expected value   The probability-weighted average of the possible outcomes of a random variable.

Expenses   Outflows of economic resources or increases in liabilities that result in decreases in equity (other than decreases because of distributions to owners); reductions in net assets associated with the creation of revenues.

Experience curve   A curve that shows the direct cost per unit of good or service produced or delivered as a typically declining function of cumulative output.

Export subsidy   Paid by the government to the firm when it exports a unit of a good that is being subsidized.

Exports   Goods and services that an economy sells to other countries.

Externality   An effect of a market transaction that is borne by parties other than those who transacted.

Extra dividend   A dividend paid by a company that does not pay dividends on a regular schedule, or a dividend that supplements regular cash dividends with an extra payment.

FIFO method   The first in, first out, method of accounting for inventory, which matches sales against the costs of items of inventory in the order in which they were placed in inventory.

FX swap   The combination of a spot and a forward FX transaction.

Face value   The amount of cash payable by a company to the bondholders when the bonds mature; the promised payment at maturity separate from any coupon payment.

Factor   A common or underlying element with which several variables are correlated.

Factor markets   Markets for the purchase and sale of factors of production.

Fair value   The amount at which an asset could be exchanged, or a liability settled, between knowledgeable, willing parties in an arm's-length transaction; the price that would be received to sell an asset or paid to transfer a liability in an orderly transaction between market participants.

Fed funds rate   The U.S. interbank lending rate on overnight borrowings of reserves.

Federal funds rate   The U.S. interbank lending rate on overnight borrowings of reserves.

Fiat money   Money that is not convertible into any other commodity.

Fibonacci sequence   A sequence of numbers starting with 0 and 1, and then each subsequent number in the sequence is the sum of the two preceding numbers. In Elliott Wave Theory, it is believed that market waves follow patterns that are the ratios of the numbers in the Fibonacci sequence.

Fiduciary call   A combination of a European call and a risk-free bond that matures on the option expiration day and has a face value equal to the exercise price of the call.

Fill or kill   See *immediate or cancel order*.

Financial account   A component of the balance of payments account that records investment flows.

Financial flexibility   The ability to react and adapt to financial adversities and opportunities.

Financial leverage The extent to which a company can effect, through the use of debt, a proportional change in the return on common equity that is greater than a given proportional change in operating income; also, short for the financial leverage ratio.

Financial leverage ratio A measure of financial leverage calculated as average total assets divided by average total equity.

Financial risk The risk that environmental, social, or governance risk factors will result in significant costs or other losses to a company and its shareholders; the risk arising from a company's obligation to meet required payments under its financing agreements.

Financing activities Activities related to obtaining or repaying capital to be used in the business (e.g., equity and long-term debt).

Firm commitment offering See *underwritten offering*.

First lien debt Debt secured by a pledge of certain assets that could include buildings, but may also include property and equipment, licenses, patents, brands, etc.

First mortgage debt Debt secured by a pledge of a specific property.

First price sealed bid auction An auction in which envelopes containing bids are opened simultaneously and the item is sold to the highest bidder.

First-degree price discrimination Where a monopolist is able to charge each customer the highest price the customer is willing to pay.

Fiscal multiplier The ratio of a change in national income to a change in government spending.

Fiscal policy The use of taxes and government spending to affect the level of aggregate expenditures.

Fisher effect The thesis that the real rate of interest in an economy is stable over time so that changes in nominal interest rates are the result of changes in expected inflation.

Fisher index The geometric mean of the Laspeyres index.

Fixed charge coverage A solvency ratio measuring the number of times interest and lease payments are covered by operating income, calculated as (EBIT + lease payments) divided by (interest payments + lease payments).

Fixed costs Costs that remain at the same level regardless of a company's level of production and sales.

Fixed price tender offer Offer made by a company to repurchase a specific number of shares at a fixed price that is typically at a premium to the current market price.

Fixed rate perpetual preferred stock Nonconvertible, non-callable preferred stock that has a fixed dividend rate and no maturity date.

Fixed-for-floating interest rate swap An interest rate swap in which one party pays a fixed rate and the other pays a floating rate, with both sets of payments in the same currency. Also called *plain vanilla swap* or *vanilla swap*.

Flags A technical analysis continuation pattern formed by parallel trendlines, typically over a short period.

Flat price The full price of a bond minus the accrued interest; also called the *quoted* or *clean* price.

Float In the context of customer receipts, the amount of money that is in transit between payments made by customers and the funds that are usable by the company.

Float factor An estimate of the average number of days it takes deposited checks to clear; average daily float divided by average daily deposit.

Float-adjusted market-capitalization weighting An index weighting method in which the weight assigned to each constituent security is determined by adjusting its market capitalization for its market float.

Floaters See *floating-rate notes*.

Floating-rate notes A note on which interest payments are not fixed, but instead vary from period to period depending on the current level of a reference interest rate.

Floor A series of put options on an interest rate, with each option expiring at the date on which the floating loan rate will be reset, and with each option having the same exercise rate. A floor in general can have an underlying other than the interest rate.

Floor traders Market makers that buy and sell by quoting a bid and an ask price. They are the primary providers of liquidity to the market.

Floorlet Each component put option in a floor.

Flotation cost Fees charged to companies by investment bankers and other costs associated with raising new capital.

Foreign currency reserves Holding by the central bank of non-domestic currency deposits and non-domestic bonds.

Foreign direct investment Direct investment by a firm in one country (the source country) in productive assets in a foreign country (the host country).

Foreign exchange gains (or losses) Gains (or losses) that occur when the exchange rate changes between the investor's currency and the currency that foreign securities are denominated in.

Foreign portfolio investment Shorter-term investment by individuals, firms, and institutional investors (e.g., pension funds) in foreign financial instruments such as foreign stocks and foreign government bonds.

Forward commitments Class of derivatives that provides the ability to lock in a price to transact in the future at a previously agreed-upon price.

Forward contract An agreement between two parties in which one party, the buyer, agrees to buy from the other party, the seller, an underlying asset at a later date for a price established at the start of the contract.

Forward curve A series of forward rates, each having the same timeframe.

Forward market For future delivery, beyond the usual settlement time period in the cash market.

Forward price The fixed price or rate at which the transaction scheduled to occur at the expiration of a forward contract will take place. This price is agreed on at the initiation date of the contract.

Forward rate The interest rate on a bond or money market instrument traded in a forward market. A forward rate can be interpreted as an incremental, or marginal, return for extending the time-to-maturity for an additional time period.

Forward rate agreement (FRA) A forward contract calling for one party to make a fixed interest payment and the other to make an interest payment at a rate to be determined at the contract expiration.

Fractile A value at or below which a stated fraction of the data lies.

Fractional reserve banking Banking in which reserves constitute a fraction of deposits.

Free cash flow The actual cash that would be available to the company's investors after making all investments necessary to maintain the company as an ongoing enterprise (also referred to as free cash flow to the firm); the internally generated funds that can be distributed to the company's investors (e.g., shareholders and bondholders) without impairing the value of the company.

Free cash flow to equity (FCFE)   The cash flow available to a company's common shareholders after all operating expenses, interest, and principal payments have been made, and necessary investments in working and fixed capital have been made.

Free cash flow to the firm (FCFF)   The cash flow available to the company's suppliers of capital after all operating expenses have been paid and necessary investments in working capital and fixed capital have been made.

Free float   The number of shares that are readily and freely tradable in the secondary market.

Free trade   When there are no government restrictions on a country's ability to trade.

Free trade areas   One of the most prevalent forms of regional integration, in which all barriers to the flow of goods and services among members have been eliminated.

Free-cash-flow-to-equity models   Valuation models based on discounting expected future free cash flow to equity.

Frequency distribution   A tabular display of data summarized into a relatively small number of intervals.

Frequency polygon   A graph of a frequency distribution obtained by drawing straight lines joining successive points representing the class frequencies.

Full price   The price of a security with accrued interest; also called the *invoice* or *dirty* price.

Fundamental analysis   The examination of publicly available information and the formulation of forecasts to estimate the intrinsic value of assets.

Fundamental value   The underlying or true value of an asset based on an analysis of its qualitative and quantitative characteristics. Also called *intrinsic value*.

Fundamental weighting   An index weighting method in which the weight assigned to each constituent security is based on its underlying company's size. It attempts to address the disadvantages of market-capitalization weighting by using measures that are independent of the constituent security's price.

Funds of hedge funds   Funds that hold a portfolio of hedge funds.

Future value (FV)   The amount to which a payment or series of payments will grow by a stated future date.

Futures commission merchants (FCMs)   Individuals or companies that execute futures transactions for other parties off the exchange.

Futures contract   A variation of a forward contract that has essentially the same basic definition but with some additional features, such as a clearinghouse guarantee against credit losses, a daily settlement of gains and losses, and an organized electronic or floor trading facility.

Futures price   The agreed-upon price of a futures contract.

G-spread   The yield spread in basis points over an actual or interpolated government bond.

GDP deflator   A gauge of prices and inflation that measures the aggregate changes in prices across the overall economy.

Gains   Asset inflows not directly related to the ordinary activities of the business.

Game theory   The set of tools decision makers use to incorporate responses by rival decision makers into their strategies.

Gamma   A numerical measure of how sensitive an option's delta is to a change in the underlying.

General equilibrium analysis   An analysis that provides for equilibria in multiple markets simultaneously.

General partner   The partner that runs the business and theoretically bears unlimited liability.

Geometric mean   A measure of central tendency computed by taking the nth root of the product of n non-negative values.

Giffen good   A good that is consumed more as the price of the good rises.

Gilts   Bonds issued by the U.K. government.

Giro system   An electronic payment system used widely in Europe and Japan.

Global depository receipt   A depository receipt that is issued outside of the company's home country and outside of the United States.

Global minimum-variance portfolio   The portfolio on the minimum-variance frontier with the smallest variance of return.

Global registered share   A common share that is traded on different stock exchanges around the world in different currencies.

Gold standard   With respect to a currency, if a currency is on the gold standard a given amount can be converted into a prespecified amount of gold.

Golden cross   A technical analysis term that describes a situation where a short-term moving average crosses from below a longer-term moving average to above it; this movement is considered bullish.

Good-on-close   An execution instruction specifying that an order can only be filled at the close of trading. Also called *market on close*.

Good-on-open   An execution instruction specifying that an order can only be filled at the opening of trading.

Good-till-cancelled order   An order specifying that it is valid until the entity placing the order has cancelled it (or, commonly, until some specified amount of time such as 60 days has elapsed, whichever comes sooner).

Goods markets   Markets for the output of production.

Goodwill   An intangible asset that represents the excess of the purchase price of an acquired company over the value of the net assets acquired.

Government equivalent yield   A yield that restates a yield-to-maturity based on 30/360 day-count to one based on actual/actual.

Greenmail   The purchase of the accumulated shares of a hostile investor by a company that is targeted for takeover by that investor, usually at a substantial premium over market price.

Grey market   The forward market for bonds about to be issued. Also called "when issued" market.

Gross domestic product   The market value of all final goods and services produced within the economy in a given period of time (output definition) or, equivalently, the aggregate income earned by all households, all companies, and the government within the economy in a given period of time (income definition).

Gross margin   Sales minus the cost of sales (i.e., the cost of goods sold for a manufacturing company).

Gross profit   Sales minus the cost of sales (i.e., the cost of goods sold for a manufacturing company).

Gross profit margin   The ratio of gross profit to revenues.

Grouping by function   With reference to the presentation of expenses in an income statement, the grouping together of expenses serving the same function, e.g. all items that are costs of goods sold.

Grouping by nature With reference to the presentation of expenses in an income statement, the grouping together of expenses by similar nature, e.g., all depreciation expenses.

Growth cyclical A term sometimes used to describe companies that are growing rapidly on a long-term basis but that still experience above-average fluctuation in their revenues and profits over the course of a business cycle.

Growth investors With reference to equity investors, investors who seek to invest in high-earnings-growth companies.

Haircut See *repo margin.*

Harmonic mean A type of weighted mean computed by averaging the reciprocals of the observations, then taking the reciprocal of that average.

Head and shoulders pattern In technical analysis, a reversal pattern that is formed in three parts: a left shoulder, head, and right shoulder; used to predict a change from an uptrend to a downtrend.

Headline inflation The inflation rate calculated based on the price index that includes all goods and services in an economy.

Hedge funds Private investment vehicles that typically use leverage, derivatives, and long and short investment strategies.

Hedge portfolio A hypothetical combination of the derivative and its underlying that eliminates risk.

Held for trading Debt or equity financial assets bought with the intention to sell them in the near term, usually less than three months; securities that a company intends to trade. Also called *trading securities.*

Held-to-maturity Debt (fixed-income) securities that a company intends to hold to maturity; these are presented at their original cost, updated for any amortization of discounts or premiums.

Herding Clustered trading that may or may not be based on information.

Hidden order An order that is exposed not to the public but only to the brokers or exchanges that receive it.

High water marks The highest value, net of fees, which a fund has reached. It reflects the highest cumulative return used to calculate an incentive fee.

Histogram A bar chart of data that have been grouped into a frequency distribution.

Historical cost In reference to assets, the amount paid to purchase an asset, including any costs of acquisition and/or preparation; with reference to liabilities, the amount of proceeds received in exchange in issuing the liability.

Historical equity risk premium approach An estimate of a country's equity risk premium that is based upon the historical averages of the risk-free rate and the rate of return on the market portfolio.

Historical simulation Another term for the historical method of estimating VAR. This term is somewhat misleading in that the method involves not a *simulation* of the past but rather what *actually happened* in the past, sometimes adjusted to reflect the fact that a different portfolio may have existed in the past than is planned for the future.

Holder-of-record date The date that a shareholder listed on the corporation's books will be deemed to have ownership of the shares for purposes of receiving an upcoming dividend; two business days after the ex-dividend date.

Holding period return The return that an investor earns during a specified holding period; a synonym for total return.

Holding period yield (HPY) The return that an investor earns during a specified holding period; holding period return with reference to a fixed-income instrument.

Homogeneity of expectations The assumption that all investors have the same economic expectations and thus have the same expectations of prices, cash flows, and other investment characteristics.

Horizon yield The internal rate of return between the total return (the sum of reinvested coupon payments and the sale price or redemption amount) and the purchase price of the bond.

Horizontal analysis Common-size analysis that involves comparing a specific financial statement with that statement in prior or future time periods; also, cross-sectional analysis of one company with another.

Horizontal demand schedule Implies that at a given price, the response in the quantity demanded is infinite.

Household A person or a group of people living in the same residence, taken as a basic unit in economic analysis.

Hurdle rate The rate of return that must be met for a project to be accepted.

Hypothesis With reference to statistical inference, a statement about one or more populations.

Hypothesis testing With reference to statistical inference, the subdivision dealing with the testing of hypotheses about one or more populations.

I-spread The yield spread of a specific bond over the standard swap rate in that currency of the same tenor.

IRR rule An investment decision rule that accepts projects or investments for which the IRR is greater than the opportunity cost of capital.

Iceberg order An order in which the display size is less than the order's full size.

If-converted method A method for accounting for the effect of convertible securities on earnings per share (EPS) that specifies what EPS would have been if the convertible securities had been converted at the beginning of the period, taking account of the effects of conversion on net income and the weighted average number of shares outstanding.

Immediate or cancel order An order that is valid only upon receipt by the broker or exchange. If such an order cannot be filled in part or in whole upon receipt, it cancels immediately. Also called *fill or kill.*

Impact lag The lag associated with the result of actions affecting the economy with delay.

Imperfect competition A market structure in which an individual firm has enough share of the market (or can control a certain segment of the market) such that it is able to exert some influence over price.

Implicit price deflator for GDP A gauge of prices and inflation that measures the aggregate changes in prices across the overall economy.

Implied forward rates Calculated from spot rates, an implied forward rate is a break-even reinvestment rate that links the return on an investment in a shorter-term zero-coupon bond to the return on an investment in a longer-term zero-coupon bond.

Implied volatility The volatility that option traders use to price an option, implied by the price of the option and a particular option-pricing model.

Import license Specifies the quantity of a good that can be imported into a country.

Imports   Goods and services that a domestic economy (i.e., house-holds, firms, and government) purchases from other countries.

In the money   Options that, if exercised, would result in the value received being worth more than the payment required to exercise.

Incentive fee (or performance fee)   Funds distributed by the general partner to the limited partner(s) based on realized profits.

Income   Increases in economic benefits in the form of inflows or enhancements of assets, or decreases of liabilities that result in an increase in equity (other than increases resulting from contributions by owners).

Income constraint   The constraint on a consumer to spend, in total, no more than his income.

Income elasticity of demand   A measure of the responsiveness of demand to changes in income, defined as the percentage change in quantity demanded divided by the percentage change in income.

Income statement   A financial statement that provides information about a company's profitability over a stated period of time. Also called *statement of operations* or *profit and loss statement*.

Income tax paid   The actual amount paid for income taxes in the period; not a provision, but the actual cash outflow.

Income tax payable   The income tax owed by the company on the basis of taxable income.

Income trust   A type of equity ownership vehicle established as a trust issuing ownership shares known as units.

Increasing marginal returns   Where the marginal product of a resource increases as additional units of that input are employed.

Increasing returns to scale   Reduction in cost per unit resulting from increased production.

Increasing-cost industry   An industry in which per-unit costs and output prices are higher when industry output is increased in the long run.

Incremental cash flow   The cash flow that is realized because of a decision; the changes or increments to cash flows resulting from a decision or action.

Indenture   Legal contract that describes the form of a bond, the obligations of the issuer, and the rights of the bondholders. Also called the *trust deed.*

Independent   With reference to events, the property that the occurrence of one event does not affect the probability of another event occurring.

Independent projects   Independent projects are projects whose cash flows are independent of each other.

Independently and identically distributed (IID)   With respect to random variables, the property of random variables that are independent of each other but follow the identical probability distribution.

Index of Leading Economic Indicators   A composite of economic variables used by analysts to predict future economic conditions.

Index-linked bond   Bond for which coupon payments and/or principal repayment are linked to a specified index.

Indexing   An investment strategy in which an investor constructs a portfolio to mirror the performance of a specified index.

Indifference curve   A curve representing all the combinations of two goods or attributes such that the consumer is entirely indifferent among them.

Indifference curve map   A group or family of indifference curves, representing a consumer's entire utility function.

Indirect format   With reference to cash flow statements, a format for the presentation of the statement which, in the operating cash flow section, begins with net income then shows additions and subtractions to arrive at operating cash flow. Also called *indirect method.*

Indirect method   See *indirect format.*

Indirect taxes   Taxes such as taxes on spending, as opposed to direct taxes.

Industry   A group of companies offering similar products and/or services.

Industry analysis   The analysis of a specific branch of manufacturing, service, or trade.

Inelastic   Insensitive to price changes.

Inelastic supply   Said of supply that is insensitive to the price of goods sold.

Inferior goods   A good whose consumption decreases as income increases.

Inflation   The percentage increase in the general price level from one period to the next; a sustained rise in the overall level of prices in an economy.

Inflation Reports   A type of economic publication put out by many central banks.

Inflation premium   An extra return that compensates investors for expected inflation.

Inflation rate   The percentage change in a price index—that is, the speed of overall price level movements.

Inflation uncertainty   The degree to which economic agents view future rates of inflation as difficult to forecast.

Inflation-linked bond   Type of index-linked bond that offers investors protection against inflation by linking the bond's coupon payments and/or the principal repayment to an index of consumer prices. Also called *linkers.*

Information cascade   The transmission of information from those participants who act first and whose decisions influence the decisions of others.

Information-motivated traders   Traders that trade to profit from information that they believe allows them to predict future prices.

Informationally efficient market   A market in which asset prices reflect new information quickly and rationally.

Initial margin   The amount that must be deposited in a clearinghouse account when entering into a futures contract.

Initial margin requirement   The margin requirement on the first day of a transaction as well as on any day in which additional margin funds must be deposited.

Initial public offering   (IPO) The first issuance of common shares to the public by a formerly private corporation.

Installment method   With respect to revenue recognition, a method that specifies that the portion of the total profit of the sale that is recognized in each period is determined by the percentage of the total sales price for which the seller has received cash.

Installment sales   With respect to revenue recognition, a method that specifies that the portion of the total profit of the sale that is recognized in each period is determined by the percentage of the total sales price for which the seller has received cash.

Intangible assets   Assets lacking physical substance, such as patents and trademarks.

Interbank market   The market of loans and deposits between banks for maturities ranging from overnight to one year.

Interbank money market   The market of loans and deposits between banks for maturities ranging from overnight to one year.

Interest   Payment for lending funds.

Interest coverage   A solvency ratio calculated as EBIT divided by interest payments.

Interest rate   A rate of return that reflects the relationship between differently dated cash flows; a discount rate.

Interest rate call   An option in which the holder has the right to make a known interest payment and receive an unknown interest payment.

Interest rate cap   A series of call options on an interest rate, with each option expiring at the date on which the floating loan rate will be reset, and with each option having the same exercise rate. A cap in general can have an underlying other than an interest rate.

Interest rate collar   A combination of a long cap and a short floor, or a short cap and a long floor. A collar in general can have an underlying other than an interest rate.

Interest rate floor   A series of put options on an interest rate, with each option expiring at the date on which the floating loan rate will be reset, and with each option having the same exercise rate. A floor in general can have an underlying other than the interest rate.

Interest rate forward   See *forward rate agreement.*

Interest rate option   An option in which the underlying is an interest rate.

Interest rate put   An option in which the holder has the right to make an unknown interest payment and receive a known interest payment.

Interest rate swap   A swap in which the underlying is an interest rate. Can be viewed as a currency swap in which both currencies are the same and can be created as a combination of currency swaps.

Intergenerational data mining   A form of data mining that applies information developed by previous researchers using a dataset to guide current research using the same or a related dataset.

Intermarket analysis   A field within technical analysis that combines analysis of major categories of securities—namely, equities, bonds, currencies, and commodities—to identify market trends and possible inflections in a trend.

Intermediate goods and services   Goods and services purchased for use as inputs to produce other goods and services.

Internal rate of return   (IRR) The discount rate that makes net present value equal 0; the discount rate that makes the present value of an investment's costs (outflows) equal to the present value of the investment's benefits (inflows).

Interpolated spread   The yield spread of a specific bond over the standard swap rate in that currency of the same tenor.

Interquartile range   The difference between the third and first quartiles of a dataset.

Interval   With reference to grouped data, a set of values within which an observation falls.

Interval scale   A measurement scale that not only ranks data but also gives assurance that the differences between scale values are equal.

Intrinsic value   See *fundamental value.*

Inventory   The unsold units of product on hand.

Inventory blanket lien   The use of inventory as collateral for a loan. Though the lender has claim to some or all of the company's inventory, the company may still sell or use the inventory in the ordinary course of business.

Inventory investment   Net change in business inventory.

Inventory turnover   An activity ratio calculated as cost of goods sold divided by average inventory.

Inverse demand function   A restatement of the demand function in which price is stated as a function of quantity.

Investing activities   Activities which are associated with the acquisition and disposal of property, plant, and equipment; intangible assets; other long-term assets; and both long-term and short-term investments in the equity and debt (bonds and loans) issued by other companies.

Investment banks   Financial intermediaries that provide advice to their mostly corporate clients and help them arrange transactions such as initial and seasoned securities offerings.

Investment opportunity schedule   A graphical depiction of a company's investment opportunities ordered from highest to lowest expected return. A company's optimal capital budget is found where the investment opportunity schedule intersects with the company's marginal cost of capital.

Investment policy statement   (IPS) A written planning document that describes a client's investment objectives and risk tolerance over a relevant time horizon, along with constraints that apply to the client's portfolio.

Investment property   Property used to earn rental income or capital appreciation (or both).

January effect   Calendar anomaly that stock market returns in January are significantly higher compared to the rest of the months of the year, with most of the abnormal returns reported during the first five trading days in January. Also called *turn-of-the-year effect.*

Joint probability   The probability of the joint occurrence of stated events.

Joint probability function   A function giving the probability of joint occurrences of values of stated random variables.

Just-in-time (JIT) method   Method of managing inventory that minimizes in-process inventory stocks.

Keynesians   Economists who believe that fiscal policy can have powerful effects on aggregate demand, output, and employment when there is substantial spare capacity in an economy.

Kondratieff wave   A 54-year long economic cycle postulated by Nikolai Kondratieff.

Kurtosis   The statistical measure that indicates the peakedness of a distribution.

LIFO layer liquidation   With respect to the application of the LIFO inventory method, the liquidation of old, relatively low-priced inventory; happens when the volume of sales rises above the volume of recent purchases so that some sales are made from relatively old, low-priced inventory. Also called *LIFO liquidation.*

LIFO method   The last in, first out, method of accounting for inventory, which matches sales against the costs of items of inventory in the reverse order the items were placed in inventory (i.e., inventory produced or acquired last are assumed to be sold first).

Labor force   The portion of the working age population (over the age of 16) that is employed or is available for work but not working (unemployed).

Labor markets   Markets for labor services.

Labor productivity   The quantity of goods and services (real GDP) that a worker can produce in one hour of work.

Laddering strategy   A form of active strategy which entails scheduling maturities on a systematic basis within the investment portfolio such that investments are spread out equally over the term of the ladder.

Lagging economic indicators   Turning points that take place later than those of the overall economy; they are believed to have value in identifying the economy's past condition.

Laspeyres index   A price index created by holding the composition of the consumption basket constant.

Law of demand   The principle that as the price of a good rises, buyers will choose to buy less of it, and as its price falls, they will buy more.

Law of diminishing returns   The smallest output that a firm can produce such that its long run average costs are minimized.

Law of one price   The condition in a financial market in which two equivalent financial instruments or combinations of financial instruments can sell for only one price. Equivalent to the principle that no arbitrage opportunities are possible.

Law of supply   The principle that a rise in price usually results in an increase in the quantity supplied.

Lead underwriter   The lead investment bank in a syndicate of investment banks and broker–dealers involved in a securities underwriting.

Leading economic indicators   Turning points that usually precede those of the overall economy; they are believed to have value for predicting the economy's future state, usually near-term.

Legal tender   Something that must be accepted when offered in exchange for goods and services.

Lender of last resort   An entity willing to lend money when no other entity is ready to do so.

Leptokurtic   Describes a distribution that is more peaked than a normal distribution.

Letter of credit   Form of external credit enhancement whereby a financial institution provides the issuer with a credit line to reimburse any cash flow shortfalls from the assets backing the issue.

Level of significance   The probability of a Type I error in testing a hypothesis.

Leverage   In the context of corporate finance, leverage refers to the use of fixed costs within a company's cost structure. Fixed costs that are operating costs (such as depreciation or rent) create operating leverage. Fixed costs that are financial costs (such as interest expense) create financial leverage.

Leveraged buyout   (LBO) A transaction whereby the target company management team converts the target to a privately held company by using heavy borrowing to finance the purchase of the target company's outstanding shares.

Liabilities   Present obligations of an enterprise arising from past events, the settlement of which is expected to result in an outflow of resources embodying economic benefits; creditors' claims on the resources of a company.

Life-cycle stage   The stage of the life cycle: embryonic, growth, shakeout, mature, declining.

Likelihood   The probability of an observation, given a particular set of conditions.

Limit down   A limit move in the futures market in which the price at which a transaction would be made is at or below the lower limit.

Limit move   A condition in the futures markets in which the price at which a transaction would be made is at or beyond the price limits.

Limit order   Instructions to a broker or exchange to obtain the best price immediately available when filling an order, but in no event accept a price higher than a specified (limit) price when buying or accept a price lower than a specified (limit) price when selling.

Limit order book   The book or list of limit orders to buy and sell that pertains to a security.

Limit up   A limit move in the futures market in which the price at which a transaction would be made is at or above the upper limit.

Limitations on liens   Meant to put limits on how much secured debt an issuer can have.

Limited partners   Partners with limited liability. Limited partnerships in hedge and private equity funds are typically restricted to investors who are expected to understand and to be able to assume the risks associated with the investments.

Line chart   In technical analysis, a plot of price data, typically closing prices, with a line connecting the points.

Linear interpolation   The estimation of an unknown value on the basis of two known values that bracket it, using a straight line between the two known values.

Linear scale   A scale in which equal distances correspond to equal absolute amounts. Also called *arithmetic scale*.

Linker   See *inflation-linked bond*.

Liquid market   Said of a market in which traders can buy or sell with low total transaction costs when they want to trade.

Liquidating dividend   A dividend that is a return of capital rather than a distribution from earnings or retained earnings.

Liquidation   To sell the assets of a company, division, or subsidiary piecemeal, typically because of bankruptcy; the form of bankruptcy that allows for the orderly satisfaction of creditors' claims after which the company ceases to exist.

Liquidity   The ability to purchase or sell an asset quickly and easily at a price close to fair market value. The ability to meet short-term obligations using assets that are the most readily converted into cash.

Liquidity premium   An extra return that compensates investors for the risk of loss relative to an investment's fair value if the investment needs to be converted to cash quickly.

Liquidity ratios   Financial ratios measuring the company's ability to meet its short-term obligations.

Liquidity trap   A condition in which the demand for money becomes infinitely elastic (horizontal demand curve) so that injections of money into the economy will not lower interest rates or affect real activity.

Load fund   A mutual fund in which, in addition to the annual fee, a percentage fee is charged to invest in the fund and/or for redemptions from the fund.

Locals   Market makers that buy and sell by quoting a bid and an ask price. They are the primary providers of liquidity to the market.

Lockbox system   A payment system in which customer payments are mailed to a post office box and the banking institution retrieves and deposits these payments several times a day, enabling the company to have use of the fund sooner than in a centralized system in which customer payments are sent to the company.

Locked limit   A condition in the futures markets in which a transaction cannot take place because the price would be beyond the limits.

Lockup period   The minimum period before investors are allowed to make withdrawals or redeem shares from a fund.

Logarithmic scale A scale in which equal distances represent equal proportional changes in the underlying quantity.

London Interbank Offered Rate (Libor or LIBOR) Collective name for multiple rates at which a select set of banks believe they could borrow unsecured funds from other banks in the London interbank market for different currencies and different borrowing periods ranging from overnight to one year.

Long The buyer of a derivative contract. Also refers to the position of owning a derivative.

Long position A position in an asset or contract in which one owns the asset or has an exercisable right under the contract.

Long-lived assets Assets that are expected to provide economic benefits over a future period of time, typically greater than one year. Also called *long-term assets*.

Long-run average total cost curve The curve describing average total costs when no costs are considered fixed.

Long-run industry supply curve A curve describing the relationship between quantity supplied and output prices when no costs are considered fixed.

Long-term contract A contract that spans a number of accounting periods.

Long-term equity anticipatory securities (LEAPS) Options originally created with expirations of several years.

Longitudinal data Observations on characteristic(s) of the same observational unit through time.

Look-ahead bias A bias caused by using information that was unavailable on the test date.

Loss severity Portion of a bond's value (including unpaid interest) an investor loses in the event of default.

Losses Asset outflows not directly related to the ordinary activities of the business.

Lower bound The lowest possible value of an option.

M^2 A measure of what a portfolio would have returned if it had taken on the same total risk as the market index.

Macaulay duration The approximate amount of time a bond would have to be held for the market discount rate at purchase to be realized if there is a single change in interest rate. It indicates the point in time when the coupon reinvestment and price effects of a change in yield-to-maturity offset each other.

Macroeconomics The branch of economics that deals with aggregate economic quantities, such as national output and national income.

Maintenance covenants Covenants in bank loan agreements that require the borrower to satisfy certain financial ratio tests while the loan is outstanding.

Maintenance margin The minimum amount that is required by a futures clearinghouse to maintain a margin account and to protect against default. Participants whose margin balances drop below the required maintenance margin must replenish their accounts.

Maintenance margin requirement The margin requirement on any day other than the first day of a transaction.

Management buy-ins Leveraged buyout in which the current management team is being replaced and the acquiring team will be involved in managing the company.

Management buyout (MBO) An event in which a group of investors consisting primarily of the company's existing management purchase all of its outstanding shares and take the company private.

Management fee A fee based on assets under management or committed capital, as applicable. Also called *base fee*.

Manufacturing resource planning (MRP) The incorporation of production planning into inventory management. A MRP analysis provides both a materials acquisition schedule and a production schedule.

Margin The amount of money that a trader deposits in a margin account. The term is derived from the stock market practice in which an investor borrows a portion of the money required to purchase a certain amount of stock. In futures markets, there is no borrowing so the margin is more of a down payment or performance bond.

Margin bond A cash deposit required by the clearinghouse from the participants to a contract to provide a credit guarantee. Also called a *performance bond*.

Margin call A request for the short to deposit additional funds to bring their balance up to the initial margin.

Margin loan Money borrowed from a broker to purchase securities.

Marginal cost The cost of producing an additional unit of a good.

Marginal probability The probability of an event *not* conditioned on another event.

Marginal product Measures the productivity of each unit of input and is calculated by taking the difference in total product from adding another unit of input (assuming other resource quantities are held constant).

Marginal propensity to consume The proportion of an additional unit of disposable income that is consumed or spent; the change in consumption for a small change in income.

Marginal propensity to save The proportion of an additional unit of disposable income that is saved (not spent).

Marginal rate of substitution The rate at which one is willing to give up one good to obtain more of another.

Marginal revenue The change in total revenue divided by the change in quantity sold; simply, the additional revenue from selling one more unit.

Marginal revenue product The amount of additional revenue received from employing an additional unit of an input.

Marginal value The added value from an additional unit of a good.

Marginal value curve A curve describing the highest price consumers are willing to pay for each additional unit of a good.

Mark to market The revaluation of a financial asset or liability to its current market value or fair value.

Market A means of bringing buyers and sellers together to exchange goods and services.

Market anomaly Change in the price or return of a security that cannot directly be linked to current relevant information known in the market or to the release of new information into the market.

Market bid–ask spread The difference between the best bid and the best offer.

Market discount rate The rate of return required by investors given the risk of the investment in a bond; also called the *required yield* or the *required rate of return*.

Market equilibrium The condition in which the quantity willingly offered for sale by sellers at a given price is just equal to the quantity willingly demanded by buyers at that same price.

Market float The number of shares that are available to the investing public.

Market liquidity risk The risk that the price at which investors can actually transact—buying or selling—may differ from the price indicated in the market.

Market mechanism   The process by which price adjusts until there is neither excess supply nor excess demand.

Market model   A regression equation that specifies a linear relationship between the return on a security (or portfolio) and the return on a broad market index.

Market multiple models   Valuation models based on share price multiples or enterprise value multiples.

Market order   Instructions to a broker or exchange to obtain the best price immediately available when filling an order.

Market structure   The competitive environment (perfect competition, monopolistic competition, oligopoly, and monopoly).

Market value   The price at which an asset or security can currently be bought or sold in an open market.

Market-capitalization weighting   An index weighting method in which the weight assigned to each constituent security is determined by dividing its market capitalization by the total market capitalization (sum of the market capitalization) of all securities in the index. Also called *value weighting*.

Market-on-close   An execution instruction specifying that an order can only be filled at the close of trading.

Market-oriented investors   With reference to equity investors, investors whose investment disciplines cannot be clearly categorized as value or growth.

Marketable limit order   A buy limit order in which the limit price is placed above the best offer, or a sell limit order in which the limit price is placed below the best bid. Such orders generally will partially or completely fill right away.

Marking to market   A procedure used primarily in futures markets in which the parties to a contract settle the amount owed daily. Also known as the *daily settlement*.

Markowitz efficient frontier   The graph of the set of portfolios offering the maximum expected return for their level of risk (standard deviation of return).

Matching principle   The accounting principle that expenses should be recognized when the associated revenue is recognized.

Matching strategy   An active investment strategy that includes intentional matching of the timing of cash outflows with investment maturities.

Matrix pricing   Process of estimating the market discount rate and price of a bond based on the quoted or flat prices of more frequently traded comparable bonds.

Maturity premium   An extra return that compensates investors for the increased sensitivity of the market value of debt to a change in market interest rates as maturity is extended.

Maturity structure   A factor explaining the differences in yields on similar bonds; also called *term structure*.

Mean absolute deviation   With reference to a sample, the mean of the absolute values of deviations from the sample mean.

Mean excess return   The average rate of return in excess of the risk-free rate.

Mean–variance analysis   An approach to portfolio analysis using expected means, variances, and covariances of asset returns.

Measure of central tendency   A quantitative measure that specifies where data are centered.

Measure of value   A standard for measuring value; a function of money.

Measurement scales   A scheme of measuring differences. The four types of measurement scales are nominal, ordinal, interval, and ratio.

Measures of location   A quantitative measure that describes the location or distribution of data; includes not only measures of central tendency but also other measures such as percentiles.

Median   The value of the middle item of a set of items that has been sorted into ascending or descending order; the 50th percentile.

Medium of exchange   Any asset that can be used to purchase goods and services or to repay debts; a function of money.

Medium-term note   A corporate bond offered continuously to investors by an agent of the issuer, designed to fill the funding gap between commercial paper and long-term bonds.

Menu costs   A cost of inflation in which businesses constantly have to incur the costs of changing the advertised prices of their goods and services.

Mesokurtic   Describes a distribution with kurtosis identical to that of the normal distribution.

Mezzanine financing   Debt or preferred shares with a relationship to common equity due to a feature such as attached warrants or conversion options and that is subordinate to both senior and high yield debt. It is referred to as mezzanine because of its location on the balance sheet.

Microeconomics   The branch of economics that deals with markets and decision making of individual economic units, including consumers and businesses.

Minimum efficient scale   The smallest output that a firm can produce such that its long run average cost is minimized.

Minimum-variance portfolio   The portfolio with the minimum variance for each given level of expected return.

Minsky moment   Named for Hyman Minksy: A point in a business cycle when, after individuals become overextended in borrowing to finance speculative investments, people start realizing that something is likely to go wrong and a panic ensues leading to asset sell-offs.

Mismatching strategy   An active investment strategy whereby the timing of cash outflows is not matched with investment maturities.

Modal interval   With reference to grouped data, the most frequently occurring interval.

Mode   The most frequently occurring value in a set of observations.

Modern portfolio theory   (MPT) The analysis of rational portfolio choices based on the efficient use of risk.

Modified duration   A measure of the percentage price change of a bond given a change in its yield-to-maturity.

Momentum oscillators   A graphical representation of market sentiment that is constructed from price data and calculated so that it oscillates either between a high and a low or around some number.

Monetarists   Economists who believe that the rate of growth of the money supply is the primary determinant of the rate of inflation.

Monetary policy   Actions taken by a nation's central bank to affect aggregate output and prices through changes in bank reserves, reserve requirements, or its target interest rate.

Monetary transmission mechanism   The process whereby a central bank's interest rate gets transmitted through the economy and ultimately affects the rate of increase of prices.

Monetary union   An economic union in which the members adopt a common currency.

Money   A generally accepted medium of exchange and unit of account.

Money convexity For a bond, the annual or approximate convexity multiplied by the full price.

Money creation The process by which changes in bank reserves translate into changes in the money supply.

Money duration A measure of the price change in units of the currency in which the bond is denominated given a change in its yield-to-maturity.

Money market The market for short-term debt instruments (one-year maturity or less).

Money market securities Fixed-income securities with maturities at issuance of one year or less.

Money market yield A yield on a basis comparable to the quoted yield on an interest-bearing money market instrument that pays interest on a 360-day basis; the annualized holding period yield, assuming a 360-day year.

Money multiplier Describes how a change in reserves is expected to affect the money supply; in its simplest form, 1 divided by the reserve requirement.

Money neutrality The thesis that an increase in the money supply leads in the long-run to an increase in the price level, while leaving real variables like output and employment unaffected.

Money-weighted return The internal rate of return on a portfolio, taking account of all cash flows.

Moneyness The relationship between the price of the underlying and an option's exercise price.

Monopolist Said of an entity that is the only seller in its market.

Monopolistic competition Highly competitive form of imperfect competition; the competitive characteristic is a notably large number of firms, while the monopoly aspect is the result of product differentiation.

Monopoly In pure monopoly markets, there are no substitutes for the given product or service. There is a single seller, which exercises considerable power over pricing and output decisions.

Monte Carlo simulation An approach to estimating a probability distribution of outcomes to examine what might happen if particular risks are faced. This method is widely used in the sciences as well as in business to study a variety of problems.

Mortgage-backed securities Debt obligations that represent claims to the cash flows from pools of mortgage loans, most commonly on residential property.

Moving average The average of the closing price of a security over a specified number of periods. With each new period, the average is recalculated.

Moving-average convergence/divergence oscillator (MACD) A momentum oscillator that is constructed based on the difference between short-term and long-term moving averages of a security's price.

Multi-factor model A model that explains a variable in terms of the values of a set of factors.

Multi-market indices Comprised of indices from different countries, designed to represent multiple security markets.

Multi-step format With respect to the format of the income statement, a format that presents a subtotal for gross profit (revenue minus cost of goods sold).

Multilateral trading facilities See *alternative trading systems*.

Multinational corporation A company operating in more than one country or having subsidiary firms in more than one country.

Multiplication rule for probabilities The rule that the joint probability of events A and B equals the probability of A given B times the probability of B.

Multiplier models Valuation models based on share price multiples or enterprise value multiples.

Multivariate distribution A probability distribution that specifies the probabilities for a group of related random variables.

Multivariate normal distribution A probability distribution for a group of random variables that is completely defined by the means and variances of the variables plus all the correlations between pairs of the variables.

Muni A type of non-sovereign bond issued by a state or local government in the United States. It very often (but not always) offers income tax exemptions.

Municipal bonds A type of non-sovereign bond issued by a state or local government in the United States. It very often (but not always) offers income tax exemptions.

Mutual fund A professionally managed investment pool in which investors in the fund typically each have a pro-rata claim on the income and value of the fund.

Mutually exclusive projects Mutually exclusive projects compete directly with each other. For example, if Projects A and B are mutually exclusive, you can choose A or B, but you cannot choose both.

n Factorial For a positive integer n, the product of the first n positive integers; 0 factorial equals 1 by definition. n factorial is written as $n!$.

NDFs See *non-deliverable forwards*.

NPV rule An investment decision rule that states that an investment should be undertaken if its NPV is positive but not undertaken if its NPV is negative.

Narrow money The notes and coins in circulation in an economy, plus other very highly liquid deposits.

Nash equilibrium When two or more participants in a non-coop-erative game have no incentive to deviate from their respective equilibrium strategies given their opponent's strategies.

National income The income received by all factors of production used in the generation of final output. National income equals gross domestic product (or, in some countries, gross national product) minus the capital consumption allowance and a statistical discrepancy.

Natural rate of unemployment Effective unemployment rate, below which pressure emerges in labor markets.

Negative externality A negative effect (e.g., pollution) of a market transaction that is borne by parties other than those who transacted; a spillover cost.

Neo-Keynesians A group of dynamic general equilibrium models that assume slow-to-adjust prices and wages.

Net book value The remaining (undepreciated) balance of an asset's purchase cost. For liabilities, the face value of a bond minus any unamortized discount, or plus any unamortized premium.

Net exports The difference between the value of a country's exports and the value of its imports (i.e., value of exports minus imports).

Net income The difference between revenue and expenses; what remains after subtracting all expenses (including depreciation, interest, and taxes) from revenue.

Net operating cycle An estimate of the average time that elapses between paying suppliers for materials and collecting cash from the subsequent sale of goods produced.

Net present value (NPV) The present value of an investment's cash inflows (benefits) minus the present value of its cash outflows (costs).

Net profit margin   An indicator of profitability, calculated as net income divided by revenue; indicates how much of each dollar of revenues is left after all costs and expenses. Also called *profit margin* or *return on sales*.

Net realisable value   Estimated selling price in the ordinary course of business less the estimated costs necessary to make the sale.

Net revenue   Revenue after adjustments (e.g., for estimated returns or for amounts unlikely to be collected).

Net tax rate   The tax rate net of transfer payments.

Netting   When parties agree to exchange only the net amount owed from one party to the other.

Neutral rate of interest   The rate of interest that neither spurs on nor slows down the underlying economy.

New Keynesians   A group of dynamic general equilibrium models that assume slow-to-adjust prices and wages.

New classical macroeconomics   An approach to macroeconomics that seeks the macroeconomic conclusions of individuals maximizing utility on the basis of rational expectations and companies maximizing profits.

New-issue DRP   Dividend reinvestment plan in which the company meets the need for additional shares by issuing them instead of purchasing them.

No-load fund   A mutual fund in which there is no fee for investing in the fund or for redeeming fund shares, although there is an annual fee based on a percentage of the fund's net asset value.

Node   Each value on a binomial tree from which successive moves or outcomes branch.

Nominal GDP   The value of goods and services measured at current prices.

Nominal rate   A rate of interest based on the security's face value.

Nominal risk-free interest rate   The sum of the real risk-free interest rate and the inflation premium.

Nominal scale   A measurement scale that categorizes data but does not rank them.

Non-accelerating inflation rate of unemployment   Effective unemployment rate, below which pressure emerges in labor markets.

Non-cumulative preference shares   Preference shares for which dividends that are not paid in the current or subsequent periods are forfeited permanently (instead of being accrued and paid at a later date).

Non-current assets   Assets that are expected to benefit the company over an extended period of time (usually more than one year).

Non-current liabilities   Obligations that broadly represent a probable sacrifice of economic benefits in periods generally greater than one year in the future.

Non-cyclical   A company whose performance is largely independent of the business cycle.

Non-deliverable forwards   Cash-settled forward contracts, used predominately with respect to foreign exchange forwards. Also called *contracts for differences*.

Non-participating preference shares   Preference shares that do not entitle shareholders to share in the profits of the company. Instead, shareholders are only entitled to receive a fixed dividend payment and the par value of the shares in the event of liquidation.

Non-renewable resources   Finite resources that are depleted once they are consumed, such as oil and coal.

Non-satiation   The assumption that the consumer could never have so much of a preferred good that she would refuse any more, even if it were free; sometimes referred to as the "more is better" assumption.

Non-sovereign bonds   A bond issued by a government below the national level, such as a province, region, state, or city.

Non-sovereign government bonds   A bond issued by a government below the national level, such as a province, region, state, or city.

Nonconventional cash flow   In a nonconventional cash flow pattern, the initial outflow is not followed by inflows only, but the cash flows can flip from positive (inflows) to negative (outflows) again (or even change signs several times).

Noncurrent assets   Assets that are expected to benefit the company over an extended period of time (usually more than one year).

Nonparametric test   A test that is not concerned with a parameter, or that makes minimal assumptions about the population from which a sample comes.

Nonsystematic risk   Unique risk that is local or limited to a particular asset or industry that need not affect assets outside of that asset class.

Normal distribution   A continuous, symmetric probability distribution that is completely described by its mean and its variance.

Normal good   A good that is consumed in greater quantities as income increases.

Normal profit   The level of accounting profit needed to just cover the implicit opportunity costs ignored in accounting costs.

Notching   Ratings adjustment methodology where specific issues from the same borrower may be assigned different credit ratings.

Notes payable   Amounts owed by a business to creditors as a result of borrowings that are evidenced by (short-term) loan agreements.

Notice period   The length of time (typically 30 to 90 days) in advance that investors may be required to notify a fund of their intent to redeem.

Notional principal   An imputed principal amount.

Number of days of inventory   An activity ratio equal to the number of days in a period divided by the inventory ratio for the period; an indication of the number of days a company ties up funds in inventory.

Number of days of payables   An activity ratio equal to the number of days in a period divided by the payables turnover ratio for the period; an estimate of the average number of days it takes a company to pay its suppliers.

Number of days of receivables   Estimate of the average number of days it takes to collect on credit accounts.

Objective probabilities   Probabilities that generally do not vary from person to person; includes a priori and objective probabilities.

Off-the-run   Seasoned government bonds are off-the-run securities; they are not the most recently issued or the most actively traded.

Offer   The price at which a dealer or trader is willing to sell an asset, typically qualified by a maximum quantity (ask size).

Official interest rate   An interest rate that a central bank sets and announces publicly; normally the rate at which it is willing to lend money to the commercial banks. Also called *official policy rate* or *policy rate*.

Official policy rate An interest rate that a central bank sets and announces publicly; normally the rate at which it is willing to lend money to the commercial banks.

Offsetting A transaction in exchange-listed derivative markets in which a party re-enters the market to close out a position.

Oligopoly Market structure with a relatively small number of firms supplying the market.

On-the-run The most recently issued and most actively traded sovereign securities.

One-sided hypothesis test A test in which the null hypothesis is rejected only if the evidence indicates that the population parameter is greater than (smaller than) θ_0. The alternative hypothesis also has one side.

One-tailed hypothesis test A test in which the null hypothesis is rejected only if the evidence indicates that the population parameter is greater than (smaller than) θ_0. The alternative hypothesis also has one side.

Open economy An economy that trades with other countries.

Open interest The number of outstanding contracts in a clearinghouse at any given time. The open interest figure changes daily as some parties open up new positions, while other parties offset their old positions.

Open market operations The purchase or sale of bonds by the national central bank to implement monetary policy. The bonds traded are usually sovereign bonds issued by the national government.

Open-end fund A mutual fund that accepts new investment money and issues additional shares at a value equal to the net asset value of the fund at the time of investment.

Open-market DRP Dividend reinvestment plan in which the company purchases shares in the open market to acquire the additional shares credited to plan participants.

Operating activities Activities that are part of the day-to-day business functioning of an entity, such as selling inventory and providing services.

Operating breakeven The number of units produced and sold at which the company's operating profit is zero (revenues = operating costs).

Operating cash flow The net amount of cash provided from operating activities.

Operating cycle A measure of the time needed to convert raw materials into cash from a sale; it consists of the number of days of inventory and the number of days of receivables.

Operating efficiency ratios Ratios that measure how efficiently a company performs day-to-day tasks, such as the collection of receivables and management of inventory.

Operating leverage The use of fixed costs in operations.

Operating profit A company's profits on its usual business activities before deducting taxes. Also called *operating income*.

Operating profit margin A profitability ratio calculated as operating income (i.e., income before interest and taxes) divided by revenue. Also called *operating margin*.

Operating risk The risk attributed to the operating cost structure, in particular the use of fixed costs in operations; the risk arising from the mix of fixed and variable costs; the risk that a company's operations may be severely affected by environmental, social, and governance risk factors.

Operational independence A bank's ability to execute monetary policy and set interest rates in the way it thought would best meet the inflation target.

Operationally efficient Said of a market, a financial system, or an economy that has relatively low transaction costs.

Opportunity cost The value that investors forgo by choosing a particular course of action; the value of something in its best alternative use.

Option A financial instrument that gives one party the right, but not the obligation, to buy or sell an underlying asset from or to another party at a fixed price over a specific period of time. Also referred to as *contingent claim* or *option contract*.

Option contract See *option*.

Option premium The amount of money a buyer pays and seller receives to engage in an option transaction.

Option price The amount of money a buyer pays and seller receives to engage in an option transaction.

Option-adjusted price The value of the embedded option plus the flat price of the bond.

Option-adjusted spread OAS = Z-spread − Option value (in basis points per year).

Option-adjusted yield The required market discount rate whereby the price is adjusted for the value of the embedded option.

Order A specification of what instrument to trade, how much to trade, and whether to buy or sell.

Order precedence hierarchy With respect to the execution of orders to trade, a set of rules that determines which orders execute before other orders.

Order-driven markets A market (generally an auction market) that uses rules to arrange trades based on the orders that traders submit; in their pure form, such markets do not make use of dealers.

Ordinal scale A measurement scale that sorts data into categories that are ordered (ranked) with respect to some characteristic.

Ordinary annuity An annuity with a first cash flow that is paid one period from the present.

Ordinary shares Equity shares that are subordinate to all other types of equity (e.g., preferred equity). Also called *common stock* or *common shares*.

Organized exchange A securities marketplace where buyers and seller can meet to arrange their trades.

Other comprehensive income Items of comprehensive income that are not reported on the income statement; comprehensive income minus net income.

Other receivables Amounts owed to the company from parties other than customers.

Out of the money Options that, if exercised, would require the payment of more money than the value received and therefore would not be currently exercised.

Out-of-sample test A test of a strategy or model using a sample outside the time period on which the strategy or model was developed.

Outcome A possible value of a random variable.

Over-the-counter (OTC) markets A decentralized market where buy and sell orders initiated from various locations are matched through a communications network.

Overbought A market condition in which market sentiment is thought to be unsustainably bullish.

Oversold A market condition in which market sentiment is thought to be unsustainably bearish.

Own-price The price of a good or service itself (as opposed to the price of something else).

Own-price elasticity of demand The percentage change in quantity demanded for a percentage change in own price, holding all other things constant.

Owner-of-record date The date that a shareholder listed on the corporation's books will be deemed to have ownership of the shares for purposes of receiving an upcoming dividend; two business days after the ex-dividend date.

Owners' equity The excess of assets over liabilities; the residual interest of shareholders in the assets of an entity after deducting the entity's liabilities. Also called *shareholders' equity*.

Paasche index An index formula using the current composition of a basket of products.

Paired comparisons test A statistical test for differences based on paired observations drawn from samples that are dependent on each other.

Paired observations Observations that are dependent on each other.

Pairs arbitrage trade A trade in two closely related stocks involving the short sale of one and the purchase of the other.

Panel data Observations through time on a single characteristic of multiple observational units.

Par curve A sequence of yields-to-maturity such that each bond is priced at par value. The bonds are assumed to have the same currency, credit risk, liquidity, tax status, and annual yields stated for the same periodicity.

Par value The amount of principal on a bond.

Parallel shift A parallel yield curve shift implies that all rates change by the same amount in the same direction.

Parameter A descriptive measure computed from or used to describe a population of data, conventionally represented by Greek letters.

Parametric test Any test (or procedure) concerned with parameters or whose validity depends on assumptions concerning the population generating the sample.

Pari passu On an equal footing.

Partial equilibrium analysis An equilibrium analysis focused on one market, taking the values of exogenous variables as given.

Participating preference shares Preference shares that entitle shareholders to receive the standard preferred dividend plus the opportunity to receive an additional dividend if the company's profits exceed a pre-specified level.

Passive investment A buy and hold approach in which an investor does not make portfolio changes based on short-term expectations of changing market or security performance.

Passive strategy In reference to short-term cash management, it is an investment strategy characterized by simple decision rules for making daily investments.

Payable date The day that the company actually mails out (or electronically transfers) a dividend payment.

Payment date The day that the company actually mails out (or electronically transfers) a dividend payment.

Payments system The system for the transfer of money.

Payoff The value of an option at expiration.

Payout Cash dividends and the value of shares repurchased in any given year.

Payout policy A company's set of principles guiding payouts.

Peak The highest point of a business cycle.

Peer group A group of companies engaged in similar business activities whose economics and valuation are influenced by closely related factors.

Pennants A technical analysis continuation pattern formed by trendlines that converge to form a triangle, typically over a short period.

Per capita real GDP Real GDP divided by the size of the population, often used as a measure of the average standard of living in a country.

Per unit contribution margin The amount that each unit sold contributes to covering fixed costs—that is, the difference between the price per unit and the variable cost per unit.

Percentage-of-completion A method of revenue recognition in which, in each accounting period, the company estimates what percentage of the contract is complete and then reports that percentage of the total contract revenue in its income statement.

Percentiles Quantiles that divide a distribution into 100 equal parts.

Perfect competition A market structure in which the individual firm has virtually no impact on market price, because it is assumed to be a very small seller among a very large number of firms selling essentially identical products.

Perfectly elastic Said of a good or service that is infinitely sensitive to a change in the value of a specified variable (e.g., price).

Perfectly inelastic Said of a good or service that is completely insensitive to a change in the value of a specified variable (e.g., price).

Performance appraisal The evaluation of risk-adjusted performance; the evaluation of investment skill.

Performance bond See *margin bond*.

Performance evaluation The measurement and assessment of the outcomes of investment management decisions.

Performance measurement The calculation of returns in a logical and consistent manner.

Period costs Costs (e.g., executives' salaries) that cannot be directly matched with the timing of revenues and which are thus expensed immediately.

Periodicity The assumed number of periods in the year, typically matches the frequency of coupon payments.

Permanent differences Differences between tax and financial reporting of revenue (expenses) that will not be reversed at some future date. These result in a difference between the company's effective tax rate and statutory tax rate and do not result in a deferred tax item.

Permutation An ordered listing.

Perpetual bonds Bonds with no stated maturity date.

Perpetuity A perpetual annuity, or a set of never-ending level sequential cash flows, with the first cash flow occurring one period from now. A bond that does not mature.

Personal consumption expenditures All domestic personal consumption; the basis for a price index for such consumption called the PCE price index.

Personal disposable income Equal to personal income less personal taxes.

Personal income A broad measure of household income that includes all income received by households, whether earned or unearned; measures the ability of consumers to make purchases.

Plain vanilla bond Bond that makes periodic, fixed coupon payments during the bond's life and a lump-sum payment of principal at maturity. Also called *conventional bond*.

Plain vanilla swap An interest rate swap in which one party pays a fixed rate and the other pays a floating rate, with both sets of payments in the same currency.

Planning horizon A time period in which all factors of production are variable, including technology, physical capital, and plant size.

Platykurtic Describes a distribution that is less peaked than the normal distribution.

Point and figure chart A technical analysis chart that is constructed with columns of X's alternating with columns of O's such that the horizontal axis represents only the number of changes in price without reference to time or volume.

Point estimate A single numerical estimate of an unknown quantity, such as a population parameter.

Point of sale (POS) Systems that capture transaction data at the physical location in which the sale is made.

Policy rate An interest rate that a central bank sets and announces publicly; normally the rate at which it is willing to lend money to the commercial banks.

Population All members of a specified group.

Population mean The arithmetic mean value of a population; the arithmetic mean of all the observations or values in the population.

Population standard deviation A measure of dispersion relating to a population in the same unit of measurement as the observations, calculated as the positive square root of the population variance.

Population variance A measure of dispersion relating to a population, calculated as the mean of the squared deviations around the population mean.

Portfolio company In private equity, the company that is being invested in.

Portfolio demand for money The demand to hold speculative money balances based on the potential opportunities or risks that are inherent in other financial instruments.

Portfolio planning The process of creating a plan for building a portfolio that is expected to satisfy a client's investment objectives.

Position The quantity of an asset that an entity owns or owes.

Position trader A trader who typically holds positions open overnight.

Positive externality A positive effect (e.g., improved literacy) of a market transaction that is borne by parties other than those who transacted; a spillover benefit.

Posterior probability An updated probability that reflects or comes after new information.

Potential GDP The level of real GDP that can be produced at full employment; measures the productive capacity of the economy.

Power of a test The probability of correctly rejecting the null—that is, rejecting the null hypothesis when it is false.

Precautionary money balances Money held to provide a buffer against unforeseen events that might require money.

Precautionary stocks A level of inventory beyond anticipated needs that provides a cushion in the event that it takes longer to replenish inventory than expected or in the case of greater than expected demand.

Preference shares A type of equity interest which ranks above common shares with respect to the payment of dividends and the distribution of the company's net assets upon liquidation. They have characteristics of both debt and equity securities. Also called *preferred stock*.

Preferred stock See *preference shares*.

Premium In the case of bonds, premium refers to the amount by which a bond is priced above its face (par) value. In the case of an option, the amount paid for the option contract.

Prepaid expense A normal operating expense that has been paid in advance of when it is due.

Present value (PV) The present discounted value of future cash flows: For assets, the present discounted value of the future net cash inflows that the asset is expected to generate; for liabilities, the present discounted value of the future net cash outflows that are expected to be required to settle the liabilities.

Present value models Valuation models that estimate the intrinsic value of a security as the present value of the future benefits expected to be received from the security. Also called *discounted cash flow models*.

Pretax margin A profitability ratio calculated as earnings before taxes divided by revenue.

Price The market price as established by the interactions of the market demand and supply factors.

Price elasticity of demand Measures the percentage change in the quantity demanded, given a percentage change in the price of a given product.

Price floor A minimum price for a good or service, typically imposed by government action and typically above the equilibrium price.

Price index Represents the average prices of a basket of goods and services.

Price limits Limits imposed by a futures exchange on the price change that can occur from one day to the next.

Price multiple A ratio that compares the share price with some sort of monetary flow or value to allow evaluation of the relative worth of a company's stock.

Price priority The principle that the highest priced buy orders and the lowest priced sell orders execute first.

Price relative A ratio of an ending price over a beginning price; it is equal to 1 plus the holding period return on the asset.

Price return Measures *only* the price appreciation or percentage change in price of the securities in an index or portfolio.

Price return index An index that reflects *only* the price appreciation or percentage change in price of the constituent securities. Also called *price index*.

Price stability In economics, refers to an inflation rate that is low on average and not subject to wide fluctuation.

Price takers Producers that must accept whatever price the market dictates.

Price to book value A valuation ratio calculated as price per share divided by book value per share.

Price to cash flow A valuation ratio calculated as price per share divided by cash flow per share.

Price to earnings ratio (P/E ratio or P/E) The ratio of share price to earnings per share.

Price to sales A valuation ratio calculated as price per share divided by sales per share.

Price value of a basis point A version of money duration, it is an estimate of the change in the full price of a bond given a 1 basis point change in the yield-to-maturity.

Price weighting An index weighting method in which the weight assigned to each constituent security is determined by dividing its price by the sum of all the prices of the constituent securities.

Priced risk Risk for which investors demand compensation for bearing (e.g. equity risk, company-specific factors, macroeconomic factors).

Primary bond markets Markets in which issuers first sell bonds to investors to raise capital.

Primary capital markets (primary markets) The market where securities are first sold and the issuers receive the proceeds.

Primary dealers   Financial institutions that are authorized to deal in new issues of sovereign bonds and that serve primarily as trading counterparties of the office responsible for issuing sovereign bonds.

Primary market   The market where securities are first sold and the issuers receive the proceeds.

Prime brokers   Brokers that provide services including custody, administration, lending, short borrowing, and trading.

Principal   The amount of funds originally invested in a project or instrument; the face value to be paid at maturity.

Principal amount   Amount that an issuer agrees to repay the debt holders on the maturity date.

Principal business activity   The business activity from which a company derives a majority of its revenues and/or earnings.

Principal value   Amount that an issuer agrees to repay the debt holders on the maturity date.

Prior probabilities   Probabilities reflecting beliefs prior to the arrival of new information.

Priority of claims   Priority of payment, with the most senior or highest ranking debt having the first claim on the cash flows and assets of the issuer.

Private equity securities   Securities that are not listed on public exchanges and have no active secondary market. They are issued primarily to institutional investors via non-public offerings, such as private placements.

Private investment in public equity   An investment in the equity of a publicly traded firm that is made at a discount to the market value of the firm's shares.

Private placement   Typically a non-underwritten, unregistered offering of securities that are sold only to an investor or a small group of investors. It can be accomplished directly between the issuer and the investor(s) or through an investment bank.

Private value auction   An auction in which the value of the item being auctioned is unique to each bidder.

Probability   A number between 0 and 1 describing the chance that a stated event will occur.

Probability density function   A function with non-negative values such that probability can be described by areas under the curve graphing the function.

Probability distribution   A distribution that specifies the probabilities of a random variable's possible outcomes.

Probability function   A function that specifies the probability that the random variable takes on a specific value.

Producer price index   Reflects the price changes experienced by domestic producers in a country.

Producer surplus   The difference between the total revenue sellers receive from selling a given amount of a good and the total variable cost of producing that amount.

Production function   Provides the quantitative link between the level of output that the economy can produce and the inputs used in the production process.

Production opportunity frontier   Curve describing the maximum number of units of one good a company can produce, for any given number of the other good that it chooses to manufacture.

Productivity   The amount of output produced by workers in a given period of time—for example, output per hour worked; measures the efficiency of labor.

Profit   The return that owners of a company receive for the use of their capital and the assumption of financial risk when making their investments.

Profit and loss (P&L) statement   A financial statement that provides information about a company's profitability over a stated period of time.

Profit margin   An indicator of profitability, calculated as net income divided by revenue; indicates how much of each dollar of revenues is left after all costs and expenses.

Profitability ratios   Ratios that measure a company's ability to generate profitable sales from its resources (assets).

Project sequencing   To defer the decision to invest in a future project until the outcome of some or all of a current project is known. Projects are sequenced through time, so that investing in a project creates the option to invest in future projects.

Promissory note   A written promise to pay a certain amount of money on demand.

Property, plant, and equipment   Tangible assets that are expected to be used for more than one period in either the production or supply of goods or services, or for administrative purposes.

Prospectus   The document that describes the terms of a new bond issue and helps investors perform their analysis on the issue.

Protective put   An option strategy in which a long position in an asset is combined with a long position in a put.

Pseudo-random numbers   Numbers produced by random number generators.

Public offer   See *public offering*.

Public offering   An offering of securities in which any member of the public may buy the securities. Also called *public offer*.

Pull on liquidity   When disbursements are paid too quickly or trade credit availability is limited, requiring companies to expend funds before they receive funds from sales that could cover the liability.

Pure discount bonds   See *zero-coupon bonds*.

Pure discount instruments   Instruments that pay interest as the difference between the amount borrowed and the amount paid back.

Pure-play method   A method for estimating the beta for a company or project; it requires using a comparable company's beta and adjusting it for financial leverage differences.

Put   An option that gives the holder the right to sell an underlying asset to another party at a fixed price over a specific period of time.

Put option   An option that gives the holder the right to sell an underlying asset to another party at a fixed price over a specific period of time.

Put/call ratio   A technical analysis indicator that evaluates market sentiment based upon the volume of put options traded divided by the volume of call options traded for a particular financial instrument.

Putable bonds   Bonds that give the bondholder the right to sell the bond back to the issuer at a predetermined price on specified dates.

Putable common shares   Common shares that give investors the option (or right) to sell their shares (i.e., "put" them) back to the issuing company at a price that is specified when the shares are originally issued.

Put–call parity   An equation expressing the equivalence (parity) of a portfolio of a call and a bond with a portfolio of a put and the underlying, which leads to the relationship between put and call prices.

Quantile   A value at or below which a stated fraction of the data lies. Also called *fractile*.

Quantitative easing An expansionary monetary policy based on aggressive open market purchase operations.

Quantity The amount of a product that consumers are willing and able to buy at each price level.

Quantity demanded The amount of a product that consumers are willing and able to buy at each price level.

Quantity equation of exchange An expression that over a given period, the amount of money used to purchase all goods and services in an economy, $M \times V$, is equal to monetary value of this output, $P \times Y$.

Quantity theory of money Asserts that total spending (in money terms) is proportional to the quantity of money.

Quartiles Quantiles that divide a distribution into four equal parts.

Quasi-fixed cost A cost that stays the same over a range of production but can change to another constant level when production moves outside of that range.

Quasi-government bonds A bond issued by an entity that is either owned or sponsored by a national government. Also called *agency bond*.

Quick assets Assets that can be most readily converted to cash (e.g., cash, short-term marketable investments, receivables).

Quick ratio A stringent measure of liquidity that indicates a company's ability to satisfy current liabilities with its most liquid assets, calculated as (cash + short-term marketable investments + receivables) divided by current liabilities.

Quintiles Quantiles that divide a distribution into five equal parts.

Quota rents Profits that foreign producers can earn by raising the price of their goods higher than they would without a quota.

Quotas Government policies that restrict the quantity of a good that can be imported into a country, generally for a specified period of time.

Quote-driven market A market in which dealers acting as principals facilitate trading.

Quoted interest rate A quoted interest rate that does not account for compounding within the year. Also called *stated annual interest rate*.

Quoted margin The specified yield spread over the reference rate, used to compensate an investor for the difference in the credit risk of the issuer and that implied by the reference rate.

Random number An observation drawn from a uniform distribution.

Random number generator An algorithm that produces uniformly distributed random numbers between 0 and 1.

Random variable A quantity whose future outcomes are uncertain.

Range The difference between the maximum and minimum values in a dataset.

Ratio scales A measurement scale that has all the characteristics of interval measurement scales as well as a true zero point as the origin.

Real GDP The value of goods and services produced, measured at base year prices.

Real income Income adjusted for the effect of inflation on the purchasing power of money.

Real interest rate Nominal interest rate minus the expected rate of inflation.

Real risk-free interest rate The single-period interest rate for a completely risk-free security if no inflation were expected.

Realizable (settlement) value With reference to assets, the amount of cash or cash equivalents that could currently be obtained by selling the asset in an orderly disposal; with reference to liabilities, the undiscounted amount of cash or cash equivalents expected to be paid to satisfy the liabilities in the normal course of business.

Rebalancing Adjusting the weights of the constituent securities in an index.

Rebalancing policy The set of rules that guide the process of restoring a portfolio's asset class weights to those specified in the strategic asset allocation.

Recession A period during which real GDP decreases (i.e., negative growth) for at least two successive quarters, or a period of significant decline in total output, income, employment, and sales usually lasting from six months to a year.

Recognition lag The lag in government response to an economic problem resulting from the delay in confirming a change in the state of the economy.

Record date The date that a shareholder listed on the corporation's books will be deemed to have ownership of the shares for purposes of receiving an upcoming dividend; two business days after the ex-dividend date.

Redemption yield See *yield to maturity*.

Redemptions Withdrawals of funds by investors.

Refinancing rate A type of central bank policy rate.

Registered bonds Bonds for which ownership is recorded by either name or serial number.

Relative dispersion The amount of dispersion relative to a reference value or benchmark.

Relative frequency With reference to an interval of grouped data, the number of observations in the interval divided by the total number of observations in the sample.

Relative price The price of a specific good or service in comparison with those of other goods and services.

Relative strength analysis A comparison of the performance of one asset with the performance of another asset or a benchmark based on changes in the ratio of the securities' respective prices over time.

Relative strength index A technical analysis momentum oscillator that compares a security's gains with its losses over a set period.

Renewable resources Resources that can be replenished, such as a forest.

Rent Payment for the use of property.

Reorganization Agreements made by a company in bankruptcy under which a company's capital structure is altered and/or alternative arrangements are made for debt repayment; U.S. Chapter 11 bankruptcy. The company emerges from bankruptcy as a going concern.

Repo A form of collateralized loan involving the sale of a security with a simultaneous agreement by the seller to buy the same security back from the purchaser at an agreed-on price and future date. The party who sells the security at the inception of the repurchase agreement and buys it back at maturity is borrowing money from the other party, and the security sold and subsequently repurchased represents the collateral.

Repo margin The difference between the market value of the security used as collateral and the value of the loan. Also called *haircut*.

Repo rate The interest rate on a repurchase agreement.

Repurchase agreement   A form of collateralized loan involving the sale of a security with a simultaneous agreement by the seller to buy the same security back from the purchaser at an agreed-on price and future date. The party who sells the security at the inception of the repurchase agreement and buys it back at maturity is borrowing money from the other party, and the security sold and subsequently repurchased represents the collateral.

Repurchase date   The date when the party who sold the security at the inception of a repurchase agreement buys the security back from the cash lending counterparty.

Repurchase price   The price at which the party who sold the security at the inception of the repurchase agreement buys the security back from the cash lending counterparty.

Required margin   The yield spread over, or under, the reference rate such that an FRN is priced at par value on a rate reset date.

Required rate of return   See *market discount rate*.

Required yield   See *market discount rate*.

Required yield spread   The difference between the yield-to-maturity on a new bond and the benchmark rate; additional compensation required by investors for the difference in risk and tax status of a bond relative to a government bond. Sometimes called the *spread over the benchmark*.

Reservation prices   The highest price a buyer is willing to pay for an item or the lowest price at which a seller is willing to sell it.

Reserve requirement   The requirement for banks to hold reserves in proportion to the size of deposits.

Residual claim   The owners' remaining claim on the company's assets after the liabilities are deducted.

Resistance   In technical analysis, a price range in which selling activity is sufficient to stop the rise in the price of a security.

Restricted payments   A bond covenant meant to protect creditors by limiting how much cash can be paid out to shareholders over time.

Retail method   An inventory accounting method in which the sales value of an item is reduced by the gross margin to calculate the item's cost.

Retracement   In technical analysis, a reversal in the movement of a security's price such that it is counter to the prevailing longterm price trend.

Return on assets (ROA)   A profitability ratio calculated as net income divided by average total assets; indicates a company's net profit generated per dollar invested in total assets.

Return on equity (ROE)   A profitability ratio calculated as net income divided by average shareholders' equity.

Return on sales   An indicator of profitability, calculated as net income divided by revenue; indicates how much of each dollar of revenues is left after all costs and expenses.

Return on total capital   A profitability ratio calculated as EBIT divided by the sum of short- and long-term debt and equity.

Return-generating model   A model that can provide an estimate of the expected return of a security given certain parameters and estimates of the values of the independent variables in the model.

Revaluation model   The process of valuing long-lived assets at fair value, rather than at cost less accumulated depreciation. Any resulting profit or loss is either reported on the income statement and/or through equity under revaluation surplus.

Revenue   The amount charged for the delivery of goods or services in the ordinary activities of a business over a stated period; the inflows of economic resources to a company over a stated period.

Reversal patterns   A type of pattern used in technical analysis to predict the end of a trend and a change in direction of the security's price.

Reverse repo   A repurchase agreement viewed from the perspective of the cash lending counterparty.

Reverse repurchase agreement   A repurchase agreement viewed from the perspective of the cash lending counterparty.

Reverse stock split   A reduction in the number of shares outstanding with a corresponding increase in share price, but no change to the company's underlying fundamentals.

Revolving credit agreements   The strongest form of short-term bank borrowing facilities; they are in effect for multiple years (e.g., 3–5 years) and may have optional medium-term loan features.

Rho   The sensitivity of the option price to the risk-free rate.

Ricardian equivalence   An economic theory that implies that it makes no difference whether a government finances a deficit by increasing taxes or issuing debt.

Risk averse   The assumption that an investor will choose the least risky alternative.

Risk aversion   The degree of an investor's inability and unwillingness to take risk.

Risk budgeting   The establishment of objectives for individuals, groups, or divisions of an organization that takes into account the allocation of an acceptable level of risk.

Risk management   The process of identifying the level of risk an entity wants, measuring the level of risk the entity currently has, taking actions that bring the actual level of risk to the desired level of risk, and monitoring the new actual level of risk so that it continues to be aligned with the desired level of risk.

Risk premium   An extra return expected by investors for bearing some specified risk.

Risk tolerance   The amount of risk an investor is willing and able to bear to achieve an investment goal.

Robust   The quality of being relatively unaffected by a violation of assumptions.

Rule of 72   The principle that the approximate number of years necessary for an investment to double is 72 divided by the stated interest rate.

Running yield   See *current yield*.

Safety stock   A level of inventory beyond anticipated needs that provides a cushion in the event that it takes longer to replenish inventory than expected or in the case of greater than expected demand.

Safety-first rules   Rules for portfolio selection that focus on the risk that portfolio value will fall below some minimum acceptable level over some time horizon.

Sales   Generally, a synonym for revenue; "sales" is generally understood to refer to the sale of goods, whereas "revenue" is understood to include the sale of goods or services.

Sales returns and allowances   An offset to revenue reflecting any cash refunds, credits on account, and discounts from sales prices given to customers who purchased defective or unsatisfactory items.

Sales risk   Uncertainty with respect to the quantity of goods and services that a company is able to sell and the price it is able to achieve; the risk related to the uncertainty of revenues.

Salvage value   The amount the company estimates that it can sell the asset for at the end of its useful life. Also called *residual value*.

Sample   A subset of a population.

Sample excess kurtosis   A sample measure of the degree of a distribution's peakedness in excess of the normal distribution's peakedness.

Sample kurtosis   A sample measure of the degree of a distribution's peakedness.

Sample mean   The sum of the sample observations, divided by the sample size.

Sample selection bias   Bias introduced by systematically excluding some members of the population according to a particular attribute—for example, the bias introduced when data availability leads to certain observations being excluded from the analysis.

Sample skewness   A sample measure of degree of asymmetry of a distribution.

Sample standard deviation   The positive square root of the sample variance.

Sample statistic   A quantity computed from or used to describe a sample.

Sample variance   A sample measure of the degree of dispersion of a distribution, calculated by dividing the sum of the squared deviations from the sample mean by the sample size minus 1.

Sampling   The process of obtaining a sample.

Sampling distribution   The distribution of all distinct possible values that a statistic can assume when computed from samples of the same size randomly drawn from the same population.

Sampling error   The difference between the observed value of a statistic and the quantity it is intended to estimate.

Sampling plan   The set of rules used to select a sample.

Saving   In economics, income not spent.

Say's law   Named for French economist J.B. Say: All that is produced will be sold because supply creates its own demand.

Scalper   A trader who offers to buy or sell futures contracts, holding the position for only a brief period of time. Scalpers attempt to profit by buying at the bid price and selling at the higher ask price.

Scenario analysis   Analysis that shows the changes in key financial quantities that result from given (economic) events, such as the loss of customers, the loss of a supply source, or a catastrophic event; a risk management technique involving examination of the performance of a portfolio under specified situations. Closely related to stress testing.

Screening   The application of a set of criteria to reduce a set of potential investments to a smaller set having certain desired characteristics.

Scrip dividend schemes   Dividend reinvestment plan in which the company meets the need for additional shares by issuing them instead of purchasing them.

Sealed bid auction   An auction in which bids are elicited from potential buyers, but there is no ability to observe bids by other buyers until the auction has ended.

Search costs   Costs incurred in searching; the costs of matching buyers with sellers.

Seasoned offering   An offering in which an issuer sells additional units of a previously issued security.

Seats   Memberships in a derivatives exchange.

Second lien   A secured interest in the pledged assets that ranks below first lien debt in both collateral protection and priority of payment.

Second price sealed bid   An auction (also known as a Vickery auction) in which bids are submitted in sealed envelopes and opened simultaneously. The winning buyer is the one who submitted the highest bid, but the price paid is equal to the second highest bid.

Second-degree price discrimination   When the monopolist charges different per-unit prices using the quantity purchased as an indicator of how highly the customer values the product.

Secondary bond markets   Markets in which existing bonds are traded among investors.

Secondary market   The market where securities are traded among investors.

Secondary precedence rules   Rules that determine how to rank orders placed at the same time.

Sector   A group of related industries.

Sector indices   Indices that represent and track different economic sectors—such as consumer goods, energy, finance, health care, and technology—on either a national, regional, or global basis.

Secured bonds   Bonds secured by assets or financial guarantees pledged to ensure debt repayment in case of default.

Secured debt   Debt in which the debtholder has a direct claim—a pledge from the issuer—on certain assets and their associated cash flows.

Securitized bonds   Bonds created from a process that involves moving assets into a special legal entity, which then uses the assets as guarantees to secure a bond issue.

Security characteristic line   A plot of the excess return of a security on the excess return of the market.

Security market index   A portfolio of securities representing a given security market, market segment, or asset class.

Security market line   (SML) The graph of the capital asset pricing model.

Security selection   The process of selecting individual securities; typically, security selection has the objective of generating superior risk-adjusted returns relative to a portfolio's benchmark.

Self-investment limits   With respect to investment limitations applying to pension plans, restrictions on the percentage of assets that can be invested in securities issued by the pension plan sponsor.

Sell-side firm   A broker or dealer that sells securities to and provides independent investment research and recommendations to investment management companies.

Semi-strong-form efficient market   A market in which security prices reflect all publicly known and available information.

Semiannual bond basis yield   An annual rate having a periodicity of two; also known as a *semiannual bond equivalent yield*.

Semiannual bond equivalent yield   See *semiannual bond basis yield*.

Semideviation   The positive square root of semivariance (sometimes called *semistandard deviation*).

Semilogarithmic   Describes a scale constructed so that equal intervals on the vertical scale represent equal rates of change, and equal intervals on the horizontal scale represent equal amounts of change.

Semivariance   The average squared deviation below the mean.

Seniority ranking   Priority of payment of various debt obligations.

Sensitivity analysis   Analysis that shows the range of possible outcomes as specific assumptions are changed.

Separately managed account (SMA) An investment portfolio managed exclusively for the benefit of an individual or institution.

Serial maturity structure Structure for a bond issue in which the maturity dates are spread out during the bond's life; a stated number of bonds mature and are paid off each year before final maturity.

Settlement The process that occurs after a trade is completed, the securities are passed to the buyer, and payment is received by the seller.

Settlement date Date when the buyer makes cash payment and the seller delivers the security.

Settlement period The time between settlement dates.

Settlement price The official price, designated by the clearinghouse, from which daily gains and losses will be determined and marked to market.

Share repurchase A transaction in which a company buys back its own shares. Unlike stock dividends and stock splits, share repurchases use corporate cash.

Shareholder wealth maximization To maximize the market value of shareholders' equity.

Shareholder-of-record date The date that a shareholder listed on the corporation's books will be deemed to have ownership of the shares for purposes of receiving an upcoming dividend; two business days after the ex-dividend date.

Shareholders' equity Assets less liabilities; the residual interest in the assets after subtracting the liabilities.

Sharpe ratio The average return in excess of the risk-free rate divided by the standard deviation of return; a measure of the average excess return earned per unit of standard deviation of return.

Shelf registration Type of public offering that allows the issuer to file a single, all-encompassing offering circular that covers a series of bond issues.

Short The seller of an asset or derivative contract. Also refers to the position of being short an asset or derivative contract.

Short position A position in an asset or contract in which one has sold an asset one does not own, or in which a right under a contract can be exercised against oneself.

Short selling A transaction in which borrowed securities are sold with the intention to repurchase them at a lower price at a later date and return them to the lender.

Short-run average total cost curve The curve describing average total costs when some costs are considered fixed.

Short-run supply curve The section of the marginal cost curve that lies above the minimum point on the average variable cost curve.

Shortfall risk The risk that portfolio value will fall below some minimum acceptable level over some time horizon.

Shutdown point The point at which average revenue is less than average variable cost.

Simple interest The interest earned each period on the original investment; interest calculated on the principal only.

Simple random sample A subset of a larger population created in such a way that each element of the population has an equal probability of being selected to the subset.

Simple random sampling The procedure of drawing a sample to satisfy the definition of a simple random sample.

Simple yield The sum of the coupon payments plus the straight-line amortized share of the gain or loss, divided by the flat price.

Simulation Computer-generated sensitivity or scenario analysis that is based on probability models for the factors that drive outcomes.

Simulation trial A complete pass through the steps of a simulation.

Single price auction A Dutch auction variation, also involving a single price, is used in selling U.S. Treasury securities.

Single-step format With respect to the format of the income statement, a format that does not subtotal for gross profit (revenue minus cost of goods sold).

Sinking fund arrangement Provision that reduces the credit risk of a bond issue by requiring the issuer to retire a portion of the bond's principal outstanding each year.

Skewed Not symmetrical.

Skewness A quantitative measure of skew (lack of symmetry); a synonym of skew.

Small country A country that is a price taker in the world market for a product and cannot influence the world market price.

Solvency With respect to financial statement analysis, the ability of a company to fulfill its long-term obligations.

Solvency ratios Ratios that measure a company's ability to meet its long-term obligations.

Sovereign bonds A bond issued by a national government.

Sovereign yield spread An estimate of the country spread (country equity premium) for a developing nation that is based on a comparison of bonds yields in country being analyzed and a developed country. The sovereign yield spread is the difference between a government bond yield in the country being analyzed, denominated in the currency of the developed country, and the Treasury bond yield on a similar maturity bond in the developed country.

Sovereigns A bond issued by a national government.

Spearman rank correlation coefficient A measure of correlation applied to ranked data.

Special dividend A dividend paid by a company that does not pay dividends on a regular schedule, or a dividend that supplements regular cash dividends with an extra payment.

Special purpose entity A non-operating entity created to carry out a specified purpose, such as leasing assets or securitizing receivables; can be a corporation, partnership, trust, limited liability, or partnership formed to facilitate a specific type of business activity. Also called *special purpose vehicle* or *variable interest entity*.

Special purpose vehicle See *special purpose entity*.

Specific identification method An inventory accounting method that identifies which specific inventory items were sold and which remained in inventory to be carried over to later periods.

Speculative demand for money The demand to hold speculative money balances based on the potential opportunities or risks that are inherent in other financial instruments. Also called *portfolio demand for money*.

Speculative money balances Monies held in anticipation that other assets will decline in value.

Speculative value The difference between the market price of the option and its intrinsic value, determined by the uncertainty of the underlying over the remaining life of the option.

Split coupon bond See *deferred coupon bond*.

Sponsored A type of depository receipt in which the foreign company whose shares are held by the depository has a direct involvement in the issuance of the receipts.

Spot curve A sequence of yields-to-maturity on zero-coupon bonds. Sometimes called *zero* or *strip curve* because coupon payments are "stripped" off of the bonds.

Spot markets Markets in which assets are traded for immediate delivery.

Spot prices The price of an asset for immediately delivery.

Spot rates A sequence of market discount rates that correspond to the cash flow dates; yields-to-maturity on zero-coupon bonds maturing at the date of each cash flow.

Spread In general, the difference in yield between different fixed income securities. Often used to refer to the difference between the yield-to-maturity and the benchmark.

Spread over the benchmark See *required yield spread.*

Spread risk Bond price risk arising from changes in the yield spread on credit-risky bonds; reflects changes in the market's assessment and/or pricing of credit migration (or downgrade) risk and market liquidity risk.

Stable With reference to an equilibrium, one in which price, when disturbed away from the equilibrium, tends to converge back to it.

Stackelberg model A prominent model of strategic decision-making in which firms are assumed to make their decisions sequentially.

Stagflation When a high inflation rate is combined with a high level of unemployment and a slowdown of the economy.

Standard cost With respect to inventory accounting, the planned or target unit cost of inventory items or services.

Standard deviation The positive square root of the variance; a measure of dispersion in the same units as the original data.

Standard normal distribution The normal density with mean (μ) equal to 0 and standard deviation (σ) equal to 1.

Standardizing A transformation that involves subtracting the mean and dividing the result by the standard deviation.

Standing limit orders A limit order at a price below market and which therefore is waiting to trade.

Stated annual interest rate A quoted interest rate that does not account for compounding within the year. Also called *quoted interest rate.*

Statement of cash flows A financial statement that reconciles beginning-of-period and end-of-period balance sheet values of cash; provides information about an entity's cash inflows and cash outflows as they pertain to operating, investing, and financing activities. Also called *cash flow statement.*

Statement of changes in equity (statement of owners' equity) A financial statement that reconciles the beginning-of-period and end-of-period balance sheet values of shareholders' equity; provides information about all factors affecting shareholders' equity. Also called *statement of owners' equity.*

Statement of financial condition The financial statement that presents an entity's current financial position by disclosing resources the entity controls (its assets) and the claims on those resources (its liabilities and equity claims), as of a particular point in time (the date of the balance sheet).

Statement of financial position The financial statement that presents an entity's current financial position by disclosing resources the entity controls (its assets) and the claims on those resources (its liabilities and equity claims), as of a particular point in time (the date of the balance sheet).

Statement of operations A financial statement that provides information about a company's profitability over a stated period of time.

Statement of owners' equity A financial statement that reconciles the beginning of-period and end-of-period balance sheet values of shareholders' equity; provides information about all factors affecting shareholders' equity. Also called *statement of changes in shareholders' equity.*

Statement of retained earnings A financial statement that reconciles beginning-of-period and end-of-period balance sheet values of retained income; shows the linkage between the balance sheet and income statement.

Statistic A quantity computed from or used to describe a sample of data.

Statistical inference Making forecasts, estimates, or judgments about a larger group from a smaller group actually observed; using a sample statistic to infer the value of an unknown population parameter.

Statistically significant A result indicating that the null hypothesis can be rejected; with reference to an estimated regression coefficient, frequently understood to mean a result indicating that the corresponding population regression coefficient is different from 0.

Statutory voting A common method of voting where each share represents one vote.

Step-up coupon bond Bond for which the coupon, which may be fixed or floating, increases by specified margins at specified dates.

Stock dividend A type of dividend in which a company distributes additional shares of its common stock to shareholders instead of cash.

Stock-out losses Profits lost from not having sufficient inventory on hand to satisfy demand.

Stop order An order in which a trader has specified a stop price condition. Also called *stop-loss order.*

Stop-loss order See *stop order.*

Store of value The quality of tending to preserve value.

Store of wealth Goods that depend on the fact that they do not perish physically over time, and on the belief that others would always value the good.

Straight-line method A depreciation method that allocates evenly the cost of a long-lived asset less its estimated residual value over the estimated useful life of the asset.

Strategic analysis Analysis of the competitive environment with an emphasis on the implications of the environment for corporate strategy.

Strategic asset allocation The set of exposures to IPS-permissible asset classes that is expected to achieve the client's long-term objectives given the client's investment constraints.

Strategic groups Groups sharing distinct business models or catering to specific market segments in an industry.

Street convention Yield measure that neglects weekends and holidays; the internal rate of return on cash flows assuming payments are made on the scheduled dates, even when the scheduled date falls on a weekend or holiday.

Stress testing A set of techniques for estimating losses in extremely unfavorable combinations of events or scenarios.

Strike The fixed price at which an option holder can buy or sell the underlying.

Strike price The fixed price at which an option holder can buy or sell the underlying.

Strike rate The fixed rate at which the holder of an interest rate option can buy or sell the underlying.

Striking price The fixed price at which an option holder can buy or sell the underlying.

Strong-form efficient market A market in which security prices reflect all public and private information.

Structural (or cyclically adjusted) budget deficit The deficit that would exist if the economy was at full employment (or full potential output).

Structural subordination Arises in a holding company structure when the debt of operating subsidiaries is serviced by the cash flow and assets of the subsidiaries before funds can be passed to the holding company to service debt at the parent level.

Subjective probability A probability drawing on personal or subjective judgment.

Subordinated debt A class of unsecured debt that ranks below a firm's senior unsecured obligations.

Substitutes Said of two goods or services such that if the price of one increases the demand for the other tends to increase, holding all other things equal (e.g., butter and margarine).

Sunk cost A cost that has already been incurred.

Supernormal profit Equal to accounting profit less the implicit opportunity costs not included in total accounting costs; the difference between total revenue (TR) and total cost (TC).

Supply The willingness of sellers to offer a given quantity of a good or service for a given price.

Supply curve The graph of the inverse supply function.

Supply function The quantity supplied as a function of price and possibly other variables.

Supply shock A typically unexpected disturbance to supply.

Support In technical analysis, a price range in which buying activity is sufficient to stop the decline in the price of a security.

Supranational bonds A bond issued by a supranational agency such as the World Bank.

Surety bond Form of external credit enhancement whereby a rated and regulated insurance company guarantees to reimburse bondholders for any losses incurred up to a maximum amount if the issuer defaults.

Survey approach An estimate of the equity risk premium that is based upon estimates provided by a panel of finance experts.

Survivorship bias The bias resulting from a test design that fails to account for companies that have gone bankrupt, merged, or are otherwise no longer reported in a database.

Sustainable growth rate The rate of dividend (and earnings) growth that can be sustained over time for a given level of return on equity, keeping the capital structure constant and without issuing additional common stock.

Sustainable rate of economic growth The rate of increase in the economy's productive capacity or potential GDP.

Swap contract An agreement between two parties to exchange a series of future cash flows.

Swaption An option to enter into a swap.

Syndicated loans Loans from a group of lenders to a single borrower.

Syndicated offering A bond issue that is underwritten by a group of investment banks.

Synthetic call The combination of puts, the underlying, and risk-free bonds that replicates a call option.

Synthetic put The combination of calls, the underlying, and risk-free bonds that replicates a put option.

Systematic risk Risk that affects the entire market or economy; it cannot be avoided and is inherent in the overall market. Systematic risk is also known as non diversifiable or market risk.

Systematic sampling A procedure of selecting every kth member until reaching a sample of the desired size. The sample that results from this procedure should be approximately random.

t-Test A hypothesis test using a statistic (t-statistic) that follows a t-distribution.

TRIN A flow of funds indicator applied to a broad stock market index to measure the relative extent to which money is moving into or out of rising and declining stocks.

Tactical asset allocation The decision to deliberately deviate from the strategic asset allocation in an attempt to add value based on forecasts of the near-term relative performance of asset classes.

Target balance A minimum level of cash to be held available—estimated in advance and adjusted for known funds transfers, seasonality, or other factors.

Target capital structure A company's chosen proportions of debt and equity.

Target independent A bank's ability to determine the definition of inflation that they target, the rate of inflation that they target, and the horizon over which the target is to be achieved.

Target semideviation The positive square root of target semivariance.

Target semivariance The average squared deviation below a target value.

Tariffs Taxes that a government levies on imported goods.

Tax base The amount at which an asset or liability is valued for tax purposes.

Tax expense An aggregate of an entity's income tax payable (or recoverable in the case of a tax benefit) and any changes in deferred tax assets and liabilities. It is essentially the income tax payable or recoverable if these had been determined based on accounting profit rather than taxable income.

Tax loss carry forward A taxable loss in the current period that may be used to reduce future taxable income.

Taxable income The portion of an entity's income that is subject to income taxes under the tax laws of its jurisdiction.

Taxable temporary differences Temporary differences that result in a taxable amount in a future period when determining the taxable profit as the balance sheet item is recovered or settled.

Technical analysis A form of security analysis that uses price and volume data, which is often displayed graphically, in decision making.

Technology The process a company uses to transform inputs into outputs.

Technology of production The "rules" that govern the transformation of inputs into finished goods and services.

Tenor The time-to-maturity for a bond or derivative contract. Also called *term to maturity*.

Term maturity structure Structure for a bond issue in which the bond's notional principal is paid off in a lump sum at maturity.

Term structure See *maturity structure*.

Term structure of credit spreads The relationship between the spreads over the "risk-free" (or benchmark) rates and times-to-maturity.

Term structure of yield volatility The relationship between the volatility of bond yields-to-maturity and times-to-maturity.

Terminal stock value The expected value of a share at the end of the investment horizon—in effect, the expected selling price. Also called *terminal value*.

Terminal value The expected value of a share at the end of the investment horizon—in effect, the expected selling price.

Termination date The date of the final payment on a swap; also, the swap's expiration date.

Terms of trade The ratio of the price of exports to the price of imports, representing those prices by export and import price indices, respectively.

Theory of the consumer The branch of microeconomics that deals with consumption—the demand for goods and services—by utility-maximizing individuals.

Theory of the firm The branch of microeconomics that deals with the supply of goods and services by profit-maximizing firms.

Theta The rate at which an option's time value decays.

Third-degree price discrimination When the monopolist segregates customers into groups based on demographic or other characteristics and offers different pricing to each group.

Time to expiration The time remaining in the life of a derivative, typically expressed in years.

Time value The difference between the market price of the option and its intrinsic value, determined by the uncertainty of the underlying over the remaining life of the option.

Time value of money The principles governing equivalence relationships between cash flows with different dates.

Time-period bias The possibility that when we use a time-series sample, our statistical conclusion may be sensitive to the starting and ending dates of the sample.

Time-series data Observations of a variable over time.

Time-weighted rate of return The compound rate of growth of one unit of currency invested in a portfolio during a stated measurement period; a measure of investment performance that is not sensitive to the timing and amount of withdrawals or additions to the portfolio.

Top-down analysis With reference to investment selection processes, an approach that starts with macro selection (i.e., identifying attractive geographic segments and/or industry segments) and then addresses selection of the most attractive investments within those segments.

Total comprehensive income The change in equity during a period resulting from transaction and other events, other than those changes resulting from transactions with owners in their capacity as owners.

Total costs The summation of all costs, where costs are classified according to fixed or variable.

Total expenditure The total amount spent over a time period.

Total factor productivity A scale factor that reflects the portion of growth that is not accounted for by explicit factor inputs (e.g. capital and labor).

Total fixed cost The summation of all expenses that do not change when production varies.

Total invested capital The sum of market value of common equity, book value of preferred equity, and face value of debt.

Total probability rule A rule explaining the unconditional probability of an event in terms of probabilities of the event conditional on mutually exclusive and exhaustive scenarios.

Total probability rule for expected value A rule explaining the expected value of a random variable in terms of expected values of the random variable conditional on mutually exclusive and exhaustive scenarios.

Total product The aggregate sum of production for the firm during a time period.

Total return Measures the price appreciation, or percentage change in price of the securities in an index or portfolio, plus any income received over the period.

Total return index An index that reflects the price appreciation or percentage change in price of the constituent securities plus any income received since inception.

Total return swap A swap in which one party agrees to pay the total return on a security. Often used as a credit derivative, in which the underlying is a bond.

Total revenue Price times the quantity of units sold.

Total surplus The difference between total value to buyers and the total variable cost to sellers; made up of the sum of consumer surplus and producer surplus.

Total variable cost The summation of all variable expenses.

Tracking error The standard deviation of the differences between a portfolio's returns and its benchmark's returns; a synonym of active risk.

Tracking risk The standard deviation of the differences between a portfolio's returns and its benchmark's returns; a synonym of active risk. Also called *tracking error*.

Trade creation When regional integration results in the replacement of higher cost domestic production by lower cost imports from other members.

Trade credit A spontaneous form of credit in which a purchaser of the goods or service is financing its purchase by delaying the date on which payment is made.

Trade diversion When regional integration results in lower-cost imports from non-member countries being replaced with higher-cost imports from members.

Trade payables Amounts that a business owes to its vendors for goods and services that were purchased from them but which have not yet been paid.

Trade protection Government policies that impose restrictions on trade, such as tariffs and quotas.

Trade receivables Amounts customers owe the company for products that have been sold as well as amounts that may be due from suppliers (such as for returns of merchandise) Also called *commercial receivables* or *accounts receivable*.

Trade surplus (deficit) When the value of exports is greater (less) than the value of imports.

Trading securities Securities held by a company with the intent to trade them. Also called *held-for-trading securities*.

Traditional investment markets Markets for traditional investments, which include all publicly traded debts and equities and shares in pooled investment vehicles that hold publicly traded debts and/or equities.

Transactions money balances Money balances that are held to finance transactions.

Transactions motive In the context of inventory management, the need for inventory as part of the routine production–sales cycle.

Transfer payments Welfare payments made through the social security system that exist to provide a basic minimum level of income for low-income households.

Transitive preferences The assumption that when comparing any three distinct bundles, A, B, and C, if A is preferred to B and simultaneously B is preferred to C, then it must be true that A is preferred to C.

Transparency Said of something (e.g., a market) in which information is fully disclosed to the public and/or regulators.

Treasury Inflation-Protected Securities A bond issued by the United States Treasury Department that is designed to protect the investor from inflation by adjusting the principal of the bond for changes in inflation.

Treasury shares   Shares that were issued and subsequently repurchased by the company.

Treasury stock   Shares that were issued and subsequently repurchased by the company.

Treasury stock method   A method for accounting for the effect of options (and warrants) on earnings per share (EPS) that specifies what EPS would have been if the options and warrants had been exercised and the company had used the proceeds to repurchase common stock.

Tree diagram   A diagram with branches emanating from nodes representing either mutually exclusive chance events or mutually exclusive decisions.

Trend   A long-term pattern of movement in a particular direction.

Treynor ratio   A measure of risk-adjusted performance that relates a portfolio's excess returns to the portfolio's beta.

Triangle patterns   In technical analysis, a continuation chart pattern that forms as the range between high and low prices narrows, visually forming a triangle.

Trimmed mean   A mean computed after excluding a stated small percentage of the lowest and highest observations.

Triple bottoms   In technical analysis, a reversal pattern that is formed when the price forms three troughs at roughly the same price level; used to predict a change from a downtrend to an uptrend.

Triple tops   In technical analysis, a reversal pattern that is formed when the price forms three peaks at roughly the same price level; used to predict a change from an uptrend to a downtrend.

Trough   The lowest point of a business cycle.

True yield   The internal rate of return on cash flows using the actual calendar including weekends and bank holidays.

Trust deed   See *indenture*.

Trust receipt arrangement   The use of inventory as collateral for a loan. The inventory is segregated and held in trust, and the proceeds of any sale must be remitted to the lender immediately.

Turn-of-the-year effect   Calendar anomaly that stock market returns in January are significantly higher compared to the rest of the months of the year, with most of the abnormal returns reported during the first five trading days in January.

Two-fund separation theorem   The theory that all investors regardless of taste, risk preferences, and initial wealth will hold a combination of two portfolios or funds: a risk-free asset and an optimal portfolio of risky assets.

Two-sided hypothesis test   A test in which the null hypothesis is rejected in favor of the alternative hypothesis if the evidence indicates that the population parameter is either smaller or larger than a hypothesized value.

Two-tailed hypothesis test   A test in which the null hypothesis is rejected in favor of the alternative hypothesis if the evidence indicates that the population parameter is either smaller or larger than a hypothesized value.

Two-week repo rate   The interest rate on a two-week repurchase agreement; may be used as a policy rate by a central bank.

Type I error   The error of rejecting a true null hypothesis.

Type II error   The error of not rejecting a false null hypothesis.

Unanticipated (unexpected) inflation   The component of inflation that is a surprise.

Unbilled revenue   Revenue that has been earned but not yet billed to customers as of the end of an accounting period. Also called *accrued revenue*.

Unclassified balance sheet   A balance sheet that does not show subtotals for current assets and current liabilities.

Unconditional probability   The probability of an event *not* conditioned on another event.

Underemployed   A person who has a job but has the qualifications to work a significantly higher-paying job.

Underlying   An asset that trades in a market in which buyers and sellers meet, decide on a price, and the seller then delivers the asset to the buyer and receives payment. The underlying is the asset or other derivative on which a particular derivative is based. The market for the underlying is also referred to as the *spot market*.

Underwriter   A firm, usually an investment bank, that takes the risk of buying the newly issued securities from the issuer, and then reselling them to investors or to dealers, thus guaranteeing the sale of the securities at the offering price negotiated with the issuer.

Underwritten offering   A type of securities issue mechanism in which the investment bank guarantees the sale of the securities at an offering price that is negotiated with the issuer. Also known as *firm commitment offering*.

Unearned fees   Unearned fees are recognized when a company receives cash payment for fees prior to earning them.

Unearned revenue   A liability account for money that has been collected for goods or services that have not yet been delivered; payment received in advance of providing a good or service. Also called *deferred revenue* or *deferred income*.

Unemployed   People who are actively seeking employment but are currently without a job.

Unemployment rate   The ratio of unemployed to the labor force.

Unexpected inflation   The component of inflation that is a surprise.

Unit elastic   An elasticity with a magnitude of 1.

Unit labor cost   The average labor cost to produce one unit of output.

Unit normal distribution   The normal density with mean (μ) equal to 0 and standard deviation (σ) equal to 1.

Unitary elastic   An elasticity with a magnitude of 1.

Units-of-production method   A depreciation method that allocates the cost of a long-lived asset based on actual usage during the period.

Univariate distribution   A distribution that specifies the probabilities for a single random variable.

Unlimited funds   An unlimited funds environment assumes that the company can raise the funds it wants for all profitable projects simply by paying the required rate of return.

Unsecured debt   Debt which gives the debtholder only a general claim on an issuer's assets and cash flow.

Unsponsored   A type of depository receipt in which the foreign company whose shares are held by the depository has no involvement in the issuance of the receipts.

Unstable   With reference to an equilibrium, one in which price, when disturbed away from the equilibrium, tends not to return to it.

Up transition probability   The probability that an asset's value moves up.

Utility function   A mathematical representation of the satisfaction derived from a consumption basket.

Utils   A unit of utility.

Validity instructions   Instructions which indicate when the order may be filled.

Valuation allowance   A reserve created against deferred tax assets, based on the likelihood of realizing the deferred tax assets in future accounting periods.

Valuation ratios   Ratios that measure the quantity of an asset or flow (e.g., earnings) in relation to the price associated with a specified claim (e.g., a share or ownership of the enterprise).

Value at risk   (VAR) A money measure of the minimum value of losses expected during a specified time period at a given level of probability.

Value investors   With reference to equity investors, investors who are focused on paying a relatively low share price in relation to earnings or assets per share.

Variable costs   Costs that fluctuate with the level of production and sales.

Variable-rate note   Similar to a floating-rate note, except that the spread is variable rather than constant.

Variance   The expected value (the probability-weighted average) of squared deviations from a random variable's expected value.

Variation margin   Additional margin that must be deposited in an amount sufficient to bring the balance up to the initial margin requirement.

Veblen good   A good that increases in desirability with price.

Vega   The relationship between option price and volatility.

Venture capital   Investments that provide "seed" or start-up capital, early-stage financing, or mezzanine financing to companies that are in the early stages of development and require additional capital for expansion.

Venture capital fund   A fund for private equity investors that provides financing for development-stage companies.

Vertical analysis   Common-size analysis using only one reporting period or one base financial statement; for example, an income statement in which all items are stated as percentages of sales.

Vertical demand schedule   Implies that some fixed quantity is demanded, regardless of price.

Volatility   As used in option pricing, the standard deviation of the continuously compounded returns on the underlying asset.

Voluntarily unemployed   A person voluntarily outside the labor force, such as a jobless worker refusing an available vacancy.

Voluntary export restraint   A trade barrier under which the exporting country agrees to limit its exports of the good to its trading partners to a specific number of units.

Vote by proxy   A mechanism that allows a designated party—such as another shareholder, a shareholder representative, or management—to vote on the shareholder's behalf.

Warehouse receipt arrangement   The use of inventory as collateral for a loan; similar to a trust receipt arrangement except there is a third party (i.e., a warehouse company) that supervises the inventory.

Warrant   Attached option that gives its holder the right to buy the underlying stock of the issuing company at a fixed exercise price until the expiration date.

Weak-form efficient market hypothesis   The belief that security prices fully reflect all past market data, which refers to all historical price and volume trading information.

Wealth effect   An increase (decrease) in household wealth increases (decreases) consumer spending out of a given level of current income.

Weighted average cost method   An inventory accounting method that averages the total cost of available inventory items over the total units available for sale.

Weighted average cost of capital   A weighted average of the aftertax required rates of return on a company's common stock, preferred stock, and long-term debt, where the weights are the fraction of each source of financing in the company's target capital structure.

Weighted mean   An average in which each observation is weighted by an index of its relative importance.

Wholesale price index   Reflects the price changes experienced by domestic producers in a country.

Winner's curse   The tendency for the winner in certain competitive bidding situations to overpay, whether because of overestimation of intrinsic value, emotion, or information asymmetries.

Winsorized mean   A mean computed after assigning a stated percent of the lowest values equal to one specified low value, and a stated percent of the highest values equal to one specified high value.

Working capital   The difference between current assets and current liabilities.

Working capital management   The management of a company's short-term assets (such as inventory) and short-term liabilities (such as money owed to suppliers).

World price   The price prevailing in the world market.

Yield   The actual return on a debt security if it is held to maturity.

Yield duration   The sensitivity of the bond price with respect to the bond's own yield-to-maturity.

Yield to maturity   Annual return that an investor earns on a bond if the investor purchases the bond today and holds it until maturity. It is the discount rate that equates the present value of the bond's expected cash flows until maturity with the bond's price. Also called *yield-to-redemption* or *redemption yield*.

Yield to redemption   See *yield to maturity*.

Yield-to-worst   The lowest of the sequence of yields-to-call and the yield-to-maturity.

Zero volatility spread (Z-spread)   Calculates a constant yield spread over a government (or interest rate swap) spot curve.

Zero-cost collar   A transaction in which a position in the underlying is protected by buying a put and selling a call with the premium from the sale of the call offsetting the premium from the purchase of the put. It can also be used to protect a floating-rate borrower against interest rate increases with the premium on a long cap offsetting the premium on a short floor.

Zero-coupon bonds   Bonds that do not pay interest during the bond's life. It is issued at a discount to par value and redeemed at par. Also called *pure discount bonds*.

Index